Repaso

A Spanish Grammar Review Worktext

SECOND EDITION

Ronni L. Gordon, Ph.D.

David M. Stillman, Ph.D.

The College of New Jersey

McGraw Hill

Boston   Burr Ridge, IL   Dubuque, IA   Madison, WI   New York
San Francisco   St. Louis   Bangkok   Bogotá   Caracas   Kuala Lumpur
Lisbon   London   Madrid   Mexico City   Milan   Montreal   New Delhi
Santiago   Seoul   Singapore   Sydney   Taipei   Toronto

Editor-in-chief: *Emily Barrosse*
Publisher: *William R. Glass*
Director of development: *Scott Tinetti*
Sponsoring editor: *Katherine Crouch*
Development editor: *Jennifer Kirk*
Executive marketing manager: *Nick Agnew*

Production editor: *Mel Valentin*
Production supervisor: *Richard DeVitto*
Design manager: *Violeta Díaz*
Interior designer: *Susan Breitbard*
Compositor: *Interactive Composition Corporation*
Printer: *RR Donnelley*

ISBN-13: 978-0-07-353436-7
ISBN-10: 0-07-353436-6

Printed in the United States of America.

9 10 CUS / CUS 19 18 17 16 15 14

About the Authors

Ronni L. Gordon, Ph.D., is a prominent author of foreign language textbooks, reference books, and materials for multimedia. She is co-author of the acclaimed *The Ultimate Spanish Review and Practice: Mastering Spanish Grammar for Confident Communication* and *The Big Red Book of Spanish Verbs*. She is Vice President of Mediatheque Publisher Services, a leader in the development of foreign language instructional materials. She received a Ph.D. in Spanish language and Spanish and Latin American literature and history from Rutgers University, and has taught at Harvard University and Boston University. She has read in foreign languages for the National Endowment for the Humanities, spoken at the U.S. Department of Education, and founded the Committee for Quality Education, an organization devoted to the improvement of academic standards in public schools. She is an education consultant specializing in curriculum development and is an associate scholar of a Philadelphia-based think tank.

David M. Stillman, Ph.D., teaches at The College of New Jersey, where he has given courses in Spanish, French, Italian, and Hebrew, and supervises conversation hours in French, German, Italian, Chinese, Japanese, and Arabic. He is a well-known writer of foreign language textbooks, multimedia courses, and reference books and is co-author of the acclaimed *The Ultimate Spanish Review and Practice: Mastering Spanish Grammar for Confident Communication* and *The Big Red Book of Spanish Verbs*. He is President of Mediatheque Publisher Services, a leader in the development of foreign language instructional materials. He received a Ph.D. in Spanish linguistics from the University of Illinois and has taught at Harvard University, Boston University, and Cornell University. He has been appointed to national committees devoted to the improvement of teacher training.

By the same authors:

The Ultimate Spanish Verb Review and Practice: Mastering Verbs and Sentence Building for Confident Communication
The Ultimate Spanish Review and Practice: Mastering Spanish Grammar for Confident Communication
The Ultimate Spanish Review and Practice: Mastering Spanish Grammar for Confident Communication, CD Edition
The Big Red Book of Spanish Verbs

The Ultimate French Verb Review and Practice: Mastering Verbs and Sentence Building for Confident Communication
The Ultimate French Review and Practice: Mastering French Grammar for Confident Communication
The Ultimate French Review and Practice: Mastering French Grammar for Confident Communication, CD Edition
The Big Blue Book of French Verbs

CONTENTS

CONTENTS

CONTENTS

PREFACE

"Like everything metaphysical the harmony between thought and reality is to be found in the grammar of the language."

—Ludwig Wittgenstein

Repaso—A Spanish Grammar Review Worktext is a powerful tool for review and progress in Spanish. This new college edition incorporates the suggestions of teachers using *Repaso* with their classes. *Repaso* is organized into 24 chapters offering intermediate through advanced learners of Spanish clear, concise, and well-organized grammar explanations with examples derived from everyday usage, most often in the format of conversational exchanges. These presentations of structure are easy to read and understand and encourage students to see grammar as a stepping-stone to communication. The activities in *Repaso* provide practice in all the grammar topics that intermediate-level Spanish students should know. *Repaso* bridges grammar practice and communication by emphasizing authentic language use in contextualized structural activities. Instructions for the activities are written in Spanish, helping to set the scene and prepare students for the task at hand.

Thematic vocabulary boxes linked to the activities provide a review of the vocabulary common to most first- and second-year Spanish textbooks and present additional current vocabulary that empowers learners to express themselves on a broad range of topics. Self-expression activities encourage learners to use the target grammar and vocabulary to express their own ideas. For convenient student reference, the Appendix of *Repaso* supplies easy-to-read verb charts. Also included in the Appendix are a review of numbers, dates, and telling time and a section on Written Conventions, which explains Spanish rules of spelling and punctuation. The Spanish-English Glossary contains most of the words used in the activities.

Repaso is ideal for use in a classroom setting or for assigned self-study outside the classroom. The clearly written grammatical explanations enable students to review on their own, saving class time for other activities. Chapters may be covered in any order allowing teachers to individualize grammar practice. The Answer Key provided at the end of the book allows students to check their work.

Practical, inviting, and easy to use, *Repaso* will help learners acquire knowledge that will increase their confidence in using and comprehending Spanish in a wide variety of contexts and situations.

Ronni L. Gordon, Ph.D.
David M. Stillman, Ph.D.

PARTE I   Verbs—Forms and Uses

PRESENT TENSE

Regular verbs

Verbs are presented in conjugation paradigms (i.e. charts) that summarize the forms of a verb in each tense. Spanish verbs change their form for person and number. The three persons are first person (the speaker), second person (the person spoken to), and the third person, referring neither to the speaker nor the person spoken to. Spanish, like English, has two numbers: singular and plural.

The persons of the verb and their corresponding pronouns in English are:

	SINGULAR	PLURAL
FIRST PERSON	*I*	*we*
SECOND PERSON	*you*	*you*
THIRD PERSON	*he/she/it*	*they*

The persons of the verb and their corresponding pronouns in Spanish are:

	SINGULAR	PLURAL
FIRST PERSON	yo	nosotros/nosotras
SECOND PERSON	tú	vosotros/vosotras
THIRD PERSON	él/ella/usted	ellos/ellas/ustedes

All Spanish verbs belong to one of three different classes, or conjugations, according to the ending of the infinitive—the verb form ending in **-ar, -er,** or **-ir,** that is unmarked for person or tense.

FIRST CONJUGATION: **-ar** verbs like **hablar** (*to speak*)

SECOND CONJUGATION: **-er** verbs like **aprender** (*to learn*)

THIRD CONJUGATION: **-ir** verbs like **escribir** (*to write*)

The present tense is formed by dropping the infinitive ending (**-ar, -er, -ir**) and adding the appropriate present-tense endings to the stem of the verb. Verbs conjugated according to the patterns below are called regular verbs.

First conjugation: -ar verbs

Verbs of the first conjugation (**-ar** verbs) are conjugated like **hablar.**

	SINGULAR	PLURAL
FIRST PERSON	yo habl**o**	nosotros/as habl**amos**
SECOND PERSON	tú habl**as**	vosotros/as habl**áis**
THIRD PERSON	él/ella/Ud. habl**a**	ellos/ellas/Uds. habl**an**

Common -ar verbs

acabar *to finish*
aceptar *to accept*
acompañar *to go with, accompany*
aconsejar *to advise*
aguantar *to put up with, tolerate*
ahorrar *to save*
alcanzar *to reach, overtake*
almacenar *to store*
alquilar *to rent*
analizar *to analyze*
andar *to walk*
apagar *to turn off, shut off*
aparcar *to park*
aprovechar *to take advantage of, utilize*
archivar *to file*
armar *to set up, put together*
arrastrar *to drag*
arreglar *to arrange, straighten up; to fix*
aumentar *to increase*
averiguar *to find out*
avisar *to tell, notify; to warn*
ayudar *to help*
bailar *to dance*
bajar *to go down; to lower; to download*
besar *to kiss*
borrar *to erase*
buscar *to look for*
calcular *to calculate, work out*
cambiar *to change*
caminar *to walk*
cantar *to sing*
cargar *to load; to upload*
celebrar *to celebrate*
cenar *to have dinner*
charlar *to chat*
cocinar *to cook*
colocar *to put, place*
comprar *to buy*
contestar *to answer*
cortar *to cut*

crear *to create*
cruzar *to cross*
cursar *to study (a subject); to take a course*
dejar *to let, leave*
desarrollar *to develop*
desayunar *to have breakfast*
descansar *to rest*
descargar *to download*
desear *to want*
dibujar *to draw*
diseñar *to design*
disfrutar *to enjoy*
doblar *to turn (change direction); to dub (film)*
durar *to last*
echar *to throw*
empujar *to push*
ensayar *to rehearse; to test, try out*
enseñar *to teach; to show*
entrar *to go/come in, enter; to input*
entregar *to hand in/over*
escuchar *to listen (to)*
esperar *to wait, hope, expect*
estacionar *to park*
estornudar *to sneeze*
estudiar *to study*
explicar *to explain*
felicitar *to congratulate*
firmar *to sign*
funcionar *to work, function (machine)*
ganar *to earn, win*
gastar *to spend, waste*
grabar *to record; to engrave*
gritar *to shout*
guardar *to keep; to put away; to save (a computer file)*
hablar *to speak*
instalar *to install*
invitar *to invite*
llamar *to call*
llegar *to arrive*
llevar *to carry; to wear*

llorar *to cry*
luchar *to fight, struggle*
mandar *to send; to order*
manejar *to drive*
marcar *to dial; to mark*
mascar *to chew*
mirar *to look at*
nadar *to swim*
navegar *to surf (the Internet)*
necesitar *to need*
pagar *to pay*
parar *to stop*
pasar *to spend (time); to pass*
patinar *to skate*
pegar *to stick, glue; to hit*
pintar *to paint*
pisar *to stand on, step on*
practicar *to practice; to play (a sport)*
preguntar *to ask (a question)*
preparar *to prepare*
presentar *to present, introduce*
programar *to program*
pulsar *to press, push (a button)*
quitar *to take away, remove*
regresar *to come back, return*
reparar *to repair, fix*
repasar *to review*
sacar *to take out*
saludar *to greet*
tardar *to take/be a long time*
telefonear *to telephone*
terminar *to finish, end*
tirar *to throw*
tocar *to play a musical instrument; to touch*
tomar *to take; to drink*
trabajar *to work*
trotar *to jog*
usar *to use; to wear*
utilizar *to use*
viajar *to travel*
visitar *to visit*

Second conjugation: -er verbs

Verbs of the second conjugation (**-er** verbs) are conjugated like **aprender.**

	SINGULAR	PLURAL
FIRST PERSON	yo aprend**o**	nosotros/as aprend**emos**
SECOND PERSON	tú aprend**es**	vosotros/as aprend**éis**
THIRD PERSON	él/ella/Ud. aprend**e**	ellos/ellas/Uds. aprend**en**

Common -er verbs

aprender *to learn*
beber *to drink*
comer *to eat*
comprender *to understand*
correr *to run*

coser *to sew*
creer *to think; to believe*
deber *to owe; ought, must, to be supposed to*
leer *to read*

meter *to put in, insert*
prender *to turn on*
romper *to break*
toser *to cough*
vender *to sell*

Third conjugation: -ir verbs

Verbs of the third conjugation (**-ir** verbs) are conjugated like **escribir.**

	SINGULAR	PLURAL
FIRST PERSON	yo escrib**o**	nosotros/as escrib**imos**
SECOND PERSON	tú escrib**es**	vosotros/as escrib**ís**
THIRD PERSON	él/ella/Ud. escrib**e**	ellos/ellas/Uds. escrib**en**

Common -ir verbs

abrir *to open*
añadir *to add*
aplaudir *to applaud*
asistir a *to attend*
compartir *to share*
cumplir *to fulfill, carry out; to turn _____ years old*
describir *to describe*

difundir *to publicize, broadcast, spread*
discutir *to discuss, argue*
escribir *to write*
imprimir *to print*
insistir (en) *to insist (on)*
interrumpir *to interrupt*
ocurrir *to happen*
permitir *to permit, allow*

recibir *to receive*
resistir *to resist, stand, endure*
subir *to go up, raise; to upload*
sufrir *to suffer*
transmitir *to transmit, broadcast*
vivir *to live*

NOTAS

- Verbs of the first conjugation (**-ar**) and the second conjugation (**-er**) are conjugated alike with the difference that **-ar** verbs have **a** in all endings except the **yo** form and **-er** verbs have **e** in all endings except the **yo** form.

- Verbs of the third conjugation (**-ir**) have **i** in the endings for **nosotros/as** and **vosotros/as.** The other persons are the same as the second conjugation (**-er**).

Uses of the present

The present-tense forms of Spanish verbs express both the English simple present (*I walk*) and the English present progressive (*I am walking*). Spanish present-tense forms also include the function of the auxiliary verb *do/does* that English uses in questions and in negative sentences. *Do/does* are not expressed by a separate auxiliary verb in Spanish.

Tocas el piano.	{ *You play* the piano. / *You're playing* the piano.
¿**Navegan Uds.** en la Red?	{ *Do you surf* the Net? / *Are you surfing* the Net?
No usamos esta computadora.	{ *We don't use* this computer. / *We're not using* this computer.

Questions can be formed in Spanish by inverting the subject and the verb or by changing intonation.

¿**Trabajan Uds.** aquí?
¿**Uds. trabajan** aquí? }   *Do you work here?*

The present tense can be used to ask for instructions.

¿**Hablamos** del tema ahora?	*Shall we talk* about the topic now?
¿**Cuándo entrego** el informe?	*When shall I hand in* the report?

The present tense can refer to the future if another element of the sentence expresses future time. English often uses the present progressive to indicate future time.

Mando el correo electrónico mañana.	*I'll send* the e-mail tomorrow.
Vera **cena** conmigo el viernes.	*Vera's having dinner* with me on Friday.

Spanish uses the present tense to refer to actions that began in the past but continue into the present. English uses a *have/has been doing something* construction for this function. The Spanish construction consists of the following elements.

To ask a question about how long something has been going on:

¿**Cuánto (tiempo) hace que** + *verb in present tense*?

The word **tiempo** can be omitted in the question.

¿**Cuánto (tiempo) hace que** Ud. vive en esta vecindad?	*How long* have you been living in this neighborhood?

To tell how long something has been going on:

Hace + *time expression* + **que** + *verb in present tense*

or

Verb in present tense + **hace** + *time expression*

¿**Cuánto tiempo hace que** Ud. vive en esta vecindad?	*How long* have you been living in this neighborhood?
Hace un año que vivo aquí.	*I've been living* here *for a year.*

or

Vivo aquí **hace un año.**	*I've been living* here *for a year.*

To specify the starting point of an action that began in the past and continues into the present, **desde** (*since*) is added.

¿**Desde cuándo** vives al lado
  de los Paz?
Somos vecinos **desde** septiembre.

*Since when have you been living next
  door to the Paz family?*
*We've been neighbors **since** September.*

When the verb is *to be,* Spanish often prefers to use the verb **llevar** to express *have been / has been* with expressions of time.

¿Cuánto tiempo **llevas** aquí?
Llevo an año en Madrid.
Llevamos más de dos años
  en esta universidad.

*How long **have you been** here?*
*I've been in Madrid **for one year.***
*We've been at this university
  for more than two years.*

Tener can also be used with this function, especially in Spanish America.

¿**Tienes mucho tiempo** con esta
  empresa?
Tienen dos años en Nueva York.

*Have you been with this company
  for a long time?*
*They've been in New York **for two years.***

Actividad 1 **En la clase de español.** Describa lo que pasa en la clase de español del profesor Sierra. Escriba oraciones usando el presente. Siga el modelo.

> MODELO los estudiantes / hablar español
> Los estudiantes hablan español.

1. Daniel / pronunciar muy bien

2. nosotros / abrir el libro de texto

3. tú / escuchar al profesor

4. los estudiantes / practicar los sonidos del español

5. vosotros / tomar apuntes

6. yo / leer el diálogo

7. Isabel y tú / aprender los verbos

Actividad 2 **¿En esta clase? ¡Qué va!** Describa las cosas que nunca pasan en la clase de la profesora Reyes. Escriba oraciones usando el presente. Siga el modelo.

> MODELO los estudiantes / gritar
> Los estudiantes nunca gritan.

Vocabulario | **Lo que no se hace en la clase**

copiar en los exámenes *to cheat*
faltar *to be absent*
mascar chicle *to chew gum*

utilizar una chuleta *to use a cheat sheet*

1. Uds. / comer

_____

2. nosotros / faltar a nuestra clase

_____

3. Juan Carlos / mascar chicle

_____

4. Laura y Carmen / hablar por teléfono celular

_____

5. tú / interrumpir

_____

6. yo / beber refrescos

_____

7. vosotros / utilizar una chuleta

_____

Actividad 3 **¿Qué hacen sus profesores?** Diga lo que sus profesores hacen o no hacen en la sala de clase escogiendo frases de la columna B para completar las frases de la columna A. Siga el modelo.

> MODELO   Mi profesor de inglés...   hablar en voz alta
> no interrumpir a sus estudiantes
> Mi profesor de inglés habla en voz alta.
> Mi profesor de inglés no interrumpe a sus estudiantes.

A
1. Mi profesor de historia...
2. Nuestra profesora de química...
3. Nuestros profesores de matemáticas...
4. Las profesoras de español...
5. Mi profesora de música...
6. El profesor de informática...

B
a. enseñar bien
b. usar la computadora portátil
c. preparar exámenes
d. esperar mucho de nosotros
e. escribir problemas en la pizarra
f. pasar lista (*to take attendance*)
g. prender los aparatos multimedia
h. calcular las notas todos los días
i. hablar de las guerras
j. navegar en la Red
k. discutir sus ideas
l. tocar el piano
m. invitar a los conferenciantes

Actividad 4 **¿Cuánto tiempo hace?** Ud. le pregunta a su amigo/a cuánto tiempo hace que sus amigos se dedican a sus aficiones. Escriba cada pregunta dos veces usando las construcciones del modelo.

> MODELO   María / escribir los correos electrónicos
> ¿Cuánto tiempo hace que María escribe los correos electrónicos?
> ¿Desde cuándo escribe María los correos electrónicos?

1. Uds. / navegar en la Red

   _____

   _____

2. Mario y Federico / correr en el equipo universitario

   _____

   _____

3. Consuelo / asistir a los conciertos

   _____

   _____

4. tú / alquilar vídeos

   _____

   _____

5. Esteban / bailar salsa en las discotecas

   _____

   _____

6. vosotros / sacar fotos con una cámara digital

   _____

   _____

Actividad 5 **Hace mucho tiempo que...** Su amigo/a contesta las preguntas de la Actividad 4 de dos modos. Siga el modelo.

> MODELO   María / escribir los correos electrónicos / seis meses
> Hace seis meses que María escribe los correos electrónicos.
> María escribe los correos electrónicos desde hace seis meses.

1. Uds. / navegar en la Red / cinco años

   _____

   _____

2. Mario y Federico / correr en el equipo universitario / un año

   _____

   _____

3. Consuelo / asistir a los conciertos / seis años

   _____

   _____

4. tú / alquilar videos / tres años

   _____

   _____

5. Esteban / bailar salsa en las discotecas / ocho meses

   _____

   _____

6. vosotros / sacar fotos con una cámara digital / tres semanas

   _____

   _____

Irregular verbs

The following verbs have an irregular first-person singular (yo) form in the present tense. All other present-tense forms are regular.

-G verbs are verbs that have an unexpected -g in the yo form.

INFINITIVE	yo FORM	OTHER FORMS OF THE PRESENT TENSE
caer *to fall*	cai**g**o	caes, cae, caemos, caéis, caen
hacer *to make, do*	ha**g**o	haces, hace, hacemos, hacéis, hacen
poner *to put*	pon**g**o	pones, pone, ponemos, ponéis, ponen
salir *to go out, leave*	sal**g**o	sales, sale, salimos, salís, salen
traer *to bring*	trai**g**o	traes, trae, traemos, traéis, traen
valer *to be worth*	val**g**o	vales, vale, valemos, valéis, valen

Verbs like **caer**

decaer *to decline, weaken, deteriorate* **recaer** *to fall again, relapse, backslide*

Verbs like **hacer**

deshacer *to undo* **rehacer** *to redo*

Verbs like **poner**

componer *to compose; to repair*
descomponer *to break, malfunction*

disponer *to dispose*
imponer *to impose*
oponer *to oppose*
posponer *to postpone*

proponer *to propose, suggest*
reponerse *to get well, recover*
suponer *to suppose*

Verbs like **traer**

atraer *to attract*   **contraer** *to contract*   **distraer** *to distract, amuse, entertain*

The following **-g** verbs are irregular in other persons besides the first person.

DECIR *to say, tell*	
digo	decimos
dices	decís
dice	dicen

OÍR *to hear*	
oigo	oímos
oyes	oís
oye	oyen

TENER *to have*	
tengo	tenemos
tienes	tenéis
tiene	tienen

VENIR *to come*	
vengo	venimos
vienes	venís
viene	vienen

Verbs like **decir**

desdecir (de) *to fall short of, be unworthy of*   **maldecir** *to curse*   **predecir** *to predict*

Verbs like **tener**

contener *to contain*
detener *to stop, detain; to arrest*

mantener *to maintain, keep; to support*
obtener *to obtain, get*

retener *to retain*
sostener *to sustain, support*

Verbs like **venir**

convenir *to agree; to be suitable, fitting*   **prevenir** *to prevent, warn*   **provenir** *to originate from*

Dar (*to give*) and **ir** (*to go*) are conjugated like **-ar** verbs except that the **yo** form ends in **-oy (doy, voy).** The stem of the verb **dar** is the letter **d,** and the stem of the verb **ir** is the letter **v.** Note that the **vosotros/as** form has no accent because it has only one syllable **(dais, vais).**

DAR			IR	
doy	damos		**voy**	vamos
das	dais		vas	vais
da	dan		va	van

Ir + a + *infinitive* is used to refer to future time like *to be going to* is used in English.

Aquí está el cine. **Voy a estacionar** el coche.

Y **yo voy a comprar** los billetes.

Here's the movie theater. **I'm going to park** *the car.*

And **I'm going to buy** *the tickets.*

Caber (*to fit*) and **saber** (*to know*) are irregular in the first person only. **Ver** (*to see*) is a regular **-er** verb except for the **yo** form (**veo**). The **vosotros/as** form has no accent because it has only one syllable (**veis**).

INFINITIVE	*yo* FORM	OTHER FORMS OF THE PRESENT TENSE
caber	**quepo**	cabes, cabe, cabemos, cabéis, caben
saber	**sé**	sabes, sabe, sabemos, sabéis, saben
ver	**veo**	ves, ve, vemos, veis, ven

In most verbs that end in a vowel + **-cer** or **-cir, -c** changes to **-zc** before **-o** and **-a.** In the present tense, the change occurs only in the first-person singular (**yo** form).

CONOCER *to know*	
cono**zco**	conocemos
conoces	conocéis
conoce	conocen

Note that the following verbs are conjugated like **conocer** in all forms.

desconocer *to be ignorant of*	**reconocer** *to recognize*

Most verbs with infinitives ending in **-ecer** have **-zco** in the **yo** form like **conocer.** The other forms of the present tense are regular.

aborrecer *to hate*
agradecer *to thank, be grateful*
amanecer *to wake up in the morning*
aparecer *to appear*

carecer *to lack*
compadecer *to feel sympathy for*
convalecer *to convalesce, recover*
crecer *to grow*

desaparecer *to disappear*
desobedecer *to disobey*
embellecer *to beautify, embellish*
enflaquecer *to lose weight, get thinner*

(continued)

enfurecer *to make furious*	**favorecer** *to favor, flatter*	**perecer** *to perish*
enloquecer *to drive crazy*	**fortalecer** *to fortify,*	**permanecer** *to remain, stay*
enriquecer *to enrich*	*strengthen*	**pertenecer** *to belong*
enternecer *to soften, move*	**humedecer** *to dampen,*	**prevalecer** *to prevail, take*
(emotionally)	*moisten*	*root*
entristecer *to sadden*	**merecer** *to deserve*	**resplandecer** *to shine, blaze,*
envejecer *to grow old*	**obedecer** *to obey*	*glow*
establecer *to establish*	**padecer** *to suffer, endure*	**restablecer** *to reestablish,*
estremecer *to shake, startle*	**palidecer** *to turn pale*	*restore*
fallecer *to die*	**parecer** *to seem*	

Verbs ending in **-ucir** also have **-zco** in the **yo** form, but they are regular in their other forms.

conducir *to drive*	**lucir** *to shine*	**reproducir** *to reproduce*
deducir *to deduce, deduct*	**producir** *to produce*	**seducir** *to tempt, charm*
inducir *to induce*	**reducir** *to reduce*	**traducir** *to translate*
introducir *to introduce*	**relucir** *to shine, glitter*	

Actividad 6   **Un viaje de negocios.** Ud. es jefe/a de una gran compañía internacional. Su secretario/a le hace unas preguntas sobre su viaje de negocios a Europa. Conteste sus preguntas. Siga el modelo.

> MODELO   ¿Hace Ud. un viaje en noviembre?
> Sí, hago un viaje en noviembre.

1. ¿Sale Ud. la semana próxima?

   _____

2. ¿Viene Ud. a la oficina el viernes?

   _____

3. ¿Va Ud. a Inglaterra y España?

   _____

4. ¿Conoce Ud. Italia?

   _____

5. ¿Sabe Ud. cuándo regresa?

   _____

6. ¿Establece Ud. una sucursal (*branch*) en Londres?

   _____

7. ¿Ve Ud. a sus clientes el viernes?

   _____

Actividad 7   **¡Cuánto trabajo tenemos!** Varias personas reciben una invitación a una fiesta, pero no saben si tienen tiempo para ir. Siga el modelo.

> MODELO   Juan
> Viene si tiene tiempo.

1. Roberto y Rebeca _____

2. Ud. _____

3. tú y yo _____

4. Sara _____

5. Uds. _____

6. yo _____

7. tú _____

8. vosotros _____

Actividad 8   **¿Oyes lo que dicen?** Aunque se habla en voz baja todo se oye. Escriba en español que todos oyen lo que dicen otras personas. Siga el modelo.

> MODELO   Anita / Mateo
> Anita oye lo que Mateo dice.

1. yo / Uds.

   _____

2. tú / nosotros

   _____

3. Guillermo / vosotros

   _____

4. Rosa y yo / Ud.

   _____

5. Uds. / yo

   _____

6. Elena y Paco / tú

   _____

Actividad 9   **Lo hago yo.** Conteste que es Ud. quien hace las siguientes cosas. Siga el modelo.

> MODELO   ¿Quién hace una pregunta?
> Yo hago una pregunta.

1. ¿Quién pone la mesa?

   _____

2. ¿Quién da un paseo?

   _____

3. ¿Quién ve televisión?

   _____

4. ¿Quién ofrece ayuda?

   _____

5. ¿Quién dice tal cosa?

   _____

6. ¿Quién sabe qué pasó?

   _____

7. ¿Quién va al supermercado?

   _____

8. ¿Quién conoce al nuevo programador?

   _____

Actividad 10 **¿Hablan en serio?** Sus amigos tienen ideas geniales. ¿O es que le toman el pelo (*they're pulling your leg*)? Escriba lo que dicen. Siga el modelo.

> MODELO Carlota, ¿qué propones? (un plan para resolver los problemas del mundo)
> Propongo un plan para resolver los problemas del mundo.

1. Luz, ¿qué mereces? (recibir el premio Nobel)

   _____

2. Juan Diego, ¿qué compones? (una obra maestra mozartiana)

   _____

3. Miguel, ¿qué obtienes? (una beca de dos millones de dólares)

   _____

4. Eugenia, ¿qué traduces? (novelas del vasco al sánscrito)

   _____

5. José Luis, ¿qué conduces? (la limosina presidencial)

   _____

6. Julio, ¿qué supones? (que yo voy a ser el presidente de los Estados Unidos)

   _____

Actividad 11 **¡Qué vanidad!** José Antonio es muy presumido. ¿Qué dice de su trabajo? Siga el modelo para saberlo.

> MODELO conocer a todo el mundo
> Conozco a todo el mundo.

1. pertenecer a la junta directiva (*board of directors*) de la empresa

   _____

2. producir productos importantes

   _____

3. traducir documentos del inglés al español

   _____

4. lucir en todo

   _____

5. siempre ofrecer ideas nuevas

   _____

6. merecer los aplausos de mis colegas

   _____

Actividad 12 **Todos ayudamos.** En mi casa todo el mundo ayuda. Use **ir a** + el infinitivo indicado para expresar lo que cada persona va a hacer hoy. Siga el modelo.

> MODELO tú / poner en orden la sala
> Tú vas a poner en orden la sala.

Vocabulario

Arreglando la casa

barrer el suelo *to sweep the floor*
cortar el césped *to mow the lawn*
hacer la cama *to make the bed*
hacer la compra *to do the shopping*
lavar la ropa *to do the laundry*
lavar los platos *to wash the dishes*
limpiar la alfombra *to clean the carpet*

pasar la aspiradora *to vacuum*
planchar *to iron*
poner en orden *to straighten up*
reciclar los periódicos *to recycle the newspapers*
sacar la basura *to take out the garbage*
sacudir los muebles *to dust the furniture*

1. mi hermano y yo / cortar el césped

   _____

2. mi abuela / lavar y planchar la ropa

   _____

3. yo / barrer el suelo

_____

4. mamá / hacer la compra

_____

5. mis hermanas / lavar los platos

_____

6. mi abuelo / sacar la basura

_____

7. Uds. / hacer las camas

_____

8. papá / pasar la aspiradora

_____

9. tú / sacudir los muebles

_____

10. vosotros / reciclar los periódicos

_____

Actividad 13 **La vida diaria.** Exprese en español algunas de las cosas que Ana y sus amigos hacen todos los días.

1. I take computer science at the university.

_____

2. We share a pizza.

_____

3. Felipe and I go to the mall.

_____

4. You (**Ud.**) surf the Net.

_____

5. Federico and I attend the history lectures.

_____

6. You (**tú**) read your e-mail.

_____

7. David and Olivia come to my house to listen to music.

_____

8. I go to an Internet café with my friends.

   _____

9. You (**Uds.**) go out to the movies.

   _____

10. You (**vosotros**) download songs on the computer.

   _____

11. Jaime and I rent films.

   _____

12. María Elena and Martín enjoy their visit to the museum.

   _____

Actividad 14   **Actividad oral—Un sondeo (*A poll*).** Pregúnteles a sus compañeros de clase lo que les gusta hacer los fines de semana y cuando están de vacaciones. Luego, calcule cuántos hacen cada cosa y presente los resultados a la clase.

> **acampar**
> **bailar**
> **comer en restaurantes**
> **dar un paseo**
> **dibujar**
> **esquiar**
> **hacer turismo**
> **ir al cine / a los conciertos / al teatro / a una discoteca / al centro
>   comercial / a un cibercafé**
> **ir de compras**
> **jugar al tenis / al béisbol / al fútbol / al baloncesto / al golf**
> **patinar sobre hielo / sobre ruedas**
> **pintar**
> **salir al campo / a las montañas / a la costa**
> **tocar el piano / la flauta / la guitarra / el violín / el saxofón / el
>   clarinete**
> **tomar tragos en un bar / café en Starbucks**
> **trotar**
> **ver un partido de béisbol / de fútbol americano**
> **visitar los museos**

CAPÍTULO 2

STEM-CHANGING VERBS AND VERBS WITH SPELLING CHANGES

Stem-changing verbs ending in -ar and -er

Stem-changing verbs that end in **-ar** or **-er** have two possible types of changes for the stem vowel: **e → ie** and **o → ue**. The stem change takes place in those forms of the present tense where the stem vowel is stressed. This includes all forms except **nosotros/as** and **vosotros/as.**

PENSAR to think	
pienso	pensamos
piensas	pensáis
piensa	**pie**nsan

QUERER to want, love	
qu**ie**ro	queremos
qu**ie**res	queréis
qu**ie**re	qu**ie**ren

PODER to be able to, can	
p**ue**do	podemos
p**ue**des	podéis
p**ue**de	p**ue**den

VOLVER to return	
v**ue**lvo	volvemos
v**ue**lves	volvéis
v**ue**lve	v**ue**lven

NOTA

• **Pensar** + *infinitive* means *to intend to.*

¿Qué **piensas hacer** hoy?   What **do you intend to do** today?

Verbs like pensar and querer

acertar *to be on target, guess right*
apretar *to squeeze, be tight; to grip*
ascender *to go up, promote*
atravesar *to cross*
cerrar *to close*
comenzar *to begin*
confesar *to confess*
defender *to defend*

descender *to go down*
despertar(se) *to wake up*
empezar *to begin*
encender *to light; to turn on (appliance)*
encerrar *to lock in, contain*
entender *to understand*
gobernar *to govern, manage, direct*
helar* *to freeze*

merendar *to have an afternoon snack, have a picnic*
nevar* *to snow*
perder *to lose; to miss (train, etc.)*
quebrar *to break*
recomendar *to recommend*
sentar(se) *to seat, sit down*

*Impersonal verbs; conjugated only in the third-person singular

Verbs like **poder** and **volver**

acordarse to remember
acostar(se) to put to bed, go
   to bed
almorzar to have lunch
colgar to hang
conmover to move
   (emotionally)
contar to count, tell
costar to cost
demostrar to show

devolver to return, give back
doler to hurt, ache
encontrar to find
envolver to wrap up
jugar (u → ue) to play
llover* to rain
mostrar to show, display
oler (o → hue) to smell
probar(se) to try, taste, try on
recordar to remember; to remind

resolver to solve, resolve,
   decide
rodar to roll; to film
soler to be accustomed
   to doing, to usually do
   something
tronar* to thunder
volar to fly

*Impersonal verbs; conjugated only in the third-person singular

NOTAS

- **Jugar** has the stem change **u → ue** and **oler** has the change **o → hue**.

   ¿A qué juegas?   *What are you playing?*
   Huele bien.   *It smells good.*

- **Jugar** is used with the preposition **a** and the definite article to indicate the game or sport played.

   jugar al tenis / al baloncesto / a las cartas   *to play tennis/basketball/ cards*

- **Jugar** is not used to mean *to play a musical instrument*. The verb **tocar** is used instead.

   tocar el piano / la flauta / la guitarra   *to play the piano/flute/ guitar*

Actividad 1   **Los deportes.** Escriba el deporte al que juega o de qué manera juega cada persona.

> MODELO   Roberto / el fútbol
> Roberto juega al fútbol.

1. yo / el tenis

   _____

2. Daniel y Luz / el béisbol

   _____

3. Carlota / el vólibol

   _____

4. tú / el baloncesto

   _____

5. Jorge y yo / el fútbol americano

   _____

6. Uds. / limpio (**jugar limpio** [*to play fairly*])

_____

7. Ud. / el golf

_____

8. vosotros / sucio (**jugar sucio** [*to play dirty, foul*])

_____

Actividad 2 **¿Dónde y a qué hora almuerzan?** Escriba dónde y a qué hora almuerzan estas personas.

> MODELO   yo / en casa / a las dos
> Yo almuerzo en casa a las dos.

1. Uds. / en la cafetería universitaria / a la una

_____

2. Eva / en un cibercafé / a las doce y media

_____

3. nosotros / en una tiendecita de sándwiches / a las tres

_____

4. Mauricio y Beatriz / en Subway / a la una y cuarto

_____

5. tú / en un restaurante de comida rápida / a las once y media

_____

6. yo / en una pizzería / a las dos y media

_____

7. Uds. / en un restaurante chino / a las dos menos cuarto

_____

8. vosotros / en el comedor de la residencia (*dorm*) / a las once cuarenta y cinco

_____

Actividad 3 **No puedo.** Escriba que nadie puede hacer nada hoy.

> MODELO   ¿Vas de compras hoy?
> No, no puedo ir de compras hoy.

1. ¿Uds. descargan las fotos de Internet hoy?

_____

2. ¿Empieza Elena a escribir su informe hoy?

   _____

3. ¿Trabajan Josefa y Leonardo en la librería hoy?

   _____

4. ¿Rueda Ud. su película hoy?

   _____

5. ¿Ud. trae su cámara digital hoy?

   _____

6. ¿Visitamos el museo hoy?

   _____

7. ¿Contestas tu correo electrónico hoy?

   _____

8. ¿Merendáis en un café hoy?

   _____

9. ¿Devuelves los libros a la biblioteca hoy?

   _____

Actividad 4   **En un almacén.** Margarita va a un almacén para comprar ropa. Termine la conversación que tiene con la dependienta. Complete el diálogo con la forma correcta de los verbos indicados.

> MODELO   Yo (pensar) <u>pienso</u> ir al almacén Macy's.

DEPENDIENTA   — Señorita, ¿en qué (poder) _____
              1
              servirle?

MARGARITA   — Es que yo no (encontrar) _____
              2
              los vestidos.

DEPENDIENTA   — Aquí están a la derecha. ¿Qué color (querer)

              _____ Ud.?
              3

MARGARITA   — (Pensar) _____ que el café o el
              4
              azul marino.

DEPENDIENTA   — Le (mostrar) _____ dos. Este azul
              5
              es muy bonito, ¿verdad?

MARGARITA   — Ah, sí. ¿(Poder) _____ mostrarme
              6
              el otro?

DEPENDIENTA — Cómo no. Aquí tiene el café. Yo (encontrar)

_____ el estilo muy elegante.
7

MARGARITA — Los dos son hermosos. ¿Cuánto (costar)

_____ ?
8

DEPENDIENTA — El azul (costar) _____ ciento
9

noventa euros y el café (costar)

_____ doscientos cinco
10

euros.

MARGARITA — De veras no sé. Creo que me (probar)

_____ los dos.
11

(*Margarita se prueba los vestidos.*)

Me llevo los dos vestidos. ¿Ud. me los (envolver)

_____ , por favor?
12

DEPENDIENTA — Con gusto. ¿Ud. sabe que (poder)

_____ pagar con tarjeta de
13

crédito?

MARGARITA — Ah, sí. Yo (soler) _____ pagar con
14

mi tarjeta.

DEPENDIENTA — Bien. Yo (volver) _____ en unos
15

minutos.

Actividad 5 **Sinónimos.** Consulte las listas de verbos que tienen cambios radicales en las páginas 18–19 y escoja sinónimos para los verbos que aparecen en las siguientes oraciones. Escriba cada oración con la forma correcta del nuevo verbo. Siga el modelo.

> MODELO El diccionario *vale* cien dólares.
> El diccionario cuesta cien dólares.

1. Uds. *solucionan* los problemas de álgebra.

_____

2. Los niños *cruzan* la calle con cuidado.

_____

3. El concierto *empieza* a las ocho.

_____

4. *Bajamos* al primer piso en ascensor.

_____

5. Yo no *comprendo* su idea.

_____

6. ¿*Regresas* el sábado o el domingo?

_____

7. Pedro nos *enseña* el apartamento.

_____

8. Los Salcedo *desean* salir a cenar esta noche.

_____

9. Yo *prendo* la luz.

_____

Actividad 6   **Un día típico.** Escriba lo que hacen estas personas en un día típico. Siga el modelo.

> MODELO   Juana / encender las luces
> Juana enciende las luces.

1. mi compañero/a de cuarto / despertarnos a todos nosotros

_____

2. tú / empezar a mandar tu correo electrónico

_____

3. Uds. / almorzar en un café

_____

4. Ud. / devolver los libros a la biblioteca

_____

5. mis amigos / volver a la residencia a las tres

_____

6. nosotros / comenzar a estudiar a las cuatro

_____

7. yo / soler hacer investigaciones en la Red

_____

8. los estudiantes / encontrar a sus profesores por el campus

_____

Actividad 7 **Hoy sí, mañana no.** Escriba oraciones conjugando el segundo verbo de la construcción *verbo conjugado + infinitivo* para indicar que la acción ocurre hoy. Siga el modelo.

> MODELO Mis tíos van a volver mañana.
> Mis tíos vuelven hoy.

1. Vas a recordar la fecha mañana.

   _____

2. Pablo y Lorenzo van a jugar al fútbol mañana.

   _____

3. Vamos a probar el nuevo plato mañana.

   _____

4. Alicia va a encontrar su secador mañana.

   _____

5. Yo voy a envolver los paquetes mañana.

   _____

6. Ud. va a resolver su problema mañana.

   _____

Actividad 8 **¿Qué tiempo hace?** Exprese en español el tiempo que hace hoy en varias ciudades.

Vocabulario

¿Qué tiempo hace?

Está nublado/despejado. *It's cloudy/clear.*
Hace buen/mal tiempo. *The weather's good/bad.*
Hace calor/frío. *It's warm/cold.*
Hace sol/viento. *It's sunny/windy.*
despejar* *to clear up*

escampar* *to clear up*
granizar* *to hail*
helar* (e→ie) *to freeze*
llover* (o→ue) *to rain*
nevar* (e→ie) *to snow*
tronar* (o→ue) *to thunder*
el relámpago *lightning*

*Impersonal verbs; conjugated only in the third-person singular

1. It's raining in San Francisco.

   _____

2. It's snowing in Geneva, Switzerland (**Ginebra, Suiza**).

   _____

3. It's thundering in Santa Fe.

   _____

4. The rain is beginning to freeze in Chicago.

_____

5. It's beginning to snow in Punta Arenas, Chile.

_____

6. It's clearing up in London **(Londres).**

_____

7. It's clear in Sevilla.

_____

8. It's hailing in New York.

_____

Stem-changing verbs ending in -ir

Stem-changing verbs that end in **-ir** have three possible types of changes for the stem vowel: **e → ie, o → ue,** and **e → i.** As in **-ar** and **-er** verbs, the stem change takes place in those forms of the present tense where the stem vowel is stressed. This includes all forms except **nosotros/as** and **vosotros/as.**

SENTIR *to regret*	
siento	sentimos
sientes	sentís
siente	sienten

DORMIR *to sleep*	
duermo	dormimos
duermes	dormís
duerme	duermen

PEDIR *to ask for, request, order*	
pido	pedimos
pides	pedís
pide	piden

Verbs like **sentir**

advertir *to notify, warn, point out*	**divertirse** *to have a good time*	**preferir** *to prefer*
convertir *to convert*	**hervir** *to boil*	**referirse (a)** *to refer (to)*
convertirse en *to become*	**mentir** *to lie*	**sentirse** *to feel*

Verbs like **pedir**

conseguir *to get, obtain; to manage to*	**impedir** *to prevent*	**repetir** *to repeat; to have a second helping*
despedir *to fire*	**medir** *to measure*	
despedirse (de) *to say good-bye*	**perseguir** *to pursue, aim for*	**seguir** *to follow, continue*
	proseguir *to pursue, proceed*	**servir** *to serve*
gemir *to groan, moan*	**reír(se)** *to laugh*	**sonreír(se)** *to smile*
	reñir *to quarrel, scold*	**vestir(se)** *to dress*

NOTA

- **Reír** and **sonreír** have **-í** as the stem vowel in all forms of the present tense except **nosotros** and **vosotros**.

(son)río	(son)reímos
(son)ríes	(son)reís
(son)ríe	(son)ríen

Actividad 9 **En el restaurante.** Escriba lo que piden estas personas que salen a comer. Siga el modelo.

> MODELO   Francisco / carne
> Francisco pide carne.

1. Ud. y José María / quesadillas

   _____

2. la familia Herrera / enchiladas

   _____

3. Pili y yo / una ensalada

   _____

4. tú / sopa y un sándwich

   _____

5. los chicos / arroz con pollo

   _____

6. yo / espaguetis con salsa de tomate

   _____

Actividad 10 **¿Quién sirve?** Escriba quién sirve cada bebida. Siga el modelo.

> MODELO   Uds. / café
> Uds. sirven café.

1. yo / cerveza

   _____

2. Susana / refrescos

   _____

3. nosotros / vino de la Rioja

   _____

4. Eduardo y Dolores / jugo de naranja

   _____

5. tú / agua mineral

_____

6. Ud. y Pepe / té helado

_____

Actividad 11 **¿Qué prefiere Ud. hacer?** Escriba lo que prefiere hacer cada persona. Siga el modelo.

> MODELO   Isabel / ir de compras
> Isabel prefiere ir de compras.

1. los primos / salir al campo

_____

2. Julia / leer novelas históricas

_____

3. nosotros / asistir a un concierto

_____

4. Uds. / ver televisión

_____

5. yo / jugar al tenis

_____

6. tú / bailar el tango

_____

7. Ud. / alquilar películas policíacas

_____

8. vosotros / navegar en la Red

_____

Actividad 12 **A dormir.** Escriba cuánto y cómo duermen estas personas. Siga el modelo.

> MODELO   Roberto / entre seis y siete horas
> Roberto duerme entre seis y siete horas.

1. tú / profundamente

_____

2. yo / mucho los fines de semana

_____

3. Uds. / bien en este dormitorio

_____

4. vosotros / muy poco

_____

5. nosotros / mal en este colchón (*mattress*)

_____

6. Ud. / diez horas los días feriados (*holidays*)

_____

Actividad 13   **En otras palabras.** Escriba lo que ocurre en las siguientes situaciones. Complete las oraciones con la forma correcta de los verbos que aparecen entre paréntesis. Siga el modelo.

> MODELO   Todos tienen hambre. Tú (servir) <u>sirves</u> la comida.

1. La abuela baña y (vestir) _____ a sus nietos antes de llevarlos al parque.

2. Va a llegar una tempestad del norte. El locutor de radio (advertir) _____ al público.

3. Las chicas dejan caer los vasos. Dicen que lo (sentir) _____.

4. Ya (hervir) _____ el agua. Ahora podemos hacer el café.

5. Ud. juega al tenis toda la mañana y siente un cansancio tremendo. Ud. (dormir) _____ toda la tarde.

6. Ramona exagera mucho. En realidad, ella (mentir) _____.

7. Diana (divertir) _____ a sus amigos con sus cuentos graciosos. Sin embargo, hay algunos de ellos que no (reír) _____, ¡ni siquiera (sonreír) _____!

8. Hace dos años que la empresa pierde dinero. Los dueños (despedir) _____ a mil empleados.

9. ¿Te gustó la torta? ¿Por qué no (repetir) _____?

10. Pablito se porta mal. Por eso su mamá lo (reñir) _____.

11. No comprendo lo que dice la profesora. ¿A qué se (referir)

_____?

12. ¿Por qué (tú) (gemir) _____? ¿Te duele algo?

Verbs ending in -uir

Verbs ending in **-uir** (but not those ending in **-guir**) add **-y** after the **-u** in all forms except **nosotros/as** and **vosotros/as.**

CONSTRUIR to build	
construyo	construimos
construyes	construís
construye	construyen

Verbs like **construir**

atribuir to attribute	**destruir** to destroy	**incluir** to include
concluir to conclude	**distribuir** to distribute	**influir** to influence
contribuir to contribute	**huir** to flee	**sustituir** to substitute

Actividad 14   **Vamos a contribuir.** Hubo un terremoto (*earthquake*) que destruyó muchas casas en la Ciudad de México. Ud. y sus amigos deciden recaudar (*to collect*) dinero para mandarles medicinas a los mexicanos afectados. Escriba la cantidad de dinero que contribuyen estas personas. Siga el modelo.

MODELO   Vera / diez dólares
Vera contribuye con diez dólares.

1. los padres de Vera / cien dólares

_____

2. mi hermano y yo / ciento cincuenta dólares

_____

3. tú / setenta dólares

_____

4. Ud. / setenta y cinco dólares

_____

5. Adriana / veinticinco dólares

_____

6. los habitantes del barrio / mil quinientos dólares

_____

7. yo / ochenta dólares

_____

Actividad 15 **Un proyecto.** Unos amigos colaboran para realizar un proyecto para la clase de biología. Escriba lo que propone incluir cada persona del grupo. Siga el modelo.

> MODELO   yo / una bibliografía
> Yo incluyo una bibliografía.

1. Roberto / sus investigaciones científicas

   _____

2. Uds. / algunas fotos

   _____

3. Laura y yo / las estadísticas

   _____

4. Ud. / una presentación de Power Point

   _____

5. tú / un resumen

   _____

6. David y Gabriela / una introducción

   _____

7. yo / un sitio Web

   _____

8. vosotros / una base de datos (*database*)

   _____

Verbs ending in -iar and -uar

Some verbs that end in **-iar** or **-uar** stress the **-i** or the **-u (-í, -ú)** in all forms except **nosotros/as** and **vosotros/as** in the present tense.

GUIAR *to guide; to drive*	
guío	guiamos
guías	guiáis
guía	guían

CONTINUAR *to continue*	
continúo	continuamos
continúas	continuáis
continúa	continúan

Verbs like **guiar**

confiar (en) *to trust, rely (on), confide (in)*
criar *to raise, bring up*
desafiar *to challenge, defy*

enviar *to send*
espiar *to spy*
esquiar *to ski*
fiarse (de) *to trust*

resfriarse *to catch cold*
vaciar *to empty*
variar *to vary*

Verbs like **continuar**

acentuar *to accentuate*	**efectuar** *to effect, carry out, execute*	**graduarse** *to graduate*
actuar *to act, perform, behave*	**evaluar** *to evaluate, assess*	**insinuar** *to hint*

Actividad 16 **¿Cuándo se resfrían Uds.?** Las personas tienen ideas diferentes sobre cómo y cuándo se resfrían. Escriba lo que creen las siguientes personas. Siga el modelo.

> MODELO   Ud. / en diciembre
> Ud. se resfría en diciembre.

1. Tomás / todos los inviernos

   _____

2. Uds. / cuando duermen poco

   _____

3. Lidia y Miguel / tres veces al año

   _____

4. Ud. / cuando come mal

   _____

5. yo / cuando bebo de los vasos ajenos (*other people's*)

   _____

6. nosotros / cuando salimos bajo la lluvia

   _____

7. tú / cuando no tomas las vitaminas

   _____

Actividad 17 **¿Cuándo es su graduación?** Escriba cuándo se gradúan Ud. y sus amigos de la universidad. Siga el modelo.

> MODELO   Daniela / en junio
> Daniela se gradúa en junio.

1. Micaela y Jorge / el año próximo

   _____

2. Ud. / dentro de dos años

   _____

3. Timoteo / en enero

   _____

4. Uds. / para el año 2010

   _____

5. tú / el 14 de mayo

   _____

6. nosotros / a principios de junio

   _____

7. yo / el mes que viene

   _____

8. vosotros / el jueves

   _____

Actividad 18 **Los espías.** Complete esta narración breve sobre el espionaje (*espionage, spying*). Escriba la forma correcta de los verbos indicados.

> MODELO   El espía (guiar) guía a sus colegas por el laberinto.

1. Los espías no (fiarse) _____ de nadie.

2. Todos los espías (enviar) _____ mensajes secretos.

3. El espía X (confiar) _____ solamente en el espía Y.

4. El espía Z (continuar) _____ su trabajo con los códigos.

5. El espía 003 (resfriarse) _____ trabajando bajo la lluvia.

6. Nosotros (espiar) _____ en todos los países del mundo.

Actividad 19 **¿Qué dice Ud.?** Conteste las preguntas personales.

1. ¿A Ud. le gustan las películas de espionaje y misterio? ¿Qué hacen los espías?

   _____

2. ¿Quiénes le envían a Ud. mensajes por correo electrónico?

   _____

3. ¿Se fía Ud. de los anuncios de televisión? ¿Por qué sí o por qué no?

   _____

4. ¿Qué hace y toma Ud. cuando se resfría?

   _____

5. ¿En quiénes confía Ud.?

   _____

6. ¿Cuándo se gradúa Ud.?

   _____

7. ¿Ud. esquía? ¿Dónde?

   _____

8. ¿Ud. actúa en obras de teatro? ¿En qué obras?

   _____

9. ¿Se fía Ud. de los desconocidos? ¿Por qué sí o por qué no?

   _____

Verbs with spelling changes in the present tense

Verbs with spelling changes are regular in speech. The changes are required by the rules of Spanish spelling.

In verbs that end in **-ger** and **-gir, -g** changes to **-j** before **-o** and **-a.** In the present tense, the change occurs only in the first-person singular (**yo** form).

ESCOGER *to choose*	
esco**j**o	escogemos
escoges	escogéis
escoge	escogen

Verbs like **escoger**

acoger *to welcome, receive (someone)*	**dirigir** *to direct; to lead, conduct*	**fingir** *to pretend*
afligir *to afflict*	**elegir (e → i)** *to choose, elect*	**proteger** *to protect*
coger *to take, grasp, catch*	**encoger** *to shrink*	**recoger** *to collect; to gather; to pick up*
corregir (e → i) *to correct*	**exigir** *to demand*	**surgir** *to arise*

In verbs that end in **-guir, -gu** changes to **-g** before **-o** and **-a.** In the present tense, the change occurs only in the first-person singular (**yo** form).

DISTINGUIR *to distinguish*	
distin**g**o	distinguimos
distingues	distinguís
distingue	distinguen

- **Extinguir** (*to extinguish*) is conjugated like **distinguir.**

- **Seguir** is conjugated like **distinguir** and also has the stem change **e → i.** This applies to related verbs ending in **-seguir.**

SEGUIR *to follow, continue*	
si**g**o	seguimos
si**g**ues	seguís
si**g**ue	si**g**uen

conseguir *to get, acquire*	**perseguir** *to pursue, persecute*	**proseguir** *to proceed*

In most verbs that end in **-cer** or **-cir, -c** changes to **-z** before **-o** and **-a.** In the present tense, the change occurs only in the first-person singular (**yo** form).

CONVENCER *to convince*	
conven**z**o	convencemos
convences	convencéis
convence	convencen

- **Ejercer** (*to exercise*), **mecer** (*to rock*), and **vencer** (*to conquer, overcome*) are conjugated like **convencer.**

- **Cocer** and **torcer** also follow this pattern and in addition have the stem change **o → ue.**

COCER *to cook*		TORCER *to twist*	
cuezo	cocemos	**tue**rzo	torcemos
cueces	cocéis	**tue**rces	torcéis
cuece	**cue**cen	**tue**rce	**tue**rcen

Verbs are marked with their spelling changes in the vocabulary list at the end of the book. See for example: **coger (j).** When the verb has a stem change and a spelling change, it is marked: **torcer (ue)(z).**

Actividad 20 **¿Qué elige Ud.?** Nuestros tíos van a celebrar su aniversario de veinticinco años el sábado. Por eso vamos al almacén para comprarles unos regalos. Escriba qué regalos elegimos. Siga el modelo.

> MODELO   Ud. / un florero
> Ud. elige un florero.

1. yo / una caja de bombones

   _____

2. mis padres / una bandeja (*tray*) de plata

   _____

3. nosotros / un certificado de regalo

   _____

4. tú / dos relojes

   _____

5. Uds. / un televisor de plasma

   _____

6. la abuela / una cámara digital

   _____

7. vosotros / una computadora portátil

   _____

8. nuestros primos / un mueble

   _____

9. Ud. / unos billetes de concierto

   _____

Actividad 21 **¿Cuál es su trabajo?** Las siguientes personas hacen cierto trabajo. Escriba lo que hace cada persona. Complete las oraciones con el verbo correcto de la lista.

cocer	extinguir	perseguir
corregir	mecer	recoger
dirigir		

1. Soy campesino. Yo _____ manzanas y tomates.

2. Soy policía. Yo _____ a los ladrones.

3. Soy bombero. Yo _____ incendios.

4. Soy cocinera. Yo _____ platos muy sabrosos.

5. Soy director de orquesta. Yo _____ una orquesta sinfónica.

6. Soy profesora. Yo _____ exámenes y composiciones.

7. Soy papá. Yo _____ a mi bebé en el columpio (*swing*).

Actividad 22 **Un misterio.** Describa el terror que experimenta el narrador completando cada oración con la forma correcta de los verbos indicados.

Es la una de la mañana. Yo (seguir) _____ por las

calles vacías y desoladas de la ciudad. Yo me (dirigir)

_____ al hotel. De repente, oigo pasos.

Tengo miedo. Me (encoger) _____ de hombros.[1]

Vuelvo la cabeza para ver quién camina detrás de mí, quizás en pos de mí.[2]

Yo (distinguir) _____ una sombra[3] de persona.

No la (reconocer) _____. La persona deja de

caminar y (fingir) _____ no verme. Yo (conseguir)

_____ ver que la persona (lucir)

_____ un vestido blanco que brilla a la luz de

la luna. Yo (proseguir) _____ mi camino al

hotel, pero ahora camino más rápido. La situación me (producir)

_____ mucha angustia,[4] pero yo (fingir)

_____ no estar nervioso. Yo (distinguir)

_____ un paquete que está a mis pies. Lo (recoger)

_____. ¡Me da un escalofrío[5] ver que yo soy el

destinatario[6]! Trato de persuadirme que esto es una pesadilla.[7] Por desgracia,

no me (convencer) _____. ¡Aunque yo (desconocer)

_____ el camino, voy corriendo por las calles como

un loco!

[1]Me... *I shrug my shoulders*   [2]en... *after me*   [3]*shadow*   [4]*distress*

[5]Me... *It makes me shudder*   [6]*addressee*   [7]*nightmare*

NOTA

- **Conseguir** + *infinitive* means *to manage to do something* or *to succeed in doing something*.

Actividad 23 **Consiguen hacer algunas cosas.** Escriba lo que consiguen hacer Ud. y sus amigos el sábado. Siga el modelo.

> MODELO   Rebeca / terminar su informe
> Rebeca consigue terminar su informe.

1. Víctor / salir al centro comercial

   _____

2. Pablo y yo / reparar el coche

   _____

3. Ud. / ver la nueva exposición

   _____

4. yo / leer *El Quijote* (Don Quixote)

   _____

5. Uds. / rodar una película

   _____

6. Beatriz y tú / colgar los cuadros

   _____

7. tú / ganar el partido de tenis

   _____

Actividad 24 **Sinónimos.** Escoja de la siguiente lista el sinónimo del verbo *en letra cursiva* de cada oración. Escriba la nueva oración con la forma correcta del verbo.

cocer	conseguir	distinguir	exigir	producir
coger	desconocer	elegir	fingir	seguir

1. *Continúa* con sus clases de pintura.

   _____

2. *Agarro* las monedas una por una.

   _____

3. *Ignoro* el motivo de los directores.

   _____

4. *Disimulo* tener interés en el proyecto.

   _____

5. *Cocinan* arroz para servirlo con el pollo.

_____

6. No *diferencio* entre el mar y el cielo en el cuadro.

_____

7. *Pido* más esfuerzos de parte de los miembros del equipo.

_____

8. *¿Seleccionas* tus clases para el próximo semestre?

_____

9. No *logro* hablar con mi jefe hoy.

_____

10. *Cultivo* maíz y trigo en la finca (*farm*).

_____

Actividad 25 **Las noticias.** Exprese en español los titulares (*headlines*) del periódico que Ud. lee. Trate de usar los verbos presentados en esta sección.

1. Ricardo Mateo is conducting the Philadelphia Orchestra **(la Orquesta de Filadelfia)** this week.

_____

2. The firefighters put out thirty fires each day.

_____

3. The citizens are demanding better schools.

_____

4. Senator Alonso is following the advice of his colleagues in the Senate.

_____

5. The Americans elect a new president this year.

_____

6. Young couple succeeds in winning the lottery!

_____

7. A new recipe: chef cooks soup with ice cream!

_____

8. The campaign against illiteracy **(el analfabetismo)** proceeds.

_____

3

SER and estar

Spanish has two verbs that are equivalent to the English verb *to be:* **ser** and **estar.** Both verbs are irregular in the present tense, and both have **-oy** in the **yo** form, like **ir (voy)** and **dar (doy).** The forms of **estar** are all stressed on the endings, and all second- and third-person forms require accent marks in the present tense. Like **dar (dais), ir (vais),** and **ver (veis),** the **vosotros** form of **ser (sois)** has no accent mark.

SER			ESTAR	
soy	somos		estoy	estamos
eres	sois		estás	estáis
es	son		está	están

Uses of ser

Ser is used before phrases beginning with **de** to express origin, possession, and the material something is made of.

Soy de los Estados Unidos.	*I'm from the United States.*
Somos de origen inglés.	*We're of English background.*
La cartera **es de Felipe.**	*The wallet is Felipe's.*
La blusa **es de seda.**	*The blouse is (made of) silk.*

Ser is used before adjectives to indicate that the condition expressed by the adjectives does not result from a change. Thus, these adjectives express inherent qualities and characteristics such as nationality, age, physical and moral attributes, personality, religion, and color.

Mis amigas **son** españolas.	*My friends are Spanish.*
El presidente **es** joven.	*The president is young.*
Carlos **es** alto y rubio.	*Carlos is tall and blond.*
Nora **es** inteligente.	*Nora is intelligent.*
Mis primos **son** graciosos.	*My cousins are funny.*
Esos señores **son** protestantes/ judíos/católicos.	*Those men and women are Protestant/ Jewish/Catholic.*
Nuestro coche **es** azul.	*Our car is blue.*
Jorge **es** republicano y Juan **es** demócrata.	*Jorge is a Republican and Juan is a Democrat.*
Beatriz **es** linda.	*Beatriz is pretty.*
Pablo **es** casado con Laura.	*Pablo is married to Laura.*
Inés **es** divorciada.	*Inés is divorced.*

- The verb **estar** may also be used with **casado** and **divorciado**.

Ser is used to link two nouns or pronouns or a noun and a pronoun. Both nouns and pronouns may appear in the sentence or merely be understood. **Ser** is therefore the verb used to indicate someone's profession. Unlike English, Spanish omits the indefinite article **un/una** before a noun expressing one's profession.

El señor Lara **es arquitecto.**	*Mr. Lara **is an architect.***
Pilar Suárez **es médica.**	*Pilar Suárez **is a doctor.***
Somos ingenieros.	***We're engineers.***

Ser is used to express time, dates, days of the week, and to indicate the place where an event takes place.

¿Qué hora **es**?	*What time **is it**?*
Son las ocho.	***It's** eight o'clock.*
¿Cuál **es** la fecha de hoy?	*What's today's date?*
Es el seis de octubre.	***It's** October sixth.*
¿Qué día **es** hoy?	*What day **is** today?*
Es miércoles.	***It's** Wednesday.*
¿El baile **es** en la universidad?	***Is** the dance at the university?*
No, **es** en el Hotel Palacio.	*No, **it's** at the Palace Hotel.*

Uses of estar

Estar is used to express location or position, whether it is permanent or temporary.

Santiago **está** en Chile.	*Santiago **is** in Chile.*
El perro **está** al lado del gato.	*The dog **is** next to the cat.*
La papelería **está** enfrente de la pastelería.	*The stationery store **is** opposite the pastry shop.*

Estar is used before adjectives to indicate that the condition expressed by the adjective results from a change. The condition may be a state of health or emotion, a temporary state of being (tired, seated), or the result of an action (a window being closed). **Estar** may also indicate that the adjective is the subjective impression of the speaker. **Estar** is therefore more common with adjectives that describe mental or physical states.

¿Cómo **está** Inés?	*How's Inés?*
La pobre **está** enferma.	*The poor girl **is** (has gotten) sick.*
¿**Están** levantados los niños?	*Are the children up?*
No, **están** acostados todavía.	*No, **they're** still in bed.*
¿**Están** abiertas las ventanas?	*Are the windows open?*
No, **están** cerradas.	*No, **they are** closed.*
¿No reconoces a Luis?	*Don't you recognize Luis?*
Apenas. **Está** muy delgado.	*Hardly. **He's** so skinny. (He's gotten very skinny. / He looks so skinny to me.)*

Estar is used in the formation of the progressive tenses: **estar** + *the gerund*. The gerund or **-ndo** form is equivalent to the *-ing* form in English. (See **Capítulo 9,** p. 122 for more detail.)

Están esperando.	*They're waiting.*
Estaba viviendo en París.	*He was living in Paris.*

Ser and **estar** are used with the past participle of a verb. **Ser** + *past participle* is passive; it can have an agent phrase introduced by **por**. **Estar** + *past participle* expresses the result of an action. (See **Capítulo 8** for more detail.)

La puerta **fue abierta por** la chica.	*The door **was opened by** the girl.*
La puerta **está abierta.**	*The door **is open.***
El trabajo **fue hecho por** él.	*The work **was done by** him.*
El trabajo **estaba hecho.**	*The work **was finished.***

The choice of **ser** or **estar** in a sentence can change the meaning.

Lola **es** delgada.	*Lola **is** thin. (Lola is a thin person.)*
Lola **está** delgada.	*Lola **is** thin. (Lola has gotten thin. / Lola looks thin to me.)*
Mario **es** nervioso.	*Mario **is** nervous. (He is a nervous person.)*
Mario **está** nervioso.	*Mario **is** feeling nervous. (Mario has gotten nervous / seems nervous to me.)*
Esos profesores **son** aburridos.	*Those professors **are** boring.*
Esos profesores **están** aburridos.	*Those professors **are** bored.*
Fernando **es** listo.	*Fernando **is** clever.*
Fernando **está** listo.	*Fernando **is** ready.*
La actriz **es** vieja.	*The actress **is** old.*
La actriz **está** vieja.	*The actress **is** (looks) old.*
Los hombres **son** vivos.	*The men **are** sharp/quick.*
Los hombres **están** vivos.	*The men **are** alive.*
Beatriz **es** pálida.	*Beatriz **is** pale-complexioned.*
Beatriz **está** pálida.	*Beatriz **is** (looks) pale.*
Es seguro.	*It's safe.*
Está seguro.	*He's sure.*
Paquito **es** bueno.	*Paquito **is** good (a good boy).*
La torta **está** buena.	*The cake **is** (tastes) good.*
Amalia **es** feliz.	*Amalia **is** happy (a happy person).*
Amalia **está** feliz.*	*Amalia **is** happy (feels happy).*
La carne **es** rica.	*Meat **is** delicious. (in general)*
La carne **está** rica.	*The meat **is** (tastes) delicious. (specific dish)*

NOTA

- Adjectives used with **ser** and **estar** must agree with the subject in number and gender.

---

*__Estar feliz__ is more common in Spanish America than in Spain.

Expressions with **ser**

¿Cómo es Ud.? *What are you like?, What do you look like?*

¿Cuál es la fecha de hoy? *What's today's date?*

¿Cuál es su nacionalidad? *What is your nationality?*

¿Cuál es su profesión? *What is your profession?*

¿De dónde es Ud.? *Where are you from?*

¿De qué color es? *What color is it?*

¿De qué es la camiseta? *What is the t-shirt made of?*

¿De qué origen es Ud.? *What is your origin/background?*

¿De quién es el iPod? *Whose iPod is it?*

Es importante/necesario/posible... *It's important/necessary/possible . . .*

Es que... *The fact is that . . .*

¿Qué hora es? *What time is it?*

Expressions with **estar**

estar a punto de + *infinitivo* *to be about to*

estar conforme *to be in agreement*

estar de acuerdo (con) *to agree (with)*

estar de vacaciones *to be on vacation*

estar de vuelta *to be back*

estar en la luna *to be out of it*

estar para + *infinitivo* *to be about to*

estar por *to be in favor of*

estar por + *infinitivo* *to be inclined to*

¿A cuánto(s) estamos hoy? *What is today's date?*

¿Cómo está Ud.? *How are you?*

Estamos a seis de junio. *It's June sixth.*

Estamos en primavera. *It's spring.*

Actividad 1 **Soy yo.** Escriba en español quién llama a la puerta. Escriba la forma correcta del verbo **ser.** Siga el modelo.

> MODELO ¿Quién es? (yo)
> Soy yo.

1. ¿Quién es? (ella)

   _____

2. ¿Quién es? (Uds.)

   _____

3. ¿Quién es? (nosotros)

   _____

4. ¿Quién es? (tú)

   _____

5. ¿Quién es? (él)

   _____

6. ¿Quién es? (ellas)

   _____

7. ¿Quién es? (Ud.)

_____

8. ¿Quién es? (vosotros)

_____

Actividad 2   **¿De dónde son? ¿De qué origen son?** Escriba de dónde son y de qué origen son los amigos del Club Internacional. Siga el modelo.

> MODELO   Clara / Inglaterra / alemán
> Clara es de Inglaterra, pero es de origen alemán.

1. Pablo / la Argentina / inglés
   Pablo es de la Argentina, pero es de origen inglés.

2. nosotros / El Salvador / ruso
   Nosotros somos del Salvador, pero somos de origen ruso.

3. vosotros / Canadá / japonés
   Vosotros sois de Canadá, pero sois de origen japonés.

4. Ud. / los Estados Unidos / irlandés
   Ud. es de los Estados Unidos, pero es de origen irlandés.

5. Ramón y Virginia / Puerto Rico / polaco
   Ramón y Virgina son de Puerto Rico, pero son de origen polaco.

6. tú / España / portugués
   Tú eres de España, pero eres de origen portugués

7. Ud. y Raquel / México / griego
   Ud. y Raquel son de México, pero son de origen griego.

8. yo / Venezuela / italiano
   Yo soy de Venezuela, pero soy de origen italiano.

Actividad 3   **Una encuesta.** Ud. prepara una encuesta y necesita hacerles unas preguntas a sus amigos hispanos. Exprese en español las preguntas que va a hacerles. Use el verbo **ser** en todas las oraciones.

1. Who are you?
   ¿Quién eres?

2. Where are you from?
   ¿De dónde eres?

3. What is your nationality?
   ¿Cual eres tu nacionalidad?

4. What is your background?

¿De que origen eres?

5. What are you like? / What do you look like?

¿Cómo eres?

6. What color are your eyes?

¿De que color son tus ojos?

7. What is your profession?

¿Cual es tu profession?

Actividad 4 **Están de vacaciones.** Escriba dónde y cómo están las siguientes personas usando el verbo **estar.** Siga el modelo.

> MODELO Alicia / Los Ángeles / ocupado
> Alicia está en Los Ángeles y está ocupada.

1. Patricio / Madrid / contento

Patricio está en Madrid y está contento

2. nosotros / Lima / cansado

Nosotros estamos en Lima, y estamos cansados

3. Ud. / París / nervioso

Ud. está en París y está nervioso

4. Consuelo y su hermana / Helsinki / aburrido

Consuelo y su hermana están en Helsinki y están aburridos

5. tú / Londres / enfermo

Tú estás en Londres y estás enfermo

6. yo / Roma / feliz

Estoy en Roma y estoy feliz.

7. Uds. / Las Vegas / preocupado

Uds. están en Las Vegas y están preocupados

8. vosotras / Beijing / triste

vosotras estáis en Beijing y estáis triste

Actividad 5 **¿Cuál fue la pregunta?** Lea lo que escribió una persona al contestar las preguntas de un formulario. Después, escriba las preguntas. Para cada pregunta use el verbo **ser.**

1. Roberto Iglesias.

    ¿Cual es tu nombre?

2. Uruguayo.

    ¿De que origen eres?

3. Programador de computadoras.

    ¿Cual es tu profesion?

4. Soltero. (estado civil)

    ¿Cual es tu estado civil?

5. El quince de febrero de 1980. (fecha de nacimiento)

    ¿Cual es tu fecha de naciemiento?

6. Alto, moreno, de ojos castaños.

    ¿Como eres?

Actividad 6 **Biografías.** Escriba la forma correcta del verbo **ser** o **estar** para completar los retratos biográficos de las siguientes personas.

Baltasar Estévez _____ director de cine. Él

_____ célebre por sus comedias. Sus películas
      2

_____ realmente muy cómicas. Estévez
      3

_____ muy gracioso. _____
      4   5

mexicano, pero _____ en Barcelona este año porque
      6

filma una comedia allí. Todos sus aficionados _____
                                           7

entusiasmados con esa nueva película.

Camila de la Vega _____ diseñadora de ropa
               8

para mujeres. Su ropa _____ de alta costura[1]
               9

y _____ muy cara. Este año los vestidos y
      10

los trajes que diseña _____ de seda y lana.
              11

_____ blancos, negros y de otros colores claros.
      12

La empresa de De la Vega _____ en Madrid,
              13

que _____ la capital de la moda.
    14

[1]alta... *haute couture*

Actividad 7 **El museo de arte.** Ud. es guía en un museo de arte y lleva a unos turistas a conocer el museo. Complete la descripción de la visita con las formas correctas de **ser** o **estar.**

Buenas tardes, señoras y señores. Aquí (nosotros)

___estamos___₁ en la entrada principal. A la derecha

___está___₂ la librería. ___es___₃

nueva y moderna. Y enfrente de la librería ___está___₄ la

sala de conferencias y conciertos. Esta noche precisamente hay una conferencia.

Va a hablar Francisco Velázquez que ___es___₅ profesor

de arte en la universidad. ___es___₆ especialista en la

pintura renacentista y ___es___₇ muy inteligente.

La conferencia ___es son___₈ a las ocho. Va a

___está ser___₉ muy interesante. Ahora vamos a subir la

escalera. Aquí a la derecha ___está___₁₀ la sala de pintura

impresionista. Esta exposición ___es___₁₁ muy importante.

Muchos de los cuadros que ___están___₁₂ colgados aquí

___están son___₁₃ de museos de otros países. Uds.

___están___₁₄ viendo unas obras maestras que nunca habían

salido de su país hasta ahora. Bueno, ya ___son___₁₅ las tres

y me parece que ___esta es___₁₆ hora de terminar nuestra visita.

Yo ___estoy___₁₇ muy contenta de haber podido enseñarles

el museo.

Actividad 8 **Un semestre en el extranjero.** Ud. está pasando un semestre en Madrid. Toma clases en la universidad y vive en casa de una familia española. Ud. les escribe un correo electrónico a sus padres en el cual describe cómo es su vida en Madrid. Complete cada oración con la forma correcta de **ser** o **estar.**

Queridos padres:

Ya hace dos meses que _____₁ en Madrid y

_____₂ muy contento. _____₃

una ciudad vieja y también moderna. Hay cafés, restaurantes, teatros, cines y

una maravillosa vida nocturna.[1] ¡Claro que asisto a mis clases también! La clase

de literatura española _____₄ un poco difícil a veces

porque el profesor habla muy rápido. El profesor _____₅

inteligente y simpático. Por desgracia,[2] la profesora de lengua

[1]vida... *night life*   [2]Por... *Unfortunately*

_____ aburrida. La casa donde vivo
       6

_____ en la calle Serrano. En frente de la casa
       7

_____ el Museo Arqueológico. Algunas tiendas
       8

_____ al lado de la casa también. La casa de
       9

la familia Ruiz _____ grande y bonita y mi cuarto
                        10

_____ muy cómodo. Los señores Ruiz tienen cuatro
       11

hijos. Esteban, el hijo mayor _____ un buen amigo
                                        12

mío. _____ listo y simpático. Estela, la hija mayor,
             13

_____ encantadora y muy guapa.
       14

   ¿Cómo _____ Uds.? Papá,
                  15

¿_____ muy ocupado en la empresa? Mamá,
         16

¿cómo _____ la nueva computadora? ¿Y mis
              17

hermanos? Todos _____ muy bien, espero. Claudia
                        18

debe _____ contenta en el colegio, ¿verdad? Espero
             19

recibir muchas noticias de Uds. Faltan dos meses y voy a

_____ de vuelta en casa con Uds. Hasta pronto.
       20

Un abrazo muy fuerte,

Miguel

Actividad 9   **¿Qué preguntó?** A continuación hay unas respuestas que dio su
amigo/a cuando hablaba por teléfono. Ud. no oyó las preguntas que le
hizo otro amigo / otra amiga. ¿Puede imaginarse cuáles son las preguntas?
Escoja entre **ser** y **estar** al formular cada pregunta. Siga el modelo.

MODELO	¿Hoy? Es el dos de mayo.
	¿Cuál es la fecha de hoy?

1. ¿La papelería? Enfrente del correo.

   _____

2. ¿Gloria? Rubia, alta y delgada.

   _____

3. ¿Los hermanos García? Brasileños.

   _____

4. ¿Juanito y Gracia? Preocupados y nerviosos.

   _____

5. ¿La familia Méndez? De origen español.

   _____

6. ¿Las primas de Paco? Encantadoras.

   _____

7. ¿El profesor Mora? En Costa Rica.

   _____

8. ¿El vestido? De algodón.

   _____

9. ¿La camisa y la corbata? Azules.

   _____

10. ¿Yo? Muy ocupado y cansado.

    _____

11. ¿Aquella casa? De los abuelos de Sara.

    _____

12. ¿Micaela? De Inglaterra.

    _____

Actividad 10 **Unos nuevos estudiantes extranjeros.** Exprese en español una conversación entre dos amigas sobre los nuevos estudiantes extranjeros en su universidad.

1. Who are the new foreign students? Do you know where they're from?

   ¿Quiénes son los nuevos estudiantes extranjeros?

2. I know María del Mar. She's in my history class. She's from Argentina.

   Yo se María del mar. Ella estó en mi classé de historia

3. I'm sure her background is Italian. She's very nice and smart.

   Estoy seguro que su origen es Italiano. Ella es muy inteligente

4. But she's sad because she wants to go back to Buenos Aires.

   Pero ella esta triste . . .

5. Lorenzo Tomé is English, but his grandparents are of Spanish origin.

   Lorenzo Tomé

6. He's clever and funny.

   _____

7. Lorenzo is studying biology and chemistry this year.

   _____

8. He says he wants to be a doctor.

   _____

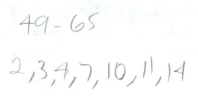

49-65

2,3,4,7,10,11,14

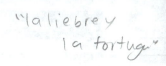

"la liebre y
la tortuga"

Regular verbs

The preterite tense is used to express events that are seen as completed in the past. The preterite is formed by adding special sets of endings to the stems of regular **-ar, -er,** and **-ir** verbs.

TOMAR *to take; to drink*		**COMER** *to eat*		**VIVIR** *to live*	
tom**é**	tom**amos**	com**í**	com**imos**	viv**í**	viv**imos**
tom**aste**	tom**asteis**	com**iste**	com**isteis**	viv**iste**	viv**isteis**
tom**ó**	tom**aron**	com**ió**	com**ieron**	viv**ió**	viv**ieron**

All preterite forms are stressed on the endings rather than on the stem.

For **-ar** verbs, the first-person singular (**yo** form) of the present tense and the third-person singular (**él, ella, Ud.** form) of the preterite are distinguished only by the stress: tom**o**/tom**ó**. The first-person plural (**nosotros/as** form) is the same in the present tense and the preterite tense: **tomamos.** The meaning is clarified by context.

Hoy **tomamos** el autobús.   *Today **we're taking** the bus.*
Ayer **tomamos** el metro.   *Yesterday **we took** the subway.*

-Er and **-ir** verbs share the same set of endings in the preterite.

For **-ir** verbs, the first-person plural (**nosotros/as** form) is the same in the present tense and the preterite tense: **vivimos.** The meaning is clarified by context.

Hoy **escribimos** un resumen.   *Today **we're writing** a summary.*
Ayer **escribimos** el informe.   *Yesterday **we wrote** the report.*

For **-er** verbs, the present and preterite of the **nosotros/as** forms are different: com**emos**/com**imos.**

Hoy **comemos** en el centro.   *Today **we're eating** downtown.*
Ayer **comimos** en casa.   *Yesterday **we ate** at home.*

Stem-changing **-ar** and **-er** verbs in the present tense do not have a stem change in any of the preterite forms. For example: p**ie**nso/p**e**nsé, v**ue**lven/v**o**lvieron.

-Ir verbs that have a stem change in the present tense also have a stem change in the preterite tense. In the preterite the vowel changes from **e → i** or from **o → u** in the third-person singular and plural.

PEDIR *to ask for, request, order*		SENTIR *to regret*		DORMIR *to sleep*	
pedí	pedimos	sentí	sentimos	dormí	dormimos
pediste	pedisteis	sentiste	sentisteis	dormiste	dormisteis
pidió	pidieron	sintió	sintieron	durmió	durmieron

Verbs like **pedir**

advertir *to point out, warn*
conseguir *to get; to manage to*
convertir *to convert*
convertirse en *to become*

divertirse *to have a good time*
medir *to measure*
mentir *to lie*
preferir *to prefer*
referirse (a) *to refer to*

repetir *to repeat*
seguir *to follow*
sentirse *to feel*
servir *to serve*
vestir(se) *to dress*

Morir(se) (*to die*) is conjugated like **dormir.**

The verbs **reír** and **sonreír** have a written accent mark on the **-i** of the endings of the **yo, tú, nosotros/as,** and **vosotros/as** forms in the preterite.

REÍR *to laugh*		SONREÍR *to smile*	
reí	reímos	sonreí	sonreímos
reíste	reísteis	sonreíste	sonreísteis
rió	rieron	sonrió	sonrieron

-Ir verbs that have **-ñ** directly before the ending drop the **-i** of the ending in the third-person singular and plural in the preterite.

gruñir (*to grunt*) → **gruñó/gruñeron**
reñir (*to scold, to quarrel*) → **riñó/riñeron**
teñir (*to dye*) → **tiñó/tiñeron**

Verbs with spelling changes

-Ar verbs whose stems end in the letters **-c, -g,** or **-z** have spelling changes in the **yo** form of the preterite. Although these verbs are regular in speech, the rules of Spanish spelling require that the sounds /k/, /g/, and /s/ (written **z**) be written differently before **-e** and **-i.**

/k/	ca, **que, qui,** co, cu
/g/	ga, **gue, gui,** go, gu
/s/ (written **z**)	za, **ce, ci,** zo, zu

Compare the spelling of the **yo** form of the present and preterite of the verbs **buscar, llegar,** and **comenzar.**

busco → **busqué**
llego → **llegué**
comienzo → **comencé**

Verbs like **buscar**

acercarse *to approach*	**embarcarse** *to embark, go on board*	**pescar** *to fish*
aparcar *to park*	**equivocarse** *to be mistaken*	**platicar** *to chat*
arrancar *to pull up/out;*	**explicar** *to explain*	**practicar** *to practice*
to start up (vehicle)	**fabricar** *to make, manufacture*	**publicar** *to publish*
atacar *to attack*	**indicar** *to indicate*	**sacar** *to take out*
chocar *to crash*	**marcar** *to dial, mark*	**secar** *to dry*
colocar *to put, place*	**mascar** *to chew*	**tocar** *to touch; to play a*
dedicarse *to devote oneself*	**masticar** *to chew*	*musical instrument*

Verbs like **llegar**

agregar *to add*	**despegar** *to take off*	**navegar** *to surf (the Internet)*
ahogarse *to drown*	**encargar** *to put in charge,*	**negar (e → ie)** *to deny*
apagar *to put out, extinguish*	*entrust, order*	**pagar** *to pay*
cargar *to load, upload*	**entregar** *to hand in, hand over*	**pegar** *to stick, beat*
castigar *to punish*	**jugar (u → ue)** *to play*	**rogar (o → ue)** *to beg, ask*
colgar (o → ue) *to hang*	**madrugar** *to get up early*	**tragar** *to swallow*

Verbs like **comenzar**

abrazar *to hug, embrace*	**aterrizar** *to land*	**realizar** *to realize, carry out,*
actualizar *to update*	**cruzar** *to cross*	*accomplish*
adelgazar *to get thin*	**deslizarse** *to slip*	**rechazar** *to reject, turn down*
alcanzar *to reach, overtake*	**empezar (e → ie)** *to begin*	**rezar** *to pray*
almorzar (o → ue) *to*	**gozar** *to enjoy*	**tranquilizarse** *to calm down*
have lunch	**lanzar** *to throw*	**tropezar (e → ie)** *to trip,*
amenazar *to threaten*	**organizar** *to organize*	*stumble*
analizar *to analyze*		

-Er and -ir verbs with stems ending in a vowel

-Er and **-ir** verbs that have a vowel immediately preceding the preterite ending change **-ió** to **-yó** in the third-person singular and **-ieron** to **-yeron** in the third-person plural in the preterite. These verbs also add a written accent to the **-i** of the **tú, nosotros/as,** and **vosotros/as** endings.

LEER *to read*	
leí	leímos
leíste	leísteis
le**yó**	le**yeron**

OÍR *to hear*	
oí	oímos
oíste	oísteis
oyó	o**yeron**

Traer does not follow the above pattern. See p. 59 for its irregular forms.

PARTE I

Verbs like **leer** and **oír**

caer *to fall*   **creer** *to think, believe*   **poseer** *to have, possess*

Verbs that end in **-uir** have a similar pattern; however, there is no written accent on the **tú, nosotros/as,** and **vosotros/as** forms of the verbs.

CONSTRUIR *to build*	
construí	construimos
construiste	construisteis
constru**yó**	constru**yeron**

Verbs like **construir**

concluir *to conclude*   **disminuir** *to reduce, diminish*   **incluir** *to include*
contribuir *to contribute*   **distribuir** *to distribute*   **intuir** *to have a sense of, feel*
destruir *to destroy*   **huir** *to flee*   **sustituir** *to substitute*

Verbs ending in **-guir** such as **seguir** and **conseguir** are conjugated like **pedir** in the preterite.

SEGUIR *to follow*	
seguí	segu**imos**
segu**iste**	segu**isteis**
si**guió**	si**guieron**

CONSEGUIR *to get, to manage to*	
conseguí	consegu**imos**
consegu**iste**	consegu**isteis**
consi**guió**	consi**guieron**

Actividad 1   ¡Tanta tarea! Escriba las cosas que Ud. y sus compañeros de clase hicieron ayer. Siga el modelo.

MODELO   Bárbara / practicar el japonés en el laboratorio
Bárbara practicó el japonés en el laboratorio.

1. Esteban / estudiar la historia de la Edad Media
   estudió

2. Rosa y Elena / solucionar los problemas de cálculo
   solucionaron

3. tú / escribir un artículo para una revista electrónica
   escribiste

4. nosotros / trabajar en la librería
   trabajamos

5. yo / visitar unos sitios Web

   visité

6. Uds. / contestar las preguntas de filosofía

   contestaron

7. Ud. / aprender las fechas de historia de memoria

   aprendió

8. vosotros / discutir varios temas

   discutisteis

Actividad 2 **¡Vaya un día de examen!** Describa lo que le pasó a Alejo el día del examen. Escriba las formas correctas del pretérito de los verbos indicados. Siga el modelo.

> MODELO   Felipe me (despertar) <u>despertó</u> a las siete.

En seguida yo me (levantar) _leventé_ ₁ y me (arreglar)
arreglé ₂. (Bajar) _Bajé_ ₃
a la cocina donde (saludar) _saludé_ ₄ a mis amigos. Yo
me (preparar) _preparé_ ₅ cereal y pan tostado. Mi amigo
Carlos (pasar) _pasó_ ₆ por mí y (desayunar)
desayunó ₇ con nosotros. Él y yo (terminar)
terminamos ₈ el desayuno y yo (coger)
cogé ₉ mi mochila de la sala. Carlos y yo (salir)
salimos ₁₀ corriendo para la parada de autobuses.
Nosotros (subir) _subimos_ ₁₁ al autobús y (viajar)
viajamos ₁₂ quince minutos hasta llegar a la universidad.
Nosotros (bajar) _bajamos_ ₁₃ casi en la puerta principal.
Tan pronto como el autobús (arrancar) _arrancó_ ₁₄,
yo (buscar) _busqué_ ₁₅ mi mochila. No la (encontrar)
encontré ₁₆. «¡No (recordar) _recordó_ ₁₇
haber cogido la mochila al bajar!». Carlos (explicar) _explicó_ ₁₈,
«Chico, no te preocupes. ¡Aquí la tienes!»

Actividad 3 **Salimos a cenar.** Escriba qué tal Ud. lo pasó cuando salió a cenar con sus amigos. Siga el modelo.

> MODELO   mis amigos y yo / salir a cenar / anoche
> Mis amigos y yo salimos a cenar anoche.

1. Felipe / escoger / el café Valencia

    escogió

2. nosotros / llegar / al restaurante a las siete

    llegamos

3. nosotros / leer / la carta

    leímos

4. el mozo / recomendar / la paella

    recomendó

5. Lorenzo / pedir / ternera y sopa

    pidió

6. Eva y Diana / pedir / pescado y ensalada

    pidieron

7. Uds. / preferir / la carne con papas

    prefirieron

8. tú / comer / torta de postre

    comiste

9. todos nosotros / tomar / café

    tomamos

10. vosotros / beber / vino

    bebisteis

11. yo / pagar / la cuenta

    pagué

12. Isabel / dejar / la propina

    dejó

13. yo / gozar / mucho de la comida

_____

14. todos nosotros / divertirse mucho

_____

Actividad 4 **Todo hecho ya.** Su amigo le pregunta si va a hacer ciertas cosas. Para responderle, escriba que ya las hizo. Siga el modelo.

> MODELO ¿Vas a apagar las luces?
> Ya apagué las luces.

1. ¿Vas a sacar los libros de la biblioteca?

_Ya saqué_____

2. ¿Vas a jugar al tenis?

_jugué_____

3. ¿Vas a tocar la flauta?

_toqué_____

4. ¿Vas a colocar los documentos en el archivo?

_coloqué_____

5. ¿Vas a arrancar la mala hierba (weeds) del jardín?

_arranqué_____

6. ¿Vas a navegar en la Red?

_navegué_____

7. ¿Vas a colgar los cuadros?

_colgué_____

8. ¿Vas a almorzar con Victoria?

_almorcé_____

9. ¿Vas a entregar el informe?

_entregué_____

10. ¿Vas a actualizar los datos?

_actualicé_____

Actividad 5 **Pasaron los años.** Hace ocho años que Ud. no ve a estas personas. Ahora tiene noticias de ellas. Escriba lo que les pasó a lo largo de los años. Siga el modelo.

MODELO Jacinta / caer / enferma
Jacinta cayó enferma.

1. los hermanos Serrat / construir / muchas casas

_____

2. el profesor Burgos / influir / mucho en la vida política

_____

3. Francisca / leer / libros para una casa editorial

_____

4. Marco e Isabel / huir / a otro pueblo por una tempestad

_____

5. doña Elvira / contribuir / con mucho dinero a las caridades (*charities*)

_____

6. Leonardo / concluir / los trámites de la empresa

_____

Actividad 6 **¡Qué mala suerte!** Ayer todo le salió mal. Complete las oraciones con las formas correctas del pretérito de los verbos indicados. Siga el modelo.

MODELO Yo me (caer) <u>caí</u> en la escalera.

Yo me (equivocar) _____1_____ de número de teléfono y

(marcar) _____2_____ mal cuatro veces. Luego

(tropezar) _____3_____ con la pared y me (pegar)

_____4_____ en el hueso de la alegría.[1] Luego me

(deslizar) _____5_____ en una cáscara de plátano. En la

cena (mascar) _____6_____ la carne demasiado rápido y

(tragar) _____7_____ mal. Para tranquilizarme,

me (bañar) _____8_____. Casi me (ahogar)

_____9_____ en la bañera. ¡Claro que no me (tranquilizar)

_____10_____!

[1]hueso... *funny bone*

Actividad 7 **Yo no hice eso.** Complete las oraciones con las formas correctas de los verbos indicados para describir lo que hicieron otras personas y lo que hizo Ud. Siga el modelo.

> MODELO Alicia <u>encargó</u> unos vestidos. (encargar)
> Yo <u>encargué</u> unas camisetas.

1. Jorge _____ la pelota en el partido. (lanzar)

   Yo _____ el bate.

2. Álvaro _____ unos cuentos. (publicar)

   Yo _____ una novela.

3. Tú te _____ a la pintura. (dedicar)

   Yo me _____ a la música.

4. Uds. _____ los datos. (cargar)

   Yo _____ los programas.

5. Los Sierra _____ un viaje a Turquía. (realizar)

   Yo _____ un viaje a Israel.

6. Ud. _____ para Lanzarote. (embarcar)

   Yo _____ para Mallorca.

Actividad 8 **Una entrevista.** Ud. acaba de volver de Puerto Rico donde pasó tres semanas con sus amigos. Ahora un periodista del periódico universitario le hace unas preguntas sobre el viaje. Contéstelas. Siga el modelo.

> MODELO ¿Qué día llegó a Puerto Rico? (el veinte de diciembre)
> Llegué el veinte de diciembre.

1. ¿Dónde aterrizaron Uds.? (el aeropuerto de San Juan)

   _____

2. ¿Qué lugares turísticos visitó? (fortalezas [*fortresses*], museos e iglesias)

   _____

3. ¿Rezó Ud. en una iglesia? (yo en la iglesia de San Juan y Sara en una sinagoga)

   _____

4. ¿Almorzó Ud. en la playa? (en varias playas de la isla)

   _____

5. ¿Avanzaron Uds. en su dominio del español? (mucho)

_____

6. ¿Qué tal el viaje que realizaron? (maravilloso)

_____

7. ¿Gozó de su estancia (_stay_) en Puerto Rico? (muchísimo)

_____

Actividad 9 **¿Cómo reaccionó la gente?** Exprese en español cómo reaccionaron estas personas a una situación o a una noticia. Siga el modelo.

> MODELO   Laura denied it.
> Laura lo negó.

1. You **(tú)** smiled.

_____

2. The boys repeated the question.

_____

3. Patricio grunted.

_____

4. We laughed.

_____

5. You **(Uds.)** fell asleep **(dormirse).**

_____

6. Daniel lied.

_____

7. Our friends warned us.

_____

8. Paquita had a good time.

_____

Irregular verbs

Many Spanish verbs have an irregular stem plus a special set of endings in the preterite. The endings for these verbs are: **-e, -iste, -o, -imos, -isteis, -ieron.** Note that the **yo** and **él** forms are stressed on the stem, not on the ending.

ANDAR *to walk*	
anduve	anduvimos
anduviste	anduvisteis
anduvo	anduvieron

CABER *to fit*	
cupe	cupimos
cupiste	cupisteis
cupo	cupieron

DECIR *to say, tell*	
dije	dijimos
dijiste	dijisteis
dijo	dijeron

ESTAR *to be*	
estuve	estuvimos
estuviste	estuvisteis
estuvo	estuvieron

HACER *to do, make*	
hice	hicimos
hiciste	hicisteis
hizo	hicieron

PODER *to be able, can*	
pude	pudimos
pudiste	pudisteis
pudo	pudieron

PONER *to put*	
puse	pusimos
pusiste	pusisteis
puso	pusieron

PRODUCIR *to produce*	
produje	produjimos
produjiste	produjisteis
produjo	produjeron

QUERER *to want; to love*	
quise	quisimos
quisiste	quisisteis
quiso	quisieron

SABER *to know*	
supe	supimos
supiste	supisteis
supo	supieron

TENER *to have*	
tuve	tuvimos
tuviste	tuvisteis
tuvo	tuvieron

TRAER *to bring*	
traje	trajimos
trajiste	trajisteis
trajo	trajeron

VENIR *to come*	
vine	vinimos
viniste	vinisteis
vino	vinieron

- For the third-person singular of **hacer** in the preterite, the stem is spelled **hiz- (hizo).** The spelling change **c → z** before **o** retains the /s/.

- Irregular preterites whose stems end in **-j,** such as **dij- (decir)** and **traj- (traer),** have **-eron** and not **-ieron** in the third-person plural form: **dijeron, produjeron, trajeron.** Other verbs ending in **-ducir** are also conjugated like **producir** in the preterite: **condujeron (conducir** *to drive*), **tradujeron (traducir** *to translate*).

- Compound forms of the verbs **hacer (rehacer, satisfacer), poner (proponer, reponerse), tener (mantener, sostener), traer (atraer, distraer),** and **venir (convenir, prevenir)** are conjugated the same way as the main verb.

- The preterite form of **hay** (*there is, there are*) is **hubo.**

Dar takes the endings of regular **-er** and **-ir** verbs in the preterite. Note that the first- and third-person singular forms are written without an accent mark. **Ver,** which is regular in the preterite, has no written accent marks, like **dar.**

DAR *to give*		VER *to see*	
di	dimos	vi	vimos
diste	disteis	viste	visteis
dio	dieron	vio	vieron

Ser and **ir** have the same forms in the preterite tense. Although isolated sentences may be ambiguous (for example, **fue** means both *he was* and *he went*), context usually clarifies the meaning.

SER *to be* / IR *to go*	
fui	fuimos
fuiste	fuisteis
fue	fueron

Some verbs have a different meaning when they are used in the preterite. The distinction in meaning will be especially important when you study the difference between the preterite tense and the imperfect tense, which are two ways of looking at past events. When these verbs are used in the preterite, they focus on the beginning or completion of an action. For example, **conocí** means *I began to know,* that is, *I met.*

VERB	SPANISH	ENGLISH
conocer *to know*	Conocimos a Carmen ayer.	*We met Carmen yesterday.*
poder *to be able to*	No pudieron salir.	*They didn't manage to go out.*
querer *to want*	No quisiste trotar.	*You refused to jog.*
saber *to know*	Supe la fecha hoy.	*I found out the date today.*
tener *to have*	Tuvo una idea.	*He got an idea.*

El pronóstico meteorológico. Su amiga está leyendo el periódico y comenta sobre el tiempo que hace en varias ciudades. Escriba qué tiempo hizo ayer. Siga el modelo.

> MODELO   Hace buen tiempo en la Ciudad de México.
> Hizo buen tiempo ayer también.

1. Llueve en Bilbao.
   llovió

2. Hace viento en Montevideo.
   Hizo

3. Está despejado en Guadalajara.
   estuvo

4. Hace fresco en Madrid.
   hizo

5. Nieva en Chicago.
   nevó

6. Está nublado en San Francisco.
   estuvo

7. Hace ochenta y dos grados en Quito.
   hizo

8. Hace mucho calor en Santa Fe.
   hizo

Escenas breves. Escriba las formas correctas del pretérito de los verbos indicados para saber lo que se dice en los diálogos breves.

1. —¿Qué (decir) _dijiste_ Ud. entonces?

   —Pues, no (decir) _dije_ nada.

2. —¿A qué hora (ir) _fuiste_ Uds. al cibercafé?

   —(Ir) _fui_ a las nueve.

3. —¿Dónde (tú: estar) _estuviste_ el sábado?

   —(Estar) _estuve_ en el centro comercial.

4. —¿Las mozas les (traer) _trajiste_ el plato principal?

   —No, una moza nos (traer) _traje_ el pan y nada más.

5. —¿Tú (poder) _pudiste_ enviar el correo electrónico anoche?

   —No, (tener) _tendré_ que salir.

6. —¿Uds. (venir) _____ en coche?

   Yo (venir) _____ en coche, pero Teri

   —(venir) _____ en tren.

7. —Yo (dar) _____ con Catalina anteayer.

   —¿Ah, sí? ¿Dónde la (ver) _____ (Ud.)?

8. —¿Clara (oír) _____ lo que pasó?

   —Sí, lo (saber) _____ la semana pasada.

9. —Tú (hacer) _____ la comida, ¿verdad?

   —Claro. Y (poner) _____ la mesa también.

10. —¿José (leer) _____ el correo basura?

    —No, no (querer) _____.

11. —¿Quién (hacer) _____ las investigaciones?

    —(Ser) _____ yo.

Actividad 12 **¿Y qué pasó después?** Para cada una de las siguientes situaciones hay una reacción. Para saber cuál es, complete las oraciones con la expresión correcta de la lista y conjugue el verbo en el pretérito. Siga el modelo.

> MODELO Yo invité a Marta a mi casa.
> Marta <u>vino a verme</u>.

decir que sí	hacerse médico	poner la mesa
estar feliz	ir tras ella	tener frío
hacerse daño	poder distinguir	

1. Matilde ganó la lotería.

   Ella _____.

2. Juan Carlos se graduó en la facultad de medicina.

   Él _____.

3. Bajó mucho la temperatura entre las cinco y las seis de la tarde.

   Los niños _____.

4. Preparamos una cena para veinte invitados.

   Nosotros _____.

5. El pintor se cayó de la escalera (*ladder*).

   Él _____.

6. Fue un día de mucha niebla.

   Yo ni _____ la carretera.

7. Uds. le pidieron prestado (*borrowed*) el coche a Rodrigo.

   Rodrigo _____ .

8. Tu novia salió de la conferencia.

   Y tú _____ .

Actividad 13   **Ayer, al contrario...** Generalmente Ud. hace cosas de cierta manera. Ayer, sin embargo, no fue así. Escriba cómo salieron sus actividades usando la información indicada. Siga el modelo.

> MODELO   Generalmente me acuesto a las diez. (las once)
> Pero ayer me acosté a las once.

1. Generalmente me despierto a las ocho. (las siete)

   _____

2. Generalmente almuerzo en el café París. (el café Atenas)

   _____

3. Generalmente voy de compras por la tarde. (por la mañana)

   _____

4. Generalmente hago un plato de pollo. (un plato de pescado)

   _____

5. Generalmente juego al tenis con Roberto. (con Ricardo)

   _____

6. Generalmente sigo por la calle Toledo. (la calle Atocha)

   _____

7. Generalmente empiezo a trabajar después del desayuno. (antes del desayuno)

   _____

8. Generalmente vengo en tren. (en taxi)

   _____

9. Generalmente navego en la Red por una hora. (dos horas)

   _____

10. Generalmente ando rápidamente. (más lentamente)

    _____

Actividad 14 **Una merienda en el campo.** Unos amigos recuerdan lo bien que lo pasaron ese domingo en julio cuando fueron a merendar en el campo. Complete las oraciones con los verbos de la lista. Escriba los verbos usando el pretérito. Se puede usar algunos verbos más de una vez.

comenzar	divertirse	ir	recoger	ver
conducir	estar	oír	tener	
dar	hacer	poder	traer	

¡Todos nosotros _____nos divertimos_____ tanto ese día! Todos

nosotros _____fuimos_____ en carro. Antonio y Francisco

_____condujeron_____ los carros. Por desgracia Juliana no

_____pudo_____ acompañarnos. _____Hizo_____

muy buen tiempo. Diego _____dio_____ un

paseo. Lila y Berta _____recogieron_____ flores. Yo

_____traje_____ sándwiches y ensaladas. Leticia y

Manuel _____trajeron_____ fruta y jugo. Los chicos

_____oyeron_____ vacas y caballos y _____

cantar los pájaros. A las cinco de la tarde _____comenzó_____

a llover y nosotros _____tuvimos_____ que volver a la ciudad.

¡Nosotros _____estuvimos_____ muy contentos ese día!

Actividad 15 **¡Qué suspenso!** Ud. es escritor/a de cuentos de misterio. Escriba un cuento de misterio expresando las oraciones en español.

1. The monster came to the city.

   _____

2. It smashed **(hacer pedazos)** cars and destroyed buildings.

   _____

3. When the people saw the monster they shouted **(dar gritos).**

   _____

4. I got **(ponerse)** pale.

   _____

5. My friend Lorenzo got a headache **(darle un dolor de cabeza a uno).**

   _____

6. My friend Marisol got a stomachache **(darle un dolor de estómago a uno).**

   _____

7. We all started (echarse a) to run.

_____

8. Some people didn't manage (poder) to escape.

_____

Actividad 16 **¿Qué dice Ud.?** Conteste las siguientes preguntas personales.

1. ¿Adónde fuiste el fin de semana pasado?

_____ fui _____

2. ¿Qué hiciste el sábado?

_____ hice _____

3. ¿Adónde fuiste para comer?

_____ fui _____

4. ¿Con quiénes fuiste?

_____ fui _____

5. ¿Qué pidieron Uds.?

_____ pedimos _____

6. ¿Qué tal estuvo la comida?

_____ estuvo _____

7. ¿Qué tal sirvieron los mozos?

_____ sirvieron _____

8. ¿Quién pagó la cuenta?

_____ pagó _____

9. ¿Quién dejó la propina?

_____ dejó _____

10. ¿Dónde pasó Ud. las vacaciones de verano (invierno)?

_____ pasé _____

11. ¿Con quiénes fue Ud.?

_____ fui _____

12. ¿Qué hicieron Uds. allí?

_____ hicimos _____

IMPERFECT TENSE

Forms of the imperfect

The imperfect tense is used to describe an ongoing condition or a repeated or incomplete action in the past. It is formed by adding the imperfect endings to the stem of the verb. The imperfect endings of **-ar** verbs have **-aba** in all forms, and the imperfect endings of all **-er** and **-ir** verbs have **-ía** in all forms.

VIAJAR *to travel*	
viaj**aba**	viaj**ábamos**
viaj**abas**	viaj**abais**
viaj**aba**	viaj**aban**

CORRER *to run*	
corr**ía**	corr**íamos**
corr**ías**	corr**íais**
corr**ía**	corr**ían**

SALIR *to go out, leave*	
sal**ía**	sal**íamos**
sal**ías**	sal**íais**
sal**ía**	sal**ían**

NOTAS

- The first- and third-person singular forms are identical for all verbs in the imperfect: **(yo/él/ella/Ud.) viajaba, corría, salía.**
- For **-ar** verbs, only the **nosotros/as** form has a written accent.
- For **-er** and **-ir** verbs, all forms have a written accent over the **-í.**
- The imperfect of **hay** is **había** (*there was, there were*).

All verbs are regular in the imperfect tense except for **ir, ser,** and **ver.**

IR *to go*	
iba	íbamos
ibas	ibais
iba	iban

SER *to be*	
era	éramos
eras	erais
era	eran

VER *to see*	
veía	veíamos
veías	veíais
veía	veían

Uses of the imperfect

The imperfect tense is used to describe conditions or actions in the past without any reference to their beginning or end. Because the imperfect does not indicate the beginning or completion of an action, it is the tense used for expressing repeated actions in past time. Adverbs and adverbial phrases such as **todos los días, siempre,** and **muchas veces** are often clues for the selection of the imperfect rather than the preterite. The imperfect is therefore also the tense used for description and expressing background in the past. Common English equivalents for the Spanish imperfect are *used to do, was doing.*

¿**Eras** estudiante entonces?
No, **yo era** ingeniero ya.

Were you a student then?
No, I was already an engineer.

¿**No querían** cantar en el coro?
No, **querían** tocar en la orquesta.

Didn't they want to sing in the choir?
No, they wanted to play in the orchestra.

¿Dónde **estaban** anoche?
Estábamos en el teatro.

Where were you last night?
We were at the theater.

Leía el periódico todos los días, ¿no?
Sólo cuando **tenía** tiempo.

You used to read the newspaper every day, didn't you?
Only when I had time.

¿Qué tiempo **hacía**?
Hacía frío y **llovía**.

What was the weather like?
It was cold, and it rained.

The imperfect tense is used to tell what time it was in the past. The preterite is never used.

¿Qué hora **era**?
Era la una en punto.

What time was it?
It was exactly one o'clock.

The imperfect tense is used in *indirect discourse* (in other words, to retell or report what someone said) after the preterite of verbs such as **anunciar, avisar, decir, escribir,** and **informar.**

Paco nos **anunció** que **se casaba**.

Paco announced to us that he was getting married.

¡Y a mí me **informó** que **pensaba** romper con su novia!

And he informed me that he intended to break up with his fiancée!

¿Qué te dijo Loli?
Me **dijo** que **venía**.

What did Loli tell you?
She told me she was coming.

¿Les escribiste?
Sí, les **escribí** que **viajaba**.

Did you write to them?
Yes, I wrote them that I was traveling.

Actividad 1 **Cuando yo era niño/a…** Ud. tiene nostalgia por esos años tan inolvidables de su niñez. Escriba sus recuerdos en su diario. Complete las oraciones usando el imperfecto de los verbos indicados. Siga el modelo.

MODELO   Yo (visitar) <u>visitaba</u> a mis amigos.

Yo (vivir) _____ en Madrid con mis padres y mis

hermanos Jaime y Marisol. Jaime (ser) _____ el mayor

de los tres. Yo (ir) _____ al colegio y (hacer)
3

_____ todas las cosas que (soler)
4

_____ hacer los niños. Mis hermanos, mis amigos y yo
5

(ir) _____ al cine, a los partidos de fútbol y a las fiestas.
6

Lo que más me (gustar) _____ de aquellos años (ser)
7

_____ la estancia[1] en la casa de campo. Allí en la
8

sierra[2] de Guadarrama mis padres, mis hermanos y yo (pasar)

_____ el mes de agosto. El aire (ser)
9

_____ tan fresco y puro y no (hacer)
10

_____ tanto calor como en Madrid. (Haber)
11

_____ un campo detrás de la casa donde mis
12

hermanos y yo (jugar) _____ al fútbol. Mi mamá
13

(cultivar) _____ rosas y buganvillas en el jardín.
14

¡Qué hermosas (ser) _____! Toda la casa (oler)
15

_____ divinamente a flores. Nosotros (salir)
16

_____ a merendar en el bosque todas las tardes.
17

(Nosotros: Subir) _____ en el monte hasta llegar a un
18

lugar desde donde se (ver) _____ todo el valle. Mamá
19

nos (servir) _____ los bocadillos[3] más sabrosos del
20

mundo. A veces papá nos (leer) _____ un cuento.
21

Nosotros siempre (ir) _____ a nadar en uno de los
22

lagos cristalinos[4] de la sierra. Al atardecer[5] (nosotros: estar)

_____ muy cansados. Mis hermanos (volver)
23

_____ caminando a la casa, pero papá me (llevar)
24

_____ a mí en brazos porque yo (ser)
25

_____ el bebé de la familia. ¡Qué felices recuerdos!
26

[1]*stay*   [2]*mountain range*   [3]*sandwiches*   [4]*crystal clear*   [5]Al... *At dusk*

Actividad 2   **Reunión de la clase del año X.** Ud. y sus compañeros de la universidad se reúnen después de no verse por muchos años. Se hacen preguntas para ponerse al día (*catch up on the news*). Escriba lo que contestan sus amigos, usando el imperfecto. Siga el modelo.

MODELO   Oye, Clara, ¿todavía estudias arte?
Antes estudiaba arte, pero ya no.

1. Oye, Manolo, ¿todavía escribes para *El tiempo*?

    _____

2. Oye, Dora, ¿todavía vas de vacaciones en junio?

    _____

3. Oye, Pepe, ¿todavía sales con Lola?

    _____

4. Oye, Jorge, ¿todavía te gusta la cocina tailandesa?

    _____

5. Oye, Ana María, ¿todavía trabajas como programadora?

    _____

6. Oye, Paco, ¿todavía juegas en un equipo de béisbol?

    _____

7. Oye, Carmen, ¿todavía vienen tú y tu marido al pueblo en invierno?

    _____

8. Oye, Paula, ¿todavía eres presidenta de la compañía?

    _____

9. Oye, Mario, ¿todavía eres socio del Club Atlántico?

    _____

10. Oye, Sofía, ¿todavía toca tu hijo la trompeta?

    _____

11. Oye, Juan, ¿todavía tienes una cadena de restaurantes?

    _____

12. Oye, Laura, ¿todavía prefieres vivir en el centro?

    _____

Actividad 3 **Un vuelo.** Ud. acaba de aterrizar (*land*) en el aeropuerto donde lo/la espera su familia. Mientras van a buscar su equipaje, Ud. les habla de los viajeros que conoció en el vuelo. Escriba qué eran y adónde iban usando el imperfecto de los verbos irregulares **ser** e **ir.** Siga el modelo.

> MODELO   Conocí al señor Torres. (abogado / Chicago)
> El señor Torres era abogado. Iba a Chicago.

1. Conocí a la señorita Fajardo. (gerente de fábrica / Miami)

   _____

2. Conocí a unos señores italianos. (dueños de una pastelería / Buenos Aires)

   _____

3. Conocí a Isabela Iriarte. (profesora de economía / Irlanda)

_____

4. Conocí a la señora Montoya. (banquera / Suiza)

_____

5. Conocí a don Pedro Domínguez. (candidato a senador / Monterrey)

_____

6. Conocí a Lorena Iglesias. (ama de casa / Costa Rica)

_____

7. Conocí a los hermanos Machado. (músicos / Nueva York)

_____

8. Conocí al señor Rubio. (cirujano / la India)

_____

Actividad 4   **¿Qué tal se veía?** Las siguientes personas no podían ver bien porque se les quedaron las gafas (*glasses*) en casa. Usando la forma correcta del imperfecto del verbo **ver**, describa lo que no podían ver. Siga el modelo.

> MODELO   Carla / el edificio suyo / la calle Mercado
> Carla no veía el edificio suyo desde la calle Mercado.

1. Carolina y Ramón / el mar Caribe / el avión

_____

2. nosotros / la cara de los actores / el anfiteatro (*balcony*) del teatro

_____

3. Federica / el embotellamiento (*traffic jam*) / la ventana del dormitorio

_____

4. Uds. / toda la cancha de fútbol / la tribuna (*stand*) del estadio

_____

5. yo / la cumbre de la montaña / el valle

_____

6. Daniel / la discoteca / la esquina

_____

7. tú / al público / la parte derecha del escenario (*stage*)

_____

Imperfect and preterite: Two aspects of past time

The imperfect and preterite tenses express different ways of looking at past actions and events. The imperfect tense designates an ongoing action in the past without any reference to its beginning or end. The preterite tense designates an action completed in the past. Spanish speakers must select one of these two tenses—imperfect or preterite—for every past action they refer to. English often does not distinguish between these two aspects of past time.

Cuando **estaba** en la universidad, **estudiaba** chino.	*When **I was** in college, **I studied** Chinese (or **I used to study** Chinese).*
Ayer **estudié** chino.	*Yesterday **I studied** Chinese.*

Sometimes English uses entirely different verbs to express the difference between the imperfect and the preterite of some Spanish verbs. For example, **tenía** means *I was in the process of having* or *I had;* **tuve** means *I began to have* or *I got, received.*

Sabía el precio.	*__I knew__ the price.*
Supe el precio.	*__I found__ out the price.*
Conocían a Sergio.	*__They knew__ Sergio.*
Conocieron a Sergio.	*__They met__ Sergio.*
No podíamos llegar para las cuatro.	*__We couldn't__ arrive by four o'clock. (Doesn't say whether we arrived by four or not.)*
No pudimos llegar para las cuatro.	*__We couldn't__ arrive by four o'clock. (We didn't arrive by four.)*
Laura **no quería** ir en metro.	*Laura __didn't want__ to take the subway.*
Laura **no quiso** ir en metro.	*Laura __refused to__ (didn't want to and didn't) take the subway.*

The imperfect and the preterite can be used in two different clauses in the same sentence. The imperfect expresses the background, a continuing action, or ongoing state, against which a completed action or event takes place.

Mientras **trabajábamos,** Julia **durmió** la siesta.	*While __we were working,__ Julia __took__ a nap.*

It is possible to have sentences with all verbs in the imperfect if the speaker sees the past actions or events as ongoing processes.

Pilar **leía** mientras Marta **jugaba** al tenis.	*Pilar __was reading__ while Marta __was playing__ tennis.*

It is also possible to have sentences with all verbs in the preterite if the speaker views the actions mentioned as a series of completed events.

Cené, me arreglé y **fui** al teatro.	*__I ate__ dinner, __got ready,__ and __went__ to the theater.*

Actividad 5 **¿Qué tiempo hacía cuándo… ?** Sus amigos quieren saber qué tiempo hacía cuando sucedieron ciertas cosas. Escriba las oraciones usando el imperfecto para hablar del tiempo y el pretérito para hablar de los sucesos. Siga el modelo.

> MODELO   hacer buen tiempo / Ud. / salir
> Hacía buen tiempo cuando Ud. salió.

1. llover / Beatriz y tú / volver

2. hacer frío / los Sorolla / levantarse

_____

3. estar despejado / tú / ir a la biblioteca

_____

4. hacer viento / José Antonio / venir a la casa

_____

5. nevar / nosotros / terminar el trabajo

_____

6. tronar / Ud. / entrar en el cine

_____

7. hacer sol / yo / llegar a la universidad

_____

8. lloviznar / Uds. / irse

_____

9. hacer calor / vosotros / ponerse en marcha

_____

Actividad 6 **¿Qué hora era cuando… ?** Su amigo quiere saber a qué hora pasaron ciertas actividades. Escriba las oraciones usando el imperfecto para hablar de la hora y el pretérito para hablar de las actividades. Siga el modelo.

> MODELO las ocho / Carmen y Víctor / llamar
> Eran las ocho cuando Carmen y Víctor llamaron.

1. las nueve y media / Consuelo y Berta / despedirse

_____

2. la una / el programa / comenzar

_____

3. mediodía / Sara / servir el almuerzo

_____

4. las diez en punto / el empleado / abrir la taquilla

_____

5. medianoche / nosotros / regresar de la discoteca

_____

6. muy tarde / Uds. / dormirse

_____

7. temprano / el cartero / traer el correo

   _____

8. las cinco y cuarto / yo / iniciar la sesión (*to log on*)

   _____

9. las tres cuarenta / tú / reunirse con tus amigos

   _____

10. las once de la noche / el avión / aterrizar

    _____

Actividad 7 **Mientras estábamos de vacaciones…** Durante las vacaciones de invierno pasaron muchas cosas. Escriba las oraciones usando el imperfecto para dar información de fondo (*background*) y el pretérito para hablar de algunas cosas que sucedieron. Siga el modelo.

> MODELO nosotros / estar de vacaciones / yo / leer cinco libros
> Mientras estábamos de vacaciones, yo leí cinco libros.

1. tú / viajar / acabar / la telenovela

   _____

2. Marta y Miguel / quedarse en un hotel / un ladrón / forzar una entrada (*to break in*)

   _____

3. Estefanía / vivir / en el extranjero / sus padres / vender su casa de campo

   _____

4. Uds. / hacer un viaje / sus vecinos / montar una nueva empresa

   _____

5. yo / ver / las siete maravillas del mundo / otras siete / añadirse a la lista

   _____

6. Benito / trabajar en San Antonio / su novia / romper con él

   _____

7. el avión de Diego / aterrizar en Los Ángeles / el de su hermana / despegar en Atlanta

   _____

8. los turistas / conocer los Estados Unidos / la guerra / estallar en su país

   _____

9. nosotros / estar en el puerto / haber / un incendio en el barco

   _____

10. vosotros / caminar al cibercafé / yo / alcanzaros

_____

11. Laura y yo / platicar / mi teléfono celular / sonar

_____

12. tú / leer / nosotros / enviar el correo electrónico

_____

Actividad 8 **Y al mismo tiempo…** Escriba las cosas que hacían las personas al mismo tiempo usando el imperfecto. Use las actividades de la siguiente lista o invente otras. Siga el modelo.

> MODELO Sara escribía mensajes de correo electrónico mientras Teresa dibujaba.

arreglarse	divertirse	ir de compras	salir
caminar	ensayar	jugar	tocar
cocinar	escribir	leer	tomar
comer	esperar el tren	navegar en la Red	trabajar
dibujar	estudiar	practicar	ver una película

1. _____
2. _____
3. _____
4. _____
5. _____
6. _____
7. _____
8. _____
9. _____
10. _____

Actividad 9 **Perspectivas.** Gabriela Godoy recuerda la primera vez que sus padres la llevaron a una ópera. Seleccione el imperfecto o el pretérito de los verbos para completar su historia.

Cuando yo (tenía/tuve) _____ once años, mis padres

me (llevaban/llevaron) _____ por primera vez a ver

una ópera. La acomodadora[1] nos (sentaba/sentó) _____

y nos (daba/dio) _____ el programa. Mientras

(leíamos/leímos) _____ las notas sobre la obra, las

[1]_usher_

luces (se apagaban/se apagaron) _____. Luego
                                                      6
(subía/subió) _____ el telón[2] y (veíamos/vimos)
                            7
_____ la escena. (Había/Hubo)
                  8
_____ un decorado[3] de palacio. Una cantante que
                  9
(hacía/hizo) _____ el papel de la reina (estaba/estuvo)
                          10
_____ sentada en el trono. Ella (llevaba/llevó)
                  11
_____ una corona[4] de oro y (vestía/vistió)
                  12
_____ una capa de terciopelo[5] verde con armiño.[6] El
                  13
cantante que (hacía/hizo) _____ el papel del rey
                                      14
(salía/salió) _____ a la escena y (se ponía/se puso)
                          15
_____ a cantar. Yo (quedaba/quedé)
                  16
_____ tan impresionada con lo que vi y oí que
                  17
(me hacía/me hice) _____ aficionada a la ópera para
                                  18
siempre.

[2]*curtain*   [3]*set*   [4]*crown*   [5]*velvet*   [6]*ermine*

Actividad 10   **La vida de un periodista.** Carlos Vega habla de su carrera y de su vida.
Seleccione el imperfecto o el pretérito de los verbos para completar su
historia.

Hace ocho años (me graduaba/me gradué) _____ en
                                                            1
la Facultad de comunicaciones. (Sacaba/Saqué) _____
                                                                  2
mi título en periodismo. (Esperaba/Esperé) _____
                                                      3
encontrar trabajo en uno de los periódicos grandes de la ciudad donde
(nacía/nací) _____. (Quería/Quise)
                          4
_____ quedarme en Texas porque mis padres y mis
                  5
hermanos vivían allí. Por desgracia, no (había/hubo)
_____ empleo en ningún periódico del estado. Por lo
                  6
tanto, yo (mandaba/mandé) _____ mi currículum[1] a
                                        7
varios periódicos por todo el país. (Tenía/Tuve) _____
                                                              8
suerte. (Encontraba/Encontré) _____ trabajo de
                                            9
reportero en un periódico que (se publicaba/se publicó)
_____ en Maine. Al principio la vida en Maine me
                  10

[1]*résumé*

(era/fue) _____ muy difícil. Yo no (conocía/conocí)
₁₁

_____ a nadie donde (vivía/viví)
₁₂

_____ y no (estaba/estuve)
₁₃

_____ acostumbrado al clima.[2] ¡(Hacía/Hizo)
₁₄

_____ un frío horrible en invierno! Pero un día yo
₁₅

(conocía/conocí) _____ a Juana quien (trabajaba/
₁₆

trabajó) _____ en el periódico también. Ella (era/fue)
₁₇

_____ editora. ¡Y (era/fue)
₁₈

_____ un flechazo![3] En fin, Juana y yo (nos
₁₉

casábamos/nos casamos) _____. Yo (llegaba/llegué)
₂₀

_____ a ser jefe de redacción[4] del periódico. Juana y
₂₁

yo (teníamos/tuvimos) _____ dos hijos. ¡Y todos
₂₂

(vivíamos/vivimos) _____ muy felices![5]
₂₃

[2]*weather*   [3]*¡Y... And it was love at first sight!*   [4]*jefe... editor-in-chief*
[5]*¡Y... And we all lived happily ever after!*

Actividad 11 **Contrastes.** Exprese las siguientes ideas en español. Los contrastes surgen de la diferencia entre el imperfecto y el pretérito.

1. Bárbara thought Tomás knew her sister Luz.

   _____

   He met Luz last night at dinner.

   _____

2. The businessmen wanted to discuss the report.

   _____

   But their lawyers refused to.

   _____

3. The bride **(la novia)** didn't have any gifts.

   _____

   Then she got twenty gifts this morning.

   _____

4. We didn't know who had the documents.

   _____

   We found out yesterday.

   _____

5. I wasn't able to assemble **(armar)** the toy.

_____

Javier (tried but) couldn't assemble it either.

_____

Actividad 12 **Castillos de España.** Describa una visita a un castillo español completando las oraciones con la forma correcta del verbo indicado. Escoja entre el pretérito y el imperfecto.

Yo siempre (querer) _____ visitar un castillo en
                                    1
España. Por eso cuando mi esposo y yo (ir) _____ a
                                                               2
hacer un viaje en mayo, yo le (decir) _____ a Rolando
                                                     3
que me (interesar) _____ visitar un castillo español.
                                 4
A Rolando le (gustar) _____ la idea porque no
                                      5
(conocer) _____ España. Rolando (comprar)
                        6
_____ los billetes electrónicos y también (hacer)
              7
_____ la reservación para el hotel. Nosotros (pensar)
              8
_____ hacer una gira[1] de tres semanas con visitas a
              9
Madrid, Toledo, Sevilla, Segovia y Santiago de Compostela. Nosotros (tomar)

_____ el avión y (llegar) _____
              10   11
a Madrid el tres de mayo. Durante las tres semanas nosotros (visitar)

_____ varios lugares históricos y naturalmente
              12
(conocer) _____ el Palacio Real[2] en Madrid, el alcázar[3]
                        13
de Sevilla, Segovia y Toledo y otros castillos y palacios. Al llegar a Santiago de

Compostela yo (tener) _____ una gran sorpresa. En
                                          14
vez de simplemente visitar un castillo, nosotros (poder)

_____ quedarnos en uno por tres días. El famoso
              15
castillo (ser) _____ un parador.[4] Los paradores, es
                            16
decir, hoteles patrocinados[5] por el gobierno español, (estar)

_____ por todas partes del país. ¡Por fin yo (realizar)
              17
_____ mi sueño de visitar un castillo en España!
              18

[1]_tour, excursion_   [2]_Royal_   [3]_fortress_   [4]_state-run hotel housed in a historic building (Sp.)_
[5]_sponsored_

Actividad 13 **Del diario de un detective.** Aquí tiene Ud. una página de la libreta (*notebook*) de apuntes del famoso detective privado Samuel Espada. Para poder leer los apuntes e intentar desenredar (*unravel*) el misterio, complete las oraciones usando el imperfecto o el pretérito de los verbos indicados.

Vocabulario

El crimen

el/la chantajista *blackmailer*
la cita *appointment*
el/la detective privado/a *private detective*
el ladrón / la ladrona *thief*
maltés/maltesa *Maltese*

la pandilla *gang*
la policía *police*
el rescate *ransom*
seguir la pista *to follow the lead*
sobresaltado/a *startled*

(Ser) _____ las diez de la mañana cuando (sonar)

_____ el teléfono en mi oficina. Yo (estar)

_____ despierto desde la noche anterior. Yo (descolgar)

_____ y (oír) _____ la voz

sobresaltada de una mujer. La mujer me (decir) _____

que una pandilla de ladrones le (robar) _____ su

estatuilla[1] del halcón[2] maltés y que ahora le (pedir)

_____ un rescate por el halcón. Además, la señorita

me (explicar) _____ que (tener)

_____ miedo de ir a la policía. Ella y yo (quedar)

_____ en vernos en el vestíbulo[3] del Hotel Casablanca.

Ya (ser) _____ las siete de la tarde cuando yo (llegar)

_____ al hotel. Toda la tarde yo (seguir)

_____ la pista de los chantajistas hasta que (llegar)

_____ la hora de la cita. En el vestíbulo yo (ver)

_____ a una señorita guapísima que (estar)

_____ sentada en un sofá. Ella (tener)

_____ el pelo castaño y largo, los ojos verdes como

dos esmeraldas[4] y (llevar) _____ una gardenia en la

chaqueta. Yo me (acercar) _____ y me (sentar)

_____ a su lado. Ella (oler)

_____ a un perfume exótico. Yo le (hablar)

[1]*figurine* [2]*falcon* [3]*lobby* [4]*emeralds*

_____ primero. «¿Es Ud. la señorita María Aster?»,

23

le (preguntar) _____ . Ella se (poner)

24

_____ a llorar y me (decir)

25

_____ sollozando:[5] «Samuel, es que tú no

26

comprendes.» Pero sí, yo (comprender) _____ muy

27

bien. ¡Esto (ir) _____ a ser otro dramón[6]!

28

[5]_sobbing_ [6]_sob story_

Imperfect with expressions of time

Remember that the Spanish construction **hace** + _expression of time_ + **que** + _verb in the present tense_ is used to label an action that began in the past and is continuing in the present. Similarly, the construction **hacía** + _expression of time_ + **que** + _verb in the imperfect tense_ is used to label an action that was continuing in the past when something else happened. The corresponding question is **¿Cuánto tiempo hacía… ?** The word **tiempo** may be omitted.

¿Cuánto (tiempo) hacía que esperabas cuando llegó el tren?	_How long had you been waiting when the train arrived?_
Hacía más de una hora que esperaba.	_I had been waiting more than an hour._

A _verb in the imperfect tense_ + **desde hacía** + _expression of time_ is also used to label an action that was continuing in the past when something else happened.

¿Desde cuándo rodaban la película cuando ocurrió el terremoto?	_How long had they been shooting the film when the earthquake happened?_
Rodaban la película **desde hacía dos días** cuando **hubo** un terremoto.	_They had been shooting the film for two days when there was an earthquake._

Actividad 14 ¿Cuánto tiempo hacía que… ? Haga preguntas usando **¿Cuánto tiempo hacía que… ?** y contéstelas usando la construcción **hacía** + _expresión de tiempo_ + **que** + _verbo en el imperfecto._ Siga el modelo.

> MODELO Leonor / estudiar inglés / salir para Inglaterra (dos años)
> ¿Cuánto tiempo hacía que Leonor estudiaba inglés cuando salió para Inglaterra?
> Hacía dos años que estudiaba inglés.

1. Montserrat Pujol / cantar ópera / firmar un contrato con la Metropolitana (ocho años)

_____

_____

_____

2. los señores Salazar / estar casados / su hija / nacer (cuatro años)

_____

_____

3. tú / vivir en Filadelfia / tus padres / mudarse a Londres (once meses)

_____

_____

4. Susana y Lía / ser amigas / Susana / quitarle el novio a Lía (doce años)

_____

_____

5. Ud. / comprar billetes de lotería / ganar el premio (quince años)

_____

_____

6. Patricio y Ud. / tocar el violonchelo / el conservatorio / darles una beca (nueve años)

_____

_____

_____

Actividad 15 **Cambios políticos y económicos.** Hubo algunos cambios en la vida política y económica del un país latinoamericano en este ejercicio. Escriba las oraciones con la construcción *verbo en imperfecto* + **desde hacía** + *expresión de tiempo* para describir los cambios. Junte las dos frases con **hasta que.** Siga el modelo.

> MODELO el gobierno / prometer muchas cosas / dos años /
> los ciudadanos / empezar a reclamar
> El gobierno prometía muchas cosas desde hacía dos años hasta que los ciudadanos empezaron a reclamar.

Política y economía

los bienes *goods*
controlar la inflación *to control inflation*
la década *decade*
el dictador *dictator*
el/la economista *economist*
establecer la democracia *to establish democracy*
explotar el petróleo *to drill for, develop oil*
el gobierno *government*
el golpe de estado *coup d'état*

intentar *to try, attempt*
la libertad *liberty*
el libre mercado *free market*
el/la obrero/a *worker*
la prensa *press*
el/la presidente/a *president*
privatizar la industria *to privatize industry*
el pueblo *the people*
reclamar *to demand*
el sindicato *union*
el sueldo *salary*

1. el gobierno / explotar el petróleo / treinta años / el presidente / privatizar la industria

   _____

   _____

   _____

2. la gente / sufrir por la inflación / cinco años / los economistas / intentar controlarla

   _____

   _____

   _____

3. la prensa / no ser libre / cincuenta años / haber / un golpe de estado

   _____

   _____

   _____

4. los obreros / no recibir un sueldo decente / cinco décadas / formarse los sindicatos

   _____

   _____

   _____

5. el país / no producir los bienes necesarios / varios años / el gobierno establecer el libre mercado

   _____

   _____

   _____

6. el pueblo / no tener ninguna libertad / cuarenta y cinco años / morir el dictador y establecerse la democracia

_____

_____

_____

Actividad 16 **¿Qué dice Ud.?** Conteste las siguientes preguntas personales.

1. ¿Cuántos años tenía cuando comenzó a vestirse solo/a?

_____

2. ¿Cuántos años tenía cuando empezó a estudiar en el colegio?

_____

3. Cuando era niño/a, ¿adónde iba de vacaciones?

_____

4. ¿Qué le gustaba hacer cuando era niño/a?

_____

5. ¿Cómo era de niño/a?

_____

6. Hable Ud. de las cosas que solía hacer todos los días cuando asistía al colegio.

_____

7. ¿Qué sueños quería realizar en la vida?

_____

8. ¿Pudo realizar algunos ya?

_____

Actividad 17 **Un viaje a México.** Exprese esta historia en español. Escoja entre el pretérito y el imperfecto para hablar del pasado.

1. The first day Beatriz and I spent in Mexico City, we went to Chapultepec Park.

_____

2. The weather was beautiful. It was sunny and warm.

_____

3. There were many people in the park.

_____

4. Children were playing on the slides **(los resbalines)** and riding their bicycles.

_____

5. As we walked through the park, we saw Moctezuma's Tree and Chapultepec Castle.

_____

6. We arrived at the National Museum of Anthropology and went in.

_____

7. We walked from room to room and saw the exhibit of pre-Columbian **(precolombino)** art.

_____

8. We spent two hours in the museum.

_____

9. Then we went to the bookstore where I bought a book about the Aztecs and the Mayas.

_____

10. We had lunch in the museum cafeteria.

_____

11. It was five o'clock when we left the museum.

_____

12. We weren't in a hurry because we were on vacation.

_____

13. That evening our Mexican friends took us to the Palacio de Bellas Artes.

_____

Actividad 18 **Actividad oral.** Prepare una lista de algunas actividades que Ud. hacía cuando era niño/a. Luego pregúnteles a sus compañeros de clase si ellos también hacían esas actividades. Algunas posibilidades:

Jugaba al fútbol.
Navegaba en la Red.
Me divertía en el parque de atracciones.
Pasaba los veranos en un campamento.
Cocinaba con mi mamá o papá.

Tocaba un instrumento musical.
Montaba en bicicleta.
Buceaba en el mar.
Iba al centro comercial.

FUTURE AND CONDITIONAL TENSES

Forms of the future

The future tense is one of several forms that Spanish uses to refer to future time. The future tense is formed by adding a special set of endings to the infinitive. These endings of the future tense are the same for all verbs in Spanish.

FIRMAR *to sign*		CORRER *to run*	
firmar**é**	firmar**emos**	correr**é**	correr**emos**
firmar**ás**	firmar**éis**	correr**ás**	correr**éis**
firmar**á**	firmar**án**	correr**á**	correr**án**

ASISTIR *to attend*	
asistir**é**	asistir**emos**
asistir**ás**	asistir**éis**
asistir**á**	asistir**án**

A small number of Spanish verbs uses a modified form of the infinitive in the future tense, thus creating an irregular future stem. For example, some verbs replace the vowel **-e** or **-i** before the **-r** of the infinitive with **-d.**

poner → **pondré**	tener → **tendré**	venir → **vendré**
salir → **saldré**	valer → **valdré**	

Some verbs drop the vowel **-e** before the **-r** of the infinitive in the future tense.

caber → **cabré**	poder → **podré**	saber → **sabré**
haber → **habré**	querer → **querré**	

Two verbs shorten the infinitive.

decir → **diré**   hacer → **haré**

-Ir verbs that have an accent mark in the infinitive drop the accent mark in the future.

oír → **oiré**	reír → **reiré**	sonreír → **sonreiré**

The future of **hay** is **habrá** (*there will be*).

Compounds of the verbs with irregular future stems have the same irregularities.

componer → **compondré**	prevenir → **prevendré**	satisfacer → **satisfaré**
contradecir → **contradiré**	retener → **retendré**	

Uses of the future

The future tense is used in Spanish and English to express future time.

¿A qué hora **llegarán Uds.**?   *At what time **will you arrive?***
Estaremos para las tres.   *We'll be there by three o'clock.*

The future tense in Spanish is often replaced by the **ir a** + *infinitive* construction. This commonly used construction refers to the immediate future, whereas the future tense refers to both the immediate and the remote future.

Esquiaré en los Pirineos.   *I'll ski in the Pyrenees.*
Voy a esquiar en los Pirineos.   *I'm going to ski in the Pyrenees.*

The future tense is often replaced by the simple present tense when there is another element of the sentence that indicates future time.

Llamo **el jueves.**   *I'll call on Thursday.*

Note that Spanish uses the present tense to ask for instructions where English uses *shall* or *should.*

¿**Doblo** aquí?   *Shall (Should) I turn here?*
¿Los **invitamos** o no?   *Shall (Should) we invite them or not?*

The future tense is commonly used in the main clause of a conditional sentence when the dependent **si** clause (*if* clause) has the verb in the present tense.

Si Juana **va,** yo **iré** también.   *If Juana goes, I'll go, too.*

NOTA

- The order of the clauses can be reversed with the **si** clause following the main clause.

  Yo **iré si** Juana **va.**

Actividad 1 **Mis planes para el futuro.** Cambie los verbos del presente al futuro en las oraciones para saber lo que hará Daniel después de graduarse. Siga el modelo.

> MODELO Trabajo en una oficina.
> Trabajaré en una oficina.

1. Me gradúo en junio.
   me graduaré

2. Mis amigos y yo celebramos con una fiesta.
   celebraremos

3. Nuestros padres están muy contentos.
   estarán

4. Yo hago un viaje a Europa en el verano.
   haré

5. Miguel me acompaña.
   me acompañará

6. Nos encanta el viaje.
   nos encantará

7. Vamos a los países de la Europa oriental.
   iremos

8. Andrés y Manuel quieren ir también.
   querrán

9. Salimos para Polonia a mediados de junio.
   saldremos

10. Pasamos dos meses viajando.
    pararemos

11. Andrés vuelve antes porque tiene que buscar empleo.
    volverán

12. Al regresar yo empiezo a trabajar en una compañía multinacional.
    empezaré

13. Miguel puede trabajar en la empresa de sus padres.
    podrá

14. Manuel sigue con sus clases en la Facultad de ingeniería.
    seguirá

15. ¡Tenemos tiempo de vernos, espero!

tendremos

Actividad 2 | **¡Qué reacciones!** ¿Cómo reaccionarán estas personas al oír las noticias que Ud. tiene? Escriba sus reacciones usando el futuro de los verbos. Siga el modelo.

> MODELO   Luisa / sonreír
> Luisa sonreirá.

1. Mari Carmen / llorar

   llorará

2. las tías / decir «¡ay de mí!»

   dirán

3. Ramón / tener vergüenza

   tendrá

4. tú / volverse loco

   te voldrás

5. Juan y Alicia / poner el grito en el cielo (*scream bloody murder*)

   pondrán

6. Uds. / enfadarse

   se enfadarán

7. vosotros / reírse a carcajadas

   se veiréis

8. Ud. / ponerse de buen humor

   se pondrá

9. nosotros / estar contento

   estaremos

Actividad 3 | **¡Qué día!** Mañana será un día sumamente ajetreado (*hectic*), con muchas ocupaciones para Ud. Diga lo que pasará, escribiendo los verbos en el futuro. Siga el modelo.

> MODELO   Estudiamos todo el día.
> Estudiaremos todo el día.

1. ¡Mañana es un ajetreo continuo (*hustle and bustle*)!

   continuará

2. ¡Tenemos un día lleno de frenética actividad!

Tendremos

3. Hay clases todo el día.

habrá

4. Tomamos exámenes también.

tomaremos

5. Además, yo voy al almacén.

iré

6. Le compro un regalo a mi hermana.

compraré

7. Sarita cumple diecisiete años mañana.

cumplirá

8. Mamá hace una comida y una torta.

hará

9. Papá y yo salimos para comprar vino.

saldremos

10. También quiero terminar mi informe.

querré

11. Mis amigos y yo trabajamos hasta muy tarde.

trabajaremos

12. Trasnochamos (*We go to bed very late*) porque tenemos exámenes pasado mañana.

Trasnocharemos

Actividad 4   **Actividad y descanso.** Ud. y sus amigos se dedicarán a ciertas cosas durante las vacaciones de invierno. Diga lo que piensan hacer, escribiendo los verbos en el futuro. Siga el modelo.

> MODELO   Felipe / escuchar CDs todo el día
> • Felipe escuchará CDs todo el día.

1. Yolanda y Ana / patinar en la pista universitaria

patinarán

2. tú / salir a la sierra para esquiar

saldrás

3. Julio / bailar en la discoteca toda la noche

   _____ *bailará* _____

4. Consuelo / querer alquilar vídeos

   _____ *querré* _____

5. yo / venir al cibercafé todas las tardes

   _____ *vendré* _____

6. vosotros / conocer el nuevo centro comercial

   _____ *conoceréis* _____

7. nosotros / hacer una fiesta

   _____ *haremos* _____

8. Ud. / poder dormir hasta las 11:00 de la mañana

   _____ *podrá* _____

Actividad 5 **Todo depende.** Ciertas cosas pasarán si pasan otras cosas. Para expresar esta idea escriba oraciones que tienen una cláusula con **si** con el verbo en el presente y otra cláusula principal con el verbo en el futuro. Siga el modelo.

> MODELO   tú / estudiar en la biblioteca / yo / trabajar allí también
> Si tú estudias en la biblioteca, yo trabajaré allí también.

1. María / querer salir / nosotros / salir con ella

   _____ *quiere* _____ *saldremos* _____

2. ellos / venir / Ud. / poder verlos

   _____ *vienen* _____ *podrá* _____

3. yo / hacer la comida / tú / venir a almorzar

   _____ *ha* _____ *vendrás* _____

4. Uds. / trabajar mucho / tener éxito

   Si Uds trabajan mucho, tendrán éxito

5. tú / no saber qué pasó / yo / decirte

   _____ *sabes* _____ *te diré* _____

6. vosotros / comprar los billetes en Internet / ahorrar mucho dinero

   _____ *compráis* _____ *ahorraréis* _____

7. hacer calor / Carlos y Pedro / ir a la playa

   _____ *Hace* _____ *irán* _____

8. llover / Celeste / querer ir al cine

   _____ *llove* _____ *querrá* _____

Expressing probability or conjecture with the future

The future tense in Spanish is also used to express probability or conjecture in the present. The English equivalents of the future of probability (*I wonder, it's probably, it might*) are usually very unlike the Spanish structures.

¿Qué hora es?	*What time is it?*
Serán las ocho.	*It's probably eight o'clock.*
¿Quién tendrá las llaves?	*I wonder who has the keys.*
Las **tendrá** Mario.	*Mario probably has them.*

Context determines whether a verb in the future tense refers to the future or to a probability in the present. For example, **¿Quién llamará?** means *Who will call?* as well as *I wonder who's calling.*

Deber de + *infinitive* is also used to express probability in the present. For example, **Deben de ser las diez** means the same thing as **Serán las diez.**

Actividad 6 **¿Qué será?** Su amiga no está segura de varias cosas. Ud. tampoco está seguro/a y por cada cosa expresa probabilidad o conjetura. Escriba los verbos en el futuro quitando la palabra o las palabras que indican probabilidad. Siga el modelo.

> MODELO   Probablemente los Hidalgo están en casa.
> Los Hidalgo estarán en casa.

1. Probablemente son las seis.

   Serán

2. ~~Me imagino que~~ Teodoro tiene catorce años.

   tendrá

3. ~~Supongo que~~ el reloj vale mucho.

   Valdrá

4. Probablemente hay problemas entre los socios.

   Habrá

5. Supongo que Teresa sabe la hora de la conferencia.

   Sabrá

6. Me imagino que Lola quiere ir a la reunión.

   querrá

7. Supongo que las muchachas vuelven pronto.

   ~~volvd~~ *volvrán*

Actividad 7 **¿Qué habrá en esa caja?** Ud. y sus amigos vieron a Juan Pedro llevando una caja enorme. Todos se mueren por saber lo que hay adentro. Uds. hacen conjeturas (*guesses*) sobre el contenido usando el futuro de probabilidad. Siga los modelos.

> MODELOS It's probably big.
> Será grande.
> I wonder if it's beautiful.
> ¿Será hermoso?

1. I wonder if it's green?
   Será verde

2. It probably has batteries.
   Tendrá

3. I wonder if there are many parts?
   Serán mucha

4. Do you think it's made of wood **(madera)**?
   estará hecho

5. Could it cost a lot?
   Costará mucho / valdrá

6. It probably makes noise.
   Hará ruido

7. It must be very big.
   Será grande

8. Could everybody have one?
   Todos lo tendrán / ~~tendrán un~~ podrán tener uno

9. I wonder if it's alive.
   ~~será~~ estará vivo

10. It probably fits in your hand.
    Cabrá en su mano

Forms of the conditional

The conditional tense (*would,* in English) expresses what might happen or what would happen if certain conditions existed. Spanish forms the conditional by adding a special set of endings to the infinitive. These endings of the conditional tense are the same for all verbs in Spanish.

COBRAR *to charge*		ENTENDER *to understand*		RECIBIR *to receive, get*	
cobra**ría**	cobra**ríamos**	entende**ría**	entende**ríamos**	recibi**ría**	recibi**ríamos**
cobra**rías**	cobra**ríais**	entende**rías**	entende**ríais**	recibi**rías**	recibi**ríais**
cobra**ría**	cobra**rían**	entende**ría**	entende**rían**	recibi**ría**	recibi**rían**

NOTA

- When *would* means *used to*, the imperfect tense rather than the conditional is used.

Cuando yo era niño, mi familia y yo **íbamos** al campo todos los veranos.	*When I was a child, my family and I **would go** to the country every summer.*

The verbs that have modified infinitives in the future tense have the same changes in the conditional tense.

caber → **cabría**	poder → **podría**	salir → **saldría**
decir → **diría**	poner → **pondría**	tener → **tendría**
haber → **habría**	querer → **querría**	valer → **valdría**
hacer → **haría**	saber → **sabría**	venir → **vendría**

The conditional of **hay** is **habría** (*there would be*).

Compounds of verbs with irregular future stems have the same irregularities in the conditional.

componer → **compondría**	prevenir → **prevendría**	satisfacer → **satisfaría**
contradecir → **contradiría**	retener → **retendría**	

Uses of the conditional

The conditional tense is commonly used in subordinate (dependent) clauses after main verbs of communication **(decir)** and knowledge or belief **(saber, creer)** when the main verb is in the past tense. There is a similar correspondence of tenses in Spanish and English: *present/future* and *past/conditional*.

Juan **dice** que **irá**.	*Juan says he will go.*
Juan **dijo** que **iría**.	*Juan said he would go.*

Sé que **llamarán**.	*I know they will call.*
Sabía que **llamarían**.	*I knew they would call.*

The conditional tense in Spanish is also used to express probability or conjecture in past time. The verbs most commonly used to express probability with the conditional are **ser, haber, tener,** and **estar.**

Sería la una.	*It was probably one o'clock.*
Habría algunas dificultades.	*There were probably some difficulties.*
El niño **tendría** nueve años.	*The boy was probably nine years old.*
¡Qué desilusionados **estarían** los aficionados!	*The fans were probably so disappointed.*
El coche **costaría** un dineral.	*The car probably cost a fortune.*

Context will determine whether a verb in the conditional tense refers to the conditional or to probability in past time. For example, **Serían las tres** means *It would be three o'clock* as well as *It was probably three o'clock.*

Deber de in the imperfect + *infinitive* may be used to express probability in past time. For example, **Debían de ser las diez** means the same thing as **Serían las diez.**

The conditional tense is used in contrary-to-fact sentences where the dependent **si** clause is expressed in the imperfect subjunctive and the main clause is expressed in the conditional. This pattern is practiced in greater depth in **Capítulo 12.**

Si Elena **saliera,** yo **saldría** también.   *If Elena were to leave, I'd leave, too.*

Actividad 8   **Y Ud., ¿qué haría?** ¿Qué harían las personas en cada una de las siguientes situaciones? Escriba los verbos usando el condicional. Siga el modelo.

> MODELO   Estás en la clase de historia. La profesora hace preguntas.
> ¿Qué harías?
>   **a.** contestar
>   Yo contestaría.
>   **b.** cambiar el tema
>   Yo cambiaría el tema.

1. Ud. está en un almacén y busca los abrigos, pero no puede encontrarlos. ¿Qué haría?

   a. hablar con la dependienta

   _____

   b. ir a otro almacén

   _____

2. Carolina cena en casa de los Cela. Le encanta el arroz con pollo. ¿Qué haría?

   a. repetir (*to have a second helping*)

   _____

   b. pedir la receta

   _____

3. Estamos en el metro. Un pasajero grita «¡fuego!». ¿Qué haríamos?

   a. salir corriendo

   _____

   b. llamar a los bomberos

   _____

4. Osvaldo está en el teatro. Mientras busca su asiento le pisa el pie a una señora. ¿Qué haría?

   a. disculparse con la señora

   _____

   b. sentarse en su regazo (*lap*)

   _____

5. La madre quiere bañar a sus hijos, pero no hay agua caliente. ¿Qué haría?

   a. acostarlos sin bañarlos

   _____

   b. llamar al fontanero (*plumber*)

   _____

6. Hay un choque de coches no muy serio. Ud. es testigo del accidente. ¿Qué haría?

   a. decirle al policía lo que pasó

   _____

   b. ponerles vendas (*bandages*) a los heridos

   _____

Actividad 9 **¡Qué bonanza!** Ud. y sus amigos acaban de comprar un billete para la lotería que esta semana llegó a veinte millones de dólares. ¿Qué harían Uds. con veinte millones de dólares? Escriba algunas ideas empleando el condicional. Siga el modelo.

> MODELO   yo / comprar un chalet (*country house*)
> Yo compraría un chalet.

1. Ud. / pagar la matrícula en la universidad

   _____

2. mi prima Celia / venir de Australia a visitarnos

   _____

3. Uds. / hacer un viaje a Barcelona

_____ *harían* _____

4. Juan Pablo y Ana María / poner el dinero en el banco

_____ *pondrían* _____

5. tú / ya / no tener deudas (*debts*)

_____ *tendrías* _____

6. mi hermano y yo / querer donar dinero a las caridades

_____ *querríamos* _____

7. nosotros / jugar a la Bolsa (*stock market*)

_____

8. vosotros / salir a comer en los restaurantes más caros

_____ *saldríais* _____

Actividad 10 **¿Qué dijeron?** Dígale a un amigo lo que cada persona prometió hacer para ayudar con los preparativos para una fiesta este fin de semana. Complete las oraciones usando el condicional de los verbos indicados en las cláusulas subordinadas. Siga el modelo.

> MODELO Pedro me dijo que (llamar) <u>llamaría</u> a los invitados.

1. Victoria nos dijo que le (gustar) _____ *ya gustaría* _____ tener una fiesta en su casa.

2. Pablo le preguntó a Victoria si ella (querer) _____ *querría* _____ planearla para el sábado.

3. Victoria nos aseguró que no (haber) _____ *habría* _____ problema con ese día.

4. Isabel quería saber lo que nosotros (poder) _____ *podríamos* _____ traer.

5. Victoria nos dejó saber que su mamá se (ocupar)

_____ *ocuparía* _____ de la comida.

6. José y yo le dijimos que (hacer) _____ *haríamos* _____ galletas y pasteles para la fiesta.

7. Marta y Carlos dijeron que (poner) _____ *pondrían* _____ la mesa antes de la fiesta.

8. Todos le prometimos a Victoria que (venir) _____ *vendrían* _____ muy temprano para ayudarla con los preparativos.

Actividad 11 **Probabilidad en el pasado.** Exprese probabilidad o conjetura en el pasado al contestar las preguntas de su amiga. Escriba los verbos usando el condicional. Siga el modelo.

> MODELO ¿Cuántos años tenía el primo de Fernando? (quince años)
> Tendría quince años.

1. ¿Qué hora era cuando Uds. volvieron a casa? (las once)

   Serían las once

2. ¿Cuántos invitados había en la fiesta? (sesenta)

   Habría sesenta

3. ¿Cómo estaban tus padres después del viaje? (cansados)

   estarían cansados

4. ¿Cuánto costaba aquel carro? (30 mil dólares)

   costaría 30 mil dólares

5. ¿Cómo eran los nuevos vecinos? (simpáticos)

   Serían simpáticas

6. ¿Dónde estaba Elena cuando fuiste a su casa? (la librería)

   estaría / en librería

Actividad 12 **Al contrario.** Si ciertas personas fueran (*were going*) a la fiesta, algunas cosas pasarían. Para saber qué pasaría, escriba los verbos indicados usando el condicional. Las formas del verbo **ir** aparecen aquí en el imperfecto de subjuntivo. Siga el modelo.

> MODELO Si fuera Matilde a la fiesta, Guillermo (ir) <u>iría</u> también.

1. Si fueran los Bello, nosotros (estar) _estaríamos_ contentos.

2. Si fueran Uds., yo (poder) _~~pered~~ podría_ llevarlos.

3. Si fuera Catalina, Tomás (querer) _querría_ bailar con ella.

4. Si fuéramos todos nosotros, los Herrera no (caber)

   cabrían en el coche.

5. Si fuera Ud., (venir) _vendría_ conmigo.

6. Si fueras, te (poner) _pondrías_ un esmoquin (*tuxedo*).

7. Si fueran todos los invitados, no (haber) _habría_ lugar en la pista de baile (*dance floor*).

Actividad 13 | **Gustos e intereses.** Use el condicional para expresar lo que le gustaría hacer y lo que a otros les gustaría hacer. Use los verbos **encantar, gustar, interesar, preferir** y **querer**.

1. I'd like to . . .

   _____

2. My parents would prefer to . . .

   _____

3. My sister would want to . . .

   _____

4. My friend _____ would love to . . .

   _____

5. My friend _____ would be interested in . . .

   _____

6. My brother would like to . . .

   _____

7. I'd love to . . .

   _____

8. Our teachers would prefer to . . .

   _____

9. My classmates would be interested in . . .

   _____

10. My family would want to . . .

    _____

Actividad 14 | **Actividad oral.** Con un compañero / una compañera de clase, haga un diálogo que tiene lugar en una oficina de la compañía donde Uds. trabajan. Uno de Uds. es el jefe y el otro es director de marketing. El director le hace preguntas al jefe sobre el viaje de negocios que va a hacer. El jefe contesta sus preguntas. Use el futuro y el condicional lo más posible. Por ejemplo:

Director:	¿Adónde iré primero? Me gustaría hacer los preparativos para el viaje lo antes posible.
Jefe:	Bueno, primero visitará la oficina en Madrid. Luego hará el viaje a Barcelona.
Director:	Tendré que comprar los billetes electrónicos. ¿Cuánto costarán?
Jefe:	Se lo podrían calcular en contabilidad (*accounting*). Ahora, en cuanto al itinerario...

Past participle and perfect tenses

Formation of the past participle

Most past participles are regular in Spanish. In **-ar** verbs, the **-ar** of the infinitive changes to **-ado:**

envi**ar**	envi**ado**	*sent*
habl**ar**	habl**ado**	*spoken*

In **-er** and **-ir** verbs, the **-er** and **-ir** of the infinitive change to **-ido:**

com**er**	com**ido**	*eaten*
viv**ir**	viv**ido**	*lived*

In **-er** and **-ir** verbs whose stems end in a vowel such as **caer, leer,** and **oír,** an accent mark is added over the **i** of the past participle ending **-ido.**

ca**er**	ca**ído**	*fallen*
cre**er**	cre**ído**	*believed*
le**er**	le**ído**	*read*
o**ír**	o**ído**	*heard*
pose**er**	pose**ído**	*possessed*
tra**er**	tra**ído**	*brought*

The following verbs have irregular past participles.

abrir	**abierto**	*opened*
cubrir	**cubierto**	*covered*
decir	**dicho**	*said*
devolver	**devuelto**	*returned*
escribir	**escrito**	*written*
freír*	**frito, freído**	*fried*
hacer	**hecho**	*done*
imprimir	**impreso**	*printed*
morir	**muerto**	*dead*
poner	**puesto**	*put*
resolver	**resuelto**	*resolved, solved*
romper	**roto**	*broken*
ver	**visto**	*seen*
volver	**vuelto**	*returned*

---

*Although both the regular past participle **freído** and the irregular past participle **frito** may be used to form the perfect tenses (**he freído, habíamos frito,** etc.), only **frito** may be used as an adjective (**papas fritas, pollo frito**).

When a prefix is added to any of the preceding verbs, the past participle shows the same irregularities.

componer	**compuesto**	*composed*
descomponer	**descompuesto**	*broken, in disrepair*
describir	**descrito**	*described*
descubrir	**descubierto**	*discovered*
deshacer	**deshecho**	*undone*
imponer	**impuesto**	*imposed*
inscribir	**inscrito**	*registered*
posponer	**pospuesto**	*postponed*
predecir	**predicho**	*predicted*
prever	**previsto**	*foreseen*
proponer	**propuesto**	*proposed, suggested*
rehacer	**rehecho**	*redone*
revolver	**revuelto**	*turned over*
satisfacer	**satisfecho**	*satisfied*

The past participle forms of **ser** and **ir** are **sido** and **ido,** respectively.

Present perfect

The perfect tenses in Spanish are similar to their English equivalents. They consist of a conjugated form of the auxiliary verb **haber** (*to have*) + *past participle*. The past participle does not change to show gender or number in compound tenses.

The present perfect consists of the present tense of the auxiliary verb **haber** + *past participle*. The English equivalent of the present perfect is *to have done something*. This tense is called **el pretérito perfecto** in Spanish.

LLEGAR/COMER/SUBIR	
(yo) **he** llegado/comido/subido	(nosotros/as) **hemos** llegado/comido/subido
(tú) **has** llegado/comido/subido	(vosotros/as) **habéis** llegado/comido/subido
(él/ella/Ud.) **ha** llegado/comido/subido	(ellos/ellas/Uds.) **han** llegado/comido/subido

The present perfect is used in Spanish, as in English, to mark or describe past events that have an influence on the present or that continue into the present.

Ya he visto esa película.	*I've already seen that movie.*
Hemos estado aquí todo el día.	*We've been here all day.*
Juan ha empezado a estudiar para el examen.	*Juan has started studying for the exam.*

NOTA

- The present perfect of **hay** is **ha habido** (*there has/have been*).

In the perfect tenses, no words are placed between the auxiliary verb and the past participle. Object pronouns precede the forms of **haber.** In questions, subject pronouns follow the past participle. They are not placed between the auxiliary verb and the past participle as they are in English.

¿**Lo** has leído?	*Have you read it?* (object pronoun)
¿Qué han visto **Uds.**?	*What have **you** seen?*
¿Todavía no se ha levantado **Ud.**?	*Haven't **you** gotten up yet?*

Actividad 1 **¿Listos para viajar?** Ud. y su familia se van de vacaciones. Antes de salir de la casa tienen que hacer ciertas cosas. Describa quién hizo cada cosa usando el pretérito perfecto. Siga el modelo.

> MODELO papá / comprar / el mapa
> Papá ha comprado el mapa.

Vocabulario

Preparándose para un viaje

el baúl *trunk (car)*
el cheque de viajero *traveler's check*
desenchufar los aparatos eléctricos *to unplug the appliances*
el equipaje *luggage*
hacer las maletas *to pack*

la linterna *flashlight*
llenar el tanque del coche *to fill the tank*
el mapa *map*
la pila *battery (flashlight)*
prepararse *to get ready*
la ventanilla *small window*

1. Pedro / apagar / las luces

   _____

2. Cecilia y Pilar / hacer / las maletas

   _____

3. papá / llenar / el tanque del coche

   _____

4. vosotros / desenchufar / los aparatos eléctricos

   _____

5. Sara y Juan Carlos / meter / el equipaje en el baúl

   _____

6. yo / decirles / a los vecinos / que nos vamos

   _____

7. mamá / poner / pilas en la linterna

   _____

8. Paco y yo / despedirse / de nuestros amigos

   _____

9. tú / limpiar / las ventanillas del coche

   _____

Actividad 2 **Una receta de cocina (*recipe*).** Ud. y unos amigos han preparado un plato especial para servir en la cena. Describa paso a paso lo que han hecho usando el pretérito perfecto. Siga el modelo.

> MODELO Vera / comprar / mariscos
> Vera ha comprado mariscos.

Vocabulario

Una receta de cocina

el aguacate *avocado*
añadir *to add*
la cacerola *saucepan*
la cebolla *onion*
cortar *to cut*
cubrir *to cover*
encender el fuego *to turn on the flame*
la ensalada *salad*

los espárragos *asparagus*
freír *to fry*
picar *to chop*
la pimienta picante *hot pepper*
el pollo *chicken*
poner al horno *to put in the oven*
quemar *to burn*
la sal *salt*
la sartén *frying pan*

1. nosotros / leer / la receta

   _____

2. Jorge / encender / el fuego

   _____

3. yo / hacer / la salsa

   _____

4. Alicia y Juan Diego / picar / las pimientas picantes

   _____

5. Ud. / freír / las cebollas

   _____

6. Estrella y yo / cortar / el pan

   _____

7. tú / lavar / los espárragos y los aguacates

   _____

8. vosotros / añadir / la sal

   _____

9. Uds. / poner / el pollo al horno

   _____

10. yo / mezclar / la ensalada

    _____

11. Martín / cubrir / la cacerola

    _____

12. Lupe y Julio / quemar / las sartenes

    _____

Actividad 3 **Una receta de cocina.** Vuelva a escribir las oraciones de la **Actividad 2,** cambiando el sustantivo por el pronombre de complemento directo correcto. Siga el modelo.

> MODELO   Vera ha comprado **mariscos.**
> Vera **los** ha comprado.

1. _____
2. _____
3. _____
4. _____
5. _____
6. _____
7. _____
8. _____
9. _____
10. _____
11. _____
12. _____

Actividad 4 **¡Nos aburrimos como ostras (*oysters*)! (*We're dying of boredom!*)** Ud. y sus amigos quieren escaparse de una fiesta muy aburrida. Describa lo que Uds. han hecho, cambiando los verbos del tiempo presente al pretérito perfecto. Siga el modelo.

> MODELO   Pablo trata de huir.
> Pablo ha tratado de huir.

1. Vosotros os dormís.

   _____

2. Ud. bosteza.

   _____

3. Yo me pongo el abrigo.

   _____

4. Carlos y Beatriz se despiden de la anfitriona (*hostess*).

   _____

5. ¡Nos matan de aburrimiento!

   _____

6. Tú te quejas que la comida te cayó mal.

_____

7. Ud. y Clara dan excusas.

_____

8. Ramón dice que se enferma.

_____

Actividad 5 **Preguntas personales.** Conteste las preguntas usando el pretérito perfecto.

1. ¿Qué materias ha tomado Ud. este año?

_____

2. ¿Qué notas ha sacado en esas materias?

_____

3. ¿Se ha hecho Ud. socio/a de (*Have you joined*) un club? ¿Del cuál?

_____

4. ¿A qué países ha viajado Ud.?

_____

5. ¿Qué planes han hecho Ud. y sus amigos para el verano?

_____

6. ¿Qué películas ha visto Ud. este año? ¿Cuál le ha gustado más?

_____

7. ¿Cómo ha celebrado Ud. su último cumpleaños?

_____

8. ¿Qué regalos ha recibido? ¿Quién le ha dado cada regalo?

_____

9. ¿Qué cosas han hecho Ud. y sus amigos hoy?

_____

10. ¿Qué libros ha leído Ud. recientemente?

_____

11. ¿Cuál le ha interesado más?

_____

Actividad 6 **Cosa hecha.** Conteste las preguntas usando el pretérito perfecto del verbo reflexivo* en la oración original para explicar que las cosas ya están hechas. Siga el modelo.

> MODELO ¿Cuándo van Uds. a mudarse?
> Nos hemos mudado ya.

1. ¿Cuándo va Cristóbal a matricularse?
   Se ha matriculado

2. ¿Cuándo van Uds. a colocarse (*to get a job*)?
   Se hemos colocado

3. ¿Cuándo vas a instalarte en la nueva casa?
   me he instalado

4. ¿Cuándo van Irene y Jaime a comprometerse (*to get engaged*)?
   se Han comprometido ya

5. ¿Cuándo va Nora a enterarse de los líos (*messes, problems*) de la familia?
   se ha enterado

6. ¿Cuándo vas a apuntarte en la lista de voluntarios?
   me He apuntado

7. ¿Cuándo van los Roldán a divorciarse?
   Se han divorciado ya

Past perfect

The past perfect consists of the imperfect of the auxiliary verb **haber** + *past participle*. The English equivalent of the past perfect is *had done something.* This tense is called **el pluscuamperfecto** in Spanish.

LLEGAR/COMER/SUBIR	
(yo) **había** llegado/comido/subido	(nosotros/as) **habíamos** llegado/comido/subido
(tú) **habías** llegado/comido/subido	(vosotros/as) **habíais** llegado/comido/subido
(él/ella/Ud.) **había** llegado/comido/subido	(ellos/ellas/Uds.) **habían** llegado/comido/subido

The past perfect, or pluperfect tense, designates an event that happened prior to another past event.

Yo ya me había despertado cuando sonó el despertador.	*I had already awakened when the alarm clock went off.*
María ya había ido al teatro cuando Pedro la llamó.	*María had already gone to the theater when Pedro called her.*
Nosotros habíamos vuelto a casa cuando empezó a nevar.	*We had gotten back home when it began to snow.*

NOTA
- The past perfect of **hay** is **había habido** (*there had been*).

*See **Capítulo 10** for a more in-depth explanation of reflexive verbs.

Actividad 7 **Sí, había pasado antes.** Explique cuándo había pasado cada una de las cosas mencionadas usando el pluscuamperfecto. Siga el modelo.

> MODELO Lorenzo/llegar/la semana pasada
> Había llegado la semana pasada.

1. Uds. / ver la exposición en el museo / hace unos meses

   _____

2. Amelia / cortarse el pelo / el sábado

   _____

3. Ricardo y Leonor / casarse / en abril

   _____

4. nosotros / hacer el asado / el 4 de julio

   _____

5. tú / celebrar tu cumpleaños / hace un mes

   _____

6. Ud. / cambiar de idea / hace varios días

   _____

7. yo / ponerme en contacto con Felipe / hace tres semanas

   _____

8. Javier / devolverme los disquetes / la semana pasada

   _____

9. vosotros / escribir los informes / en noviembre

   _____

10. Marcos / romperse el codo / hace casi un año

   _____

Actividad 8 **Tomás, el holgazán (*loafer*).** Los amigos de Tomás no pueden contar con él porque no le gusta trabajar y siempre llega tarde. Escriba oraciones en las cuales Ud. explica lo que ya habían hecho los amigos de Tomás cuando él llegó por fin. Siga el modelo.

> MODELO Cuando Tomás llegó por fin / los amigos / lavar el carro
> Cuando Tomás llegó por fin, los amigos ya habían lavado
>   el carro.

1. Cuando Tomás llegó por fin / Raúl / hacer la pizza

   _____

2. Cuando Tomás llegó por fin / Uds. / poner la mesa

   _____

3. Cuando Tomás llegó por fin / Diana y Judit / ver el sitio Web

   _____

4. Cuando Tomás llegó por fin / Ud. / sacar la basura

   _____

5. Cuando Tomás llegó por fin / yo / subir las cajas a la buhardilla (*attic*)

   _____

6. Cuando Tomás llegó por fin / tú / ir de compras

   _____

7. Cuando Tomás llegó por fin / Plácido y yo / volver de la tienda de vídeos

   _____

Actividad 9 **Ya habíamos hecho muchas cosas.** Explique lo que Ud. y otras personas habían hecho ya cuando pasaron ciertas cosas. Escriba oraciones usando el pretérito para la primera frase y el pluscuamperfecto para la segunda. Siga el modelo.

> MODELO sonar el teléfono / ellos / cenar
> Cuando sonó el teléfono, ellos ya habían cenado.

1. Julia / venir a buscarnos / nosotros / hacer ejercicio

   _____

2. yo / ir a su casa / Virginia / dar una vuelta

   _____

3. Ud. / levantarse / sus padres / desayunar

   _____

4. nosotros / volver a casa / Juanita / escribir su composición

   _____

5. los bomberos / llegar / Uds. / apagar el incendio en la cocina

   _____ llegaron _____

6. los bisnietos / lograr ver a su bisabuelo / el bisabuelo / enfermarse

   _____ lograron _____ se ~~cate~~ ____

   se ya había enfermado

Actividad 10   **Nunca habíamos visto…**   Ud. y su familia vuelven mañana a Estados Unidos después de pasar seis semanas en España. Ahora que Uds. se van, se ponen a pensar en las cosas que no habían visto ni hecho en los viajes anteriores. Escriba oraciones en el pluscuamperfecto en las cuales Uds. describen las cosas que no habían visto ni hecho antes. Siga el modelo.

> MODELO   mamá / visitar la catedral de Burgos
> Mamá no había visitado la catedral de Burgos hasta este viaje.

1. Laura / ver una corrida de toros (*bullfight*) en Madrid

   _____

2. Rodolfo y Eva / dar un paseo por Santiago de Compostela

   _____

3. yo / hacer una excursión a El Escorial

   _____

4. tú y Susana / pasearse por el barrio de Santa Cruz

   _____

5. mamá, papá y yo / subir al monte Tibidabo

   _____

6. Jaime / conocer la Alhambra

   _____

7. tú / pasar Semana Santa en Sevilla

   _____

8. nosotros / conocer lugares tan impresionantes

   _____

9. yo / interesarse tanto en la arquitectura gótica

   _____

10. vosotros / ir a tantos restaurantes y discotecas

   _____

Future perfect

The future perfect consists of the future tense of the auxiliary verb **haber** + *past participle.* The English equivalent of the future perfect is *will have done something.* This tense is called **el futuro perfecto** or **el futuro compuesto** in Spanish.

LLEGAR/COMER/SUBIR	
(yo) **habré** llegado/comido/subido	(nosotros/as) **habremos** llegado/comido/subido
(tú) **habrás** llegado/comido/subido	(vosotros/as) **habréis** llegado/comido/subido
(él/ella/Ud.) **habrá** llegado/comido/subido	(ellos/ellas/Uds.) **habrán** llegado/comido/subido

In Spanish, as in English, the future perfect tense designates an event that will be completed in the future before another event occurs or before a specific point of time in the future.

Habrán vuelto para finales del mes.
They'll have returned by the end of the month.

Lo habré terminado todo antes de irme.
I'll have finished everything before I leave.

The future perfect is also used to express probability in past time. The future perfect of probability corresponds to the preterite or the present perfect.

Habrá pasado algo.
Probablemente pasó algo.
Probablemente ha pasado algo.
} *Something probably happened.*

Deber de + *perfect infinitive* (the infinitive **haber** + *past participle*) can be used instead of the future perfect to express probability in past time.

Marta **debe de haber llamado.**
Marta must have (probably) called.

Actividad 11 **Mirando hacia el futuro.** Escriba oraciones usando el futuro perfecto para explicar cuándo habrán ocurrido ciertas cosas. Siga el modelo.

> MODELO nosotros / almorzar / para las dos
> Nosotros habremos almorzado para las dos.

1. Elena / graduarse / para el año próximo
   se habrá graduado

2. Alfredo y Armando / mejorarse / antes de regresar a la universidad
   se habrían mejorado

3. nosotros / ahorrar dinero / antes de las vacaciones de invierno
   habremos ahorrado

4. yo / darte tu regalo / antes de tu fiesta de cumpleaños
   me habré dado

5. Ud. y Laura / mudarse / para mediados del mes
   se habrán mudado

6. tú / sacar un pasaporte / para julio

   tú habrás sacado

7. Uds. / volver del centro comercial / para las ocho

   habrán vuelto

8. vosotros / abrir una cuenta bancaria / antes de empezar el trabajo nuevo

   habréis abierto

Actividad 12 **¿Qué habrá ocurrido?** Exprese sus conjeturas sobre lo que pasó. Escriba las oraciones usando el futuro perfecto para expresar probabilidad en el pasado. Siga el modelo.

> MODELO   Probablemente llegó el cartero.
> Habrá llegado el cartero.

1. Su coche probablemente le costó un ojo de la cara (*an arm and a leg*).

   _____

2. Clara probablemente escribió la carta.

   _____

3. Felicia y Eduardo probablemente ganaron la regata.

   _____

4. Uds. probablemente tomaron la merienda (*snack*).

   _____

5. Martín y yo probablemente no entendimos el motivo.

   _____

6. Ud. probablemente no hizo cola por mucho tiempo.

   _____

Conditional perfect

The conditional perfect consists of the conditional tense of the auxiliary verb **haber** + *past participle*. It corresponds to the English *would have done something*. This tense is called **el condicional perfecto** or **el condicional compuesto** in Spanish.

LLEGAR/COMER/SUBIR	
(yo) **habría** llegado/comido/subido	(nosotros/as) **habríamos** llegado/comido/subido
(tú) **habrías** llegado/comido/subido	(vosotros/as) **habríais** llegado/comido/subido
(él/ella/Ud.) **habría** llegado/comido/ subido	(ellos/ellas/Uds.) **habrían** llegado/comido/ subido

The conditional perfect is used to designate an action or event that would have been completed in the past or when there is a real or implied condition.

| Yo no lo **habría dicho.** | *I wouldn't have said it.* |
| Nosotros **nos habríamos quedado** más tiempo. | *We would have stayed longer.* |

The conditional perfect is also used to express probability in past time. It corresponds to the past perfect + *probably*.

| Ya **se habría ido,** me imagino. | *He had probably left, I imagine.* |

NOTA

The perfect infinitive (the infinitive **haber** + *past participle*) is used after prepositions and as the complement of some verbs.

| Lorenzo ha sacado excelentes notas **por haber estudiado** tanto. | *Lorenzo has gotten excellent grades for having studied so much (because he studied so much).* |
| No recuerdo **haberlo visto.** | *I don't remember having seen him.* |

Actividad 13   **No lo habríamos hecho.** Escriba oraciones que expresan que Ud. y otras personas no habrían hecho las cosas que hicieron algunas personas. Siga el modelo.

> MODELO   Gregorio pidió el plato de langosta (*lobster*) con salsa de chocolate. (yo)
>   Yo no lo habría pedido.

1. Diego y Jaime salieron a la calle durante la tormenta. (Patricia y yo)

   Nosotros no lo habríamos salido

2. Tere rompió su compromiso con su novio. (Sofía)

   Sofía no lo habría roto

3. Uds. hicieron el viaje a California en autobús. (los turistas venezolanos)

   los turistas venezolanos no lo habrían hecho

4. Ariana se cortó el pelo en la peluquería Melenas. (tú)

   Tú no lo habrías cortado

5. Nosotros creímos lo que nos dijo Cecilia. (Ud.)

   Usted no lo habría creído

6. Te reíste cuando se te cayeron los vasos. (yo)

   Yo no me habría reído

Actividad 14 **Allá en el rancho grande.** Exprese en español sus conjeturas sobre el rancho o la estancia que tenía su familia hace muchos años. Escriba oraciones de probabilidad usando el condicional perfecto.

1. The ranch had probably been very big.

   _____

2. The farmers had probably had hens in a henhouse.

   _____

3. The farm workers had probably picked cherries and strawberries.

   _____

4. The landscape of the countryside had probably been beautiful.

   _____

5. The people had probably made barbecues every Sunday.

   _____

6. My great-grandfather had probably gone fishing in the lake that was nearby.

   _____

7. My great-grandmother had probably cooked fresh fruits and vegetables from the harvest.

   _____

8. There had probably been horses and cows on the ranch.

   _____

9. The farmers had probably sowed seeds in the vegetable garden.

   _____

10. We probably would have loved life on the ranch.

    _____

Actividad 15 **¡Felicidades!** Ud. es el maestro / la maestra de ceremonias del programa del premio Óscar. Les presenta la estatuilla del Óscar a los ganadores de las diferentes categorías artísticas de las películas del año. Practique el uso del infinitivo compuesto (*perfect infinitive*) tras (*after*) **por.** Siga el modelo.

> MODELO   Maribel Sánchez / trabajar en «Alma y corazón»
> A Maribel Sánchez por haber trabajado en «Alma y corazón».

1. Lope Cernuda / dirigir «Plátanos y cerezas»

   _____

2. Ernesto del Olmo / componer la música de «Mosquitos mágicos»

   _____

Past participle and perfect tenses   **111**

3. Ela Pantoja y Roberto Campillo / escribir el guión de «Agua hervida»

_____

4. Agustín Domingo / cantar en «Después de haber bailado»

_____

5. Beatriz Perales / ser primera actriz en «Salchichas al sol»

_____

6. Mateo de León y Diana Duque / producir «Grapadora en la mesa»

_____

7. Silvia Siles / hacer la escenografía de «Narices al aire»

_____

8. Memo Morado / actuar en «Langostas en el cielo»

_____

9. Edit Revueltas / diseñar el vestuario de «Tijeras de poliéster»

_____

10. Pepe del Oeste / maquillar a los actores de «Tamales quemados»

_____

Actividad 16   **Actividad oral.** Trabaje con un compañero / una compañera para discutir las cosas que Uds. **han hecho** este año y las cosas que **habrían hecho.** Por ejemplo, Ud. dice: **Yo he estudiado latín este año.** Su compañero/a responde: **Yo habría estudiado griego.** Se puede hablar de las materias, los deportes, los amigos, los pasatiempos, las vacaciones y otros temas.

PASSIVE CONSTRUCTIONS

Passive voice

The passive voice in Spanish is similar to the passive voice in English. It consists of a subject, a form of **ser** + *past participle*. (See **Capítulo 7** for the formation of the past participle.) This is often followed by an agent phrase introduced by the preposition **por.** In the passive voice, the past participle functions like an adjective, agreeing in number and gender with the subject of the sentence.

La cena fue servida **por Margarita.**	*Dinner was served **by Margarita.***
Los paquetes serán entregados **por el cartero.**	*The packages will be delivered **by the letter carrier.***
El coche ha sido reparado **por los mecánicos.**	*The car has been repaired **by the mechanics.***

The passive voice is used in Spanish when the speaker wishes to deemphasize the performer of the action. In the passive construction, the speaker can focus on the direct object by making it the subject of the passive sentence.

(*active voice*)	Los asesores escribirán el informe.
(*passive voice*)	El informe será escrito por los asesores.

NOTAS

- The direct object of the active sentence, **el informe,** becomes the subject of the passive sentence. The subject of the active sentence, the performer of the action, **los asesores,** appears in the *agent phrase* introduced by **por.** In the rephrasing of the active sentence into a passive sentence, the speaker focuses on **el informe** and on its **being written** rather than on the performer of the action, **los asesores.**

- The passive voice in Spanish is more common in writing and formal speech. It is not as common in everyday spoken Spanish as it is in English.

Actividad 1 **En la oficina.** Vuelva a escribir las oraciones cambiando la construcción activa a la construcción pasiva para describir las actividades que ocurren en la oficina. Mantenga el tiempo verbal de la oración en voz activa. Siga el modelo.

> MODELO El secretario arregló los papeles.
> Los papeles fueron arreglados por el secretario.

Vocabulario

La oficina

actualizar *to update*
el/la administrador(a) de Web
  webmaster
el folleto *brochure, pamphlet*
el formulario *form*

el/la gerente *manager*
la impresora *printer*
el ordenador *computer (Sp.)*
la pantalla *screen*
el/la programador(a) *programmer*

1. La recepcionista leyó el correo electrónico.
   El correo electrónico fue leído

2. Los empleados llenarán los formularios.
   fueron llenarado

3. El diseñador gráfico ha preparado el folleto.
   fue preparado

4. La programadora hizo la base de datos en su nuevo ordenador.
   fue hecho

5. El administrador de Web actualizará el sitio Web.
   fue actualizado

6. Los agentes de viajes compraron los billetes electrónicos.
   fueron comprado

7. El técnico reparó la pantalla.
   fue reparado

8. Los gerentes han resuelto los problemas.
   fue resuelto

Actividad 2 **Día de mudanza.** Escriba oraciones usando la voz pasiva y el pretérito para describir lo que pasó en casa de los Pidal el día de su mudanza de San Salvador a Nueva York. Siga el modelo.

> MODELO   los muebles / llevar / los cargadores (*movers*)
> Los muebles fueron llevados por los cargadores.

1. las camas / subir a los dormitorios / tres hombres
   fueron subiert

2. la alfombra de la sala / correr / la señora Pidal
   ~~fueron~~ fue corrido

3. los cuadros / colgar en las paredes / Benita y Ramona
   fueron colgado

4. la secadora / bajar al sótano / un cargador

    _____fue bajado_____

5. el sillón azul / colocar al lado de la ventana / el señor Pidal

    _____fue colocado_____

6. las lámparas / poner en las mesas / la abuela

    _____fue puesto_____

Se constructions with passive meaning

Spanish uses the construction **se** + *verb* in the third-person singular or plural to deemphasize the performer of the action. The agent phrase beginning with **por** cannot be used in this construction. Notice that this **se** construction (**se** + *verb*) can be translated into English in many different ways, including by the passive voice. The verb in this construction is either third-person singular or third-person plural, depending on whether the grammatical subject is singular or plural.

Se dieron los premios.	*The prizes **were given out (awarded).***
Se sabe el motivo.	*The reason **is known.** (**We/You/They/ People** know the reason.) (**One** knows the reason.)*
Se entregó el informe.	*The report **was handed in.***
Se entregaron los informes.	*The reports **were handed in.***

For intransitive verbs, that is, those that do not take a direct object, the verb is always in the third-person singular.

Se sale por aquí.	*You **go out** this way. (This **is the way out.**)*
Se vive bien en este país.	*People **live** well in this country.*
Se trabaja con entusiasmo.	*We/You/They/People **work** enthusiastically.*

When an infinitive is the subject of a **se** construction, the verb is conjugated in the third-person singular.

¿Por dónde **se puede entrar**?	*Which way **can you enter**?*
¿**Se puede ir** en autobús?	*Can one go by bus?*
Se prohíbe fumar.	*Smoking **is forbidden.***
No se permite mascar chicle.	*Gum-**chewing is not allowed.***

Note that reflexive verbs such as **divertirse** and **despertarse** can only show an unidentified or deemphasized subject with the addition of **uno** (or **una** if the reference is feminine) to a third-person singular verb.

Uno se divierte mucho en esta la discoteca.	*You have a lot of fun at this dance club.*
Uno se despierta más tarde los domingos.	*People wake up later on Sundays.*

Spanish also uses **la gente** with a third-person singular verb to label an indefinite subject. Compare this usage to the use of *people* in English. This Spanish construction is less common than its English equivalent.

Para divertirse, **la gente** va a un concierto.	*To have a good time, **people** go to a concert.*

Spanish also uses the third-person plural of the verb to label an indefinite subject. In this case, the subject pronouns **ellos/ellas** cannot be used.

Dicen que va a llover.	***They say*** *it's going to rain.*
Me **van** a invitar a la boda.	***They're going*** *to invite me to the wedding. (I'm going to be invited to the wedding.)*
Lo **entrevistaron** la semana pasada.	***They interviewed*** *him last week. (He was interviewed last week.)*

Actividad 3   **¡Se están instalando todavía!** A los Pidal les quedan muchas cosas que hacer para instalarse. Diga cuáles son estas cosas escribiendo oraciones con la construcción con **se** + *verbo en el futuro*. Fíjese que esta vez no hay agente en las oraciones. Siga el modelo.

> MODELO   correr / las cortinas
> Se correrán las cortinas.

1. enchufar / la nevera

   _____Se enchufara_____

2. encender / las lámparas

   _____Se encenderán_____

3. guardar / las cajas

   _____Se guardarán_____

4. poner / el sofá / en la sala

   _____Se pon_____

5. colocar / el lavaplatos / en la cocina

   _____

6. meter / las sábanas / en el armario

   _____

7. poner / las sillas / con la mesa del comedor

   _____

8. subir / el escritorio / al dormitorio

   _____

Actividad 4   **Titulares y anuncios del periódico.** Escriba oraciones usando la construcción con el sujeto indefinido **se** + *verbo*. Mantenga el tiempo verbal de la oración original. Siga el modelo.

> MODELO   Los políticos estudian los problemas económicos.
> Se estudian los problemas económicos.

1. La empresa busca programadores de computadoras.

   _____

2. La ley prohíbe el fumar en los restaurantes.

   _____

3. Los contadores (*accountants*) calculaban los impuestos.

   _____

4. Los inquilinos (*tenants*) alquilaron el condominio en la playa.

   _____

5. El restaurante chino entrega comida a la casa hasta la una de la mañana.

   _____

6. Los clientes pagan con cheque o tarjeta de crédito.

   _____

7. Esta sucursal del Banco de Barcelona solicitará gerentes.

   _____

8. La compañía necesita asesores bilingües.

   _____

Actividad 5 **Una excursión al zoológico.** Cambie las siguientes oraciones sobre una excursión al zoológico de la voz pasiva a la voz activa usando los sujetos indicados. Siga el modelo.

> MODELO   Se visita el zoológico. (nosotros)
> Visitamos el zoológico.

1. Se hace una excursión al zoológico. (mis amigos y yo)

   _____

2. Para llegar al zoológico, se toma el autobús en la calle Azorín. (nosotros)

   _____

3. Se ven leones, tigres, leopardos y panteras. (yo)

   _____

4. Se da de comer a los animales. (los guardianes)

   _____

5. Se come bambú. (los pandas)

   _____

6. Se tiran cacahuetes a los elefantes. (tú)

   _____

7. Se juega tirando plátanos. (un mono)

   _____

8. Se compran palomitas y refrescos. (vosotros)

   _____

Uses of the past participle

The Spanish past participle enters into a number of constructions. It is used with the auxiliary verb **haber** to form the perfect tenses (see **Capítulo 7**). When used with **haber,** the past participle is invariable.

La profesora **nos ha dado** mucha tarea.	*The teacher **has given us** a lot of homework.*
¿Ya **habrán llegado** las chicas?	*I wonder if the girls **have arrived.***

The past participle can also be used as an adjective, either modifying a noun directly or following **ser, estar,** or other verbs such as **parecer.**

un papel **roto**	*a **torn** piece of paper*
una puerta **cerrada**	*a **closed** door*
coches recién **pintados**	*freshly **painted** cars*
máquinas **descompuestas**	***broken** machines*

La clase **es aburrida.**	*The class **is boring.***
Los estudiantes **están aburridos.**	*The students **are bored.***
Él **parece cansado.**	*He **seems tired.***

The past participle as a predicate adjective is more commonly used after **estar** than after **ser.**

El papel **está roto.**	*The piece of paper **is torn.***
La puerta **está cerrada.**	*The door **is closed.***
Los coches **están recién pintados.**	*The cars **are freshly painted.***
Las máquinas **están descompuestas.**	*The machines **are broken.***

Ser and **estar** may contrast with each other when used with the past participle. Passive sentences use **ser** + *past participle* and usually have an agent phrase introduced by **por.** Whereas these sentences focus on the action itself, sentences that use **estar** + *past participle* focus on the result of the action. These sentences do not have an agent phrase introduced by **por.**

La torta **fue hecha** por el cocinero.	*The cake **was made** by the chef.*
La torta **estaba hecha.**	*The cake **was made** (done, completed, finished).*

Actividad 6   **Todo estaba hecho.** Cuando Ud. llegó todo estaba hecho ya. Explíqueselo a su amiga. Siga el modelo.

> MODELO   ¿Quién abrió las ventanas?
> No sé. Cuando yo llegué, las ventanas ya estaban abiertas.

1. ¿Quién arregló el cuarto?

   _____

2. ¿Quién preparó el almuerzo?

   _____

3. ¿Quién cerró la puerta?

   _____

4. ¿Quién apagó el microondas?

   _____

5. ¿Quién puso la mesa?

_____

6. ¿Quién rompió los vasos?

_____

7. ¿Quién mandó el fax?

_____

8. ¿Quién prendió las luces?

_____

Actividad 7 **Observaciones.** Escriba estos intercambios en los cuales una persona confirma la observación de la otra. Siga el modelo.

> MODELO tu camisa / romper (*to break, tear*) / sí, tengo
> Tu camisa está rota.
> Sí, tengo la camisa rota.

1. tus papeles / estrujar (*to crush, crumple*) / sí, tengo

_____

_____

2. esta torta / quemar / sí, tiremos esta

_____

_____

3. tus regalos / envolver (*to wrap*) / sí, traigo

_____

_____

4. tu informe / terminar / sí, hoy entrego

_____

_____

5. tus papeles / archivar / sí, tengo

_____

_____

6. la tortilla / recalentar (*to warm up, reheat*) / sí, hoy sirvo

_____

_____

Passive constructions 119

Actividad 8 **¿Qué significa?** Su amigo español está pasando las vacaciones de verano en su casa. Mientras Uds. se pasean por la ciudad, su amigo le pregunta qué quieren decir los letreros que ve. Explíquele lo que dicen en español usando la construcción con **se.**

1. Newspapers and magazines sold here.

   _____

2. Park here.

   _____

3. Turn right.

   _____

4. Enter this way.

   _____

5. Spanish is spoken here.

   _____

6. Travelers checks cashed.

   _____

Actividad 9 **¿Qué dice Ud.?** Un nuevo estudiante en su departamento académico le hace unas preguntas sobre la vida diaria. Conteste sus preguntas usando la construcción con **se.**

1. ¿Qué materias toman en el departamento?

   _____

2. ¿A qué hora almuerzan?

   _____

3. ¿Cómo llegan a la universidad?

   _____

4. ¿Dónde compran sus libros de texto?

   _____

5. ¿Cómo pueden sacar buenas notas?

   _____

6. ¿Qué hacen para divertirse los fines de semana?

   _____

7. ¿En qué restaurantes comen cerca del campus?

_____

8. ¿A qué deportes juegan en la universidad?

_____

Actividad 10 **Actividad oral.** En este juego de adivinanza Ud. y sus compañeros de clase intentan adivinar quién escribió una famosa obra literaria. Uno de Uds. dice el título de la obra, por ejemplo, *Don Quijote,* y los otros estudiantes tienen que decir lo más rápido posible quién lo escribió. Contesten empleando la voz pasiva, por ejemplo, **Fue escrito por Cervantes.**

CAPÍTULO 9

GERUND AND PROGRESSIVE TENSES

Formation of the gerund (present participle)

The gerund, or **-ndo** form in Spanish, corresponds to the *-ing* form in English. The gerund (present participle) is called **el gerundio (el participio presente)** in Spanish. To form the gerund of **-ar** verbs add the ending **-ando** to the stem of the verb. Add the ending **-iendo** to the stem of **-er** and **-ir** verbs.

INFINITIVE	STEM	GERUND
ensayar	ensay-	ensay**ando**
tomar	tom-	tom**ando**
aprender	aprend-	aprend**iendo**
comer	com-	com**iendo**
abrir	abr-	abr**iendo**
escribir	escrib-	escrib**iendo**

-Er and **-ir** verbs whose stems end in a vowel use **-yendo,** not **-iendo,** to form the gerund.

INFINITIVE	STEM	GERUND
caer	ca-	ca**yendo**
construir	constru-	constru**yendo**
creer	cre-	cre**yendo**
leer	le-	le**yendo**
oír	o-	o**yendo**
traer	tra-	tra**yendo**

-Ir verbs that have a change in the vowel of the stem in the third-person singular of the preterite and **-ir** verbs with irregular preterite stems have the same change in the gerund.

INFINITIVE	PRETERITE	GERUND
decir	dijo	**diciendo**
dormir	durmió	**durmiendo**
morir	murió	**muriendo**
pedir	pidió	**pidiendo**
repetir	repitió	**repitiendo**
sentir	sintió	**sintiendo**
servir	sirvió	**sirviendo**
venir	vino	**viniendo**

Ir and **poder** also have irregular gerunds.

ir → **yendo**
poder → **pudiendo**

Object and reflexive pronouns are attached to the present participle in writing, and an accent mark is written over the **-a** or **-e** of the gerund ending.

esperando + lo → **esperándolo**
dando + me + los → **dándomelos**
viendo + las → **viéndolas**
levantando + se → **levantándose**
sintiendo + se → **sintiéndose**

The gerund in Spanish is usually equivalent to an English clause or gerund phrase beginning with *by, while, if, when,* or *because.*

Se aprende mucho **estudiando** con la profesora Padilla.
*You learn a lot **studying (when you study)** with Professor Padilla.*

Viajando en marzo, Nicolás ahorró mucho dinero.
***By traveling** in March, Nicolás saved a lot of money.*

With verbs of perception, such as **escuchar, mirar, oír,** and **ver,** either the infinitive or the gerund can be used, as in English.

Los oímos **cantar.**
Los oímos **cantando.**
*We heard them **sing/singing.***

Actividad 1 **La vecina entremetida (*busybody*).** Su vecina se mete en todo. Ahora quiere saber lo que Ud. y otras personas hicieron hoy porque no los vio durante todo el día. Contéstele usando **pasar** + *el gerundio*. Siga el modelo.

> MODELO   ¿Trabajó Ud. en la oficina hoy?
> Sí, pasé el día trabajando en la oficina.

1. ¿Habló Ud. por teléfono celular hoy?

_____

2. ¿Tomaron Carlos y Celeste café en el cibercafé hoy?

_____

3. ¿Durmió la siesta hoy Paquito?

_____

4. ¿Leyeron hoy Ud. y su hermano?

_____

5. ¿Oíste las noticias hoy?

_____

6. ¿Imprimisteis los documentos hoy?

_____

Actividad 2 **¡Cómo va volando el tiempo!** (*How time flies!*) Ud. piensa en las cosas que hizo ayer y en cuánto tiempo le llevó cada cosa. ¡Qué rápido se le fue el día! Escriba oraciones usando **pasar** + *el gerundio* para describir su horario de ayer. Siga el modelo.

> MODELO   yo / desayunar (media hora)
> Pasé media hora desayunando.

1. yo / arreglarse (cuarenta y cinco minutos)

_____

2. Estrella y yo / andar en bicicleta (una hora y media)

_____

3. yo / escribir un informe (dos horas)

_____

4. Fernando, Chelo y yo / comprar cosas en el centro comercial
   (un par de horas)

_____

5. mis amigos y yo / vestirse (una hora y cuarto)

_____

6. yo / ver un documental (una hora)

_____

Progressive tenses

The progressive tenses consist of the present, imperfect, preterite, future, or conditional forms of the verb **estar** followed by the present participle.

PRESENTE PROGRESIVO (*present progressive*)
Estoy oyendo música.   *I'm listening to* music.

IMPERFECTO PROGRESIVO (*imperfect progressive*)
Estaba oyendo música.   *I was listening to* music.

PRETÉRITO PROGRESIVO (*preterite progressive*)

Estuve oyendo música hasta que salimos.

I was listening to music until we went out.

FUTURO PROGRESIVO (*future progressive*)

Estaré oyendo música toda la tarde.

I'll be listening to music all afternoon.

CONDICIONAL PROGRESIVO (*conditional progressive*)

Estaría oyendo música si tuviera un radio.

I'd be listening to music if I had a radio.

The verbs **estar, ir,** and **venir** are not commonly used in the gerund form in the progressive tenses.

The present, imperfect, and future progressive are different from the corresponding simple tenses in that they emphasize that the action is or was in progress. They may also suggest that the action is temporary, not habitual, or represents a change from the usual pattern.

Miguel juega al fútbol.

Miguel plays soccer.
    (habitual action)

Miguel está jugando al fútbol.

Miguel's playing soccer.
    (He's playing soccer right now *or* He's begun to play soccer.)

The preterite progressive is used to show an action that was in progress in the past but is now completed. Sentences with the preterite progressive usually have a time phrase or a clause with **hasta (que)** that indicates the end of the action.

Estuvieron viajando en coche **hasta el anochecer.**

They were driving until nightfall.

Estuvimos estudiando Latín **hasta que Óscar vino a buscarnos.**

We were studying Latin until Óscar came to get us.

Estuve hablando con él **dos horas.**

I was speaking with him for two hours.

The imperfect progressive, like the simple imperfect tense, indicates that an action was in progress in the past without focusing on the beginning or end of that action.

Estábamos estudiando Latín **cuando Óscar vino a buscarnos.**

We were studying Latin when Óscar came to get us.

Estaba hablando con él **y los dos nos reíamos mucho.**

I was talking with him and both of us were laughing a lot.

Estaban viajando en un coche que no tenía aire acondicionado.

They were driving in a car that didn't have air-conditioning.

The present progressive in Spanish can never refer to the future as the present progressive in English does. To express future time, Spanish uses the simple present, the **ir a** + *infinitive* construction, or the future tense.

Sacamos los boletos mañana.
Vamos a sacar los boletos mañana. }
Sacaremos los boletos mañana.

We're buying the tickets tomorrow.

In the progressive tenses, object and reflexive pronouns may either precede the form of **estar** or be attached to the end of the present participle, in which case a written accent is added.

Isabel y Juan **se** están paseando. }
Isabel y Juan están paseándo**se**. }   *Isabel and Juan are taking a walk.*

The verb **seguir** is used with the present participle to mean *to be still doing something, to keep on doing something.*

Marta **sigue despertándose** antes de las seis.   *Marta is still waking up before six o'clock.*

Sigan buscando la llave.   *Keep on looking for the key.*

Ir is commonly used with the gerund as well. It is used to convey the idea of *gradually* or *little by little.*

La empresa **va prosperando.**   *The company is gradually prospering.*

Las flores **se fueron secando** poco a poco.   *The flowers withered away little by little.*

Actividad 3 **En el campamento (*camp*) de verano.** Escriba lo que están haciendo los niños en un día típico en el campamento usando el presente progresivo. Siga el modelo.

> MODELO   Eva y Ángela trabajan en un campamento.
> Eva y Ángela están trabajando en un campamento.

En el campamento

Vocabulario

acampar *to camp*
la araña *spider*
asar *to roast*
desenvolver (o → ue) *to unroll*
encender (e → ie) el fuego *to light the fire*
la hormiga *ant*
el hormiguero *anthill*

el lago *lake*
la mochila *backpack, knapsack*
nadar *to swim*
el perro caliente *hot dog*
la picadura *bite*
el saco de dormir *sleeping bag*
la tienda de campaña *tent*

1. Los niños acampan en la sierra.
   están acampando

2. Ricardo nada en el lago.
   está nando nadando

3. Lupe y yo llenamos la mochila.
   estamos llenando

4. Ester desenvuelve el saco de dormir.

está desenvolviendo

5. Pablo se acuesta en el saco de dormir.

está se acostándose / se está acostando

6. Yo observo las hormigas en el hormiguero.

estoy observiendo

7. Tú enciendes el fuego para asar los perros calientes.

estás encendiendo

8. Pepe y Lucía meten las pilas en la linterna.

_____

9. Todos nosotros nos quejamos de las picaduras de los mosquitos.

_____

10. Ud. se asusta al ver las arañas en la tienda de campaña.

_____

Actividad 4 **Acciones en progreso.** Escriba oraciones usando el presente, el imperfecto o el futuro progresivo. Cuando sea posible, cambie los sustantivos a pronombres de complemento directo. Siga el modelo.

> MODELO   Carlos practica el ruso.   _Ca_
> Carlos está practicándolo.
> Carlos lo está practicando.   _carlos lo está practrando_

1. Leíamos los periódicos.

estamos _Nosotros los leyendo_
estamos _nosotros leyendolo_

2. Uds. harán las maletas.

las están hiciendo
están hiciendolas

3. Me pongo el traje.

estoy pusiéndolo poniéndolo
estoy lo pusiendo me lo estoy poniendo

4. Ud. se lavaba el pelo.

usted se está lavándolo lavándoselo
usted se lo está lavando

Roshina

5. Nos dirás los planes.

estarás ~~estás~~ diciéndonoslos

nos los estarás diciendo

6. Rita busca el sitio Web.

está buscandolo

lo está buscando

Actividad 5 **Cuando estalló (*broke out*) el fuego,...** Cuando estalló el fuego en la cocina del Hotel Dos Reyes los huéspedes y los empleados del hotel estaban haciendo varias cosas. Describa lo que estaban haciendo usando el imperfecto progresivo. Escriba cada oración de dos maneras cuando sea posible. Siga el modelo.

MODELO la señora Escudero / bañarse
La señora Escudero estaba bañándose.
La señora Escudero se estaba bañando.

En el hotel

Vocabulario

el ascensor *elevator*
el botones *bellhop*
el equipaje *luggage*
flameado/a *flambéed*
el/la gerente *manager*
el huésped / la huéspeda *guest* (*in a hotel*)
jactarse (de) *to brag about*

el lavado *wash*
el/la lavandero/a *laundry worker*
el/la mozo/a *server*
el noveno piso *ninth floor*
la recepción *check-in desk*
registrarse *to check in*
tocar el timbre *to ring the bell*

1. los señores Sotomayor / registrarse

_____

_____

2. el botones / subirles el equipaje a unos huéspedes

_____

_____

3. los mozos / servirles la cena a los clientes

_____

_____

4. el gerente / prender el aire acondicionado

_____

_____

5. la lavandera / devolverle el lavado a la señora Casona

_____

_____

6. los huéspedes del noveno piso / bajar en el ascensor

_____

_____

7. los turistas ingleses / tocar el timbre en la recepción

_____

_____

8. los cocineros / jactarse de los plátanos flameados que habían preparado

_____

_____

Actividad 6 **¡Qué va! Siguen haciéndolo.** Su amiga acaba de volver de Bogotá donde pasó un semestre estudiando español. Ella supone que ha habido muchos cambios mientras estaba en el extranjero. Ud. le dice que todo sigue siendo igual. Escriba oraciones usando **seguir** + *el gerundio*. Cuando sea posible, cambie los sustantivos a pronombres de complemento directo. Siga el modelo.

> MODELO Ya no estudias química, ¿verdad?
> ¡Qué va! Sigo estudiándola.

1. Elena ya no dice chismes (*gossip*), ¿verdad?
   _____Sigue diciéndolos_____

2. Ya no construyen la autopista, ¿verdad?
   _____Siguen construiéndola_____

3. Ya no lees ciencia ficción, ¿verdad?
   _____sigo leyendola_____

4. Tus hermanos ya no tocan el violín, ¿verdad?
   _____siguen tocandolo_____

5. Ud. ya no asiste a los conciertos de jazz, ¿verdad?
   _____sigue asistiéndolos_____

6. Nosotros, los Gatos Azules, ya no jugamos al fútbol en el estadio, ¿verdad?
   _____

Actividad 7 **Nosotros, los trasnochadores** (*night owls*). A Ud. y a sus amigos les gusta trasnochar (*stay up late*). Escriba oraciones usando el futuro progresivo para describir lo que Uds. estarán haciendo a esas horas. Siga el modelo.

> MODELO yo / hablar por teléfono móvil / a la una de la mañana
> Yo estaré hablando por teléfono móvil a la una de la mañana.

1. Luisa / ver televisión / a las dos y media

   _____

2. Ud. / ducharse / a medianoche

   _____

3. mis amigos y yo / morirnos de sueño / a las cuatro

   _____

4. Pablo y Ramona / jugar vídeojuegos / a las doce y media

   _____

5. yo / oír música / a la una y media

   _____

6. tú / comerse unos bocadillos / a las tres

   _____

7. Uds. / enviarme un correo electrónico / a las seis cuarenta

   _____

8. vosotros / bailar en una discoteca / a la una

   _____

Progressive tenses with **llevar**

In addition to **hace** + *expression of time* + **que** + *verb in present tense* (and *verb in present tense* + **desde hace** + *expression of time*), Spanish expresses actions that begin in the past and that continue into the present with the present tense of **llevar** + *gerund*.

Llevo tres años **estudiando** español. ⎫
Hace tres años que estudio español. ⎬ *I've been studying Spanish for three years.*
Estudio español desde hace tres años. ⎭

The gerund of **estar** is not used in the **llevar** + *gerund* construction. In this case, **llevar** is used by itself.

> **Llevo** dos horas aquí. *I've been here for two hours.*

Actividad 8 **Una entrevista.** Un periodista le entrevista al famoso pintor-escultor peruano Pablo de Lima. Conteste las preguntas usando la construcción **llevar** + *el gerundio*. Siga el modelo.

> MODELO ¿Cuánto tiempo hace que Ud. hace esculturas? (quince años)
> Llevo quince años haciendo esculturas.

Vocabulario

La pintura

el autorretrato *self-portrait*
la cerámica *ceramics, pottery*
colgar (u → ue) *to hang*
el cuadro *painting*
dibujar *to draw*
el/la escultor(a) *sculptor*
la escultura *sculpture*
exhibir *to exhibit*
la galería *gallery*

el/la modelo *model*
el mural *mural*
el paisaje *landscape*
el pincel *paintbrush*
pintar *to paint*
el/la pintor(a) *painter*
la pintura *painting, paint*
el retrato *portrait*

1. ¿Cuánto tiempo hace que Ud. pinta retratos? (doce años)

   Llevo doce años pintando retratos

2. ¿Cuánto tiempo hace que Ud. usa estos pinceles? (unos meses)

   Llevo uno meses usando estos pinceles

3. ¿Cuánto tiempo hace que Ud. dibuja con modelos? (varios años)

   Llevo varios años dibujando con modelos

4. ¿Cuánto tiempo hace que Ud. se dedica a la pintura? (toda la vida)

   Llevo todo la vida se dedicando a la pintura

5. ¿Cuánto tiempo hace que la galería Olmo cuelga sus cuadros de paisajes? (un año)

   llevo un año colgando mis cuadros de paisajes

6. ¿Cuánto tiempo hace que Ud. se interesa en los murales? (poco tiempo)

   interesandome

7. ¿Cuánto tiempo hace que Ud. trabaja en cerámica? (nueve años)

   trabajando

8. ¿Cuánto tiempo hace que Ud. vive en Nueva York? (cinco años)

   viviendo

9. ¿Cuánto tiempo hace que su esposa lo ayuda? (un par de años)

10. ¿Cuánto tiempo hace que Ud. escribe libros sobre el arte? (tres años)

11. ¿Cuánto tiempo hace que Ud. pinta autorretratos? (muchos años)

12. ¿Cuánto tiempo hace que Ud. exhibe en el Museo de Arte Moderno? (once meses)

Capítulo 9

Actividad 9 **Un partido de fútbol.** Un locutor de televisión describe un partido de fútbol. Complete las oraciones usando el presente progresivo de los verbos indicados.

1. Los aficionados (animar[a]) _____ a sus equipos.

2. Redondo (robar) _____ el balón.[b]

3. Nosotros (ver) _____ un partido emocionante.

4. Manrique (marcar[c]) _____ un gol.

5. Los entrenadores[d] (salir) _____ al campo de fútbol.

6. Martínez (regatear[e]) _____ el balón.

7. Los técnicos[f] (pedirles) _____ un gran esfuerzo a los jugadores.

8. Los aficionados (entusiasmarse) _____.

9. Uds., los televidentes,[g] (oír) _____ los gritos de los aficionados.

10. Este partido de campeonato (atraer) _____ mucha atención.

[a]to cheer   [b]ball   [c]to score   [d]trainers   [e]to dribble   [f]managers   [g]television viewers

Actividad 10 **¡En español!** Exprese las oraciones en español usando los tiempos progresivos.

1. We're having a wonderful time!

   _____

2. You (Ud.) were jogging until it began to rain.

   estuvo corriendo hace que empezó a llovar

3. They're still serving dinner at the Hotel Palacio.

   _____

4. I'm getting to know Madrid little by little.

   Voy conociendo Madrid poco a poco.

5. Mateo and Victoria will be playing tennis all afternoon.

   _____

6. Pedro and I kept on reading.

   seguimos leyendo

Actividad 11 **Actividad oral.** Trabaje con un compañero / una compañera de clase para describir lo que están haciendo los amigos durante sus horas libres en la universidad.

Reflexive verbs

Reflexive verbs

Reflexive verbs always appear with a reflexive pronoun that refers back to the same person or thing that serves as the subject. Most Spanish reflexive verbs correspond to English intransitive verbs that don't have a direct object or English verb phrases consisting of *to be* or *to get + adjective* or *past participle.* The infinitives of reflexive verbs have the reflexive pronoun **se** attached to the end of each word: **acostarse, lavarse, sentarse, vestirse.**

In the conjugations below, note that the reflexive pronoun **se** changes to agree with the subject of the verb, and that reflexive pronouns precede the conjugated verb.

ACOSTARSE *to go to bed (present tense)*	
me acuesto	nos acostamos
te acuestas	os acostáis
se acuesta	se acuestan

VESTIRSE *to get dressed (preterite)*	
me vestí	nos vestimos
te vestiste	os vestisteis
se vistió	se vistieron

LAVARSE *to wash (imperfect)*	
me lavaba	nos lavábamos
te lavabas	os lavabais
se lavaba	se lavaban

For most reflexive verbs there is a corresponding transitive verb in which the subject and direct object refer to different things or people. (Transitive verbs are those that take a direct object.)

Lavo el carro.	*I wash the car. (I = subject; car = direct object)*
Me lavo.	*I wash myself. (subject and direct object refer to* **yo***)*
Acuestas a los niños.	*You put the children to bed. (you = subject; children = direct object)*
Te acuestas.	*You go to bed. (subject and direct object refer to* **tú***)*

When the infinitive of a reflexive verb is used with another verb, such as **ir a, deber, poder,** or **querer,** the reflexive pronoun agrees with the subject. The reflexive pronoun may be placed either before the first verb of these constructions or after the infinitive. When placed after the infinitive, the reflexive pronoun is attached to the end of the infinitive.

QUEDARSE *to stay, remain*	
Me quiero **quedar.**	Quiero **quedarme.**
Te quieres **quedar.**	Quieres **quedarte.**
Se quiere **quedar.**	Quiere **quedarse.**
Nos queremos **quedar.**	Queremos **quedarnos.**
Os queréis **quedar.**	Queréis **quedaros.**
Se quieren **quedar.**	Quieren **quedarse.**

Reflexive pronouns as indirect objects

With some verbs the reflexive pronoun is an indirect object rather than a direct object. These verbs, such as **ponerse** + *article of clothing,* have a direct object (the article of clothing) in addition to the reflexive pronoun.

Los niños se ponen **el abrigo.**
Y se ponen **las botas** también.

*The children put on **their coats.***
*And they put on **their boots** also.*

Marta se lavó **las manos.**
Nos lavamos **la cara.**

*Marta washed **her hands.***
*We washed **our faces.***

NOTAS

- Spanish uses a singular noun for articles of clothing and parts of the body, even with plural subjects. It is assumed that each person has one item. Only if each person has more than one item does Spanish use a plural noun.

- In these reflexive constructions the Spanish definite article is the equivalent of a possessive adjective in English.

Common reflexive verbs and expressions

abrocharse (los zapatos, el cinturón de seguridad) *to button; to tie (one's shoelaces); to buckle, fasten (seat belt)*

acostarse (o → ue) *to go to bed*

afeitarse *to shave*

arreglarse *to get ready to go out*

atarse los zapatos *to tie one's shoelaces*

bañarse *to take a bath*

cansarse *to get tired*

cepillarse los dientes / el pelo *to brush one's teeth / one's hair*

cortarse el pelo *to cut one's hair*

cuidarse *to take care of oneself*

desabrocharse (los zapatos, el cinturón de seguridad) *to unbutton; to untie (one's shoelaces); to unbuckle, unfasten (seat belt)*

desatarse los zapatos *to untie one's shoelaces*

despertarse (e → ie) *to wake up*

ducharse *to take a shower*

lastimarse *to hurt oneself*

lavarse *to wash up*

lavarse el pelo *to wash one's hair*

limarse las uñas *to file one's nails*

limpiarse los dientes *to brush one's teeth*

maquillarse, pintarse *to put on makeup*

peinarse *to comb one's hair*

(continued)

pintarse los labios *to put on lipstick*	quemarse + *part of the body* *to burn*	secarse el pelo *to dry one's hair*
ponerse + *article of clothing* *to put on*	quitarse + *article of clothing* *to take off*	torcerse (o → ue) el tobillo *to twist one's ankle*
probarse (o → ue) *to try on*	romperse + *article of clothing* *to tear*	vestirse (e → i) *to get dressed*
quebrarse (e → ie) + *part of the body* *to break*	romperse + *part of the body* *to break*	

Actividad 1 **¿Reflexivo o no?** Complete las oraciones escogiendo la forma transitiva o reflexiva del verbo indicado. Use el tiempo verbal indicado. Siga el modelo.

> MODELO Rosita <u>bañó</u> a los niños y después se <u>bañó</u> ella. (bañar—*preterite*)

1. Mañana yo <u>me despierto</u> a las siete y <u>despierto</u> a mi hermana a las siete y cuarto. (despertar—*present*)

2. Aunque el profesor Vélez <u>aburría</u> a sus estudiantes, Miguel y Carlota no <u>se aburría</u>. (aburrir—*imperfect*)

3. Los novios <u>se casaron</u> en la catedral de Burgos. El cura de la novia los <u>casó</u>. (casar—*preterite*)

4. Nosotros ya <u>nos paseamos</u> y <u>paseamos</u> al perro también. (pasear—*preterite*)

5. La carta que Carmen recibió ayer no la <u>tranquilizó</u>. Sin embargo Martín al leerla <u>se tranquilizó</u>. (tranquilizar—*preterite*)

6. Yo <u>me divertí</u> durante el primer acto de la obra, pero los otros dos actos no me <u>divirtieron</u>. (divertir—*preterite*)

7. Pepe me hacía tantas preguntas que francamente yo <u>me mareaba</u>. ¡Ese chico <u>mareaba</u> a todo el mundo! (marear—*imperfect*)

8. Daniela no tiene ganas de hacer nada. A ver si nosotros la <u>nos animamos</u>. Vamos a invitarla a jugar al tenis. A ver si ella _____. (animar—*present*)

9. Cuando Pablo y Laura eran niños _____ al ver las películas de terror. Las películas con fantasmas (*ghosts*) los

_____ más que nada. (asustar—*imperfect*)

10. Uds. _____ por cualquier cosa. Menos mal que

no _____ a otras personas. (ofender—*present*)

Actividad 2   **Todavía no, abuelita.** La abuela llama desde Buenos Aires para hablar con sus nietos gemelos (*twins*) en Filadelfia. Ella les pregunta si pueden hacer ciertas cosas solos (*by themselves*). Los niños le explican a su abuela que no pueden hacerlas solos todavía, que se las hace su mamá. Practique los verbos como verbos transitivos y reflexivos. Siga el modelo.

MODELO   bañarse
abuelita: ¿Uds. ya se bañan solos?
nietos: No, abuelita. Nos baña mamá.

1. despertarse

   abuelita: _____

   nietos: _____

2. lavarse el pelo

   abuelita: _____

   nietos: _____

3. peinarse

   abuelita: _____

   nietos: _____

4. atarse los zapatos

   abuelita: _____

   nietos: _____

5. prepararse el desayuno

   abuelita: _____

   nietos: _____

6. acostarse

   abuelita: _____

   nietos: _____

Actividad 3 **Una excursión al campo.** Ud. y sus amigos pasaron un día en el campo. Escriba lo que cada persona llevó ese día. Practique el uso del verbo reflexivo **ponerse** en el pretérito. Siga el modelo.

MODELO tú / los zapatos de tenis
Te pusiste los zapatos de tenis.

Vocabulario

La ropa

el abrigo *overcoat*	**los jeans, los vaqueros** *jeans*
la blusa *blouse*	**las medias** *socks (L. Am.);*
las botas *boots*	*stockings (Sp.)*
la bufanda *scarf*	**los pantalones** *pants*
los calcetines *socks (Sp.)*	**el saco** *jacket*
la camisa *shirt*	**las sandalias** *sandals*
la camiseta *T-shirt*	**el smoking, el esmoquin** *tuxedo*
el chaleco *vest*	**el suéter** *sweater*
la chaqueta *jacket*	**el traje** *suit*
el cinturón *belt*	**el traje de baño** *bathing suit*
la corbata *tie*	**el vestido** *dress*
el gorro *cap*	**los zapatos de tacón alto**
los guantes *gloves*	*high-heeled shoes*
el impermeable *raincoat*	

1. Marina y yo / los jeans

   _____

2. Arturo / un traje de baño

   _____

3. Uds. / un impermeable

   _____

4. yo / un suéter de lana

   _____

5. Víctor y Paz / un gorro

   _____

6. vosotros / una camiseta

   _____

7. tú / las sandalias

   _____

8. Ud. / una chaqueta

   _____

Actividad 4 **¿Qué se llevarán para ir al trabajo?** Escriba lo que llevarán estas personas para ir al trabajo. Practique el uso del verbo reflexivo **ponerse** en el futuro. Siga el modelo.

> MODELO   Alberto / un saco
> Alberto se pondrá un saco.

1. yo / las medias

   _____

2. Alicia / una blusa

   _____

3. nosotros / los zapatos

   _____

4. Uds. / una camisa

   _____

5. los jefes / un traje

   _____

6. tú / una corbata

   _____

7. Ud. / un cinturón

   _____

8. vosotros / una bufanda

   _____

Actividad 5 **¡Ya llega el baile de gala (*the big dance*)!** Ud. y sus amigos están emocionados porque el baile de gala es el sábado. Todos Uds. necesitan probarse la ropa que van a llevar. Practique el uso del verbo reflexivo **probarse** en el presente. Siga el modelo.

> MODELO   nosotros / los zapatos de charol
> Nos probamos los zapatos de charol.

Vocabulario

¿De qué es? Las telas

el algodón *cotton*	**el nailon** *nylon*
el cuero *leather*	**el poliéster** *polyester*
el charol *patent leather*	**la seda** *silk*
la lana *wool*	**el terciopelo** *velvet*

1. Pilar y Luz / el traje largo de lana

   _____

2. yo / el abrigo de cuero

    _____

3. Lorenzo / el smoking de seda

    _____

4. Uds. / los zapatos de tacón alto

    _____

5. tú / la blusa de algodón

    _____

6. Antonio y Esteban / la corbata de seda

    _____

7. nosotros / el chaleco de poliéster

    _____

8. vosotros / los guantes de nailon

    _____

Actividad 6 **¡Qué malas noticias!** Un amigo / una amiga que acaba de volver de México pregunta por sus amigos. Le toca a Ud. (*It's your job*) darle las malas noticias. Escriba los verbos reflexivos en el pretérito. Siga el modelo.

> MODELO   Alfonso / caerse / cruzando la calle
> Alfonso se cayó cruzando la calle.

1. Miguel / romperse la pierna / montando a caballo
    Miguel se rompió la pierna montando a caballo

2. Ana / quemarse la mano / cocinando
    Ana se quemó la mano cocinando

3. el perro de Bernardo / perderse / corriendo en las afueras
    El perro de Bernardo se pierdió corriendo en las afueras
    Perdió

4. Alicia / torcerse el tobillo / patinando sobre hielo
    se torció

5. todos nosotros / enfermarse / comiendo hamburguesas poco hechas
    nos enfermamos

6. yo / hacerse daño / cortando el césped
    me hice

7. los hermanos de Anita / quebrarse el dedo / jugando al baloncesto
    se quebraron

Actividad 7 **Estimados televidentes.** Ud. es locutor/a de televisión. Por desgracia, las noticias de hoy son todas malas. Escriba los verbos reflexivos en el pretérito. Siga el modelo.

> MODELO   dos panaderos / quemarse las manos / cuando hubo una explosión en el horno
> Dos panaderos se quemaron las manos cuando hubo una explosión en el horno.

1. la actriz Ramona Taylor / lastimarse / en el rodaje (*filming*) de su nueva película

   _____

2. el futbolista Diego Suárez / romperse el pie / en el partido de hoy

   _____

3. unos turistas norteamericanos / caerse / en la escalera mecánica del metro

   _____

4. un carpintero / cortarse la mano / serrando (*sawing*) madera

   _____

5. diez arqueólogos / hacerse daño / en una excavación en las pirámides

   _____

6. un bombero / quemarse / apagando un incendio

   _____

7. los esposos / divorciarse / después de veinte años de matrimonio

   _____

Actividad 8 **El aseo personal (*personal hygiene*).** Escriba oraciones explicando cuándo y cómo algunas personas hacen su aseo personal. Practique el uso de los verbos reflexivos en el presente. Siga el modelo.

> MODELO   Guillermo / limpiarse los dientes / dos veces al día
> Guillermo se limpia los dientes dos veces al día.

1. vosotros / lavarse el pelo / todos los días

   _____

2. yo / vestirse / rápidamente por la mañana

   _____

3. Uds. / ducharse / por la noche

   _____

4. Carlos / afeitarse / con una maquinilla de afeitar

_____

5. Laura y Teresa / limarse las uñas / antes de ponerse el esmalte de uñas
(*nail polish*)

_____

6. tú / peinarse / con peine y cepillo

_____

7. Benjamín y yo / arreglarse / en el dormitorio

_____

8. Ud. / cepillarse los dientes / antes de maquillarse

_____

Actividad 9   **Hay que hacerlo.** Escriba oraciones en las cuales se expresan los deseos,
intenciones y necesidades de las siguientes personas usando el verbo entre
paréntesis. Practique la construcción del verbo conjugado con el verbo
reflexivo en el infinitivo. Escriba las oraciones de dos maneras. Siga el
modelo.

> MODELO   Guillermo se afeita todos los días. (necesitar)
> Guillermo necesita afeitarse todos los días.
> Guillermo se necesita afeitar todos los días.

1. Ud. se coloca (*get a position*) en una sucursal (*branch*) de la empresa. (querer)

_____

_____

2. Nosotros nos despertamos antes de las ocho. (deber)

_____

_____

3. Vosotros os reunís en casa de Felipe esta noche. (pensar)

_____

_____

4. Teresa se pesa todas las semanas. (necesitar)

_____

_____

5. Yo me voy de vacaciones en julio. (ir a)

_____

_____

6. Las señoras se aprovechan de las liquidaciones (*sales*). (acabar de)

_____

_____

7. ¿Te sientas en esta fila? (querer)

_____

_____

8. Uds. se secan el pelo. (tener que)

_____

_____

Reflexive pronouns with the progressive tenses

In the progressive tenses, the reflexive pronouns may either precede the forms of **estar** or follow the present participle (gerund). When they follow, they are attached to the gerund and a written accent is added to the vowel before the **-ndo** ending.

Me estoy vistiendo.	*I'm getting dressed.*
Estoy vistiéndome.	
Ana **se está arreglando.**	*Ana is getting ready.*
Ana **está arreglándose.**	

Here are some commonly used reflexive verbs that refer to motion or to a change in position. In most cases, the corresponding nonreflexive verb is transitive. Note the prepositions that accompany certain verbs.

acercarse (a) *to come closer, approach*	**acercar** *to bring something closer, over*
alejarse (de) *to move away from*	**alejar** *to move something away*
caerse *to fall down*	**caer** *to fall (usually figurative)*
correrse *to move over, make room for*	**correr** *to move (an object)*
detenerse *to stop, come to a halt*	**detener** *to stop, bring to a halt*
instalarse *to move in*	**instalar** *to install*
irse *to go away*	**ir** *to go*
levantarse *to get up, rise*	**levantar** *to lift*
moverse (o → ue) *to move, stir, budge*	**mover (o → ue)** *to move (put in motion)*
pararse *to stand up (L. Am.)*	**parar** *to stop*
pasearse *to take a walk*	**pasear** *to take for a walk, walk*
perderse (e → ie) *to get lost*	**perder (e → ie)** *to lose*
quedarse *to stay, remain*	**quedar** *to remain, be left*
sentarse (e → ie) *to sit down*	**sentar (e → ie)** *to seat*
tirarse *to jump, throw oneself / lie down*	**tirar** *to throw*
volcarse (o → ue) *to get knocked over*	**volcar (o → ue)** *to knock over*

The following verbs of motion or change of position are used primarily as reflexives.

apresurarse de *to hurry*	**mudarse** *to move (change residence)*
echarse *to lie down*	**ponerse de pie** *to stand up (Sp.)*
escaparse *to escape*	**recostarse (o → ue)** *to lie down*
inclinarse *to bend over*	

Here are some verbs that are used primarily or exclusively as reflexives in Spanish for the meanings given. Verbs marked with an asterisk exist only as reflexives.

acordarse (o → ue) (de) *to remember*	**figurarse** *to imagine*
apoderarse (de) *to take possession (of)*	**fijarse (en)** *to notice*
aprovecharse (de) *to take advantage (of)*	**llevarse bien/mal (con)** *to get along well/poorly (with)*
apuntarse (a/para) *to register, sign up (for)*	
arrepentirse (e → ie) (de) *to regret, repent*	***jactarse (de)** *to boast about*
***atreverse (a)** *to dare to do something*	**negarse (e → ie) (a)** *to refuse to*
avergonzarse (o → ue) (de) *to be ashamed (of)*	**ocuparse (de)** *to take care of*
burlarse (de) *to laugh at, make fun of*	**ofrecerse a + infinitivo** *to offer to do something*
casarse (con) *to get married (to)*	**olvidarse (de)** *to forget*
comprometerse *to get engaged*	**oponerse (a)** *to oppose, be against*
***desmayarse** *to faint*	**parecerse (a)** *to resemble*
***divorciarse** *to get divorced*	**portarse bien/mal** *to behave well/badly*
empeñarse (en) *to insist (on), persist (in)*	***quejarse (de)** *to complain about*
enamorarse (de) *to fall in love (with)*	**reírse (e → i) (me río) (de)** *to laugh at*
enterarse (de) *to find out (about)*	**sentirse (e → ie)** *to feel*
fiarse (me fío) (de) *to trust*	

NOTAS

- **Olvidar** is followed by a direct object. **Olvidarse** is followed by the preposition **de**.

  Olvidaron el número.
  Se olvidaron del número. } *They forgot the number.*

- **Olvidarse** is also used with the indirect object pronoun. See **Capítulo 19** on unplanned occurrences.

  Se les olvidó el número.   *They forgot the number.*

- The verb **desayunar** (*to have breakfast*) is used as a reflexive, **desayunarse,** in some countries.

  Todavía **no (me) he desayunado.**   *I still **haven't had breakfast.***

Actividad 10 ¡**Haciendo diabluras!** (*Making mischief!*) En una reunión familiar, los niños están haciendo sus diabluras como siempre. Y los adultos están reaccionando como siempre. Escriba oraciones usando el presente progresivo para describir la escena. Escriba cada oración de dos maneras. Siga los modelos.

> MODELOS Sarita / mojarse con la sopa
> Sarita está mojándose con la sopa.
> Sarita se está mojando con la sopa.
>
> la hermana de Sarita / quejarse
> La hermana de Sarita está quejándose.
> La hermana de Sarita se está quejando.

1. Luisito / portarse mal

   _____

   _____

2. los abuelos de Luisito / enfadarse

   _____

   _____

3. Fernandito / esconderse en un armario

   _____

   _____

4. el tío de Fernandito / asustarse

   _____

   _____

5. los gemelos / escaparse de su padre

   _____

   _____

6. el padre de los gemelos / enojarse

   _____

   _____

7. Mari Carmen / ensuciarse con el helado

   _____

   _____

8. la madre de Mari Carmen / avergonzarse

   _____

   _____

Actividad 11 **Están en movimiento.** Hay mucha actividad en el barrio hoy. Use el presente progresivo para decir lo que está haciendo cada persona. Escriba cada oración de dos maneras. Siga el modelo.

> MODELO ¿Qué hace Juan Pedro? (levantarse)
> Se está levantando.
> Está levantándose.

1. ¿Qué hace tu mamá? (apresurarse para salir)

   está

   _____

2. ¿Qué hacen los Pereira? (mudarse a otro barrio)

   _____

   _____

3. ¿Dónde están los niños? (acercarse a la escuela)

   se están

   _____

4. ¿Qué hacen tus abuelos? (pasearse por el centro)

   _____

   _____

5. ¿Qué haces tú? (divertirse)

   _____

   _____

6. ¿Qué hacen Uds.? (reunirse en casa de Pepe)

   _____

   _____

7. ¿Qué hace Elena? (vestirse para ir a un baile)

   _____

   _____

8. ¿Qué hace Nicolás? (instalarse en su nuevo apartamento)

   _____

   _____

Imperative of reflexive verbs*

Reflexive pronouns precede negative command forms but follow affirmative commands and are attached to them in writing.

Acuéstense ahora, chicos.
No se levanten hasta las ocho.

Go to bed now, kids.
Don't get up until eight.

NOTA
- A written accent mark is added to affirmative command forms of more than one syllable when the reflexive pronoun is added.

Here are some common reflexive verbs that refer to the daily routine. Corresponding nonreflexive verbs are usually transitive.

acostarse (o → ue) *to go to bed*	**acostar (o → ue)** *to put (someone) to bed*
afeitarse *to shave*	**afeitar** *to shave (someone)*
arreglarse *to get ready (fix hair, clothing)*	**arreglar** *to arrange, fix*
bañarse *to bathe, take a bath*	**bañar** *to bathe (someone)*
cansarse *to get tired*	**cansar** *to tire (someone)*
colocarse *to get a job*	**colocar** *to place, put*
cortarse *to cut oneself*	**cortar** *to cut*
cuidarse *to take care of oneself*	**cuidar** *to take care of someone*
despedirse (e → i) de *to say good-bye to*	**despedir (e → i)** *to fire, dismiss*
despertarse (e → ie)† *to wake up*	**despertar (e → ie)** *to wake someone up*
dormirse (o → ue) *to fall asleep*	**dormir (o → ue)** *to sleep*
enfermarse *to get sick*	**enfermar** *to make ill*
lastimarse *to hurt oneself*	**lastimar** *to hurt*
lavarse *to wash up*	**lavar** *to wash someone, something*
levantarse *to get up*	**levantar** *to raise, pick up*
maquillarse *to put on makeup*	**maquillar** *to put makeup on someone*
peinarse *to comb one's hair*	**peinar** *to comb someone's hair*
reunirse (con) *to get together (with)*	**reunir** *to join, gather*
vestirse (e → i) *to dress, get dressed*	**vestir (e → i)** *to dress (someone)*

†**Despertarse** may also be used nonreflexively with the meaning *to wake up.*

Here are some common reflexive verbs expressing feelings and emotions. Corresponding nonreflexive verbs are usually transitive.

aburrirse *to get, be bored*	**aburrir** *to bore someone*
alegrarse *to be glad, happy*	**alegrar** *to make someone happy*
animarse *to cheer up, feel like doing something*	**animar** *to cheer someone up, encourage someone*
asustarse *to get scared*	**asustar** *to frighten someone*
calmarse *to calm down*	**calmar** *to calm someone down*
decidirse a *to make up one's mind*	**decidir** *to decide*
divertirse (e → ie) *to have a good time*	**divertir (e → ie)** *to amuse (someone)*
emocionarse *to be moved, touched, be/get excited*	**emocionar** *to move, touch, excite*

(continued)

*See **Capítulo 14** for a more in-depth explanation of the imperative (commands).

enfadarse *to get angry*	**enfadar** *to make (someone) angry*
enojarse *to get angry*	**enojar** *to make (someone) angry*
entusiasmarse *to get excited, feel thrilled*	**entusiasmar** *to excite, thrill, stir*
exasperarse *to get exasperated, lose one's patience*	**exasperar** *to exasperate, make (someone) lose his/her patience*
interesarse en *to be interested in*	**interesar** *to interest*
involucrarse *to be involved, implicated*	**involucrar** *to involve*
irritarse *to get irritated*	**irritar** *to irritate*
marearse *to get, feel dizzy*	**marear** *to make (someone) dizzy*
molestarse *to get annoyed*	**molestar** *to annoy, bother*
ofenderse *to get offended, insulted; feel hurt*	**ofender** *to offend, insult, hurt someone*
preocuparse *to worry*	**preocupar** *to worry someone*
relajarse *to relax*	**relajar** *to relax*
sorprenderse *to be surprised*	**sorprender** *to surprise someone*
tranquilizarse *to calm down, stop worrying*	**tranquilizar** *to calm someone down, reassure*

Actividad 12   **Dando consejos.** Lea las situaciones y luego dé algunos consejos. Escriba los verbos indicados con la forma formal e informal singular del mandato. Siga el modelo.

> MODELO   Tengo calor. (quitarse el suéter)
> formal: Quítese el suéter.
> informal: Quítate el suéter.

1. Me gustan los dos trajes. (probarse los dos)

   formal: _pruebese_

   informal: _pruebate_

2. Tengo muchísimo sueño. (acostarse temprano)

   formal: _acuestese_

   informal: _acuestate_

3. ¡Tengo cita a las tres y ya son las tres menos cuarto! (darse prisa)

   formal: _dése_

   informal: _date_

4. Empieza a llover. (ponerse el impermeable)

   formal: _pongase_

   informal: _ponte_

5. Voy a ver la nueva película española esta noche. (divertirse mucho)

   formal: _diviertase_

   informal: _diviertete_

6. Me encanta Sevilla. (quedarse otra semana entonces)

   formal: _____

   informal: _____

Actividad 13 **¡No lo haga!** Déle a la persona un mandato negativo empleando el verbo indicado. Escriba la forma formal e informal singular. Siga el modelo.

> MODELO Me gusta el pelo largo. (no cortarse el pelo entonces)
> formal: No se corte el pelo entonces.
> informal: No te cortes el pelo entonces.

1. Tengo fiebre. (no levantarse todavía)

   formal: _____

   informal: _____

2. Tengo los pies mojados por la lluvia. (no enfermarse)

   formal: _____

   informal: _____

3. A Roberta se le rompió mi reloj. (no enfadarse con ella)

   formal: _____

   informal: _____

4. Voy a coger el tren de las ocho. (no despertarse tarde)

   formal: _____

   informal: _____

5. Necesito estudiar para el examen de biología. (no dormirse antes de terminar)

   formal: _____

   informal: _____

6. Yo no quiero a José Antonio. (no casarse con él)

   formal: _____

   informal: _____

7. Voy a hacer alpinismo en diciembre. (no caerse)

   formal: _____ no se caiga _____

   informal: _____ no te caigas _____

Actividad 14 **¡Niños, hagan esto!** Déles mandatos a los niños escribiendo la forma del mandato de los verbos indicados. Dígales las cosas que deben hacer. Siga el modelo.

> MODELO ducharse ahora
> Niños, dúchense ahora.

1. vestirse para salir

   _____

2. cepillarse los dientes

   _____

3. atarse los cordones

   _____

4. ponerse serios

   _____

5. lavarse las manos

   _____

6. peinarse

   _____

7. levantarse

   _____

8. probarse los zapatos

   _____

Actividad 15 **¡Niños, pórtense bien!** Déles mandatos a los niños escribiendo la forma del mandato de los verbos indicados. Esta vez, dígales las cosas que no deben hacer. Siga el modelo.

MODELO	no quitarse los guantes
	Niños, no se quiten los guantes.

1. no ensuciarse la cara

   _____

2. no hacerse los sordos (*turn a deaf ear*)

   _____

3. no caerse patinando

   _____

4. no olvidarse de guardar sus juguetes

   _____

5. no irse del jardín

   _____

6. no quebrarse el pie jugando al fútbol

   _____

7. no quejarse tanto

_____

8. no hacerse daño

_____

Reciprocal reflexive verbs

The plural forms of reflexive verbs are used to express reciprocal action corresponding to the English phrase *each other*. Because **se ven** means either *they see each other* or *they see themselves* (e.g., in the mirror), the meaning must be inferred from the context.

Jacinto y Laura **se quieren** mucho.   *Jacinto and Laura **love each other** very much.*

Se ven todos los días.   *They **see each other** every day.*
¿Dónde **se conocieron Uds.**?   *Where **did you meet each other**?*
Nos conocimos en una conferencia.   *We **met** at a lecture.*

Spanish uses the phrase **el uno al otro** (or **uno a otro**) to focus on or to clarify the meaning *each other*. This phrase agrees with the gender and number of the people referred to: **el uno al otro / la una a la otra / los unos a los otros / las unas a las otras.**

Mis hermanos se ayudan **el uno al otro.**   *My brothers help **each other**.*

Las chicas se miran **la una a la otra.**   *The girls look at **each other**.*

The reflexive pronoun is not used to express *each other* with prepositions other than **a.**

Diana y Felisa nunca quieren ir de compras **la una sin la otra.**   *Diana and Felisa never want to shop **without each other**.*

Actividad 16 **Mi mejor amigo/a y yo.** Escriba oraciones en las cuales describe cómo es la relación entre Ud. y su mejor amigo/a. Practique el uso del reflexivo con el significado *each other*. Use el tiempo presente del verbo. Siga el modelo.

> MODELO Pablo y yo / conocer muy bien
> Pablo y yo nos conocemos muy bien.

1. Marisol y yo / hablar por teléfono cuatro veces al día
   nos hablamos

2. Jorge y yo / entender perfectamente
   nos entendemos

3. María y yo / ver todos los días
   nos vemos

4. Consuelo y yo / escribir correos electrónicos
   nos escribimos

5. Alicia y yo / ayudar con la tarea

   nos ayudamos

6. Victoria y yo / prestar la ropa

   prestamos

7. Claudia y yo / querer mucho

   queremos

8. Daniel y yo / tutear (*address each other as* tú [*informally*])

   tuteamos

Actividad 17 **Un gran amor.** ¿Cómo llegaron Alejandra y Claudio a comprometerse? Escriba oraciones usando el <u>pretérito</u> con la forma recíproca del reflexivo para explicarlo. Siga el modelo.

> MODELO ver por primera vez hace un año
> Se vieron por primera vez hace un año.

1. conocer en una fiesta

   Se conocieron

2. llamar a menudo

   Se llamaron

3. escribir mensajes por correo electrónico

   se escribieron

4. hablar constantemente

   se hablaron

5. comprar regalos

   se compraron

6. comprender muy bien

   se comprendieron

7. dar la mano

   se dieron

8. decir muchas cosas importantes

   se dijeron

9. hacer promesas

   _se_

10. llegar a querer

    se llegaron

How to say *become* in Spanish

The English verb *to become* has several different translations in Spanish. When *to become* is followed by an adjective, the most common Spanish expression is **ponerse** + *adjective*. It is used for physical or emotional changes, where no effort is implied.

Esteban **se puso bravo** al leer la carta.	*Esteban **got angry** when he read the letter.*
Lidia y María **se pusieron pálidas** del susto.	*Lidia and María **turned pale** from fright.*
Juanita **se pone roja** porque es tímida.	*Juanita **blushes** because she's shy.*

Volverse + *adjective* is used to express a sudden, involuntary change, most commonly seen in the expression **volverse loco** (*to go crazy, mad*). Changes indicated by **ponerse** may be superficial whereas those indicated by **volverse** are more profound.

Daniela **se volvió loca** al recibir la noticia.	*Daniela **went crazy** when she received the news.*
Los políticos **se volvieron muy arrogantes**.	*The politicians **got very arrogant**.*
¡Ese niño **se ha vuelto imposible**!	*That child **has become impossible**!*

Hacerse and **llegar a ser** also mean *to become* and are used with nouns expressing profession or adjectives expressing social status. They imply effort on the part of the subject. **Pasar a ser,** stressing the process of change, is also used.

Manolo **se hizo abogado**.	*Manolo **became a lawyer**.*
Lola **llegó a ser abogada** también.	*Lola **became a lawyer** also.*
Pedro y yo **nos hicimos amigos**.	*Pedro and I **became friends**.*
Pedro y Tomás nunca **llegaron a ser amigos**.	*Pedro and Tomás never **got to be friends**.*
Laura **pasó a ser directora ejecutiva** de la compañía.	*Laura **became executive director** of the company.*
Y **se hizo rica** también.	*And **she got rich,** too.*

The idioms **convertirse en (e → ie)** and **transformarse en** also express ideas related to the verb *to become*.

Atlanta **se convirtió en** una ciudad importante.	*Atlanta **became** an important city.*
El príncipe **se transformó en** sapo.	*The prince **turned into** a toad.*

Very often the idea of *to become* or *to get* is expressed by a reflexive verb in Spanish.

alegrarse *to become happy*	**deprimirse** *to get depressed*	**enojarse** *to get angry*
asustarse *to get frightened*	**emocionarse** *to become excited*	**enredarse** *to get entangled,*
cansarse *to get tired*	**enfadarse** *to become angry*	*involved*

Actividad 18 *To become y to get.* Exprese las oraciones en español usando la expresión correcta para *become* o *get* en cada caso.

1. Ricardo became a millionaire.

   ~~Se puso~~ Se hizo

2. The archaeologists got excited when they saw the ruins.

   _____

3. Magdalena often blushes because she's very shy.

   Se pone ro

4. They became furious when they found out the truth.

   Se pusieron furiosos

5. Carlitos has become impossible!

   se ha vuelto

6. Felisa is getting very fat because of the cake and ice cream she eats every day.

   _____

7. The region became an important technological center.

   se convirtió

8. Isabela became a programmer.

   se hizo ~~otra~~ una p

Other reflexive verbs

There are cases of reflexive verbs that do not fit exactly into the preceding categories and that require special attention.

Equivocarse has a basic meaning of *to be mistaken, be wrong.*

Si crees que Paula te va a devolver el dinero, **te equivocas.**	*If you think Paula is going to return the money to you, **you're mistaken.***

Equivocarse means *to be wrong* only when the subject is a person. **Estar equivocado** means *to be wrong* both for persons and things.

El físico **se equivocó.**	*The physicist **was wrong.***
El físico **estuvo equivocado.**	*The physicist **was wrong.***
La respuesta **está equivocada.**	*The answer **is wrong.***

The expression **equivocarse de** can be used for other uses of the English word *wrong.*

Ud. **se ha equivocado** de casa.	*You've come to the **wrong** house.*
Nos equivocamos de carretera.	*We took the **wrong** highway.*

Quedarse has a basic meaning of *to remain, stay.*

Quédate en casa si no te sientes bien.	***Stay at home** if you don't feel well.*
Pensamos quedarnos en un parador en Segovia.	*We **intend to stay** at a government-run inn in Segovia.*

Quedarse can express *to become* to indicate a new state, either physical or emotional.

Todos **se quedaron atónitos.**	*Everyone **was astonished.***
Dos víctimas del terremoto **se quedaron ciegas y sordas.**	*Two victims of the earthquake **became blind and deaf.***

Nonreflexive **quedar** is used to mean different things.

El cuarto **queda bien/mal** con las nuevas cortinas.	*The room **looks good/bad** with the new curtains.*
Tu corbata roja **queda bien** con tu camisa azul.	*Your red tie **goes well** with your blue shirt.*
Paco **quedó bien** regalándole flores a su suegra.	*Paco **made a good impression** giving flowers to his mother-in-law.*
El director de la orquesta **quedó mal** con los músicos.	*The conductor **made a bad impression** on the musicians.*
El soldado **quedó inválido.**	*The soldier **became disabled.***
Quedamos en ir al cine.	*We **agreed** to go to the movies.*

Hacerse, when followed by a definite article and an adjective, means *to pretend to be; to act like.*

El ladrón **se hizo el desentendido** al ser encontrado por la policía.	*The thief **played dumb (pretended not to understand)** when he was found by the police.*
Lola **se hizo la sorda** cuando su hermana le pidió prestado el coche.	*Lola **turned a deaf ear** when her sister asked to borrow the car.*
Berta **se hizo la dormida** para no tener que hacer las labores domésticas.	*Berta **pretended to be asleep** so that she wouldn't have to do the household chores.*
Nicolás **se hacía el tonto** en la fiesta.	*Nicolás **was acting silly (playing the fool)** at the party.*

Both **acordarse (de)** and **recordar** mean *to remember.*

Si no **me acuerdo** mal... } Si no **recuerdo** mal... }	*If **I remember** correctly . . .*

Recordar also means *to remind.*

Les recuerdo que mañana tenemos ensayo.	*I'm **reminding them** that we have a rehearsal tomorrow.*
Me recuerdas a tu mamá.	*You **remind me** of your mother.*

Expressions with reflexive verbs

darse cuenta de *to realize*	**ponerse de acuerdo** *to come to an agreement*
darse prisa *to hurry*	**quedarse con** *to keep, hold onto*
echarse a + *infinitivo* *to begin to*	**referirse a** *to refer to*
hacerse daño *to hurt oneself*	**servirse de** *to use*
hacerse tarde *to get/grow late*	**tratarse de** *to be about, be a question of*
ponerse a + *infinitivo* *to begin to*	**valerse de** *to use*

Certain verbs are made reflexive to stress participation by the subject or to convey an intensification of the action.

Compré un coche.   *I bought* a car.
Me compré un coche.   *I bought* (*myself*) a car.

Leo **comió** los pasteles.   *Leo ate the pastries.*
Leo **se comió** los pasteles.   *Leo gobbled up the pastries.*

Actividad 19   **Preposiciones con verbos reflexivos.** Complete las oraciones con las preposiciones correctas.

1. Este niño malcriado (*spoiled*) no se lleva bien _____con_____ nadie.

2. Los turistas se fijaron _____en_____ la arquitectura de los castillos.

3. No debemos aprovecharnos _____de_____ las demás personas.

4. Gabriela se arrepiente _____de_____ haberles mentido a sus padres.

5. Yo me intereso mucho _____en_____ la historia europea.

6. Los Cela se negaron _____a_____ hacer cola en la taquilla.

7. ¿No te fías _____de_____ tu abogado?

8. El vecino se ofreció _____a_____ cortarnos el césped.

9. La abuela siempre se jacta _____de_____ sus nietos.

10. Ud. se olvidó _____de_____ desenchufar los aparatos eléctricos.

11. Daniel se casará _____con_____ Luz en mayo.

12. No nos atrevemos _____a_____ viajar de noche sin linterna.

13. Ponte _____a_____ contestar el correo electrónico.

14. ¿Por qué se empeñan _____en_____ llamarnos todos los días?

Actividad 20   **En otras palabras.** Vuelva a escribir las oraciones usando un sinónimo de los verbos o expresiones que aparecen *en letra cursiva*.

1. *Si me acuerdo bien*, los Aranda se mudaron a Los Ángeles.

   _____

2. Ud. *no tiene razón*. Lima es la capital de Perú, no de Ecuador.

   _____

3. Dos personas *perdieron la vista* a causa del accidente.

    _____

4. *Parece que* la niña *está dormida, pero no lo está.*

    _____

5. Juan Carlos *ha bajado mucho de peso.*

    _____

6. Creíamos que íbamos a *volvernos locos* por el desorden de la casa.

    _____

7. Todos los habitantes *están enfureciéndose* por el número de robos en el barrio.

    _____

8. Diego *se ponía pálido* corriendo la última milla de la carrera.

    _____

9. *Te lastimaste* esquiando.

    _____

10. Uds. *se apresuraron* por llegar al aeropuerto.

    _____

11. *Es cuestión de* hacer una base de datos primero.

    _____

Actividad 21   **Actividad oral.** Con sus compañeros de clase describa su día típico. Hable de sus actividades diarias y a qué hora las hace. Por ejemplo: **despertarse, levantarse, ducharse, peinarse, vestirse, reunirse con los amigos, acostarse.**

CAPÍTULO 11 — Subjunctive: Present and present perfect

1,2,3,4,8,9,13

Forms of the present subjunctive of regular verbs

The present subjunctive (**el presente de subjuntivo**) is formed by changing the vowel **-a** of the present indicative of **-ar** verbs to **-e** and the vowels **-e** and **-i** of the present indicative of **-er** and **-ir** verbs to **-a**. Regular **-er** and **-ir** verbs have identical endings in all persons of the subjunctive.

ESTUDIAR			
Quiere que	estudi**e**	idiomas.	*He wants me to study languages.*
	estudi**es**		*He wants you to study languages.*
	estudi**e**		*He wants him/her to study languages.*
	estudi**emos**		*He wants us to study languages.*
	estudi**éis**		*He wants you to study languages.*
	estudi**en**		*He wants them to study languages.*

COMPRENDER		
Espera que	comprend**a**.	*She hopes I'll understand.*
	comprend**as**.	*She hopes you'll understand.*
	comprend**a**.	*She hopes he'll/she'll understand.*
	comprend**amos**.	*She hopes we'll understand.*
	comprend**áis**.	*She hopes you'll understand.*
	comprend**an**.	*She hopes they'll understand.*

VIVIR			
Prefieren que	viv**a**	aquí.	*They prefer that I live here.*
	viv**as**		*They prefer that you live here.*
	viv**a**		*They prefer that he/she live here.*
	viv**amos**		*They prefer that we live here.*
	viv**áis**		*They prefer that you live here.*
	viv**an**		*They prefer that they live here.*

In the present subjunctive, the first-person singular **(yo)** form and the third-person singular **(él/ella/Ud.)** forms are identical.

-Ar and **-er** verbs that have changes in the vowel of the stem in the present indicative have these same changes in the present subjunctive.

Le aconsejan que p**ie**nse más.	*They advise her to think more.*
Nos aconsejan que pensemos más.	*They advise us to think more.*
Espera que yo enc**ue**ntre las llaves.	*He hopes that I find the keys.*
Espera que encontremos las llaves.	*He hopes that we find the keys.*

-Ir verbs that have the change **e → ie** or **e → i** in the present indicative have the same changes in the present subjunctive. However, unlike the present indicative, these verbs also have the **e → i** stem change in the **nosotros/as** and **vosotros/as** forms in the present subjunctive. **Dormir** and **morir** have the regular **o → ue** change in the present subjunctive, but also have the **o → u** stem change in the **nosotros/as** and **vosotros/as** forms.*

SENTIR		SEGUIR	
s**ie**nta	s**i**ntamos	s**i**ga	s**i**gamos
s**ie**ntas	s**i**ntáis	s**i**gas	s**i**gáis
s**ie**nta	s**ie**ntan	s**i**ga	s**i**gan

DORMIR	
d**ue**rma	d**u**rmamos
d**ue**rmas	d**u**rmáis
d**ue**rma	d**ue**rman

Verbs that end in **-iar** or **-uar** that have an accent mark on the **-i** or **-u** in the present indicative in all forms except **nosotros/as** and **vosotros/as** have an accent mark in the same persons of the present subjunctive.*

ENVIAR		CONTINUAR	
env**í**e	enviemos	contin**ú**e	continuemos
env**í**es	enviéis	contin**ú**es	continuéis
env**í**e	env**í**en	contin**ú**e	contin**ú**en

Actividad 1 **Pero yo sí quiero.** Un amigo suyo le menciona varias cosas que no suceden. Ud. le dice que sí quiere que pasen. Escriba los verbos usando el presente del modo *(mood)* subjuntivo. Siga el modelo.

> MODELO   Alicia no estudia química.
> Pero yo quiero que estudie química.

1. Marcos no trabaja en el informe.
   Pero yo quiero que trabaje en el informe

*See **Capítulo 2** for more information on stem-changing verbs.

2. Yo no consigo empleo.

    pero yo quiero que consigas empleo

3. Federico y Paula no nos escriben.

    Pero yo quiero que nos escriban

4. Juanita no sigue nuestros consejos.

    pero yo quiero que siga nuestros consejos

5. Nosotros no comemos fuera hoy.

    pero yo quiero que comamos fuera hoy.

6. Yo no vuelvo temprano.

    Pero yo quiero que vuelvas temprano

7. Los niños no duermen por la tarde.

    pero yo quiero que duerman por la tarde

8. Tú y yo no pedimos taxi.

    _____

9. Los dueños no abren la tienda hoy.

    _____

10. Vosotros no entendéis.

    _____

11. Amalia no piensa en nosotros.

    _____

12. La oficina no envía el paquete.

    _____

13. Yo no cierro las ventanas.

    _____

14. Tú y yo no nos divertimos.

    _____

15. Vosotros no repetís el vocabulario.

    _____

Forms of the present subjunctive of irregular verbs

Verbs that have an irregularity such as **-g** or **-zc** in the **yo** form of the present indicative have that irregularity in all persons of the present subjunctive. These irregularities occur only in **-er** and **-ir** verbs and therefore all the present subjunctive endings have the vowel **-a.** Note the following **-g** verbs:

INFINITIVE	PRESENT INDICATIVE (*yo* FORM)	PRESENT SUBJUNCTIVE
caer	**caig**o	caiga, caigas, caiga, caigamos, caigáis, caigan
decir	**dig**o	diga, digas, diga, digamos, digáis, digan
hacer	**hag**o	haga, hagas, haga, hagamos, hagáis, hagan
oír	**oig**o	oiga, oigas, oiga, oigamos, oigáis, oigan
poner	**pong**o	ponga, pongas, ponga, pongamos, pongáis, pongan
salir	**salg**o	salga, salgas, salga, salgamos, salgáis, salgan
tener	**teng**o	tenga, tengas, tenga, tengamos, tengáis, tengan
traer	**traig**o	traiga, traigas, traiga, traigamos, traigáis, traigan
venir	**veng**o	venga, vengas, venga, vengamos, vengáis, vengan

Note the present subjunctive of other verbs that are irregular in the **yo** form.

INFINITIVE	PRESENT INDICATIVE (*yo* FORM)	PRESENT SUBJUNCTIVE
caber	**quep**o	quepa, quepas, quepa, quepamos, quepáis, quepan
conocer	**conozc**o	conozca, conozcas, conozca, conozcamos, conozcáis, conozcan
nacer	**nazc**o	nazca, nazcas, nazca, nazcamos, nazcáis, nazcan
parecer	**parezc**o	parezca, parezcas, parezca, parezcamos, parezcáis, parezcan
construir	**construy**o	construya, construyas, construya, construyamos, construyáis, construyan
destruir	**destruy**o	destruya, destruyas, destruya, destruyamos, destruyáis, destruyan
ver	**ve**o	vea, veas, vea, veamos, veáis, vean

Dar and **estar** are regular in the present subjunctive except for the accent marks. The first- and third-person singular forms of **dar** have the written accent (**dé**) and all of the present subjunctive forms of **estar** have the written accent, except the first-person plural form **estemos.**

DAR		ESTAR	
dé	demos	**esté**	estemos
des	deis	**estés**	estéis
dé	den	**esté**	**estén**

Haber, ir, saber, and **ser** have irregular stems in the present subjunctive; however, their endings are regular.

INFINITIVE	SUBJUNCTIVE STEM	PRESENT SUBJUNCTIVE
haber	**hay-**	haya, hayas, haya, hayamos, hayáis, hayan
ir	**vay-**	vaya, vayas, vaya, vayamos, vayáis, vayan
saber	**sep-**	sepa, sepas, sepa, sepamos, sepáis, sepan
ser	**se-**	sea, seas, sea, seamos, seáis, sean

Actividad 2 **Le parece muy bien.** Su amiga María se alegra de muchas cosas. Dígalo usando el presente de subjuntivo. Siga el modelo.

> MODELO ¿Sabe María que viene Juan Carlos?
> Sí. Se alegra de que venga.

1. ¿Sabe María que conoces a Pedro?

   _____

2. ¿Sabe María que tenemos un día libre?

   _____

3. ¿Sabe María que Alfredo le trae flores?

   _____

4. ¿Sabe María que los Ibáñez construyen una casa?

   _____

5. ¿Sabe María que vosotros salís juntos?

   _____

6. ¿Sabe María que su hermanito obedece a su profesora?

   _____

7. ¿Sabe María que Raquel compone música?

   _____

8. ¿Sabe María que la fiesta es mañana?

   _____

9. ¿Sabe María que hay reunión la semana que viene?

   _____

10. ¿Sabe María que sus primos van a España?

   _____

Spelling changes in the present subjunctive

-Ar verbs whose stems end in **-c, -g,** or **-z** change those letters as follows in the present subjunctive.

c → qu	Bus**c**amos casa.	Es necesario que bus**qu**emos casa.
g → gu	Lle**g**an el lunes.	Espero que lle**gu**en el lunes.
z → c	Almor**z**amos aquí.	Prefiero que almor**c**emos aquí.

-Er and **-ir** verbs whose stems end in **-g, -gu,** or **-c** change those letters as follows in the present subjunctive.

g → j	Esco**g**es otro plato.	Queremos que esco**j**as otro plato.
gu → g	Si**gu**en andando.	Es posible que si**g**an andando.
c → z	Te conven**c**e.	Espero que te conven**z**a.

-Ar verbs whose stems end in **-j** do not require a spelling change in the subjunctive.

Tra**baj**o los domingos.   Quieren que tra**baj**e los domingos.

Irregular verbs such as **conocer** and **hacer** (see page 160) don't follow the spelling change in the second rule above but instead have irregularities in the **yo** form of the present indicative.

Cono**c**en a Marta.   No creo que cono**zc**an a Marta.
Ha**c**es la cena.   Quiero que ha**g**as la cena.

Actividad 3   **Ortografía (Spelling).** Escriba los verbos indicados usando el presente de subjuntivo. Recuerde los cambios ortográficos.

1. Espero que tú (realizar) _____ tus planes.

2. Es necesario que Uds. (acercarse) _____ más.

3. ¡Qué lástima que (comenzar) _____ a llover!

4. Se alegran de que yo (dirigir) _____ la orquesta.

5. Es probable que los chicos (sacar) _____ muy buenas notas.

6. Nos piden que (recoger) _____ las manzanas.

7. Es importante que Ud. (dedicarse) _____ a los negocios.

8. Te aconsejamos que (entregar) _____ el informe mañana.

9. Ojalá que Daniel (conseguir) _____ el puesto.

10. Tal vez Uds. (organizar) _____ la reunión.

11. No creo que Bárbara (almorzar) _____ antes de las dos.

12. Es difícil que yo los (convencer) _____.

13. Tenemos miedo que nuestros jugadores no (vencer)

_____ al otro equipo.

Uses of the present subjunctive in noun clauses

A noun clause is a clause that functions as a noun, that is, it can serve as either the subject or the object of a verb. Noun clauses that are incorporated into a longer sentence are called "dependent" or "subordinate" clauses and are introduced in Spanish by the conjunction **que**.

All the Spanish tenses studied so far belong to the indicative mood. Verbs in the indicative mood express events or states that are considered factual, definite, or part of reality as experienced by the speaker. The following examples have dependent noun clauses in the indicative. They show events perceived as part of reality because they are the objects of verbs such as **oír, parecer, saber,** and **ver.**

He oído **que hay una buena noticia.**	*I've heard **there's good news.***
Nos parece **que está lloviendo.**	*We think **it's raining.***
Sabes **que lo hizo Sandra.**	*You know **that Sandra did it.***
Verán **que Juan no entiende.**	*You'll see **that Juan doesn't understand.***

The present subjunctive in Spanish is used in dependent noun clauses that mark events or states that the speaker considers not part of reality or of his or her experience. These dependent noun clauses follow main clauses that express expectation, skepticism, doubt, uncertainty, demands, wants, needs, insistence, advice, impositions of will, negated facts. The verbs in the main clauses are in the present, present perfect, future, or imperative.

Dudo que Uds. **lleguen** para las tres.	*I doubt you'll arrive by three o'clock.*
Paula **quiere** que la **visites.**	*Paula **wants you to visit** her.*
No es cierto que **nos quedemos.**	***It's not certain** that **we'll stay.***

Verbs such as **desear** (*to want*), **esperar** (*to hope*), **insistir en** (*to insist*), **necesitar** (*to need*), **preferir** (*to prefer*), and **querer** (*to want*) are followed by a dependent noun clause in the subjunctive unless the subjects of both clauses are the same. In that case, the verb in the dependent clause should be in the infinitive.

Verb in main clause + dependent noun clause in subjunctive (two clauses: two different subjects)

Espero que Roberto **vaya.**	*I hope Roberto goes.*
Quieren que **salgamos.**	*They want us to go out.*
Insistimos en que Uds. **se queden.**	*We insist that you stay.*

Verb in main clause + infinitive (the same subject in both parts of the sentence)

Espero ir.	*I hope to go.*
Quieren salir.	*They want to go out.*
Insistimos en quedarnos.	*We insist on staying.*

The verbs **decir** (*to tell someone to do something*) and **pedir** (*to ask someone to do something*) are followed by a subjunctive clause. They may occur with an indirect object.

Le dicen a Felipe que **tenga** cuidado.	*They tell Felipe to be careful.*
Susana **nos pide** que **traigamos** el periódico.	*Susana asks us to bring the newspaper.*

Decir is followed by a dependent clause in the indicative when the dependent clause reports what someone said. For example, **José les dice: Leo mucho.** **Decir** is followed by a dependent clause in the subjunctive when it introduces a command, such as **José les dice: lean mucho.** Contrast the use of the indicative and subjunctive after **decir**.

José les dice que **lee** mucho.	*José tells them he reads a lot.*
José les dice que **lean** mucho.	*José tells them to read a lot.*

Some verbs can be followed either by a noun clause in the subjunctive or by an infinitive without a change in meaning. An indirect object pronoun is optional if these verbs are followed by a subjunctive clause, but it is obligatory when these verbs are followed by the infinitive. These verbs include **aconsejar** (*to advise*), **exigir** (*to demand*), **impedir** (*to prevent*), **mandar** (*to order*), **permitir** (*to permit*), **prohibir** (*to forbid*), **recomendar** (*to recommend*), **rogar** (*to request, beg*), and **sugerir** (*to suggest*).

(Les) aconsejo que **tomen** el tren. **Les aconsejo tomar** el tren.	*I advise you to take the train.*
(Le) exigimos a Beatriz que **regrese.** **Le exigimos** a Beatriz **regresar.**	*We demand that Beatriz return.*

The verb **dejar** (*to let, allow*) can also be followed by a noun clause in the subjunctive or by an infinitive without a change in meaning. A direct object pronoun is optional if the verb is followed by a subjunctive clause, but it is obligatory when the verb is followed by an infinitive.

(Los) **dejan** que **entren.** Los **dejan entrar.**	*They let them come in.*

Some verbs that express an emotional state, an attitude, or a bias are followed by dependent noun clauses in the subjunctive. These verbs include **alegrarse (de)** (*to be glad, happy*), **extrañar** (*to surprise*), **gustar** (*to like*), **sentir** (*to regret*), **sorprender** (*to surprise*), **temer** (*to fear*), and **tener miedo (de),** (*to be afraid [of]*).

Me alegro (de) que Uds. **visiten** Lima.	*I'm glad that you're visiting Lima.*
¿No **te extraña** que Claudia no **llame**?	*Aren't you surprised that Claudia doesn't call?*
Los Ayala **temen** que sus hijos no **saquen** buenas notas.	*Mr. and Mrs. Ayala are afraid their children won't get good grades.*

NOTA **Extrañar, gustar,** and **sorprender** are commonly used with an indirect object pronoun (See **Capítulo 19**).

Actividad 4 **¿Indicativo o subjuntivo?** Complete las oraciones usando el presente de indicativo o el presente de subjuntivo de los verbos indicados. Siga los modelos.

> MODELOS Creo que Fernando (llegar) <u>llega</u> el miércoles.
> Prefiero que Fernando (llegar) <u>llegue</u> el miércoles.

1. Daniel quiere que nosotros le (decir) _____ lo que pasó.

2. Vemos que estas chicas (aprender) _____ muchas fechas de memoria.

3. Siento que Anita no (graduarse) _____ este año.

4. Piensan que tú (quejarse) _____ de todo.

5. Mis padres insisten en que yo (matricularse)

   _____ lo antes posible.

6. Me alegro de que vosotros (ir) _____ a casaros.

7. Parece que Ud. no (salir) _____ hasta más tarde.

8. Isabel comprende que nosotros no (poder) _____ ayudarla.

9. Le aconsejamos a Diego que (ser) _____ más responsable.

10. Les gusta que ya no (haber) _____ problemas con la casa.

11. Todo el mundo entiende que Uds. (estar) _____ ocupadísimos.

12. Yo exijo que tú me (hacer) _____ caso.

13. Mercedes cree que yo lo (saber) _____ todo.

14. Debes darte cuenta que ya no se (conseguir) _____ ese libro.

Actividad 5 **¡Viva México!** Ud. y sus amigos están emocionados pensando en el viaje que van a hacer a México durante el verano. Escriba oraciones que expresen lo que quieren hacer en México. El sujeto de la cláusula principal y el de la subordinada (dependiente) deben ser el mismo. Use el modelo de *verbo conjugado + infinitivo*. Siga el modelo.

> MODELO   yo / querer / ver las pirámides de San Juan de Teotihuacán
> Yo quiero ver las pirámides de San Juan de Teotihuacán.

1. Laura / esperar / perfeccionar su español

   _____

2. Ricardo y Beti / preferir / visitar la catedral del Zócalo

   _____

3. Ud. / deber / conocer Taxco

   _____

4. Pablo y yo / desear / ir a Puebla

_____

5. tú / preferir / hacer una excursión a la Ciudad Universitaria

_____

6. yo / sentir / no poder quedarme más tiempo en la Ciudad de México

_____

7. Uds. / insistir en / escaparse un par de días a Mérida

_____

8. todos nosotros / alegrarse de / estar en Oaxaca

_____

Actividad 6 **Con los amigos en México.** Ahora escriba oraciones que expresen lo que Uds. quieren que hagan los otros amigos en México. El sujeto de la cláusula principal es diferente del de la subordinada. Use el subjuntivo. Siga el modelo.

MODELO   yo / querer / Paco y Mari / ver las pirámides de San Juan de Teotihuacán
Yo quiero que Paco y Mari vean las pirámides de San Juan de Teotihuacán.

1. Laura / esperar / nosotros / perfeccionar nuestro español

_____

2. Ricardo y Beti / preferir / Ud. / visitar la catedral del Zócalo

_____

3. Ud. / necesitar / Leo / conocer Taxco

_____

4. Pablo y yo / desear / Uds. / ir a Puebla

_____

5. tú / preferir / yo / hacer una excursión a la Ciudad Universitaria

_____

6. yo / sentir / nosotros / no poder quedarse más tiempo en la Ciudad de México

_____

7. Uds. / insistir en / los amigos / escaparse un par de días a Mérida

_____

8. todos nosotros / alegrarse de / tú / estar en Oaxaca

_____

Actividad 7 **Una familia unida** (*close*). Los miembros de la familia Ayala son muy unidos. Todos se quieren mucho y comparten sus pensamientos y sentimientos. Escriba oraciones que expresen lo que quieren para los demás miembros de la familia. Use el subjuntivo. Siga el modelo.

> MODELO el abuelo / desear / su familia / vivir bien
> El abuelo desea que su familia viva bien.

Vocabulario

Lazos familiares (*family ties*)

el/la ahijado/a *godson, goddaughter*
el/la bisabuelo/a *great-grandfather, great-grandmother*
el/la cuñado/a *brother-in-law, sister-in-law*
los familiares *relatives*

el/la nieto/a *grandson, granddaughter*
el/la novio/a *groom/bride, fiancé/fiancée*
el/la padrino/a *godfather, godmother*
el/la suegro/a *father-in-law, mother-in-law*

1. Elena / esperar / sus cuñados / tener éxito

2. el señor Ayala / pedirles / sus suegros / venir a verlos los domingos

3. la madrina / alegrarse / su ahijado / sacar buenas notas en la universidad

4. los padres / querer / sus hijos / ganarse la vida (*to earn a living*)

5. a la señora Ayala / gustarle / los bisabuelos / ser felices en la tercera edad (*old age*)

6. yo / aconsejarle / la nieta / hacerse arquitecta

7. Terencio / prohibirles / las ahijadas / ir solas al extranjero

8. tú / sentir / tu cuñado / no estar contento con el nuevo empleo

9. la suegra / preferir / los novios / mudarse con ella

10. Uds. / rogarles / los padrinos / aceptar su regalo

11. Ricardo y yo / necesitar / los nietos / darnos muchos besos y abrazos

_____

12. los hijos / no dejar / sus padres / trabajar demasiado manteniéndolos

_____

Actividad 8   **El correo electrónico.** Ana María Vázquez vive en Bogotá, Colombia. Le escribe un correo electrónico a su amiga Isabel García que vive en Los Ángeles. Complete las oraciones usando el presente de subjuntivo o el presente de indicativo de los verbos indicados.

Querida Isabel:

Espero que tú (encontrarse) _____ bien.
                                              1

Mis papás, hermanos y yo (estar) _____
                                                    2

perfectamente. Recibí tu correo electrónico ayer. Me alegro que tú (poder)

_____ venir a verme durante las vacaciones. Creo
              3

que yo (ir) _____ a ir a la playa con mi familia todo
                        4

el mes de julio. Por eso es mejor que tú (llegar) _____
                                                                        5

a principios de agosto. Mis padres quieren que tus papás y hermanos (pasar)

_____ el mes con nosotros también. Les recomiendo
              6

que (comprar) _____ los boletos de avión lo antes
                          7

posible. Les aconsejo también que (traer) _____
                                                              8

ropa un poco gruesa,[a] un impermeable y un paraguas porque (hacer)

_____ fresco, (estar) _____
              9   10

nublado y (llover) _____. Tú (deber)
                                11

_____ recordar que Bogotá queda en las
              12

montañas. Yo (saber) _____ que tú no (ir)
                                    13

_____ a aburrirte en Bogotá. Tú
              14

(ir) _____ a ver que (haber)
                15

_____ muchas cosas que ver y hacer aquí.
              16

Voy a insistir en que Uds. (despertarse) _____ muy
                                                                17

temprano todos los días aunque vamos a trasnochar oyendo música y bailando

en la discoteca. Así yo (poder) _____ enseñarles las
                                                    18

muchas cosas que hay en la ciudad y en las afueras.[b] Bueno, querida amiga,

yo (tener) _____ muchas ganas de[c] volver a verte.
                        19

[a]_heavy_   [b]las... _the outskirts of town_   [c]tener... _to really look forward to_

168   _Verbs—Forms and Uses_

¡Espero que tú me (escribir) _____ con la buena noticia [20]

de que (venir) _____ tu familia también! [21]

Cariños de Ana María

Uses of the present subjunctive with impersonal expressions; Subjunctive-indicative contrasts

Impersonal expressions (expressions with no specific subject) are similar to other types of main clauses that take the subjunctive. They require the subjunctive in dependent noun clauses if they suggest that the event or state mentioned in the dependent clause is not yet part of reality. For example, **es importante que** (*it's important that*), **es imposible que** (*it's impossible that*), **es improbable que** (*it's improbable that*), **es necesario que** (*it's necessary that*), **es posible que** (*it's possible that*), **es preciso que** (*it's necessary that*), **es probable que** (*it's probable that*), **Ojalá (que)** (*I hope [that]*), **quizás** (*perhaps, maybe*), and **tal vez** (*perhaps, maybe*) are all followed by the subjunctive.

Es necesario que discutamos el asunto.	*It's necessary that we discuss the matter.*
Es posible que yo no tenga tiempo hoy.	*It's possible I won't have time today.*
Pero **es importante que resolvamos** el problema.	*But it's important that we resolve the problem.*
De acuerdo. **Es probable que podamos** discutirlo mañana.	*Agreed. **It's probable we can** discuss it tomorrow.*
Tal vez sea posible.	***Maybe it will be** possible.*
Ojalá que tengas razón.	*I hope you're right.*

Impersonal expressions that show the speaker's emotional attitude or bias toward the event or state of the dependent clause also require the subjunctive. **Es bueno que** (*it's good that*), **es inútil que** (*it's useless that*), **es malo que** (*it's bad that*), **es mejor que** (*it's better that*), **es peor que** (*it's worse that*), **es triste que** (*it's sad that*), **es útil que** (*it's useful that*), **más vale que** (*it's better that*), **es una lástima que** (*it's a pity that*) and **¡qué lástima que!** (*what a pity that!*). **Es una lástima que** and **¡qué lástima!** are sometimes followed by the indicative.

Es bueno que José Luis **tenga** correo de voz.	*It's good that José Luis **has** voice mail.*
Es útil que **naveguemos** en la Red.	*It's useful for us to surf the Internet.*
Es una lástima que no **encuentres** tu teléfono celular.	*It's a pity you can't find your cell phone.*

When the speaker does not identify a specific subject in the dependent clause, the impersonal expression is followed by an infinitive. Study the following pairs of sentences.

Es preciso saber la fecha.	*It's necessary to know the date.*
Es preciso que sepamos la fecha.	*It's necessary that we know the date.*
Es útil hacer investigaciones.	*It's useful to do research.*
Es útil que hagas investigaciones.	*It's useful for you to do research.*

There are certain verbs and expressions in Spanish that require the subjunctive in the dependent clause only when they are negative, that is, when they suggest that the event or state in the dependent clause is a negated fact. For example: **no creer que, no es cierto que, no es evidente que, no es obvio que, no es que, no es/está seguro que, no es verdad que,** and **no pensar que.** When they are not negative, they are followed by the indicative.

Creo que Lola y Víctor **van** al cine.	*I think Lola and Víctor are going to the movies.*
No creo que Lola y Víctor **vayan** al cine.	*I don't think Lola and Víctor are going to the movies.*
Es cierto que la clase **es** interesante.	*It's true that the class is interesting.*
No es cierto que la clase **sea** interesante.	*It's not true that the class is interesting.*
Es evidente que Juana **sabe** quién lo hizo.	*It's evident that Juana knows who did it.*
No es evidente que Juana **sepa** quién lo hizo.	*It's not evident that Juana knows who did it.*
Estamos seguros de que Paco **viene** hoy.	*We're sure that Paco is coming today.*
No estamos seguros de que Paco **venga** hoy.	*We're not sure that Paco is coming today.*

NOTA

Sometimes the indicative is used after **no creer que, no pensar que, quizás,** and **tal vez.** The choice of the indicative indicates a greater degree of certainty about the action on the part of the speaker. The use of the subjunctive is always correct after these expressions, however.

No creo que ella se **dé** cuenta de lo que pasa.	*I don't think she realizes what's happening.*
No creo que ella se **da** cuenta de lo que pasa.	*I really don't think she realizes what's happening.*
Quizás vengan.	*Maybe they will come. (I have no idea whether or not they are coming.)*
Quizás vendrán.	*Maybe they will come. (I think there is a good chance that they are coming.)*
Tal vez estén enfadados.	*Maybe they're angry. (Who knows?)*
Tal vez están enfadados.	*Maybe they're angry. (There is a good chance they are.)*

When used in the affirmative, **dudar** (*to doubt*) and **es dudoso** (*it's doubtful*), require the use of the subjunctive in the dependent clause. Conversely, when **dudar** and **es dudoso** appear in the negative, the verb in the dependent clause is in the indicative.

Dudamos que Andrés **vuelva** hoy.	*We doubt Andrés is coming back today.*
No dudamos que Andrés **vuelve** hoy.	*We don't doubt Andrés is coming back today.*
Es dudoso que Andrés **vuelva** hoy.	*It's doubtful Andrés is coming back today.*
No es dudoso que Andrés **vuelve** hoy.	*It's not doubtful Andrés is coming back today.*

Actividad 9 **¡Qué desorden! Y vienen los padres.** Ud. comparte un apartamento con tres compañeras de cuarto. Este fin de semana vienen los padres a visitarlas. Uds. están contentas de ver a sus padres, pero están un poco preocupadas porque ellos van a ver que el apartamento es una pocilga (*pigsty*). Escriba las oraciones usando las expresiones impersonales indicadas con el subjuntivo para describir la situación. Siga el modelo.

> MODELO   Vienen mis papás. (es bueno)
> Es bueno que vengan mis papás.

Haciendo la limpieza

Vocabulario

el desorden *mess*
fregar (e → ie) las cacerolas *to scour the pans*
guardar *to put away*
limpiar el polvo *to dust*
meterse en *to get involved in*

ordenar *to clean up*
el producto para la limpieza *cleaning product*
la telaraña *cobweb, spiderweb*
el trapo *cleaning rag*

1. Ellos ven el desorden. (es malo)

_____

2. Hacemos la limpieza del apartamento. (es necesario)

_____

3. Lupe friega las cacerolas. (es importante)

_____

4. Uds. recogen las cajas de pizza. (es probable)

_____

5. Los padres traen trapos y productos para la limpieza. (más vale que)

_____

6. Yo limpio el polvo. (es preciso)

_____

7. Los padres se meten en todo esto. (es dudoso)

_____

8. María y Diana guardan su ropa sucia en la cómoda. (es posible)

_____

9. Tú quitas las telarañas del techo. (es mejor)

_____

10. No nos relajamos en todo el día. (¡qué lástima que!)

_____

Actividad 10 **Reacciones.** Ud. reacciona a unas afirmaciones. Al reaccionar, escoja entre el presente de subjuntivo y el presente de indicativo, según la expresión indicada. Siga los modelos.

> MODELOS   Manuela trabaja de mesera. (es verdad)
> Es verdad que Manuela trabaja de mesera.
>
> Manuela trabaja de mesera. (no es verdad)
> No es verdad que Manuela trabaje de mesera.

1. Lorenzo sigue enfermo. (no estoy seguro)

   _____

2. Teresa y Jesús se quieren mucho. (es obvio)

   _____

3. Uds. tienen problemas con el coche. (no es cierto)

   _____

4. Julia llega el sábado. (es que)

   _____

5. Carmen es de origen ruso. (no es seguro)

   _____

6. Los niños están aburridos. (no es evidente)

   _____

7. Tú lo sabes todo. (no creo que)

   _____

8. Martín renuncia a su puesto. (es cierto)

   _____

Actividad 11 **Pereza del fin de año.** Ahora que termina el año escolar y hace tan buen tiempo, sus amigos prefieren jugar al béisbol en vez de estudiar. Le toca a Ud. convencerlos que deben trabajar más. Escriba las oraciones usando el presente de subjuntivo. Siga el modelo.

> MODELO   Pedro: No quiero asistir a la clase de química hoy. (es necesario)
> Ud.: Oye, Pedro, es necesario que asistas a la clase de química hoy.

1. Anita: No voy a estudiar para los exámenes finales. (insisto en que)

   _____

2. Miguel: No deseo trabajar en la librería. (me sorprende)

   _____

3. Rebeca: No pienso escribir el informe para sociología. (más vale que)

   _____

4. Tomás: No me gusta practicar chino en el laboratorio de lenguas. (es útil)

_____

5. Graciela: No me interesa tomar apuntes en historia. (es importante)

_____

6. Alfredo: Prefiero no hacer la tarea. (te ruego)

_____

7. Carolina: No me importa sacar buenas notas. (espero)

_____

8. Ana: Voy a jugar al béisbol todo el día. (te prohíbo)

_____

Actividad 12 **En un coloquio (*discussion*).** Exprese en español las ideas de los participantes de un coloquio sobre el mundo a principios del siglo veintiuno. Use el presente de subjuntivo cuando sea necesario.

1. It's good there are so many technological advances **(adelantos).**

_____

2. We prefer to use nuclear energy even more.

_____

3. Everyone's happy to have the computer.

_____

4. It's evident that wars continue to break out **(estallar).**

_____

5. It's probable that environmental pollution is doing much harm.

_____

6. It's obvious that people want to live in a democratic society.

_____

7. We advise the political leaders to spend money more responsibly.

_____

8. I hope there will be free elections in every country.

_____

9. It's important that there be more new technology in the twenty-first century.

_____

Forms and uses of the present perfect subjunctive

The present perfect subjunctive consists of the present subjunctive of **haber** + *past participle*.

Esperan que lo	**haya visto.**	*They hope I saw him.*
	hayas visto.	*They hope you saw him.*
	haya visto.	*They hope he/she saw him.*
	hayamos visto.	*They hope we saw him.*
	hayáis visto.	*They hope you saw him.*
	hayan visto.	*They hope they saw him.*

The present perfect subjunctive is used in the same kinds of dependent clauses as the present subjunctive. It is used to indicate that the action of the dependent clause happened before the action of the main clause.

Me alegro de que Uds. **vengan.**   *I'm glad you **are coming.***
(two actions in the present)

Me alegro de que **hayan venido Uds.**   *I'm glad you **came.***
(dependent clause action happened prior to action of main clause)

Actividad 13   **¿Qué les parece?** Escriba oraciones empleando la frase indicada en la cláusula principal y cambiando el verbo del pretérito al perfecto de subjuntivo. Siga el modelo.

> MODELO   Los Fernández llegaron. (es bueno)
> Es bueno que los Fernández hayan llegado.

1. Uds. no vieron la exposición de arte. (Clara siente)

   _____

2. Vosotros escribisteis la revista electrónica. (dudamos)

   _____

3. Carlos se hizo ciudadano. (me alegro)

   _____

4. Viste la nueva película policíaca. (esperan)

   _____

5. Murió el bisabuelo de Martín. (es una lástima)

   _____

6. Las chicas no dijeron nada. (es mejor)

   _____

7. Hubo un incendio en el metro. (nos sorprende)

   _____

8. Luz se puso brava. (no piensan)

   _____

9. Me gustó el concierto. (no creen)

_____

Actividad 14 **Expresar en español.** Exprese las oraciones en español.

1. I'm glad Julia and Paco got married.

_____

2. It's good that we saw those Web sites.

_____

3. They doubt that the Tigers won the soccer game.

_____

4. We hope Fernando got rich.

_____

5. Are you (**Ud.**) surprised that the Núñez family moved?

_____

6. Ana doesn't think the boys broke the window.

_____

Actividad 15 **Actividad oral.** Con un compañero / una compañera de clase hable de las cosas que le mandan hacer y que Ud. manda que hagan los demás (sus padres, sus amigos, sus profesores, etcétera). Diga en cada caso quién manda y lo que le dice a Ud. que haga. ¿A su compañero/a le mandan hacer las mismas cosas que a Ud.?

Subjunctive: Imperfect and past perfect

Forms of the imperfect subjunctive

The forms of the imperfect subjunctive (**el imperfecto de subjuntivo**) are derived from the third-person plural form of the preterite. Any irregularity or vowel change in the stem of the third-person plural of the preterite occurs in all persons of the imperfect subjunctive.

hablaron → que yo **hablara**　　　　**fueron** → que yo **fuera**
comieron → que yo **comiera**　　　　**hicieron** → que yo **hiciera**
escribieron → que yo **escribiera**　　**pidieron** → que yo **pidiera**
durmieron → que yo **durmiera**　　　**pudieron** → que yo **pudiera**
estuvieron → que yo **estuviera**　　　**trajeron** → que yo **trajera**

The preterite ending **-ron** is replaced by the following endings in all verbs.

		HABLAR	COMER	ESCRIBIR
-ra		hablara	comiera	escribiera
-ras		hablaras	comieras	escribieras
-ra	Querían que	hablara	comiera	escribiera
-ramos		habláramos	comiéramos	escribiéramos
-rais		hablarais	comierais	escribierais
-ran		hablaran	comieran	escribieran

Meaning: *They wanted me/you/him/her/us/you/them to speak/eat/write.*

The first-person singular **(yo)** and the third-person singular **(él/ella/Ud.)** forms are identical in the imperfect subjunctive, and the **nosotros/as** form has a written accent mark on the vowel before the **-r** of the ending **habláramos, comiéramos, escribiéramos.**

There is an alternate form of the imperfect subjunctive that has endings in **-se.** The **-ra** and **-se** forms are interchangeable, but the **-se** forms are less common in colloquial speech. In the **-se** form of the imperfect subjunctive, as in the **-ra** form, the first- and third-person singular forms are identical, and the **nosotros/as** form has a written accent on the vowel before the **-s** of the ending.

		HABLAR	COMER	ESCRIBIR
-se		hablase	comiese	escribiese
-ses		hablases	comieses	escribieses
-se	Querían que	hablase	comiese	escribiese
-semos		hablásemos	comiésemos	escribiésemos
-seis		hablaseis	comieseis	escribieseis
-sen		hablasen	comiesen	escribiesen

Actividad 1 **Imperfecto de subjuntivo.** Complete las oraciones con los verbos indicados en el imperfecto de subjuntivo. Escriba cada verbo con las dos desinencias (*endings*) (**-ra** y **-se**).

1. Yo esperaba que Manolo (darse) _____ /

   _____ cuenta.

2. Nos alegramos que Lorna (encontrar) _____ /

   _____ su collar de perlas.

3. Rita insistió en que los niños (ponerse) _____ /

   _____ las botas.

4. No era cierto que nosotros lo (saber) _____ /

   _____.

5. Ojalá que (haber) _____ /

   _____ pescado en la carta.

6. Te aconsejaron que (seguir) _____ /

   _____ derecho.

7. Dudaban que Ud. (dormir) _____ /

   _____ la siesta.

8. No fue posible que yo los (ver) _____ /

   _____ hasta el jueves.

9. Habíamos querido que Uds. (reunirse) _____ /

   _____ con nosotros.

10. Le gustaría que nosotros (oír) _____ /

    _____ esta sinfonía.

11. Preferiríamos que vosotros nos lo (decir) _____ /

    _____.

12. No creían que los turistas (ser) _____ /

    _____ de Inglaterra.

13. Era preciso que se (construir) _____ /

    _____ nuevas casas en las afueras.

14. Yo querría que tú (traer) _____ /

    _____ los documentos.

15. Le dijeron a Mateo que no (irse) _____ /

    _____.

Imperfect subjunctive in noun clauses; The sequence of tenses

The imperfect subjunctive is used in dependent noun clauses requiring the subjunctive when the verb in the main clause is in the imperfect, preterite, past perfect, or conditional.

imperfect
Queríamos que lo **hicieras.**   *We wanted you to do it.*

preterite
Quisimos que lo **hicieras.**   *We wanted you to do it.*

past perfect
Habíamos querido que lo **hicieras.**   *We had wanted you to do it.*

conditional
Querríamos que lo **hicieras.**   *We would want you to do it.*

The present subjunctive is used when the verb in the main clause is in the present, present perfect, future, or imperative.

Queremos que lo **hagas.**   *We want you to do it.*
Hemos querido que lo **hagas.**   *We've wanted you to do it.*
Querremos que lo **hagas.**   *We'll want you to do it.*

The English equivalents of many noun clauses in Spanish are in the infinitive so the English sentences do not show the tense distinctions seen in the Spanish subjunctive clauses.

Queremos que lo **hagas.**   *We want you **to do** it.*
Queríamos que lo **hicieras.**   *We wanted you **to do** it.*

Remember that in Spanish, if the subjects of the main clause and the dependent clause are the same, the infinitive is used rather than the subjunctive.

Queremos **hacerlo.**   *We want **to do it.***
Queríamos **hacerlo.**   *We wanted **to do it.***

Ojalá used with the present subjunctive means *I hope*. **Ojalá** used with the imperfect subjunctive means *I wish*.

Ojalá que **saquen** boletos.   *I hope they'll get tickets.*
Ojalá que **sacaran** boletos.   *I wish they'd get tickets.*

Spanish uses the imperfect subjunctive, as well as the conditional, to soften a request or suggestion. The imperfect subjunctive of **deber, poder,** and **querer** is more courteous than the conditional, which can be used with any verb. In English, *would* is also used to soften a request: ¿Me lo **explicarías**? *Would you explain it to me?*

Uds. debieran volver a casa.   *You ought to return home.*
¿**Pudiera** prestármelo?   *Could you lend it to me?*
Quisiera hablar con Ud.   *I'd like to speak with you.*

Actividad 2 **Un caso de celos.** Narre la historia de dos chicos que quieren a Angélica. Cambie el verbo de la cláusula independiente según los verbos indicados, y cambie el verbo de la cláusula dependiente al imperfecto de subjuntivo. Siga el modelo.

> MODELO Felipe les dice a sus amigos que lo acompañen. (dijo)
> Felipe les dijo a sus amigos que lo acompañaran.

1. Felipe les sugiere que vayan a una discoteca. (sugirió)

   _____

2. Felipe espera que Angélica baile con él y nadie más. (esperaba)

   _____

3. Teodoro también desea que Angélica salga con él. (deseaba)

   _____

4. Angélica teme que los chicos tengan celos. (temía)

   _____

5. Es posible que Felipe y Teodoro se peleen por Angélica. (Era)

   _____

6. Felipe no cree que sea una buena idea ir a la discoteca. (no creía)

   _____

7. Felipe le propone a Angélica que vean una película. (propuso)

   _____

8. A Angélica le agrada que Felipe y Teodoro la quieran, ¡pero ella estaba enamorada de Julio! (agradaba)

   _____

Actividad 3 **Expectativas.** Cuando Timoteo fue a pasar un semestre en la Ciudad de Guatemala para estudiar español, tenía ciertas expectativas y preocupaciones sobre cómo iba a ser su experiencia. Lea lo que pensaba y escriba los verbos indicados usando el imperfecto de subjuntivo. Siga el modelo.

> MODELO Timoteo deseaba que la casa donde iba a vivir (quedar)
> quedara cerca de la universidad.

1. Timoteo esperaba que (haber) _____habera_____ un chico de su edad en la familia.

2. Sentía que su mejor amigo no (ir) _____fuera_____ a la Ciudad de Guatemala también.

3. Temía que nadie (poder) _____pudiera_____ comprender su español.

4. Era posible que Timoteo no (llevarse) _____se llevara_____ bien con sus compañeros de clase.

5. Tenía miedo que la comida le (caer) _____cayera_____ mal.

6. Dudaba que sus profesores le (aprobar) _____aprobaran_____ en todas las materias.

7. Era probable que Timoteo (querer) _____quisiera_____ mudarse a un hotel.

Actividad 4 **¿Qué tal le fue a Timoteo?** Para saber cómo le fue, complete las oraciones usando el imperfecto de subjuntivo. Siga el modelo.

> MODELO   Los señores de la casa insistían en que Timoteo (quedarse) <u>se quedara</u> con ellos un mes más.

1. Era bueno que sus clases (ser) _____fueran_____ tan interesantes.

2. Los señores permitían que Timoteo (salir) _____saliera_____ con su hija Aurora.

3. La madre le pidió a Timoteo que los (acompañar) _____acompañara_____ a la sierra.

4. Los hijos de la familia le rogaron a Timoteo que (jugar) _____jugara_____ al fútbol con ellos.

5. La señora dejó que Timoteo (conducir) _____condujera_____ el coche.

6. A Timoteo le sorprendió que todos lo (tratar) _____tratara_____ tan bien.

Actividad 5 **Vida de familia.** Describa lo que los padres esperaban que sus hijos hicieran. Complete las oraciones con los verbos indicados usando el imperfecto de subjuntivo. Siga el modelo.

> MODELO   Mis papás querían que nosotros (estudiar) <u>estudiáramos</u> mucho.

1. Papá esperaba que yo (hacerse) _____me hiciera_____ ingeniera.

2. Mamá insistía en que nosotros (seguir) _____siguiéramos_____ sus tradiciones.

3. Nuestros papás nos aconsejaban que (tener) _____tuviéramos_____ valores tradicionales.

4. Papá prefería que Pepe (trabajar) _____trajara_____ con él en la empresa familiar.

5. Nuestros padres deseaban que mis hermanos y yo (casarse) _____se casáramos_____.

6. A nuestros papás les era importante que nosotros (ser)

   _____ responsables, honrados y trabajadores.

7. Mamá nos pedía que (dedicarse) _____ a nuestra familia.

8. Papá nos decía que (ayudarse) _____ los unos a los otros.

9. A nuestros padres les era necesario que mis hermanas (vivir)

   _____ cerca.

Actividad 6 **Me sobra tiempo. (*I have plenty of time.*)** Sus padres le pidieron que hiciera unas cosas para ayudarlos. Ud. creía que le sobraba tiempo para hacerlas y fue a jugar al béisbol con sus amigos. Al regresar a casa, sus padres ven que todo ha quedado sin hacer. Complete las oraciones usando el imperfecto de subjuntivo de los verbos indicados. Siga el modelo.

> MODELO   Hijo, yo quería que (buscar) <u>buscaras</u> el correo.

1. Hijo, te pedí que (cortar) _____ el césped.[a]

2. Hijo, ¿no te dijimos que (descongelar) _____ la carne?

3. Hijo, te exigí que (regar[b]) _____ los arbustos.[c]

4. Hijo, esperábamos que (hacer) _____ la compra.

5. Hijo, yo quería que (bañar) _____ al perro.

6. Hijo, te rogamos que (poner) _____ el garaje en orden.

7. Hijo, yo deseaba que (guardar) _____ las herramientas.[d]

8. Hijo, insistíamos en que (sacar) _____ la basura.

9. Hijo, tu hermanito necesitaba que le (reparar)

   _____ su bicicleta.

[a]*lawn, grass*   [b]*to water*   [c]*bushes*   [d]*tools*

Actividad 7 **¡Qué pesada! (*What a pain!*)** A Josefina no le queda ni un solo amigo porque se porta mal con todo el mundo. Para saber lo que pasó con sus amigos, complete las oraciones usando el imperfecto de subjuntivo de los verbos indicados. Siga el modelo.

> MODELO   Josefina le pidió al novio de Lola que la (llevar) <u>llevara</u> al baile.

1. A los amigos no les gustaba que Josefina les (mentir)

   _____.

2. Josefina le aconsejó a Paquita que (romper) _____ con su novio.

3. Sus amigos sentían que Josefina (tener) _____ mala lengua.[a]

4. Josefina exigió que Pedro (hacer) _____ la tarea de cálculo por ella.

5. Josefina insistió en que los chicos la (invitar)

   _____ a todas sus reuniones.

6. Los amigos no querían que Josefina les (tomar)

   _____ el pelo.

7. Josefina les impidió a los amigos que (ir) _____ al cine sin ella.

8. A nadie le gustaba que Josefina (meter) _____ a los amigos en líos.[b]

[a]mala... *vicious tongue*   [b]*messes, trouble*

Actividad 8   **¡Ojalá!** Ud. quiere que sucedan ciertas cosas, pero duda que vayan a pasar. Exprese sus deseos usando el imperfecto de subjuntivo. Siga el modelo.

> MODELO   los primos / venir a visitarme
> Ojalá que los primos vinieran a visitarme.

1. yo / ir / de vacaciones / en abril

   _____

2. Uds. / recibir / un iPod

   _____

3. Diana / no quejarse / de todo

   _____

4. nuestro equipo / ganar / el campeonato

   _____

5. Bernardo y Marta / no discutir / tanto

   _____

6. tú / no preocuparse / por nada

   _____

7. tú y yo / poder asistir / al congreso (*conference*) en San Diego

   _____

8. vosotros / invitarnos / a vuestra hacienda

   _____

Past perfect (or pluperfect) subjunctive

The past perfect subjunctive (**el pluscuamperfecto de subjuntivo**) consists of the imperfect subjunctive of **haber** + *past participle*. The most common use of the past perfect subjunctive is in conditional sentences. The past perfect subjunctive is also used to express a contrary-to-fact wish in the past after **ojalá (que)**.

Ojalá (que)	**hubiera sabido.**	*I wish I had known.*
	hubieras sabido.	*I wish you had known.*
	hubiera sabido.	*I wish he/she had known.*
	hubiéramos sabido.	*I wish we had known.*
	hubierais sabido.	*I wish you had known.*
	hubieran sabido.	*I wish they had known.*

The past perfect subjunctive is also used in clauses requiring the subjunctive to indicate that the action of the dependent clause happened before the action of the main clause when the main clause is in the preterite, imperfect, or conditional.

Yo me alegré de que ella **hubiera llegado.**	*I was glad that she had arrived.*
Dudábamos que tú **hubieras podido** hacerlo.	*We doubted that you could have done it.*
Fue poco probable que el avión **hubiera despegado.**	*It was improbable that the plane had taken off.*

Actividad 9 ¿**Qué les parecía?** Escriba las oraciones empleando las frases indicadas en la cláusula principal y el verbo de la cláusula dependiente en el pluscuamperfecto de subjuntivo. Siga el modelo.

> MODELO Néstor había ganado la lotería. (esperábamos)
> Esperábamos que Néstor hubiera ganado la lotería.

1. Rebeca había llegado a ser arquitecta. (era bueno)

   _____

2. Las hermanas Cela habían hecho un viaje a Santo Domingo. (nos gustó)

   _____

3. Uds. se habían quedado tanto tiempo. (me extrañó)

   _____

4. Tú habías comprado una computadora nueva. (era necesario)

   _____

5. Yo había conocido Roma. (era importante)

   _____

6. Juan y yo nos habíamos comprometido. (todos se alegraron)

   _____

Actividad 10 **Expresar en español.** Exprese las oraciones en español.

1. You **(tú)** were hoping that they had been successful.

   _____

2. They were afraid that someone had told me.

   _____

3. We were sorry that you **(Ud.)** hadn't heard what happened.

   _____

4. Sarita doubted that we had come back from the country.

   _____

5. I was glad that it had been warm and sunny.

   _____

6. I wish you **(Uds.)** had seen the Web site.

   _____

Conditional sentences

In Spanish and English, conditional sentences consist of two clauses: a **si** clause (*if clause*) and a main clause. Both languages use similar tenses for the two clauses. The **si** clause may come before or after the main clause.

Possible conditions are expressed in both languages by using the present in the **si** clause and the future in the main clause.

si CLAUSE	MAIN CLAUSE	
PRESENT	FUTURE	
Si vas,	**yo iré** también.	*If you go, I'll go, too.*

To express a condition that is contrary to a fact or situation in present time, Spanish uses the imperfect subjunctive in the **si** clause and the conditional in the main clause.

si CLAUSE	MAIN CLAUSE	
IMPERFECT SUBJUNCTIVE	CONDITIONAL	
Si fueras,	**yo iría** también.	*If you were going, I'd go, too.*

The sentence **Si fueras, yo iría también.** expresses a condition that is contrary to fact. The fact is that **tú no vas** and the result is that **yo no voy.** The meaning is **Si fueras** (*If you were going, which you're not*), **yo iría** también (*I'd go, too*).

Spanish expresses a condition that is contrary to a fact or situation in past time by using the past perfect subjunctive in the **si** clause and the conditional perfect or the past perfect subjunctive in the main clause.

si CLAUSE	MAIN CLAUSE
Si hubieras ido,	**yo habría ido** también.
Si hubieras ido,	**yo hubiera ido** también.

} *If you had gone, I would have gone, too.*

The main clause may precede the **si** clause, but the use of the tenses remains the same.

Yo habría/hubiera ido también, si tú hubieras ido.   *I would have gone too, if you had gone.*

Como si...

The imperfect subjunctive is used after **como si** (*as if*) to express an action contemporaneous with the action of the main clause.

Él habla **como si fuera** profesor.	*He speaks **as if he were** a teacher.*
Se abrazarán **como si no estuvieran** enfadados.	*They'll hug each other **as if they weren't** angry.*
Actúa **como si quisieras** estar con ellos.	*Act **as if you wanted** to be with them.*
Entraron **como si tuvieran miedo.**	*They came in **as if they were afraid.***

The pluperfect subjunctive is used after **como si** to express an action that occurred prior to the action of the main clause.

Trabajaban **como si no hubieran entendido** las intrucciones.	*They were working **as if they hadn't understood** the instructions.*
Contestó **como si no hubiera leído** el libro.	*He answered **as if he hadn't read the book.***
Él nos aconseja **como si hubiera estudiado** derecho.	*He advises us **as if he had studied** law.*

Actividad 11   **Todo está pendiente (*up in the air*).** Complete las oraciones con la forma correcta de los verbos indicados. Use el presente de indicativo en las cláusulas que empiezan con **si.** Siga el modelo.

> MODELO   Si Uds. (ir) <u>van</u>, yo los (ver) <u>veré</u>.

1. Si yo (poder) _____, los (visitar)

   _____.

2. Si ellos le (ofrecer) _____ el puesto a Daniel, él lo

   (aceptar) _____.

3. Pepita y yo (salir) ___Saldremos___ si (tener)

   ___tenemos___ tiempo.

4. Si Mario me (llamar) ___llama___, yo se lo (decir)

   ___di___.

5. Si tú (poner) _____ la mesa, Isabel y Leo (hacer)

   _____ la cena.

6. Si Uds. no se lo (preguntar) _____ a Marisol, no

(saber) _____ qué pasó.

7. Todos nosotros (venir) _____ en taxi si no

(haber) _____ lugar en el coche de Carolina.

Actividad 12 **Si fuera posible...** Complete las oraciones con la forma correcta de los verbos indicados. Use el imperfecto de subjuntivo en las cláusulas que empiezan con **si.** Siga el modelo.

> MODELO   Si (ser) <u>fuera</u> posible, nosotros (ir) <u>iríamos</u>.

1. Si yo (tener) __tuviera__ tiempo, (hacer) __haría__ un viaje a todos los países del mundo.

2. Los Madariaga (venir) __veniera__ a visitarnos si nosotros los (invitar) __invitaríamos__.

3. Laura (ver) __~~viera~~ vería__ esa obra de teatro si (haber) __hubiera__ entradas.

4. Si Diego (ganar) __ganara__ más dinero, (comprarse) __se compraría__ un coche deportivo.

5. Si (hacer) __hiciera__ mucho viento, nosotros (salir) __saldríamos__ con la cometa (*kite*).

6. Daniel (dormir) __dormiría__ la siesta si (sentirse) __se sentiera__ cansado.

7. Si tú (poder) __pudieras__, (resolver) __resolverías__ el problema.

8. Uds. (salir) __saldrían__ más temprano si (ser) __fueran__ posible, ¿no?

9. Si Ana María y Esteban (saber) __supieran__ los motivos, se los (decir) __dirían__ a Uds.

Actividad 13 **Cuentos de hadas (*fairy tales*).** Recuerde lo que pasa en estos cuentos de hadas. Complete las oraciones con la forma correcta de los verbos indicados. Use el imperfecto de subjuntivo en las cláusulas que empiezan con **si.** Siga el modelo.

> MODELO   «Si yo no (tener) <u>tuviera</u> sueño, no (acostarse) <u>me acostaría</u> en la cama del osito», pensó Ricitos de Oro.

1. «Si yo (encontrar) _____ a la señorita que perdió la zapatilla de cristal,[a] (casarse) _____ con ella», pensó el príncipe.

2. «Si una princesa me (besar) _____, yo (dejar) _____ de ser sapo[b] y (convertirse) _____ en príncipe.»

3. «Si (haber) _____ un guisante[c] debajo de mi colchón, yo lo (notar) _____», se dijo la princesa.

4. «Si Hansel y Gretel (venir) _____ a mi casa, yo me los (comer) _____», pensó la bruja.[d]

5. «Si yo no (mentir) _____, no se me (crecer) _____ la nariz», se dijo Pinocho.

6. «Si yo le (dar) _____ un beso a la Bella Durmiente,[e] ella (despertarse) _____», se dijo el príncipe.

7. «Si la reina no (tener) _____ celos de mí, no (tener) _____ que vivir con los siete enanos[f]», pensó Blancanieves.[g]

[a]zapatilla... *glass slipper*   [b]*toad*   [c]*pea*   [d]*witch*   [e]Bella... *Sleeping Beauty*
[f]*dwarves*   [g]*Snow White*

Actividad 14 **Viajes soñados.** Complete las oraciones con la forma correcta de los verbos indicados. Use el imperfecto de subjuntivo en la cláusula que empieza con **si** y el condicional en la cláusula principal.

1. Si yo (ir) _____ a Costa Rica, me (gustar) _____ hacer ecoturismo en los bosques nacionales.

2. Si Graciela y Miguel (hacer) _____ un viaje a Brasil, (ir) _____ a Río de Janeiro para ver el Carnaval.

3. Si Uds. (poder) _____ visitar Uruguay, (quedarse) _____ en Punta del Este.

4. Si nosotros (pasar) _____ las vacaciones en Puerto Rico, (tomar) _____ el sol en la playa de Dorado.

5. Si tú (visitar) _____ Chile, (probar)

   _____ vinos del Valle Central.

6. Si Felipe (querer) _____ viajar al Ecuador,

   (conocer) _____ Quito.

Actividad 15 **Si hubiera sido posible...** Complete las oraciones con la forma correcta de los verbos indicados. Use el pluscuamperfecto de subjuntivo en la cláusula que empieza con **si** y el condicional compuesto (*conditional perfect*) o el pluscuamperfecto de subjuntivo en la cláusula principal. Siga el modelo.

> MODELO Si (ser) hubiera sido posible, nosotros (ir)
> habríamos / hubiéramos ido.

1. Si Uds. nos (preguntar) _____, se lo (decir)

   _____ / _____.

2. Yo te (devolver) ___habría___ /

   ___habría___ la cartera si te (ver)

   _____.

3. Si Jaime (hacerse) _____ médico, (estar)

   _____ / _____ más
   contento.

4. Eva y yo (llamar) _____ /

   _____ en seguida si lo (saber)

   _____.

5. Si yo (jugar) _____ béisbol en el parque, no

   (romper) _____ / _____
   la ventana de la casa.

6. Si tú (leer) _____ tú correo electrónico,

   (entender) _____ / _____
   el problema.

Actividad 16 **¿Campo o ciudad?** Pablo se crió en el campo y su prima Amelia se crió en la ciudad. Hablan de las maneras en las cuales hubiera sido diferente su vida si Pablo se hubiera criado en la ciudad y Amelia en el campo. Use el pluscuamperfecto de subjuntivo en la cláusula que empieza con **si** y el condicional compuesto o el pluscuamperfecto de subjuntivo en la cláusula principal. Siga el modelo.

> MODELO Pablo / estudiar en un colegio grande / criarse en la ciudad
> Pablo habría / hubiera estudiado en un colegio grande si se
> hubiera criado en la ciudad.

1. Pablo / asistir al teatro / vivir en la ciudad

   _____

2. Amelia / ordeñar (*to milk*) las vacas / nacer en una finca

   _____

3. Pablo / ponerse más nervioso / oír tanto ruido todos los días

   _____

4. Amelia / respirar aire no contaminado / vivir en el campo

   _____

5. Pablo / tomar el metro y los taxis / trabajar en la ciudad

   _____

6. Amelia / aprender a montar a caballo / pasar su vida en el campo

   _____

7. Pablo / comprar toda la comida en el supermercado / hacer la compra en la ciudad

   _____

8. Amelia / comer frutas y legumbres muy frescas / criarse en el campo

   _____

9. Pablo / llevar un traje, camisa y corbata / ganarse la vida trabajando en una empresa

   _____

10. Amelia usar un sombrero de paja (*straw*) / cultivar la tierra

    _____

Actividad 17   **Julio el tardón (*slow poke*).** A Julio le lleva tanto tiempo hacer cosas que siempre llega tarde a sus citas. Acaba de llegar a la fiesta de sus amigos pero no ve a nadie. Despierta a su amigo Memo que le explica que la fiesta terminó a las dos de la mañana. Julio piensa en cómo le habría salido si hubiera llegado antes. Use el pluscuamperfecto de subjuntivo en la cláusula que empieza con **si** y el condicional compuesto o el pluscuamperfecto de subjuntivo en la cláusula principal.

1. Si yo (terminar) _____ mi trabajo para las diez,

   (poder) _____ llegar a tiempo.

2. Si yo (planear) _____ mejor mi horario, no me

   (perder) _____ la fiesta.

3. Si yo (hacer) _____ mi trabajo más eficazmente,

   (bailar) _____ con Julieta, la mujer de mis sueños.

4. Si yo no (gastar) _____ tanto tiempo echándome

    agua de colonia, (disfrutar) _____ de una
    comida rica.

5. Si yo (manejar) _____ más rápido, no

    (atrasarse) _____.

6. Si mis amigos (divertirse) _____ más, ellos

    (quedarse) _____ hasta las tres de la mañana.

7. Si Memo no (acostarse) _____ de inmediato, yo

    no (tener) _____ que tocar el timbre cien veces.

Actividad 18 **Expresar en español.** Exprese las oraciones en español.

1. If Victoria had had the key, she would have opened the suitcase.

    _____

2. If you **(Ud.)** were to take a trip this summer, where would you go?

    _____

3. If they had been more careful, they wouldn't have lost their cell phone.

    _____

4. If you **(Uds.)** turn right at the corner, you'll see the museum.

    _____

5. I would pay attention to Roberto if he gave good advice.

    _____

6. If you **(tú)** had surfed the Web more, you would have found the Web site.

    _____

Actividad 19 **Como si lo dijera.** Complete las oraciones con la forma correcta del imperfecto de subjuntivo de los verbos indicados.

> MODELO   Aurelia nos habla de Mallorca como si (conocer) <u>conociera</u>
> la isla.

1. Uds. se despiden como si (ser) _____ por última
    vez.

2. Los Madariaga me describían la casa como si (vivir)

    _____ en ella.

3. Laura se ríe como si no (tener) _____ ninguna
    preocupación.

4. Felipe te pedirá tu dirección electrónica como si (pensar)

    _____ escribirte.

5. Dígale a Ester la razón como si ella no la (saber)

    _____ ya.

6. Hablas como si no (oír) _____ nada de la conversación.

7. Ud. anda como si le (doler) _____ los pies.

8. Vosotros contestáis como si no (comprender)

    _____ la pregunta.

Actividad 20   **Como si lo hubiera dicho.** Complete las oraciones con la forma correcta del pluscuamperfecto de subjuntivo de los verbos indicados.

> MODELO   Raimundo los saludó como si (estar) <u>hubiera estado</u> muy preocupado.

1. Los niños comían como si no (comer) _____ en todo el día.

2. Raquela está temblando como si (ver) _____ un fantasma.

3. Uds. reprendieron a Sara como si ella (ser) _____ la culpable.

4. Te quejabas de la fiesta como si no (divertirse)

    _____.

5. Gregorio gritó como si (hacerse) _____ daño.

6. Me hicieron unas preguntas como si yo (poder)

    _____ contestarlas.

Actividad 21   **Actividad oral.** Converse con otros estudiantes sobre lo que harían en cada caso. Pregúnteles, por ejemplo: **¿Qué harías si tuvieras un millón de dólares?** o **Si tuvieras un año de vacaciones, ¿adónde irías?**

Subjunctive in adverb and adjective clauses

1, 2, 6, 7, 9

Adverb clauses that require the subjunctive

A clause that modifies a verb the way an adverb does is called an *adverb clause*. Compare the use of adverbs and adverb clauses in the following pairs of sentences.

Salimos **temprano**.	*We went out **early**.*
Salimos **cuando terminamos**.	*We went out **when we finished**.*
Cantaron **bien**.	*They sang **well**.*
Cantaron **como les habían enseñado**.	*They sang **as they had been taught**.*

Adverb clauses are introduced by conjunctions, such as **como** and **cuando** in the previous examples. The following conjunctions introduce adverb clauses in which the verb must be in the subjunctive: **a condición de que** (*on the condition that*), **a fin de que** (*in order that, so that*), **a menos (de) que** (*unless*), **antes (de) que** (*before*), **con tal (de) que** (*provided that*), **en caso de que** (*in case*), **para que** (*so that*), **sin que**, (*without*). The same sequence-of-tense rules apply in adverb clauses as in noun clauses.

Saldré **antes de que** vuelvan.	*I'll leave **before** they get back.*
Salí **antes de que** volvieran.	*I left **before** they got back.*
Tito va a comprar huevos **para que** hagamos la torta.	*Tito's going to buy eggs **so that** we can make the cake.*
Tito compró los huevos **para que** hiciéramos la torta.	*Tito bought eggs **so that** we might make the cake.*
Escondemos el regalo **sin que** Olga sepa dónde.	*We're hiding the gift **without** Olga knowing where.*
Escondimos el regalo **sin que** Olga supiera dónde.	*We hid the gift **without** Olga knowing where.*

A menos (de) que and **con tal (de) que** are followed by the present subjunctive if the action of the dependent (subordinate) clause occurs at the same time as the action of the main clause. They are followed by the present perfect subjunctive if the action of the dependent clause occurs before the action of the main clause.

Hará su tarea de matemáticas con tal que le **devuelvas** su libro.	*He'll do his math homework provided that **you return** his book to him.*
Hará su tarea de matemáticas con tal que le **hayas devuelto** su libro.	*He'll do his math homework provided that **you've returned** his book to him.*

Adverb clauses with indicative or subjunctive

Certain conjunctions are followed by the indicative when the action of the dependent (subordinate) clause is considered a known or established fact. They are followed by the subjunctive when the action of the dependent clause is considered uncertain or indefinite. The English equivalents of these subjunctive clauses often begin with conjunctions ending in -ever: *however, whenever, wherever.* These conjunctions include **aunque** (*although, even though*), **como** (*how*), **de manera que** (*so that*), **de modo que** (*so that*), **donde** (*where*), **mientras** (*while*), **según** (*according to*).

Aunque va Elena, yo no voy.	***Even though Elena is going,** I'm not going. (I know Elena is going.)*
Aunque vaya Elena, yo no voy.	***Even though Elena may go,** I'm not going.*
Hágalo **como** ellos **dicen.**	*Do it **how (the way)** they say. (I know the way they say.)*
Hágalo **como** ellos **digan.**	*Do it **however** they say. (I don't know the way they say.)*
Iremos **donde** tú **quieres.**	*We'll go **where** you want. (We know where you want to go.)*
Iremos **donde** tú **quieras.**	*We'll go **wherever** you want to go. (We don't know yet where you want to go.)*

Adverb clauses introduced by conjunctions of time such as **así que** (*so*), **cuando** (*when*), **después (de) que** (*after*), **en cuanto** (*as soon as*), **hasta que** (*until*), **luego que** (*as soon as*), and **tan pronto (como)** (*as soon as*) are followed by the subjunctive when the main clause refers to the future or is a command.

Díselo **cuando lleguen.**	*Tell it to them **when they arrive.***
Hablaremos **después de que se vayan** los invitados.	*We'll talk **after the guests leave.***
Me quedaré **hasta que terminemos.**	*I'll stay **until we finish.***
Avísame **tan pronto como te llamen.**	*Let me know **as soon as they call you.***

If the action of the dependent clause is considered to be a habitual occurrence, the indicative, not the subjunctive, is used.

Se lo das **cuando llegan.**	*You (usually) give it to them **when they arrive.***
Los niños se levantan de la mesa **en cuanto terminan de comer.**	*The children (usually) leave the table **as soon as they finish eating.***
Me quedo **hasta que terminamos.**	*I (usually) stay **until we finish.***

When the sentence relates a past action, the indicative is used after the conjunction of time since the event in the adverbial clause is considered to be part of reality.

Se lo di **cuando llegaron.**	*I gave it to them **when they arrived.***
Los niños se levantaron de la mesa **en cuanto terminaron de comer.**	*The children left the table **as soon as they finished eating.***
Me quedé **hasta que terminamos.**	*I stayed **until we finished.***

The conjunction of time **antes (de) que** is an exception because it is followed by the subjunctive even when the verb of the main clause is in a past tense.

Nora **mandó** el correo electrónico **antes que** Pablo la **llamara.**

*Nora **sent** the e-mail **before** Pablo called her.*

If the subject of the main clause and the dependent clause is the same, the dependent clause is replaced by an infinitive.

Estudien hasta que Beti lo **entienda.**
Estudien hasta **entender**lo.

Study until Beti understands it.
Study until you understand it.

Voy a leer antes que **juguemos** tenis.
Voy a leer antes de **jugar** tenis.

I'm going to read before we play tennis.
I'm going to read before I play (playing) tennis.

Salimos sin que Uds. **almorzaran.**
Salimos sin **almorzar.**

We went out without your having lunch.
We went out without having lunch.

Actividad 1 **No se sabe todavía.** Ud. no sabe cómo son las cosas mencionadas. Exprésalo completando las cláusulas adverbiales con el presente de subjuntivo de los verbos indicados.

1. Lo haré según Uds. (mandar) _____.

2. Viviremos donde Pepita (aconsejar) _____.

3. Aunque (llover) _____ habrá un partido de fútbol.

4. Guillermo quiere pintar los cuadros donde (haber)

   _____ mucha luz.

5. Realizarán el proyecto como tú (querer) _____.

6. Voy a leer el informe aunque no (ser) _____ muy interesante.

7. Anabel comerá donde Ud. (preferir) _____.

8. Prepara el plato según nosotros (decir) _____.

9. Van al cine aunque yo no (ir) _____.

Actividad 2 **Haciendo las diligencias (*Running errands*).** Explique que algunas personas hicieron ciertas cosas antes de que otras personas hicieran otras cosas usando el pretérito para el verbo de la cláusula principal y el imperfecto de subjuntivo para la cláusula adverbial. Siga el modelo.

> MODELO Marta / ir a la pastelería / yo / ir a la carnicería
> Marta fue a la pastelería antes de que yo fuera a la carnicería.

1. Elena y Mario / salir del cibercafé / nosotros / entrar en la zapatería

   _____

2. Ud. / alquilar una película en la tienda de vídeos / yo / volver de la farmacia

   _____

3. Uds. / comprar los sellos en el supermercado / Miguel / poder ir al correo

   _____

4. Fernando y yo / estacionar en el centro comercial / tú / llegar a la discoteca

   _____

5. yo / sacar la ropa de la tintorería / Juana / tener su cita en la peluquería

   _____

6. tú / ir a la joyería / Arturo y Bárbara / buscar una librería

   _____

7. vosotros / llegar a la gasolinera / Pedro y yo / regresar de la universidad

   _____

Actividad 3   **¿Indicativo o subjuntivo?** Complete las oraciones con la forma correcta de los verbos indicados. Escoja entre el indicativo y el subjuntivo (en presente o imperfecto). Siga el modelo.

> MODELO   No queremos ir al museo sin que tú (ir) <u>vayas</u>.

1. Llamaré a Julio para que él (saber) _____*sepa*_____ lo que está pasando.

2. Se quedaron hasta que Federico (venir) _____~~venga~~ *vinó*_____.

3. Iremos al centro comercial a menos que Uds. nos (necesitar) _____*necesiten*_____ aquí.

4. Le presté el dinero a Marisol para que (poder) _____~~pude~~ *pudiera*_____ comprarse el vestido.

5. Tú puedes venir a la casa sin que nosotros te (invitar) _____*invitemos*_____.

6. Los vimos tan pronto como nosotros (entrar) *we saw them as soon as we entered*
   (pretérito) _____*entramos*_____ en la librería.

7. Carmen se puso de pie en cuanto (terminar) _____*terminó*_____ la conferencia.

8. Hazme saber cuando (llegar) _____*lleguen* ?_____ los paquetes.

Actividad 4 **Expresar en español.** Exprese las oraciones en español.

1. I'll call them when I get to the airport.

   los llamaré cuando llegue

2. Consuelo set the table an hour before her friends arrived.

   _____

3. They stood in line at the box office after they had lunch.

   después de almorzar

4. You (**Ud.**) didn't want to go shopping without our going too.

   _____

5. Do it (**Uds.**) whichever way they want.

   _____

6. Even though it's cold out, we should take a walk.

   _____

7. I'll lend you (**tú**) the book so that you won't have to take it out of the library.

   _____

8. Carlos is going to study for his exam before playing tennis.

   _____

Adjective clauses that require the subjunctive

An *adjective clause* modifies a noun the way an adjective does. All relative clauses are adjective clauses. In the example, **una obra que se titula** *Don Quijote,* **"que se titula** *Don Quijote***"** modifies **obra** the way that **"maravillosa"** does in **una obra maravillosa.** The noun modified by an adjective clause is called the *antecedent.* Thus, **obra** is the antecedent of the **que** clause.

In Spanish, there are two types of antecedents—those considered part of reality, definite or existent, and those that are not part of reality, indefinite or nonexistent. When the antecedent is something or someone that exists and that the speaker can identify, the verb of the adjective clause appears in the indicative. For example, in the sentence **Tenemos un profesor que habla chino,** the antecedent, **un profesor,** is a definite person who can be identified by name. Therefore, the indicative **habla** is used. However, in adjective clauses that modify antecedents that are not part of reality or the speaker's experience, the subjunctive is used. These include clauses that refer to indefinite, undetermined, and negative antecedents.

Buscamos un profesor que **hable** chino.	*We're looking for a professor who speaks Chinese.*
Queremos un profesor que **hable** chino.	*We want a professor who speaks Chinese.*
Necesitamos un profesor que **hable** chino.	*We need a professor who speaks Chinese.*

No conozco a nadie que **hable** vasco.   *I don't know anyone who speaks Basque.*
No hay revista que le **guste**.   *There's no magazine he likes.*

Note that **buscar, necesitar, querer,** and other such verbs may also have direct objects that are definite and identifiable. In this case, adjective clauses that modify these objects are in the indicative. In the example below, the professor being sought is known to the speakers.

Buscamos a la profesora que **habla** chino.   *We're looking for **the** professor who speaks Chinese.*
Necesitamos a la profesora que **habla** chino.   *We need **the** professor who speaks Chinese.*

The sequence-of-tense rules also apply in adjective clauses.

Quiero una novela que **tenga** un buen argumento.   *I **want** a novel that **has** a good plot.*
Quería una novela que **tuviera** un buen argumento.   *I **wanted** a novel that **had** a good plot.*

No hay casa que les **guste**.   ***There's no** house they **like**.*
No había casa que les **gustara**.   ***There was no** house they **liked**.*

In addition to **que,** other relative adverbs and pronouns such as **donde** and **quien** can introduce adjective clauses.

Buscan una florería **donde vendan** tulipanes.   *They're looking for a flower shop **where they sell** tulips.*
Tere quería una amiga **con quien pudiera** jugar al tenis.   *Tere wanted a friend **with whom she could** play tennis.*

Adjective clauses with indicative or subjunctive

In Spanish, a noun may be followed by a relative clause beginning with **que** that has a verb either in the indicative or the subjunctive. If the indicative is used, it suggests that the antecedent has already been identified. If the relative clause is in the subjunctive, it suggests that the antecedent has not been identified.

Traigo la torta que **quieres**.   *I'll bring the cake you want.*
   (I know which of the cakes you liked.)

Escoge la torta que **quieras**.   *Choose the cake you want.*
   (I don't know your tastes.)

Podemos comer **donde ellos prefieren**.   *We can eat at (the place) they prefer.*
   (We know where they prefer to eat.)
Podemos comer **donde ellos prefieran**.   *We can eat wherever they prefer.*
   (We don't yet know where they prefer to eat.)

The meaning of the subjunctive in these adjective clauses can be conveyed in English by words ending in *-ever.*

Iremos a la hora que tú **digas**.   *We'll go at **whatever** time you say.*
Ceno en el restaurante que ellos **quieran**.   *I'll have dinner at **whichever** restaurant they want.*

Actividad 5 **Se busca apartamento.** Describa el apartamento que Ud. y sus amigas esperan encontrar. Escriba las oraciones usando el presente de subjuntivo en la cláusula adjetival y el presente de indicativo en la cláusula principal. Siga el modelo.

> MODELO nosotros / buscar un apartamento / tener cuatro dormitorios
> Nosotros buscamos un apartamento que tenga cuatro dormitorios.

1. tú / querer un apartamento / tener dos baños

   _____

2. Marta / necesitar un apartamento / donde / haber aire acondicionado

   _____

3. Juana y yo / buscar un apartamento / estar cerca de la universidad

   _____

4. Uds. / necesitar un apartamento / no costar un ojo de la cara[a]

   _____

5. yo / querer un apartamento / no necesitar renovación

   _____

6. Adela y Leonor / desear un apartamento / ser moderno y fácil de limpiar

   _____

7. vosotras / buscar un apartamento / dar a una calle poco transitada[b]

   _____

8. Ud. / necesitar un apartamento / donde / caber todos los fiesteros[c]

   _____

[a]costar... *cost an arm and a leg*   [b]poco... *with little traffic*   [c]*party-goers*

Actividad 6 **Mi novio ideal.** Sara le cuenta a su amiga Raquel cómo es el hombre ideal. Para saber lo que busca en un hombre, complete las cláusulas adjetivales usando el presente de subjuntivo de los verbos indicados.

1. Busco un novio que (saber) _____ ser un buen amigo.

2. Quiero un chico con quien (poder) _____ hablar fácilmente.

3. Me hace falta un hombre que me (comprender)

   _____.

4. Quiero tener un novio con quien yo (divertirse)

   _____.

5. Necesito un chico que (ser) _____ inteligente.

6. Estoy buscando un novio que (tener) _____ un buen sentido del humor.

Actividad 7 ¡**No hay candidatas para el puesto (*job*)!** Por desgracia, Felipe no puede ayudar a Esteban porque no tiene amigas que tengan las cualidades que su amigo exige. Complete las cláusulas adjetivales de las oraciones usando el presente de subjuntivo de los verbos indicados.

1. No conozco a ninguna chica que (reunir) _____ todas estas características.

2. No hay nadie que (ser) _____ tan perfecta.

3. No conozco a ninguna mujer con quien tú (querer)

   _____ salir.

4. No hay ninguna que te (ir) _____ a interesar mucho.

5. No conozco a ninguna muchacha que (tener)

   _____ un cociente intelectual (*I.Q.*) tan alto como el tuyo.

6. ¡No hay ninguna chica que (enamorarse) _____ de ti tan fácilmente!

Actividad 8 **En la cumbre (*At the top*).** Ahora Isabel Soriano es presidenta de su propia empresa multinacional y conoce el éxito y la prosperidad. Pero a veces Isabel se pone a pensar en el pasado. Complete las cláusulas adjetivales usando el imperfecto de subjuntivo de los verbos indicados para saber cómo era su vida antes de que llegara a la cumbre.

Vocabulario

Los negocios

la compañía *company*
compartir *to share*
confiar en *to trust*
el dineral *fortune, a lot of money*
la empresa *firm, company*
esforzarse por (o → ue) *to strive to, try hard to*
el éxito *success*
la fama *name, reputation*

el horario de trabajo *work schedule*
invertir (e → ie) *to invest*
los peldaños del éxito *ladder of success*
la prosperidad *prosperity*
realizar *to achieve*
trepar *to climb*
el valor *value*

1. Yo buscaba una profesión que me (dar) _____
   un dineral, fama y felicidad.

2. No había nadie que (esforzarse) _____ más que
   yo por conseguir el éxito.

3. Yo quería tener un horario de trabajo que me (permitir)

   _____ pasar mucho tiempo con mi familia.

4. Yo necesitaba un esposo que (compartir) _____
   mis ideas y valores sobre la vida.

5. No conocía a nadie que (invertir) _____ más
   dinero en su compañía que yo.

6. No había ninguna persona que (ir) _____ de
   vacaciones menos que yo.

7. Me hacían falta unos empleados en quienes (poder)

   _____ confiar.

8. Mi esposo y yo buscábamos una casa donde (haber)

   _____ mucho lugar para mi oficina y para
   los niños.

9. Yo quería tener una empresa que me (dejar)

   _____ realizar mis ambiciones.

Actividad 9 **Expresar en español.** Exprese las oraciones en español.

1. Mario and Carmen are looking for a house that has nine rooms.

   _____

2. There's no food that he likes.

   _____

3. I wanted a friend who would go to museums with me.

   _____

4. Don't you (Ud.) know anyone who's arriving before three o'clock?

   _____

5. Rosa will prepare whatever dish we choose.

   _____

6. They needed a secretary who worked on Saturdays.

   _____

7. We'll take the class with whichever professor teaches best.

   _____

8. I'll take the train at whatever time it arrives.

   _____

9. Roberto was looking for a Web site that had all the necessary information.

   _____

10. We'll stay at whatever hotel you **(Uds.)** like.

    _____

11. There was no Internet café that was open at 1:00 in the morning.

    _____

12. They're looking for the programmers who work on the weekends.

    _____

Actividad 10   **Actividad oral.** Con tres o cuatro compañeros de clase, complete oraciones con cláusulas adjetivales como: **Busco unos profesores / unas profesoras que... , Quiero un novio / una novia que... , Necesito unos amigos que... , Deseo un empleo que... , Busco una casa que... , Deseo una computadora que...**

14 Commands

Command forms for **Ud.** and **Uds.**

The command forms of a verb are used to tell someone to do or not to do something. The formal command forms for **Ud.** and **Uds.** are the same as the corresponding present subjunctive forms.

Escriban el informe.	*Write the report.*
Escuche el ruido.	*Listen to the noise.*
Lea el libro.	*Read the book.*
Traigan el periódico.	*Bring the newspaper.*

Negative formal commands for **Ud.** and **Uds.** are formed by the addition of **no** before the affirmative command.

No escriban el informe.	***Don't write** the report.*
No escuche los rumores.	***Don't listen** to the rumors.*

A polite tone can be given to the command to soften it by the addition of **Ud.** or **Uds.** This is similar to the addition of *please* in English commands.

Espere.	*Wait.*
Espere Ud.	*Please wait.*
No griten.	*Don't shout.*
No griten Uds.	*Please don't shout.*

Actividad 1 **Una receta: La tortilla española.** Póngase el gorro de cocinero y aprenda a preparar este plato español típico. Escriba las oraciones cambiando el infinitivo de los verbos al imperativo formal. Siga el modelo.

> MODELO calentar el aceite de oliva en una sartén
> Caliente el aceite de oliva en una sartén.

Vocabulario

La cocina

a fuego lento *over low heat*
añadir *to add*
batir *to beat*
calentar (e → ie) *to heat*
la cebolla *onion*
cocinar *to cook*
darle la vuelta *to flip over*
dorar *to brown*
espolvorear *to sprinkle*

la fuente *serving dish*
la patata *potato (Sp.)*
pegar *to stick*
pelar *to peel*
picar *to chop*
la pimienta *pepper*
la sal *salt*
salpimentar *to season*
la/el sartén *frying pan*

1. añadir las patatas y cebollas peladas y picadas

   _____

2. cocinar a fuego lento

   _____

3. espolvorear con sal

   _____

4. batir los huevos

   _____

5. poner los huevos en la sartén

   _____

6. hacer dorar los huevos

   _____

7. darle la vuelta a la tortilla con cuidado

   _____

8. no dejar que se pegue la tortilla

   _____

9. servir en una fuente

   _____

Actividad 2 **Una formación profesional.** Unos jóvenes ingenieros comienzan un programa de formación profesional con la empresa de alta tecnología que acaba de contratarlos. Como jefe/a del programa, Ud. les dice lo que tienen que hacer. Escriba las oraciones usando el imperativo. Siga el modelo.

> MODELO llegar a las ocho menos cuarto todos los días
> Lleguen a las ocho menos cuarto todos los días.

1. asistir a la reunión semanal en la oficina del director

   _____

2. traer la calculadora

   _____

3. crear una base de datos

   _____

4. enviar el correo electrónico

   _____

5. seguir los consejos del gerente

   _____

6. actualizar (*update*) el sitio Web

_____

7. leer el manual sobre el programa de gráficas

_____

8. hacer copias de seguridad (*backup*)

_____

Actividad 3 **Trámites de banco (*Bank transactions*).** Ud. está de vacaciones en Santiago de Chile. Mientras Ud. cambia unos cheques de viajero en el banco, oye algunas conversaciones. Escriba los verbos que aparecen en las preguntas usando el imperativo. Cuando sea posible cambie los sustantivos a pronombres de complemento directo.* Siga el modelo.

> MODELO ¿Debo abrir la cuenta?
> Sí, ábrala.
> No, no la abra.

Vocabulario

En el banco

la banca electrónica *electronic, on-line banking*
el cajero automático *ATM*
calcular *to compute*
el cheque de viajero *traveler's check*
la clave personal *PIN (personal identification number)*
la cuenta *(bank) account*
la cuenta corriente *checking account*

firmar *to sign*
el formulario *form (paper)*
el interés *interest*
llenar *to fill out*
el peso *monetary unit of Chile and other Latin American countries*
la planilla de retiro *withdrawal form, slip*
la plata *money*
seleccionar *to select, choose*

1. ¿Debo buscar el cajero automático?

_____

_____

2. ¿Tengo que firmar la planilla de retiro?

_____

_____

3. ¿Debo llenar el formulario?

_____

_____

*See page 213 for a more in-depth explanation of the position of object pronouns with command forms.

4. ¿Le doy la plata en pesos?

_____

_____

5. ¿Puedo seleccionar una clave personal?

_____

_____

6. ¿Le calculo los intereses?

_____

_____

7. ¿Cierro la cuenta corriente?

_____

_____

8. ¿Le cobro los cheques de viajero?

_____

_____

9. ¿Debo probar la banca electrónica?

_____

_____

Command forms for nosotros

The present subjunctive forms for **nosotros/as** are used as commands.

Tomemos el tren.	*Let's take the train.*
No hagamos nada.	*Let's not do anything.*

The affirmative **nosotros/as** command is often replaced by **vamos a** + *infinitive*. **Vamos a estudiar** may mean either *We're going to study* or *Let's study*. Because this does not apply to negative **nosotros** commands, **No vamos a estudiar** can only mean *We're not going to study*.

Vamos a salir esta noche. ⎫
Salgamos esta noche. ⎭   *Let's go out tonight.*

Vamos is used instead of **vayamos** for *let's go*. However, the regular present subjunctive form is used for the negative: **no vayamos.**

Vamos al centro.	*Let's go downtown.*
No vayamos al cine.	*Let's not go to the movies.*

In affirmative **nosotros/as** commands the final **-s** of the verb ending is dropped when the reflexive pronoun **nos** or the indirect object pronoun **se** is added and attached to the end. An accent mark is written over the stressed syllable.

Enseñémosela.	(Enseñemos + se + la)	*Let's show it to them.*
Hagámoselos.	(Hagamos + se + los)	*Let's make them for him.*
Lavémonos.	(Lavemos + nos)	*Let's wash up.*
Prestémoselo.	(Prestemos + se + lo)	*Let's lend it to her.*
Quedémonos.	(Quedemos + nos)	*Let's stay.*
Sentémonos.	(Sentemos + nos)	*Let's sit down.*
Vámonos.	(Vamos + nos)	*Let's go.*

Actividad 4   **Veámoslo todo en Perú.** Ud. y sus amigos están pasando las vacaciones en Perú. Recién llegados a Lima, Uds. hablan de sus planes. Escriba las oraciones usando la primera persona del plural del imperativo. Siga el modelo.

> MODELO   viajar a Nazca
> Viajemos a Nazca.
> Vamos a viajar a Nazca.

1. dar un paseo por la zona de la Plaza de Armas

   _____

   _____

2. ir de compras en el Jirón de la Unión

   _____

   _____

3. conocer la Universidad de San Marcos

   _____

   _____

4. hacer una excursión a Machu Picchu

   _____

   _____

5. visitar la catedral y unas iglesias de Cuzco

   _____

   _____

6. quedarse en Miraflores

   _____

   _____

Actividad 5 **¡Cómo no!** Sus amigos le dicen que quieren hacer ciertas cosas hoy. Ud. les dice que está dispuesto/a a acompañarlos. Escriba las oraciones usando el imperativo de **nosotros/as** de las dos maneras. Siga el modelo.

> MODELO Quiero comprarle un regalo a Elisa.
> Cómo no. Comprémoselo.
> Cómo no. Vamos a comprárselo.

1. Quiero darle a Maximiliano los CDs.

   _____

   _____

2. Me encantaría sacar entradas para el concierto de la Sinfónica.

   _____

   _____

3. Me gustaría ir al museo por la tarde.

   _____

   _____

4. Sería agradable caminar por el parque.

   _____

   _____

5. Quiero inscribirme en la clase de computación.

   _____

   _____

6. Me gustaría jugar al tenis.

   _____

   _____

7. Me interesa conocer el nuevo centro comercial.

   _____

   _____

8. Me encantaría enseñarle el cibercafé a nuestros amigos.

   _____

   _____

9. Sería lindo tumbarse (*lie down*) en la playa.

   _____

   _____

Command forms for **tú** and **vosotros**

Like formal commands, negative informal commands for **tú** and **vosotros/as** are derived from the present subjunctive.

tú	**No comas** tanto.	*Don't eat so much.*
	No compres más.	*Don't buy more.*
	No digas eso.	*Don't say that.*
	No pidas ese plato.	*Don't order that dish.*
vosotros(as)	**No comáis** tanto.	*Don't eat so much.*
	No compréis más.	*Don't buy more.*
	No digáis eso.	*Don't say that.*
	No pidáis ese plato.	*Don't order that dish.*

Affirmative informal commands for **tú** and **vosotros/as** have their own endings. The affirmative informal commands are derived from the present indicative **tú** form minus the person ending **-s.**

PRESENT INDICATIVE	COMMAND	
Abres la ventana.	**Abre** la ventana.	***Open** the window.*
Contestas el teléfono.	**Contesta** el teléfono.	***Answer** the telephone.*
Sirves la cena.	**Sirve** la cena.	***Serve** dinner.*
Vendes el coche.	**Vende** el coche.	***Sell** the car.*

The following verbs have irregular affirmative **tú** commands. Note that the negative **tú** commands of these verbs are regular. They are derived from the present subjunctive forms.

	AFFIRMATIVE	NEGATIVE
decir →	di	**no digas**
hacer →	haz	**no hagas**
ir →	ve*	**no vayas**
poner →	pon	**no pongas**
salir →	sal	**no salgas**
ser →	sé	**no seas**
tener →	ten	**no tengas**
venir →	ven	**no vengas**

Affirmative **vosotros/as** commands are formed by replacing the **-r** of the infinitive with **-d.** They lose their final **-d** when the reflexive pronoun **os** is attached: **acordaos** (*remember*). The one exception to this rule is **idos** (*go away*).

Abri**d** la ventana.	*Open the window.*
Arregl**aos.**	*Get ready.*
Contesta**d** el teléfono.	*Answer the telephone.*
Servi**d** la cena.	*Serve dinner.*
Vende**d** el coche.	*Sell the car.*

---

*The affirmative **tú** commands for **ir** and **ver** are the same: **ve.**

Actividad 6 **Venid a la fiesta.** Vosotros estáis en España donde estáis organizando una fiesta para esta noche. Decid lo que los demás tienen que hacer usando la segunda persona plural (**vosotros/as**) del imperativo. Seguid el modelo.

> MODELO   preparar las ensaladas / no cocinar la carne todavía
> Preparad las ensaladas, pero no cocinéis la carne todavía.

1. hacer la torta / no ponerle el glaseado (*icing*) todavía

   _____

2. abrir las botellas de vino / no cortar las rebanadas (*slices*) de naranja todavía

   _____

3. sacar los platitos para las tapas / no preparar el chorizo y el pulpo (*octopus*) todavía

   _____

4. poner la mesa / no colocar los claveles (*carnations*) todavía

   _____

5. salir a comprar aceitunas (*olives*) / no ir todavía

   _____

6. remover (*stir*) la sangría / no servirlo en un jarro todavía

   _____

7. invitar a Pilar / no decirle nada a Consuelo

   _____

8. traer discos compactos / no traer vídeos

   _____

Actividad 7 **Tengo los nervios de punta. (*I'm on edge.*)** Manuela está nerviosísima estos días por los exámenes y el trabajo, y además se peleó con su novio. Dígale lo que debe hacer y no hacer para calmarse usando el imperativo. Siga los modelos.

> MODELOS   hacer mucho ejercicio   no hacer mucho ejercicio
> Haz mucho ejercicio.   No hagas mucho ejercicio.

1. dar un paseo todos los días

   _____

2. salir a divirtirse

   _____

3. tomar una infusión de manzanilla (*chamomile tea*)

   _____

4. tranquilizarse escuchando música

_____

5. no beber mucha cafeína

_____

6. no ponerse pesimista

_____

7. reunirse con tus amigos

_____

8. no preocuparse por tonterías

_____

9. buscarse otro novio más compasivo

_____

Actividad 8 **Paquito, ¡no seas así!** Ud. está cuidando a un niño mimado (*spoiled*) que hace diabluras. Escriba las oraciones usando el imperativo para decirle que haga o no haga ciertas cosas. Siga el modelo.

> MODELO   limpiar la mancha del jugo
>   Limpia la mancha del jugo.

1. portarse bien

_____

2. no hacer payasadas (*to clown around*)

_____

3. no ser terco (*stubborn*)

_____

4. dejar al perro en paz (*to leave alone*)

_____

5. recoger las migas (*crumbs*) de las galletas

_____

6. no derramar (*to spill*) el perfume de tu mamá

_____

7. hacerme caso (*pay attention to what I tell you*)

_____

8. no encerrarse en el baño

_____

9. venir acá inmediatamente

_____

Actividad 9 **Expresar en español.** Exprese en español los mandatos usando la segunda persona plural del imperativo **(vosotros/as).**

vos, tu, ud, uds

1. Be patient.

   Sed pacientes, sé paciente, sea paciente, sean

seg

2. Go away.

   Idos, vete, váyase, váyanse

3. Tell the truth.

   decid la verdad, di, diga, digan

4. Don't be unpleasant.

   no seáis, seas, sea, sean pesados

5. Don't get angry.

   no os enfadeis, no te enfades, no se enfade, no se enfaden

6. Write an e-mail.

   escribid un correo, escribe, escriba, escriban

7. Attend the lecture.

   asistid a la conferencia, asiste, asista, asistan

8. Play the piano.

   tocad, toca, toque, toquen el piano

9. Go to bed early.

   acostaos, acuéstate, acuéstese acuéstense

Actividad 10 **Tito el desgraciado (*unlucky guy*).** Pobre Tito tiene mala suerte. Déle consejos para ayudarlo. Escriba las oraciones usando el imperativo de los verbos indicados. Siga los modelos.

MODELOS	Tito, <u>mira.</u> (mirar)
	Tito, <u>no corras.</u> (no correr)

1. Tito, _____. (darse prisa)

2. Tito, _____. (no lastimarse)

3. Tito, _____. (no cortarse el dedo)

4. Tito, _____. (tener cuidado)

5. Tito, _____. (no romperse el pie)

6. Tito, _____. (no encender los fósforos)

7. Tito, _____. (conducir más lentamente)

8. Tito, _____. (ponerse una armadura[a])

[a]*suit of armor*

Actividad 11 **El médico aconseja…** Carlitos se quebró el tobillo jugando al fútbol. Su mamá lo lleva al consultorio donde el médico les da consejos a Carlitos y a su mamá. Complete las oraciones usando el imperativo de los verbos indicados para saber los consejos del médico. Siga los modelos.

MODELOS   Señora, (ponerle) <u>póngale</u> esta crema.
Carlitos, (andar) <u>anda</u> con cuidado.

Las fracturas

Vocabulario

escayolado/a *in a plaster cast*
la muleta *crutch*
la pastilla *pill*
la quebradura *fracture, break*

quebrarse (e → ie) *to break*
la receta *prescription*
el tobillo *ankle*
el vendaje *bandage*

1. Señora, (dejarlo) _____ ir al colegio.

2. Carlitos, no (mojarse) _____ la pierna escayolada.

3. Señora, (darle) _____ estas pastillas si le duele el tobillo.

4. Carlitos, no (jugar) _____ deportes por ahora.

5. Señora, (hacerle) _____ una sopa de pollo.

6. Carlitos, no (quitarse) _____ el vendaje.

7. Señora, (traerlo) _____ al consultorio la semana próxima.

8. Carlitos, (venir) _____ a verme el miércoles o el jueves.

9. Carlitos, (salir) _____ a la calle con muletas.

Position of object pronouns with commands

In negative commands, object pronouns (direct, indirect, reflexive) are placed in their usual position before the verb.

No **se lo** digas. *Don't tell it to him.*
No **lo** hagas. *Don't do it.*
No **te los** pongas. *Don't put them on.*
No **se** preocupen Uds. *Please don't worry.*
No **nos** sentemos. *Let's not sit down.*
No **me la** traiga. *Don't bring it to me.*

On the other hand, object pronouns follow affirmative commands and are attached to them. When pronouns are attached, an accent mark is placed over the stressed syllable, except when a single object pronoun is added to a one-syllable command form: **dime** (*tell me*); **dímelo** (*tell me it*).

NOTA

Dé, and **está, esté** may keep their accent marks when a single object pronoun is added: **deme** or **déme**.

Díselo. *Tell it to him.*
Hazlo. *Do it.*
Póntelos. *Put them on.*
Quédense Uds. *Please stay.*
Sentémonos. *Let's sit down.*
Tráigamela. *Bring it to me.*
Vete. *Go away.*

Actividad 12 **Sí, hágalo.** Conteste las preguntas con la forma correcta del imperativo. Cuando sea posible, cambie los sustantivos a pronombres de complemento directo y haga todos los cambios necesarios. Siga el modelo.

MODELO ¿Quieres que yo te traiga las revistas?
Sí, tráemelas.

1. ¿Quieres que yo les dé los informes a los jefes?
   Sí, díselos (No, no se lo des)

2. ¿Uds. quieren que yo les mande las cartas (a Uds.)?
   Sí, mándenoslas (no, no nos las mande)

3. ¿Ud. necesita que le entreguemos la tarea (a Ud.)?
   Sí, entréguenmela

4. ¿Quieres que te ponga el abrigo?
   Sí, pónmelo

5. ¿Uds. necesitan que yo les prepare los sándwiches (a ellos)?
   Sí, prepáraselos

6. ¿Uds. quieren que les sirvamos el postre (a ellas)?
   Sí, sírvanselo

   Sí, explícamela

   Sí, díganmelos

7. ¿Prefieres que te explique la idea?

_____

8. ¿A Ud. le interesa que le diga los motivos? (a Ud.)

_____

Actividad 13 **No, no lo haga.** Ahora, conteste las preguntas de la **Actividad 12** con imperativos negativos. Siga el modelo.

> MODELO ¿Quieres que yo te traiga las revistas?
> No, no me las traigas.

1. ¿Quieres que yo les dé los informes a los jefes?

_____

2. ¿Uds. quieren que yo les mande las cartas (a Uds.)?

_____

3. ¿Ud. necesita que le entreguemos la tarea (a Ud.)?

_____

4. ¿Quieres que te ponga el abrigo?

_____

5. ¿Uds. necesitan que yo les prepare los sándwiches (a ellos)?

_____

6. ¿Uds. quieren que les sirvamos el postre (a ellas)?

_____

7. ¿Prefieres que te explique la idea?

_____

8. ¿A Ud. le interesa que le diga los motivos (a Ud.)?

_____

Indirect commands

Indirect commands in Spanish consist of **que** + *present subjunctive.* Object and reflexive pronouns are placed before the verb. English equivalents are *Let* or *Have him/her/it/them do something.* Sometimes *I hope* is suggested in these sentences.

Que pase.	*Have him come in.*
Que espere.	*Let her wait.*
Que me llamen.	*Have them call me.*
Que se matriculen.	*Let them register.*
Que no se lo dé.	*Don't let him give it to them.*

Subject pronouns are added to indirect commands for emphasis.

Que lo haga **él.**	*Let **him** do it.*
Que salga **ella.**	*Let **her** go out.*
Que nos ayuden **ellos.**	*Have **them** help us.*
Que no se queden **ellas.**	*Don't let **them** stay.*

Indirect commands of **se** constructions with indirect object pronouns (see **Capítulo 19**—unplanned occurrences) are usually the equivalents of regular commands in English.

Que no se te olvide el carnet.	***Don't forget** your driver's license.*
Que no se les acaben los cheques de viajero.	***I hope you don't run out of** traveler's checks.*

Actividad 14 **Que lo hagan los otros.** Rosario se niega a colaborar con sus compañeros de clase en el proyecto de ciencias. Incluso manda que los otros se ocupen de todo. Escriba lo que Rosario propone que los otros hagan usando el imperativo indirecto. Siga el modelo.

> MODELO   No quiero participar en el proyecto. (los demás)
> Que participen los demás.

1. No voy a leer los libros de consulta (*reference books*). (Manolo)

   _____

2. No me interesa dibujar tablas (*charts*). (Terencio y Elena)

   _____

3. No quiero observar los experimentos en el laboratorio. (Paulina)

   _____

4. Me niego a hacer los gráficos (*plot graphs*). (los otros)

   _____

5. No tengo ganas de investigar estas teorías. (Samuel)

   _____

6. No quiero dedicarme a las ciencias. (mis amigos)

   _____

7. No pienso escribir un informe. (Celinda)

   _____

Actividad 15 **Expresar en español.** Exprese los mandatos indirectos en español.

1. Have her give the check to you **(Ud.).**

   _____

2. Let them go away.

   _____

3. Have him send the cards to her.

_____

4. I hope you (tú) don't lose your wallet. (*use* ***se*** *construction with indirect object pronoun*)

_____

5. Let them come back in the afternoon.

_____

6. I hope you (Uds.) don't run out of soft drinks. (*use* ***se*** *construction with indirect object pronoun*)

_____

Other ways of giving commands

Often in newspaper ads for employment, recipes, notices, and instructions the infinitive of the verb is used as an imperative rather than the command form. This type of command is only used in written form.

Interesados **mandar** currículum vitae.	*Interested persons,* ***send*** *your curriculum vitae.*
Enviar historial con fotografía a...	***Send*** *résumé with photograph to . . .*
Interesados **llamar** al teléfono...	*Interested persons,* ***call*** *. . .*
Secar las berenjenas, **pasarlas** por harina y **freírlas** en aceite hirviendo.	***Dry*** *the eggplants,* ***dip them*** *into flour, and* ***fry them*** *in boiling oil.*

The infinitive rather than the command form is used with the following expressions that convey formality and politeness. They are the English equivalent of asking something with *please,* and may be used in written or spoken language.

Favor de llamarme mañana.	*Please call me tomorrow.*
Favor de esperar.	*Please wait.*
Tenga la bondad de sentarse.	*Please sit down.*
Haga el favor de firmar el documento.	*Please sign the paper.*
Hágame el favor de enviar el cheque.	*Please send the check.*

Actividad 16 **Libro de cocina.** Escriba los verbos usando el infinitivo como imperativo. Siga el modelo.

> MODELO   Limpie el pollo.
> Limpiar el pollo.

1. Córtelos a tiritas (*in strips*).

_____

2. Caliente el aceite.

_____

3. Pártalos en trozos.

   _____

4. Seque los tomates.

   _____

5. Añádalas a la salsa.

   _____

6. Remuévalo (*stir*).

   _____

7. Póngala en una fuente.

   _____

Actividad 17 **El primer día de clase.** El profesor / La profesora de español pide que sus estudiantes hagan algunas cosas. Cambie el imperativo al infinitivo usando las expresiones indicadas. Siga el modelo.

> MODELO   Estudien el primer capítulo del libro. (Favor de)
> Favor de estudiar el primer capítulo del libro.

1. Vayan al laboratorio de lenguas. (Hagan el favor de)

   _____

2. Aprendan los diálogos de memoria. (Tengan la bondad de)

   _____

3. Traigan el diccionario. (Favor de)

   _____

4. Matricúlense si no lo han hecho. (Tengan la bondad de)

   _____

5. Compren el libro de texto y el cuaderno de trabajo. (Háganme el favor de)

   _____

6. Apúntense en esta lista. (Favor de)

   _____

7. Hagan hincapié (*emphasize*) en los ejercicios de fonética todos los días. (Hagan el favor de)

   _____

8. Busquen sitios Web en español. (Tengan la bondad de)

   _____

9. Vean películas y lean periódicos en español. (Favor de)

   _____

Actividad 18 **Busque empleo.** Los anuncios para varios empleos aparecen en el periódico. Complételos usando el infinitivo de los verbos indicados como el imperativo. Elija entre: **adjuntar, concertar, dirigirse, enviar, escribir, llamar, mandar, ponerse en contacto, presentarse, remitir.**

MODELO Interesados (*send*) <u>enviar</u> currículum vitae.

1. Interesados (*call*) _____ lunes día 3 al teléfono (91) 742–42–63.

2. (*Send*) _____ historial y fotografía al Apto. (**apartado** = *box*) 36492, 28080 Madrid.

3. Interesados (*write*) _____ a: ARA Publicidad, 08008 Barcelona.

4. Interesados (*apply*) _____, lunes 3 de 9,30 a 14 horas y de 15,30 a 17,30 horas, en C/Alcalá, 54, Srta. Núñez.

5. Interesados (*go to*) _____ a: PAR-7. Avda. del Mediterráneo, 22, 28007 Madrid.

6. Interesados (*attach*) _____ fotografía reciente al apartado de Correos número 2.059 de Madrid.

7. Los interesados deben (*get in touch*) _____ con Ignacio Doncel llamando de 9 a 14 horas y de 16 a 18 horas al teléfono (91) 585–83–64.

8. Las personas interesadas, (*arrange*) _____ entrevista en el teléfono (91) 653–95–00.

Actividad 19 **Actividad oral.** Dos o tres estudiantes crean escenas en las cuales los personajes emplean el imperativo. Por ejemplo: en el consultorio, el médico les aconseja a sus pacientes sobre sus problemas de salud; los padres les dicen a sus hijos que arreglen su cuarto; un profesor / una profesora de computación enseña a sus estudiantes cómo hacer funcionar la computadora.

15 Infinitives

Conjugated verb + infinitive

In Spanish, an important function of the infinitive of the verb is to serve as a complement or completion form in *verb + infinitive* constructions. Many verbs can be followed directly by an infinitive.

Debe cursar algo durante el verano.	*He should take courses during the summer.*
Necesitamos tomar una decisión.	*We have to make a decision.*
Querían salir a cenar.	*They wanted to go out to have dinner.*
¿Has podido encontrarlos?	*Have you been able to find them?*
Prefiero ir al concierto.	*I prefer to go to the concert.*
Procure llegar para las siete.	*Try to arrive by seven o'clock.*
Creo poder tenerlo listo para mañana.	*I think I can have it ready for tomorrow.*

Verbs commonly followed directly by an infinitive

conseguir (e → i) *to succeed in, manage to*
creer *to think, believe*
deber *should, ought to*
decidir *to decide*
dejar *to let, allow*
desear *to want*
esperar *to hope, expect, wait*
extrañar *to surprise*
hacer *to make*
impedir (e → i) *to prevent from*
intentar *to try to*
lograr *to succeed in*
mandar *to order to*

merecer *to deserve to*
necesitar *to need, have to*
ofrecer *to offer*
oír *to hear*
olvidar *to forget*
ordenar *to order*
parecer *to seem to*
pedir (e → i) *to ask to*
pensar (e → ie) *to intend*
permitir *to allow*
poder (o → ue) *to be able to, can*
preferir (e → ie) *to prefer*
pretender *to try to*
procurar *to try to*

prohibir *to prohibit*
prometer *to promise to*
querer (e → ie) *to want*
recordar (o → ue) *to remember to*
resolver (o → ue) *to resolve to*
saber *to know how to*
sentir (e → ie) *to regret, be sorry*
soler (o → ue) *to be used to, accustomed to*
sorprender *to surprise*
temer *to be afraid to*
ver *to see*

Infinitives may also function as the subject of a verb. Many verbs that usually appear with indirect objects (see **Capítulo 19,** page 318) commonly have an infinitive as a subject. When the infinitive is the subject of a verb, that verb appears in the third-person singular. Here are some common examples.

Me agrada **leer** revistas.	*I like **reading** magazines.*
Le conviene **madrugar**.	*It's suitable/good for him **to wake up early**.*
Te encanta **correr**.	*You love **running**.*
Les entusiasma **bailar** salsa.	*They're excited **to dance** salsa.*
Nos fascina **aprender**.	*We love **learning**.*
Me gusta **andar** en bicicleta.	*I like **riding** my bike.*
Os hace falta **hacer** la tarea.	*You need **to do** your homework.*
Le importa **reunirse** con sus amigos.	*It's important to her **to get together** with her friends.*
Les interesa **escalar** montañas.	*You're interested in mountain **climbing**.*
Me toca **ser** líder del grupo.	*It's my turn **to lead** the group.*

The infinitive is also used after **se me olvidó, se me pasó** (*I forgot*).

Se nos olvidó reservar una mesa.	*We forgot to reserve a table.*
Se me pasó decírtelo.	*I forgot to tell you.*

Actividad 1 **Fiestas y celebraciones.** Practique la construcción del *verbo conjugado + infinitivo*. Vuelva a escribir las oraciones añadiendo los verbos indicados a las oraciones originales. Mantenga el tiempo verbal de la oración original. Siga el modelo.

> MODELO Los Arriaga pasan la Nochebuena en casa. (preferir)
> Los Arriaga prefieren pasar la Nochebuena en casa.

1. Los españoles celebraron el santo del Rey Juan Carlos el 24 de junio. (querer)

    _____

2. Uds. siempre iban de vacaciones en Semana Santa. (procurar)

    _____

3. Paco no salió con su novia el Día de los Enamorados. (poder)

    _____

4. Preparas una barbacoa el Día de la Independencia. (soler)

    _____

5. Alejandra y Pepita no asistieron a la Misa del Gallo[a] este año. (conseguir)

    _____

6. Los niñitos recibían muchos regalos lindos el Día de Reyes.[b] (esperar)

    _____

7. Hay unos desfiles[c] grandes el Día de la Raza. (deber)

    _____

8. Les traje flores y bombones a los tíos por el Año Nuevo. (decidir)

    _____

[a]Misa... *midnight mass*   [b]Día... *Epiphany*   [c]*parades*

Actividad 2 **Expansión de oraciones.** Practique la construcción del *verbo conjugado +* *infinitivo*. Vuelva a escribir las oraciones añadiendo los verbos indicados a las oraciones originales. Mantenga el tiempo verbal de la oración original. Siga el modelo.

> MODELO Sirvió la comida. (mandar)
> Mandó servir la comida.

1. Nadabais muy bien. (saber)

   _____

2. Terminé el proyecto. (lograr)

   _____

3. Se sale por esa puerta. (prohibir)

   _____

4. Han tocado un vals. (ofrecer)

   _____

5. Limpiábamos la casa. (hacer)

   _____

6. No escuchaste los discos compactos. (dejar)

   _____

Conjugated verb + preposition + infinitive

Some verbs require a preposition before an infinitive. The most common prepositions are **a** and **de,** but some verbs require **en** or **por.**

Van a pedir paella.	*They're going to order paella.*
Comenzó a llover hace media hora.	*It began to rain half an hour ago.*
Yo me encargué de hacer las investigaciones.	*I took charge of doing the research.*
No insistas en sentarte en la primera fila.	*Don't insist on sitting in the first row.*
¿Uds. no se interesaban por coleccionar sellos?	*Weren't you interested in collecting stamps?*

Verbs that require **a** before an infinitive

acercarse a *to approach*	**comenzar a (e → ie)** *to begin to*	**empezar a (e → ie)** *to begin to*
acostumbrarse a *to be accustomed to*	**cuidar a/de** *to take care of*	**enseñar a** *to show how, teach to*
animar a *to encourage to*	**decidirse a** *to decide to*	**invitar a** *to invite to*
aprender a *to learn to*	**dedicarse a** *to devote oneself to*	**ir a** *to be going to*
atreverse a *to dare to*	**disponerse a** *to get ready to*	**llegar a** *to get to, succeed in*
ayudar a *to help*	**echar(se) a** *to begin to*	**llevar a** *to lead to*
bajar a *to go down to*		

(continued)

meterse a *to start to*	**ponerse a** *to begin to*	**volver a (o → ue)** *to do*
negarse a (e → ie) *to*	**prepararse a** *to get ready to*	*(something) again*
refuse to	**renunciar a** *to give up doing*	
obligar a *to force, compel to*	*something, quit*	
persuadir a *to persuade to*		

¿Te **decidiste a seguir** trabajando en esta oficina?	*Did you **make up your mind to continue** working in this office?*
Sí. Ya **me he acostumbrado a trabajar** aquí.	*Yes. **I've already gotten used to working** here.*
Mañana **empiezo a estudiar** en serio.	*Tomorrow **I'll start studying** seriously.*
Yo también **debo ponerme a trabajar.**	*I also **ought to begin working.***
¿**Volvieron a pedirte** dinero?	***Did they ask you** for money **again**?*
No. **No se atrevieron a pedirme** nada.	*No. **They didn't dare ask me** for anything.*

Verbs of motion are connected to a following infinitive by the preposition **a.** The preposition **a** indicates the purpose of the action.

Bajo/Subo **a** ayudarte.	*I'm coming downstairs/upstairs **(in order) to** help you.*

Verbs that require **de** before an infinitive

acabar de *to have just (done something)*	**avergonzarse de (o → üe)** *to be ashamed of*	**hartarse de** *to get fed up with*
acordarse de (o → ue) *to remember*	**cuidar de/a** *to take care of*	**jactarse de** *to boast about*
alegrarse de *to be glad*	**dejar de** *to stop*	**olvidarse de** *to forget*
arrepentirse de (e → ie) *to regret*	**encargarse de** *to take charge of*	**presumir de** *to boast about*
		terminar de *to stop*
		tratar de *to try to*

No te olvides de venir a cenar el jueves.	***Don't forget to come** have dinner on Thursday.*
No te preocupes. **Acabo de anotar** el día y la hora.	*Don't worry. **I've just written down** the day and the time.*

Verbs that require **en** before an infinitive

consentir en (e → ie) *to consent, agree to*	**empeñarse en** *to insist on, be determined to*	**interesarse en/por** *to be interested in*
consistir en *to consist of*	**esforzarse (o → ue) en/por** *to strive, try hard, make an effort*	**quedar en** *to agree to*
demorar en *to delay, put off, take a long time to*	**insistir en** *to insist on*	**tardar en** *to delay in, take a long time to*
dudar en *to hesitate over*		**vacilar en** *to hesitate over*

Carlos **se interesa** mucho **en hablarme.**	*Carlos **is** very **interested in talking** to me.*
¿**Consentiste en verlo?**	***Did you agree to see** him?*
Sí. **Quedamos en vernos** mañana.	*Yes. **We agreed to see** each other tomorrow.*

Verbs that require **con** before an infinitive

amenazar con *to threaten to*	**contar con (o → ue)** *to count on, rely on*	**soñar con (o → ue)** *to dream of, about*

En vez de trabajar, Juanita **sueña todo el día con hacerse** actriz. Por eso el jefe **amenazó con despedirla.**	*Instead of working, Juanita **dreams all day of becoming** an actress. That's why the boss **threatened to fire her.***

The verb **tener** is followed by **que** before an infinitive. **Tener que** means *to have to do something.*

Teníamos que estacionar el coche.	*We **had to park** the car.*

Hay is also followed by **que** before an infinitive when it means *to have to do something.*

Hay que buscar un cajero automático.	*We **have to** / One **has to** look for an ATM.*

Many of the preceding verbs take the same preposition before a noun object as they do before an infinitive.

¿Se dedica la señora Gómez **a su familia**?	*Does Mrs. Gómez devote herself to her family?*
Sí, se encarga **de la casa** y **de sus hijos.**	*Yes, she's in charge of the house and her children.*
¿Juan renunció **a su puesto de contable**?	*Did Juan quit his job as an accountant?*
Sí, se metió **a profesor.**	*Yes, he became a teacher.*

Actividad 3 ¿**Qué hacen los estudiantes?** Practique el uso de las preposiciones. Complete las oraciones con las preposiciones correctas. Siga el modelo.

> MODELO   Empiezan ___a___ estudiar portugués.

1. Carolina y Miguel quedaron _____ verse en la clase de física.

2. Jorge se empeña _____ sacar buenas notas este semestre.

3. Isabel se ha dedicado _____ hacer investigaciones.

4. Marco presume _____ saberlo todo.

5. Fernanda volverá _____ cursar biología.

6. Tú y yo nos encargaremos _____ organizar los archivos.

7. Teresa se decidió _____ matricularse en la escuela de verano.

8. Pancho cuenta _____ terminar la carrera (*course of study*) este año.

9. Julia y Lorenzo acaban _____ completar sus requisitos (*requirements*).

10. Nosotros tendríamos _____ buscar otras optativas (*electives*).

Actividad 4 **Expresar en español.** Exprese las oraciones en español usando la construcción del *verbo conjugado + infinitivo*.

1. We were accustomed to having dinner at 9:00 P.M.

   _____

2. Why did they take so long in calling us?

   _____

3. Patricia refused to lend Diego money.

   _____

4. Try (**Ud.**) to pay with a credit card.

   _____

5. Sing (**Uds.**) that song again.

   _____

6. I'm going to attend the lecture.

   _____

7. Silvia threatened to leave immediately.

   _____

8. They dream about becoming millionaires.

   _____

Actividad 5 **Sinónimos.** Escoja un sinónimo de las listas de verbos con y sin preposiciones para cada expresión escrita *en letra cursiva.* Siga el modelo.

> MODELO Los miembros del comité *acuerdan* reunirse el martes.
> Los miembros del comité convienen en reunirse el martes.

1. Pedro *logró* hacerse presidente de la empresa.

   _____

2. Consuelo *se jacta de* ser la mejor futbolista del equipo.

   _____

3. El profesor *mandó* cerrar los libros.

   _____

4. Uds. *sintieron* perderse la boda.

   _____

5. Yo no *recordé* recoger los pasteles.

   _____

6. ¿Cómo es que *te pusiste a* hacer la tarea a las dos de la mañana?

   _____

7. No se *dejaba* entrar en las salas de escultura.

   _____

8. Están *dudando en* invertir dinero en la compañía.

   _____

Infinitive after prepositions

English uses the present participle (the verb form ending in *-ing*) after most prepositions. Spanish, however, does not allow the use of the present participle (the verb form ending in **-ndo**) after a preposition, and requires the infinitive. The infinitive is used after many prepositions, such as: **a, al, a pesar de, antes de, con el objeto de, con tal de, después de, en caso de, en lugar de, en vez de, hasta, para, por** y **sin.** Study the contrasting usage in English and Spanish in the last two examples below.

Almorcemos **después de montar** en bicicleta.	*Let's have lunch **after we go for a** bicycle **ride.***
Estudie más **para aprender** más.	*Study more **(in order) to learn** more.*
Me alegré **al oír** la buena noticia.	*I became happy **when I heard** the good news.*
Mario irá **con tal de ver** a Susana.	*Mario will go **provided that he sees** Susana.*
Llenen el formulario **antes de firmarlo.**	*Fill out the form **before signing it**.*
¿Entraste **sin vernos**?	*Did you come in **without seeing us**?*

Actividad 6 **Expresar en español.** Exprese las oraciones en español. Practique usando el infinitivo después de las preposiciones.

1. We'll call you (**tú**) before we go out.

   _____

2. They traveled to Ponce by car without stopping.

   _____

3. Children, go to bed (**Uds.**) after you brush your teeth.

   _____

4. Bernardo should read a book instead of watching television.

   _____

5. I'll be in the library until I come home.

   _____

6. Elena will skate provided that Daniel skates, too.

   _____

7. Invite (**Ud.**) them in case you see them.

_____

8. When we got to the party we started to dance.

_____

Al + _infinitive_

The construction **al** + _infinitive_ can replace an adverbial clause beginning with **cuando** when the subject of both clauses is the same.

Lo vieron cuando entraron. → Lo vieron **al entrar.**	_They saw him when they came in._
Lo perdí cuando me fui. → Lo perdí **al irme.**	_I lost it when I left._

The construction **al** + _infinitive_ can also replace a clause beginning with **cuando** that refers to future time and is in the subjunctive.

Te lo diremos cuando lleguemos. → Te lo diremos **al llegar.**	_We'll tell you when we get there._
Muéstrame el informe cuando lo termines. → Muéstrame el informe **al terminarlo.**	_Show me the report when you finish it._

The **al** + _infinitive_ phrase may also occur at the beginning of a sentence.

Al entrar, lo vieron.	_When they came in, they saw him._
Al llegar, te lo diremos.	_When we get there, we'll tell you._

The English equivalent to the **al** + _infinitive_ construction is _upon doing something_, but this construction is literary and formal whereas **al** + _infinitive_ is part of everyday speech in Spanish. Thus, **Lo vieron al entrar** may be translated as _They saw him upon entering_, but this English translation is much less common, especially in speech.

In everyday language, including in much modern writing, the **al** + _infinitive_ construction may be used even when the subjects of the two verbs are different. The subject of the infinitive is merely placed after it.

Lo vieron cuando él entró en el café. → Lo vieron **al entrar él** en el café.	_They saw him when he came into the café._
Me devolvió el libro cuando tú se lo recordaste. → Me devolvió el libro **al recordárselo tú.**	_She returned the book to me when you reminded her about it._
Decidimos mudarnos cuando papá consiguió un ascenso. → Decidimos mudarnos **al conseguir papá** un ascenso.	_We decided to move when Dad got a promotion._

Saldremos para la playa cuando
salga el sol.
→ Saldremos para la playa **al salir
el sol.**

*We'll leave for the beach when the sun
comes out.*

Avíseme Ud. cuando los
programadores terminen el
proyecto.
→ Avíseme Ud. **al terminar los
programadores** el proyecto.

*Let me know when the programmers
finish the project.*

Note the difference in meaning in the following pairs of sentences.

Lo vieron **al entrar** en el café.

*They saw him when they came into
the café.*

Lo vieron **al entrar él** en el café.

They saw him when he came into the café.

Al llegar, te lo diremos.
Al llegar ellos, te lo diremos.

We'll tell you when we get there.
We'll tell you when they get there.

Actividad 7 **La salud ante todo.** Explique lo que hacen estas personas para mantenerse
en forma. Reemplace las cláusulas que empiecen con **cuando** con la
construcción **al** + *infinitivo*. Siga el modelo.

> MODELO Hago ejercicios cuando me levanto.
> Hago ejercicios al levantarme.

Para estar en forma

Vocabulario

los alimentos naturales *health
foods*
el gimnasio *gym(nasium)*

levantar pesas *to lift weights*
sentirse en forma *to feel fit*
trotar *to jog*

1. Mis padres toman sus vitaminas cuando desayunan.

   _____

2. Mi amigo Pablo y yo siempre salimos a trotar cuando acabamos la tarea.

   _____

3. Cuando salen del trabajo, Teresa y Laura van al gimnasio.

   _____

4. Tú levantarás pesas cuando te sientas en forma.

   _____

5. Vosotros camináis cuando termináis de almorzar.

   _____

6. Cuando tomo café, yo no como pasteles.

   _____

7. Llámenme cuando salgan para la piscina.

_____

8. Y cuando vaya a la tienda de alimentos naturales, yo los avisaré.

_____

Actividad 8 **¡Qué oficina!** Cuente lo que pasa en la oficina del señor Montalbán. Reemplace las cláusulas que empiecen con **cuando** con la construcción **al** + *infinitivo*. Fíjese que en algunas de las oraciones los sujetos son diferentes en las dos cláusulas. Siga el modelo.

> MODELO   El señor Montalbán se enoja cuando sus empleados no cumplen con su deber.
> El señor Montalbán se enoja al no cumplir sus empleados con su deber.

El mundo del trabajo

Vocabulario

chismear *to gossip*
convocar una reunión *to call a meeting*
cumplir con su deber *to do one's duty, do what one is supposed to*

gruñón/gruñona *grumpy, grouchy*
molestarse *to get annoyed*
ponerse + adjetivo *to become*
reinar *to reign, prevail*

1. Los empleados se quejan cuando el señor Montalbán exige demasiado.

_____

2. Cuando ve un problema grande, el señor Montalbán convoca una reunión.

_____

3. Los empleados se ponen gruñones cuando reciben el aviso de la reunión.

_____

4. En la reunión, todo el mundo se calló cuando entró el señor Montalbán.

_____

5. El señor Montalbán se puso muy serio cuando se dirigió a sus empleados.

_____

6. Pero cuando salió el señor Montalbán, todos empezaron a chismear.

_____

Infinitive after verbs of perception

The infinitive is used after verbs of perception such as **oír** and **ver** to signal a completed action. The gerund, rather than the infinitive, is used to show an incomplete or in-progress action, but the gerund of verbs of motion is not common.

Los **oí cantar**.	*I heard them sing.*
Los oí **cantando**.	*I heard them singing.*

¿Uds. no nos **vieron entrar**?	*Didn't you see us come in?*
¿Uds. no los vieron **haciendo** las maletas?	*Didn't you see them packing?*

The gerund is often replaced by **que** + *imperfect* in everyday Spanish.

Los oí **que cantaban**.	*I heard them singing.*
Los vimos **que leían**.	*We saw them reading.*

The construction consisting of **que** + *imperfect* is preferred for verbs of motion.

Te vi **que salías**.	*I saw you going out.*
Los oímos **que caminaban** arriba.	*We heard them walking upstairs.*

Actividad 9 **¿Qué oyó?** Lorenzo tiene problema del oído y va con una audioprotesista (*hearing aid specialist*) porque necesita un aparato. La especialista le pregunta lo que oyó. Siga el modelo.

> MODELO ¿Oyó Ud. el ruido de los coches? (frenar)
> Sí, los oí frenar.

Vocabulario

Los ruidos

el aterrizaje *landing*	**maullar** *to meow*
aterrizar *to land*	**el maullido** *meow*
despegar *to take off*	**roncar** *to snore*
el despegue *takeoff*	**los ronquidos** *snoring*
frenar *to break*	**susurrar** *to whisper*
ladrar *to bark*	**el susurro** *whisper*
el ladrido *(dog) barking*	

1. ¿Oyó Ud. el ladrido de los perros? (ladrar)

   _____

2. ¿Oyó Ud. el maullido del gato? (maullar)

   _____

3. ¿Oyó Ud. el despegue y el aterrizaje de los aviones? (despegar/aterrizar)

   _____

4. ¿Oyó Ud. el susurro de las hojas? (susurrar)

   _____

5. ¿Oyó Ud. los gritos de sus hijos? (gritar)

_____

6. ¿Oyó Ud. los ronquidos de su mujer? (roncar)

_____

Actividad 10 **¿Qué vieron Uds.?** Escriba oraciones usando el verbo de percepción **ver.** Siga el modelo.

> MODELO   María / bailar
> La vimos bailar.

1. José y Pablo / trotar

_____

2. vosotros / hacer ejercicio

_____

3. Roberto / entrar en la discoteca

_____

4. la señorita Barba / dictar una conferencia

_____

5. Uds. (*masc.*) / hablar por teléfono celular

_____

6. tu / escanear los documentos

_____

7. Ud. (*fem.*) / salir de la tienda de deportes

_____

Infinitive preceded by **que**

The infinitive is often preceded by **que;** however, the **que** + *infinitive* construction cannot be used with verbs of searching, needing, and requesting. In these cases **para** is used.

Me queda mucho **que hacer.**	*I have a lot left to do.*
Nos han dado tantas cosas **que/para hacer.**	*They've given us so many things to do.*
Compra algo **que/para leer.**	*Buy something to read.*
Pidió algo **para aplacar** su sed.	*He ordered something to quench his thirst.*
Queríamos algo **para comer.**	*We wanted something to eat.*

Actividad 11   **¿Qué o para?** Complete las oraciones usando **que** o **para** antes del infinitivo.

1. Teníamos mucho _____ hacer.

2. Están buscando algo _____ comer.

3. Compraré algo _____ leer.

4. Hay muchas cosas _____ ver.

Adjective + de + infinitive

The construction *adjective* + **de** + *infinitive* is used when the infinitive of a transitive verb is not followed by object or a clause. The **de** is omitted when an object or a clause appears.

El vasco es muy difícil **de** aprender.	*Basque is very difficult to learn.*
Es muy difícil aprender vasco.	*It's very difficult to learn Basque.*
Su teoría es imposible **de** comprobar.	*His/Her theory is impossible to prove.*
Es imposible comprobar su teoría.	*It's impossible to prove his/her theory.*

Actividad 12   **¿De o nada?** Complete las oraciones con **de** antes del infinitivo cuando sea necesario. Si no es necesario usar la preposición, escriba una X.

1. No es posible _____ comprenderlo.

2. Eso es fácil _____ ver.

3. Es triste _____ pensar que ya no vuelven.

4. El japonés no es difícil _____ aprender.

Actividad 13   **Actividad oral.** Se juega entre dos equipos de estudiantes. Uno de los equipos da una oración y un verbo para expandirla al otro equipo como en la **Actividad 2** de este capítulo. Cada respuesta correcta vale un punto. Se juega hasta que uno de los equipos consiga diez puntos.

PARTE II

Nouns and Their Modifiers; Pronouns

16 Nouns and articles

Gender of nouns

In Spanish, all nouns are either masculine or feminine. There are ways to determine the gender of most nouns.

Most nouns that end in **-o** or that refer to males are masculine.

Masculine nouns

el banco *bank*	**el hombre** *man*	**el piano** *piano*
el doctor *doctor*	**el laboratorio** *laboratory*	**el profesor** *professor*
el duque *duke*	**el libro** *book*	**el señor** *gentleman*
el hijo *son*	**el padre** *father*	**el toro** *bull*

Most nouns that end in **-a** or that refer to females are feminine.

Feminine nouns

la computadora *computer*	**la librería** *bookstore*	**la profesora** *professor*
la duquesa *duchess*	**la madre** *mother*	**la revista** *magazine*
la flauta *flute*	**la mujer** *woman*	**la señora** *lady*
la hija *daughter*	**la oficina** *office*	**la vaca** *cow*

There are many nouns that end in **-a** and **-ma** that are masculine, and some nouns that end in **-o** that are feminine. The gender of these words must be memorized.

Masculine nouns ending in -a

el clima *climate*	**el mediodía** *midday, noon*	**el problema** *problem*
el día *day*	**el panda** *panda*	**el programa** *program*
el idioma *language*	**el planeta** *planet*	**el sistema** *system*
el mapa *map*	**el poema** *poem*	**el tranvía** *streetcar*

Feminine nouns ending in -o

la foto (*abbrev. of* **la fotografía**) *photo(graph)*
la mano *hand*

la moto (*abbrev. of* **la motocicleta**) *motorcycle*
la radio *radio*

The gender of most nouns that end in **-e** or a consonant cannot be predicted and must therefore be memorized.

Nouns ending in -e or consonant

MASCULINE		FEMININE
el aceite *oil*	**el disfraz** *disguise*	**la base** *base*
el alfiler *pin*	**el disquete** *diskette*	**la clase** *class*
el arroz *rice*	**el examen** *test*	**la gente** *people*
el billete *ticket*	**el informe** *report*	**la llave** *key*
el cine *movie theater*	**el lápiz** *pencil*	**la luz** *light*
el cobre *copper*	**el papel** *paper*	**la piel** *skin*
el desván *attic*	**el plan** *plan*	**la Red** *the Web, the Internet*
		la torre *tower*

Nouns that have endings in **-dad, -tad, -tud, -umbre, -ión, -ie, -cia, -ez, -eza, -nza, -sis,** and **-itis** are usually feminine.

Nouns feminine by suffix

la certidumbre *certainty*
la ciudad *city*
la crisis *crisis*
la cumbre *mountain top*
la diferencia *difference*
la dirección *address*
la esperanza *hope*

la felicidad *happiness*
la juventud *youth*
la libertad *liberty, freedom*
la multitud *multitude, crowd*
la nación *nation*
la pereza *laziness*
la presencia *presence*

la reunión *meeting*
la sencillez *simplicity*
la serie *series*
la superficie *surface*
la tesis *thesis*
la verdad *truth*

Nouns that end in **-aje, -ambre, -or, -án,** or a stressed vowel are usually masculine.

Nouns masculine by suffix

el amor *love*
el calambre *cramp*
el champú *shampoo*

el equipaje *luggage*
el paisaje *landscape*
el refrán *proverb*

el rubí *ruby*
el valor *value*

Nouns that refer to people (and some animals) that end in **-or, -és -ón,** and **-ín** are usually masculine and add **-a** to make the feminine form. The accent mark of the masculine form is dropped in the feminine.

Nouns referring to people

MASCULINE		FEMININE	
el anfitrión *host*	**el doctor** *doctor*	**la anfitriona** *hostess*	**la doctora** *doctor*
el bailarín *dancer*	**el francés** *Frenchman*	**la bailarina** *dancer*	**la francesa**
el campeón *champion*	**el profesor** *professor*	**la campeona** *champion*	*Frenchwoman*
el consultor *consultant*		**la consultora** *consultant*	**la profesora** *professor*

In forming the feminine, some nouns that refer to people (or some animals) change only their article but not their form. Many of these nouns end in **-e, -a, -ista, -nte,** or a consonant.

Nouns feminine by articles

el/la agente *agent*	**el/la dependiente** *clerk*	**el/la líder** *leader*
el/la artista *artist*	**el/la estudiante** *student*	**el/la mártir** *martyr*
el/la atleta *athlete*	**el/la intérprete** *interpreter*	**el/la tigre** (*also,* **tigresa**)
el/la cantante *singer*	**el/la joven** *young man/*	*tiger*
el/la dentista *dentist*	*woman*	**el/la turista** *tourist*

Some speakers change **-nte** to **-nta** for the feminine (**la dependienta, la estudianta**), but this is more characteristic of colloquial speech.

Sometimes the feminine form of a noun is not predictable from the masculine.

MASCULINE		FEMININE	
el actor	*actor*	**la actriz**	*actress*
el emperador	*emperor*	**la emperatriz**	*empress*
el príncipe	*prince*	**la princesa**	*princess*
el rey	*king*	**la reina**	*queen*

The days of the week are masculine.

Iremos a la sierra **el jueves** y volveremos **el lunes.**

*We'll go to the mountains **on Thursday** and we'll come back **on Monday.***

The months of the year are masculine.

el enero más frío
el agosto más caluroso

the coldest January
the hottest August

The names of languages are masculine.

El español se habla en más de veinte países.

Spanish is spoken in more than twenty countries.

El inglés es la lengua de muchos países también.

English is the language of many countries also.

Compound nouns that consist of a verb and a noun are masculine.

Compound nouns

el abrelatas *can opener*
el cumpleaños *birthday*
el lavaplatos *dishwasher*
el limpiaparabrisas *windshield wiper*

el parabrisas *windshield*
el parachoques *bumper*
el paraguas *umbrella*
el portaaviones *aircraft carrier*

el saltamontes *grasshopper*
el salvavidas *lifeguard, life preserver*

Numbers **(los números)** are masculine.

El veintisiete de enero es el cumpleaños de Mozart.

*January **twenty-seventh** is Mozart's birthday.*

Mi número de suerte es **el quince.**

*My lucky number is **fifteen.***

Colors are masculine when used as nouns.

Me gusta **el azul** más que **el marrón.**

*I like **blue** more than **brown.***

Many names of trees are masculine, although their fruit is often feminine.

EL ÁRBOL	
el almendro	*almond tree*
el castaño	*chestnut tree*
el cerezo	*cherry tree*
el ciruelo	*plum tree*
el limonero	*lemon tree*
el manzano	*apple tree*
el melocotonero	*peach tree*
el naranjo	*orange tree*
el peral	*pear tree*

LA FRUTA	
la almendra	*almond*
la castaña	*chestnut*
la cereza	*cherry*
la ciruela	*plum*
el limón	*lemon*
la manzana	*apple*
el melocotón	*peach*
la naranja	*orange*
la pera	*pear*

All infinitives used as nouns are masculine.

El fumar hace daño.

***Smoking** is harmful.*

El navegar en la Red es divertido.

***Surfing** the Web is fun.*

Nouns that begin with stressed **-a** or **-ha** are feminine but take the masculine article in the singular; these nouns take the feminine article **las** in the plural. This rule does not apply where the first vowel is not stressed (**la alfombra, la ambición**) or when referring to the name of the letter *a* (**la a**) and the letter *h* (**la hache**).

Nouns beginning with stressed -a or -ha

el agua *water*
el agua fría del lago *the cold water of the lake*
el águila *eagle*

el alma *soul*
el área *area*
el ave *bird*
el hacha *hatchet*

el hambre *hunger*
las aguas tibias del Caribe *the warm waters of the Caribbean*

The names of rivers, seas, and oceans are masculine.

Los Estados Unidos tiene costa en **el (océano) Atlántico** y **el Pacífico.**
El (río) Amazonas atraviesa Brasil.

*The United States has coasts on **the Atlantic Ocean** and on **the Pacific.** **The Amazon River** passes through Brazil.*

Some Spanish nouns have both a masculine and feminine gender, but with a difference in meaning.

Nouns: gender determining meaning

MASCULINE		FEMININE	
el busca *beeper, pager*	**el mañana** *tomorrow*	**la busca** *the search*	**la mañana** *morning*
el capital *money*	**el orden** *order*	**la capital** *capital city*	**la orden** *order*
el coma *coma*	(*tidiness*)	**la coma** *comma*	(*command*)
el cometa *comet*	**el policía** *police officer*	**la cometa** *kite*	**la policía** *police*
el frente *front*		**la frente** *forehead*	*officer, police force*
(*weather, military*)			

The word **arte** is masculine in the singular but feminine in the plural.

el arte español   *Spanish art*
las bellas artes   *fine arts*

Some nouns do not vary in gender and are applied to males and females, in some cases with a change in article.

Nouns referring to males and females

el ángel *angel*
el/la bebé *baby*
el/la genio *genius*
el/la modelo *model*

la persona *person*
el personaje *character (in a book, play)*

el/la testigo *witness*
la víctima *victim*

Thus you say **Juan fue *la* víctima más joven del accidente** but **Marta es *la* testigo más importante.**

Spanish has borrowed many words from English in various technical and cultural fields. These borrowings are almost always masculine.

Nouns borrowed from English

el campus	el login/logon/logoff	el poster
el fax	el marketing	el ranking
el jazz	el módem	el software

The borrowed word **Web** can be either masculine or feminine. The use of the feminine **la Web** is conditioned by the Spanish term for the Worldwide Web, **la Red.**

When words are borrowed from a language that has a feminine gender, especially other Romance languages, the feminine may be preserved in Spanish.

la pizza (*from Italian*)
la suite (*from French*)

Many speakers change **la radio** to **el radio** under the influence of the ending **-o.** For other speakers, **el radio** refers to a radio receiver and **la radio** refers to the medium of mass communication.

Se me descompuso **el radio.**	*My radio broke.*
Siempre escucho **la radio** mexicana.	*I always listen to Mexican radio.*

El mar often becomes feminine when referring to conditions of the sea.

mar brava	*very rough sea*
mar gruesa	*rough sea*
mar llena	*high tide*
mar rizada	*choppy sea*

Sometimes an inanimate feminine noun can be applied to a male person with a change in meaning. In this case, the new noun is masculine.

FEMININE			MASCULINE	
la cámara	*camera*		**el** cámara	*cameraperson*
las medias	*socks*		**los** Medias Rojas	*the Red Sox*
la trompeta	*trumpet*		**el** trompeta	*trumpet player*

Actividad 1 ¿**Masculino o femenino?** Escriba la forma masculina o femenina del artículo definido para cada sustantivo de la lista.

1. _____ concierto
2. _____ sistema
3. _____ escritor
4. _____ tierra
5. _____ drama
6. _____ mano

7. _____ natación
8. _____ día
9. _____ natalidad
10. _____ legumbre
11. _____ guión
12. _____ capital (*capital city*)

13. _____ computadora	17. _____ verde
14. _____ rompecabezas	18. _____ frente (*forehead*)
15. _____ dirección	19. _____ ascensor
16. _____ escocés	20. _____ parabrisas

Actividad 2 **Por parejas.** Escriba quién es la pareja femenina (*counterpart*) de cada hombre. Practique usando la forma femenina de los sustantivos. Escriba el artículo también.

1. el profesor _____

2. el rey _____

3. el artista _____

4. el abogado _____

5. el príncipe _____

6. el gobernador _____

7. el representante _____

8. el bailarín _____

9. el emperador _____

10. el actor _____

11. el estadista _____

12. el holandés _____

13. el cliente _____

14. el atleta _____

15. el programador _____

Actividad 3 **Expresar en español.** Exprese las oraciones en español.

1. Ms. Galíndez is leaving on a business trip on Tuesday and will return on Thursday.

   _____

2. Don't put **(Ud.)** the frying pan in the dishwasher.

   _____

3. English and French are the official languages of Canada.

   _____

4. Beethoven was born on December 16, 1770.

   _____

5. My favorite colors are green and blue.

    _____

6. Let's pick apples from that (apple) tree.

    _____

7. The official bird of the United States is the eagle.

    _____

8. Did they like the cruise **(crucero)** in the Mediterranean or the Caribbean better?

    _____

9. Reading is so pleasant.

    _____

10. A tropical front will arrive tomorrow.

    _____

11. We'll invest our capital in an international company.

    _____

12. What are the names of the characters in the novel?

    _____

13. The cameraman lost his camera.

    _____

14. In the film we saw, the angels saved the baby.

    _____

15. The witnesses talked to the victim of the accident.

    _____

Number of nouns

In Spanish, nouns that end in a vowel form the plural by adding **-s.**

Nouns plural in -s

SINGULAR		PLURAL	
el café *coffee, café*	**el espejo** *mirror*	los cafés	los espejos
el carretera *highway*	**el hermano** *brother*	las carreteras	los hermanos
el clarinete *clarinet*	**la placa** *license plate*	los clarinetes	las placas

Nouns that end in a consonant, including **-y,** form the plural by adding **-es.**

<table>
<tr><td colspan="2">**Nouns plural in -es**</td></tr>
<tr><td colspan="2" align="center">SINGULAR</td><td colspan="2" align="center">PLURAL</td></tr>
<tr><td>**el examen** *test*</td><td>**la opinión** *opinion*</td><td>**los exámenes**</td><td>**las opiniones**</td></tr>
<tr><td>**el huracán** *hurricane*</td><td>**el origen** *origin*</td><td>**los huracanes**</td><td>**los orígenes**</td></tr>
<tr><td>**el inglés** *English*</td><td>**el país** *country*</td><td>**los ingleses**</td><td>**los países**</td></tr>
<tr><td>**el lápiz** *pencil*</td><td>**el peatón** *pedestrian*</td><td>**los lápices**</td><td>**los peatones**</td></tr>
<tr><td>**la ley** *law*</td><td>**el pez** *fish*</td><td>**las leyes**</td><td>**los peces**</td></tr>
<tr><td>**el limón** *lemon*</td><td>**el titular** *headline*</td><td>**los limones**</td><td>**los titulares**</td></tr>
<tr><td>**el mes** *month*</td><td>**la voz** *voice*</td><td>**los meses**</td><td>**las voces**</td></tr>
</table>

Nouns with a written accent on the last syllable in the singular lose their accent mark in the plural: **autobús → autobuses, inglés → ingleses, limón → limones, opinión → opiniones.** Exception: **país → países.**

Lápices and all nouns that have a written accent on the next-to-the last syllable in the singular retain that accent in the plural: **azúcar → azúcares.**

Examen, joven, and **origen** have an accent mark in the plural: **exámenes, jóvenes,** and **orígenes.**

A few common nouns shift their stress in the plural: **el carácter → los caracteres, el espécimen → los especímenes, el régimen → los regímenes.**

When **-es** is added to a word that ends in **-z,** the **-z** is changed to **-c:** **lápiz → lápices, pez → peces, voz → voces.**

The plural of a noun that ends in **-í** or **-ú** is formed by adding **-es: el rubí → los rubíes, tabú → los tabúes.**

Nouns of more than one syllable ending in an unstressed vowel plus **-s** do not add a plural ending.

el abrelatas	→	los abrelatas
el atlas	→	los atlas
la crisis	→	las crisis
el miércoles	→	los miércoles
el paraguas	→	los paraguas
el viernes	→	los viernes

The masculine plural of nouns referring to people can refer to a group of males or a group of males and females.

los hermanos	*brothers and sisters*
los hijos	*children, sons and daughters*
los Reyes de España	*The King and Queen of Spain*
los tíos	*aunt and uncle*

These words can also refer to males only. The context clarifies the exact meaning.

los hermanos	*brothers*
los hijos	*sons*
los reyes	*kings*
los tíos	*uncles*

PARTE II

If a proper name refers to a family, it has no plural form. If a group of individuals happens to have the same name, a plural form is used. Names that end in **-z** are usually invariable.

Los Prado viven en esta calle.	*The Prado family lives on this street.*
La guía telefónica tiene tantos **Morelos** y **Blancos.**	*The telephone book has so many Morelos and Blancos (people named Morelo and Blanco).*
¿No conoces a **los Fernández**?	*Don't you know the Fernándezes?*

Some nouns are always plural in Spanish. Many of their English equivalents are always plural as well.

Nouns always used in the plural

las afueras *outskirts*	**los bienes** *goods*	**los gemelos** *twins, binoculars, cuff links*
los alrededores *surroundings*	**las cosquillas** *tickling*	
los anteojos *eyeglasses*	**las gafas** *eyeglasses*	**las tijeras** *scissors*
los auriculares *earphones*	**las ganas** *urge, desire*	**las vacaciones** *vacation*

Many of these words appear in set expressions, for example: **hacerle cosquillas a alguien** *to tickle someone*. Note that **las ganas** appears in the singular in **No me da la gana** *I don't feel like it*.

The Spanish equivalent of *They washed their hair* is **Se lavaron la cabeza.** Notice that Spanish uses the singular noun **la cabeza** implying there is one for each person.

Se cortaron **la rodilla.**	*They cut their knees.*
Se pusieron **la chaqueta.**	*They put on their jackets.*
¿Tienen Uds. **novia**?	*Do you have girlfriends?*

Actividad 4 **En plural.** Escriba la forma plural de los sustantivos.

1. guante _____

2. lavaplatos _____

3. religión _____

4. origen _____

5. color _____

6. amistad _____

7. rey _____

8. tos _____

9. martes _____

10. irlandés _____

11. paréntesis _____

12. luz _____

13. té _____

Actividad 5 **El arca de Noé.** No se olvide que hay dos animales de cada especie que suben al arca de Noé. Practique usando el plural de los sustantivos. Siga el modelo.

> MODELO   caballo <u>caballos</u>

1. vaca   _____

2. orangután   _____

3. elefante   _____

4. avestruz (*ostrich*)   _____

5. león   _____

6. castor (*beaver*)   _____

7. loro (*parrot*)   _____

8. cóndor   _____

9. delfín (*dolphin*)   _____

10. faisán (*pheasant*)   _____

11. pantera (*panther*)   _____

12. tigre   _____

13. oveja (*sheep*)   _____

14. mono (*monkey*)   _____

Actividad 6 **Sobre gustos no hay nada escrito. (*Everyone to his or her own taste.*)** Escriba oraciones en las cuales Ud. explica lo que a cada persona le gusta comer. Cambie el sustantivo al plural. Siga el modelo.

> MODELO   Carlos / comer / haba
> Carlos come habas.

Vocabulario

Los alimentos

el aguacate *avocado*
el espárrago *asparagus*
el chile *chile (chili) pepper*
el frijol *kidney bean*

el guisante *pea*
el haba *bean*
el camarón *shrimp*

1. Lucía / pedir / guisante

_____

2. yo / preferir / espárrago

_____

3. tú / ordenar / papa frita

_____

4. Claudia y Jesús / querer / chile

_____

5. nosotros / tener ganas de comer / aguacate

_____

6. Ud. y Luis / pedir / frijol

_____

7. Ud. / querer / camarón

_____

Actividad 7 ¡Que toque la orquesta! Escriba estos instrumentos en la forma plural con el artículo definido.

1. piano   _____
2. flauta   _____
3. viola   _____
4. clarinete   _____
5. violonchelo   _____
6. violín   _____
7. trompeta   _____
8. trombón   _____
9. arpa   _____
10. oboe   _____
11. tambor   _____
12. tuba   _____

Forms and uses of definite articles

In Spanish, the definite article, which in English is the word *the*, changes its form to agree with the noun in gender (masculine/feminine) and number (singular/plural).

	MASCULINE	FEMININE			MASCULINE	FEMININE
SINGULAR	el	la		**SINGULAR**	el cuerpo	la cabeza
PLURAL	los	las		**PLURAL**	los cuerpos	las cabezas

In Spanish, unlike in English, the definite article is used before a noun to refer to something in a general way (mass or uncountable nouns) or to refer to all the members of its class. Colors, like abstract nouns, also require the article.

La democracia es el mejor sistema de gobierno.	**Democracy** is the best system of government.
El agua mineral es buena para la digestión.	**Mineral water** is good for digestion.
El verde es el color que más me gusta.	**Green** is the color I like best.
No le gustan **las espinacas**.	She doesn't like **spinach**.

Note that the sentence **No le gustan las espinacas** is ambiguous out of context because it can mean she doesn't like all spinach, that is, spinach in general, or she doesn't like a particular spinach already mentioned in the conversation.

The definite article **el** is used before the names of languages except directly after **hablar** and after the prepositions **de** and **en.** It is also commonly omitted directly after the verbs **aprender, enseñar, estudiar, leer, practicar,** and **saber.**

Escribió la carta **en** alemán.	He wrote the letter in German.
Hablamos bien **el** español.	We speak Spanish well.
Hablamos español.	We speak Spanish.
Os presto el diccionario **de** chino.	I'll lend you the Chinese dictionary.
Saben hebreo y estudian japonés.	They know Hebrew, and they're studying Japanese.

The definite article is used before titles except when the person is being addressed directly. It is not used before **don/doña** and **San/Santo/Santa.**

El señor Lerma está bien.	**Mr.** Lerma is well.
Señor Lerma, ¿cómo está Ud.?	**Mr.** Lerma, how are you?
José nació el día de **San José.**	José was born on **San José's** day.

The definite article is used to express the time of day.

Son **las cuatro y media.**	It's **four-thirty.**
Se acostaron a **la una** de la mañana.	They went to bed at **one** A.M.

The definite article is used with the days of the week.

Nos vemos **el jueves,** entonces.	We'll see each other **on Thursday,** then.
Los lunes el museo está cerrado.	**On Mondays** the museum is closed.
¿Quién enseña la clase **del martes**?	Who's teaching **Tuesday's** class?

The definite article is omitted after forms of **ser.**

Hoy es **miércoles.**	Today is **Wednesday.**

However, the definite article is used after forms of **ser** when **ser** means *to happen; to take place.*

Eso fue **el domingo.**	That was (happened) **on Sunday.**
El concierto fue **el sábado.**	The concert was **on Saturday.**

The definite article is omitted before the names of the days of the week when a date follows.

viernes, cinco de agosto	**Friday,** August fifth

The definite article is used with the names of the seasons. It can be omitted after the preposition **en** when it is suggested that the event mentioned occurs in that season every year.

Me encanta **el verano.**	*I love **summer.***
Alano va a Madrid **en el otoño.**	*Alano is going to Madrid **in the fall.***
Gonzalo viaja a Barcelona **en invierno.**	*Gonzalo travels to Barcelona **in winter.***

Spanish uses the definite article rather than the possessive adjective commonly used in English with parts of the body and articles of clothing, especially with reflexive verbs.

Mauricio está cepillándose **los dientes.**	*Mauricio is brushing **his teeth.***
Sofi se puso **los jeans.**	*Sofi put on **her jeans.***

The definite article is used before infinitives that function as nouns. The article is often omitted when the infinitive is the subject of the sentence.

(El) robar es malo.	***Stealing** is bad.*
El estafar es también un vicio.	***Swindling** is also a vice.*

The definite article is used with the names of rivers, oceans, and mountains.

El Sena pasa por París y **el Támesis** por Londres.	***The Seine** flows through Paris and **the Thames** through London.*
Los Pirineos quedan entre España y Francia.	***The Pyrenees** are between Spain and France.*

The definite article is traditionally used before the names of some countries, although it tends to be omitted more and more in contemporary Spanish. However, the definite article must be used before the name of a country, city, or continent that is modified.

por **(la)** Argentina *through Argentina*	**la** España medieval *Medieval Spain*	**la** Europa central *Central Europe*
a través de **(del)** Canadá *through Canada*	en **(los)** Estados Unidos *in the United States*	sobre **(el)** Japón *about Japan*
		hacia **(el)** Perú *toward Peru*

When the definite article is part of the name of a country or city, it is not omitted.

Los Ángeles *Los Angeles*	**La Paz** *La Paz (capital of Bolivia)*	**El Salvador** *El Salvador*
El Cairo *Cairo*		
La Coruña *La Coruña (city in northwestern Spain)*	**La República Dominicana** *The Dominican Republic*	

Some place names always take the definite article.

la India	*India*
el Reino Unido	*the United Kingdom*
los Países Bajos	*the Netherlands*

The definite article is used before nouns of measurement.

un dólar **la libra**   *a dollar per pound*
cincuenta centavos **el kilo** *fifty cents per kilo*

In Spanish, many set phrases that require the definite article do not usually have it in their English equivalents.

a/en/de **la** iglesia   *to/in/from church*
en **la** televisión   *on television*
en **el** mar   *at sea, on/in the sea*

Actividad 8 **El artículo definido.** Complete la tabla con la forma correcta del artículo definido en singular. Luego, escriba el sustantivo y el artículo definido en la forma plural.

ARTÍCULO DEFINIDO

SINGULAR		PLURAL
1. _____	aceituna	_____
2. _____	ensayo	_____
3. _____	agua	_____
4. _____	árbol	_____
5. _____	sal	_____
6. _____	pasaporte	_____
7. _____	volcán	_____
8. _____	actividad	_____
9. _____	origen	_____
10. _____	mes	_____
11. _____	serpiente	_____
12. _____	lápiz	_____
13. _____	francés	_____
14. _____	vez	_____
15. _____	sacapuntas	_____
16. _____	jugador	_____

Actividad 9 **Retrato de la heroína romántica.** Armando, un pintor romántico, pinta el retrato de su mujer ideal. ¿Cómo es? Complete las frases con la forma correcta del artículo definido y el sustantivo.

MODELO Para mí la mujer ideal tiene: (*feet*) <u>los pies</u> pequeños

1. (*eyes*) _____ azules

2. (*cheeks*) _____ rosadas

3. (*hands*) _____ suaves

4. (*lips*) _____ como cerezas

5. (*teeth*) _____ como perlas

6. (*hair*) _____ como el oro

7. (*neck*) _____ como cisne[a]

8. (*ears*) _____ bien formadas

[a]*swan*

Actividad 10 **¿Artículo definido o no?** Complete las oraciones con la forma correcta del artículo definido cuando sea necesario. Si no es necesario escriba una X.

1. Bogotá, ___X___ capital de Colombia, se encuentra en las montañas.

2. Nos interesa ___el___ cine.

3. Laura y Pedro saben perfectamente ___el___ ruso.

4. Hay multa por ___X___ ensuciar las calles.

5. —¿Adónde va Ud., ___X___ Señor Maldonado?

6. Volvimos a casa a ___la___ diez y cuarto.

7. Estas revistas están escritas en ___X___ catalán.

8. La comida fue ___el___ miércoles.

9. ___Las___ legumbres son buenas para ___la___ salud.

10. ___El___ verano es la estación más agradable del año.

11. Hoy es ___X___ domingo.

12. Hicimos investigaciones sobre ___la___ España contemporánea.

13. ___Los___ duraznos se venden a dos dólares ___la___ libra en verano.

14. ¿Habrá algo interesante en ___la___ televisión?

15. ___La___ señorita Suárez llega de ___la___ iglesia.

Actividad 11 **Expresar en español.** Exprese las oraciones en español.

1. The Sánchez family is going to Florida in the spring.

   _____

2. Florencia put on her socks.

   _____

3. Give (**Ud.**) us the Latin books.

   _____

4. Juli and Nicolás love swimming.

   _____

5. What did the tourists do at sea?

   _____

6. The twins washed their faces.

   _____

7. Elías knows Portuguese, speaks Italian, reads Russian, and is learning German.

   _____

8. The dance was on Saturday. It began at 9:30 P.M.

   _____

Omission of definite articles

The definite article is omitted before mass or count nouns that do not refer to the whole of their class but only to some of it or a part of it (an unspecified quantity).

Guadalupe tiene **paciencia.**	*Guadalupe is patient.*
Toman **aspirinas.**	*They're taking aspirin.*
Amparo compró **carne.**	*Amparo bought meat.*

Spanish usually omits the definite article after forms of **haber.**

Hay gente en el comedor.	*There are people in the dining room.*

When two nouns are joined by **de** to form a compound noun, the definite article is omitted before the second noun. Note that in these compound nouns, the order of the nouns is the reverse of their English equivalents.

la chuleta de ternera *veal chop*	**el libro de historia** *history book*
el cinturón de seguridad *seat belt*	**el objeto de valor** *valuable object*
el dolor de cabeza *headache*	**la sala de espera** *waiting room*

To pluralize a compound noun joined by **de,** only the first noun is made plural.

las chuletas de ternera *veal chops*	**los libros de historia** *history books*
los cinturones de seguridad *seat belts*	**los objetos de valor** *valuable objects*
los dolores de cabeza *headaches*	**las salas de espera** *waiting rooms*

In some compound nouns joined by **de,** the second element is always plural.

la base de datos	*database*
la bolsa de valores	*stock exchange*
la tienda de muebles	*furniture store*
el traje de luces	*bullfighter's costume*

The plural of these nouns is made by pluralizing the first noun.

las bases de datos	*databases*
las bolsas de valores	*stock exchanges*
las tiendas de muebles	*furniture stores*
los trajes de luces	*bullfighter's costumes*

The definite article is usually omitted in apposition.

Caracas, capital de Venezuela *Caracas, the capital of Venezuela*
Mario Vargas Llosa, novelista *Mario Vargas Llosa, the novelist*

Santa Fe, capital de Nuevo México *Santa Fe, the capital of New Mexico*
Simón Bolívar, libertador de Sudamérica *Simón Bolívar, the liberator of South America*

The definite article is omitted before ordinal numbers with kings and other rulers.

Alfonso X (décimo)	*Alfonso X (the tenth)*
Carlos V (quinto)	*Charles V (the fifth)*

In Spanish, there are many set adverbial phrases that do not take the definite article, whereas their English equivalents usually do.

en nombre de	*in the name of*
a corto/largo plazo	*in the short/long term*
en camino	*on the way*

Actividad 12 **¿Falta el artículo definido?** Complete las oraciones con el artículo definido cuando sea necesario. Cuando no es necesario escriba una X.

1. Plácido Domingo, _____ tenor, y Montserrat

   Caballé, _____ soprano, son españoles.

2. Juan Carlos _____ I (primero) subió al trono español en 1975.

3. Alfonsito tiene dolor de _____ estómago y

   Luisito tiene dolor de _____ muelas por los bombones que se comieron.

4. Los anfitriones compraron _____ vinos más caros para la fiesta.

5. Aurelia no está en casa porque ya está en _____ camino.

6. No hay _____ sillones en la sala todavía.

7. Tomamos _____ vitaminas para tener

   _____ energía.

Neuter article lo

Spanish has a neuter article **lo,** which is placed before an adjective used as a noun to express an abstract idea or a certain quality. The form **lo** is invariable and is used with masculine and feminine and singular and plural *adjectives* + **que** to express *how.* **Lo** is also used with adverbs and adverbial phrases.

lo bueno	*the good part, what's good*
lo fácil	*the easy part, what's easy*
Oí **lo graciosos/as** que son.	*I heard **how witty they** are.*
Lo importante es que nosotros pensamos **lo mismo.**	***The important thing** is that we think **the same.***
Vi **lo listo/a** que es.	*I saw **how clever** he/she is.*
Pensaban en **lo bien** que lo iban a pasar.	*They were thinking about **the good time** they were going to have.*

Lo is used before a **de** phrase, which means *the matter concerning.*

lo del ingeniero	***the matter concerning** the engineer*
lo de tus documentos	***the business about** your papers*

Lo is also used in the phrases **lo más/menos posible** *as much as possible / as little as possible* and **lo antes posible** *as soon as possible.*

Actividad 13   **Artículos en el museo.** Cuando Ud. fue al museo con su amiga vieron muchas cosas interesantes. Complete las oraciones con la forma correcta del artículo cuando sea necesario. Escoja entre el artículo neutro **lo** y el artículo definido o indefinido (para más información sobre los artículos indefinidos, véase la siguiente página). No se olvide de escribir las contracciones **al** y **del** cuando sean necesarias. Si el artículo no es necesario, escriba una X.

_____El_____₁ viernes yo fui con Edita a _____un / al_____₂ museo de _____X_____₃ arte. Todo _____lo_____₄ de _____del_____₅ arte nos interesa mucho. _____lo_____₆ bello de _____del_____₇ museo son _____las_____₈ salas de _____X_____₉ escultura. Hay tantos artículos y piezas de _____X_____₁₀ gran valor. No pudimos ver _____las_____₁₁ esculturas porque _____el_____₁₂ mes pasado hubo _____un_____₁₃ robo en _____el_____₁₄ museo. Parece que _____los_____₁₅ ladrones entraron a _____al_____₁₆ museo a _____las_____₁₇ tres de _____la_____₁₈ mañana. Se llevaron _____las / unas_____₁₉ estatuas preciosas. _____un_____₂₀ guardia muy simpático nos dijo que _____lo_____₂₁ de _____la_____₂₂ seguridad en _____el_____₂₃ museo es _____un_____₂₄ problema. Edita y yo decidimos ir a ver _____las_____₂₅ salas de _____X_____₂₆ pintura. Subimos a _____al_____₂₇ segundo piso y entramos primero a _____la_____₂₈ sala de pintura de _____del_____₂₉ Renacimiento. Vimos _____unas_____₃₀ obras realmente impresionantes. Después

bajamos a _____la_____ tienda donde yo compré _____un_____ libro y
             31   32

_____unos_____ carteles y Edita compró _____una_____ pulsera de
     33   34

_____X_____ plata.
    35

Forms, uses, and omissions of indefinite articles

The Spanish indefinite article (English *a, an*) appears as **un** before a masculine noun and as **una** before a feminine noun. Like the definite article, the indefinite article changes to agree with the noun in gender (masculine/feminine) and number (singular/plural).

	MASCULINE	FEMININE
SINGULAR	un	una
PLURAL	unos	unas

The plural indefinite articles **unos/unas** are the equivalent of the English *some, a few,* or *a couple of.*

El and **un** are always used (instead of **la** and **una**) before feminine nouns that begin with a stressed **a-** or **ha-**. The plural of these nouns always uses **las** and **unas**. This rule does not apply where the first vowel is not stressed (**la alfombra, la ambición**) or when referring to the name of the letter *a* (**la a**) and the letter *h* (**la hache**).

Feminine nouns with stressed -a, -ha

SINGULAR		PLURAL	
el/un agua *water*	**el/un** arpa *harp*	**las/unas** aguas	**las/unas** arpas
el/un águila *eagle*	**el/un** ave *bird*	**las/unas** águilas	**las/unas** aves
el/un alma *soul*	**el/un** haba *bean*	**las/unas** almas	**las/unas** habas
el/un arca *ark*	**el/un** habla *language*	**las/unas** arcas	**las/unas** hablas
el/un área *area*	**el/un** hacha *axe*	**las/unas** áreas	**las/unas** hachas
el/un arma *arm, weapon*	**el/un** hambre *hunger*	**las/unas** armas	**las/unas** hambres

Since the change of **la** and **una** to **el** and **un** before these nouns is conditioned by the stressed /a/ sound, if another word comes between the article and noun, **el** and **un** revert to **la** and **una,** respectively. Note that adjectives have their expected feminine forms before these feminine nouns.

    una nueva arma
    la vieja arca
    una buena alma
    la joven águila

Other determiners such as demonstratives, possessives, and quantifying adjectives use the expected feminine forms before these nouns.

    esta área
    aquella agua
    nuestra habla
    mucha/tanta hambre

The indefinite article is omitted before predicate nouns that denote profession, occupation, nationality, religion, social status, and gender. If, however, the noun is modified by a phrase or an adjective, the indefinite article is expressed.

Amparo es violinista.	*Amparo is a violinist.*
Es una violinista brillante.	*She's a brilliant violinist.*
Francisco es carpintero.	*Francisco is a carpenter.*
Esos chicos son argentinos.	*Those kids are Argentine.*
Ester es judía/católica/protestante.	*Ester is Jewish/Catholic/Protestant.*

The indefinite article is usually omitted after the verbs **buscar, comprar, llevar, sacar, tener,** and **usar.**

Compra pasteles.	*Buy pastries.*
Asunción tiene jardín.	*Asunción has a garden.*
Nieves y Julián usan anteojos.	*Nieves and Julián wear glasses.*

The indefinite article is omitted in phrases with **¡qué... !** (*what a . . . !*) and before **cierto/a** (*a certain*), **medio/a** (*half a*), **otro/a** (*another*), **tal** (*such a*), **cien** (*a hundred*), and **mil** (*a thousand*). The English equivalents of these words and phrases have the indefinite article.

¡Qué día!	*What a day!*
cierta persona	*a certain person*
medio kilo	*half a kilo*
otro color y otro estilo	*another color and another style*
tal problema	*such a problem*
cien dólares	*a hundred dollars*
mil dólares	*a thousand dollars*

Actividad 14   **El artículo indefinido.** Complete la tabla con la forma correcta del artículo indefinido en singular. Luego, escriba el sustantivo y el artículo indefinido en la forma plural.

ARTÍCULO INDEFINIDO

SINGULAR		PLURAL
1. _____	mar	_____
2. _____	verdad	_____
3. _____	nariz	_____
4. _____	parador	_____
5. _____	olor	_____
6. _____	oboe	_____
7. _____	área	_____
8. _____	mochila	_____
9. _____	joven	_____
10. _____	papel	_____
11. _____	irlandés	_____
12. _____	paraguas	_____
13. _____	voz	_____
14. _____	desfile	_____

PARTE II

15. _____ nación _____

16. _____ lavaplatos _____

17. _____ sucursal _____

18. _____ ascensor _____

19. _____ habla _____

20. _____ agua _____

21. _____ aula _____

22. _____ mapa _____

23. _____ programa _____

24. _____ crisis _____

Actividad 15   **En el taller.** El pintor Dionisio está pintando en su taller donde se encuentran las siguientes cosas. Escriba la forma correcta del artículo indefinido al lado del sustantivo.

1. _____ cuadro

2. _____ caballete (*m.*) (*easel*)

3. _____ pinceles (*brushes*)

4. _____ mural

5. _____ modelos (*f.*)

6. _____ colección

7. _____ paisajes

8. _____ escultura

9. _____ retratos (*portraits*)

10. _____ pinturas

11. _____ naturaleza muerta (*still life*)

12. _____ marco (*frame*)

Actividad 16   **¿Artículo indefinido o no?** Complete cada oración con la forma correcta del artículo indefinido cuando sea necesario. Si no es necesario, escriba una X.

1. Sergio es _____ ingeniero.

2. Es _____ día muy caluroso.

3. Gabriel es _____ judío y Carmen es _____ católica.

4. Verónica tiene entre _____ cien y _____ mil sellos en su colección.

5. ¿Puede Ud. enseñarme _____ otro estilo de abrigo, por favor?

6. Simón Colón es _____ pianista muy talentoso.

7. La nueva vecina es _____ mexicana.

8. Todos los niños de esa familia usan _____ gafas.

9. No se puede encontrar _____ paraguas grande.

10. Nosotros no dijimos tal _____ cosa.

11. El cocinero preparó _____ cierto postre.

12. ¡Qué _____ idea!

Contractions del and al

There are two contractions in Spanish. The masculine article **el** combines with the preposition **de** to form **del** (*of the*) and with **a** to form **al** (*to the*). These prepositions do not contract with the other forms of the definite article **la, los,** or **las.** The contractions are not used if the definite article is part of a proper name.

Mateo es el gerente **del hotel.**	Mateo is the manager **of the hotel.**
Álvaro fue **al museo.**	Álvaro went **to the museum.**
Cervantes es el autor **de El Quijote.**	Cervantes is the author **of El Quijote.**
Sol fue **a El Prado.**	Sol went **to El Prado.**
Teresa y Ramón regresaron a **El Salvador.**	Teresa and Ramón went back **to El Salvador.**

Actividad 17 **¿Dónde están todos?** Exprese que las personas no están porque fueron a distintos lugares. Use la contracción **al** cuando sea necesario. Siga el modelo.

> MODELO Nieves / teatro
> Nieves fue al teatro.

1. Concepción y Simón / puesto de periódicos

   _____

2. yo / ayuntamiento (*town hall*)

   _____

3. vosotros / supermercado

   _____

4. Ud. / parque de atracciones

   _____

5. Lourdes / iglesia

   _____

6. mi hermano / bolsa (*stock exchange*)

   _____

7. nosotros / estación de tren

   _____

PARTE II

8. tú / centro comercial

_____

9. Uds. / cibercafé

_____

10. Juan Diego / facultad

_____

Actividad 18 **¿De dónde salieron?** Diga de qué lugares salieron o volvieron estas personas. Use la contracción **del** cuando sea necesario. Siga el modelo.

> MODELO Ud. / salir / restaurante mexicano
> Ud. salió del restaurante mexicano.

1. tú y yo / volver / banco

_____

2. Mercedes y Julio / salir / cine

_____

3. yo / regresar / librería

_____

4. Uds. / volver / tienda de vídeos

_____

5. Pedro / salir / apartamento

_____

6. tú / regresar / galería de arte

_____

7. vosotros / salir / museo de ciencias naturales

_____

8. Ud. / volver / aeropuerto

_____

Possession

In Spanish, possession is expressed by the use of a prepositional phrase with **de.** Spanish titles such as **señor** and **profesora** must be preceded by the definite article when referring to the specific person.

Leí el informe **de Jacinta.**	*I read **Jacinta's** report.*
Leí todos los capítulos **del libro.**	*I read all the chapters **of the book.***
Hoy es el día **del** examen final.	*Today is the day **of the** final exam.*
Cenaron en el restaurante **del** hotel.	*They had dinner **in the** hotel restaurant.*
¿Conoces el comercio **del** señor Bermúdez?	*Are you familiar with **Mr. Bermúdez'** store?*

In Spanish, **¿De quién?** followed by **ser** is equivalent to the English *Whose*.

¿De quién es el cinturón?　　　*Whose belt **is** it?*
¿De quién son estos pendientes?　*Whose earrings **are** these?*
¿De quién son estas postales?　　*Whose postcards **are** these?*

A form **¿De quiénes?** also exists to refer to a plural possessor, but it is not common in the spoken language.

¿De quién(es) es el barco?　　　*Whose boat **is** it?*

Actividad 19　**¿De quién es?** Escriba preguntas y respuestas que demuestran posesión. Siga el modelo.

> MODELO　los libros de texto / el profesor
> ¿De quién son los libros de texto?
> Son del profesor.

1. el almacén / el señor Acosta

   _____

   _____

2. los peines / Adela y Matilde

   _____

   _____

3. el equipaje / las turistas

   _____

   _____

4. los discos compactos / el pianista

   _____

   _____

5. este llavero / la empleada

   _____

   _____

6. las sartenes / el cocinero

   _____

   _____

7. las raquetas / estas tenistas

   _____

   _____

8. el reloj / el doctor Villanueva

   _____

   _____

¿De quiénes son estas cosas? Exprese las frases en español.

1. Mr. Valle's florist shop

   _____

2. the president's (*m.*) office

   _____

3. the programmer's (*f.*) disks

   _____

4. the dentist's (*f.*) schedule

   _____

5. Dr. (*m.*) Arriaga's employees (*m.*)

   _____

6. the students' Web sites

   _____

7. Professor (*f.*) Salas' lectures

   _____

8. the engineer's (*m.*) project

   _____

9. Mr. and Mrs. Manrique's children

   _____

10. the boss's (*f.*) report

    _____

Actividad 21 **Actividad oral.** El presentador del programa lee sustantivos a los dos equipos que luego tienen que ponerles el artículo definido o indefinido correcto. Se puede variar con frases de posesión, las contracciones **al** y **del**, etcétera. Al final se calculan los puntos ganados por cada equipo para saber quiénes sacaron el premio gordo (*grand prize*).

Agreement of adjectives

Spanish adjectives agree in gender and number with the nouns they modify.
Adjectives that have a masculine singular form ending in **-o** have four forms.

	MASC.	FEM.		MASC.	FEM.
SINGULAR	bonito	bonita	**SINGULAR**	maravilloso	maravillosa
PLURAL	bonitos	bonitas	**PLURAL**	maravillosos	maravillosas

Adjectives that have a masculine singular ending in a consonant or in **-e** have
only two forms, a singular and a plural. They do not change for gender.

	MASC. AND FEM.		MASC. AND FEM.
SINGULAR	difícil	**SINGULAR**	triste
PLURAL	difíciles	**PLURAL**	tristes

A small number of adjectives of nationality end in **-a** or in stressed **-í** or **-ú.**
These also have only two forms.

belga *Belgian*

	MASC. AND FEM.
SINGULAR	belga
PLURAL	belgas

israelí *Israeli*

	MASC. AND FEM.
SINGULAR	israelí
PLURAL	israelíes

hindú *Hindu, Indian*

	MASC. AND FEM.
SINGULAR	hindú
PLURAL	hindúes

Other similar adjectives are **azteca** (*Aztec*), **inca** (*Incan*), **iraní** (*Iranian*), **iraquí**
(*Iraqi*), **marroquí** (*Moroccan*), **maya** (*Mayan*), **pakistaní** (*Pakistani*), and **bantú**
(*Bantu*). There are also adjectives ending in **-ista, -sta,** and **-ita** that follow the
same pattern as **azteca** (above): **entusiasta, cosmopolita, realista, nacionalista.**

Adjectives ending in the suffixes **-dor, -ón,** and **-án** add **-a** to form the feminine and therefore have four forms like adjectives ending in **-o.** These adjectives form their masculine plural by adding **-es** and their feminine plural by adding **-as.** Those suffixes that are accented lose their accent mark when an ending is added.

hablador *talkative*

	MASC.	FEM.
SINGULAR	hablador	hablador**a**
PLURAL	hablador**es**	hablador**as**

preguntón *inquisitive*

	MASC.	FEM.
SINGULAR	preguntón	pregunton**a**
PLURAL	pregunton**es**	pregunton**as**

holgazán *lazy*

	MASC.	FEM.
SINGULAR	holgazán	holgazan**a**
PLURAL	holgazan**es**	holgazan**as**

Spanish adjectives usually follow the nouns they modify.

En esa tienda de ropa venden **cosas maravillosas.**	*In that clothing store they sell **wonderful things.***
Sí. Veo que te has comprado unos **vestidos** muy **bonitos.**	*Yes. I see that you've bought yourself some very **pretty dresses.***

Actividad 1 **¿Cómo están?** Su amigo/a le pregunta cómo están varias personas. Contéstele las preguntas usando los adjetivos indicados. Haga las concordancias necesarias. Siga el modelo.

> MODELO ¿Cómo está tu hermana? (ocupado)
> Está ocupada.

1. ¿Cómo están tus padres? (feliz)

   _____

2. ¿Cómo estás? (contento)

   _____

3. ¿Cómo se encuentra Raquel? (nervioso)

   _____

4. ¿Cómo se siente Claudio? (deprimido)

   _____

5. ¿Cómo se encuentran las hermanas de Augusto? (triste)

   _____

6. ¿Cómo están Uds.? (cansado)

   _____

7. ¿Cómo os sentís vosotros? (enfermo)

   _____

Actividad 2 **Don de gentes.** Jacobo y su hermana Luisa son estudiantes de intercambio que llegaron de Tegucigalpa, Honduras, el año pasado. Viven con una familia norteamericana y se llevan muy bien con todo el mundo. ¿Qué piensa la gente de los hermanos hondureños? Escriba oraciones usando los adjetivos indicados para saber lo que opinan de ellos. Haga las concordancias necesarias. Siga el modelo.

MODELO   Elena creer / Luisa / honesto
          Elena cree que Luisa es honesta.

Carácter y personalidad

Vocabulario

cortés *courteous*
el don de gentes *charm, getting on well with people*
encantador(a) *charming*
generoso/a *generous*
gracioso/a *witty*
honesto/a *honest*
independiente *independent*
inteligente *intelligent*

listo/a *clever*
responsable *reliable*
serio/a *serious*
simpático/a *nice, pleasant*
sincero/a *sincere*
tener personalidad *to have personality or character*
trabajador(a) *hard-working*

1. Paco creer / Jacobo / listo

   _____

2. la señora Alvarado pensar / Luisa / encantador

   _____

3. el profesor de cálculo encontrar / a los hermanos / inteligente y trabajador

   _____

4. Nieves creer / Jacobo / sincero

   _____

5. el señor Alvarado decir / Luisa / gracioso y generoso

   _____

6. las profesoras de computación encontrar / a Jacobo / serio y responsable

   _____

7. los hijos de los Alvarado creer / Luisa / independiente y simpático

_____

8. todo el mundo decir / Jacobo y Luisa / cortés

_____

Actividad 3   **¿Qué se piensa de ellos?** Juan y Teresa no le caen bien a nadie. ¿Qué piensa la gente de ellos? Complete las oraciones usando los adjetivos indicados. Haga las concordancias necesarias. Siga el modelo.

> MODELO   Laura dice: No soporto a Juan porque es (antipático)
> __antipático__ .

Vocabulario   ## Más carácter y personalidad

aguantar _to stand_
antipático/a _unpleasant_
desleal _disloyal_
engañoso/a _deceitful_
Me cae mal. _I don't like him/her._
mentiroso/a _lying_

molesto/a _annoying_
No los puedo ver. _I can't stand them._
odiar _to hate_
soportar _to stand_
tacaño/a _mean_
tonto/a _silly, stupid_

1. Ramón dice: Creo que Teresa es muy

   (arrogante) _____.

2. Patricio dice: No aguanto a Juan porque es

   (molesto) _____.

3. Matilde dice: Los encuentro

   (tacaño) _____.

4. Ana dice: No los puedo ver porque son

   (tonto) _____.

5. Luisa dice: Teresa me cae mal porque es

   (mentiroso) _____.

6. Joaquín dice: Yo odio a los dos porque son

   (desleal) _____.

7. Adán dice: Yo encuentro a los dos

   (engañoso) _____.

8. Bárbara dice: No los soporto porque son

   (gruñón) _____.

Actividad 4 **El Príncipe Azul** (*Prince Charming*). El Príncipe Azul estudia su ropa. Escriba lo que tiene en su armario empleando los adjetivos de color. Fíjese bien si tiene ropa apropiada para encontrar a su princesa.

Para montar a caballo

1. una chaqueta (rojo) _____

2. unos pantalones (amarillo) _____

3. unas botas (marrón) _____

4. unos guantes (negro) _____ o

   (rojo) _____

5. un sombrero con plumas (amarillo) _____

   (anaranjado) _____ y

   (verde) _____

Para ir a un baile de etiqueta (*formal ball*)

6. un esmoquin (negro) _____

7. un sombrero de copaª (negro) _____

8. una fajaᵇ (morado) _____

9. unos calcetines (morado) _____ y

   (gris) _____

ªsombrero... *top hat*   ᵇ*cummerbund*

Position of adjectives and shortened forms of adjectives

Although descriptive adjectives in Spanish usually follow the noun they modify, descriptive and other adjectives can also appear before nouns in certain cases.

An adjective can precede a noun when it expresses an inherent characteristic of the noun that is known to all and does not add any new information about the noun.

la **blanca nieve**	*white snow*
el **tímido cordero**	*the timid lamb*
una **olorosa rosa**	*a fragrant rose*

An adjective can precede a noun when it expresses a subjective judgment of the speaker. **Bueno, malo,** and their comparatives **mejor** and **peor** fall into this category.

Vivimos en una **pequeña ciudad.**	*We live in a small city.*
Tenemos que leer una **larga novela.**	*We have to read a long novel.*
Sobrevolaron la **enorme selva.**	*They flew over the huge jungle.*
Es el **peor libro** que leímos.	*It's the worst book that we read.*
Prepararon una **buena comida.**	*They prepared a good meal.*

PARTE II

Adjectives that express quantity precede the noun: **alguno, ambos** (*both*), **bastante, cuánto, mucho, ninguno, poco, suficiente,** and **varios** (*several*).

¿Hay **alguna farmacia** por aquí?	*Is there a (any) drugstore around here?*
Alberto siempre tiene **muchas ideas.**	*Alberto always has a lot of ideas.*
No ganan **suficiente dinero.**	*They don't earn enough money.*

Adjectives can precede nouns in exclamations beginning with **¡Qué!**

¡Qué **mala** suerte!	*What bad luck!*
¡Qué **hermosa** plaza!	*What a beautiful square!*

When an adverb such as **más, muy,** or **tan** modifies the adjective, the adjective usually follows the noun.

¡Qué plaza **más hermosa**!	*What a beautiful square!*
Prepararon una comida **muy buena.**	*They prepared a very good meal.*
Fue una clase **tan interesante.**	*It was an especially interesting class.*

The adjectives **bueno, malo, primero, tercero, uno, alguno,** and **ninguno** lose their final **-o** before a masculine singular noun. **Alguno** and **ninguno** add an accent mark when shortened **(algún, ningún).** The cutting off of the last sound or syllable(s) of a word is called *apocope* **(el apócope).**

¿No conoces a **ningún** estudiante?	*Don't you know any students?*
No conozco a nadie todavía. Es mi **primer** día aquí.	*I don't know anyone yet. It's my first day here.*
¿Hay **algún** consejo que te pueda dar?	*Is there any advice that I can give you?*
No, he tenido un **mal** día, nada más.	*No, I've had a bad day, that's all.*

The adjectives **cualquiera** (*any*) and **grande** shorten to **cualquier** and **gran** before any singular noun.

Cualquier restaurante por aquí es un **gran** restaurante.	*Any restaurant around here is a great restaurant.*

Cualquiera has its full form in the phrases **cualquiera de los/las dos** (*either one of the two*).

The adjective **Santo** shortens to **San** before all masculine saints' names except those that begin with **To-** and **Do-** as in **Santo Tomás** and **Santo Domingo.** For example, **San Francisco** and **San Antonio.** The feminine form **Santa** has no shortened form, as in **Santa Bárbara** and **Santa María.**

Some adjectives have different English equivalents depending on whether they precede or follow the nouns they modify.

nuestro **antiguo** jefe	*our **former** boss*
una ciudad **antigua**	*an **old, ancient** city*
cierto país	*a **certain** country, **some** countries*
una cosa **cierta**	*a **sure** thing, a **true** thing*
Me interesa **cualquier** película española.	*I'm interested in **any** Spanish film.*
Alquilemos una película **cualquiera.**	*Let's rent **any old** film.*
diferentes libros	***various** books*
libros **diferentes**	***different** books*
un **gran** presidente	*a **great** president*
un hombre **grande**	*a **large** man*

Paco es **medio** español.	*Paco is **half** Spanish.*
el español **medio**	*the **average** Spaniard*
la **misma** profesora	*the **same** teacher*
la profesora **misma**	*the teacher **herself***
una **nueva** casa	***another** house*
una casa **nueva**	*a **new** house*
un **pobre** hombre	*a **poor, unfortunate** man*
un hombre **pobre**	*a **poor, penniless** man*
Este café es **pura** agua.	*This coffee is **nothing but** water.*
Prefiero beber agua **pura**.	*I prefer to drink **pure** water.*
Juan es un **simple** camarero.	*Juan is **just** a waiter.*
Juan es un muchacho **simple**.	*Juan is a **simple** boy.*
María es la **única** mexicana aquí.	*María is the **only** Mexican here.*
María es una chica **única**.	*María is a **unique** girl.*

Actividad 5   **Adjetivos pre- y pospuestos.** Complete las oraciones con los adjetivos indicados poniéndolos o antes o después de los sustantivos. Haga los cambios necesarios.

1. ¡Éste es el ___mejor___ día _____ de mi vida! (mejor)

2. Hay ___algunos___ discos compactos _____ en el escritorio. (alguno)

3. Ha habido ___muchos___ días _____ de lluvia este año. (mucho)

4. Los estudiantes leyeron unos _____ poemas ___renacentistas___. (renacentista)

5. El profesor dará el examen a ___ambas___ clases _____ el miércoles. (ambos)

6. Pili tiene los _____ ojos ___castaño___. (castaño)

7. No retiraron ___suficiente___ plata _____ de su cuenta de ahorros. (suficiente)

8. Pedro tomó la ___peor___ decisión _____ posible. (peor)

9. Miguel y Paloma se dedican al análisis de _____ teorías ___políticas___. (político)

Actividad 6 **¡Qué exclamación!** Amplíe cada exclamación con la forma correcta de los adjetivos indicados. Haga los cambios necesarios. Siga el modelo.

> MODELO ¡Qué casa! (más lindo)
> ¡Qué casa más linda!

1. ¡Qué situación! (absurdo)

   _____

2. ¡Qué clima! (tan perfecto)

   _____

3. ¡Qué partido! (más emocionante)

   _____

4. ¡Qué paella! (tan rico)

   _____

5. ¡Qué ideas! (más estupendo)

   _____

6. ¡Qué problemas! (más complicado)

   _____

7. ¡Qué niños! (cariñoso)

   _____

8. ¡Qué reunión! (tan animado)

   _____

Actividad 7 **Adjetivos: ¿apócope o no?** Complete las oraciones con la forma correcta de los adjetivos indicados.

1. El cinco de septiembre es el (primero) _____ día del semestre.

2. No es (malo) _____ idea llevar el paraguas hoy.

3. Estos estadistas[a] son (grande) _____ hombres.

4. Unas canicas[b] son un (bueno) _____ juguete para Juanita.

5. Ya es la (tercero) _____ vez que me han invitado a salir.

6. Esperamos que vengan a vernos (alguno) _____ día.

7. No hemos hecho (ninguno) _____ plan hasta ahora.

[a]statesmen   [b]marbles

8. Yo nací el día de (Santo) _____ Juan.

9. Albéniz fue un (grande) _____ compositor[c] español.

10. No les gustó (ninguno) _____ bicicleta.

11. Pruebe (alguno) _____ recetas de este libro de cocina italiana.

12. (Cualquiera) _____ librería tendrá el libro que buscas.

13. Carlos es el (tercero) _____ rey de la dinastía.

14. ¡No des (malo) _____ ejemplo para los niños!

[c]composer

Actividad 8 **Adjetivos: antes o después del sustantivo.** Complete las oraciones usando los adjetivos indicados poniéndolos antes o después de los sustantivos.

1. Beti y yo vamos al ___mismo___ dentista _____. (same)

2. Atenas es una _____ ciudad ___Antigua___. (ancient)

3. La fecha de su boda es una _____ cosa ___cierta___. (sure)

4. Tino es ___medio___ portugués _____ y ___medio___ mexicano _____. (half/half)

5. Bolívar fue un ___gran___ general _____. (great)

6. ¡El _____ dramaturgo ___mismo___ no aguanta su obra! (himself)

7. La sopa que pedí es ___pura___ agua _____. (nothing but)

8. Benita es una _____ persona ___única___. (unique)

9. ___Una cierta___ empresa _____ sigue perdiendo dinero. (a certain)

10. La ___Antigua___ casa _____ de Daniela y Pablo quedaba en las afueras de la ciudad. (former)

11. Mi biblioteca tiene _____ libros

    _____ sobre el _____

    tema _____. (*several/same*)

12. A Leonor le va a encantar _____ regalo

    _____ que le demos. (*any*)

Adjectives of nationality

Adjectives of nationality that end in **-o** in the masculine singular have the expected four forms that all adjectives whose masculine singular ends in **-o** have.

chileno *Chilean*

	MASC.	FEM.
SINGULAR	chilen**o**	chilen**a**
PLURAL	chilen**os**	chilen**as**

mexicano *Mexican*

	MASC.	FEM.
SINGULAR	mexican**o**	mexican**a**
PLURAL	mexican**os**	mexican**as**

Adjectives of nationality or of origin that end in a consonant also have four forms. An **-a** is added to form the feminine. The masculine plural ends in **-es,** not **-os.** Adjectives of nationality that have an accent mark on the last syllable of the masculine singular lose that accent mark when an ending is added.

español *Spanish*

	MASC.	FEM.
SINGULAR	español	español**a**
PLURAL	español**es**	español**as**

inglés *English*

	MASC.	FEM.
SINGULAR	inglés	ingles**a**
PLURAL	ingles**es**	ingles**as**

alemán *German*

	MASC.	FEM.
SINGULAR	alemán	aleman**a**
PLURAL	aleman**es**	aleman**as**

andaluz *Andalusian*

	MASC.	FEM.
SINGULAR	andaluz	andaluz**a**
PLURAL	andaluc**es**	andaluz**as**

Adjectives of nationality or of origin that end in a vowel other than **-o** have only two forms. Many of these have the suffix **-ense** such as **bonaerense** (*from Buenos Aires*), **canadiense** (*Canadian*).

Adjetivos gentilicios:*Los continentes

CONTINENTE	GENTILICIO	CONTINENTE	GENTILICIO
África	**africano/a**	**Australia**	**australiano/a**
la Antárdida	**antártico/a**	**Europa**	**europeo/a**
el Ártico	**ártico/a**	**Norteamérica**	**norteamericano/a**
Asia	**asiático/a**	**Sudamérica**	**sudamericano/a**

*El **gentilicio** is the name of an inhabitant of a country, city, or region.

Países y regiones

PAÍS/REGIÓN	GENTILICIO	PAÍS/REGIÓN	GENTILICIO
Afganistán	afgano/a	Irak	iraquí
Alemania (*Germany*)	alemán/alemana	Irán	iraní
Andorra	andorrano/a	Irlanda	irlandés/irlandesa
Arabia Saudita	saudí/saudita	Israel	israelí
Argelia (*Algeria*)	argelino/a	Italia	italiano/a
(la) Argentina	argentino/a	Jamaica	jamaicano/a
Australia	australiano/a	(el) Japón	japonés/japonesa
Austria	austríaco/a	Jordania	jordano/a
Bélgica (*Belgium*)	belga	Kuwait	kuwaití
Bolivia	boliviano/a	Líbano (*Lebanon*)	libanés/libanesa
Brasil	brasileño/a	Madagascar	malgache
Cachemira (*Kashmir*)	cachemir(a)	Marruecos (*Morocco*)	marroquí
Camboya (*Cambodia*)	camboyano/a	México	mexicano/a
(el) Canadá	canadiense	Nicaragua	nicaragüense
Chile	chileno/a	Noruega (*Norway*)	noruego/a
China	chino/a	Nueva Zelanda	neocelandés/ neocelandesa
Colombia	colombiano/a		
Corea (del Norte/Sur)	coreano/a	los Países Bajos (*The Netherlands*)	holandés/holandesa
Costa Rica	costarricense		
Cuba	cubano/a	Panamá	panameño/a
Dinamarca (*Denmark*)	danés/danesa	Paraguay	paraguayo/a
(el) Ecuador	ecuatoriano/a	(el) Perú	peruano/a
Egipto	egipcio/a	Polonia (*Poland*)	polaco/a
El Salvador	salvadoreño/a	Portugal	portugués/portuguesa
Escocia (*Scotland*)	escocés/escocesa	Puerto Rico	puertorriqueño/a
España	español(a)	la República Dominicana	dominicano/a
(los) Estados Unidos	estadounidense, norteamericano/a		
Finlandia	finlandés/finlandesa	Rumania	rumano/a
Francia	francés/francesa	Rusia	ruso/a
Gales (*Wales*)	galés/galesa	Serbia	serbio/a
Gibraltar	gibraltareño/a	Siria	sirio/a
Gran Bretaña (*Great Britain*)	británico/a	Sudáfrica (*S. Africa*)	sudafricano/a
		Sudán	sudanés/sudanesa
Grecia	griego/a	Suecia (*Sweden*)	sueco/a
Guatemala	guatemalteco/a	Suiza (*Switzerland*)	suizo/a
Guinea Ecuatorial	guineoecuatoriano/a	Tailandia	tailandés/tailandesa
Haití	haitiano/a	Taiwán	taiwanés/taiwanesa
Holanda	holandés/holandesa	Túnez (*Tunisia*)	tunecino/a
Honduras	hondureño/a	Turquía (*Turkey*)	turco/a
Hungría	húngaro/a	Ucrania (*Ukraine*)	ucraniano/a, ucranio/a
(la) India	indio/a, hindú	(el) Uruguay	uruguayo/a
Indonesia	indonesio/a	Venezuela	venezolano/a
Inglaterra (*England*)	inglés/inglesa	Vietnám	vietnamés/vietnamesa
		Yemen	yemení

PARTE II

Islas

ISLA(S)	GENTILICIO	ISLA(S)	GENTILICIO
las Antillas	antillano/a	las Filipinas	filipino/a
las Bahamas	bahamiano/a	Mallorca	mallorquín/mallorquina
las Baleares	balear	las Malvinas	malvinense, malvinero/a
las Canarias	canario/a	(Falkland Islands)	

Ciudades

CIUDAD	GENTILICIO	CIUDAD	GENTILICIO
Barcelona	barcelonés/barcelonesa	Madrid	madrileño/a
Berlín	berlinés/berlinesa	Málaga	malagueño/a
Bilbao	bilbaíno/a	Moscú	moscovita
Bogotá	bogotano/a	Nueva York	neoyorquino/a
Buenos Aires	bonaerense, porteño/a	París	parisiense, parisino/a
		Quito	quiteño/a
Caracas	caraqueño/a	Rio de Janeiro	carioca
Florencia	florentino/a	Roma	romano/a
Kosovo	kosovano/a	Santiago	santiaguino/a
La Habana	habanero/a	Sevilla	sevillano/a
Lima	limeño/a	Toledo	toledano/a
Londres	londinense	Valencia	valenciano/a

Actividad 9 **¿De dónde son?** Ud. y su amiga están preparando una lista de los estudiantes extranjeros de la Facultad de Ingeniería. Su amiga le pregunta si son de cierto país y Ud. lo confirma con el adjetivo de nacionalidad. Siga el modelo.

> MODELO   Catalina es de Italia, ¿verdad?
> Sí, es italiana.

1. Miguel es de Rusia, ¿verdad?

   _____

2. Rosalinda y Arturo son de Canadá, ¿verdad?

   _____

3. David es de Israel, ¿verdad?

   _____

4. Mercedes es de Costa Rica, ¿verdad?

   _____

5. Hugo es de Guatemala, ¿verdad?

   _____

6. Alano es de Japón, ¿verdad?

   _____

7. Bárbara es de la India, ¿verdad?

   _____

8. Manolo y Lucía son de Egipto, ¿verdad?

   _____

9. Margarita es de Inglaterra, ¿verdad?

   _____

10. Gerardo es de Corea del Sur, ¿verdad?

    _____

11. Cristina y Oliverio son de Francia, ¿verdad?

    _____

Actividad 10 **¡De muchos uno solo!** Los Estados Unidos es un país de habitantes de miles de orígenes distintos. Escriba oraciones que dicen de qué origen son estos norteamericanos usando el adjetivo del nombre del país. Siga el modelo.

> MODELO   Josefa e Ignacio / Panamá
> Josefa e Ignacio son de origen panameño.

1. yo / Estados Unidos

   _____

2. Teodoro e Irene / El Salvador

   _____

3. Uds. / Corea del Sur

   _____

4. Gabriel / Vietnám

   _____

5. Adela y Rosa / la India

   _____

6. vosotros / Grecia

   _____

7. tú / México

_____

8. Ud. y yo / Taiwán

_____

9. Gualterio / Hungría

_____

More on the agreement of adjectives

Adjectives modifying two plural nouns of the same gender are in the plural of that gender.

libros y periódicos argentin**os**   *Argentine books and newspapers*
ciudades y provincias argentin**as**   *Argentine cities and provinces*

If two nouns of different genders, whether singular or plural, are modified by a single adjective, the adjective is masculine plural.

pantalones y chaquetas barat**os**   *inexpensive pants and jackets*
un colegio y una universidad urban**os**   *an urban school and university*

When a noun is used as an adjective, it usually does not agree in gender and number with the noun it modifies.

una visita **relámpago** (*lightning*)   *a quick visit*
la luz **piloto** (*pilot*)   *pilot light (stove)*
apartamentos **piloto**   *model apartments*

Actividad 11 **Sustantivos en plural.** Complete las oraciones usando la forma plural de los adjetivos indicados.

1. Hay (bueno) _____ almacenes y restaurantes en el centro comercial.

2. Conocimos varios pueblos y aldeas (español)
_____.

3. Queremos manzanas y cerezas recién (recogido)
_____.

4. Tengo mapas y guías (inglés) _____.

5. Compre pan y torta (fresco) _____.

6. José Luis necesita una camisa y unos calcetines (rojo)
_____.

7. Busquen un lavaplatos y una máquina de lavar (rebajado)

_____.

8. Después del choque tuvieron que poner un parachoques y una puerta

(nuevo) _____.

9. Hay ofertas y liquidaciones (magnífico) _____ toda esta semana.

10. Clara tiene el pelo y las pestañas (negro) _____.

11. Tecnolandia tiene computadoras y teléfonos celulares (caro) _____.

12. El administrador de Web y la programadora eran muy (creativo) _____.

Two or more adjectives modifying a noun

Typically, if two adjectives modify a noun, they both follow it and are joined by **y.**

una chica inteligente **y** simpática	*a nice, intelligent girl*
un día caluroso **y** agradable	*a warm, pleasant day*

If **y** is left out, the adjective that the speaker wishes to emphasize comes last.

artistas europeos **modernos**	*modern European artists (out of all European artists, the modern ones)*
artistas modernos **europeos**	*modern **European** artists (out of all modern artists, the European ones)*

However, if one of the two adjectives usually precedes the noun, it is placed there.

cierto país europeo	*a certain European country*
el único estudiante español	*the only Spanish student*
diferentes libros científicos	*various scientific books*
otra ciudad moderna	*another modern city*
ese **pobre** hombre enfermo	*that poor sick man*

Actividad 12 **El rodaje de una película (*shooting of a film*).** Comente sobre el rodaje de una película del director de cine Federico Felino, poniendo los elementos de cada grupo en su orden correcto. Cada grupo consiste en un sustantivo, un adjetivo que debe aparecer antes del sustantivo y un adjetivo descriptivo. Escriba la oración completa haciendo los cambios necesarios.

1. Federico Felino es director de cine / mejor / joven

   _____

2. «El tango rojo» es su film / primero / doblado (*dubbed*)

   _____

3. Será una película / grande / extranjero

   _____

4. Hay efectos / diferente / coreográfico

   _____

5. Escribieron guión (*script*) / uno / inteligente

   _____

6. Trabajaron en el film intérpretes (*actors*) (*m. and f.*) / alguno / principal (*star, lead*)

_____

7. La película tiene argumento (*plot*) / uno / interesante

_____

8. La película ganará un premio / importante / cinematográfico

_____

Past participle as an adjective

The past participle **(el participio pasado)** of most verbs can function as an adjective.

El ladrón entró por la **ventana abierta.**	*The thief got in through the **open window.***
Quiero dominar la **lengua escrita** y **hablada.**	*I want to master the **written** and **spoken language.***
Encontré los **documentos perdidos.**	*I found the **lost documents.***
¡Trato **hecho**!	*It's a deal! (Done deal!)*

The Spanish past participle is used to describe positions of people and objects where the present participle is used in English.

Todos están **sentados** en el comedor.	*Everyone is **sitting/seated** in the dining room.*
A estas horas hay mucha gente **parada** en el metro.	*At this hour there are a lot of people **standing** in the subway.*

Actividad 13 **Diálogos.** Complete los siguientes diálogos usando la forma correcta del participio pasado como adjetivo. El adjetivo se encuentra en el modismo (*idiom*) o se deriva del modismo presentado antes de cada diálogo. Siga el modelo.

> MODELO **estar mojado(a) hasta los huesos** *to be soaking wet*
> Felipe —Mírame. Estoy <u>mojado</u> hasta los huesos.
> Isabel —Si yo saliera sin paraguas, yo también estaría <u>mojada</u> hasta los huesos.

1. **estar frito** *to be done for*

   Diana   —¡Qué mala nota saqué en el examen!

   ¡Estoy _____!

   Mateo   —Yo también. ¡Los dos estamos _____!

2. **estar hecho una sopa** *to be soaking wet*

   Raúl   —¡Está lloviendo a cántaros!ª

   Estoy _____ una sopa.

ª¡Está... *It's raining cats and dogs!*

Sara   —¡Gregorio y yo estamos _____ una

sopa también.

3. **morirse de risa** *to die laughing*

Roberto   —Mira a Clara e Inés. Están _____ de

risa.

Dorotea   —Fíjate que Pepe y Esteban también están

_____ de risa.

4. **comerse de envidia** *to be consumed by envy*

Julia   —¿Sabes que Aurelia está _____ de

envidia porque yo salgo con Matías?

Anita   —¡No sólo Aurelia sino todas las chicas están

_____ de envidia!

5. **meterse en lo que no le importa** *to butt into someone else's business*

Lola   —Como siempre, Raúl está _____ en

lo que no le importa.

Paco   —Así son sus hermanos también, siempre

_____ en lo que no les importa.

6. **estar muy pagado de sí mismo** *to have a high opinion of oneself*

Alfredo   —Chico, ya no salgo con Brígida porque está muy

_____ de sí misma.

Marco   —Haces muy bien. ¡Yo rompí con Tere, Eva y Paloma porque

están muy _____ de sí mismas!

7. **dormirse en los laureles** *to rest on one's laurels*

Tito   —Veo que no te esfuerzas porque estás

_____ en los laureles.

José   —Cuando logres algo como yo, tú también estarás

_____ en los laureles.

8. **estar hecho una lástima** *to be a sorry sight, in a sad state*

Leonor   —¿Qué les pasa a Paula y Dora? Están

_____ una lástima.

Alicia   —A lo mejor tienen lo que tiene Mari que también está

_____ una lástima.

Actividad 14   **¿Qué están haciendo?** Use participios pasados como adjetivos para explicar la posición de las siguientes personas. Complete las oraciones usando la forma correcta del adjetivo y del verbo **estar**. Siga el modelo.

> MODELO   Mario (levantar) <u>está levantado</u> ya.

1. Rosario (echar) _____ en el sofá.

2. Clemente (parar) _____ en la puerta de la casa esperando a su novia.

3. Los García (sentar) _____ a la mesa todavía por la sobremesa.

4. Pili (asomar) _____ a la ventana.

5. Los niños (arrodillar) _____ en el suelo jugando con sus cochecitos.

6. Adolfo y Javier (tirar) _____ en el suelo por los puñetazos que se dieron.

7. Paloma (inclinar) _____ mientras el público le aplaude.

Actividad 15   **¡Preparados! ¡Listos! ¡Ya!** (*Ready! Set! Go!*) Su amigo le pregunta cuándo Ud. y otras personas van a hacer ciertas cosas porque tiene prisa por salir. Explíquele que Uds. están listos porque esas cosas ya están hechas. Practique usando el participio pasado como adjetivo. Siga el modelo.

> MODELO   ¿Cuándo van Uds. a arreglarse?
> Ya estamos arreglados/as.

1. ¿Cuándo va Gerardo a bañarse?

   _____

2. ¿Cuándo van Elías e Isaac a afeitarse?

   _____

3. ¿Cuándo va Juliana a maquillarse?

   _____

4. ¿Cuándo van Uds. a vestirse?

   _____

5. ¿Cuándo va Ud. a peinarse?

   _____

6. ¿Cuándo vais a ducharos?

   _____

7. ¿Cuándo vas a pintarte?

   _____

Actividad 16 ¡A comer pues! Ya es hora de comer. Su mamá quiere que Ud. y los otros miembros de su familia hagan ciertas cosas. Pero parece que todo está hecho ya. Explique eso derivando el adjetivo del verbo en el mandato. Siga el modelo.

> MODELO   Polo, prende el horno, por favor.
>   Ya está prendido.

1. Margarita, pon los cubiertos (*place settings*), por favor.

_____

2. Benjamín, sirve el agua, por favor.

_____

3. Abuela, prepara el dulce de leche, por favor.

_____

4. Pancho, rompe los huevos, por favor.

_____

5. Pepe y Nano, corten el pan, por favor.

_____

6. Trini, haz la ensalada, por favor.

_____

7. Tía, fríe el pollo, por favor.

_____

8. Toni, pela unos dientes de ajo (*garlic cloves*), por favor.

_____

Adjectives used as nouns

Spanish adjectives can be used as nouns when the noun they modify is deleted.

Las camisas verdes son más caras que **las rojas.**	*The green shirts are more expensive than the red ones.*
De acuerdo. Pero prefiero **las verdes.**	*Agreed. But I prefer the green ones.*
La casa vieja es más grande que **la moderna.**	*The old house is bigger than the modern one.*
Por eso vamos a comprar **la vieja.**	*That's why we're going to buy the old one.*

When the noun is deleted, the masculine singular indefinite article changes from **un** to **uno**: un libro nuevo → **uno nuevo,** un profesor comprensivo → **uno comprensivo.**

Él tiene dos carros, un carro grande y **uno** pequeño.	*He has two cars, a big car and a small one.*
Ella se compró dos suéteres azules y **uno** negro.	*She bought herself two blue sweaters and one black one.*

Opciones y preferencias. Sus amigos le preguntan qué cosas prefiere. Explíqueles que aunque Ud. prefiere una de las cosas también le gusta la otra. Use los adjetivos como sustantivos cuando sea posible. Siga el modelo.

> MODELO ¿Cuál prefieres, la novela histórica o la novela fantástica?
> Prefiero la histórica, pero me gusta la fantástica también.

1. ¿Cúal te gusta más, la música instrumental o la música vocal?

   _____

2. ¿Cuáles prefieres, los programas serios o los programas cómicos?

   _____

3. ¿Dónde prefieres comer, en el restaurante chino o en el restaurante francés?

   _____

4. ¿Prefieres el apartamento moderno o el apartamento viejo?

   _____

5. ¿Cuál te gusta más, la universidad privada o la universidad estatal?

   _____

6. ¿Cuáles prefieres, las películas norteamericanas o las películas extranjeras?

   _____

7. ¿Dónde quieres vivir, en la ciudad grande o en la ciudad pequeña?

   _____

8. ¿Cuál te interesa más, las ciencias políticas o las ciencias naturales?

   _____

Comparative of adjectives

An object or person may be seen as having more, less, or the same amount of a characteristic as another. To express this, Spanish and English use the comparative construction.

Comparison of superiority (**más** + *adjetivo* + **que**):

| La avenida es **más ancha que** nuestra calle. | *The avenue is **wider than** our street.* |

Comparison of inferiority (**menos** + *adjetivo* + **que**):

| Pero la avenida es **menos ancha que** la autopista. | *But the avenue is **less wide than** the highway.* |

Comparison of equality (**tan** + *adjetivo* + **como**):

| La avenida es **tan ancha como** el Paseo de Miraflores. | *The avenue is **as wide as** Miraflores Boulevard.* |

The English comparison of inferiority is usually expressed as *not as*: The avenue is *not as wide as* the highway.

The adjectives **bueno** and **malo** have irregular comparative forms.

bueno *good* → **mejor** *better*
malo *bad* → **peor** *worse*

| Este restaurante es **mejor** que el otro. | *This restaurant is **better** than the other one.* |
| El ruido aquí es **peor** que en el barrio mío. | *The noise is **worse** here than in my neighborhood.* |

The phrases **más bueno** and **más malo** are used to refer to moral qualities.

Grande and **pequeño** have irregular comparative forms when they refer to age.

grande *big* → **mayor** *older*
pequeño *small* → **menor** *younger*

| Mi hermano **menor** es más alto que mi hermana **mayor.** | *My **younger** brother is taller than my **older** sister.* |

Adverbs are compared in the same way as adjectives.

Ella contesta **más cortésmente que** él.	*She answers **more politely than** he does.*
Ella contesta **menos cortésmente que** él.	*She answers **less politely than** he does.*
Ella contesta **tan cortésmente como** él.	*She answers **as politely as** he does.*

Some common adverbs have irregular comparative forms:

bien *well* → **mejor** *better*
mal *badly* → **peor** *worse*
poco *little, not much* → **menos** *less*
mucho *much, a lot* → **más** *more*

When **mejor** and **peor** are adverbs they are invariable.

In comparing verbs and nouns, **tan** changes to **tanto. Tanto** is invariable with verbs, but agrees with the nouns that follow it.

Comparing verbs:
Yo trabajo **más que** tú.	*I work **more than** you do.*
Yo trabajo **menos que** tú.	*I work **less than** you do.*
Yo trabajo **tanto como** tú.	*I work **as much as** you do.*

Comparing nouns:
| Creo que tú tienes **menos exámenes que** Amalia. | *I think you have **fewer exams than** Amalia.* |
| Te equivocas. Yo tengo **tantos exámenes como** ella, y **más trabajos escritos.** | *You're mistaken. I have **as many exams as** she does, and **more papers.*** |

Que (*than*) is followed by subject pronouns unless the pronoun is the direct or indirect object of the verb. In that case, **que** is followed by **a** + *stressed pronoun.*

| Yo estudio más **que tú.** | *I study more **than you do.*** |
| A mí me gusta más **que a ti.** | *I like it more **than you do.*** |

Que is followed by **nada, nadie,** and **nunca** where English uses *anything, anyone,* and *ever.*

El curso es difícil, más **que nada.**	*The course is hard, more **than anything.***
Luis Alberto baila mejor **que nadie.**	*Luis Alberto dances better **than anyone.***
Trabajamos más **que nunca.**	*We're working harder **than ever.***

Que is replaced by **de** before a numeral.

Ganan más **de** dos mil dólares por semana.	*They earn more **than** two thousand dollars per week.*

Que is replaced by **de lo que** before a clause implying a standard for comparison.

Este libro es más difícil **de lo que** cree el profesor.	*This book is more difficult **than** the teacher thinks. (How difficult the teacher thinks the book is the basis for comparison.)*
Y menos interesante **de lo que** yo me imaginaba.	*And less interesting **than** I imagined. (How interesting I imagined the book was is the basis for comparison.)*

Que is replaced by **de** before **el que, la que, los que, las que.** The article represents a deleted noun.

Necesito más plata **de la que** me prestaste. (la que = la plata que)	*I need more money than (the money) you lent me.*
Encontramos menos problemas **de los que** esperábamos. (los que = los problemas que)	*We found fewer problems than (the problems) we expected.*

Actividad 18 **En comparación.** Combine las dos oraciones de cada grupo en una sola oración que exprese una comparación. Escriba dos oraciones de comparación para cada grupo. Siga el modelo.

> MODELO   Loren es listo. / Julio es más listo.
> Julio es <u>más</u> listo que Loren.
> Loren es <u>menos</u> listo que Julio.

1. Ana es astuta. / Luisa es más astuta.

   _____

   _____

2. El museo de arte es bueno. / El museo de historia natural es mejor.

   _____

   _____

3. Mi novio/a es inteligente. / Yo soy más inteligente.

   _____

   _____

4. El cuarto de Elena es hermoso. / Tu cuarto es más hermoso.

_____

_____

5. La película inglesa es aburrida. / La película francesa es más aburrida.

_____

_____

6. Los bailarines son talentosos. / Los cantantes son más talentosos.

_____

_____

Actividad 19   **Comparación de adverbios.** Escriba oraciones comparativas usando adverbios de tres maneras: **más, menos** y **tan.** Siga el modelo.

> MODELO   Él corrió <u>más</u> rápidamente <u>que</u> ella.
> Ella corrió <u>menos</u> rápidamente <u>que</u> él.
> Él corrió <u>tan</u> rápidamente <u>como</u> ella.

1. José / hablar / francamente / Consuelo

_____

_____

_____

2. los enfermeros / trabajar / cuidadosamente / los médicos

_____

_____

_____

3. Virginia / resolver los problemas / fácilmente / Mario

_____

_____

_____

Actividad 20   **Adjetivos: Igualdad.** Escriba oraciones que demuestren la comparación de igualdad de los dos sustantivos.

> MODELO   Eduardo / diligente / Mercedes
> Eduardo es tan diligente como Mercedes.

1. la obra de teatro / divertida / la película

_____

2. las clases de física / fáciles / las clases de cálculo

_____

3. los documentales / artísticos / los reportajes

_____

4. los platos griegos / sabrosos / los platos húngaros

_____

5. esta actriz / célebre / ese actor

_____

6. el arroz / bueno / el maíz

_____

Actividad 21 **Sustantivos: Igualdad.** Escriba oraciones que demuestren la comparación de igualdad.

1. Alejandro / mandar / correo electrónico / Felipe

_____

2. Miriam / tener / paciencia / Catalina

_____

3. ellos / pasar / horas / en línea / nosotros

_____

4. ella / comer / comida rápida / tú

_____

5. sus amigos / ver / programas de realidad / Uds.

_____

6. los asesores / demostrar / interés en el proyecto / vosotros

_____

7. a él / quedarle / dinero / a ti

_____

8. yo / conocer / clubes de jazz / Marcos

_____

Superlative of adjectives and absolute superlative

Spanish has no special superlative form. Usually, the definite article (or possessive adjective) is used with the noun that the adjective modifies to imply a superlative. Compare the following comparative and superlative sentences.

Quiero ver **una película más emocionante.**   *I want to see **a more exciting film.***
(*comparative*)

Ésta es **la película más emocionante** que alquilé. (*superlative*)

*This is **the most exciting film** that I rented.*

After a superlative, *in* is translated as **de.**

Estamos en la ciudad más importante **del** país.
Y ésta es la calle más elegante **de** la ciudad.

*We're in the most important city **in** the country.*
*And this is the most elegant street **in** the city.*

Spanish has a suffix **-ísimo** called the absolute superlative **(el superlativo absoluto),** that is added to adjectives. This suffix adds the idea of *very* to the adjective. Note that **-c** and **-g** change to **-qu** and **-gu,** and **-z** changes to **-c** when **-ísimo** is added. Adjectives ending in **-ísimo** are four-form adjectives.

lindo → lind**ísimo**
fácil → facil**ísimo**
feo → fe**ísimo**
rico → ri**quísimo**
largo → lar**guísimo**
feliz → feli**císimo**

Actividad 22 **¿Cómo son los estudiantes?** Use los signos aritméticos para escribir oraciones usando superlativos que describan a los estudiantes de la clase. Haga los cambios necesarios. Siga el modelo.

> MODELO Carlos / – atento
> Carlos es el estudiante menos atento.

1. Juan Pablo / + aplicado

   _____

2. Daniel y Arturo / – obediente

   _____

3. Silvia / + simpático

   _____

4. Irene y María / – trabajador

   _____

5. Verónica / + inteligente

   _____

6. Íñigo y Marisol / + hablador

   _____

7. Sergio / + encantador

   _____

8. Rosa y Jacinto / – preparado

   _____

Actividad 23 **¡Qué parque más precioso!** Confirme las observaciones de su amigo respecto al parque que están visitando. Escriba las oraciones usando el superlativo absoluto del adjectivo. Siga el modelo.

> MODELO El parque es lindo.
> Sí. Es <u>lindísimo</u>.

1. La vegetación es interesante.

   _____

2. Ese árbol es viejo.

   _____

3. Esas flores son hermosas.

   _____

4. El zoológico del parque es grande.

   _____

5. Ese león parece feroz.

   _____

6. Los monos son simpáticos.

   _____

7. Las veredas (*paths*) son largas.

   _____

8. El lago es bello.

   _____

Actividad 24 **Visitando la ciudad.** Raquel les enseña su ciudad a sus amigos. Escriba lo que les dice a los amigos usando superlativos y haciendo los cambios necesarios. Siga el modelo.

> MODELO aquí está / museo / importante / ciudad
> Aquí está el museo más importante de la ciudad.

1. allí se encuentra / plaza / imponente / ciudad

   _____

2. aquí ven / centro comercial / moderno / estado

   _____

3. en frente hay / universidad / conocido / país

   _____

4. ésta es / calle / largo / ciudad

   _____

5. en esta calle hay / tiendas / hermoso / zona

_____

6. allí está / tienda de comestibles / estimado / barrio

_____

7. delante de nosotros hay / hotel / internacional / país

_____

8. en este barrio se encuentran / restaurantes / concurrido (*busy, much frequented*) / ciudad

_____

9. aquí ven / casa / viejo / ciudad

_____

10. pronto veremos / estadio / grande / región

_____

Actividad 25 **La clase de literatura.** El profesor y los estudiantes describen las obras que estudian con superlativos. Escriba lo que dicen. Haga los cambios necesarios. Siga el modelo.

> MODELO novela / interesante / siglo
> Es la novela más interesante del siglo.

1. poema / conocido / literatura europea

_____

2. obra de teatro / presentado / año

_____

3. comedia / aplaudido / teatro nacional

_____

4. novela / vendido / literatura moderna

_____

5. tragedia / estimado / nuestro teatro

_____

6. poeta / respetado / su siglo

_____

7. novelista (*f.*) / leído / mundo

_____

8. dramaturgo / apreciado / nuestra época

_____

Expresar en español. Exprese las ideas en español.

1. I read more than you (**Ud.**) do.

   Yo leo más que Usted

2. They know less than we do.

   Saben menos que nosotros

3. Ignacio complains as much as his wife does.

   Ignacio se queja tanto como su esposa

4. I have more compact discs than Federico.

   Tengo más discos compactos que Federico

5. Eva sees fewer films than Margarita.

   Eva ve menos películas que Margarita

6. We take as many trips as they do.

   Hacemos tantas viajes como ellos

7. We have more than ten thousand books in our library.

   Tenemos

8. The soccer game was more exciting than they expected.

   _____

9. Ruiz is the best programmer in the company.

   _____

10. This is the most beautiful beach in the country.

    Esta es la playa más hermosa de país.

11. You (**vosotros**) live in the most elegant neighborhood in the city.

    _____

12. She liked the film more than we did.

    A elle le gustó la película más que a nosotros

13. Rolando surfs the Web more than anyone.

    Rolando navega en internet más que nadie

14. You (**Uds.**) get together more than ever.

    Ustedes se reúnen más que nunca

Actividad oral. Converse con un compañero / una compañera con el fin de describir a sus parientes y a sus amigos. Describa cómo son (carácter, personalidad, lo físico), cómo están, de dónde son, de qué origen son. Compárelos con otros familiares y amigos.

Capítulo 17

DEMONSTRATIVES AND POSSESSIVES

Demonstrative adjectives

Spanish has three demonstrative adjectives (**adjetivos demostrativos**): **este** *this* (*near the speaker*), **ese** *that* (*near the person spoken to*), and **aquel** *that* (*removed from both the speaker and the person spoken to*). The demonstrative adjectives agree in gender and number with the noun they modify.

	MASC.	FEM.
SINGULAR	este	esta
PLURAL	estos	estas

	MASC.	FEM.
SINGULAR	ese	esa
PLURAL	esos	esas

	MASC.	FEM.
SINGULAR	aquel	aquella
PLURAL	aquellos	aquellas

Este apartamento tiene más habitaciones que **aquellas** casas.
Préstame **ese** bolígrafo que tienes. **Este** bolígrafo que tengo ya no escribe.

This apartment has more rooms than those houses (over there).
Lend me that pen that you have. This pen that I have doesn't write any more.

Note that the three demonstratives correspond to specific place words for *here* and *there*.

este → **aquí/acá***
ese → **ahí**
aquel → **allí/allá**†

The demonstrative **ese** can also be placed after a noun to convey a note of contemptuousness.

No sé por qué una muchacha tan inteligente como Margarita saldría con el chico **ese**.

I don't know why a girl as intelligent as Margarita would go out with a guy like that.

Actividad 1 | **Útiles de escuela.** Cambie el artículo definido o indefinido a la forma correcta del adjetivo demostrativo para hablar de sus útiles de escuela. Escriba cada oración de tres maneras. Siga el modelo.

> MODELO   Necesito un cuaderno.
> Necesito este cuaderno.
> Necesito ese cuaderno.
> Necesito aquel cuaderno.

Acá often replaces **aquí** in Latin American Spanish.
†**Allá** often conveys the idea of *far away*.

1. Los libros de texto están bien escritos.

_____

_____

_____

2. Prefiero los disquetes.

_____

_____

_____

3. La marca de agenda electrónica *(PDA)* es conocida.

_____

_____

_____

4. Me gusta el diccionario de español.

_____

_____

_____

5. Usé la calculadora de bolsillo.

_____

_____

_____

6. Las enciclopedias no tienen información sobre el tema.

_____

_____

_____

Actividad 2 **De compras en El Corte Inglés.** Complete los diálogos entre unos amigos que van de compras. Use la forma correcta del adjetivo demostrativo.

En la sección de ropa para mujeres

Irene —Oye, Trini, ¿qué te parece *(this)* _____
             1
traje?

Trini —¿Cuál? ¿*(That)* _____ traje azul?
                                        2

Irene —Sí. ¿Verdad que *(this)* _____ color es muy
                                                      3
bonito?

Trini —Francamente me gusta más (*that over there*)

_____ traje verde.
₄

Irene —Pero me gustan (*these*) _____ blusas y no
₅

hacen juego con el traje verde.

Trini —Bueno chica, llévate (*that*) _____ traje azul
₆

y (*those*) _____ blusas entonces. Y si te
₇

queda dinero todavía, cómprate el traje verde con (*that over there*)

_____ blusa negra. ¡El conjunto te
₈

quedará fenómeno!

En la sección de ropa para hombres

Lupe —Bueno Tito, ayúdame. ¿Qué le regalo a Mateo por su cumpleaños?

¿(*This*) _____ corbata roja o (*that*)
₉

_____ cinturón negro?
₁₀

Tito —Querida hermana, no me gustan ni (*these*)

_____ corbatas ni (*those*)
₁₁

_____ cinturones. Mateo es un gran chico.
₁₂

(*This*) _____ novio tuyo se merece algo
₁₃

más interesante e importante. Mira (*this*)

_____ sección de deportes... (*that over*
₁₄

there) _____ bate, o (*that*)
₁₅

_____ guante para jugar béisbol... o quizás
₁₆

(*this*) _____ raqueta de tenis, o...
₁₇

Lupe —Tito, yo comprendo lo que estás haciendo. Quieres que Mateo te

preste su nuevo bate o guante o raqueta. ¡Es mejor que escoja el

regalo yo!

Demonstrative pronouns

Demonstrative pronouns in Spanish have the same form as demonstrative
adjectives except that an accent mark is added over the stressed vowel of the
pronoun. Demonstrative pronouns refer to a specific noun.

Estas tortas son más ricas que **aquéllas.**	*These cakes are more delicious than* **those (over there).**
Pero aquellas galletas no son tan buenas como **éstas.**	*But those cookies (over there) aren't as good as* **these.**

¿Qué camisa prefiere Ud.? **¿Ésta** o **ésa?**	Which shirt do you prefer? **This one** or **that one?**
Creo que me gusta más **aquélla** que está en el otro mostrador.	I think that I like **that one** on the other counter best.
Aquellos anteojos son más bonitos que **ésos.**	Those eyeglasses (over there) are prettier than **those.**
Puede ser, pero **éstos** tienen la montura que más me gusta.	That may be, but **these** have the frame I like best.
¿Quiénes son los dos muchachos que figuran en la foto?	Who are the two boys in the photo?
Éste es mi primo Carlos y **ése** es su amigo.	**This one** is my cousin Carlos and **that one** is his friend.

NOTA

In modern usage, the written accent is sometimes left off demonstrative pronouns.

Spanish has three neuter demonstrative pronouns ending in **-o: esto, eso, aquello.** These never have a written accent. They refer to situations or ideas, not to specific nouns.

Dicen que Pedro toma y que después maneja.	They say that Pedro drinks and then drives.
No hay nada más peligroso que **eso.**	There's nothing more dangerous than **that.** (**eso** = drinking and driving)
La tía María tenía antes una tienda de ropa en el centro.	Aunt María used to have a clothing store downtown.
Aquello fue hace muchos años, ¿verdad?	**That** was many years ago, wasn't it? (**aquello** = that she had a clothing store downtown)

The neuter demonstratives can be followed by **de** to express *this/that situation regarding* or *this/that matter of/about*. Compare with **lo de,** page 252.

Esto de trabajar demasiado no te hace ningún bien.	**This situation of (your) working too much** is not doing you any good.
Aquello de tu hermano Íñigo me puso triste.	**That business about your brother Íñigo** made me sad.

Esto de, eso de, and **aquello de** can be understood as referring to relative time differences. **Esto de** means *the matter I was just talking about.* **Eso de** means *the matter you were just talking about* or *the thing you just said.* **Aquello de** refers to a matter discussed in the past.

Actividad 3 **Un crítico de restaurantes.** Ud. es crítico/a de restaurantes. Alguien le hace una entrevista sobre ciertas comidas que probó. Contéstele usando los pronombres demostrativos en su respuesta. Siga el modelo.

> MODELO ¿Qué queso le gustó más? ¿Este queso o ese queso?
> Me gustó éste más que ése. *or*
> Me gustó ése más que éste.

1. ¿Qué salsa de champiñones (*mushrooms*) le gustó más? ¿Esa salsa o aquella salsa?

   _____

2. ¿Qué fideos (*noodles*) le gustaron más? ¿Aquellos fideos o estos fideos?

   _____

3. ¿Qué bizcocho (*cake*) le gustó más? ¿Este bizcocho o ese bizcocho?

   _____

4. ¿Qué salchichas le gustaron más? ¿Esas salchichas o aquellas salchichas?

   _____

5. ¿Qué guisado (*stew*) le gustó más? ¿Este guisado o ese guisado?

   _____

6. ¿Qué panes le gustaron más? ¿Estos panes o aquellos panes?

   _____

7. ¿Qué sopa de legumbres le gustó más? ¿Esta sopa de legumbres o esa sopa de legumbres?

   _____

Possessive adjectives

Possessive adjectives in Spanish agree with the noun they modify. Possessive adjectives referring to the singular pronouns and to the third-person plural have only two forms: a singular and a plural. The possessives **nuestro/a** and **vuestro/a** are four-form adjectives because they agree in gender as well as in number.

(yo)	**mi/mis**	(nosotros)	**nuestro/a/os/as**
(tú)	**tu/tus**	(vosotros)	**vuestro/a/os/as**
(él/ella/Ud.)	**su/sus**	(ellos/ellas/Uds.)	**su/sus**

¿Has visto **mis** libros?
Sí, aquí están **tus** libros.

*Have you seen **my** books?*
*Yes, here are **your** books.*

¿Venís a **nuestra** casa?
Sí, vamos a **vuestra** casa.

*Are you coming to **our** house?*
*Yes, we're going to **your** house.*

The possessive adjective **su/sus** means *his, her, its, your,* and *their.* To clarify the person(s) to whom **su/sus** refers, a phrase consisting of **de** + *pronoun* may be added.

¡Qué bueno! Allí están Sergio y Marisa. Necesito su libro.
¿El libro **de él** o el libro **de ella**?

Great! There are Sergio and Marisa. I need (his/her/their) book.
His book or her book?

¿Qué computadora te gustó más?	*Which computer did you like best?*	
La computadora **de Uds.** La computadora **de ellos** no me gustó tanto.	*Your computer. I didn't like their computer so much.*	

Spanish has a set of long-form or stressed possessive adjectives that can be used to contrast one possessor with another (*It's **my** book, not **your** book*). These are all four-form adjectives and follow the noun they modify.

(yo)	el libro **mío**	la casa **mía**
	los libros **míos**	las casas **mías**
(tú)	el libro **tuyo**	la casa **tuya**
	los libros **tuyos**	las casas **tuyas**
(él/ella/Ud.)	el libro **suyo**	la casa **suya**
	los libros **suyos**	las casas **suyas**
(nosotros/as)	el libro **nuestro**	la casa **nuestra**
	los libros **nuestros**	las casas **nuestras**
(vosotros/as)	el libro **vuestro**	la casa **vuestra**
	los libros **vuestros**	las casas **vuestras**
(ellos/ellas/Uds.)	el libro **suyo**	la casa **suya**
	los libros **suyos**	las casas **suyas**

The phrases consisting of **de** + *pronoun* clarify the person to whom **suyo** refers.

Rogelio y Paula escribieron muchos artículos.	*Rogelio and Paula wrote a lot of articles.*
Los artículos **de él** se publicaron en España y **los** artículos **de ella** en México.	***His** articles were published in Spain and **her** articles in Mexico.*
El teléfono celular **mío** no funciona. ¿Me prestas el teléfono celular **tuyo**?	***My** cell phone doesn't work. Can you lend me **your** cell phone?*
Lo siento. **El** teléfono celular **mío** no funciona tampoco.	*I'm sorry. **My** cell phone doesn't work either.*

The long-form possessive adjectives can also occur with the indefinite article.

unos amigos **míos**	*some friends of mine*
una idea **tuya**	*an idea of yours*

After **ser** the definite article is frequently omitted after long-form possessives.

Este coche es **mío.**	*This car is mine.*
Esas maletas son **nuestras.**	*Those suitcases are ours.*

When the definite article does appear with a long-form possessive after forms of **ser,** there is a difference in meaning that is difficult to express in English.

Esta casa es **mía.**	*This house is mine. (I own it. The focus is on ownership.)*
En esta calle hay varias casas. ¿Cuál es **la tuya**?	*There are several houses on this street. Which one is yours? (The focus is on which one of many belongs to someone.)*
Esta casa es **la mía.**	*This house is mine.*

Actividad 4 **En el depósito de artículos perdidos (*lost and found*).** A sus amigos siempre se les pierden sus cosas. Ud. y su amiga buscan esos artículos en el depósito donde suelen acabar. Dígale a su amiga de quiénes serán las cosas. Use un adjetivo posesivo en su respuesta. Siga el modelo.

> MODELO Esta raqueta de tenis será de Paco, ¿no? (Jorge)
> No, no es suya. Será de Jorge.

1. Este guante será de Rebeca, ¿no? (Martina)

   _____

2. Estas llaves serán de Carlos y Pepe, ¿no? (nosotros)

   _____

3. Este disquete será de Amparo, ¿no? (Enrique)

   _____

4. Estos apuntes de historia serán del nuevo estudiante, ¿no? (Uds.)

   _____

5. Estas calculadoras serán de Fernando y Graciela, ¿no? (tú)

   _____

6. Esta bolsa será de Anita, ¿no? (la profesora Márquez)

   _____

7. Esta agenda electrónica será de Uds., ¿no? (Eduardo)

   _____

Actividad 5 **Viajes.** ¿Qué se lleva en un viaje? Escriba frases usando un adjetivo posesivo de forma larga. Siga el modelo.

> MODELO la bolsa / (yo)
> la bolsa mía

1. las maletas / (tú)

   _____

2. el equipaje de mano / (nosotros)

   _____

3. los cheques de viajero / (ellos)

   _____

4. la computadora portátil / (Ud.)

   _____

5. los maletines / (tú y yo)

_____

6. la mochila / (Uds.)

_____

7. el pasaporte / (yo)

_____

8. las visas / (vosotras)

_____

9. los billetes electrónicos / (tú)

_____

Possessive pronouns

Spanish possessive pronouns consist of the definite article plus the long-form possessive adjective. The noun is deleted.

Javier se compró un coche espléndido.	_Javier bought himself a terrific car._
Sí, **el suyo** costó mucho más que **el nuestro.**	_Yes, **his** cost much more than **ours** did._
Los estudiantes **míos** son muy buenos este semestre. ¿Y **los suyos**?	_**My** students are very good this semester. What about **yours**?_
Los míos también son excelentes.	_**Mine** are excellent, too._
Mira mi computadora nueva.	_Look at my new computer._
Es fabulosa. Creo que **la tuya** tiene más memoria que **la mía.**	_It's fabulous. I think **yours** has more memory than **mine**._

The masculine plural of the possessive pronoun can refer to family members or to teams.

¿Cómo están **los tuyos**?	_How's **your family**?_
¿Los míos? Perfectamente, gracias.	_**My family**? Just fine, thanks._
Espero que ganen **los nuestros.**	_I hope **our team** wins._
Ya veremos. Los otros son muy buenos también.	_We'll see. The others are very good, too._

The neuter article **lo** + _the masculine singular of the long-form possessive_ forms a neuter possessive pronoun meaning _whose part_, or _whose task._

Denme **lo mío** y me voy.	_Give me **my share** and I'll leave._
Lo tuyo son veinte dólares.	_**Your part** is twenty dollars._
Lo suyo es crear la base de datos.	_**His task** is to create the data base._
No encontramos **lo nuestro.**	_We can't find **our things**._

Actividad 6 **Fernando el fanfarrón (*braggart*).** Cada vez que alguien dice que tiene algo bueno, Fernando se jacta de tener algo mejor. Escriba lo que dice Fernando usando los pronombres posesivos. Siga el modelo.

> MODELO Martín   —Mi coche es muy lujoso.
> Fernando —¡Pero el mío es más lujoso que el tuyo!

1. Lucia   —Mi iPod es muy moderno.

    Fernando —_____

2. Patricia   —Mis discos compactos son nuevos.

    Fernando —_____

3. Ricardo   —Mi novia es muy simpática.

    Fernando —_____

4. Dalia   —Mi computadora funciona muy bien.

    Fernando —_____

5. Carlos   —Mis revistas de deportes son muy interesantes.

    Fernando —_____

6. Clara   —Mis ideas son muy buenas.

    Fernando —_____

7. Leo   —Mi perro es sumamente inteligente.

    Fernando —_____

Actividad 7 **¿Dónde está?** Explique dónde Ud. cree que están las siguientes cosas. Conteste las preguntas usando los pronombres posesivos. Siga el modelo.

> MODELO ¿Dónde está el anillo de Virginia? (en el dormitorio)
> El suyo estará en el dormitorio.

1. ¿Dónde están los manuales de José? (en la mesa)

    _____

2. ¿Dónde está tu permiso de manejar? (en mi cartera)

    _____

3. ¿Dónde están las pulseras de Lola y Nieves? (en la cómoda)

    _____

4. ¿Dónde están sus sellos (de Uds.)? (en el escritorio)

    _____

PARTE II

5. ¿Dónde está nuestra agenda electrónica? (en la computadora)

   _____

6. ¿Dónde están vuestros frascos de agua de colonia? (en el baño)

   _____

7. ¿Dónde está su (de Ud.) guitarra? (encima del piano)

   _____

Actividad 8 ¡**Qué niño más repipí!** (*What a brat!*) Angelito siempre se sale con la suya (*gets his own way*). ¿Y estas otras personas? ¿Siempre se salen con la suya? Escriba oraciones usando el pronombre posesivo apropiado en decir que sí o que no. Siga el modelo.

> MODELO   la hermanita de Angelito (sí)
>   Sí, se sale con la suya.

1. las hermanas grandes de Angelito (no)

   _____

2. Rafaelito (no)

   _____

3. Ud. (sí)

   _____

4. Bárbara (no)

   _____

5. Uds. (no)

   _____

6. tú (sí)

   _____

7. vosotros (sí)

   _____

Actividad 9 **Expresar en español.** Exprese las oraciones en español.

1. This business about the company is difficult to understand.

   _____

2. That situation regarding our trip has to be resolved.

   _____

3. We'll have to talk about that matter of buying a new car.

   _____

4. An old friend of mine is arriving on Saturday.

   _____

5. How's your **(tú)** family? (use a possessive pronoun)

   _____

6. We hope our team wins. (use a possessive pronoun)

   _____

7. Your **(Ud.)** part (task) is to bring the flowers.

   _____

8. My task is to make copies.

   _____

Actividad 10 **Actividad oral.** Practique usando los demostrativos y los posesivos. Pregúnteles a otros estudiantes a quiénes pertenecen ciertas cosas. Por ejemplo, Ud. pregunta «¿De quién es este libro de texto?» Un compañero / Una compañera contesta: «Es mío» o «Es suyo», señalando a otro compañero / otra compañera.

PRONOUNS: Subject, object, prepositional

Subject pronouns

The subject pronouns in Spanish are:

SINGULAR	PLURAL
yo *I*	**nosotros/as** *we*
tú *you (informal singular)*	**vosotros/as** *you (informal plural, Spain only)*
él *he, it*	**ellos** *they (masculine)*
ella *she, it*	**ellas** *they (feminine)*
Ud. (usted) *you (formal singular)*	**Uds. (ustedes)** *you (formal and informal plural in Latin America, formal plural in Spain)*

Each of the four forms of *you* in Spanish is used to distinguish number and politeness. All Spanish-speaking countries use the singular forms **tú** (informal) and **Ud.** (formal), and the plural form **Uds.*** (formal/informal), which can be used for any group of two or more people. In addition to these three forms, the plural **vosotros** (informal) replaces the informal use of **Uds.** in Spain.

Since all Spanish nouns are either masculine or feminine, **él** and **ella** refer to things as well as to people.

Subject pronouns are less common in Spanish than in English because the verb endings show who is performing the action. They are used, however, to contrast or emphasize the subject of the verb.

¿Qué hac**es** mañana?	*What are **you** doing tomorrow?*
Trabaj**o.**	*I am working.*
¿Qué hac**en** (Uds.) mañana?	*What are **you** doing tomorrow?*
Ella tiene el día libre, pero **yo** trabajo.	*She has the day off, but **I**'m working.*

Note the following use of the subject pronouns with **ser** (colloquial English translations appear in parentheses).

Soy yo. *It is I. (It's me.)*	**Somos nosotros/as.** *It is we. (It's us.)*
Eres tú. *It is you.*	**Sois vosotros/as.** *It is you.*
Es él. *It is he. (It's him.)*	**Son ellos.** *It is they (masculine). (It's them.)*
Es ella. *It is she. (It's her.)*	**Son ellas.** *It is they (feminine). (It's them.)*
Es Ud. *It is you.*	**Son Uds.** *It is you.*

*Note that **Ud.** and **Uds.** are often abbreviated **Vd.** and **Vds.** in Spain.

Actividad I **El sujeto.** Escriba el pronombre sujeto al lado de la oración. Si hay más de una posibilidad, escriba todos los pronombres posibles. Siga el modelo.

MODELO   Lees una cantidad de libros. _____tú_____

1. Estacionemos en esta calle. _____

2. Es español. _____

3. Sois simpáticas. _____

4. Buscaban casa. _____

5. Tengo razón. _____

6. Está contentísima. _____

7. Cenasteis a las nueve. _____

8. Lo verás. _____

9. Eran bellas. _____

10. Es inglesa. _____

Actividad 2 **Yo… pero tú…** Practique usando el pronombre sujeto combinando las dos oraciones en una. Siga el modelo.

MODELO   Estudias español. Estudia (ella) francés.
         Tú estudias español, pero ella estudia francés.

1. Trabajo de lunes a viernes. Trabajas los fines de semana.

   _____

2. Estudiamos en una universidad particular. Estudian (Uds.) en una universidad estatal.

   _____

3. Viven (ellas) en pleno centro. Vive (Ud.) en las afueras.

   _____

4. Vas de compras el sábado. Vamos de compras el jueves.

   _____

5. Es (él) abogado. Soy profesor.

   _____

6. Escuchan (ellos) música clásica. Escucháis rock.

   _____

Pronouns after prepositions

After a preposition, Spanish uses the subject pronouns, except for **yo** and **tú**.

para **mí**	para **nosotros/as**
para **ti**	para **vosotros/as**
para **él**	para **ellos**
para **ella**	para **ellas**
para **Ud.**	para **Uds.**

NOTA **Mí** has a written accent but **ti** does not.

Three irregular forms exist with the preposition **con: conmigo** (*with me*), **contigo** (*with you*) (*informal singular*), and **consigo** (*with himself, with herself, with yourself* [Ud.], *with yourselves* [Uds.], *with themselves*).

¿Puedes ir **conmigo**?	*Can you go **with me**?*
Hoy no. Mañana voy **contigo**.	*Not today. Tomorrow I'll go **with you**.*
Alicia está enojada **con nosotros**.	*Alicia is angry **with us**.*
Debería estar enojada **consigo** misma. Ella tiene la culpa de todo.	*She should be angry **with herself**. She's to blame for everything.*

After the prepositions **como** (*like*), **entre** (*between, among*), **excepto** (*except*), **menos** (*except*), **salvo** (*except*), and **según** (*according to*), subject pronouns are used even in the first- and second-person singular forms.

No quiero que haya problemas **entre tú y yo**.	*I don't want there to be any problems **between you and me**.*
Vamos todos al cine **menos tú**.	*Everyone but you is going to the movies.*
Don Quijote es el mejor libro del mundo, **según yo**.	Don Quijote *is the best book in the world, **according to me** (in my opinion).*

Yo and **tú** replace **mí** and **ti** after **y** with other prepositions as well.

Lo dijo **delante de Ud. y yo**.	*He said it **in front of you and me**.*

Actividad 3 **Pronombres preposicionales.** Escriba la forma correcta del pronombre. Haga los cambios necesarios. Siga el modelo.

> MODELO de __mí__ (yo)

1. para   _____ (él)

2. con   _____ (tú)

3. según   _____ (tú)

4. por   _____ (nosotros)

5. salvo   _____ (yo)

6. sobre   _____ (Ud.)

7. con   _____ (yo)

8. de   _____ (vosotros)

9. para   _____ (ellas)

10. por   _____ (tú)

11. menos   _____ (tú)

12. como   _____ (yo)

13. en   _____ (ella)

14. entre   _____ y yo (tú)

Actividad 4 **Más pronombres preposicionales.** Conteste las preguntas usando los pronombres preposicionales correctos. Siga el modelo.

> MODELO   ¿Trajiste algo para Elenita?
> Sí, traje algo para ella.

1. ¿Vive Ud. cerca de las tiendas?

   _____

2. ¿Trabajaba Timoteo en esa oficina?

   _____

3. ¿Lograron Uds. hablar sobre esos asuntos?

   _____

4. ¿Pagaste un dineral (*fortune*) por el televisor plasma?

   _____

5. ¿Salió Ud. con Isabel y Alfonso?

   _____

6. ¿Hay mucho trabajo para la clase de filosofía?

   _____

7. ¿Se casó María Elena con el pintor?

   _____

8. ¿Felicitaste a los jugadores por la victoria?

   _____

Actividad 5 **Te equivocas.** Conteste las preguntas de su amigo diciéndole que Ud. no hizo las cosas ni con las personas que él cree ni para ellas. Escriba oraciones usando los pronombres preposicionales. Siga el modelo.

> MODELO   Saliste con Gabriela, ¿verdad?
> No, con ella, no.

PARTE II

1. Almorzaste con Paquita y Laura, ¿verdad?

_____

2. Fuiste al cine con Víctor, ¿verdad?

_____

3. Hiciste el informe para la profesora Godoy, ¿verdad?

_____

4. Trabajaste en la librería por tu hermana, ¿verdad?

_____

5. Compraste un regalo para tus padres, ¿verdad?

_____

6. Escribiste el trabajo por Daniel, ¿verdad?

_____

7. Jugaste tenis con los Villa, ¿verdad?

_____

8. Preparaste el almuerzo para mí, ¿verdad?

_____

Personal **a** and direct objects

A direct object noun in Spanish is joined directly to its verb, without a preposition, if it refers to a thing. Direct object nouns that refer to specific people are preceded by **a.** This is called the *personal a.*

No veo **a tu abuela.**	*I don't see **your grandmother.***
Está en la cocina ayudando a **mi madre.**	*She's in the kitchen helping **my mother.***
¿Alquilaste **la película**?	*Did you rent **the film?***
Sí, y compré **palomitas de maíz.**	*Yes, and I bought **popcorn.***

In the preceding examples, the nouns **abuela, madre, película,** and **palomitas de maíz** are direct objects. Only the direct objects that refer to people use the personal **a.**

The personal **a** is not used before nouns referring to people unless they are specific.

Este restaurante busca **camareros.**	*This restaurant is looking for waiters.*
También necesitan **un cajero.**	*They also need a cashier.*
La empresa necesita **programadores.**	*The firm needs programmers.*
Admiten **cientos de estudiantes.**	*They admit hundreds of students.*

Nouns preceded by numbers are not considered specific and usually do not take the personal **a.**

Contrataron **(a) cien empleados nuevos.**	*They hired one hundred new employees.*
Conozco **(a) diez primos suyos.**	*I know ten cousins of his.*

However, the personal **a** is required before **alguien** and **nadie**, and before **alguno, ninguno,** and **cualquiera** when they modify a noun referring to people or are used as pronouns referring to people.

¿**A quién** llamas?	**Whom** are you calling?
No puedo llamar **a nadie.** El teléfono está descompuesto.	I can't call **anyone.** The phone is out of order.
¿Despidieron **a alguien**?	Did they fire **anyone**?
Creo que despidieron **a algunos empleados.**	I think they fired **a few employees.**
¿Conoces **a algunos profesores** en Madrid?	Do you know **any professors** in Madrid?
No, no conozco **a ningún profesor.**	No, I don't know **any.**
¿Invitaste **a alguien**?	Did you invite **anyone**?
No, no invité **a nadie.**	No, I didn't invite **anyone.**
Nunca he visto **a nadie** que hable tanto como él.	I've never seen **anyone** who talks as much as he does.
Sí, él es capaz de marear **a cualquiera.**	Yes, he can make **anyone** dizzy.
Laura está dispuesta a ayudar **a cualquier amigo.**	Laura is willing to help **any friend.**
Sí, ella siempre ayuda **a todo el mundo.**	Yes, she always helps **everyone.**

The personal **a** is also used before other pronouns that refer to people.

Hoy llevo **a los míos** al centro.	Today I'm taking **my family** downtown.
¿Puedo ir con Uds.? Me encantaría conocer **a los tuyos.**	Can I go with you? I would love to meet **your family.**

The personal **a** is generally used before **¿cuántos?** when it refers to people but, as mentioned on p. 303, is often omitted before the number that may appear in the answer to the question.

¿**A cuántos** conociste?	**How many of them** did you meet?
Conocí **(a)** siete.	I met **seven.**
¿**A cuántos candidatos** eligieron?	**How many candidates** did they elect?
Eligieron **(a)** doce.	They elected **twelve.**

The personal **a** is not usually used after **tener.**

¿**Qué profesora** tienes para sicología?	**Which teacher** do you have for psychology?
Tengo **la mejor profesora** que hay.	I have **the best teacher** there is.

When the personal **a** is used after **tener** it implies having a person in a certain condition or in a certain role.

Tiene **a su mujer** como asistenta.	He has **his wife** as his assistant.
Tengo **a mi hija** en la universidad ahora.	I've got **my daughter** in college now.

The personal **a** is also used after **tener** when **tener** means to hold.

La mujer **tenía a su bebé** en brazos.	The woman **held her baby** in her arms.

When the personal **a** is used after **querer,** the verb means *to love, like.* When the personal **a** is omitted after **querer,** the verb means *to want.*

Ricardo quiere **a** Sofía.	*Ricardo loves Sofía.*
No quieren **a su cocinero.**	*They don't like their cook.*
Quieren **otro cocinero.**	*They want another cook.*

Actividad 6 **La *a* personal.** Complete las oraciones con la **a** personal. Si no es necesario añadirla, escriba una X. No se olvide de escribir la contracción **al (a + el)** cuando haga falta.

1. Yo buscaba _____ los sobres.

2. Encontré _____ las niñas en el patio.

3. Busquen _____ los documentos en el escritorio.

4. Encontraron _____ el arquitecto en su oficina.

5. Paco conoció _____ su novia hace seis meses.

6. ¿_____ quién viste en el teatro?

7. Llevamos _____ nuestros amigos a la sierra.

8. ¿No comprendes _____ el problema todavía?

9. Me gustaría conocer _____ la ciudad.

10. Llévate _____ el paquete.

11. No he encontrado _____ el número de teléfono.

12. Jesús y Tito llevan _____ la camiseta de su equipo.

13. Ayuda _____ tu hermana.

14. Voy a ver _____ mis tíos mañana.

15. Nadie comprende _____ el profesor Delgado.

16. ¿_____ quiénes llamaste?

Actividad 7 **¡Un flechazo! (*Love at first sight!*)** Simón le explica a su amigo Pedro cómo se enamoró de una chica durante su semestre en Palma de Mallorca. Complete las oraciones con la **a** personal. Si no es necesario añadirla, escriba una X.

Pedro —Entonces, ¿ya conocías _____ algunos estudiantes de la
                                              1
Facultad de Ciencias Sociales?

Simón —Por desgracia, las primeras semanas no conocí _____
                                                                            2
ninguno de los estudiantes.

| Pedro | —¿Pero no viste _____ muchos chicos en la universidad? |
| | 3 |

Simón   —Claro que los vi, pero no me presenté _____ ellos
4

porque no dominaba el español.

Pedro   —¿Cómo es que cambió la situación entonces?

Simón   —Bueno, después de un mes más o menos conocí _____
5

alguien de la facultad de ingeniería que me llevó a una fiesta.

Pedro   —Seguro que invitó _____ estudiantes de la facultad. Allí
6

conociste _____ mucha gente, ¿verdad?
7

Simón   —_____ muchas personas, no, pero _____ una
8   9

muy especial, sí. Es que vi _____ tantas chicas muy
10

lindas.

Pedro   —Y querías sacar a bailar _____ todas, ¿no?
11

Simón   —Sí, al principio. ¡Hasta que me fijé en una que me dejó boquiabierto!

Pedro   —¡Un flechazo! No invitaste _____ ninguna a salir…
12

Simón   —¡Excepto _____ Josefa!
13

Forms and position of direct object pronouns

Direct object nouns can be replaced by direct object pronouns. The direct object pronouns in Spanish are:

me	nos
te	os
lo/la	los/las

NOTAS

- **Lo, la, los, las** refer to both people and things.
- **Lo, la, los, las** are also the direct object pronouns for **Ud.** and **Uds.,** so they mean *you* as well as *him, her, it, them.*
- In Spain, **lo** is usually replaced by **le** when referring to people.

Direct object pronouns precede the conjugated verb in Spanish, whereas in English they follow the conjugated verb.

¿Dónde estarán los niños? Hace
   quince minutos que **los** busco y
   no **los** encuentro.
Los vi en el parque.

Where can the children be? I've been
   *looking for **them** for fifteen minutes*
   *and I can't find **them**.*
*I saw **them** in the park.*

¡Ay! No tengo el libro de química. **Lo** dejé en el aula.	*Oh! I don't have the chemistry book. I left **it** in the classroom.*
Aquí tengo el mío. ¿**Lo** quieres?	*I have mine here. Do you want **it**?*
Me avisará si hay un cambio en el horario de mañana.	*You'll inform **me** if there's a change in tomorrow's schedule.*
Cómo no, señora. Cualquier cosa y **la** llamo en seguida.	*Of course, Madam. If anything comes up, I'll call **you** immediately.*
¿Vas al centro ahora? ¿**Nos** llevas?	*Are you going downtown now? Will you take **us**?*
Con mucho gusto. **Los** dejo delante del correo. ¿Está bien?	*Gladly. I'll leave **you** in front of the post office. Is that all right?*

In compound tenses the direct object pronouns are placed before the auxiliary verb **haber.**

Carlos, ¡qué milagro! No **te** hemos visto por tanto tiempo.	*Carlos, what a surprise! We haven't seen **you** for such a long time.*
Es que **me** han contratado en una empresa de las afueras.	*That's because they've hired **me** at a firm in the suburbs.*

In *verb + infinitive* constructions, the direct object pronoun may either precede the first verb or be attached to the infinitive.

¿Has visto la nueva película española?	*Have you seen the new Spanish film?*
No, pero **la** quiero ver.	*No, but I want to see **it**.*
or	
No, pero quiero ver**la**.	

In the progressive tenses, the direct object pronoun can be placed either before the form of **estar** or be attached to the present participle. When the pronoun is attached to the present participle, an accent mark is added to the vowel before the **-ndo.**

¿Y los vasos?	*What about the glasses?*
Los estoy lavando ahora mismo.	*I'm washing **them** right now.*
or	
Estoy lav**á**ndo**los** ahora mismo.	
¿Has leído la nueva novela de Atienza?	*Have you read the new novel by Atienza?*
La estoy leyendo ahora.	*I'm reading **it** now.*
or	
Estoy ley**é**ndo**la** ahora.	
Antes los chicos no comían legumbres.	*The children didn't use to eat vegetables.*
Ahora **las** están comiendo.	*Now they eat **them**.*
or	
Ahora están comi**é**ndo**las**.	

The direct object pronoun is also attached to affirmative command forms. An accent mark is added to the stressed vowel of the command form, except in the case of one-syllable commands. In negative commands, the direct object pronoun precedes the verb.

Éstas son las palabras nuevas, chicos. Apréndan**las** de memoria.	*These are the new words, kids. Learn **them** by heart.*
Por favor, repáse**las** con nosotros, profesor.	*Please, review **them** with us, sir.*
¿No tienes el periódico? Bú**scalo**.	*Don't you have the newspaper? Look for **it**.*
No, có**gelo** tú y llé**valo** arriba.	*No, you get **it** and take **it** upstairs.*
Ese archivo puede estar contaminado. No **lo** abras.	*That file may be contaminated. Don't open **it**.*

To emphasize or contrast direct object pronouns referring to people, a phrase consisting of **a** + *the corresponding prepositional pronoun* is added to the sentence.

¿Reconociste a Laura y a Marcos?	*Did you recognize Laura and Marcos?*
La reconocí **a ella,** pero no **lo** vi **a él.**	*I recognized **her,** but I didn't see **him.***
Parece que las secretarias son más simpáticas que la jefa.	*It seems that the secretaries are nicer than the boss.*
Sí, **a ellas las** encuentro encantadoras, pero **a ella** no **la** aguanto.	*Yes, I find **them** charming, but I can't stand **her.***

When a direct object noun precedes the verb, the direct object pronoun must be present. This is true even if the direct object is a thing.

Veo **a Juan.**	**A Juan lo** veo.
Dejé **los libros** en la mesa.	**Los libros los** dejé en la mesa.

Actividad 8 **Mi coche.** Conteste las preguntas sobre el cuidado de su coche cambiando el sustantivo a un pronombre de complemento directo. Escriba la respuesta de dos maneras. Siga el modelo.

> MODELO ¿Compraste la bomba de aire (*air pump*)?
> No, no la compré. Voy a comprarla.

Vocabulario

El coche

la caja de herramientas *toolbox*
el faro *headlight*
el gato *jack*
el parachoques *bumper*
las piezas de repuesto *spare parts*

la placa de matrícula *license plate*
el silenciador *muffler*
el volante *steering wheel*

1. ¿Cambiaste el aceite?

   _____

   _____

2. ¿Reparaste el parachoques?

   _____

   _____

3. ¿Pediste las placas de matrícula?

_____

_____

4. ¿Llevaste una caja de herramientas y piezas de repuesto?

_____

_____

5. ¿Usaste el gato?

_____

_____

6. ¿Arreglaste el volante?

_____

_____

7. ¿Instalaste el silenciador?

_____

_____

Actividad 9 **María y los coches.** María acaba de sacar su licencia de conducir y piensa mucho en su coche. Escriba oraciones sobre la afición de María cambiando el sustantivo a un pronombre de complemento directo. Escriba la respuesta de dos maneras. Siga el modelo.

> MODELO María quiere limpiar el baúl.
> María quiere limpiarlo. / María lo quiere limpiar.

Vocabulario

El coche

la avería *breakdown*
el baúl *trunk*
cargar la batería *to charge the battery*
el coche descapotable *convertible*

el coche todo terreno *SUV*
el pinchazo *blowout*
la señal de tráfico *road sign*

1. Piensa comprar el coche todo terreno.

_____

_____

2. Tiene que llenar el tanque de gasolina.

_____

_____

3. Trata de leer todas las señales de tráfico.

   _____

   _____

4. Prefiere conducir un coche descapotable.

   _____

   _____

5. Debe cargar la batería.

   _____

   _____

6. Teme tener un pinchazo.

   _____

   _____

7. Procura evitar las averías.

   _____

   _____

Actividad 10 **Lo significa** *you.* El complemento directo **lo, la, los, las** también reemplaza **Ud.** y **Uds.** Conteste las preguntas usando el complemento directo en su respuesta. Siga el modelo.

> MODELO   ¿Me conoce Ud.?
> Sí, señor, lo conozco.

1. ¿Me conoce Ud.?

   Sí, señorita, _____.

2. ¿Nos comprende Ud.?

   Sí, señores, _____.

3. ¿Me llama Ud.?

   No, arquitecta, no _____.

4. ¿Nos busca Ud.?

   No, señoras, no _____.

5. ¿Me lleva Ud.?

   Sí, señor, _____.

6. ¿Nos conoce Ud.?

   No, señoritas, no _____.

7. ¿Me ayuda Ud.?

   Sí, profesor, _____.

8. ¿Nos ve Ud.?

   No, señores, no _____.

Actividad 11   **¡Míralo!** Dé mandatos a varias personas diciéndoles lo que deben hacer y no hacer en ciertos deportes. Escriba mandatos afirmativos y negativos colocando el pronombre de complemento directo en su posición correcta. Siga el modelo.

> MODELO   ver / Ud. / los Juegos Olímpicos
> Véalos. / No los vea.

1. marcar / Ud. /goles

   _____

   _____

2. llamar / tú / al árbitro (*umpire*)

   _____

   _____

3. recoger / Uds. / esos bates

   _____

   _____

4. saltar / Ud. / vallas (*hurdles*)

   _____

   _____

5. hacer / tú / gimnasia

   _____

   _____

6. lanzar / tú / la pelota

   _____

   _____

7. ser / Ud. / plusmarquista (*m.*) (*record holder*)

   _____

   _____

8. levantar / Uds. / las pesas

   _____

   _____

Capítulo 19

Actividad 12 **¿Lo ha visto Ud.?** Unos amigos quieren saber si Ud. ha visto a ciertas personas y cosas hoy. Conteste usando el pronombre de complemento directo. Siga el modelo.

> MODELO ¿Ha visto a Paulina hoy? (sí/no)
> Sí, la he visto.
> No, no la he visto.

1. ¿Has visto al señor Domínguez hoy? (sí)

   _____

2. ¿Ha visto Ud. a los decanos de la universidad? (no)

   _____

3. ¿Han visto Uds. la cámara digital? (sí)

   _____

4. ¿Ha visto Ud. los alicates (*pliers*)? (no)

   _____

5. ¿Has visto a las hermanas Moya? (no)

   _____

6. ¿Han visto Uds. las tarjetas de crédito? (sí)

   _____

7. ¿Ha visto Ud. el recibo? (sí)

   _____

8. ¿Has visto a la ortodontista? (no)

   _____

Actividad 13 **La catedral de Sevilla.** La catedral se remonta (*dates back*) al siglo quince cuando se empezó a construir. Ud. vive en la Edad Media y es testigo de la construcción. Describa las actividades que está viendo. Escriba las oraciones de dos maneras cambiando el sustantivo al pronombre de complemento directo. Siga el modelo.

> MODELO Yo estoy viendo la construcción.
> Yo estoy viéndola.
> Yo la estoy viendo.

Vocabulario

La catedral de Sevilla: Su construcción

el albañil *bricklayer*
los andamios *scaffolding*
la argamasa *mortar*
el/la dibujante *draftsperson*
echar los cimientos *to lay the foundation*

el fraile *monk*
el/la maestro/a de obras *master builder*
la mezquita *mosque*
la monja *nun*
rezar las oraciones *to say prayers*

1. Los arquitectos están empleando el estilo gótico.

   _____

   _____

2. Los constructores van cubriendo la mezquita.

   _____

   _____

3. Los dibujantes están dibujando las ventanas.

   _____

   _____

4. Los maestros de obras están echando los cimientos.

   _____

   _____

5. Los frailes y las monjas siguen rezando sus oraciones.

   _____

   _____

6. Los trabajadores siguen colocando los andamios.

   _____

   _____

7. Los albañiles van trayendo piedras.

   _____

   _____

8. Los obreros están poniendo argamasa.

   _____

   _____

Actividad 14 **Pili lo arregla todo.** David vuelve a casa después de un viaje de negocios. Le hace varias preguntas a su sobrina Pili para saber dónde están sus cosas y los miembros de su familia. ¿Qué le dice Pili a su tío David? Use el complemento directo en primer lugar. Siga el modelo.

> MODELO   ¿Dónde está tu tía? (ver salir hace una hora)
> A mi tía la vi salir hace una hora.

1. ¿Dónde está mi calculadora de bolsillo? (poner en tu mesa de trabajo)

   _____

2. ¿Dónde están los chicos? (llevar al cine)

   _____

3. ¿Dónde está mi teléfono celular? (dejar en el jardín)

   _____

4. ¿Dónde están tus padres? (ver en la sala)

   _____

5. ¿Dónde están mis libros? (arreglar en tu oficina)

   _____

6. ¿Dónde están las cartas que escribí? (echar al correo)

   _____

7. ¿Dónde está mi abrigo? (colgar en el armario)

   _____

8. ¿Dónde están las galletas que compré? (comer)

   _____

Forms and position of indirect object pronouns

Indirect object nouns are joined to the verb by the preposition **a.** Indirect objects most commonly refer to people.

The indirect object pronouns in Spanish are:

me	nos
te	os
le	les

Indirect object pronouns follow the same rules of position as direct object pronouns (See pp. 306–308).

Te dije la verdad.

Le debo decir la verdad. *or* Debo decir**le** la verdad.

Les estoy diciendo la verdad. *or* Estoy diciéndo**les** la verdad.

Nos han dicho la verdad.

Díga**me** la verdad.

An indirect object noun in Spanish is usually accompanied by the corresponding indirect object pronoun (**le** or **les,** depending on whether the noun is singular or plural).

¿Les escribiste **a tus padres?**
Sí, y también **le** mandé un correo electrónico **a mi hermana.**

Did you write to your parents?
Yes, and I also sent my sister an e-mail.

Some verbs that take an indirect object in Spanish take a direct object in English.

contestarle a uno *to answer someone*	**preguntarle a uno** *to ask someone*
pedirle algo a uno *to ask someone for something*	**recordarle a uno** *to remind someone*

Many verbs take an indirect object of the person (**le... a uno**) and a direct object that is a thing (**algo**).

contarle algo a uno *to relate, recount something to someone*	**mandarle algo a uno** *to send something to someone*
darle algo a uno *to give something to someone*	**mostrarle algo a uno** *to show something to someone*
decirle algo a uno *to tell, say something to someone*	**ofrecerle algo a uno** *to offer something to someone*
devolverle algo a uno *to return something to someone*	**pedirle algo a uno** *to ask someone for something*
enseñarle algo a uno *to show something to someone*	**recordarle algo a uno** *to remind someone of something*
entregarle algo a uno *to hand over something to someone*	**regalarle algo a uno** *to give something to someone as a gift*
enviarle algo a uno *to send something to someone*	**servirle algo a uno** *to serve something to someone*
escribirle algo a uno *to write something to someone*	**traerle algo a uno** *to bring something to someone*
explicarle algo a uno *to explain something to someone*	**venderle algo a uno** *to sell something to someone*

The indirect object is often the equivalent of the English *from* with verbs meaning *take away, steal,* and *remove*.

arrebatarle algo a uno *to snatch, grab something from someone*	**pedirle prestado algo a uno** *to borrow something from someone*
comprarle algo a uno *to buy something from someone*	**quitarle algo a uno** *to take something away from someone*
esconderle algo a uno *to hide something from someone*	**robarle algo a uno** *to steal something from someone*
exigirle algo a uno *to demand something of/from someone*	**sacarle algo a uno** *to get something out of/from someone*
ganarle algo a uno *to win something from someone*	**solicitarle algo a uno** *to ask, request something of/from someone*
ocultarle algo a uno *to hide something from someone*	**suspenderle algo a uno** *to revoke, cancel something of someone's*

¿**A quién le** compraste el coche?	*Whom did you buy the car from?*
Me exigieron mis documentos de identidad.	*They demanded my identification papers (of/from me).*
Le solicité trabajo **al padre de Lucas.**	*I applied for work with/from Lucas' father.*
Al turista le quitaron el pasaporte.	*They took the tourist's passport from him.*

To emphasize or contrast indirect object pronouns, a phrase consisting of **a** + *the corresponding prepositional pronoun* is added to the sentence.

¿Qué **les** pidieron los aduaneros **a Uds.**?

*What did the customs officers ask **you** for?*

A mí me pidieron el pasaporte, pero **a ella le** pidieron todos los documentos.

*They asked **me** for **my** passport, but they asked **her** for all of **her** documents.*

¿**A Uds. les** regalaron algo?
A nosotros nos regalaron muchas cosas, pero **a ellos no les** dieron nada.

*Did they give **you** anything as a gift?*
*They gave **us** many things, but they didn't give **them** anything.*

Actividad 15   **El complemento indirecto.** Vuelva a escribir las oraciones cambiando el pronombre de complemento indirecto. Siga el modelo.

> MODELO   Yo le pedí unas revistas. (a ellos)
> Yo les pedí unas revistas.

1. Les traje los refrescos. (a ti)

   _____

2. Me dieron flores. (a nosotros)

   _____

3. Le mandó una tarjeta postal. (a mí)

   _____

4. Nos dijeron los precios. (a Ud.)

   _____

5. Te ofrecimos el escritorio. (a él)

   _____

6. Les preguntó la hora. (a ella)

   _____

7. Le expliqué mis ideas. (a vosotros)

   _____

8. Me recordaron el cumpleaños de Leo. (a Uds.)

   _____

Actividad 16   **Salir ganando o salir perdiendo.** Complete las oraciones con una frase que consiste en **a** + *el pronombre enfático*. Siga el modelo.

> MODELO   __A mí__ me enviaron mucha plata, pero __a ella__ (Roberta) no le enviaron nada.

1. _____ nos mostraron el castillo, pero

_____ (Ud. y Felipe) les mostraron solamente el

establo de caballos.

2. Marta me contó _____ la pura verdad, pero

_____ te contó puras mentiras.

3. Yo le escribí una carta de amor _____ (Daniel),

pero le escribí una carta de odio _____ (su novia).

4. _____ te dimos la llave de la casa, pero

_____ (Catarina y Jorge) les dimos una carta de

despedida.

5. _____ os regalaron unos discos compactos

fabulosos, pero _____ nos regalaron unos discos

rayados (*scratched*).

6. _____ (Elena y Margarita) les trajo unos bom-

bones, pero _____ (Ud.) le trajo una caja vacía.

Actividad 17 **Titulares de periódico.** Componga estos titulares para el periódico de hoy. Debe haber un pronombre de complemento indirecto en cada titular. Escriba las oraciones usando el presente de indicativo. Siga el modelo.

> MODELO (ellos) / a una señora / robarle el carro / mientras compra leche en una tienda
> A una señora le roban el carro mientras compra leche en una tienda.

1. (ellos) / a tres jóvenes / suspender el permiso de manejar

_____

2. (los políticos) / a nosotros / ocultar los problemas económicos del país

_____

3. (ellos) / al pueblo / exigir más sacrificios

_____

4. (nuestro país) / a España / ir a comprar barcos

_____

5. (el gobierno) / a tres extranjeros / quitar la visa

_____

Verbs usually appearing with an indirect object pronoun

Certain verbs in Spanish are almost always used with an indirect object pronoun. This construction is different from the English equivalents of these verbs. The most common of these is **gustar**.

Me gusta la torta. *I like the cake.*	**Nos gusta** la torta. *We like the cake.*
Me gustan las galletas. *I like the cookies.*	**Nos gustan** las galletas. *We like the cookies.*
Te gusta la torta. *You like the cake.*	**Os gusta** la torta. *You like the cake.*
Te gustan las galletas. *You like the cookies.*	**Os gustan** las galletas. *You like the cookies.*
Le gusta la torta. *He, She likes / You like the cake.*	**Les gusta** la torta. *They/You like the cake.*
Le gustan las galletas. *He, She likes / You like the cookies.*	**Les gustan** las galletas. *They/You like the cookies.*

NOTA The verb agrees with the subject of the Spanish sentence, **torta** or **galletas**.

When the grammatical subject of a verb like **gustar** is an infinitive, **gustar** is always conjugated in third-person singular.

Me encanta patinar sobre el hielo.	*I love to ice skate.*
A mí **me gusta** más **esquiar.**	*I like skiing better.*

Verbs like **gustar**

agradarle a uno *to like something*
caerle bien/mal a uno *to like/dislike (usually a person)*
convenirle a uno *to suit someone, be good for someone*
desagradarle a uno *to dislike something, find something unpleasant*
encantarle a uno *to love something*
entusiasmarle a uno *to be excited about something*
faltarle a uno *to be missing something, not to have something*

fascinarle a uno *to love something, be fascinated by something*
hacerle falta a uno *to need something*
importarle a uno *to care about something, to mind*
interesarle a uno *to be interested in something*
quedarle a alguien *to have something left*
sobrarle a uno *to have more than enough of something*
tocarle a uno *to be someone's turn*
urgirle a uno *to be urgent for someone to do something*

¿Te interesa acompañarme a la exposición de arte?	*Would you be interested in accompanying me to the art show?*
Me encantaría. Me fascina mucho la pintura.	*I'd love to. I like painting a lot.*
Creo que **te convendría** salir un poco.	*I think it would be good for you to go out a little.*
Sé que **me hace falta,** pero **me sobra** trabajo.	*I know I need to, but I have too much work.*
Parece que no **te entusiasman** mucho estos juegos.	*It seems that you're not very excited about these games.*
Cada vez que **me toca a mí,** pierdo.	*Every time it's my turn, I lose.*

| ¿**Les hace falta** verla? | *Do you need to see her?* |
| Sí, **nos urge.** | *Yes, it is urgent that we do.* |

Phrases consisting of **a** + *the corresponding prepositional pronouns that emphasize or contrast indirect object pronouns* (see p. 316) are also used as short responses.

¿Cuánto dinero nos queda?	*How much money do we have left?*
A mí me quedan doscientos dólares. **¿Y a ti?**	*I have two hundred dollars left.* **How about you?**
Chicos, ¿a quién le gusta la torta de chocolate?	*Kids, who likes chocolate cake?*
¡A mí! ¡A mí! ¡A mí!	*I do! I do! I do!*

In the preceding examples, the phrase **¿Y a ti?** is short for **Y a ti, ¿cuánto dinero te queda?,** and the phrase **¡A mí!** is short for **A mí me gusta la torta de chocolate.**

Actividad 18 **En plural.** Cambie el sujeto de las oraciones al plural. Todos los verbos son del tipo **gustar.** No se olvide de hacer todos los cambios necesarios. Siga el modelo.

> MODELO Me gusta ese suéter.
> Me gustan esos suéteres.

1. Le encanta ese perfume.

   _____

2. Nos interesa esta novela.

   _____

3. Les queda un examen.

   _____

4. Te entusiasma la comedia.

   _____

5. Os importa la idea.

   _____

6. Me hace falta una guía.

   _____

7. Les fascina esta materia.

   _____

8. Le falta un cuaderno.

   _____

9. Nos agrada su plan.

   _____

En el futuro. Vuelva a escribir las oraciones con verbos como **gustar** usando la construcción **ir a** + *infinitivo*. Siga los modelos.

> MODELOS   Me gusta esa película.
> Me va a gustar esa película.
>
> Me gustan esas películas.
> Me van a gustar esas películas.

1. Nos importan sus problemas.

   _____

2. No les queda mucho dinero.

   _____

3. Le encanta visitar a sus abuelos.

   _____

4. No les sobra comida.

   _____

5. Os conviene viajar en tren.

   _____

6. Te fascinan esos cuadros.

   _____

7. Me entusiasman sus obras.

   _____

8. No le interesan esos programas.

   _____

Actividad 20 **¿Quién y a quién?** Conteste las preguntas escogiendo entre los pronombres sujetos y las frases con **a.** Siga el modelo.

> MODELO   ¿Quién estudia chino? (Yo. / A mí.)
> Yo.

1. ¿A quién le gusta jugar al baloncesto? (Él. / A él.)

   A él

2. ¿Quiénes vieron a los niños? (Ellos. / A ellos.)

   Ellos

3. ¿A Juana le quedan cincuenta dólares? (Ella no. / A ella no.)

   A ella no

4. ¿Conociste a Diana? (Yo no. / A mí no.)

   _Yo no_

5. ¿Comprendieron al profesor? (Nosotros sí. / A nosotros sí.)

   Nosotros sí

6. ¿A quién le interesan estos poemas? (Ud. / A Ud.)

   _A Ud._

7. ¿Te hace falta manejar? (Yo sí. / A mí sí.)

   A mí me hace falta. (A mí sí)

8. ¿Devolvieron los libros a la biblioteca? (Yo sí. / A mí sí.)

   _Yo sí_

Actividad 21 **Los Castellón planean un viaje.** Exprese en español la conversación que tienen los señores Castellón y sus tres hijos sobre el viaje que piensan hacer en el verano. Escriba oraciones usando los verbos como **gustar.**

1. Alicia: I'd like to take a trip to Spain.

   _____

2. Rafael: I'd love to visit my relatives in Venezuela and Argentina.

   _____

3. Lorenzo: I'd be interested in going camping in New Mexico or Arizona.

   _____

4. Nora: And I'd be fascinated to see Italy.

   _____

5. Carla: I'd be very enthusiastic about doing water sports.

   _____

6. Rafael: It would suit us to make a decision as soon as possible.

   _____

7. Lorenzo: We have more than enough suggestions. Let's draw lots! **(echar suertes)**

   _____

8. Nora: It's my turn first!

   _____

Other uses of the indirect object

The indirect object in Spanish is often the equivalent of the English possessive with parts of the body and articles of clothing. This is also true of reflexive pronouns.

¿**Te quito** el abrigo?	*Shall I help you take off your overcoat?*
No, gracias. Siempre **me haces daño** en el brazo cuando me lo quitas.	*No, thank you. You always hurt my arm when you help me take it off.*
Ven, Carlitos. **Te lavo** las manos.	*Come, Carlitos. I'll wash your hands.*
No, no. Yo mismo **me las lavo.**	*No, no. I'll wash them myself.*

The indirect object tells for whose benefit or for whose disadvantage something is done.

¿**Me haces** el almuerzo, mamá?	*Can you make my lunch for me, Mom?*
Sí, si **me llevas** las bolsas de comida a la cocina.	*Yes, if you carry the bags of food to the kitchen for me.*
Espero que no **nos** caiga otra vez la vecina con sus dos hijos.	*I hope the neighbor doesn't drop in on us again with her two children.*
Sí, la última vez esos dos diablos casi **nos** destruyeron la casa.	*Yes, the last time those two rascals almost destroyed our house.*
¡Y **nos** comieron todas las galletas que teníamos!	*And they ate up all the cookies that we had!*

The indirect object pronouns can be added to certain impersonal expressions.

Es difícil caminar cuando nieva.	*It's hard to walk when it snows.*
Me es difícil caminar cuando nieva.	*It's hard for me to walk when it snows.*
Es necesario estudiar más.	*It's necessary to study more.*
Nos es necesario estudiar más.	*It's necessary for us to study more.*

The indirect object pronoun can be added to a **se** construction with certain verbs to express *unplanned occurrences*. These constructions focus on the object affected rather than on the person involved.

acabársele a uno *to run out of*	**olvidársele a uno** *to forget*
caérsele a uno *to drop*	**perdérsele a uno** *to lose*
descomponérsele a uno *to have something break down*	**quebrársele a uno** *to break*
	quedársele a uno *to leave something behind*
hacérsele tarde a uno *to get/grow late*	**rompérsele a uno** *to break*
ocurrírsele a uno *to dawn on, get the idea of*	

Veo que **se te rompieron** los anteojos.	*I see that you broke your glasses.*
Sí, **se me cayeron** en la calle.	*Yes, I dropped them in the street.*
¿Cómo **se les ocurrió** venir ayer?	*How did they get the idea to come yesterday?*
Se les había olvidado que la reunión era mañana.	*They had forgotten that the meeting was tomorrow.*
Se nos está acabando la gasolina. Tenemos que comprar más.	*We're running out of gas. We have to buy some more.*
Pero **se me quedó** la tarjeta de crédito en casa.	*But I left my credit card at home.*

Sucesos inesperados. Complete las oraciones con los verbos indicados. Todas las oraciones expresan la idea de un suceso inesperado. Use el pretérito de los verbos indicados y *el complemento directo + construcción con* **se.**

1. No pudimos hacer los sándwiches. (acabársele)

   _____ el pan.

2. Plácido no pudo entrar en su casa. (perdérsele)

   _____ las llaves.

3. No le mandé una tarjeta a Beatriz. (olvidársele)

   _____ la fecha de su cumpleaños.

4. ¡Pero estáis mojadísimos! (quedársele)

   ¿_____ el paraguas en casa?

5. ¡Cuidado de no cortarte la mano! (rompérsele)

   ¿Cómo _____ los vasos?

6. ¡Pasando por Madrid, Uds. no visitaron a los tíos! (ocurrírsele)

   ¿Ni _____ llamarlos?

7. Los niños están recogiendo todos los papeles en el suelo. (caérsele)

   ¿Cómo _____?

Prevenir contra lo inesperado. Escriba las oraciones previniendo a unas personas contra ciertas cosas. Fíjese que el imperativo de los verbos como **acabársele** es un mandato indirecto. Siga el modelo.

> MODELO   tú / no caérsele / los platos
> Que no se te caigan los platos.

1. Uds. / no olvidársele / asistir a la conferencia

   _____

2. él / no perdérsele / los anteojos

   _____

3. Ud. / no acabársele / la paciencia

   _____

4. vosotros / no quedársele / los cheques de viajero en el hotel

   _____

5. ella / no rompérsele / las estatuillas de porcelana (*china figurines*)

   _____

6. tú / no ocurrírsele / tales cosas

_____

7. ellos / no caérsele / la torta de chocolate

_____

Expresar en español. Exprese los diálogos en español usando la construcción del suceso inesperado.

1. Did you **(Ud.)** lose your wallet?
   No, I had left it at home.

_____

_____

2. They're running out of pastries at the bake shop.
   Didn't it occur to you **(tú)** to buy them this morning?

_____

_____

3. Be **(Uds.)** careful! You're going to drop your iPod!
   We already broke it!

_____

_____

4. I forgot to pick Tere and Leo up.
   Didn't it dawn on you **(tú)** that they were waiting all night?

_____

_____

Double object pronouns

In Spanish a direct object pronoun and an indirect object pronoun can appear together with a verb. The indirect object pronoun precedes the direct object pronoun.

Necesito mil pesos. ¿**Me los** prestas?	_I need a thousand pesos. Will you lend_ **_them to me_**_?_
Te los presto con tal de que **me los** devuelvas la semana que viene.	_I'll lend **them to you** as long as you return **them to me** next week._
Nos interesa tu colección de sellos. ¿**Nos la** enseñas?	_We're interested in your stamp collection. Will you show **it to us**?_
Claro. Ahora **se la** traigo.	_Of course. I'll bring **it to you** right now._

When a third-person indirect object pronoun (**le** or **les**) precedes a third-person direct object pronoun (**lo, la, los, las**), the indirect object pronoun changes to **se**.

le/les + **lo**   → **se lo**

le/les + **la**   → **se la**

le/les + **los** → **se los**

le/les + **las** → **se las**

Double object pronouns cannot be separated from each other. They follow the same rules of position as single object pronouns. When double object pronouns are added to an infinitive, present participle, or affirmative command, an accent mark is always added, even to infinitives and command forms of one syllable: **Quiero dártelo, Dámelo.**

¿Cuándo le va a entregar Ud. el informe al jefe?	*When are you going to submit the report to the boss?*
Ya **se lo** he entregado.	*I've already submitted **it to him**.*
Hay un problema que no comprendo.	*There's a problem that I don't understand.*
Muéstramelo. A ver si **te lo** puedo explicar.	*Show **it to me**. Let's see if I can explain **it to you**.*
or	
A ver si puedo **explicártelo.**	
¿Dónde están nuestras maletas?	*Where are our suitcases?*
El botones **nos las** está subiendo ahora.	*The bellhop is bringing **them** up **for us** now.*
or	
El botones está subié**ndonoslas** ahora.	

Sentences with **se** out of context can be ambiguous. Context or a phrase consisting of **a** + *prepositional pronoun* clarifies to whom **se** refers.

¿La niñita se puso los zapatos?	*Did the little girl put on her shoes?*
Sí, **se los** puso. (**se** = reflexive pronoun referring to **la niña**)	*Yes, she put **them** on.*
¿La niñita se puso los zapatos?	*Did the little girl put on her shoes?*
No, **yo se los puse.** (**se** = indirect object pronoun referring to **la niña**)	*No, I put **them** on (**for her**).*
¿El gerente y la directora tienen la copia del informe?	*Do the manager and the director have the copy of the report?*
Sí, **a él se la** mandé por correo electrónico y **a ella se la** di personalmente.	*Yes, I sent **it to him** by e-mail, and I gave **it to her** personally.*

Actividad 25 **Dos pronombres de complemento directo e indirecto.** Escriba las oraciones cambiando el sustantivo de complemento directo a un pronombre y haga todos los cambios necesarios. Algunas oraciones tienen dos respuestas posibles. Siga el modelo.

> MODELO Les entregaré las cartas el martes.
> Se las entregaré el martes.

1. Me dijeron los motivos.

   _____

2. Le hemos puesto los zapatos.

   _____

3. Está explicándoles la idea.

   _____

4. Os muestro el paquete.

   _____

5. ¿Te darían una beca?

   _____

6. Les cuentas los chismes.

   _____

7. Nos ha hecho las chuletas de cordero.

   _____

8. Devuélvame el cortacésped (*lawn mower*).

   _____

9. Me estaban enseñando las fotos.

   _____

10. ¿A quién le vendiste tu velero (*sailboat*)?

    _____

11. Os había escrito una tarjeta postal (*postcard*).

    _____

12. ¿Nos prestarás los DVDs?

    _____

13. Apréndanse las fechas de memoria.

    _____

14. ¿Estáis preguntándole el por qué?

    _____

15. Le pusieron una multa.

    _____

16. Les preparó carne y arroz.

    _____

17. Estará bajándome el equipaje.

    _____

18. Vendámosles la casa.

    _____

19. Estuvimos trayéndole los periódicos ingleses.

    _____

20. Te apagaré la televisión.

    _____

Actividad 26 **Algo pasará. / Algo pasó.** Vuelva a escribir las oraciones usando la construcción **ir a** + *infinitivo* o **acabar de** + *infinitivo*. Haga los cambios necesarios respecto a los verbos y a los pronombres de complemento directo e indirecto. Escriba cada oración de dos maneras. Siga los modelos.

MODELOS	Se los doy. (ir a)	(acabar de)
	Voy a dárselos.	Acabo de dárselos.
	Se los voy a dar.	Se los acabo de dar.

1. Me la traen. (ir a)

   _____

   _____

2. Te lo dice. (acabar de)

   _____

   _____

3. Se los hacemos. (ir a)

   _____

   _____

4. Os las pongo. (acabar de)

   _____

   _____

5. Se lo muestra. (ir a)

   _____

   _____

6. Nos la compráis. (acabar de)

   _____

   _____

7. Me los cuentas. (ir a)

   _____

   _____

8. Se las arreglo. (acabar de)

   _____

   _____

9. Te la suben. (ir a)

   _____

   _____

10. Os lo damos. (acabar de)

_____

_____

11. Se lo describimos. (ir a)

_____

_____

12. Se la prueba. (acabar de)

_____

_____

13. Te los limpia. (ir a)

_____

_____

14. Se las encuentro. (acabar de)

_____

_____

15. Me la piden. (ir a)

_____

_____

Actividad 27 **¡Mami, papi, cómprenmelo!** Esta niña Rita vuelve loca a toda su familia. No deja de pedir cosas y, por desgracia, sus familiares se lo conceden todo. Por eso es una niña mal criada (*spoiled brat*). Escriba diálogos entre Rita y sus familiares en los cuales Ud. emplea los pronombres de complemento directo e indirecto con mandatos y con los verbos en el presente. Siga el modelo.

MODELO	Mami / comprarme / una bicicleta
Rita	—Mami, cómpramela.
Mamá	—Sí, hijita, te la compro.

1. Papi / darme / bombones

   Rita   —Papi, _____.

   Papá   —Sí, hijita, _____.

2. Mami / comprarme / canicas (*marbles*)

   Rita   —Mami, _____.

   Mamá   —Sí, hijita, _____.

3. Juan / prestarme / tu patineta (*scooter*)

   Rita   —Juan, _____.

   Juan   —Sí, hermanita, _____.

4. Amparo / comprarme / un televisor de plasma

   Rita   —Amparo, _____.

   Amparo   —Sí, hermanita, _____.

5. Abuelo / regalarme / un caballo

   Rita   —Abuelo, _____.

   Abuelo   —Sí, hijita, _____.

6. Elvira / servirme / todo el helado de chocolate

   Rita   —Elvira, _____.

   Elvira   —Sí, hermanita, _____.

7. Tía / ponerme / tus joyas de oro

   Rita   —Tía, _____.

   Tía   —Sí, hijita, _____.

8. Abuela / traerme / mi muñeca

   Rita   —Abuela, _____.

   Abuela   —Sí, hijita, _____.

Actividad 28   **¿Las cosas claras?** Exprese las oraciones en inglés aclarando a quién(es) se refiere el ambiguo **se.** Unas oraciones pueden tener más de una sola traducción.

1. **a.** Se la dio Adela.

   _____

   b. Se la dio a Adela.

   _____

2. **a.** Se lo dijeron los profesores.

   _____

   b. Se lo dijeron a los profesores.

   _____

3. **a.** Se las prestó el vecino.

   _____

   b. Se las prestó al vecino.

   _____

4. **a.** Se los pidieron mis colegas.

   _____

   b. Se los pidieron a mis colegas.

   _____

5. **a.** Se la devolvió Laura.

_____

b. Se la devolvió a Laura.

_____

Special uses of the object pronouns

The object pronoun **lo** is used to replace a clause or an adjective or a predicate noun of both genders and numbers. This **lo** has no equivalent in English.

Los Ochoa se mudaron a Ecuador. | *The Ochoas moved to Ecuador.*
Sí, **lo sé.** (**lo** = que se mudaron a Ecuador) | *Yes, I know.*

¿María Elena es simpática? | *Is María Elena nice?*
Sí, **lo es.** (**lo** = simpática) | *Yes, she is.*

¿Son profesoras Marta y Sara? | *Are Marta and Sara teachers?*
Lo fueron. Ahora son abogadas. (**lo** = profesoras) | *They were. Now they're lawyers.*

Nouns that follow forms of **hay** are considered direct objects and must be replaced by direct object pronouns.

¿Hay **papel**? | *Is there any paper?*
Sí, **lo** hay. | *Yes, there is.*

¿Hay **manzanas**? | *Are there any apples?*
No, no **las** hay. | *No, there aren't any.*

The object pronouns **la** and **las** appear in many idioms without any antecedent. They must be memorized as part of the idiom.

---

apañárselas *to manage, get by*
arreglárselas *to manage, get by*
componérselas *to manage, get by*
echárselas de + *adjetivo, sustantivo* *to boast of being*

habérselas con *to be up against, face, have to deal with*
tenérsela jurada a uno *to have it in for someone*
vérselas con *to explain oneself to*

Creo que el profesor Méndez **me la tiene jurada.** | *I think Professor Méndez **has it in for me.***

No te preocupes. **Te las arreglarás** bien en su clase. | *Don't worry. **You'll manage** fine in his class.*

Óscar siempre **se las echa de rico.** | *Óscar always **boasts of being rich.***
Y no tiene dónde caerse muerto. No sé cómo **se las apaña.** | *And he doesn't have a penny. I don't know how **he manages.***

Esta profesora tiene que **habérselas con** una clase mediocre. | *This teacher has **to face** a class of mediocre students.*
Y si no hacen progreso, tiene que **vérselas con** el director. | *And if they don't do well, she has to **explain why** to the principal.*

Actividad 29   **Expresar en español.**   Exprese las oraciones en español.

1. —Do you **(tú)** know if the stores are open?
    —I couldn't **(sabría)** tell you.

    —_____

    —_____

2. I don't know how Raúl manages. He thinks that everyone has it in for him.

    _____

3. Any student who behaves badly will have to explain himself or herself to me.

    _____

4. —Are Ramón and Serena engineers?
    —No, they're not. They're programmers.
    —I think they're very intelligent.
    —Yes, they are.

    —_____

    —_____

    —_____

    —_____

5. Mariana couldn't put on her coat, so I helped her with it.

    _____

6. —Should I ask Alicia and Pablo for their history notes?
    —Ask **(tú)** him for them. Don't ask her for them.

    —_____

    —_____

7. —Javier, please lend me your physics notes.
    —Pili, I gave them to you on Thursday.
    —I'm sorry. I lost them.

    —_____

    —_____

    —_____

Actividad 30   **Actividad oral.**   Hable de este año escolar con unos compañeros. Háganse preguntas sobre libros, exámenes, tareas, amigos y actividades. Usen pronombres de complemento directo e indirecto en las respuestas.

332-345

1A, 5, 6, 7, 9, 10

The relative pronoun que

Relative pronouns are used to join two sentences into a single sentence. The clause introduced by the relative pronoun is the relative clause. A relative clause modifies a noun in the same way that an adjective does. This is why it is also called an adjective clause. The noun that the relative clause refers to is called the *antecedent*.

The relative pronoun **que** can refer to persons or things and can be either the subject or direct object of the verb of the relative clause it introduces. **Que** can refer to both singular and plural nouns and is the most common relative pronoun in everyday conversation.

el hombre **que** trabaja aquí (*que refers to* **hombre** *and is the subject of the clause*)	*the man **who** works here*
los paquetes **que** están en la mesa (*que refers to* **paquetes** *and is the subject of the clause*)	*the packages **that** are on the table*
los abogados **que** conozco (*que refers to* **abogados** *and is the direct object of the clause*)	*the lawyers **whom** I know*
la casa **que** compré (*que refers to* **casa** *and is the direct object of the clause*)	*the house **that** I bought*

In English, the relative pronoun can be omitted when it is the object of the verb: *the lawyers I know, the house I bought*. In Spanish, **que** is never omitted.

When **nadie** or **alguien** is the antecedent of a relative clause, **que** is used as the subject or direct object of the clause. When **todo** is the antecedent, it is followed by **lo que** to express *all that*.

Si hay **alguien que** comprende, es él.	*If there's **someone who** understands, it is he.*
No, él no comprende tampoco. No hay **nadie que** comprenda.	*No, he doesn't understand either. There's **no one who** understands.*
Esto es **todo lo que** tengo.	*This is **all (everything)** I have.*

Actividad 1 **Seamos precisos.** Conteste las preguntas de su amiga con una cláusula relativa para que ella sepa de qué objeto o persona se trata. Siga los modelos.

> MODELOS ¿Qué libro quieres? (El libro está en la estantería.)
> Quiero el libro que está en la estantería.
>
> ¿Qué suéter lleva Paula? (Su novio le compró el suéter en Ecuador.)
> Lleva el suéter que su novio le compró en Ecuador.

1. ¿A qué médico ves? (Tiene su consulta en aquel edificio.)

   _____

2. ¿Qué película quieres ver? (La película se rodó en Perú.)

   _____

3. ¿Qué revistas te gustan más? (Las revistas se publican en Asunción.)

   _____

4. ¿Qué restaurante prefieres? (El restaurante sirve comida del Caribe.)

   _____

5. ¿A qué peluquería vas? (La peluquería está en la calle del Conde.)

   _____

6. ¿Qué libros queréis comprar? (La profesora nos recomendó los libros.)

   _____

7. ¿Qué ordenador usas? (Mis padres me regalaron el ordenador para Navidad.)

   _____

8. ¿Con qué secretaria hablaban Uds.? (Contratamos a esa secretaria la semana pasada.)

   _____

9. ¿Qué mecánico repara tu coche? (El vecino conoce al mecánico.)

   _____

10. ¿Qué carta estás leyendo? (Silvia me mandó esta carta ayer.)

    _____

11. ¿A qué tienda de vídeos van Mirián y Alejo? (La tienda de vídeos queda al lado de la pizzería.)

    _____

12. ¿Qué discos compactos escuchan Uds.? (Claudia nos prestó los discos compactos.)

    _____

Actividad 2 **Más precisiones.** La persona que habla usa cláusulas relativas para indicar exactamente a qué objeto o persona se refiere. Siga el modelo.

> MODELO ¿Qué computadora?
> (Olivia la usa.) La computadora que usa Olivia.
> (Tiene mucha memoria.) La computadora que tiene mucha memoria.

1. ¿Qué profesora?

   (Todos los estudiantes la admiran.)

   _____

   (Enseña francés y español.)

   _____

   (Acaba de casarse.)

   _____

   (Mis padres la conocen.)

   _____

2. ¿Qué casa?

   (Juana y Rafael la compraron.)

   _____

   (Tiene patio y piscina.)

   _____

   (La construyeron en 2005.)

   _____

   (Es de ladrillos.)

   _____

3. ¿Qué regalo?

   (Mis hermanos y yo lo recibimos hace dos días.)

   _____

   (Mis tíos nos lo mandaron.)

   _____

   (Te lo enseñé ayer.)

   _____

   (Nos gustó tanto.)

   _____

4. ¿Qué restaurante?

   (Nuestros amigos cubanos lo abrieron el año pasado.)

   _____

   (Sirve comida cubana auténtica.)

   _____

   (Tiene fotos de La Habana.)

   _____

   (Se encuentra en la Calle Ocho.)

   _____

5. ¿Qué senadora?

   (Era jefa de una empresa.)

   _____

   (Prometió reducir los impuestos.)

   _____

   (Es casada con un ingeniero.)

   _____

   (La eligieron hace dos años.)

   _____

The relative pronoun **quien**

When **que** is the direct object of the verb in the relative clause and it has an antecedent that is a person, it can be replaced by **a quien** or, if the antecedent is plural, **a quienes. A quien, a quienes** are somewhat more formal than **que.**

El empleado **a quien** conocíamos ya no trabaja aquí.	*The employee (**whom**) we knew doesn't work here any longer.*
Busqué a los estudiantes **a quienes** vi ayer, pero no los encontré.	*I looked for the students (**whom**) I saw yesterday, but I couldn't find them.*

Quien and **quienes** can also serve as the subject of a relative clause if that clause is set off by commas (nonrestrictive clause).

José Pedro fue a hablar con la profesora Umbral, **quien** siempre tiene tiempo para sus estudiantes.	*José Pedro went to speak with Professor Umbral, **who** always has time for her students.*

Actividad 3 ...**a quien** / ...**a quienes.** Combine las oraciones en una con **a quien** o **a quienes** para describir a ciertas personas. Siga el modelo.

> MODELO Las chicas vinieron a vernos. / Las conocimos en el teatro.
> Las chicas a quienes conocimos en el teatro vinieron a vernos.

1. Mis primos están de vacaciones en Estados Unidos. / Los vi en Caracas hace dos años.

   _____

   _____

2. La pintora sólo pinta acuarelas. / La vieron en la exposición.

   _____

   _____

3. La muchacha me dio las gracias hoy. / Yo le di un regalo ayer.

   _____

   _____

4. Los amigos no quisieron salir. / Los llamamos a la una de la mañana.

   _____

   _____

5. Los vecinos se habían mudado. / Los buscábamos.

   _____

   _____

6. El dependiente ya no trabaja en esta tienda. / Ud. lo conoció el año pasado.

   _____

   _____

7. El señor es mi profesor de cálculo. / Lo encontraste en la calle.

   _____

   _____

Actividad 4 **El profesor, quien...** Combine las oraciones con **quien/quienes** para describir a algunas personas que están en la universidad. Siga el modelo.

> MODELO Cajal, Toledano y Puche aprobaron sus exámenes. / Ellos son compañeros de cuarto en una residencia universitaria.
> Cajal, Toledano y Puche, quienes son compañeros de cuarto en una residencia universitaria, aprobaron sus exámenes.

Vocabulario

La universidad

aprobar (o → ue) *to pass*
los archivos *files*
el/la ayudante *assistant*
el congreso *conference*
el/la decano/a *dean*
dictar una conferencia *to deliver
a lecture*

jubilarse *to retire*
el salón de actos *assembly hall,
auditorium*
el/la secretario/a general
registrar
el tribunal de exámenes *board
of examiners*

1. La señora Mora es secretaria general de la universidad. / Ella se encarga de los archivos.

   _____

   _____

2. El profesor Uriarte enseña química. / Él asistió a un congreso en Boston.

   _____

   _____

3. Los estudiantes tienen que entregar una tesis. / Ellos se gradúan en junio.

   _____

   _____

4. La doctora Arrieta tiene dos ayudantes de laboratorio. / Ella figura en el tribunal de exámenes.

   _____

   _____

5. Estos decanos trabajan en la Facultad de Ingeniería. / Ellos planean el programa.

   _____

   _____

6. El rector de la universidad es abogado. / Él dicta conferencias de ciencias políticas.

   _____

   _____

7. Algunos estudiantes de medicina fueron a hablar con el profesor Quijano. / Él estaba ya en el salón de actos.

   _____

   _____

8. La profesora Arenas se jubila el año que viene. / Ella hace investigaciones de biología.

_____

_____

Actividad 5 **¿Sujeto u objeto?** Complete las oraciones escogiendo **quien/es** si se refiere al sujeto de una cláusula relativa o **a quien/es** si se refiere al complemento directo del verbo. Subraye su respuesta.

1. Te presento al señor (quien / a quien) conocimos ayer.

2. Llamemos a aquella señorita (quien / a quien) siempre está dispuesta a ayudarnos.

3. Voy a la casa de los señores (a quienes / quienes) compraron la casa de enfrente.

4. ¿Conocéis a los chicos (a quienes / quienes) invité a la fiesta?

5. Esos arquitectos, (a quienes / quienes) trabajan en el rascacielos nuevo, son mis cuñados.

6. ¿Comprende Ud. a la locutora (quien / a quien) yo no comprendo bien?

7. Jorge llama a su novia (a quien / quien) quiere muchísimo.

8. La novia de Jorge está enamorada de Alfredo (quien / a quien) es el mejor amigo de Jorge.

The relative pronouns **el que, el cual**

The relative pronouns **el que** and **el cual** have four forms each: **el que, la que, los que, las que; el cual, la cual, los cuales, las cuales.** They can replace **que** or **a quien / a quienes** when the antecedent is animate and the relative pronoun is the object of the verb.

los españoles **a los que** he conocido	_the Spaniards_ (**whom**) _I met_
el electricista **al que** he llamado	_the electrician_ (**whom**) _I called_
la vecina **a la que** no soportamos	_the neighbor_ (**whom**) _we can't stand_

In nonrestrictive clauses (those set off by commas), **el que** and **el cual** can function as both subject and object and can refer to either people or things. Since **el que** and **el cual** show gender and number distinctions, they are used to avoid confusion when there is more than one possible antecedent for **que** or **quien.**

El amigo de mi prima, **el cual / el que** estudia física, llega mañana de Caracas.	_My cousin's friend,_ **who** (_refers to the male friend_) _studies physics, is arriving from Caracas tomorrow._
El amigo de mi prima, **la cual / la que** estudia física, llega mañana de Caracas.	_My cousin's friend,_ **who** (_refers to the female cousin_) _studies physics, is arriving from Caracas tomorrow._

The neuter relative pronouns **lo que** and **lo cual** refer to a preceding clause or idea. They only occur in clauses set off by commas (nonrestrictive clauses).

Su hija le dijo que no quería seguir estudiando biología, **lo que / lo cual** no le gustó para nada al señor Lara.

*His daughter told him that she didn't want to continue studying biology, **which** Mr. Lara didn't like at all.*

Actividad 6 **¿El que o lo que?** Complete las oraciones con la forma correcta del pronombre **el que** o **lo que.**

1. Me cayeron muy bien los turistas a _____ conocimos en la excursión.

2. Los Merino nos invitaron a pasar el fin de semana en su barco, _____ nos agradó mucho.

3. La hermana de Federico, _____ vive en Bogotá, estudiará administración de empresas en Estados Unidos.

4. Nadie vio llegar a Isabel, _____ nos sorprendió.

5. ¡Por fin subimos en la montaña rusa, _____ nos dejó medio muertos!

6. El amigo de mi hermano, _____ trabaja en Barcelona, se casará en mayo.

7. Esas chicas tan antipáticas con _____ saliste son mis primas.

Actividad 7 **¿El cual o lo cual?** Ahora reemplace los pronombres relativos de la **Actividad 6** con la forma correcta de **el cual** o **lo cual.**

1. Me cayeron muy bien los turistas a _____ conocimos en la excursión.

2. Los Merino nos invitaron a pasar el fin de semana en su barco, _____ nos agradó mucho.

3. La hermana de Federico, _____ vive en Bogotá, estudiará administración de empresas en Estados Unidos.

4. Nadie vio llegar a Isabel, _____ nos sorprendió.

5. ¡Por fin subimos en la montaña rusa, _____ nos dejó medio muertos!

6. El amigo de mi hermano, _____ trabaja en Barcelona, se casará en mayo.

7. Esas chicas tan antipáticas con _____ saliste son mis primas.

Relative pronouns after prepositions

Que may be used after the prepositions **a, de,** and **con** when the antecedent is not a person.

Éste es el tema **a que** nos limitamos.	*This is the subject to **which** we will limit ourselves.*
¿Comprendes los problemas **de que** te hablé?	*Do you understand the problems **that** I spoke to you about?*
Mi abuelo me mostró el bastón **con que** camina.	*My grandfather showed me the cane he walks with.*

En que is common after expressions of time and to express imprecise location.

el mes **en que** se fueron	*the month they went away*
un siglo **en que** la vida era muy difícil	*a century **in which** life was very difficult*
el edificio **en que** trabajamos	*the building we work **in***
la materia **en que** se interesa	*the subject she's interested **in***

The **en** of **en que** can be omitted after expressions of time.

El día **(en) que** la vi.	*The day I saw her.*

When **en** expresses physical location inside an object, **en el que / en la que / en los que / en las que** is used.

Abrió la gaveta **en la que** había metido las llaves.	*He opened the drawer **in which** he had put the keys.*

Donde can replace **en** + *relative pronoun* to express location. See page 342 of this chapter.

Abrió la gaveta **donde** había metido las llaves.	*He opened the drawer **in which** he had put the keys.*

Quien/Quienes or **el que** are used after prepositions for human antecedents. Some speakers also use **el cual.**

el tío **a quien / al que** Pablito se parece	*the uncle **(whom)** Pablito looks like*
la chica **con quien / con la que** se casó mi hermano	*the girl **(whom)** my brother married*
los amigos **de quienes / de los que** me fío	*the friends **(whom)** I trust*

The relative pronoun **que** is not used after prepositions other than **a, de, con,** and **en. Quien/Quienes** may be used for people. **El que** and **el cual** may be used for both people and things. **El cual** is especially common after prepositions of more than one syllable (**contra, desde, durante, hacia, mediante, para, según, sobre**) and with compound prepositions (**a causa de, delante de, detrás de, encima de, debajo de, por medio de, en frente de, al frente de, antes de, después de**).

una guerra **durante la cual** cayeron muchos soldados	*a war **during which** many soldiers died*
el edificio **delante del cual** la vi	*the building **in front of which** I saw her*
los problemas **a causa de los cuales** dejé de estudiar	*the problems **because of which** I stopped studying*
los señores **para quienes (para los que / para los cuales)** trabajo	*the men **for whom** I work*
las ancianas al lado **de quienes (al lado de las cuales)** vivimos	*the elderly women next door **to whom** we live*

Actividad 8 **Les enseño mi ciudad.** Ud. les enseña su ciudad a unos amigos extranjeros. Usando la información indicada complete las oraciones con una cláusula relativa. Siga el modelo.

> MODELO Hay un festival de teatro durante el verano.
> El verano es la estación <u>durante la cual hay un festival de teatro.</u>

1. Hay varias líneas de metro debajo de estas calles.

   Éstas son las calles _____.

2. Vivimos cerca de la facultad.

   Allí ven la facultad _____.

3. Hay un restaurante en frente de ese cine.

   Allí está el cine _____.

4. Solemos pasar los domingos aquí.

   Ven y te presento a los muchachos _____.

5. Hay una exposición de arte en medio de la plaza.

   Ésta es la plaza _____.

6. Hay un mercado al aire libre detrás de aquellos edificios.

   Aquéllos son los edificios _____.

7. Ahora caminamos hacia un barrio muy antiguo.

   El barrio _____.

8. Unas tiendas elegantes se encuentran al otro lado de este río.

   Éste es el río _____.

Actividad 9 **«En» de varios significados.** Complete las frases con el pronombre relativo correcto. Recuerde que hay una diferencia entre el **en** concreto que significa **dentro de** y el **en** que expresa una relación abstracta.

1. los libros _____ me intereso (en que / en los que)

2. el armario _____ cuelgo mi ropa (en que / en el que)

3. la exactitud _____ insiste el profesor (en que / en la que)

4. el arreglo _____ quedaron (en que / en el que)

5. el bolsillo _____ tengo mis llaves (en que / en el que)

6. los cuadernos _____ escribo (en que / en los que)

7. los métodos _____ creemos (en que / en los que)

8. las bolsas _____ llevaban la comida (en que / en las que)

The relative pronoun **cuyo**

Cuyo means *whose*. It agrees in gender and number with the following noun.

La doctora Paredes es la profesora **cuyas clases** cursé con mucho provecho.	*Dr. Paredes is the teacher **whose classes** I took and benefited greatly from.*
Ése es el autor **cuyos libros** leemos en la clase de literatura.	*That's the author **whose books** we read in literature class.*
Él es un hombre sobre **cuya vida** se comenta mucho.	*He's a man about **whose life** people comment a lot.*

Donde as a relative pronoun

Donde is used after prepositions to refer to a place. It can also replace **en el que** when the relative pronoun refers to a concrete place. As a relative pronoun, **donde** does not take a written accent.

la avenida **donde** hay muchos cibercafés	*the avenue **on which / where** there are many Internet cafés*
la puerta **por donde** salieron	*the door **through which** they went out*
la playa **hacia donde** caminábamos	*the beach **toward which** we were walking*

Actividad 10 **Cuyo.** Complete las oraciones usando la forma correcta del pronombre relativo **cuyo.**

1. Ésta es la nueva cantante _____ canciones han ganado muchos premios.

2. Éstos son los señores _____ hijos asisten a la universidad con los nuestros.

3. Tengo que buscar a la persona _____ coche está estacionado delante de mi garaje.

4. Quieren conocer al compositor _____ sinfonía será estrenada (*premiered*) el sábado.

5. Habla con tu vecino _____ perro ladra toda la noche.

6. Se habla mucho de la profesora de arqueología

   _____ clases son tan interesantes.

7. Es un país _____ historia no se estudia lo suficiente.

8. Ésos son los técnicos _____ equipos han llegado al campeonato.

Actividad 11   **Expresar en inglés.** Exprese las oraciones en inglés.

1. Ahora sabes la razón por la cual me enfadé.

   _____

2. Vivíamos en un barrio donde había muchas tiendas.

   _____

3. Allí a la derecha está la puerta por donde entran y salen los actores.

   _____

4. Yo no entiendo los motivos por los cuales el sindicato (*union*) declaró la huelga (*strike*).

   _____

5. Mis amigos no me dijeron para donde iban.

   _____

6. Son las horas durante las cuales Menchu hace su tarea.

   _____

7. Aquí está el quiosco detrás del cual Sergio y Sol quedaron en verse.

   _____

8. ¿Uds. conocen a los amigos con quienes salí anoche?

   _____

9. Te presentaré al joven cuyo padre era mi profesor de mercadeo.

   _____

10. Raquela no nos invitó a su fiesta, lo cual nos sorprendió.

    _____

Actividad 12   **Actividad oral.** Invente un acertijo (*riddle*) para un compañero / una compañera de clase. Las pistas (*hints*) se formularán con cláusulas relativas: **Es algo que... , Es alguien quien... , Es un lugar donde... , Es una persona con quien...** Dé cinco pistas. ¡A ver si su compañero/a adivina!

PARTE III

Adverbs and Prepositions

21 Adverbs

Forms of adverbs

Most Spanish adverbs are formed by adding **-mente** to the feminine form of the adjective. The Spanish suffix **-mente** corresponds to the English adverbial suffix *-ly*.

MASCULINE	FEMININE	ADVERB
histórico *historic*	histórica	históricamente *historically*
intenso *intense*	intensa	intensamente *intensely*
lento *slow*	lenta	lentamente *slowly*
cariñoso *loving*	cariñosa	cariñosamente *lovingly*
profundo *deep*	profunda	profundamente *deeply*
serio *serious*	seria	seriamente *seriously*

Adjectives that do not have a distinct feminine form add **-mente** to the masculine/feminine singular.

amable *kind*	→ amablemente *kindly*
fácil *easy*	→ fácilmente *easily*
feliz *happy*	→ felizmente *happily*
inteligente *intelligent*	→ inteligentemente *intelligently*
triste *sad*	→ tristemente *sadly*

Several adverbs either have irregular forms or are identical to the corresponding adjectives.

bueno(a) *good*	→	bien *well*
malo(a) *bad*	→	mal *badly*
mejor *better*	→	mejor *better*
peor *worse*	→	peor *worse*

Many adverbs of quantity have no suffix but are identical to the masculine singular form of the adjective.

mucho	demasiado	más
poco	tanto	menos

Adverbs referring to loudness and softness have no ending but are identical to the masculine singular form of the adjective.

hablar alto/bajo *to speak loudly, softly*
hablar fuerte *to speak loudly*

Some adverbs have alternate forms that are the same as the masculine singular form of the adjective.

El tren corre rápidamente. ⎫
El tren corre rápido. ⎭ *The train moves quickly.*

Masculine singular adjectives that function as adverbs are more commonly used in Latin America than in Spain.

La niña dibuja muy bonito. *The girl draws very beautifully.*
¡Qué lindo juegan los niños! *How nicely the children play!*

NOTA

Solamente *only* has the alternate form **sólo.**

Sólo a ti te lo digo. *I'm telling only you.*

Actividad I **Para describir acciones.** Escriba los adverbios que corresponden a los adjetivos. Siga el modelo.

MODELO	maravilloso
	maravillosamente

1. alegre _____

2. descuidado _____

3. cruel _____

4. artístico _____

5. normal _____

6. abierto _____

7. franco _____

8. nervioso _____

9. evidente _____

10. responsable _____

11. débil _____

12. verdadero _____

13. torpe (*clumsy*) _____

14. violento _____

15. perspicaz (*perceptive*) _____

16. burlón (*mocking*) _____

17. comercial   _____

18. sagaz (*wise*)   _____

19. honrado   _____

20. humilde   _____

21. difícil   _____

22. admirable   _____

23. estupendo   _____

24. afectuoso   _____

25. vulgar   _____

Actividad 2   **¿Cómo hablaron?** Escriba oraciones que describan cómo algunas personas hablaron en ciertas situaciones. Siga el modelo.

> MODELO   Marisol habló. ¿Fue sincera?
> Sí, habló sinceramente.

1. Hernán explicó el motivo. ¿Estaba nervioso?

    _____

2. Matías pidió disculpas. (*apologized*) ¿Fue honesto?

    _____

3. Anita y Bárbara contaron sus problemas. ¿Estaban tristes?

    _____

4. Ud. se enojó con un compañero de clase. ¿Estuvo furioso?

    _____

5. La señorita Cortés se quejó. ¿Estaba malhumorada (*in a bad mood*)?

    _____

6. Uds. contestaron la pregunta. ¿Estuvieron incómodos (*embarrassed*)?

    _____

7. Hablaste por teléfono. ¿Estabas distraído?

    _____

8. Gladis habló después del accidente. ¿Estuvo incoherente?

    _____

PARTE III

Adverbs of manner

Adverbs of manner (adverbs that tell how something is done), such as the ones presented in the previous section, come right after the verbs they modify or as close after the verb as possible.

Hiciste **mal** el trabajo.	*You did the work **poorly.***
¿Qué dices? Lo hice **bien.** De todas formas, lo hice **mejor** que tú.	*What are you talking about? I did it **well.** Anyway, I did it **better** than you did.*
Mentira. Yo trabajé **cuidadosamente.**	*Not true. I worked **carefully.***
A mí me parece que no hiciste nada **sistemáticamente.**	*I think you didn't do anything **systematically.***

Adverbs cannot come between an auxiliary verb and the main verb, as they often do in English.

El huracán ha destruido el pueblo **totalmente.**	*The hurricane has **totally** destroyed the town.*
El enfermo está mejorando **rápidamente.**	*The patient is **rapidly** improving.*

Direct objects, including negative and indefinite words such as **algo, nada, nadie,** and neuter demonstratives, often come between the verb and the adverb.

Leyó **el artículo** atentamente.	*He read **the article** attentively.*
No explicó **nada** claramente.	*She didn't explain **anything** clearly.*
Dijo **eso** torpemente.	*He said **that** awkwardly.*

When two or more adverbs ending in **-mente** modify the same verb, the suffix **-mente** is dropped from all but the last adverb.

Nos habló **franca** y **abiertamente.**	*He spoke to us **frankly** and **openly.***
Hicieron su trabajo **diligente** y **cuidadosamente.**	*They did their work **diligently** and **carefully.***

Adverbs ending in **-mente** can often be replaced by **con** + *corresponding noun.*

alegremente	→	con alegría
claramente	→	con claridad
cuidadosamente	→	con cuidado
elegantemente	→	con elegancia
inteligentemente	→	con inteligencia
torpemente	→	con torpeza

Adverbs as intensifiers

Intensifiers, or adverbs that modify adjectives and other adverbs, such as **completamente, muy, tan,** etc., precede the adjective or adverb they modify.

completamente inútil *completely useless*	**muy bonito** *very pretty*	**sumamente bien** *extremely well*
elegantemente vestido *elegantly dressed*	**tan fácilmente** *so easily*	**totalmente ridículo** *totally ridiculous*
extremadamente inteligente *extremely intelligent*	**muy rápidamente** *very quickly*	

In colloquial speech the words **súper** and **medio** are used as adverbs that modify adjectives.

Es una carrera **súper** interesante.
Nos llevaron a un restaurante **súper** caro.

It's a really interesting course of study.
They took us to a really expensive restaurant.

Es un tipo **medio** cínico.
Vivimos en una zona **medio** árida.

He's a pretty cynical guy.
We live in a pretty arid region.

Actividad 3 **Cada adverbio en su lugar.** Ordene los elementos para escribir oraciones colocando los adverbios en su lugar correcto. Siga el modelo.

> MODELO   problema / claramente / el / explicó
> Explicó el problema claramente.

1. las / mal / frases / pronunciaron

_____

2. responsablemente / trabajaron / muy

_____

3. bien / cosas / las / andaban

_____

4. hijos / que / felizmente / mis / quiero / vivan

_____

5. su / interesante / última / fue / película / muy

_____

6. esos / sumamente / Patricia / difíciles / encontró / problemas

_____

7. totalmente / proyecto / encontramos / ridículo / el

_____

8. súper / mi madre / ocupada / está / estos días

_____

Actividad 4 **En otras palabras.** Vuelva a escribir las oraciones cambiando el sustantivo a la forma verbal y el adjetivo al adverbio correspondiente. Siga el modelo.

> MODELO   Juan es un hablador apasionado.
> Juan habla apasionadamente.

1. Martín y Fernando son unos trabajadores responsables.

_____

2. Celia es una cantante maravillosa.

_____

PARTE III

3. Carmen y Pilar son escritoras hábiles.

   _____

4. Paquito es un compositor estupendo.

   _____

5. Luisa es una estudiante diligente.

   _____

6. Margarita es una pintora divina.

   _____

7. Carla y Pedro son viajeros frecuentes.

   _____

8. Alfonso es un jugador enérgico.

   _____

Actividad 5 **Con + sustantivo = adverbio.** Cambie el adverbio que termina en **-mente** a una frase que consiste en la preposición **con** + *sustantivo*. Siga el modelo.

> MODELO   claramente → con claridad

1. inteligentemente _____

2. armónicamente _____

3. elegantemente _____

4. diligentemente _____

5. cariñosamente _____

6. alegremente _____

7. fuertemente _____

8. felizmente _____

9. tristemente _____

10. calurosamente _____

Actividad 6 **Un adverbio más otro.** Escriba frases con dos adverbios para describir cómo se hicieron ciertas cosas. Cambie los adjetivos a la forma correcta del adverbio. Siga el modelo.

> MODELO   ellos / hacer su trabajo / diligente y cuidadoso
> Hicieron su trabajo diligente y cuidadosamente.

1. ella / bailar / elegante y fácil

   _____

2. tú / cantar / lento y suave

_____

3. Uds. / recibirnos / cariñoso y caluroso

_____

4. él / contestar su correo electrónico / oportuno y apasionado

_____

5. nosotros / hacer la limpieza / ligero y perezoso

_____

6. Ud. / servirles / fiel y leal

_____

7. yo / darle consejos / sabio y astuto

_____

8. vosotros / despedirnos / deprimido y triste

_____

Adverbs of time and place

Ya means *already, now, right now.* **Ya no** means *no longer, not anymore.*

Tocan a la puerta.	*Someone's at the door.*
Ya voy.	*I'll be **right** there.*
¿**Ya** has visto la nueva película?	*Have you **already** seen the new film?*
No, **ya no** voy al cine.	*No, I don't go to the movies **anymore.***

The adverb **recién** appears before past participles with the meaning *newly, just, recently.* This is especially common in South American Spanish.

un niño **recién** nacido	*a newborn child*
los **recién** casados	*the recently married couple*
una casa **recién** construida	*a newly built house*

Common adverbs of time

ahora *now*	**después** *after, afterward*	**posteriormente** *subsequently*
ahora mismo *right now*	**en seguida** *right away*	**siempre** *always*
anteriormente *formerly*	**entonces** *then, afterward*	**tarde** *late*
antes *before*	**luego** *then, afterward*	**temprano** *early*
apenas *hardly, scarcely*	**mucho antes** *a long time*	**todavía** *still, yet*
aún *still, yet*	*before*	**todavía no** *not yet*

¿**Ya** han llegado los invitados?	*Have the guests arrived already?*
No, **todavía no.**	*No, not yet.*
¿Carlos salió **en seguida**?	*Did Carlos leave right away?*
No, salió **mucho después.**	*No, he left much later.*

Tenías que llamar **temprano**, a las nueve.	*You were supposed to call early, at nine.*	
Sí, pero llamé **mucho antes.**	*Yes, but I called much before that.*	

Spanish has several words meaning *even*. **Incluso** and **inclusive** are the most common, although **inclusive** is more widely used in the Americas than in Spain. The words **aun** and **hasta** are also used with the meaning of *even*. (Don't confuse **aún** [*still, yet*] and **aun** [*even*].) The phrase **ni siquiera** means *not even*.

Incluso en los países ricos hay pobreza.	*Even in rich countries there is poverty.*
Inclusive me prestaron dinero.	*They even lent me money.*
Hasta mi hijo de dos años lo sabía.	*Even my two-year-old son knew it.*
Aun si nos invitan, no iremos.	*Even if they invite us, we won't go.*
Ni siquiera nos saludaron.	*They didn't even say hi to us.*

The basic adverbs of place in Spanish are **aquí** (*here*), **ahí** (*there [near the person spoken to]*), and **allí** (*there [not near the speaker or the person spoken to]*). **Allá** means *way over there, somewhere over there*. In Spanish America, **acá** often replaces **aquí**.

Aquí hay excelentes escuelas.	*There are excellent schools **here**.*
Allá en mi país también.	***Back** in my country also.*
¿Qué veo **ahí** en tu impresora?	*What do I see **there** on your printer?*
Es mi cartera.	*It's my wallet.*

Common adverbs of place

a la derecha/izquierda *on the right/left*	**al lado** *next door, next to it*	**encima** *on top*
a mano derecha/izquierda *on the right/left*	**arriba** *up, upstairs; above*	**fuera, afuera** *outside*
	atrás *behind*	**lejos** *far off, far away*
abajo *down, downstairs; underneath*	**cerca** *close, nearby*	**por algún sitio/lado** *somewhere*
	delante *in front*	
al fondo *in back, at the bottom*	**en lo alto** *up, up there, up high*	**por ningún sitio/lado** *nowhere*

Adverbs of place can combine with various prepositions and with each other.

allí arriba *up there*	**hasta allí** *up to there*	**por allá** *around there (far away)*
aquí abajo *down here*	**para atrás** *backward, to the back*	
aquí cerca *near here*		**por allí** *around there*
desde aquí *from here*	**por ahí** *around there*	**por aquí** *around here*
hacia allá *toward that place far away*		

Actividad 7 **Expresar en español.** Exprese los diálogos en español. Tenga presente especialmente el uso de los adverbios.

1. Did you **(Ud.)** go to the supermarket already?

   _____

   Not yet. I haven't gotten dressed yet.

   _____

Capítulo 21

2. I'll be back right away.

_____

Come **(tú)** here right now!

_____

3. Mariana can't find her cat anywhere.

_____

Look **(Ud.)** up there! The cat's in the tree.

_____

4. Are the boys around here?

_____

They're probably in the house.

_____

Do you **(tú)** know if they're upstairs or downstairs?

_____

They're probably hiding behind some piece of furniture.

_____

They may even be in the garden.

_____

5. Is the video store far away?

_____

No, it's nearby. And there's a wonderful ice cream store next to it.

_____

Comparison of adverbs

Adverbs are compared much the way adjectives are (see **Capítulo 17,** pp. 279–280).

Él habla **más claramente que** tú.	_He speaks more clearly than you do._
Él habla **menos claramente que** tú.	_He speaks less clearly than you do._
Él habla **tan claramente como** tú.	_He speaks as clearly as you do._

The superlative of adverbs does not use the definite article and therefore has no special form. Its meaning is inferred from context.

El que **más claramente** habla soy yo.	_The one who speaks most clearly is I._

Adverbs can also be formed from the feminine form of the absolute superlatives of adjectives (see **Capítulo 17**, pp. 283–284).

MASCULINE	FEMININE	ADVERB
clarísimo	clarísima	clarísimamente *very clearly*
malísimo	malísima	malísimamente *very badly*
tontísimo	tontísima	tontísimamente *very foolishly*

Actividad 8 **Comparaciones.** Escriba oraciones de comparación usando los elementos indicados. Siga los modelos.

> MODELOS   Luisa / trabajar / + hábil / sus compañeras
> Luisa trabaja más hábilmente que sus compañeras.
>
> Luisa / trabajar / – hábil / sus compañeras
> Luisa trabaja menos hábilmente que sus compañeras.
>
> Luisa / trabajar / = hábil / sus compañeras
> Luisa trabaja tan hábilmente como sus compañeras.

1. él / escribir / + sarcástico / tú

_____

2. tú / analizar el artículo / – crítico / yo

_____

3. ellos / hacerlo / = fácil / nosotros

_____

4. Ana / hablar / + franco / Lucía

_____

5. este niño / jugar / – alegre / aquél

_____

6. ella / expresarse / = lógico / tú

_____

7. nosotros / mandar correo electrónico / + frecuente / ellos

_____

8. vosotros / recibirnos / = afectuoso / Pablo y Lucero

_____

Actividad 9 **Actividad oral.** Un/a estudiante le pregunta a otro/a cómo se hicieron ciertas acciones. Por ejemplo: «¿Cómo hablaste con el profesor?» Su compañero/a le contesta usando un adverbio: «Hablé francamente». Luego, los dos estudiantes cambian de papel para que tengan la oportunidad de preguntar y contestar.

The preposition **a**

A preposition is a word that links a noun to a verb, an adjective, or another noun. Prepositions can also link verbs to each other (See **Capítulo 15,** pp. 221–222).

el libro **de** Paula

entra **en** la cocina

darle el dinero **a** Pablo

dejar **de** fumar

The preposition **a** has many uses in Spanish. Remember its contraction **a + el → al.**

The preposition **a** indicates motion toward a place.

ir **a** la ciudad	*to go to the city*
llegar **a** la oficina	*to arrive at the office*
regresar **a** casa	*to return home*

The preposition **a** labels the animate, specific direct object—this is also known as the personal **a** (See **Capítulo 19,** pp. 303–305).

ver **a** Consuelo	*to see Consuelo*
ayudar **a** los niños	*to help the children*

The preposition **a** labels the indirect object noun and is usually accompanied by the corresponding indirect object pronoun, especially in Spanish America.

Le di el paquete **a** Carla.	*I gave Carla the package.*
Les compré helado **a** los chicos.	*I bought the children ice cream.*

The preposition **a** connects verbs of motion to infinitives (*conveys the idea of purpose*).

salir **a** comer	*to go out to eat*
venir **a** vernos	*to come to see us*

The preposition **a** labels a rate or price.

¿**A** cuánto está el dólar hoy?	*What's the exchange rate of the dollar today?*
Condujimos **a** sesenta millas por hora.	*We drove at sixty miles per hour.*
Estos coches se venden **a** cuarenta mil dólares.	*These cars sell at / for forty thousand dollars.*
Voy al gimnasio dos veces **al** día / **a** la semana.	*I go to the gym twice a day / a week.*

The preposition **a** labels the manner in which something is done

a caballo *on horseback*
a doble espacio *double-spaced*
a la española *Spanish-style*
a pie *on foot*

a regañadientes *reluctantly*
andar a gatas *to crawl on all fours*

escribir a lápiz *to write in pencil*
hecho/a a mano *made by hand*

The preposition **a** expresses location

a dos kilómetros de aquí *two kilometers from here*
a la izquierda/derecha, a mano izquierda/derecha *on the left/right*
a la salida del pueblo *at the edge of town*
a la salida del trabajo *upon leaving work*

a la vuelta de la esquina *around the corner*
a las dos de la tarde *at two in the afternoon*
a nuestra llegada *upon our arrival*
al final de la calle *at the end of the street*

estar a dieta, a régimen *to be on a diet*
estar sentado/a a la mesa *to be seated at the table*
tocar a la puerta *to knock at the door*

The preposition **a** in idiomatic expressions

a escondidas *stealthily, behind someone's back*
a espaldas de uno *behind someone's back*

a mi juicio, a mi parecer *in my opinion*
a veces *sometimes*

al mes de trabajar aquí *after working here for one month*
paso a paso *step-by-step*
uno a uno *one by one*

Actividad 1   **¿A, al o nada?** Complete las oraciones con la preposición **a** donde sea necesaria. No se olvide de la contracción **al.** Si no es necesario usar la preposición, escriba una X.

1. Les envié un correo electrónico _____ a _____ mis amigos.

2. ¿Conociste _____ X _____ la Alhambra?

3. No pudimos ir _____ a _____ verlos.

4. Leonardo habló con nosotros _____ X _____ dos veces.

5. Llegué _____ al _____ el pueblo _____ a la _____ la una.

6. Viajaban _____ a _____ cien millas por hora.

7. ¿_____ a _____ cuánto está el euro hoy?

8. Ya son _____ X _____ las ocho.

9. La parada queda _____ a _____ seis cuadras de mi casa.

The preposition de

Like **a**, the preposition **de** has many uses in Spanish. Remember the contraction **de** + **el** → **del.**

The preposition **de** indicates motion from a place.

El avión llega **de** Colombia.	*The plane is arriving from Colombia.*
Vengo **de** la farmacia.	*I'm coming from the drugstore.*
Salgo **de** casa a las ocho menos diez.	*I leave home at ten to eight.*

De indicates origin and possession.

Son **de** Venezuela.	*They're from Venezuela.*
el tren **de** Buenos Aires	*the train from Buenos Aires*
la mochila **de** Pedrito	*Pedrito's backpack*

De indicates the material of which something is made or the contents of a container.

una casa **de** ladrillos	*a brick house*
un reloj **de** oro	*a gold watch*
un vaso **de** agua	*a glass of water*
una caja **de** juguetes	*a box of toys*

De is often the equivalent of English *with* or *in* in descriptive expressions.

lleno/a **de** agua	*filled with water (also: full of water)*
cubierto/a **de** nieve	*covered with snow*
forrado/a **de** plumón	*down-lined, lined with down*
vestido/a **de** negro	*dressed in black*
pintado/a **de** azul	*painted (in) blue*

De forms noun phrases that are the equivalent of *noun + noun* or *present participle + noun* constructions in English.

una exposición **de** arte	*an art show*
un programa **de** televisión	*a television program*
la máquina **de** lavar	*the washing machine*
la Facultad **de** Medicina	*the medical school*
el cuarto **de** baño	*the bathroom*
el libro **de** biología	*the biology book*

De indicates a characteristic of a noun.

una persona **de** dinero	*a wealthy person*
la mujer **del** sombrero rojo	*the woman in the red hat*
una chica **de** talento	*a talented girl*
un hombre **de** porte medio	*a man of medium build*

De indicates a limitation or restriction on a verb or adjective.

Trabajo **de** programador.	*I work as a programmer.*
ciego/a **del** ojo izquierdo	*blind in one's left eye*
alto/a **de** estatura	*tall*
ancho/a **de** espaldas	*broad-shouldered*
un metro **de** largo / **de** ancho / **de** alto	*a meter long/wide/high*

De indicates time in certain fixed expressions.

trabajar **de** día / **de** noche	*to work days/nights*
muy **de** mañana	*very early in the morning*

De indicates the manner in which something is done.

ponerse **de** pie / **de** rodillas	*to stand up / get on one's knees*
estar **de** luto	*to be in mourning*
Se viste / Se disfraza **de** policía.	*He dresses as / He disguises himself as a police officer.*
servir **de** intérprete	*to serve / act as interpreter*
hacer algo **de** buena fe / **de** mala gana	*to do something in good / bad faith*
beber algo **de** un trago	*to drink something in one gulp*

De connects nouns in humorous or mocking descriptions of people.

el loco **de** Pedro	*crazy Pedro*
la muy tonta **de** Marta	*silly Marta*
el pobre **de** mi cuñado	*my poor brother-in-law*
aquel burro **de** recepcionista	*that jerk of a receptionist*

De indicates the cause or reason.

saltar **de** alegría	*to jump for joy*
gritar **de** dolor	*to scream in pain, because of the pain*
morir **de** hambre	*to starve to death*
estar loco **de** alegría	*to be insanely happy*
no poder moverse **de** miedo	*to be paralyzed with fear*

De indicates the topic (English *about*).

hablar **de** filosofía	*to talk about philosophy*
saber poco **de** aquella familia	*to know little about that family*

Actividad 2   **¿De, del o nada?** Complete las oraciones con la preposición **de** donde sea necesario. No se olvide de la contracción **del**. Si no es necesario usar la preposición escriba una X.

1. ¡Qué hermosa es tu blusa _____de_____ seda!

2. Esos turistas son _____X_____ chilenos.

3. Diana lleva un vestido _____X_____ azul.

4. Estos son los documentos _____del_____ el ingeniero.

5. La niñita saltó _____X_____ alegremente.

6. Salieron _____de_____ casa a las diez y cuarto.

7. Pedro tomará su lección _____de_____ piano el jueves.

8. Sírvame una taza _____de_____ té, por favor.

The preposition en

The basic meaning of the preposition **en** is to express location. It may be the equivalent of the English *in, on,* or *at*.

The preposition **en** indicates location (English *in, on, at*).

en el comedor	*in the dining room*
en la mesa	*on the table*
en el aeropuerto	*at the airport*

En indicates extent of time.

Vuelvo **en** unos minutos.	*I'll be back in a few minutes.*
Roma no se construyó **en** un día.	*Rome wasn't built in a day.*

En is used in some expressions of manner.

en serio	*seriously*
en broma	*not seriously, as a joke*
estar **en** contra	*to be against something*

En labels the amount by which measured quantities differ.

Los precios han aumentado **en** un 20 por ciento.	*Prices have gone up (by) 20 percent.*
más alto que yo **en** una cabeza	*a head taller than I*

En can label price.

Te lo doy **en** diez dólares.	*I'll give it to you for ten dollars.*

En labels the means by which an action occurs.

Te reconocí **en** la voz.	*I recognized you by your voice.*
ir **en** avión / **en** coche / **en** tren / **en** barco	*to go by plane / by car / by train / by boat*

Actividad 3 **Expresar en español.** Exprese las oraciones en español.

1. We plan to go by plane.

   _____

2. I'll pick you **(Uds.)** up at the airport.

   _____

3. Miguel is taller than Juan by a head.

   _____

4. Are you **(Ud.)** saying this seriously or as a joke?

   _____

5. Paula will arrive in a week.

   _____

The preposition **con**

The preposition **con** expresses the idea of accompaniment or the means by which something is done. Its most common English equivalent is *with*.

The preposition **con** expresses accompaniment.

salir **con** los amigos	*to go out with friends*
llegar **con** un ramillete de flores	*to arrive with a bouquet of flowers*
té **con** limón	*tea with lemon*

Con expresses attitude.

Es muy amable **con**migo.	*He's very nice to me.*
insolente **con** el/la maestro/a	*fresh to the teacher*

Con labels the means by which something is done.

abrir la puerta **con** una llave	*to open the door with a key*
atar el paquete **con** cuerda	*to tie the package with string*

When preceding an infinitive, **con** labels the action as a means.

Con pulsar esta tecla, se guarda el archivo.	*By pushing this key, you save the file.*

Con labels the manner in which something is done.

Nos recibió **con** una sonrisa.	*She received us with a smile.*
Lo hice **con** mucho esfuerzo.	*I did it with a great deal of effort.*

Con expresses the phrases *in spite of* or *notwithstanding*.

Con todos sus problemas, se hizo abogado.	*In spite of all his problems, he became a lawyer.*
Con tener tanto dinero de su tío, acabó sin un centavo.	*Notwithstanding all the money he had from his uncle, he wound up penniless.*

Con can label the content of a container and is less ambiguous than **de.**

una cesta **con** ropa	*a basket of clothing*
una bolsa **con** cebollas	*a bag of onions*

Actividad 4 **¿Con qué?** Complete las oraciones con una de las expresiones de la lista.

con caramelos	con esfuerzo	con leche
con cuerda	con gusto	con llave

1. Tomó cafe _____.

2. Abrieron la puerta _____.

3. Se ató el paquete _____.

4. Nos saludó _____.

5. Búscame la caja _____.

6. Porque están enfermos, lo hacen todo _____.

Actividad 5 **¿Qué falta?** Complete las oraciones con la preposición correcta. Escoja entre **a, de, en** y **con.** No se olvide de escribir las contracciones **al** y **del** donde sean necesarias.

1. ¿Viste a la señora _____del_____ el vestido rojo?

2. _____con_____ todos sus defectos, José me parece una buena persona.

3. Vivo _____a_____ dos cuadras de la oficina.

4. ¿Hablas _____en_____ serio?

5. Tengo que terminar mi tesis _____en_____ una semana.

6. El señor Salas es muy cariñoso _____con_____ sus hijos.

7. Es una mujer _____de_____ estatura media.

8. El dólar está _____ a _____ veintiocho pesos.

9. Las calles están cubiertas _____ de _____ nieve.

10. Limpio el suelo _____ con _____ un trapo.

11. ¿Me puedes dar agua _____ con _____ hielo?

12. Hay un buen restaurante _____ en _____ la estación de trenes.

13. Vengan a sentarse _____ a _____ la mesa.

14. La reconocí _____ en _____ el modo de andar.

15. El inocente _____ de _____ mi hermano se compró un coche usado que no funciona.

16. Este jarro fue hecho _____ a _____ máquina.

17. Hace frío. Ponte el gorro _____ de _____ lana.

18. La sala es grande. Tiene cinco metros _____ de _____ largo.

19. _____ al _____ mes de trabajar en la empresa, Víctor renunció a su puesto.

20. _____ al _____ principio, no nos gustaba la casa.

The prepositions **para** and **por**

The prepositions **para** and **por** are often difficult for English-speakers because both correspond to English *for* in many cases. It is most useful to consider the different relationships each expresses.

The preposition **para** labels destination, the time by which something will occur, or the figurative goal.

Tomaron el tren para Córdoba.	*They took the train for Córdoba. (destination)*
Los chicos salieron para el colegio.	*The kids left for school. (destination)*
Terminaré para el martes.	*I'll finish by Tuesday. (time)*
El regalo es para ti.	*The gift is for you. (figurative goal)*
Estudio para médico.	*I'm studying to be a doctor. (figurative goal)*
Es un honor para nosotros.	*It's an honor for us. (figurative goal)*
Leo para perfeccionar mi español.	*I read to improve my Spanish. (infinitive as figurative goal)*

Para labels the standard for comparison.

Para profesor, tiene poca paciencia.	*For a teacher, he doesn't have much patience.*
Para médica, sabe poco.	*For a doctor, she doesn't know much.*

Para labels the information in the sentence as someone's opinion.

Para mí, la obra fue excelente.	*In my opinion, the play was excellent.*
Para ella, el precio es bueno.	*In her opinion, the price is good.*

Para appears in some common expressions and idioms.

para entonces	*by that time*
para siempre	*forever*
para variar	*just for a change*
ser tal para cual	*to be two of a kind*
estar para	*to be about to*

The preposition **por** expresses motion through a place or an imprecise location.

Salga por esa puerta.	*Go out through that door.* (*motion through*)
Hay varios restaurantes por este barrio.	*There are several restaurants in this neighborhood.* (*imprecise location*)
No lo he visto por aquí.	*I haven't seen him around here.* (*imprecise location*)
¡En primavera hay flores por todas partes!	*In the spring there are flowers everywhere!* (*imprecise location*)

Por expresses duration of time or an imprecise point in time.

Trabajó por muchos años.	*She worked for many years.* (*duration*)
Tuve que hacer cola por tres horas.	*I had to stand in line for three hours.* (*duration*)
Se reunieron ayer por la tarde.	*They got together yesterday afternoon.* (*imprecise point in time*)
Nos veremos por Navidad.	*We'll see each other around Christmas time.* (*imprecise point in time*)

Por designates a cause or reason.

Se ofenden por cualquier cosa.	*They get insulted at/over any little thing.*
Te felicito por tus buenas notas.	*I congratulate you on your good grades.*
Lo pasé mal en Panamá por el calor.	*I had a bad time of it in Panama because of the heat.*

Por designates the means by which something is done.

Mándeme un mensaje por correo electrónico.	*Send me a message by e-mail.*

Por designates motivation or incentive. It also designates the person for whose sake something is done.

Brindaron por el equipo vencedor.	*They toasted the winning team.*
Todo lo hice por mi familia.	*Everything I did was for my family.*
Me callé por ti.	*I kept quiet for your sake.*

Por expresses exchange or substitution.

Pagamos mucho dinero por la computadora.	*We paid a lot of money for the computer.*
Enseñé la clase por el profesor.	*I taught the class for the teacher.* (*instead of him*)

Por adds the idea of motion to prepositions of location.

El caballo saltó por encima de la valla.	*The horse jumped over the hurdle.*
El mesero pasó por detrás de las sillas.	*The waiter passed behind the chairs.*
El perro corrió por debajo de la mesa.	*The dog ran under the table.*

Por labels the agent in passive constructions (see **Capítulo 8**).

El libro fue escrito por un historiador inglés.

The book was written by an English historian.

El sitio Web será creado por la administradora de Web.

The website will be created by the Web master.

Common expressions with **por**

por acá/ahí/allá/aquí *around here/there/there/here*
por ahora *for now*
por añadidura *in addition*
por aquel entonces *at that time*
por casualidad *by chance*
por cierto *certainly*
por completo *completely*
por consecuencia *consequently*
por consiguiente *consequently*
por culpa de *the fault of*
por dentro y por fuera *inside and outside*
por desgracia *unfortunately*

por ejemplo *for example*
por esa época *around that time*
por escrito *in writing*
por eso *therefore, that's why*
por favor *please*
por fin *finally*
por lo común *usually*
por lo demás *furthermore*
por lo general *generally*
por lo menos *at least*
por lo mismo *for that very reason*
por lo pronto *for the time being*
por lo tanto *therefore*
por lo visto *apparently*

por medio de *by means of*
por mi parte *as far as I'm concerned*
por poco *almost*
por primera vez *for the first time*
por si acaso *just in case*
por su cuenta *on one's own*
por su parte *as far as one is concerned*
por supuesto *of course*
por todas partes *everywhere*
por todos lados *everywhere*
por último *finally*
por un lado, por otro *on the one hand, on the other*

Idioms with **por**

dar gato por liebre (*hare*) *to put something over on someone*
(de) una vez por todas *once and for all*
en un dos por tres *in a jiffy*
escaparse por un pelo *to have a narrow escape, escape by the skin of one's teeth*

estar por *to be in the mood for something*
pasar un examen por los pelos *to barely get through an exam*
poner por las nubes *to praise to the skies*
por las buenas o por las malas *whether one likes it or not*
por los cuatro costados *on both sides (of the family)*

por motivo de *on account of*
por si las moscas *just in case*
siete por dos son catorce *seven times two are fourteen (mathematical)*
trabajar por cuatro *to work like a slave*
traído por los pelos *far-fetched*

Por and **para** contrast with each other in certain contexts.

por esa época — *around that time*
para esa época — *by that time*

Por algo lo hizo. — *She did it for some reason or other.*
Para algo lo hizo. — *She did it for some purpose.*

¿Para quién trabaja Ud.?	*For whom are you working?*
Trabajo para el señor Domínguez.	*I'm working for Mr. Domínguez.*
	(he's my boss)

¿Por quién trabaja Ud.?	*For whom are you working?*
Trabajo por el señor Domínguez.	*I'm working for Mr. Domínguez.*
	(in his place)

Actividad 6 **Pepita la preguntona (busybody).** Pepita pregunta muchas cosas por ser curiosa. Conteste sus preguntas usando la preposición **por** en sus respuestas. Siga el modelo.

> MODELO ¿Por qué se durmió Ud. tan temprano? (un tremendo sueño)
> Me dormí tan temprano por un tremendo sueño.

1. ¿Por qué fue Ud. al almacén? (un par de zapatos)

   _____

2. ¿Por qué felicitaron Uds. a Verónica? (su cumpleaños)

   _____

3. ¿Por qué te duele la espalda? (jugar al tenis / cuatro horas)

   _____

4. ¿Por qué no terminó Javier el informe? (pereza)

   _____

5. ¿Cuándo veremos a Carlos y Elena? (la tarde)

   _____

6. ¿Cómo salieron los Salcedo de la ciudad? (el puente más céntrico)

   _____

7. ¿Por qué cosas irán Uds. a la bodega? (salchicha y queso)

   _____

8. ¿Cómo tendrás que hacer la tarea? (escrito)

   _____

Actividad 7 **¿Una película encantadora?** A su amigo le gustó tanto la película «Mangos del Caribe» que la vio cinco veces. Ud. quiere saber por qué le gustó tanto porque Ud. la encontró francamente aburrida. Escriba sus respuestas usando la preposición **por.** Siga el modelo.

> MODELO ¿Por qué te gustó la película tanto? (los actores principales)
> Por los actores principales.

1. ¿Por qué la viste cinco veces? (la fotografía)

   _____

2. ¿Por qué te interesa tanto? (el argumento)

_____

3. ¿Por qué quedaste tan impresionado? (la dirección)

_____

4. ¿Por qué te llamó la atención? (el guión)

_____

5. ¿Por qué estás tan entusiasmado por el film? (el diálogo)

_____

Actividad 8 **¿Para qué?** Ud. es el hermano modelo para su hermanito. Por eso él tiene interés en saber todo lo que Ud. hace y por qué lo hace. Ud. le contesta dándole muy buenos consejos. Use la preposición **para** + *infinitivo* en su respuesta. Siga el modelo.

MODELO ¿Para qué estudias tanto? (sacar buenas notas)
Para sacar buenas notas.

1. ¿Para qué trabajas en la biblioteca? (ganar plata)

_____

2. ¿Para qué lees tantos libros? (aprender mucho)

_____

3. ¿Para qué te quedas en casa los sábados hasta las tres? (ayudar a mamá y a papá)

_____

4. ¿Para qué le compras flores y bombones a tu novia? (demostrarle mi cariño)

_____

5. ¿Para qué practicas español cuatro horas al día todos los días? (perfeccionarlo)

_____

Actividad 9 **¡Una semana muy ocupada!** Hay tantas cosas que hacer y tan poco tiempo para hacerlas. Escriba para cuándo todas las cosas se tienen que hacer. Conteste las preguntas usando la preposición **para.** Siga el modelo.

MODELO ¿Para cuándo te cortas el pelo? (el jueves)
Para el jueves.

1. ¿Para cuándo tienes que entregar el informe? (pasado mañana)

_____

2. ¿Para cuándo arreglaste cita con el dentista? (la semana entrante)

   _____

3. ¿Para cuándo vas a entrevistarte para el empleo? (el martes)

   _____

4. ¿Para cuándo necesitas devolver los libros a la biblioteca? (finales del mes)

   _____

5. ¿Para cuándo precisas el regalo para el aniversario de tus papás?
   (el mes próximo)

   _____

Actividad 10 **¿Por o para?** Complete los diálogos escogiendo **por** o **para.**

1. —¿Cuándo sale el tren de Madrid _____
   Barcelona?

   —Sale _____ la mañana pasando

   _____ Zaragoza

   _____ la tarde.

2. —¿Van tú y Mari Carmen al centro comercial

   _____ ver los escaparates?

   —Ah, sí, vamos una vez _____ semana.

3. —_____ peluquera, Teresa no sabe cortar el pelo.

   —_____ eso ya no voy a esa peluquería.

4. —Hagamos una excursión _____ la sierra

   _____ mediados de julio.

   —_____ variar, viajemos

   _____ las islas _____

   principios de agosto.

5. —¿_____ quién es este hermoso traje hecho a la
   medida?

   —Es _____ mi hermana Rosa. Fue hecho

   _____ Gabriela, la famosa diseñadora.

6. —¿Le dijiste a Juan lo de Armando _____ teléfono?

   —¡Qué va! _____ darle esta noticia tengo que

   hacerlo _____ escrito.

   —¿Vas a enviarle un mensaje _____ correo electrónico?

   —Claro que sí. Así llega en un dos _____ tres.

7. —Parece que el ladrón se escapó _____ los pelos.

   ¿_____ dónde entró en la tienda?

   —_____ lo que leí en el periódico, entró

   _____ una ventana del sótano.

8. —Rodrigo estuvo enfermo _____ la leche estropeada que tomó.

   —Yo sé. Él me llamó _____ pedirme que fuera

   al trabajo _____ él.

Actividad 11 **¡Vivan los fiesteros!** Les toca a los estudiantes hacer una fiesta del fin de curso. Cada persona salió a comprar algo y ahora cuenta lo que compró y cuánto costó. Escriba oraciones usando la preposición **por.** Siga el modelo.

> MODELO   yo / ir / los manteles : pagar / doce dólares
> Yo fui por los manteles. Pagué doce dólares por ellos.

1. Beatriz / ir / ensalada de fruta : pagar / treinta dólares

   _____

2. Carlos y Leo / ir / refrescos : pagar / cincuenta y cinco dólares

   _____

3. Paula y yo / ir / servilletas : pagar / siete dólares

   _____

4. tú / ir / los bocadillos : pagar / ciento setenta y nueve dólares

   _____

5. yo / ir / torta : pagar / dieciocho dólares

   _____

6. Uds. / ir / vino : pagar / cuarenta y tres doláres

   _____

Other simple prepositions

Other simple prepositions

desde *from*	**hacia** *toward*	**según** *according to*
durante *during*	**hasta** *until*	**sin** *without*
entre *between, among*	**menos** *except*	**sobre** *above, about*
excepto *except*	**salvo** *except*	

Desde is more specific than **de** in labeling a starting point.

Lo vi desde la ventana.	*I saw him from the window.*
Desde aquel día hemos sido buenos amigos.	*From that day on we have been good friends.*

Hacia can refer to attitudes and feelings as well as direction.

Siente mucho cariño hacia sus sobrinos.	*He feels deep affection toward his nieces and nephews.*

Note the following combinations of **hacia** + *adverb.*

hacia atrás	*backward; toward the rear*
hacia adelante	*toward the front*
hacia arriba	*upward*
hacia abajo	*downward*

Hasta can mean *even* as well as *until.*

Hasta mis abuelos vinieron a la fiesta.	*Even my grandparents came to the party.*

Sin + *infinitive* has a variety of English equivalents.

El trabajo quedó sin hacer.	*The work remained undone.*
Las calles están sin pavimentar.	*The streets are unpaved.*
Habla sin parar.	*She talks nonstop.*
Quedamos sin comer.	*We ended up not eating.*

Sobre means *about* as well as *above, on top of.* It can also mean *about* in the sense of *approximately.*

Leí un artículo sobre la industria mexicana.	*I read an article on (about) Mexican industry.*
Vamos a comer sobre las siete.	*We'll eat at about seven o'clock.*

Actividad 12   **En español, por favor.** Exprese las oraciones en español.

1. My report is unfinished.

    Mi informe sin terminar

2. I put one book on top of the other.

    Puse un libro sobre el otro
    encima del

3. I saw him go out toward the rear.

Lo vi salir atrás

4. She lived for (during) many years among the indigenous people.

Vivió durante mucho años entre los pueblos indígenas

5. It's hot even in the mountains.

Hace h

6. The immigrants feel love for their new country.

_____

7. They followed us from the door of the movie theater.

_____

8. I'm reading a book about Puerto Rico.

_____

Sets of prepositions and compound prepositions

Sets of prepositions and compound prepositions

a causa de *because of*	**bajo, debajo de** *under*	**frente a, en frente de** *across from*
a lo largo de *along*	**cerca de** *near; about (approximately)*	**junto a** *close to, right next to*
a pesar de *in spite of*	**contra, en contra de** *against*	**lejos de** *far from*
a través de *through*	**delante de** *in front of*	**respecto a** *about (concerning)*
acerca de *about (concerning)*	**dentro de** *inside of*	
(a)fuera de *outside of*	**encima de** *on, upon, on top of*	**tras, detrás, después de** *behind, after*
al lado de *next to*		
ante, antes de *before*		

Antes de is used to mean *before* with time expressions, whereas **ante** is figurative. **Delante de** expresses physical location.

antes de su llegada	*before your arrival*
antes del verano	*before the summer*
antes de las ocho	*before eight o'clock*
comparecer ante el juez	*to appear before the judge*
ante todo	*first of all, above all*
No sé qué hacer ante tantas posibilidades.	*I don't know what to do faced with so many possibilities.*
Hay un jardín delante de la casa.	*There's a garden in front of the house.*

Bajo is generally figurative, whereas **debajo de** is usually literal.

bajo la administración de González	*under the González government*
bajo Carlos V	*under Charles the Fifth*
bajo ningún concepto	*in no way*
diez grados bajo cero	*ten degrees below zero*
bajo llave	*under lock and key*
bajo juramento	*under oath*
debajo del puente	*under the bridge*

En contra de usually expresses being against someone's ideas, policies, or political views. **Contra** means *against* in most other contexts.

escribir un artículo en contra de la guerra	*to write an article against (opposing) the war*
Los hechos van en contra de sus ideas.	*The facts run counter to your ideas.*
apoyarse contra el árbol	*to lean against the tree*
pastillas contra la gripe	*pills for the flu*
luchar contra el enemigo	*to fight against the enemy*

Frente a and **enfrente de** (*opposite, facing, across from*) are synonyms. Note that **delante de** should be used to mean *in front of*.

Hay una parada de autobuses enfrente de / frente a nuestra casa.	*There's a bus stop across from our house.*

Tras means *behind, after* in certain set expressions. Generally, **detrás de** means *behind* and **después de** means *after*.

año tras año	*year after year*
un artículo tras otro	*one article after another*
detrás de la casa	*behind the house*
después de la clase	*after class*

The prepositions **a** and **de** in compound prepositions contract with the definite article **el** when **el** follows directly.

junto al parque	*right next to the park*
cerca del teatro	*near the theater*

Actividad 13 **Actividad de conjunto.** Complete las oraciones con la respuesta correcta.

1. No pudieron lanzar el nuevo cohete _____ mal tiempo que hacía.

   a. por medio del   **b.** junto al   **c.** a causa del

2. Todo lo que sé lo supe _____ noticiero del canal 7.

   a. encima del   **b.** sobre el   **c.** a través del

3. No puedo salir de la oficina a las cinco. Por eso, llegaré al restaurante

   _____ las seis.

   a. a pesar de   **b.** respecto a   **c.** después de

4. El señor Aranda tuvo un ataque de nervios _____ la perspectiva de perder su empleo.

   a. ante   **b.** para   **c.** al lado de

5. Marta mandó carta _____ carta y nunca recibió una respuesta.

   a. tras   **b.** atrás   **c.** detrás de

6. Si alquilas un apartamento tan _____ la oficina, tendrás que viajar por lo menos una hora para llegar al trabajo.

   a. junto a   **b.** lejos de   **c.** por medio de

7. En la radio están hablando constantemente _____ peligro de un ciclón.

   a. sobre el   **b.** encima del   **c.** cerca del

8. El coche resbaló, salió de la carretera y fue _____ por la cuesta.

   a. afuera   **b.** hacia abajo   **c.** cerca

9. Miré por la ventanilla mientras el avión volaba _____ Nueva York.

   a. entre   **b.** por encima de   **c.** antes de

10. El tren de alta velocidad viaja _____ 270 kilómetros _____ hora.

    a. por, de   **b.** en, para   **c.** a, por

11. _____ culpa de él, el proyecto quedó _____ terminar.

    a. Para, en   **b.** Con, hasta   **c.** Por, sin

12. A mi amiga traviesa la quiero _____ todo.

    a. a pesar de   **b.** a lo largo de   **c.** frente a

13. Los ciclistas tienen que pasar _____ los coches cuando hay mucho tráfico.

    a. por entre   **b.** ante   **c.** después de

14. Varios senadores se expresaron _____ tratado.

    a. por medio del   **b.** en contra del   **c.** dentro del

15. Todos estos sarapes están hechos _____ mano.

    a. a   **b.** con   **c.** de

16. Pedro Camacho es el señor _____ traje gris.

    a. con el   **b.** dentro del   **c.** del

17. —¿No vino Zenaida?

    —No. Vinieron todos _____ ella.

    a. con   **b.** después de   **c.** menos

18. Este autor vivió _____ los Reyes Católicos.

    a. debajo de   **b.** sin   **c.** bajo

Actividad 14   **Actividad oral.** Dos o más equipos tratan de ganar puntos expresando en español o en inglés ciertas expresiones y oraciones presentadas por un presentador/mediador. Las expresiones y oraciones se deben sacar de las listas de este capítulo.

PARTE III

PARTE IV   INTERROGATIVES AND NEGATIVES

CAPÍTULO 23 — INTERROGATIVE WORDS AND QUESTION FORMATION

Interrogative words

Questions that begin with an interrogative word **(palabra interrogativa)** such as **¿Cuándo?** or **¿Quién?** ask for a piece of information (When is the party?, Who is your teacher?, Which one do you want?). They are called *information questions*. In Spanish, interrogative words have a written accent.

Important interrogative words

¿cuál?, ¿cuáles? *which one(s)?*
¿cuándo? *when?*
¿cuánto(a)? *how much?*
¿cuántos(as)? *how many?*
¿cómo? *how?*
¿dónde? *where? (at what place?)*

¿adónde? *where? (to what place?)*
¿de dónde? *from where?*
¿qué? *what?, which?*
¿para qué? *for what purpose?*
¿por qué? *why?*

¿quién?, ¿quiénes? *who? (subject)*
¿a quién?, ¿a quiénes? *whom? (object)*
¿de quién?, ¿de quiénes? *whose?*

Some of the interrogatives are not used exactly like their English equivalents.

¿Cómo? has different meanings depending on whether it is used with **ser** or **estar.**

¿Cómo está tu hermano?	*How is your brother? (asks about health or mental state)*
¿Cómo es tu hermano?	*What does your brother look like? or What is your brother like? (character, personality)*

¿Cómo? can be used to ask for repetition of something you didn't understand or to express surprise at something you have just heard (English uses *what* for this purpose).

Hay examen de física hoy. ¿Cómo?	*There's a physics exam today. What?*

Unlike English *how* in questions such as *How heavy is the package?*, *How wide is the river?*, *How fast does he run?*, **¿cómo?** cannot precede adjectives or adverbs directly. Here are the ways Spanish asks for measurements.

¿Cuánto pesa el paquete?	
¿Cómo es de pesado el paquete?	*How heavy is the package?*
¿Cuánto es de pesado el paquete?	

¿Cómo es el río de ancho?	
¿Cuánto es el río de ancho?	
¿Cuánto tiene el río de ancho?	*How wide is the river?*
¿Qué anchura tiene el río?	
¿Cuánto mide el río de ancho?	

¿Con qué rapidez corre?	*How fast does he run?*

NOTA

In Spanish America, the colloquial form **¿Qué tan ancho es el río?** is also common.

¿Cuál? and **¿Cuáles?** are replaced by **¿Qué?** before a noun in standard Spanish.

¿Qué libros leíste?	*Which books did you read?*
¿Qué materias escogiste?	*Which subjects did you choose?*

In parts of Spanish America, such as Mexico and Cuba, sentences such as **¿Cuáles materias escogiste?** are acceptable.

¿Cuál? is used for English *what* when an identification is asked for.

¿Cuál es la diferencia?	*What's the difference?*
¿Cuál es la capital de Nicaragua?	*What's the capital of Nicaragua?*
¿Cuál es la fecha de hoy?	*What's today's date?*
¿Cuál fue el resultado?	*What was the result?*
¿Cuál fue el año de la crisis económica?	*What was the year of the crisis in the economy?*

Note that **¿qué?** before **ser** asks for a definition.

¿Qué es la programación?	*What is programming?*
¿Qué es un nanosegundo?	*What is a nanosecond?*

¿Dónde? is used to ask about location. **¿Adónde?** asks direction and is used with verbs of motion.

¿Dónde trabaja Jimena?	*Where does Jimena work?*
¿Adónde va Jimena?	*Where is Jimena going?*

NOTAS

- Many speakers use **¿dónde?** instead of **¿adónde?** with verbs of motion.
- **¿Para dónde?** and **¿hacia dónde?** mean *toward where?*

Questions beginning with **¿De quién/es?** have a different word order than their English equivalents.

¿De quién es el libro?	*Whose book is this?*

Prepositions always precede the interrogative word in Spanish.

¿Con cuántas personas llegó?	*How many people did he arrive with?*
¿Para quiénes es el regalo?	*Whom is the gift for?*
¿Sobre qué habló el profesor?	*What did the teacher talk about?*
¿En qué casa vive Nélida?	*Which house does Nélida live in?*

Actividad 1 **Los detalles, por favor.** Cuando su amiga le habla de lo que hacen unas personas, Ud. le pide más detalles usando las palabras interrogativas con las preposiciones apropiadas. Siga el modelo.

> MODELO Francisca se lamenta de todo.
> ¿De qué se lamenta?

1. Monserrat se quejaba de todo.

_____

2. Jorge y Maribel se interesan en todo.

_____

3. Eduardo se jacta de todo.

_____

4. Carlota se casará con Octavio.

_____

5. Luz se fija en todo.

_____

6. Elvira se enamoró de Roberto.

_____

7. Pablo soñó con muchas personas.

_____

Actividad 2 **¿Quiénes son?** Lea la información dada sobre cada persona y derive preguntas con palabras interrogativas de ella. Escriba más preguntas cuando sea posible. Siga el modelo.

> MODELO Es venezolano.
> ¿De dónde es? *or* ¿De qué nacionalidad es?

A. Leonardo Gustavo Saénz

(1) Es argentino. (2) Es ingeniero. (3) Trabaja para una compañía argentina con sucursales en Estados Unidos. (4) Vive en Nueva York. (5) Es casado con una norteamericana. (6) Tiene tres hijos.

1. _____
2. _____
3. _____
4. _____
5. _____
6. _____

PARTE IV

B. Delmira Danielo

(7) Nació en Francia. (8) Sus abuelos son de España. (9) Se mudó a Canadá cuando tenía cuatro años. (10) Hace estudios posgraduados en química en una universidad canadiense. (11) Estudia para química. (12) Vive con sus padres y hermanos en las afueras de Montreal.

7. _____

8. _____

9. _____

10. _____

11. _____

12. _____

C. Claudio del Mundo

(13) Ganó la gran carrera de bicicletas. (14) Es un héroe nacional en España. (15) Fue condecorado por el rey español. (16) Tiene cuarenta y dos bicicletas. (17) Le gusta más su bicicleta italiana amarilla. (18) Quiere descansar. (19) Irá de vacaciones al Caribe. (20) Llevará a su mujer y a sus dos hijas.

13. _____

14. _____

15. _____

16. _____

17. _____

18. _____

19. _____

20. _____

Actividad 3 ¿**Cómo? ¡Habla más fuerte!** Su amiga llama para invitarlo/la a ir de compras con ella. Por desgracia, hay interferencias en la línea y Ud. le pregunta lo que dijo usando las palabras interrogativas apropiadas. Escriba más de una pregunta cuando sea posible. Siga el modelo.

> MODELO —Voy al centro comercial.
> —¿Adónde vas?

1. —Pienso ir al centro comercial que queda en la carretera de Salamanca.

   — _____

2. —Hay ochenta y siete tiendas en el centro comercial.

   — _____

3. —Hay unos veintiséis restaurantes y cafés en el centro comercial.

   — _____

4. —Voy a comprar dos pares de zapatos.

   — _____

5. —Necesito comprarle un regalo a mi cuñada.

   — _____

6. —Trataré de gastar menos de cien dólares.

   — _____

7. —Quizás le compre una blusa de seda.

   — _____

8. —No sé si le gusta más la blusa azul o la verde.

   — _____

9. —Pagaré con tarjeta de crédito o con cheque.

   — _____

10. —Voy a llegar al centro comercial en coche.

   — _____

Actividad 4 **Estudiantes.** Complete las oraciones con las palabras interrogativas correctas.

A.

1. Nati —¿_____Cuantas_____ materias estás tomando este semestre?

   Sergio —Estoy tomando cinco.

2. Nati —¿_____cuales_____ son?

   Sergio —Historia de los Estados Unidos, literatura inglesa, física, español y el arte latino de los Estados Unidos.

3. Nati —¿_____Quien_____ enseña la clase de arte?

   Sergio —El profesor Durán.

4. Nati —¿_____Como_____ es la clase?

   Sergio —¡Excelente y fuerte! El profe es estupendo. No hay cosa que no sepa. Se aprende mucho sobre los artistas de origen hispánico de hoy.

5. Nati —¿_____Cuantos_____ estudiantes hay en la clase?

6. Sergio —Creo que somos veintidós. ¿_____Por que_____ te interesa tanto?

7. Nati   —Es que soy aficionada a la historia norteamericana. Es posible que tome la clase de oyente.[a]

      ¿_____Dónde_____ se reúnen Uds.?

  Sergio   —En el edificio de ciencias políticas, aula número 387.

8. Nati   —¿_____Qué_____ hora?

  Sergio   —De las diez y media hasta las doce.

B.

9. Diana   —Oye, Paco, ¿_____De quién_____ es esta carpeta[b]? ¿De Adriana?

10. Paco   —¿_____ dice adentro? ¿No tiene nombre ni papeles?

11. Diana   —¿_____? Yo no veo nada. Mira.

12. Paco   —¿_____ color es la de Jaime? ¿No tiene él una así?

13. Diana   —No me acuerdo. Vamos a llamarlo. ¿_____ es su número de teléfono?

  Paco   —No creo que lo encontremos en la casa porque lo vi hace poco por aquí.

14. Diana   —¿_____ iba?

  Paco   —No tengo la menor idea.

15. Diana   —¿Con _____ estaba?

  Paco   —Ni te puedo decir porque yo hablaba con Aurelia.

16. Diana   —¿_____ dices? ¿Tú y Aurelia otra vez?

17. Paco   —Ay, chica, ¿_____ quieres que yo haga? La quiero mucho. ¿Pero _____ me hablas de esto ahora?

18. Diana   —Bueno, es tema para otro día. Por ahora, ¿_____ no llamamos a Jaime en su celular?

[a]tome... *I'll audit the class*   [b]*briefcase*

Actividad 5   **Un testigo.** Ud. está paseándose por la calle cuando ve un choque de coches. Un policía acaba de llegar a la escena del accidente y quiere hacerle unas preguntas. Escriba las preguntas usando las palabras interrogativas correctas.

1. ¿_____ estaba Ud. cuando vio ocurrir el accidente?

2. ¿_____ pasó? Déme todos los detalles.

3. ¿_____ pasó? Dígame la hora exacta.

4. ¿_____ pasó la luz roja sin parar?

5. ¿_____ iba el conductor del coche blanco?

6. ¿_____ venía el conductor del coche rojo?

7. ¿_____ personas se acercaron a la escena?

8. ¿_____ minutos pasaron entre el choque y la llegada de la policía?

Actividad 6 **Una conversación telefónica.** Ud. está escuchando lo que dice su amiga mientras ella habla por teléfono. Porque no oye lo que dice la otra persona, Ud. tiene que imaginarse lo que ésta le pregunta a su amiga. Escriba las preguntas que se habrán hecho. Siga el modelo.

> MODELO —¿Qué tiempo hace?
> —Hace calor.

1. —_____

—De parte de Jaime Vega.

2. —_____

—La casa queda en la calle Olmo.

3. —_____

—El coche es de Roberto.

4. —_____

—Es verde oscuro.

5. —_____

—Voy a llevar a Ofelia.

6. —_____

—Llegaremos a las nueve.

7. —_____

—Tengo veinte y un años.

8. —_____

—Pienso ver a Inés y a Matilde.

9. —_____

—Será el sábado.

10. —_____

—Llegan mis primos.

11. —_____

—Gasté mucha plata.

12. —_____

—Está lloviendo.

13. —_____

—Tito y Josefa se encuentran muy bien.

14. —_____

—Me quedo hasta el domingo.

15. —_____

—No quiero ninguno de los dos.

Actividad 7 **¡Maravillas naturales de las Américas!** Escriba preguntas acerca de la magnitud de estos lugares tan conocidos.

> MODELO el río Grande / ser 1900 millas / largo
> ¿Cómo/Cuánto es el río Grande de largo?

1. el río Iguazú / tener 1.320 kilómetros / largo

_____

2. el río Amazonas / tener 6.500 kilómetros / longitud

_____

3. el río Misisipí / medir 2.350 millas / largo

_____

4. el lago Titicaca / ser 3.815 metros / ancho

_____

5. el desierto Atacama / tener 600 millas / largo

_____

6. el monte McKinley / tener 20.320 pies / altura

_____

7. la cumbre Aconcagua / medir 6.959 metros / alto

_____

Actividad 8 **¿Cuál es?** Complete las oraciones con las palabras interrogativas correctas. Escoja **¿cuál?, ¿cómo?** o **¿qué?**

1. ¿_____ es la capital de Costa Rica?

2. ¿_____ es la computación?

3. ¿_____ son tus hermanos?

4. ¿_____ fue el problema?

5. ¿_____ están por tu casa?

6. ¿_____ es la fecha de hoy?

7. ¿_____ es el guacamole?

Actividad 9 **¿De qué se habla?** Escriba preguntas derivadas de las oraciones. Tenga presente que la preposición precede la palabra interrogativa. Siga el modelo.

> MODELO Van *para el mar*.
> ¿Para dónde van?

1. Estas rosas son *para Susana*.

_____

2. Los ingenieros hablaron *sobre el nuevo puente*.

_____

3. Celeste trabaja *en aquella oficina*.

_____

4. Alberto fue *con otras siete personas*.

_____

5. Los CDs son *de Uds*.

_____

6. Fernando caminaba *hacia el río*.

_____

7. Jeremías entró *por aquí*.

_____

8. Sol jugará al tenis *con su hermana*.

_____

9. Se metieron *en un lío*.

_____

10. Vienen *del centro comercial*.

_____

Yes/no questions

Questions that do not begin with a question word require either *yes* or *no* as an answer. These *yes/no* questions are referred to in Spanish as **preguntas generales.**

To make a statement into a *yes/no* question in Spanish, the intonation changes from falling to rising at the end of the sentence without changing the word order.

¿Los chicos tienen juguetes?   *Do the children have toys?*
¿Alfonsina trabaja mañana?   *Is Alfonsina working tomorrow?*
¿Martín sacó las entradas?   *Did Martín buy the tickets?*

Yes/no questions can also be formed from statements by inverting the subject and the verb.

¿Tienen los chicos juguetes?   *Do the children have toys?*
¿Trabaja Alfonsina mañana?   *Is Alfonsina working tomorrow?*
¿Sacó Martín las entradas?   *Did Martín buy the tickets?*

The subject can also be placed at the end of the sentence to emphasize it. This is not very common.

¿Trabaja Alfonsina mañana?   *Is Alfonsina working* tomorrow?
                                     (*focus on* tomorrow)
¿Trabaja mañana Alfonsina?   *Is* Alfonsina *working tomorrow?*
                                     (*focus on* Alfonsina)

In *yes/no* questions consisting of just a subject and verb, either the subject or the verb may come at the end of the sentence, depending on which element is the focus of the question. Thus, the questions **¿Carlos se va?** and **¿Se va Carlos?** require different answers, since their focus is different.

¿Carlos se va?   *Is Carlos* leaving? (*focus on the verb*)
No, se queda.   *No, he's* staying.

¿Se va Carlos?   *Is Carlos* leaving? (*focus on Carlos*)
No, Carlos no. Se va Raúl.   *No, not* Carlos. Raúl *is leaving.*

Statements consisting of a subject, **ser** or **estar,** and an adjective are usually made into *yes/no* questions by placing the subject at the end of the sentence, not right after the verb as in English.

El coche es caro.   *The car is expensive.*
¿Es caro el coche?   *Is the car expensive?*

Las tiendas están cerradas.   *The stores are closed.*
¿Están cerradas las tiendas?   *Are the stores closed?*

Spanish can add phrases such as **¿verdad?, ¿no es verdad?, ¿no es cierto?,** and **¿no?** to statements to turn them into questions. The added phrases are called *tags*. These tag questions signal that the speaker expects the answer *yes*. If the statement is negative, only **¿verdad?** can be used as a tag.

Vienen con nosotros, ¿no es cierto? *You're coming with us, aren't you?*
Les gustó la clase, ¿no?   *They liked the class, didn't they?*
No tienes hambre, ¿verdad?   *You're not hungry, are you?*

Capítulo 23

Actividad 10 ¿**Cuál es la pregunta?** Escriba preguntas generales derivadas de las siguientes oraciones colocando el sujeto inmediatamente después del verbo. Siga el modelo.

> MODELO   Raúl estudia arquitectura.
> ¿Estudia Raúl arquitectura?

1. Gustavo y Melinda aprenden francés.

   ¿Aprenden Gustavo y Melinda francés?

2. Pepe trabaja en una tienda de vídeos.

   ¿Trabaja Pepe en una tienda de vídeos?

3. Ud. toca piano.

   _____

4. Los niños se han vestido.

   _____

5. Cristóbal jugará al béisbol.

   _____

6. Elena se matriculó anteayer.

   _____

7. Uds. deben quedarse unos días más.

   _____

8. Ramona está a dieta.

   _____

Actividad 11 ¿**Ser/estar +** *adjetivo* **+** *sujeto*? Escriba preguntas generales derivadas de las oraciones. Ponga el verbo **ser** o **estar** primero, seguido del adjetivo y al final el sujeto. Siga el modelo.

> MODELO   El edificio es alto.
> ¿Es alto el edificio?

1. Estos niños son traviesos.

   _____

2. Las margaritas (*daisies*) son bonitas.

   _____

3. El televisor estaba descompuesto.

   _____

4. El museo está abierto.

_____

5. La revista es italiana.

_____

6. Las joyas fueron robadas.

_____

7. Los pantalones están rotos (*torn*).

_____

8. Esta marca es buena.

_____

9. El espectáculo fue impresionante.

_____

Actividad 12 **Para hacer un picnic.** Unos amigos quieren hacer un picnic y necesitan hacer ciertas cosas para que resulte bien. ¿Quién se ocupa de cada cosa? Para saberlo, conteste las preguntas generales usando los nombres indicados. Siga el modelo.

> MODELO   ¿Trae la carne Marianela? (Clarita)
> No, Marianela no. La trae Clarita.

1. ¿Compra los panes Pedro? (Memo)

_____

2. ¿Domingo y Toni nos llevan en coche? (Salvador y Soledad)

_____

3. ¿Dora va a preparar las ensaladas? (Leonor)

_____

4. ¿Traerá Jorge el bate y la pelota? (Miguel)

_____

5. ¿Piensa Carmen llevar los manteles? (Marcos)

_____

6. ¿Harán Uds. los sándwiches? (Olivia y Nacho)

_____

7. ¿Jesús y Marta invitarán a los amigos? (tú)

_____

8. ¿Te ocupas tú de la fruta? (Mari)

_____

Questions in indirect speech

When a question is not asked directly, but incorporated into a larger sentence as a dependent clause, it is called an *indirect question*. Compare the following examples. The first one has a question quoted directly; the second one has the same question reported indirectly by being incorporated into a larger sentence.

She asked me, "Where is the post office?"
She asked me where the post office was.

Information questions are turned into indirect questions as subordinate clauses. The question word retains its accent mark.

Me preguntaron: —**¿De dónde vienes?**	*They asked me, "Where are you coming from?"*
Me preguntaron **de dónde venía.**	*They asked me where I was coming from.*
Te pregunté: —**¿Cuándo regresarás?**	*I asked you, "When will you return?"*
Te pregunté **cuándo regresarías.**	*I asked you when you would return.*
Siempre nos preguntan: —**¿Qué quieren?**	*They always ask us, "What do you want?"*
Siempre nos preguntan **qué queremos.**	*They always ask us what we want.*

Yes/no questions are turned into indirect questions by means of the word **si,** the equivalent of the English *whether, if.*

DIRECT QUESTION: ¿Sales, Juan?	*Are you going out, Juan?*
INDIRECT QUESTION: Le pregunté a Juan si salía.	*I asked Juan if he was going out.*

If **preguntar** is in the present or future, then the tense of the direct question is kept in the indirect question.

DIRECT: Me pregunta —**¿Para qué lo haces?**	*He asks me, "Why do you do it?"*
INDIRECT: Me pregunta **para qué lo hago.**	*He asks me why I do it.*
DIRECT: Nos pregunta —**¿Cuándo vendrá Marta?**	*He asks us, "When will Marta come?"*
INDIRECT: Nos pregunta **cuándo vendrá Marta.**	*He asks us when Marta will come.*
DIRECT: Me preguntará —**¿Quiénes regresaron?**	*She will ask me, "Who returned?"*
INDIRECT: Me preguntará **quiénes regresaron.**	*She'll ask me who returned.*

The following table sums up the tense changes in indirect questions.

If the verb of the main clause is in the:		The tense of the original question changes to:	
PRESENT	¿Para qué lo haces?	IMPERFECT	Me preguntó para qué lo hacía.
FUTURE	¿Cuándo vendrá Marta?	CONDITIONAL	Me preguntó cuándo vendría Marta.
PRETERITE	¿Quiénes regresaron?	PLUPERFECT	Me preguntó quiénes habían regresado.
		OR	
		PRETERITE	Me preguntó quiénes regresaron.

Actividad 13 **¡Cuántas preguntas!** Unas personas le hicieron tantas preguntas hoy que Ud. se encuentra mareado/a (*dizzy*). Ahora Ud. le cuenta a un amigo / una amiga lo que le preguntaron usando la pregunta indirecta. Siga el modelo.

> MODELO Anita me preguntó: —¿Adónde vas?
> Anita me preguntó adónde iba.

1. Felipe me preguntó: —¿Qué harás en la tarde?

   _____

2. Isabel me preguntó: —¿Con quiénes saliste?

   _____

3. Carlos me preguntó: —¿Por qué no quieres jugar al baloncesto?

   _____

4. Sol me preguntó: —¿A qué hora volviste a casa?

   _____

5. Claudio me preguntó: —¿Para cuándo necesitas escribir el informe?

   _____

6. Mi hermanita me preguntó: —¿Cuándo me llevas a una discoteca?

   _____

7. Mis primos me preguntaron: —¿Por qué no nos invitas al parque de atracciones?

   _____

8. Mi mamá me preguntó: —¿Por qué tienes dolor de cabeza?

   _____

9. Yo me pregunté a mí mismo/a: —¿Por qué te levantaste de la cama hoy?

   _____

10. Mis amigos me preguntaron: —¿De dónde vienes?

_____

11. Mirián me preguntó: —¿Cómo vas a llegar al centro?

_____

12. Alejo me preguntó: —¿Cuándo piensas regresar a Madrid?

_____

Actividad 14 **Actividad oral.** Uno/a de los estudiantes piensa en una persona, una cosa o un acontecimiento histórico. Los otros estudiantes tienen que hacerle preguntas hasta adivinar lo que es. Le toca al / a la estudiante que lo adivina pensar en otra persona, cosa o acontecimiento.

NEGATIVE AND indefinite words

Negative words and expressions

Study the following list of Spanish negative words and expressions and their affirmative counterparts.

nada *nothing*	**algo** *something*
nadie *no one, nobody*	**alguien** *someone, somebody*
	alguna vez *sometime*
	algunas veces *sometimes*
nunca, jamás *never*	**a veces** *sometimes*
	muchas veces, a menudo *often*
	siempre *always*
nunca más *never again*	**otra vez** *again*
tampoco *neither, not either*	**también** *also*
ni, ni siquiera *not even*	**o** *or*
ni... ni *neither . . . nor*	**o... o** *either . . . or*
en/por ningún lado/sitio/lugar *nowhere*	**en/por algún lado/sitio/lugar** *somewhere*
en/por ninguna parte *nowhere*	**en/por alguna parte** *somewhere*
de ninguna manera, de ningún modo *in no way*	**de alguna manera, de algún modo** *somehow, in some way*
ya no *no longer*	**todavía** *still*

When negative words follow the verb, **no** precedes it.

No hice **nada** hoy.	*I didn't do **anything** today.*
Catalina **no** hizo **nada tampoco**.	*Catalina didn't do **anything either**.*
No vamos **nunca** a esquiar.	*We **never** go skiing.*

However, if a negative word precedes the verb, then **no** is not used.

Nunca voy al cine.	*I **never** go to the movies.*
Yo **tampoco** voy mucho.	*I don't go much **either**.*

Spanish also has negative and affirmative adjectives **ninguno** (*no, not a*) and **alguno** (*some*). **Ninguno** and **alguno** are shortened to **ningún** and **algún** before a masculine singular noun.

Laura trabaja en **algún** edificio del centro.	*Laura works in **some** building downtown.*
Guillermo trabaja en **alguna** oficina.	*Guillermo works in **some** office.*
Hay **algunos** anuncios en el periódico.	*There are **some** ads in the newspaper.*
Conozco **algunas** tiendas elegantes por aquí.	*I know **some** elegant stores around here.*

Ninguno is not used in the plural unless the noun it modifies is always used in the plural such as **anteojos, tijeras,** or **vacaciones.**

No hay **ningún** hospital aquí.	*There is **no** hospital here. (There are no hospitals . . .*)
No recibí **ninguna** respuesta.	*I didn't receive **any** answer.*
Este año no tenemos **ningunas** vacaciones.	*This year we don't have **any** vacation.*

Personal **a** is used before **nadie** and **alguien** when they are direct objects and also before forms of **ninguno** and **alguno** when they refer to people and are direct objects.

¿Viste **a alguien** en la plaza?	*Did you see **anyone** in the square?*
No, no vi **a nadie.**	*No, I didn't see **anyone.***
¿Invitaste **a alguno** de los vecinos?	*Did you invite **any** of the neighbors?*
No, no llamé **a ninguno.**	*No, I didn't call **any** (of them).*

When words joined by **o... o** are the subject of a sentence, the verb is usually singular.

Alquilará la película **o Esteban o Elena.**	***Either Esteban or Elena** will rent the film.*

When words joined by **ni... ni** are the subject of a sentence, the verb generally appears in the plural. In English, the singular is preferred with *neither... nor.*

No salen **ni marcos ni Emilia.**	***Neither marcos nor Emilia** is going out.*

A single **ni** means *not even.* **Ni siquiera** is a more emphatic form.

¿Cuántos asistieron a la reunión?	*How many attended the meeting?*
Ni uno. / **Ni siquiera** uno.	*Not even one.*
¿Te ofrecieron algo?	*Did they offer you anything?*
Ni un vaso de agua.	*Not even a glass of water.*

Actividad 1 ¡**No!** Conteste las preguntas negativamente usando **no** y las palabras negativas que corresponden a las palabras *en letra cursiva.* Siga el modelo.

> MODELO ¿Quieres tomar *algo*?
> No, no quiero tomar nada.

1. ¿Fuiste *alguna vez* a la Isla de Pascua?

   _____

2. ¿Aprendieron Uds. chino *también*?

   _____

3. *¿Alguien* ha llamado esta tarde?

   _____

4. ¿Va Isabel a tomar álgebra *otra vez*?

   _____

5. ¿Leerás *o* la novela *o* el guión de la película?

   _____

6. ¿*Algunos* jefes renunciaron su puesto?

_____

7. ¿Conoció Osvaldo *a alguien* por fin?

_____

8. ¿*Siempre* limpias la casa los sábados?

_____

Actividad 2 **Angustias, la aguafiestas (*the wet blanket*).** Angustias lo ve todo negro, es decir, es muy pesimista. Lea sus comentarios sobre una fiesta y cambie el orden de la oración. Siga el modelo.

> MODELO Nadie se divierte.
> No se divierte nadie.

1. Nada queda de la comida.

_____

2. Tampoco hay refrescos.

_____

3. Ni los chicos ni las chicas bailan.

_____

4. Ningún cantante canta bien.

_____

5. Nadie tiene ganas de quedarse.

_____

6. Nunca dan fiestas divertidas.

_____

Actividad 3 **¡Qué iluso! (*What a dreamer!*)** Humberto pasa la vida soñando, pero son sueños imposibles. Dígale que no puede ser. Escriba las oraciones usando las palabras negativas apropiadas. Siga el modelo.

> MODELO Siempre gano becas.
> ¡Qué va! Nunca ganas becas.

1. Alguien me regaló dos millones de dólares.

_____

2. Algunas chicas dicen que soy un Adonis.

_____

3. Muchas veces saco una A en mis exámenes.

_____

4. Los reyes de España me mandaron algo.

_____

5. Yo también voy a la luna.

_____

6. Conchita va a salir conmigo otra vez.

_____

7. Mis padres me van a regalar o un Jaguar o un Ferrari.

_____

Further uses of negative words

Spanish, unlike English, allows two or more negative words in a sentence.

Nadie trae **nada nunca.**	*Nobody ever brings **anything.***

Alguno can have an emphatic negative meaning when placed after the noun.

No hay problema **alguno.**	*There is no problem **at all.***
No recibimos carta **alguna.**	*We received no letter **at all.***

In Spanish, negative words are used in some constructions where English uses indefinite words.

Spanish uses negatives after **que** (*than*) in comparative sentences.

La lluvia fue peor **que nada.**	*The rain was worse **than anything.***
Sí, y yo me mojé más **que nadie.**	*Yes, and I got wetter **than anyone.***
Se ha sufrido más aquí **que en ningún otro lugar.**	*People have suffered more here **than anywhere else.***
Hoy habló la profesora mejor **que nunca.**	*Today the teacher spoke better **than ever.***
Y aprendimos más cosas **que en ningún otro momento.**	*And we learned more **than at any other time.***

Spanish uses negatives after **antes de, antes que,** and **sin.**

Antes de hacer **nada,** lee las instrucciones.	*Before doing **anything,** read the instructions.*
Has llegado **antes que nadie.**	*You've arrived **before anyone else.***
Lo hizo **sin** pedir **nada a nadie nunca.**	*He did it **without ever** asking **anything of anyone.***

Spanish uses negatives after **imposible, inútil, poco probable,** expressions of doubt, and other similar words that imply negation.

Es **imposible** hacer **nada** aquí.	*It's **impossible** to do **anything** here.*
Es **inútil** pedirle **nada.**	*It's **useless** to ask him for **anything.***
Dudo que venga **nadie.**	*I **doubt** that **anyone** will come.*

PARTE IV

The conjunction **pero** is replaced by **sino** after a negative clause.

No viene ella, **sino** él.   *Not she, **but** he, is coming.*
No solamente viene ella, **sino**   *Not only is she coming, **but** he is, too.*
  también viene él.

Actividad 4   **Hay que ser negativo.** Complete las oraciones con las expresiones negativas
o indefinidas apropiadas.

1. Es imposible decirle _____nada_____ a este chiquillo
   porque no le hace caso a _____a nadie_____.

2. ¡_____Nunca_____ he oído tantas barbaridades!

3. El programa no fue _____nada_____ bueno, pero los
   locutores sí fueron _____algo_____ interesantes.

4. ¿No probaste la sopa? Y salió mejor que _____nunca_____.

5. No sólo visitamos Córdoba, _____sino también_____ nos quedamos
   ocho días en Granada.

6. ¡Qué señora más distinguida! Será _____alguien_____
   importante.

7. ¡Están más contentos ahora que en _____ningún otro momento_____ de su
   vida.

8. Mauricio es siempre el primero en llegar. Llega antes que
   _____nadie_____.

9. —¿Vino Alicia Delgado?
   —Sí, y _____no solamente_____ ella, _____sino también_____
   su hermano Francisco.

10. Muchos dicen que Toledo es más interesante por su arte e historia que
    _____ninguna_____ otra ciudad española.

Negative words in conversation

Negative words frequently serve as one-word answers to questions.

¿Vas a menudo al café estudiantil?   *Do you often go to the student café?*
Nunca.   *Never.*

¿Quién te ayudó con el trabajo?   *Who helped you with the work?*
Nadie.   *Nobody.*

Negative words, including **no,** often appear with subject pronouns or with
phrases consisting of **a** + *prepositional pronoun* as short answers to questions.

¿Cursan tú y Carla español?   *Are you and Carla taking Spanish?*
Yo, sí. **Ella, no.**   *I am. **She's not.***

No voy a la fiesta hoy. ¿Y tú?   *I'm not going to the party today. What
                                              about you?*
Yo tampoco.   *Neither am I.*

A mí no me gusta este plato.	*I don't like this dish.*
A nosotros tampoco.	***We don't either.***
A mí siempre me escriben.	*People are always writing to me.*
A nosotros nunca.	***Never to us.***

Some non-negative expressions such as **en absoluto** and **en la vida** can function as negatives.

En la vida he visto un espectáculo tan bueno.	*I have **never in my life** seen such a good show.*
Yo tampoco.	*Neither have I.*
¿Contrataría Ud. a ese señor?	*Would you hire that man?*
En absoluto.	***Absolutely not.***

Algo and **nada** can function as adverbs and modify adjectives and verbs.

El discurso fue **algo** confuso.	*The speech was **somewhat** confusing.*
Y no fue **nada** interesante.	*And it **wasn't at all** interesting.*
Tomás trabaja **algo.**	*Tomás works **a little.***
Pero no se concentra **nada.**	*But he doesn't concentrate **at all.***

Para nada is an emphatic replacement for **nada: No se concentra para nada.**

Algo de and **nada de** are used before nouns. **Algo de** is a synonym for **un poco de.**

¿Quieres **algo de** chocolate?	*Do you want **a little** chocolate?*
No, no debo comer **nada de** dulces.	*No, I'm not supposed to eat **any** sweets.*

Negative and indefinite words appear in many idiomatic expressions.

Expressions with **nunca** and **jamás**

casi nunca *hardly ever*	**¡Hasta nunca!** *Good-bye forever!*	**nunca jamás** *never ever*
el cuento de nunca acabar *the never-ending story*	**jamás de los jamases** *never ever*	**nunca más** *never again, no more*

Expressions with **ni**

ni hablar, ni modo *nothing doing*	**No lo puedo ver ni en pintura.** *I can't stand him at all.*	**No tengo ni idea.** *I haven't the slightest idea.*
¡Ni lo pienses! *Don't even think about it!*		

Expressions with **nada**

casi nada *hardly*
como si nada *as if it were nothing at all*
¡De eso nada, monada! *(slang) None of that!, No way!*
De nada. / Por nada. *You're welcome., Don't mention it.*
dentro de nada *in a moment*
más que nada *more than anything*
nada de eso *nothing of the sort*

nada de extraordinario *nothing unusual*
nada de nada *nothing at all*
¡Nada de salir antes de terminar la tarea! *Forget about going out before you finish your homework!*
nada más *that's all*
No me conoce de nada. *He doesn't know me from Adam.*
No por nada le llaman «tonto». *They don't call him "dumb" for nothing.*

no servir para nada *to be useless*
no tener nada de + *sustantivo* *to not be _____ at all*
no tener nada de particular *to have nothing special about*
no tener nada que ver con *to have nothing to do with*
por nada del mundo *for nothing in the world*
tener en nada *to think very little of; take no notice of*

Expressions with **nadie**

Es un don nadie. *He's a nobody.*

nadie más *nobody else*

Tú no eres nadie para quejarte. *You have no right to complain.*

Expressions with **indefinite words**

a la hora de siempre *at the usual time*
algo así *something like that*
Algo es algo. / Más vale algo que nada. *Something is better than nothing.*

De algo lo conozco. *I know you from somewhere.*
lo de siempre *the same old story*
para siempre *forever*
¡Por algo será! *There must be a reason!*

ser alguien *to be somebody*
tener algo que ver con *to have something to do with*
Ya es algo. *That's something at least. / It's a start.*

Actividad 5 **¿Cómo se dice en inglés?** Exprese las oraciones en inglés. Tenga en cuenta especialmente las expresiones con palabras negativas e indefinidas.

1. ¡No la puedo ver ni en pintura!

   _____

2. Van a verse a la hora de siempre.

   _____

3. No por nada la llaman encantadora.

   _____

4. Guillermo dice que no tiene ni idea.

   _____

5. Al fin y al cabo todo el discutir no sirvió para nada.

   _____

6. Lo que dices no tiene nada que ver con la situación actual.

   _____

7. Me parece que el proyecto es algo desorganizado.

   _____

8. Si Laura te dijo eso por algo será.

   _____

Other indefinite words and constructions

The pronoun **cualquiera** means *anyone* or *any one* and can refer to people or things.

¿Cuál de los dos pasteles quieres? **Cualquiera** de los dos.	*Which of the two pastries do you want?* *Any one (either one) of the two.*
No cualquiera podría hacer esto.	*Not just anyone would be able to do this.*
Al contrario. **Cualquiera** lo habría hecho mucho mejor.	*On the contrary. Anyone would have done it much better.*

NOTA There is an idiomatic use of **cualquiera** as a noun.

Él es un cualquiera.	*He's a nobody.*

When used as an adjective, **cualquiera** becomes **cualquier.**

El tren puede llegar en **cualquier** momento.	*The train can arrive at any moment.*
La vida es más fácil en **cualquier** otro lugar.	*Life is easier anywhere else.*
Está contento con **cualquier** cosa.	*He's happy with anything.*

Spanish also indicates uncertainty by the subjunctive. English often uses *whatever* or *wherever* in these cases. Compare the following pairs of sentences.

Lee el libro que recomiendan.	*Read the book that they recommend. (indicative: speaker knows which book it is)*
Lee el libro que **recomienden.**	*Read whatever book they recommend. (subjunctive: speaker does not know which book it is)*
Haga lo que quiere.	*Do what you want. (indicative: we already know what you want to do)*
Haga lo que **quiera.**	*Do whatever you want. (subjunctive: we don't know what you want to do)*

Todo is usually followed by a definite article and noun.

Por **todo el** país.	*Throughout **the whole** country.*
Toda la casa.	***The whole** house.*
Todos los estudiantes.	***All the** students.*
Todas las calles.	***Every** street.*

Todo followed by the indefinite article means *quite the, a real, just like a.*

Él es **todo un** cocinero.	*He's quite the cook.*
Ella es **toda una** reina.	*She's just like a queen.*

When **todo** is followed directly by a singular noun it means *every* or *any.*

Todo jugo de fruta es bueno.	***Any** fruit juice is good.*
Todo estudiante tiene computadora.	***Every** student has a computer.*
Nos sirvieron **toda** clase de fruta.	*They served us **every** kind of fruit.*

Note also the use of **todo** with place names.

Hay paradores por **toda España.**	*There are government inns **all over Spain.***
En casi **todo Santiago** hay servicio de metro.	*The subway serves almost **all of Santiago.***

Todo can also be used as a pronoun or in pronominal phrases.

Todo es interesante en España.	***Everything** is interesting in Spain (**Todo** takes a singular verb.)*
Todos son amables.	***Everyone** is nice. (**Todos** takes a plural verb.)*
Todo el mundo trata de ayudar.	***Everyone, everybody** tries to help. (**Todo el mundo** takes a singular verb.)*

Actividad 6   **¡En español, por favor!** Exprese las oraciones en español. Tenga en cuenta especialmente las expresiones con palabras negativas o indefinidas.

1. He had good reason to quit his job.

   _____

2. They'll call at any moment.

   _____

3. We walked the whole day through the whole city.

   _____

4. Anyone could help us with the work.

   _____

5. Every avenue is blocked during rush hour.

   _____

6. There are Roman ruins all over Spain.

   _____

Actividad 7 **Finales dramáticos o «Lo que el viento se llevó» (*Gone With the Wind*).**
Le toca a Ud. como guionista (*script writer*) escribir las últimas palabras de unas películas. Escríbalas en español. Tenga en cuenta las expresiones con palabras negativas e indefinidas.

1. Although I'll love you forever, I must say: "good-bye forever!"

   _____

2. Something is better than nothing.

   _____

3. Forget (**tú**) about going to Mars before you graduate!

   _____

4. And here ends the never-ending story!

   _____

5. I know you (**Ud.**) from somewhere. You must be somebody.

   _____

6. Do (**tú**) whatever you want! Go wherever you want! I shall never ever forget you!

   _____

7. This ending? That ending? I'm happy with either one.

   _____

8. That's all. Tomorrow is another day!

   _____

9. I won't leave you for anything in the world.

   _____

10. I can't stand her at all.

    _____

11. We'll get together at the usual time.

    _____

12. Stop (**Uds.**) crying. It's useless.

    _____

Actividad 8 **Actividad oral.** Un/a estudiante de cada pareja afirma algo. El otro / la otra contesta haciendo negativa la afirmación. Luego, se hace al inverso: un/a estudiante dice algo usando palabras o expresiones negativas y el otro / la otra contesta con una respuesta afirmativa.

APÉNDICE

NUMBERS; DATES; TIME

Cardinal numbers

Cardinal numbers are used for counting.

The Spanish cardinal numbers from 1–99

0	cero	13	trece	26	veintiséis
1	uno/a	14	catorce	27	veintisiete
2	dos	15	quince	28	veintiocho
3	tres	16	dieciséis	29	veintinueve
4	cuatro	17	diecisiete	30	treinta
5	cinco	18	dieciocho	31	treinta y uno/a
6	seis	19	diecinueve	32	treinta y dos
7	siete	20	veinte	40	cuarenta
8	ocho	21	veintiuno/a	50	cincuenta
9	nueve	22	veintidós	60	sesenta
10	diez	23	veintitrés	70	setenta
11	once	24	veinticuatro	80	ochenta
12	doce	25	veinticinco	90	noventa

Numbers ending in *one* agree in gender with the noun that follows. **Uno** shortens to **un** before a masculine noun. The number **veintiún** has a written accent in the masculine.

veintiún libros	*twenty-one books*
veintiuna revistas	*twenty-one magazines*
cincuenta y un estudiantes	*fifty-one students*
cincuenta y una profesoras	*fifty-one female teachers*

Una also shortens to **un** before a noun beginning with a stressed **a** sound.

un águila	*one eagle*
veintiún aulas	*twenty-one lecture halls*
cuarenta y un hachas	*forty-one axes*

Numbers ending in **uno** are used in counting and when no masculine noun follows directly.

¿Cuánto es? ¿Treinta y dos pesos?	*How much is it? Thirty-two pesos?*
No, treinta y uno.	*No, thirty-one.*

The numbers from sixteen to nineteen and from twenty-one to twenty-nine can be written as three words: **diez y seis, diez y siete, diez y ocho, diez y nueve, veinte y uno/a, veinte y dos, veinte y tres.** No accent marks are used when these numbers are spelled as three words. Compare **veintiséis** and **veinte y seis.**

Spanish numbers from 100 to 999

100	cien	200	doscientos/as	600	seiscientos/as
101	ciento uno/a	300	trescientos/as	700	setecientos/as
110	ciento diez	400	cuatrocientos/as	800	ochocientos/as
167	ciento sesenta y siete	500	quinientos/as	900	novecientos/as

NOTAS

- **Cien** becomes **ciento** before another number: **ciento sesenta** (*one hundred sixty*).

- Spanish does not use **y** to connect hundreds to tens or ones the way English often uses the word *and:* **doscientos cuarenta** (*two hundred **and** forty*).

- The hundreds from two hundred to nine hundred agree in gender with the noun they modify. This agreement takes place even when other numbers come between the hundreds and the noun.

doscient**os** edifici**os**	*two hundred buildings*
doscient**as** cas**as**	*two hundred houses*
doscient**as** treinta y cuatro casas	*two hundred thirty-four houses*

- The masculine plural is used when the same number counts both masculine and feminine nouns.

trescientos cajas y cajones	*three hundred boxes and cases*

Spanish numbers above 1,000

1.000	mil	10.000	diez mil	1.000.000	un millón
2.000	dos mil	100.000	cien mil	2.000.000	dos millones
6.572	seis mil quinientos setenta y dos	250.000	doscientos cincuenta mil		

NOTAS

- Numerals ending in **-cientos** agree across the word **mil**
  seiscientas cincuenta mil compañías 650,000 *companies*

- Spanish uses the period to separate thousands in writing numbers and the comma as a decimal point: $7.560 = **siete mil quinientos sesenta dólares**; $7,50 = **siete dólares cincuenta centavos.**

- Spanish does not count by hundreds above 1,000. Thus, *seventeen hundred* must be rendered **mil setecientos**, *thirty-two hundred* as **tres mil doscientos.**

- **Millón** is a noun and is followed by **de** when it appears before another noun unless another number comes between **millón** and the noun that follows it: **un millón de pesos; dos millones de pesos; un millón doscientos mil pesos.**

- *A billion* in Spanish is **mil millones. Un billón** means *a trillion.*

- The Spanish word **o** is written **ó** between numerical figures to avoid confusion with zero: **5 ó 6.**

Ordinal numbers

Ordinal numbers are used for ranking (*first, second, third*). Usually in Spanish conversation, only the ordinal numbers through *tenth* are used. Spanish ordinal numbers are adjectives that agree with the noun they modify in gender and number.

primero/a *first*	**quinto/a** *fifth*	**octavo/a** *eighth*
segundo/a *second*	**sexto/a** *sixth*	**noveno/a** *ninth*
tercero/a *third*	**séptimo/a** *seventh*	**décimo/a** *tenth*
cuarto/a *fourth*		

Ordinal numbers usually precede the noun. **Primero** and **tercero** become **primer** and **tercer** before a masculine singular noun.

el **primer** día	*the first day*
la **segunda** hija	*the second daughter*
el **tercer** capítulo	*the third chapter*
la **séptima** sinfonía	*the seventh symphony*

Ordinals often follow nouns such as **siglo** and the names of kings and queens. The definite article is not used after names of royalty.

el siglo segundo	*the second century*
Carlos V (Quinto)	*Charles the Fifth*

Above *tenth*, Spanish generally uses the cardinal numbers after the noun instead of the ordinals. Sometimes the cardinal numbers are used even below *tenth*.

Vive en el piso quince.	*He lives on the fifteenth floor.*
Vamos a leer el capítulo tres.	*We're going to read the third chapter.*

Days, dates, and years

The days of the week and the months of the year are not capitalized in Spanish. Note that the Hispanic week begins with Monday.

Days of the week

lunes *Monday*	**jueves** *Thursday*	**domingo** *Sunday*
martes *Tuesday*	**viernes** *Friday*	
miércoles *Wednesday*	**sábado** *Saturday*	

Months of the year

enero *January*	**mayo** *May*	**septiembre** *September*
febrero *February*	**junio** *June*	**octubre** *October*
marzo *March*	**julio** *July*	**noviembre** *November*
abril *April*	**agosto** *August*	**diciembre** *December*

Seasons

la primavera *spring*	**el otoño** *fall, autumn*
el verano *summer*	**el invierno** *winter*

In Spanish there are several patterns for using the preceding words in expressions of time. The singular definite article **el** means *on* before the days of the week.

| Nos vamos **el** lunes. | *We're leaving **on** Monday.* |

The plural definite article **los** indicates a repeated action or regular occurrence.

| Van a la iglesia **los** domingos. | *They go to church **on** Sundays.* |

The preposition **en** is used before months of the year and the names of the seasons: **en enero, en otoño.** The definite article is sometimes used after **en** with the names of seasons: **en la primavera.**

To express dates, Spanish uses cardinal numbers except for **el primero.** The definite article **el** precedes the date. The order is day-month-year and the preposition **de** is placed before the month and also the year, if it is given. Note that as with days of the week, no preposition is used for *on*.

| Creía que tus primos llegaban el treinta de noviembre. | *I thought your cousins were arriving on November thirtieth.* |
| No, vienen el primero de diciembre. | *No, they're coming December first.* |

Note the following useful expressions for talking about days and dates or that use the days and months in idiomatic ways.

¿Qué fecha es hoy?	*What's the date today?*
¿Cuál es la fecha de hoy?	*What's the date today?*
¿A cuántos estamos hoy?	*What's the date today?*
Es el primero de junio.	*It's June first.*
Estamos a diez de octubre.	*It's October tenth.*
¿Qué día es hoy?	*What day is it today?*
Hoy es jueves.	*Today is Thursday.*
pasando un día, un día de por medio	*every other day*
a principios de marzo	*at/toward the beginning of March*
a mediados de julio	*at/toward the middle of July*
a finales/últimos de septiembre	*at/toward the end of September*
martes trece	*Tuesday the thirteenth (equivalent of Friday the thirteenth)*

Telling time

To ask the time say, **¿Qué hora es?** In Spanish America **¿Qué horas son?** is also very common.

Es la una.	*It's one o'clock.*
Son las tres.	*It's three o'clock.*
Son las tres y diez.	*It's ten after three.*
Son las tres y cuarto/quince.	*It's a quarter after three / It's three-fifteen.*
Son las tres y media/treinta.	*It's three-thirty.*
Son las cuatro menos veinte.	*It's twenty to four.*
Son las cuatro menos cuarto/quince.	*It's a quarter to four.*

An alternative system for expressing the times between the half hour and the following hour is very common in Spanish America. The verbs used are **faltar** and **ser.**

Faltar:

Faltan veinte (minutos) para las cuatro.	*It's twenty to four.*
Faltan quince (minutos) para las cuatro.	*It's a quarter to four.*

Ser:

Son diez (minutos) para las cuatro.	*It's ten to four.*
Son cinco (minutos) para las cuatro.	*It's five to four.*

It is also acceptable to use digital clock time as in English.

Son las tres cincuenta.	*It's three fifty.*
Son las tres cincuenta y cinco.	*It's three fifty-five.*

The equivalents of English A.M. and P.M. in Spanish are the phrases **de la mañana, de la tarde, de la noche** added to the expression of time. Spanish-Americans often use A.M. and P.M. as in English. For noon and midnight, people say **Son las doce del día, Son las doce de la noche** or **Es (el) mediodía, Es (la) medianoche.**

Son las diez de la mañana.	*It's 10 A.M.*
Son las seis de la tarde.	*It's 6 P.M.*
Son las once y media de la noche.	*It's 11:30 P.M.*

To express the time when something occurs, Spanish uses the preposition **a.**

A las ocho de la mañana.	*At 8 A.M.*
A veinte para las siete.	*At twenty to seven.*

In Spanish-speaking countries, a 24-hour clock is used for official purposes such as train and plane schedules and show times. In the 24-hour clock, the minutes past the hour are counted from one to fifty-nine. **Cuarto** and **media** are replaced by **quince, treinta,** and **cuarenta y cinco;** and the phrases **de la mañana, de la tarde, de la noche** are not used.

Mi avión sale a las trece treinta.	*My plane leaves at 1:30 P.M.*
La película es a las veinte cuarenta.	*The film is at 8:40 P.M.*

The word **horas** often appears when using the 24-hour clock.

El programa es a las dieciocho horas.	*The program is at 6 P.M.*

Arithmetic operations, fractions, percentages

The basic arithmetic operations are read as follows in Spanish.

$15 + 12 = 27$	quince **más** doce **son / es igual a** veintisiete
$40 - 24 = 16$	cuarenta **menos** veinticuatro **son / es igual a** dieciséis
$10 \times 15 = 150$	diez **por** quince **son / es igual a** ciento cincuenta
$120 \div 12 = 10$	ciento veinte **dividido por** doce **son / es igual a** diez

NOTA

For division, the preposition **entre** is also used to mean *divided by:* **ciento veinte** *entre* **doce son diez.** Some Spanish-speaking countries use **para** in this meaning: **ciento veinte** *para* **doce son diez.**

Except for **un medio** (*one-half*) and **un tercio** (*one-third*), fractions have the same form as masculine ordinal numbers.

un cuarto	*one-fourth*
tres quintos	*three-fifths*

Above one-tenth, the suffix **-avo** is added to the cardinal number to form the corresponding fraction: **un onceavo** (*one-eleventh*), **tres veinteavos** (*three-twentieths*). Note also the fractions **un centavo** or **un centésimo** (*one-hundredth*) and **un milésimo** (*one-thousandth*).

Percentages in Spanish usually have an article (either **un** or **el**) before the figure.

Dan un veinte por ciento de descuento.	*They give a twenty percent discount.*
El diez por ciento de la población habla español.	*Ten percent of the population speaks Spanish.*

Words for mathematical operations

calcular *to calculate, estimate*	**multiplicar** *to multiply*	**el quebrado** *fraction*
computar *to compute, calculate*	**por ciento** *percent*	**restar** *to subtract*
dividir *to divide*	**el porcentaje** *percentage*	**sumar** *to add*

WRITTEN CONVENTIONS

Spanish has several written conventions that are different from those we observe in English.

Capitalization

Spanish capitalizes proper names (**México, Chile, Estados Unidos**) but does not capitalize adjectives derived from these names: **mexicano, chileno, estadounidense.** Spanish does not capitalize names of religions or the words referring to believers in those religions: **el catolicismo, católico/a, el protestantismo, protestante, el judaísmo, judío/a.** Spanish also does not capitalize titles of government officials: **el presidente de México, el rey / la reina de España.**

The names of the months and the days of the week are not capitalized in Spanish: **jueves, 23 de agosto.** In Spanish book and movie titles, all words except the first one are written with lowercase letters unless there are proper names in the title: *Como agua para chocolate, Mujeres al borde de una crisis de nervios, La historia oficial, Lo que se llevó el viento.* But Spanish does capitalize the words in the titles of newspapers and magazines: **El Vocero, El Mundo, La Prensa.**

Punctuation

Questions in Spanish begin with an inverted question mark ¿ and end with a question mark identical to the one used in English. Exclamations in Spanish begin with an inverted exclamation point ¡ and end with an exclamation point identical to the one used in English. The Spanish treatment of questions and exclamations in writing parallels the English treatment of quotations, in which quotation marks are placed at both the beginning and end of the quote.

> **¿Quién es ese muchacho?**

> **¡Qué artículo más interesante!**

Within certain sentences, the inverted question mark or exclamation point is placed not at the beginning of the sentence but at the beginning of the actual question or exclamation.

> **Pero, ¡qué bueno!**

> **Entonces, dime, ¿cuándo sales para Europa?**

Accent marks

Spanish uses diacritics, or accent marks, over certain letters (**acento** or **tilde** in Spanish).

The **tilde** over the letter **n** creates a different letter **ñ** (called **eñe**) with its own sound.

> **año   peña   sueño**

The accent mark (´) is placed over a vowel to show that the word it appears in violates one of the rules of Spanish stress.

The rules for stress in Spanish are simple. Words ending in a vowel or the consonants **-n** or **-s** are stressed on the next-to-the-last syllable, also called the *penultimate* syllable. These words are called **palabras llanas.**

> admi**nis**tran
>
> aprendi**za**je
>
> desco**nec**tas
>
> dis**que**te
>
> per**mi**tido
>
> rea**li**zan

Words ending in a consonant other than **-n** or **-s** are stressed on the final syllable. These words are called **palabras agudas.**

> capa**taz**
>
> celu**lar**
>
> digi**tal**
>
> grati**tud**
>
> internacio**nal**
>
> Inter**net**
>
> represen**tar**
>
> us**ted**

In order to calculate the position of stress you have to understand the Spanish classification of vowels. The vowels **a, e, o** are considered strong vowels. The vowels **i, u** are considered weak vowels. When two strong vowels appear in succession, they constitute separate syllables.

co-rre-o

le-al

ma-es-tro

pa-se-ar

pe-o-res

po-e-ma

ro-er

to-a-lla

When a strong and a weak vowel appear together they constitute a *diphthong*. A diphthong is a combination of two vowels pronounced in the same syllable. In diphthongs, the weak vowels **i** and **u** have the sound values /y/ and /w/. These diphthongs count as single vowels for the purpose of determining stress.

aurora

b**ai**le

b**oi**na

c**au**sa

c**ie**nc**ia**

d**eu**da

g**ai**ta

p**ei**ne

p**ue**s

s**ie**nto

s**ua**ve

v**ue**lto

When a word violates one of the above rules of stress, a written accent mark is placed over the vowel of the stressed syllable.

Words that end in a vowel or the consonants **-n** or **-s** but are not stressed on the penultimate syllable but instead on the final syllable or on the third-from-the-last syllable require a written accent mark to indicate this deviation from the rule. Words stressed on the third-from-the-last syllable are called **palabras esdrújulas.** The

third-from-the-last syllable is called the *antepenultimate* syllable in English.

abrir**ás**

an**á**lisis

ánimo

cibercaf**é**

eli**gió**

habla**rán**

lev**án**tate

matem**á**ticas

Panam**á**

sic**ó**logo

química

raz**ón**

Tom**ás**

vínculo

Words ending in a consonant other than **-n** or **-s** that are not stressed on the final syllable but instead on the penultimate syllable or on the antepenultimate syllable require a written accent mark to indicate this deviation from the rule.

az**ú**car

álbum

béisbol

fácil

lápiz

módem

When a strong and a weak vowel in succession are pronounced not as a diphthong but as two separate syllables, a written accent is placed over the weak vowel.

act**ú**a

ata**úd**

ba**úl**

l**í**o

pa**ís**

re**ú**ne

r**í**e

tecnolog**í**a

The accent mark in Spanish is also used to distinguish in writing words that are otherwise identical in speech. Usually one member of each of these pairs of words can carry stress in the phrase or sentence it occurs in, and that is the member of the pair that is written with an accent mark. For instance, the definite article **el** is not stressed but the subject pronoun **él** can carry stress.

UNSTRESSED WORD	STRESSED WORD
de *of, from*	**dé** *give!*
el *the*	**él** *he*
mas *but (literary)*	**más** *more*
mi *my*	**mí** *me (object of a preposition)*
que *relative pronoun*	**qué** *interrogative pronoun*
se *pronoun*	**sé** *I know; be!*
si *if*	**sí** *yes*
solo *alone*	**sólo** *only*
te *you (object pronoun)*	**té** *tea*
tu *your*	**tú** *you (subject pronoun)*

Interrogative words in Spanish are written with an accent mark. They retain this accent mark even when incorporated into a larger sentence.

| ¿**Cuándo** sale Juan? | *When is Juan leaving?* |
| No sé **cuándo** sale. | *I don't know when he is leaving.* |

When interrogative words are written without accents, they are conjunctions or relative pronouns.

| Lo veré **cuando** llegue. | *I'll see him when he gets here.* |
| Es el muchacho con **quien** trabajo. | *It's the boy whom I work with.* |

Most publications distinguish demonstrative adjectives from demonstrative pronouns by placing an accent mark over the stessed vowel of the pronoun. In modern usage, the written accent is sometimes left off demonstrative pronouns.

A él le gusta **aquel** libro, pero a mí me gusta **éste (este).**	*He likes **that** book, but I like **this one.***
¿**Qué** te parece **esta** cartera, señora?	*How do you like **this** handbag, ma'am?*
Ésa (Esa) no tanto. **Aquéllas (Aquellas)** me gustan más.	*I don't like **that one** so much. I like **those over there** more.*

VERB CHARTS

Regular Verbs

-ar verbs

CANTAR *to sing*	
Indicative mood	
PRESENT	canto, cantas, canta, cantamos, cantáis, cantan
IMPERFECT	cantaba, cantabas, cantaba, cantábamos, cantabais, cantaban
PRETERITE	canté, cantaste, cantó, cantamos, cantasteis, cantaron
FUTURE	cantaré, cantarás, cantará, cantaremos, cantaréis, cantarán
CONDITIONAL	cantaría, cantarías, cantaría, cantaríamos, cantaríais, cantarían
PRESENT PERFECT	he cantado, has cantado, ha cantado, hemos cantado, habéis cantado, han cantado
PLUPERFECT	había cantado, habías cantado, había cantado, habíamos cantado, habíais cantado, habían cantado
PRETERITE PERFECT	hube cantado, hubiste cantado, hubo cantado, hubimos cantado, hubisteis cantado, hubieron cantado
FUTURE PERFECT	habré cantado, habrás cantado, habrá cantado, habremos cantado, habréis cantado, habrán cantado
CONDITIONAL PERFECT	habría cantado, habrías cantado, habría cantado, habríamos cantado, habríais cantado, habrían cantado
Subjunctive mood	
PRESENT	cante, cantes, cante, cantemos, cantéis, canten
IMPERFECT	cantara, cantaras, cantara, cantáramos, cantarais, cantaran cantase, cantases, cantase, cantásemos, cantaseis, cantasen
PRESENT PERFECT	haya cantado, hayas cantado, haya cantado, hayamos cantado, hayáis cantado, hayan cantado
PLUPERFECT	hubiera/hubiese cantado, hubieras/hubieses cantado, hubiera/hubiese cantado, hubiéramos/hubiésemos cantado, hubierais/hubieseis cantado, hubieran/hubiesen cantado
Imperative mood	
	canta / no cantes (tú), cante (Ud.), cantemos (nosotros), cantad / no cantéis (vosotros), canten (Uds.)

-er verbs

COMER *to eat*

Indicative mood

PRESENT	como, comes, come, comemos, coméis, comen
IMPERFECT	comía, comías, comía, comíamos, comíais, comían
PRETERITE	comí, comiste, comió, comimos, comisteis, comieron
FUTURE	comeré, comerás, comerá, comeremos, comeréis, comerán
CONDITIONAL	comería, comerías, comería, comeríamos, comeríais, comerían
PRESENT PERFECT	he comido, has comido, ha comido, hemos comido, habéis comido, han comido
PLUPERFECT	había comido, habías comido, había comido, habíamos comido, habíais comido, habían comido
PRETERITE PERFECT	hube comido, hubiste comido, hubo comido, hubimos comido, hubisteis comido, hubieron comido
FUTURE PERFECT	habré comido, habrás comido, habrá comido, habremos comido, habréis comido, habrán comido
CONDITIONAL PERFECT	habría comido, habrías comido, habría comido, habríamos comido, habríais comido, habrían comido

Subjunctive mood

PRESENT	coma, comas, coma, comamos, comáis, coman
IMPERFECT	comiera, comieras, comiera, comiéramos, comierais, comieran comiese, comieses, comiese, comiésemos, comieseis, comiesen
PRESENT PERFECT	haya comido, hayas comido, haya comido, hayamos comido, hayáis comido, hayan comido
PLUPERFECT	hubiera/hubiese comido, hubieras/hubieses comido, hubiera/hubiese comido, hubiéramos/hubiésemos comido, hubierais/hubieseis comido, hubieran/hubiesen comido

Imperative mood

	come / no comas (tú), coma (Ud.), comamos (nosotros), comed / no comáis (vosotros), coman (Uds.)

-ir verbs

VIVIR *to live*

Indicative mood

PRESENT	vivo, vives, vive, vivimos, vivís, viven
IMPERFECT	vivía, vivías, vivía, vivíamos, vivían
PRETERITE	viví, viviste, vivió, vivimos, vivisteis, vivieron
FUTURE	viviré, vivirás, vivirá, viviremos, viviréis, vivirán
CONDITIONAL	viviría, vivirías, viviría, viviríamos, viviríais, vivirían
PRESENT PERFECT	he vivido, has vivido, ha vivido, hemos vivido, habéis vivido, han vivido
PLUPERFECT	había vivido, habías vivido, había vivido, habíamos vivido, habíais vivido, habían vivido
PRETERITE PERFECT	hube vivido, hubiste vivido, hubo vivido, hubimos vivido, hubisteis vivido, hubieron vivido
FUTURE PERFECT	habré vivido, habrás vivido, habrá vivido, habremos vivido, habréis vivido, habrán vivido
CONDITIONAL PERFECT	habría vivido, habrías vivido, habría vivido, habríamos vivido, habríais vivido, habrían vivido

Subjunctive mood

PRESENT	viva, vivas, viva, vivamos, viváis, vivan
IMPERFECT	viviera, vivieras, viviera, viviéramos, vivierais, vivieran viviese, vivieses, viviese, viviésemos, vivieseis, viviesen
PRESENT PERFECT	haya vivido, hayas vivido, haya vivido, hayamos vivido, hayáis vivido, hayan vivido
PLUPERFECT	hubiera/hubiese vivido, hubieras/hubieses vivido, hubiera/hubiese vivido, hubiéramos/hubiésemos vivido, hubierais/hubieseis vivido, hubieran/hubiesen vivido

Imperative mood

vive / no vivas (tú), viva (Ud.), vivamos (nosotros), vivid / no viváis (vosotros), vivan (Uds.)

Verbs with changes in the vowel of the stem

PENSAR (e → ie) *to think*

PRESENT INDICATIVE	pienso, piensas, piensa, pensamos, penséis, piensan
PRESENT SUBJUNCTIVE	piense, pienses, piense, pensemos, penséis, piensen
IMPERATIVE	piensa / no pienses, piense, pensemos, pensad / no penséis, piensen

Other tenses and forms have no changes in the vowel of the stem.

ENTENDER (e → ie) *to understand*

PRESENT INDICATIVE	entiendo, entiendes, entiende, entendemos, entendéis, entienden
PRESENT SUBJUNCTIVE	entienda, entiendas, entienda, entendamos, entendáis, entiendan
IMPERATIVE	entiende / no entiendas, entienda, entendamos, entended / no entendáis, entiendan

Other tenses and forms have no changes in the vowel of the stem.

RECORDAR (o → ue) *to remember*

PRESENT INDICATIVE	recuerdo, recuerdas, recuerda, recordamos, recordáis, recuerdan
PRESENT SUBJUNCTIVE	recuerde, recuerdes, recuerde, recordemos, recordéis, recuerden
IMPERATIVE	recuerda / no recuerdes, recuerde, recordemos, recordad / no recordéis, recuerden

Other tenses and forms have no changes in the vowel of the stem.

VOLVER (o → ue) *to return*

PRESENT INDICATIVE	vuelvo, vuelves, vuelve, volvemos, volvéis, vuelven
PRESENT SUBJUNCTIVE	vuelva, vuelvas, vuelva, volvamos, volváis, vuelvan
IMPERATIVE	vuelve / no vuelvas, vuelva, volvamos, volved / no volváis, vuelvan

Other tenses and forms have no changes in the vowel of the stem.

Stem-changing **-ir** verbs have three types of possible changes in the vowel of the stem: **e → ie, e → i, o → ue.** In addition to the expected changes in the present subjunctive and imperative, verbs having the change **e → ie** and **e → i** have **-i** as the stem vowel, and verbs having the change **o → ue** have **-u** as the stem vowel in the following forms:

a. the **nosotros/as** and **vosotros/as** forms of the present subjunctive
b. the **nosotros/as** command and the negative **vosotros/as** commands
c. the third-person singular and third-person plural forms of the preterite
d. all persons of the imperfect subjunctive (both **-ra** and **-se** forms)
e. the present participle

Sample conjugations

SENTIR (e → ie)   *to feel, regret*

PRESENT INDICATIVE	siento, sientes, siente, sentimos, sentís, sienten
PRESENT SUBJUNCTIVE	sienta, sientas, sienta, sintamos, sintáis, sientan
IMPERATIVE	siente / no sientas, sienta, sintamos, sentid / no sintáis, sientan
PRETERITE	sentí, sentiste, sintió, sentimos, sentisteis, sintieron
IMPERFECT SUBJUNCTIVE	sintiera, sintieras, sintiera, sintiéramos, sintierais, sintieran sintiese, sintieses, sintiese, sintiésemos, sintieseis, sintiesen
PRESENT PARTICIPLE	sintiendo

Other tenses and forms have no changes in the vowel of the stem.

PEDIR (e → i)   *to ask for*

PRESENT INDICATIVE	pido, pides, pide, pedimos, pedís, piden
PRESENT SUBJUNCTIVE	pida, pidas, pida, pidamos, pidáis, pidan
IMPERATIVE	pide / no pidas, pida, pidamos, pedid / no pidáis, pidan
PRETERITE	pedí, pediste, pidió, pedimos, pedisteis, pidieron
IMPERFECT SUBJUNCTIVE	pidiera, pidieras, pidiera, pidiéramos, pidierais, pidieran pidiese, pidieses, pidiese, pidiésemos, pidieseis, pidiesen
PRESENT PARTICIPLE	pidiendo

Other tenses and forms have no changes in the vowel of the stem.

DORMIR (o → ue) *to sleep*

PRESENT INDICATIVE	duermo, duermes, duerme, dormimos, dormís, duermen
PRESENT SUBJUNCTIVE	duerma, duermas, duerma, durmamos, durmáis, duerman
IMPERATIVE	duerme / no duermas, duerma, durmamos, dormid / no durmáis, duerman
PRETERITE	dormí, dormiste, durmió, dormimos, dormisteis, durmieron
IMPERFECT SUBJUNCTIVE	durmiera, durmieras, durmiera, durmiéramos, durmierais, durmieran
	durmiese, durmieses, durmiese, durmiésemos, durmieseis, durmiesen
PRESENT PARTICIPLE	durmiendo

Other tenses and forms have no changes in the vowel of the stem.

Verbs with spelling changes

These changes occur in the first-person singular of the preterite, in all persons of the present subjunctive, and in imperative forms derived from the present subjunctive.

Verbs ending in **-car (c → qu** before **-e)**

TOCAR *to play an instrument; to touch*

PRETERITE	toqué, tocaste, tocó, tocamos, tocasteis, tocaron
PRESENT SUBJUNCTIVE	toque, toques, toque, toquemos, toquéis, toquen
IMPERATIVE	toca / no toques, toque, toquemos, tocad / no toquéis, toquen

Verbs ending in **-gar (g → gu** before **-e)**

LLEGAR *to arrive*

PRETERITE	llegué, llegaste, llegó, llegamos, llegasteis, llegaron
PRESENT SUBJUNCTIVE	llegue, llegues, llegue, lleguemos, lleguéis, lleguen
IMPERATIVE	llega / no llegues, llegue, lleguemos, llegad / no lleguéis, lleguen

Verbs ending in **-zar (z → c** before **-e)**

CRUZAR *to cross*

PRETERITE	crucé, cruzaste, cruzó, cruzamos, cruzasteis, cruzaron
PRESENT SUBJUNCTIVE	cruce, cruces, cruce, crucemos, crucéis, crucen
IMPERATIVE	cruza / no cruces, cruce, crucemos, cruzad / no crucéis, crucen

Verbs ending in **-ger** and **-gir (g → j** before **-a** and **-o)**

RECOGER *to pick up*	
PRESENT INDICATIVE	recojo, recoges, recoge, recogemos, recogéis, recogen
PRESENT SUBJUNCTIVE	recoja, recojas, recoja, recojamos, recojáis, recojan
IMPERATIVE	recoge / no recojas, recoja, recojamos, recoged / no recojáis, recojan

EXIGIR *to demand*	
PRESENT INDICATIVE	exijo, exiges, exige, exigimos, exigís, exigen
PRESENT SUBJUNCTIVE	exija, exijas, exija, exijamos, exijáis, exijan
IMPERATIVE	exige / no exijas, exija, exijamos, exegid / no exijáis, exijan

Verbs ending in **-guir (gu → g** before **-a** and **-o)**

SEGUIR *to follow*	
PRESENT INDICATIVE	sigo, sigues, sigue, seguimos, seguís, siguen
PRESENT SUBJUNCTIVE	siga, sigas, siga, sigamos, sigáis, sigan
IMPERATIVE	sigue / no sigas, siga, sigamos, seguid / no sigáis, sigan

Verbs ending in a consonant + **-cer, -cir (c → z** before **-a** and **-o)**

CONVENCER *to convince*	
PRESENT INDICATIVE	convenzo, convences, convence, convencemos, convencéis, convencen
PRESENT SUBJUNCTIVE	convenza, convenzas, convenza, convenzamos, convenzáis, convenzan
IMPERATIVE	convence / no convenzas, convenza, convenzamos, convenced / no convenzáis, convenzan

-Er verbs having stems ending in a vowel

*These verbs change the **-i** of the preterite endings **-ió** and **-ieron** and the **-i** of the present participle ending **-iendo** to **-y**. The **-y** appears in all persons of the imperfect subjunctive. These verbs also add written accents to the endings of the second-person singular and the first- and second-persons plural of the preterite and the past participle.*

CREER *to believe*	
PRETERITE	creí, creíste, creyó, creímos, creísteis, creyeron
IMPERFECT SUBJUNCTIVE	creyera (creyese), creyeras, creyera, creyéramos, creyerais, creyeran
PRESENT PARTICIPLE	creyendo
PAST PARTICIPLE	creído

-Ar verbs having stems ending in **-i** or **-u** where those letters represent a full syllable, not part of a diphthong

*These verbs have a written accent over the **-i** or **-u** in all persons of the singular and in the third-person plural of the present indicative and present subjunctive and all imperative forms except **nosotros/as** and **vosotros/as.***

ENVIAR *to send*

PRESENT	envío, envías, envía, enviamos, enviáis, envían
PRESENT SUBJUNCTIVE	envíe, envíes, envíe, enviemos, enviéis, envíen
IMPERATIVE	envía / no envíes, envíe, enviemos, enviad / no enviéis, envíen

CONTINUAR *to continue*

PRESENT	continúo, continúas, continúa, continuamos, continuáis, continúan
PRESENT SUBJUNCTIVE	continúe, continúes, continúe, continuemos, continuéis, continúen
IMPERATIVE	continúa / no continúes, continúe, continuemos, continuad / no continuéis, continúen

Irregular verbs

Only irregular forms are shown.

Verbs ending in a vowel + **-cer** or **-ucir**

*These verbs change the final **c** of the stem to **-zc** before **-a** and **-o**. The **zc** appears in the first-person singular of the present indicative, in all persons of the present subjunctive, and in imperative forms derived from the present subjunctive. The verb **mecer** (to rock a child, a cradle) is conjugated like **convencer,** and not like **conocer**: present **mezo, meces,** etc.; present subjunctive **meza, mezas,** etc. The verb **cocer** is also conjugated like **convencer** and in addition has the stem change **o → ue**: present **cuezo, cueces,** etc.; present subjunctive **cueza, cuezas,** etc.*

CONOCER *to know*

PRESENT INDICATIVE	conozco, conoces, conoce, conocemos, conocéis, conocen
PRESENT SUBJUNCTIVE	conozca, conozcas, conozca, conozcamos, conozcáis, conozcan

CONDUCIR *to drive*

PRESENT INDICATIVE	conduzco, conduces, conduce, conducimos, conducís, conducen
PRESENT SUBJUNCTIVE	conduzca, conduzcas, conduzca, conduzcamos, conduzcáis, conduzcan

Verbs ending in **-uir** (not including those ending in **-guir**)

*These verbs add **y** before a vowel other than **i** and change the unaccented **i** between vowels to **y**. The **y** appears in all singular forms and the third-person plural of the present, in the third-person singular and plural of the preterite, in all persons of the present and imperfect subjunctive, and in all imperative forms except the affirmative **vosotros/as** command.*

CONSTRUIR *to build*

PRESENT INDICATIVE	construyo, construyes, construye, construimos, construís, construyen
PRETERITE	construí, construiste, construyó, construimos, construisteis, construyeron
IMPERATIVE	construye / no construyas, construya, construyamos, construid / no construyáis, construyan
PRESENT SUBJUNCTIVE	construya, construyas, construya, construyamos, construyáis, construyan
IMPERFECT SUBJUNCTIVE	construyera (construyese), construyeras, construyera, construyéramos, construyerais, construyeran

Other irregular verbs

Only irregular forms are shown.

ANDAR *to walk*

PRETERITE	anduve, anduviste, anduvo, anduvimos, anduvisteis, anduvieron
IMPERFECT SUBJUNCTIVE	anduviera (anduviese), anduvieras, anduviera, anduviéramos, anduvierais, anduvieran

CABER *to fit*

PRESENT INDICATIVE	quepo, cabes, cabe, cabemos, cabéis, caben
PRETERITE	cupe, cupiste, cupo, cupimos, cupisteis, cupieron
FUTURE	cabré, cabrás, cabrá, cabremos, cabréis, cabrán
CONDITIONAL	cabría, cabrías, cabría, cabríamos, cabríais, cabrían
IMPERATIVE	cabe / no quepas, quepa, quepamos, cabed / no quepáis, quepan
PRESENT SUBJUNCTIVE	quepa, quepas, quepa, quepamos, quepáis, quepan
IMPERFECT SUBJUNCTIVE	cupiera (cupiese), cupieras, cupiera, cupiéramos, cupierais, cupieran

CAER *to fall*

PRESENT INDICATIVE	caigo, caes, cae, caemos, caéis, caen
PRETERITE	caí, caíste, cayó, caímos, caísteis, cayeron
IMPERATIVE	cae / no caigas, caiga, caigamos, caed / no caigáis, caigan
PRESENT SUBJUNCTIVE	caiga, caigas, caiga, caigamos, caigáis, caigan
IMPERFECT SUBJUNCTIVE	cayera (cayese), cayeras, cayera, cayéramos, cayerais, cayeran
PRESENT PARTICIPLE	cayendo
PAST PARTICIPLE	caído

DAR *to give*

PRESENT INDICATIVE	doy, das, da, damos, dais, dan
PRETERITE	di, diste, dio, dimos, disteis, dieron
IMPERATIVE	da / no des, dé, demos, dad / no deis, den
PRESENT SUBJUNCTIVE	dé, des, dé, demos, deis, den
IMPERFECT SUBJUNCTIVE	diera (diese), dieras, diera, diéramos, dierais, dieran

DECIR *to say, tell*

PRESENT INDICATIVE	digo, dices, dice, decimos, decís, dicen
PRETERITE	dije, dijiste, dijo, dijimos, dijisteis, dijeron
FUTURE	diré, dirás, dirá, diremos, diréis, dirán
CONDITIONAL	diría, dirías, diría, diríamos, diríais, dirían
IMPERATIVE	di / no digas, diga, digamos, decid / no digáis, digan
PRESENT SUBJUNCTIVE	diga, digas, diga, digamos, digáis, digan
IMPERFECT SUBJUNCTIVE	dijera (dijese), dijeras, dijera, dijéramos, dijerais, dijeran
PRESENT PARTICIPLE	diciendo
PAST PARTICIPLE	dicho

ESTAR *to be*

PRESENT INDICATIVE	estoy, estás, está, estamos, estáis, están
PRETERITE	estuve, estuviste, estuvo, estuvimos, estuvisteis, estuvieron
IMPERATIVE	está / no estés, esté, estemos, estad / no estéis, estén
PRESENT SUBJUNCTIVE	esté, estés, esté, estemos, estéis, estén
IMPERFECT SUBJUNCTIVE	estuviera (estuviese), estuvieras, estuviera, estuviéramos, estuvierais, estuvieran

HABER *to have (auxiliary verb)*

PRESENT INDICATIVE	he, has, ha, hemos, habéis, han
PRETERITE	hube, hubiste, hubo, hubimos, hubisteis, hubieron
FUTURE	habré, habrás, habrá, habremos, habréis, habrán
CONDITIONAL	habría, habrías, habría, habríamos, habríais, habrían
PRESENT SUBJUNCTIVE	haya, hayas, haya, hayamos, hayáis, hayan
IMPERFECT SUBJUNCTIVE	hubiera (hubiese), hubieras, hubiera, hubiéramos, hubierais, hubieran

HACER *to do, make*

PRESENT INDICATIVE	hago, haces, hace, hacemos, hacéis, hacen
PRETERITE	hice, hiciste, hizo, hicimos, hiciste, hicieron
FUTURE	haré, harás, hará, haremos, haréis, harán
CONDITIONAL	haría, harías, haría, haríamos, haríais, harían
IMPERATIVE	haz / no hagas, haga, hagamos, haced / no hagáis, no hagan
PRESENT SUBJUNCTIVE	haga, hagas, haga, hagamos, hagáis, hagan
IMPERFECT SUBJUNCTIVE	hiciera (hiciese), hicieras, hiciera, hiciéramos, hicierais, hicieran
PAST PARTICIPLE	hecho

IR *to go*

PRESENT INDICATIVE	voy, vas, va, vamos, vais, van
PRETERITE	fui, fuiste, fue, fuimos, fuisteis, fueron
IMPERATIVE	ve / no vayas, vaya, vamos / no vayamos, id / no vayáis, vayan
PRESENT SUBJUNCTIVE	vaya, vayas, vaya, vayamos, vayáis, vayan
IMPERFECT SUBJUNCTIVE	fuera (fuese), fueras, fuera, fuéramos, fuerais, fueran
PRESENT PARTICIPLE	yendo

OÍR *to hear*

PRESENT INDICATIVE	oigo, oyes, oye, oímos, oís, oyen
PRETERITE	oí, oíste, oyó, oímos, oísteis, oyeron
IMPERATIVE	oye / no oigas, oiga, oigamos, oíd / no oigáis, oigan
PRESENT SUBJUNCTIVE	oiga, oigas, oiga, oigamos, oigáis, oigan
IMPERFECT SUBJUNCTIVE	oyera (oyese), oyeras, oyera, oyéramos, oyerais, oyeran
PRESENT PARTICIPLE	oyendo
PAST PARTICIPLE	oído

PODER *to be able, can*

PRESENT INDICATIVE	puedo, puedes, puede, podemos, podéis, pueden
PRETERITE	pude, pudiste, pudo, pudimos, pudisteis, pudieron
FUTURE	podré, podrás, podrá, podremos, podréis, podrán
CONDITIONAL	podría, podrías, podría, podríamos, podríais, podrían
PRESENT SUBJUNCTIVE	pueda, puedas, pueda, podamos, podáis, puedan
IMPERFECT SUBJUNCTIVE	pudiera (pudiese), pudieras, pudiera, pudiéramos, pudierais, pudieran
PRESENT PARTICIPLE	pudiendo

PONER *to put*

PRESENT INDICATIVE	pongo, pones, pone, ponemos, ponéis, ponen
PRETERITE	puse, pusiste, puso, pusimos, pusisteis, pusieron
FUTURE	pondré, pondrás, pondrá, pondremos, pondréis, pondrán
CONDITIONAL	pondría, pondrías, pondría, pondríamos, pondríais, pondrían
IMPERATIVE	pon / no pongas, ponga, pongamos, poned / no pongáis, pongan
PRESENT SUBJUNCTIVE	ponga, pongas, ponga, pongamos, pongáis, pongan
IMPERFECT SUBJUNCTIVE	pusiera (pusiese), pusieras, pusiera, pusiéramos, pusierais, pusieran
PAST PARTICIPLE	puesto

PRODUCIR *to produce*

PRESENT INDICATIVE	produzco, produces, produce, producimos, producís, producen
PRETERITE	produje, produjiste, produjo, produjimos, produjisteis, produjeron
IMPERATIVE	produce / no produzcas, produzca, produzcamos, producid / no produzcáis, produzcan
PRESENT SUBJUNCTIVE	produzca, produzcas, produzca, produzcamos, produzcáis, produzcan
IMPERFECT SUBJUNCTIVE	produjera (produjese), produjeras, produjera, produjéramos, produjerais, produjeran

QUERER *to want*

PRESENT INDICATIVE	quiero, quieres, quiere, queremos, queréis, quieren
PRETERITE	quise, quisiste, quiso, quisimos, quisisteis, quisieron
FUTURE	querré, querrás, querrá, querremos, querréis, querrán
CONDITIONAL	querría, querrías, querría, querríamos, querríais, querrían
IMPERATIVE	quiere / no quieras, quiera, queramos, quered / no queráis, quieran
PRESENT SUBJUNCTIVE	quiera, quieras, quiera, queramos, queráis, quieran
IMPERFECT SUBJUNCTIVE	quisiera (quisiese), quisieras, quisiera, quisiéramos, quisierais, quisieran

SABER *to know*

PRESENT INDICATIVE	sé, sabes, sabe, sabemos, sabéis, saben
PRETERITE	supe, supiste, supo, supimos, supisteis, supieron
FUTURE	sabré, sabrás, sabrá, sabremos, sabréis, sabrán
CONDITIONAL	sabría, sabrías, sabría, sabríamos, sabríais, sabrían
IMPERATIVE	sabe / no sepas, sepa, sepamos, sabed / no sepáis, sepan
PRESENT SUBJUNCTIVE	sepa, sepas, sepa, sepamos, sepáis, sepan
IMPERFECT SUBJUNCTIVE	supiera (supiese), supieras, supiera, supiéramos, supierais, supieran

SALIR *to go out*

PRESENT INDICATIVE	salgo, sales, sale, salimos, salís, salen
FUTURE	saldré, saldrás, saldrá, saldremos, saldréis, saldrán
CONDITIONAL	saldría, saldrías, saldría, saldríamos, saldríais, saldrían
IMPERATIVE	sal / no salgas, salga, salgamos, salid / no salgáis, salgan
PRESENT SUBJUNCTIVE	salga, salgas, salga, salgamos, salgáis, salgan

SER *to be*

PRESENT INDICATIVE	soy, eres, es, somos, sois, son
PRETERITE	fui, fuiste, fue, fuimos, fuisteis, fueron
IMPERATIVE	sé / no seas, sea, seamos, sed / no seáis, sean
PRESENT SUBJUNCTIVE	sea, seas, sea, seamos, seáis, sean
IMPERFECT SUBJUNCTIVE	fuera (fuese), fueras, fuera, fuéramos, fuerais, fueran

TENER *to have*

PRESENT INDICATIVE	tengo, tienes, tiene, tenemos, tenéis, tienen
PRETERITE	tuve, tuviste, tuvo, tuvimos, tuvisteis, tuvieron
FUTURE	tendré, tendrás, tendrá, tendremos, tendréis, tendrán
CONDITIONAL	tendría, tendrías, tendría, tendríamos, tendríais, tendrían
IMPERATIVE	ten / no tengas, tenga, tengamos, tened / no tengáis, tengan
PRESENT SUBJUNCTIVE	tenga, tengas, tenga, tengamos, tengáis, tengan
IMPERFECT SUBJUNCTIVE	tuviera (tuviese), tuvieras, tuviera, tuviéramos, tuvierais, tuvieran

TRAER *to bring*

PRESENT INDICATIVE	traigo, traes, trae, traemos, traéis, traen
PRETERITE	traje, trajiste, trajo, trajimos, trajisteis, trajeron
IMPERATIVE	trae / no traigas, traiga, traigamos, traed / no traigáis, traigan
PRESENT SUBJUNCTIVE	traiga, traigas, traiga, traigamos, traigáis, traigan
IMPERFECT SUBJUNCTIVE	trajera (trajese), trajeras, trajera, trajéramos, trajerais, trajeran
PRESENT PARTICIPLE	trayendo
PAST PARTICIPLE	traído

VALER *to be worth*

PRESENT INDICATIVE	valgo, vales, vale, valemos, valéis, valen
FUTURE	valdré, valdrás, valdrá, valdremos, valdréis, valdrán
CONDITIONAL	valdría, valdrías, valdría, valdríamos, valdríais, valdrían
IMPERATIVE	vale / no valgas, valga, valgamos, valed / no valgáis, valgan
PRESENT SUBJUNCTIVE	valga, valgas, valga, valgamos, valgáis, valgan

VENIR *to come*

PRESENT INDICATIVE	vengo, vienes, viene, venimos, venís, vienen
PRETERITE	vine, viniste, vino, vinimos, vinisteis, vinieron
FUTURE	vendré, vendrás, vendrá, vendremos, vendréis, vendrán
CONDITIONAL	vendría, vendrías, vendría, vendríamos, vendríais, vendrían
IMPERATIVE	ven / no vengas, venga, vengamos, venid / no vengáis, vengan
PRESENT SUBJUNCTIVE	venga, vengas, venga, vengamos, vengáis, vengan
IMPERFECT SUBJUNCTIVE	viniera (viniese), vinieras, viniera, viniéramos, vinierais, vinieran
PRESENT PARTICIPLE	viniendo

VER *to see*

PRESENT INDICATIVE	veo, ves, ve, vemos, veis, ven
PRETERITE	vi, viste, vio, vimos, visteis, vieron
IMPERFECT INDICATIVE	veía, veías, veía, veíamos, veíais, veían
IMPERATIVE	ve / no veas, vea, veamos, ved / no veáis, vean
PRESENT SUBJUNCTIVE	vea, veas, vea, veamos, veáis, vean
IMPERFECT SUBJUNCTIVE	viera (viese), vieras, viera, viéramos, vierais, vieran
PAST PARTICIPLE	visto

ANSWER KEY

PARTE UNO

Capítulo 1

Actividad 1 **1.** Daniel pronuncia muy bien. **2.** Nosotros abrimos el libro de texto. **3.** Tú escuchas al profesor. **4.** Los estudiantes practican los sonidos del español. **5.** Vosotros tomáis apuntes. **6.** Yo leo el diálogo. **7.** Isabel y tú aprenden los verbos.

Actividad 2 **1.** Uds. nunca comen. **2.** Nosotros nunca faltamos a nuestra clase. **3.** Juan Carlos nunca masca chicle. **4.** Laura y Carmen nunca hablan por teléfono celular. **5.** Tú nunca interrumpes. **6.** Yo nunca bebo refrescos. **7.** Vosotros nunca utilizáis una chuleta.

Actividad 3 *Answers will vary.*

Actividad 4 **1.** ¿Cuanto tiempo hace que Uds. navegan en la Red? ¿Desde cuándo navegan Uds. en la Red? **2.** ¿Cuánto tiempo hace que Mario y Federico corren en el equipo universitario? ¿Desde cuándo corren Mario y Federico en el equipo universitario? **3.** ¿Cuánto tiempo hace que Consuelo asiste a los conciertos? ¿Desde cuándo asiste Consuelo a los conciertos? **4.** ¿Cuánto tiempo hace que alquilas vídeos? ¿Desde cuándo alquilas vídeos? **5.** ¿Cuánto tiempo hace que Esteban baila salsa en las discotecas? ¿Desde cuándo baila Esteban salsa en las discotecas? **6.** ¿Cuánto tiempo hace que sacáis fotos con una cámara digital? ¿Desde cuándo sacáis fotos con una cámara digital?

Actividad 5 **1.** Hace cinco años que Uds. navegan en la Red. Uds. navegan en la Red desde hace cinco años. **2.** Hace un año que Mario y Federico corren en el equipo universitario. Mario y Federico corren en el equipo universitario desde hace un año. **3.** Hace seis años que Consuelo asiste a los conciertos. Consuelo asiste a los conciertos desde hace seis años. **4.** Hace tres años que alquilas vídeos. Alquilas vídeos desde hace tres años. **5.** Hace ocho meses que Esteban baila salsa en las discotecas. Esteban baila salsa en las discotecas desde hace ocho meses. **6.** Hace tres semanas que sacáis fotos con una cámara digital. Sacáis fotos con una cámara digital desde hace tres semanas.

Actividad 6 **1.** Sí, salgo la semana próxima. **2.** Sí, vengo a la oficina el viernes. **3.** Sí, voy a Inglaterra y España. **4.** Sí, conozco Italia. **5.** Sí, sé cuándo regreso. **6.** Sí, establezco una sucursal en Londres. **7.** Sí, veo a mis clientes el viernes.

Actividad 7 **1.** (Roberto y Rebeca) Vienen si tienen tiempo. **2.** (Ud.) Viene si tiene tiempo. **3.** (Tú y yo) Venimos si tenemos tiempo. **4.** (Sara) Viene si tiene tiempo. **5.** (Uds.) Vienen si tienen tiempo. **6.** (Yo) Vengo si tengo tiempo. **7.** (Tú) Vienes si tienes tiempo. **8.** (Vosotros) Venís si tenéis tiempo.

Actividad 8 **1.** Yo oigo lo que Uds. dicen. **2.** Tú oyes lo que nosotros decimos. **3.** Guillermo oye lo que vosotros decís. **4.** Rosa y yo oímos lo que Ud. dice. **5.** Uds. oyen lo que yo digo. **6.** Elena y Paco oyen lo que tú dices.

Actividad 9 **1.** Yo pongo la mesa. **2.** Yo doy un paseo. **3.** Yo veo televisión. **4.** Yo ofrezco ayuda.

5. Yo digo tal cosa. **6.** Yo sé qué pasó. **7.** Yo voy al supermercado. **8.** Yo conozco al nuevo programador.

Actividad 10 **1.** Merezco recibir el premio Nobel. **2.** Compongo una obra maestra mozartiana. **3.** Obtengo una beca de dos millones de dólares. **4.** Traduzco novelas del vasco al sánscrito. **5.** Conduzco la limosina presidencial. **6.** Supongo que yo voy a ser el presidente de los Estados Unidos.

Actividad 11 **1.** Pertenezco a la junta directiva de la empresa. **2.** Produzco productos importantes. **3.** Traduzco documentos del inglés al español. **4.** Luzco en todo. **5.** Siempre ofrezco ideas nuevas. **6.** Merezco los aplausos de mis colegas.

Actividad 12 **1.** Mi hermano y yo vamos a cortar el césped. **2.** Mi abuela va a lavar y planchar la ropa. **3.** Yo voy a barrer el suelo. **4.** Mamá va a hacer la compra. **5.** Mis hermanas van a lavar los platos. **6.** Mi abuelo va a sacar la basura. **7.** Uds. van a hacer las camas. **8.** Papá va a pasar la aspiradora. **9.** Tú vas a sacudir los muebles. **10.** Vosotros vais a reciclar los periódicos.

Actividad 13 **1.** Yo curso informática en la universidad. **2.** Nosotros compartimos una pizza. **3.** Felipe y yo vamos al centro comercial. **4.** Ud. navega en la Red. **5.** Federico y yo asistimos a las conferencias de historia. **6.** Tú lees tu correo electrónico. **7.** David y Olivia vienen a mi casa para escuchar música. **8.** Yo voy a un cibercafé con mis amigos. **9.** Uds. salen al cine. **10.** Vosotros bajáis (descargáis) canciones en la computadora. **11.** Jaime y yo alquilamos películas. **12.** María Elena y Martín disfrutan su visita al museo.

Actividad 14 *Answers will vary.*

Capítulo 2

Actividad 1 **1.** Yo juego al tenis. **2.** Daniel y Luz juegan al béisbol. **3.** Carlota juega al vólibol. **4.** Tú juegas al baloncesto. **5.** Jorge y yo jugamos al fútbol americano. **6.** Uds. juegan limpio. **7.** Ud. juega al golf. **8.** Vosotros jugáis sucio.

Actividad 2 **1.** Uds. almuerzan en la cafetería universitaria a la una. **2.** Eva almuerza en un cibercafé a las doce y media. **3.** Nosotros almorzamos en una tiendecita de sándwiches a las tres. **4.** Mauricio y Beatriz almuerzan en Subway a la una y cuarto. **5.** Tú almuerzas en un restaurante de comida rápida a las once y media. **6.** Yo almuerzo en una pizzería a las dos y media. **7.** Uds. almuerzan en un restaurante chino a las dos menos cuarto. **8.** Vosotros almorzáis en el comedor de la residencia a las once cuarenta y cinco.

Actividad 3 **1.** No, no podemos descargar las fotos de Internet hoy. **2.** No, no puede empezar a escribir su informe hoy. **3.** No, no pueden trabajar en la librería hoy. **4.** No, no puedo rodar mi película hoy. **5.** No, no puedo traer mi cámara digital hoy. **6.** No, no podemos visitar el museo hoy. **7.** No, no puedo contestar mi correo electrónico hoy. **8.** No, no podemos merendar en un café hoy. **9.** No, no puedo devolver los libros a la biblioteca hoy.

Actividad 4 **1.** puedo **2.** encuentro **3.** quiere **4.** Pienso **5.** muestro **6.** Puede **7.** encuentro **8.** cuestan **9.** cuesta

10. cuesta 11. pruebo 12. envuelve 13. puede 14. suelo
15. vuelvo

Actividad 5 1. resuelven 2. atraviesan 3. comienza
4. Descendemos 5. entiendo 6. Vuelves 7. muestra
8. quieren 9. enciendo

Actividad 6 1. Mi compañero/a de cuarto nos despierta a
todos nosotros. 2. Tú empiezas a mandar tu correo electrónico.
3. Uds. almuerzan en un café. 4. Ud. devuelve los libros a la
biblioteca. 5. Mis amigos vuelven a la residencia a las tres.
6. Nosotros comenzamos a estudiar a las cuatro. 7. Yo suelo
hacer investigaciones en la Red. 8. Los estudiantes encuentran
a sus profesores por el campus.

Actividad 7 1. Recuerdas la fecha hoy. 2. Pablo y Lorenzo
juegan al fútbol hoy. 3. Probamos el nuevo plato hoy.
4. Alicia encuentra su secador hoy. 5. Yo envuelvo los
paquetes hoy. 6. Ud. resuelve su problema hoy.

Actividad 8 1. Llueve (Está lloviendo) en San Francisco.
2. Nieva (Está nevando) en Ginebra, Suiza. 3. Truena (Está
tronando) en Santa Fe. 4. La lluvia empieza a helar en
Chicago. 5. Empieza a nevar en Punta Arenas, Chile.
6. Escampa (Despeja) en Londres. 7. Está despejado (claro) en
Sevilla. 8. Graniza (Está granizando) en Nueva York.

Actividad 9 1. Ud. y José María piden quesadillas. 2. La
familia Herrera pide enchiladas. 3. Pili y yo pedimos una
ensalada. 4. Tú pides sopa y un sándwich. 5. Los chicos piden
arroz con pollo. 6. Yo pido espaguetis con salsa de tomate.

Actividad 10 1. Yo sirvo cerveza. 2. Susana sirve refrescos.
3. Nosotros servimos vino de la Rioja. 4. Eduardo y Dolores
sirven jugo de naranja. 5. Tú sirves agua mineral. 6. Ud. y
Pepe sirven té helado.

Actividad 11 1. Los primos prefieren salir al campo. 2. Julia
prefiere leer novelas históricas. 3. Nosotros preferimos asistir a
un concierto. 4. Uds. prefieren ver televisión. 5. Yo prefiero
jugar al tenis. 6. Tú prefieres bailar el tango. 7. Ud. prefiere
alquilar películas policíacas. 8. Vosotros preferís navegar en
la Red.

Actividad 12 1. Tú duermes profundamente. 2. Yo duermo
mucho los fines de semana. 3. Uds. duermen bien en
este dormitorio. 4. Vosotros dormís muy poco. 5. Nosotros
dormimos mal en este colchón. 6. Ud. duerme diez horas los
días feriados.

Actividad 13 1. viste 2. advierte 3. sienten 4. hierve
5. duerme 6. miente 7. divierte, ríen, sonríen 8. despiden
9. repites 10. riñe 11. refiere 12. gimes

Actividad 14 1. Los padres de Vera contribuyen con cien
dólares. 2. Mi hermano y yo contribuimos con ciento
cincuenta dólares. 3. Tú contribuyes con setenta dólares.
4. Ud. contribuye con setenta y cinco dólares. 5. Adriana
contribuye con veinticinco dólares. 6. Los habitantes del barrio
contribuyen con mil quinientos dólares. 7. Yo contribuyo con
ochenta dólares.

Actividad 15 1. Roberto incluye sus investigaciones científicas.
2. Uds. incluyen algunas fotos. 3. Laura y yo incluimos las
estadísticas. 4. Ud. incluye una presentación de Power Point.
5. Tú incluyes un resumen. 6. David y Gabriela incluyen una
introducción. 7. Yo incluyo un sitio Web. 8. Vosotros incluís
una base de datos.

Actividad 16 1. Tomás se resfría todos los inviernos. 2. Uds.
se resfrían cuando duermen poco. 3. Lidia y Miguel se
resfrían tres veces al año. 4. Ud. se resfría cuando come mal.
5. Yo me resfrío cuando bebo de los vasos ajenos. 6. Nosotros

nos resfriamos cuando salimos bajo la lluvia. 7. Tú te resfrías
cuando no tomas las vitaminas.

Actividad 17 1. Micaela y Jorge se gradúan el año próximo.
2. Ud. se gradúa dentro de dos años. 3. Timoteo se gradúa en
enero. 4. Uds. se gradúan para el año 2010. 5. Tú te gradúas
el 14 de mayo. 6. Nosotros nos graduamos a principios de
junio. 7. Yo me gradúo el mes que viene. 8. Vosotros os
graduáis el jueves.

Actividad 18 1. se fían 2. envían 3. confía 4. continúa
5. se resfría 6. espiamos

Actividad 19 *Answers will vary.*

Actividad 20 1. Yo elijo una caja de bombones. 2. Mis padres
eligen una bandeja de plata. 3. Nosotros elegimos un
certificado de regalo. 4. Tú eliges dos relojes. 5. Uds. eligen
un televisor de plasma. 6. La abuela elige una cámara digital.
7. Vosotros elegís una computadora portátil. 8. Nuestros
primos eligen un mueble. 9. Ud. elige unos billetes de
concierto.

Actividad 21 1. recojo 2. persigo 3. extingo 4. cuezo
5. dirijo 6. corrijo 7. mezo

Actividad 22 1. sigo 2. dirijo 3. encojo 4. distingo
5. reconozco 6. finge 7. consigo 8. luce 9. prosigo
10. produce 11. finjo 12. distingo 13. recojo 14. convenzo
15. desconozco

Actividad 23 1. Víctor consigue salir al centro comercial.
2. Pablo y yo conseguimos reparar el coche. 3. Ud. consigue
ver la nueva exposición. 4. Yo consigo leer El Quijote.
5. Uds. consiguen rodar una película. 6. Beatriz y tú
consiguen colgar los cuadros. 7. Tú consigues ganar el
partido de tenis.

Actividad 24 1. Sigue 2. Cojo 3. Desconozco 4. Finjo
5. Cuecen 6. distingo 7. Exijo 8. Eliges 9. consigo
10. Produzco

Actividad 25 1. Ricardo Mateo dirige la Orquesta de
Filadelfia esta semana. 2. Los bomberos extinguen treinta
fuegos cada día. 3. Los ciudadanos exigen mejores escuelas.
4. El senador Alonso sigue los consejos de sus colegas en el
senado. 5. Los americanos/estadounidenses eligen un nuevo
presidente este año. 6. ¡Joven pareja consigue ganar la lotería!
7. Una nueva receta: ¡cocinero cuece una sopa con helado!
8. La campaña contra el analfabetismo prosigue.

Capítulo 3

Actividad 1 1. Es ella. 2. Son Uds. 3. Somos nosotros.
4. Eres tú. 5. Es él. 6. Son ellas. 7. Es Ud. 8. Sois vosotros.

Actividad 2 1. Pablo es de la Argentina, pero es de origen
inglés. 2. Nosotros somos de El Salvador, pero somos de origen
ruso. 3. Vosotros sois de Canadá, pero sois de origen japonés.
4. Ud. es de los Estados Unidos, pero es de origen irlandés.
5. Ramón y Virginia son de Puerto Rico, pero son de origen
polaco. 6. Tú eres de España, pero eres de origen portugués.
7. Ud. y Raquel son de México, pero son de origen griego.
8. Yo soy de Venezuela, pero soy de origen italiano.

Actividad 3 1. ¿Quién eres? 2. ¿De dónde eres? 3. ¿De qué
nacionalidad eres? (¿Cuál es tu nacionalidad?) 4. ¿De qué
origen eres? 5. ¿Cómo eres? 6. ¿De qué color son tus ojos?
7. ¿Cuál es tu profesión?

Actividad 4 1. Patricio está en Madrid y está contento.
2. Nosotros estamos en Lima y estamos cansados. 3. Ud. está
en París y está nervioso. 4. Consuelo y su hermana están en

Helsinki y están aburridas. **5.** Tú estás en Londres y estás enferma. **6.** Yo estoy en Roma y estoy feliz. **7.** Uds. están en Las Vegas y están preocupados. **8.** Vosotras estáis en Beijing y estáis tristes.

Actividad 5 **1.** ¿Cuál es su nombre? **2.** ¿Cuál es su nacionalidad? **3.** ¿Cuál es su profesión? **4.** ¿Cuál es su estado civil? **5.** ¿Cuál es su fecha de nacimiento? **6.** ¿Cómo es Ud.?

Actividad 6 **1.** es **2.** es **3.** son **4.** es **5.** Es **6.** está **7.** están **8.** es **9.** es **10.** es **11.** son **12.** Son **13.** está **14.** es

Actividad 7 **1.** estamos **2.** está **3.** Es **4.** está **5.** es **6.** Es **7.** es **8.** es **9.** ser **10.** está **11.** es **12.** están **13.** son **14.** están **15.** son **16.** es **17.** estoy

Actividad 8 **1.** estoy **2.** estoy **3.** Es **4.** es **5.** es **6.** es **7.** está **8.** está **9.** están **10.** es **11.** es **12.** es **13.** Es **14.** es **15.** están **16.** estás **17.** es **18.** están **19.** estar **20.** estar

Actividad 9 **1.** ¿Dónde está la papelería? **2.** ¿Cómo es Gloria? **3.** ¿De dónde son los hermanos García? (¿De qué nacionalidad son los hermanos García?) **4.** ¿Cómo están Juanito y Gracia? **5.** ¿De qué origen es la familia Méndez? **6.** ¿Cómo son las primas de Paco? **7.** ¿Dónde está el profesor Mora? **8.** ¿De qué es el vestido? **9.** ¿De qué color son la camisa y la corbata? **10.** ¿Cómo está(s)? **11.** ¿De quién/es es aquella casa? **12.** ¿De dónde es Micaela?

Actividad 10 **1.** ¿Quiénes son los nuevos estudiantes extranjeros? ¿Sabes de dónde son? **2.** Yo conozco a María del Mar. Está en mi clase de historia. Es de la Argentina. **3.** Estoy seguro/a de que es de origen italiano. Es muy simpática e inteligente. **4.** Pero está triste porque quiere volver a Buenos Aires. **5.** Lorenzo Tomé es inglés, pero sus abuelos son de origen español. **6.** Él es listo y gracioso. **7.** Lorenzo estudia biología y química este año. **8.** Él dice que quiere ser médico.

Capítulo 4

Actividad 1 **1.** Esteban estudió la historia de la Edad Media. **2.** Rosa y Elena solucionaron los problemas de cálculo. **3.** Tú escribiste un artículo para una revista electrónica. **4.** Nosotros trabajamos en la librería. **5.** Yo visité unos sitios Web. **6.** Uds. contestaron las preguntas de filosofía. **7.** Ud. aprendió las fechas de historia de memoria. **8.** Vosotros discutisteis varios temas.

Actividad 2 **1.** levanté **2.** arreglé **3.** Bajé **4.** saludé **5.** preparé **6.** pasó **7.** desayunó **8.** terminamos **9.** cogí **10.** salimos **11.** subimos **12.** viajamos **13.** bajamos **14.** arrancó **15.** busqué **16.** encontré **17.** recordé **18.** explicó

Actividad 3 **1.** Felipe escogió el Café Valencia. **2.** Nosotros llegamos al restaurante a las siete. **3.** Nosotros leímos la carta. **4.** El mozo recomendó la paella. **5.** Lorenzo pidió ternera y sopa. **6.** Eva y Diana pidieron pescado y ensalada. **7.** Uds. prefirieron la carne con papas. **8.** Tú comiste torta de postre. **9.** Todos nosotros tomamos café. **10.** Vosotros bebisteis vino. **11.** Yo pagué la cuenta. **12.** Isabel dejó la propina. **13.** Yo gocé mucho de la comida. **14.** Todos nosotros nos divertimos mucho.

Actividad 4 **1.** Ya saqué los libros de la biblioteca. **2.** Ya jugué al tenis. **3.** Ya toqué la flauta. **4.** Ya coloqué los documentos en el archivo. **5.** Ya arranqué la mala hierba del jardín. **6.** Ya navegué en la Red. **7.** Ya colgué los cuadros. **8.** Ya almorcé con Victoria. **9.** Ya entregué el informe. **10.** Ya actualicé los datos.

Actividad 5 **1.** Los hermanos Serrat construyeron muchas casas. **2.** El profesor Burgos influyó mucho en la vida política. **3.** Francisca leyó libros para una casa editorial. **4.** Marco e Isabel huyeron a otro pueblo por una tempestad. **5.** Doña Elvira contribuyó con mucho dinero a las caridades. **6.** Leonardo concluyó los trámites de la empresa.

Actividad 6 **1.** equivoqué **2.** marqué **3.** tropecé **4.** pegué **5.** deslicé **6.** masqué **7.** tragué **8.** bañé **9.** ahogué **10.** tranquilicé

Actividad 7 **1.** lanzó, lancé **2.** publicó, publiqué **3.** dedicaste, dediqué **4.** cargaron, cargué **5.** realizaron, realicé **6.** embarcó, embarqué

Actividad 8 **1.** Aterrizamos en el aeropuerto de San Juan. **2.** Visité fortalezas, museos e iglesias. **3.** Yo recé en la iglesia de San Juan y Sara rezó en una sinagoga. **4.** Almorcé en varias playas de la isla. **5.** Avanzamos mucho en nuestro dominio del español. **6.** Realizamos un viaje maravilloso. **7.** Gocé muchísimo de mi estancia en Puerto Rico.

Actividad 9 **1.** Tú sonreíste. **2.** Los chicos repitieron la pregunta. **3.** Patricio gruñó. **4.** Nosotros reímos. **5.** Uds. se durmieron. **6.** Daniel mintió. **7.** Nuestros amigos nos advirtieron. **8.** Paquita se divirtió.

Actividad 10 **1.** Llovió ayer también. **2.** Hizo viento ayer también. **3.** Estuvo despejado ayer también. **4.** Hizo fresco ayer también. **5.** Nevó ayer también. **6.** Estuvo nublado ayer también. **7.** Hizo ochenta y dos grados ayer también. **8.** Hizo mucho calor ayer también.

Actividad 11 **1.** dijo, dije **2.** fueron, Fuimos **3.** estuviste, Estuve **4.** trajeron, trajo **5.** pudiste, tuve **6.** vinieron, vine, vino **7.** di, vio **8.** oyó, supo **9.** hiciste, puse **10.** leyó, quiso **11.** hizo, Fui

Actividad 12 **1.** estuvo feliz **2.** se hizo médico **3.** tuvieron frío **4.** pusimos la mesa **5.** se hizo daño **6.** pude distinguir **7.** dijo que sí **8.** fuiste tras ella

Actividad 13 **1.** Pero ayer me desperté a las siete. **2.** Pero ayer almorcé en el café Atenas. **3.** Pero ayer fui de compras por la mañana. **4.** Pero ayer hice un plato de pescado. **5.** Pero ayer jugué al tenis con Ricardo. **6.** Pero ayer seguí por la calle Atocha. **7.** Pero ayer empecé a trabajar antes del desayuno. **8.** Pero ayer vine en taxi. **9.** Pero ayer navegué en la Red por dos horas. **10.** Pero ayer anduve más lentamente.

Actividad 14 **1.** nos divertimos **2.** fuimos **3.** condujeron **4.** pudo **5.** Hizo **6.** dio **7.** recogieron **8.** hice **9.** trajeron **10.** vieron **11.** oyeron **12.** comenzó **13.** tuvimos **14.** estuvimos

Actividad 15 **1.** El monstruo llegó (vino) a la ciudad. **2.** Hizo pedazos a los coches y destruyó edificios. **3.** Al ver el monstruo la gente dio gritos. (Cuando la gente vio el monstruo dio gritos.) **4.** Me puse pálido/a. **5.** A mi amigo Lorenzo le dio un dolor de cabeza. **6.** A mi amiga Marisol le dio un dolor de estómago. **7.** Todos nos echamos a correr. **8.** Algunas (Unas) personas no pudieron escaparse.

Actividad 16 *Answers will vary.*

Capítulo 5

Actividad 1 **1.** vivía **2.** era **3.** iba **4.** hacía **5.** solían **6.** íbamos **7.** gustaba **8.** era **9.** pasábamos **10.** era **11.** hacía **12.** Había **13.** jugábamos **14.** cultivaba **15.** eran **16.** olía **17.** salíamos **18.** Subíamos **19.** veía **20.** servía **21.** leía **22.** íbamos **23.** estábamos **24.** volvían **25.** llevaba **26.** era

Actividad 2   1. Antes escribía para *El tiempo,* pero ya no. 2. Antes iba de vacaciones en junio, pero ya no.   3. Antes salía con Lola, pero ya no.   4. Antes me gustaba la cocina tailandesa, pero ya no.   5. Antes trabajaba como programadora, pero ya no.   6. Antes jugaba en un equipo de béisbol, pero ya no. 7. Antes veníamos al pueblo en invierno, pero ya no. 8. Antes era presidenta de la compañía, pero ya no.   9. Antes era socio del Club Atlántico, pero ya no.   10. Antes mi hijo tocaba la trompeta, pero ya no.   11. Antes tenía una cadena de restaurantes, pero ya no.   12. Antes prefería vivir en el centro, pero ya no.

Actividad 3   1. La señorita Fajardo era gerente de fábrica. Iba a Miami.   2. Unos señores italianos eran dueños de una pastelería. Iban a Buenos Aires.   3. Isabela Iriarte era profesora de economía. Iba a Irlanda.   4. La señora Montoya era banquera. Iba a Suiza.   5. Don Pedro Domínguez era candidato a senador. Iba a Monterrey.   6. Lorena Iglesias era ama de casa. Iba a Costa Rica.   7. Los hermanos Machado eran músicos. Iban a Nueva York.   8. El señor Rubio era cirujano. Iba la India.

Actividad 4   1. Carolina y Ramón no veían el mar Caribe desde el avión.   2. Nosotros no veíamos la cara de los actores desde el anfiteatro del teatro.   3. Federica no veía el embotellamiento desde la ventana del dormitorio.   4. Uds. no veían toda la cancha de fútbol desde la tribuna del estadio.   5. Yo no veía la cumbre de la montaña desde el valle.   6. Daniel no veía la discoteca desde la esquina.   7. Tú no veías al público desde la parte derecha del escenario.

Actividad 5   1. Llovía cuando Beatriz y tú volvieron (volvisteis).   2. Hacía frío cuando los Sorolla se levantaron. 3. Estaba despejado cuando fuiste a la biblioteca.   4. Hacía viento cuando José Antonio vino a la casa.   5. Nevaba cuando nosotros terminamos el trabajo.   6. Tronaba cuando Ud. entró en el cine.   7. Hacía sol cuando yo llegué a la universidad. 8. Lloviznaba cuando Uds. se fueron.   9. Hacía calor cuando vosotros os pusisteis en marcha.

Actividad 6   1. Eran las nueve y media cuando Consuelo y Berta se despidieron.   2. Era la una cuando el programa comenzó.   3. Era mediodía cuando Sara sirvió el almuerzo. 4. Eran las diez en punto cuando el empleado abrió la taquilla.   5. Era medianoche cuando regresamos de la discoteca.   6. Era muy tarde cuando Uds. se durmieron. 7. Era temprano cuando el cartero trajo el correo.   8. Eran las cinco y cuarto cuando yo inicié la sesión.   9. Eran las tres cuarenta cuando te reuniste con tus amigos.   10. Eran las once de la noche cuando el avión aterrizó.

Actividad 7   1. Mientras tú viajabas, acabó la telenovela. 2. Mientras Marta y Miguel se quedaban en un hotel, un ladrón forzó una entrada.   3. Mientras Estefanía vivía en el extranjero, sus padres vendieron su casa de campo.   4. Mientras Uds. hacían un viaje, sus vecinos montaron una nueva empresa. 5. Mientras yo veía las siete maravillas del mundo, se añadieron otras siete a la lista.   6. Mientras Benito trabajaba en San Antonio, su novia rompió con él.   7. Mientras el avión de Diego aterrizaba en Los Ángeles, el de su hermana despegó en Atlanta. 8. Mientras los turistas conocían los Estados Unidos, la guerra estalló en su país.   9. Mientras nosotros estábamos en el puerto, hubo un incendio en el barco.   10. Mientras vosotros caminabais al cibercafé, yo os alcancé.   11. Mientras Laura y yo platicábamos, mi teléfono celular sonó.   12. Mientras tú leías, nosotros enviamos el correo electrónico.

Actividad 8   *Answers will vary.*

Actividad 9   1. tenía   2. llevaron   3. sentó   4. dio 5. leíamos   6. se apagaron   7. subió   8. vimos   9. Había

10. hacía   11. estaba   12. llevaba   13. vestía   14. hacía 15. salió   16. se puso   17. quedé   18. me hice

Actividad 10   1. me gradué   2. Saqué   3. Esperaba 4. nací   5. Quería   6. había   7. mandé   8. Tuve 9. Encontré   10. se publicaba   11. fue   12. conocía 13. vivía   14. estaba   15. Hacía   16. conocí   17. trabajaba 18. era   19. fue   20. nos casamos   21. llegué   22. tuvimos 23. vivimos

Actividad 11   1. Bárbara creía que Tomás conocía a su hermana Luz. Él conoció a Luz anoche en la cena.   2. Los hombres de negocios querían hablar del informe. Pero sus abogados no quisieron.   3. La novia no tenía regalos. Entonces tuvo veinte regalos esta mañana.   4. No sabíamos quién tenía los documentos. Lo supimos ayer.   5. Yo no podía armar el juguete. Javier no pudo armarlo tampoco.

Actividad 12   1. quería   2. íbamos   3. dije   4. interesaba 5. gustó   6. conocía   7. compró   8. hizo   9. pensábamos 10. tomamos   11. llegamos   12. visitamos   13. conocimos 14. tuve   15. podíamos   16. era   17. estaban   18. realicé

Actividad 13   1. Eran   2. sonó   3. estaba   4. descolgué 5. oí   6. dijo   7. robó   8. pidió   9. explicó   10. tenía 11. quedamos   12. eran   13. llegué   14. seguía   15. llegó 16. vi   17. estaba   18. tenía   19. llevaba   20. acerqué 21. senté   22. olía   23. hablé   24. pregunté   25. puso 26. dijo   27. comprendí   28. iba

Actividad 14   1. ¿Cuánto tiempo hacía que Montserrat Pujol cantaba ópera cuando firmó un contrato con la Metropolitana? Hacía ocho años que cantaba ópera.   2. ¿Cuánto tiempo hacía que los señores Salazar estaban casados cuando nació su hija? Hacía cuatro años que estaban casados.   3. ¿Cuánto tiempo hacía que vivías en Filadelfia cuando tus padres se mudaron a Londres? Hacía once meses que yo vivía en Filadelfia. 4. ¿Cuánto tiempo hacía que Susana y Lía eran amigas cuando Susana le quitó el novio a Lía? Hacía doce años que eran amigas. 5. ¿Cuánto tiempo hacía que Ud. compraba billetes de lotería cuando ganó el premio? Hacía quince años que yo compraba billetes de lotería.   6. ¿Cuánto tiempo hacía que Patricio y Ud. tocaban el violonchelo cuando el conservatorio les dio una beca? Hacía nueve años que tocábamos el violonchelo.

Actividad 15   1. El gobierno explotaba el petróleo desde hacía treinta años hasta que el presidente privatizó la industria. 2. La gente sufría por la inflación desde hacía cinco años hasta que los economistas intentaron controlarla.   3. La prensa no era libre desde hacía cincuenta años hasta que hubo un golpe de estado.   4. Los obreros no recibían un sueldo decente desde hacía cinco décadas hasta que se formaron los sindicatos. 5. El país no producía los bienes necesarios desde hacía varios años hasta que el gobierno estableció el libre mercado.   6. El pueblo no tenía ninguna libertad desde hacía cuarenta y cinco años hasta que murió el dictador y se estableció la democracia.

Actividad 16   *Answers will vary.*

Actividad 17   1. El primer día que Beatriz y yo pasamos en la Ciudad de México, fuimos al Bosque de Chapultepec.   2. Hacía muy buen tiempo. Hacía sol y calor.   3. Había mucha gente en el parque (el bosque).   4. Los niños jugaban en los resbalines y montaban en bicicleta.   5. Mientras caminábamos por el parque (el bosque) vimos el Árbol de Moctezuma y el Castillo de Chapultepec.   6. Llegamos al Museo Nacional de Antropología y entramos.   7. Caminábamos de una sala a otra y vimos la exposición de arte precolombino.   8. Pasamos dos horas en el museo.   9. Entonces fuimos a la librería donde yo compré un libro sobre los aztecas y los mayas.   10. Almorzamos (Tomamos el almuerzo) en la cafetería del museo.   11. Eran las cinco cuando salimos del museo.   **12.** No teníamos prisa porque estábamos de vacaciones.   **13.** Esa noche nuestros amigos mexicanos nos llevaron al Palacio de Bellas Artes.

Actividad 18   *Answers will vary.*

Capítulo 6

Actividad 1   **1.** Me graduaré en junio.   **2.** Mis amigos y yo celebraremos con una fiesta.   **3.** Nuestros padres estarán muy contentos.   **4.** Yo haré un viaje a Europa en el verano.
5. Miguel me acompañará.   **6.** Nos encantará el viaje.
7. Iremos a los países de la Europa oriental.   **8.** Andrés y Manuel querrán ir también.   **9.** Saldremos para Polonia a mediados de junio.   **10.** Pasaremos dos meses viajando.
11. Andrés volverá antes porque tendrá que buscar empleo.
12. Al regresar yo empezaré a trabajar en una compañía multinacional.   **13.** Miguel podrá trabajar en la empresa de sus padres.   **14.** Manuel seguirá con sus clases en la Facultad de Ingeniería.   **15.** ¡Tendremos tiempo de vernos, espero!

Actividad 2   **1.** Mari Carmen llorará.   **2.** Las tías dirán «¡ay de mí!».   **3.** Ramón tendrá vergüenza.   **4.** Tú te volverás loco.
5. Juan y Alicia pondrán el grito en el cielo.   **6.** Uds. se enfadarán.   **7.** Vosotros os reiréis a carcajadas.   **8.** Ud. se pondrá de buen humor.   **9.** Nosotros estaremos contentos.

Actividad 3   **1.** ¡Mañana será un ajetreo continuo!
2. ¡Tendremos un día lleno de frenética actividad!   **3.** Habrá clases todo el día.   **4.** Tomaremos exámenes también.
5. Además, yo iré al almacén.   **6.** Le compraré un regalo a mi hermana.   **7.** Sarita cumplirá diecisiete años mañana.
8. Mamá hará una comida y una torta.   **9.** Papá y yo saldremos para comprar vino.   **10.** También querré terminar mi informe.   **11.** Mis amigos y yo trabajaremos hasta muy tarde.   **12.** Trasnocharemos porque tendremos exámenes pasado mañana.

Actividad 4   **1.** Yolanda y Ana patinarán en la pista universitaria.   **2.** Tú saldrás a la sierra para esquiar.
3. Julio bailará en la discoteca toda la noche.   **4.** Consuelo querrá alquilar vídeos.   **5.** Yo vendré al cibercafé todas las tardes.   **6.** Vosotros conoceréis el nuevo centro comercial.
7. Nosotros haremos una fiesta.   **8.** Ud. podrá dormir hasta las 11:00 de la mañana.

Actividad 5   **1.** Si María quiere salir, nosotros saldremos con ella.   **2.** Si ellos vienen, Ud. podrá verlos.   **3.** Si yo hago la comida, tú vendrás a almorzar.   **4.** Si Uds. trabajan mucho, tendrán éxito.   **5.** Si tú no sabes qué pasó, yo te diré.
6. Si vosotros compráis los billetes en Internet, ahorraréis mucho dinero.   **7.** Si hace calor, Carlos y Pedro irán a la playa.
8. Si llueve, Celeste querrá ir al cine.

Actividad 6   **1.** Serán las seis.   **2.** Teodoro tendrá catorce años.
3. El reloj valdrá mucho.   **4.** Habrá problemas entre los socios.
5. Teresa sabrá la hora de la conferencia.   **6.** Lola querrá ir a la reunión.   **7.** Las muchachas volverán pronto.

Actividad 7   **1.** ¿Será verde?   **2.** Tendrá pilas.   **3.** ¿Habrá muchas partes?   **4.** ¿Será de madera?   **5.** ¿Costará (Valdrá) mucho?   **6.** Hará un ruido.   **7.** Será muy grande.   **8.** ¿Todo el mundo tendrá uno? (¿Todos tendrán uno?)   **9.** ¿Estará vivo?
10. Cabrá en la mano.

Actividad 8   **1.** a. Yo hablaría con la dependienta. b. Yo iría a otro almacén.   **2.** a. Carolina repetiría. b. Carolina pediría la receta.   **3.** a. Nosotros saldríamos corriendo. b. Nosotros llamaríamos a los bomberos.   **4.** a. Osvaldo se disculparía con la señora. b. Osvaldo se sentaría en su regazo.   **5.** a. La madre los acostaría sin bañarlos. b. La madre llamaría al fontanero.

6. a. Yo le diría al policía lo que pasó. b. Yo les pondría vendas a los heridos.

Actividad 9   **1.** Ud. pagaría la matrícula en la universidad.
2. Mi prima Celia vendría de Australia a visitarnos.   **3.** Uds. harían un viaje a Barcelona.   **4.** Juan Pablo y Ana María pondrían el dinero en el banco.   **5.** Tú ya no tendrías deudas.
6. Mi hermano y yo querríamos donar dinero a las caridades.
7. Nosotros jugaríamos a la Bolsa.   **8.** Vosotros saldríais a comer en los restaurantes más caros.

Actividad 10   **1.** gustaría   **2.** querría   **3.** habría   **4.** podríamos
5. ocuparía   **6.** haríamos   **7.** pondrían   **8.** vendríamos

Actividad 11   **1.** Serían las once cuando volvimos a casa.
2. Habría sesenta invitados en la fiesta.   **3.** Estarían cansados después del viaje.   **4.** Aquel carro costaría treinta mil dólares.
5. Los nuevos vecinos serían simpáticos.   **6.** Estaría en la librería cuando fui a su casa.

Actividad 12   **1.** estaríamos   **2.** podría   **3.** querría
4. cabrían   **5.** vendría   **6.** pondrías   **7.** habría

Actividad 13   *Answers will vary.*   **1.** Me gustaría...
2. Mis padres preferirían...   **3.** Mi hermana querría...
4. A mi amigo/a _____ le encantaría...   **5.** A mi amigo/a
_____ le interesaría...   **6.** A mi hermano le gustaría...
7. Me encantaría...   **8.** Nuestros/as profesores/as preferirían...
9. A mis compañeros/as de clase les interesaría...
10. Mi familia querría...

Actividad 14   *Answers will vary.*

Capítulo 7

Actividad 1   **1.** Pedro ha apagado las luces.   **2.** Cecilia y Pilar han hecho las maletas.   **3.** Papá ha llenado el tanque del coche.   **4.** Vosotros habéis desenchufado los aparatos eléctricos.
5. Sara y Juan Carlos han metido el equipaje en el baúl.
6. Yo les he dicho a los vecinos que nos vamos.   **7.** Mamá ha puesto pilas en la linterna.   **8.** Paco y yo nos hemos despedido de nuestros amigos.   **9.** Tú has limpiado las ventanillas del coche.

Actividad 2   **1.** Nosotros hemos leído la receta.   **2.** Jorge ha encendido el fuego.   **3.** Yo he hecho la salsa.   **4.** Alicia y Juan Diego han picado las pimientas picantes.   **5.** Ud. ha freído/frito las cebollas.   **6.** Estrella y yo hemos cortado el pan.   **7.** Tú has lavado los espárragos y los aguacates.   **8.** Vosotros habéis añadido la sal.   **9.** Uds. han puesto el pollo al horno.
10. Yo he mezclado la ensalada.   **11.** Martín ha cubierto la cacerola.   **12.** Lupe y Julio han quemado las sartenes.

Actividad 3   **1.** Nosotros la hemos leído.   **2.** Jorge lo ha encendido.   **3.** Yo la he hecho.   **4.** Alicia y Juan Diego las han picado.   **5.** Ud. las ha freído/frito.   **6.** Estrella y yo lo hemos cortado.   **7.** Tú los has lavado.   **8.** Vosotros la habéis añadido.
9. Uds. lo han puesto al horno.   **10.** Yo la he mezclado.
11. Martín la ha cubierto.   **12.** Lupe y Julio las han quemado.

Actividad 4   **1.** Vosotros os habéis dormido.   **2.** Ud. ha bostezado.   **3.** Yo me he puesto el abrigo.   **4.** Carlos y Beatriz se han despedido de la anfitriona.   **5.** ¡Nos han matado de aburrimiento!   **6.** Tú te has quejado que la comida te cayó mal.
7. Ud. y Clara han dado excusas.   **8.** Ramón ha dicho que se enferma.

Actividad 5   *Answers will vary.*

Actividad 6   **1.** Cristóbal se ha matriculado ya.   **2.** Nos hemos colocado ya.   **3.** Yo me he instalado en la nueva casa ya.
4. Irene y Jaime se han comprometido ya.   **5.** Nora se ha enterado de los líos de la familia ya.   **6.** Yo me he apuntado en la lista de voluntarios ya.   **7.** Los Roldán se han divorciado ya.

Actividad 7 **1.** Uds. habían visto la exposición en el musco hace unos meses. **2.** Amelia se había cortado el pelo el sábado. **3.** Ricardo y Leonor se habían casado en abril. **4.** Habíamos hecho el asado el 4 de julio. **5.** Habías celebrado tu cumpleaños hace un mes. **6.** Ud. había cambiado de idea hace varios días. **7.** Yo me había puesto en contacto con Felipe hace tres semanas. **8.** Javier me había devuelto los disquetes la semana pasada. **9.** Habíais escrito los informes en noviembre. **10.** Marcos se había roto el codo hace casi un año.

Actividad 8 **1.** Cuando Tomás llegó por fin, Raúl ya había hecho la pizza. **2.** Cuando Tomás llegó por fin, Uds. ya habían puesto la mesa. **3.** Cuando Tomás llegó por fin, Diana y Judit ya habían visto el sitio Web. **4.** Cuando Tomás llegó por fin, Ud. ya había sacado la basura. **5.** Cuando Tomás llegó por fin, yo ya había subido las cajas a la buhardilla. **6.** Cuando Tomás llegó por fin, tú ya habías ido de compras. **7.** Cuando Tomás llegó por fin, Plácido y yo ya habíamos vuelto de la tienda de vídeos.

Actividad 9 **1.** Cuando Julia vino a buscarnos, nosotros ya habíamos hecho ejercicio. **2.** Cuando yo fui a su casa, Virginia ya había dado una vuelta. **3.** Cuando Ud. se levantó, sus padres ya habían desayunado. **4.** Cuando volvimos a casa, Juanita ya había escrito su composición. **5.** Cuando los bomberos llegaron, Uds. ya habían apagado el incendio en la cocina. **6.** Cuando los bisnietos lograron ver a su bisabuelo, el bisabuelo ya se había enfermado.

Actividad 10 **1.** Laura no había visto una corrida de toros en Madrid hasta este viaje. **2.** Rodolfo y Eva no habían dado un paseo por Santiago de Compostela hasta este viaje. **3.** Yo no había hecho una excursión a El Escorial hasta este viaje. **4.** Tú y Susana no se habían paseado por el barrio de Santa Cruz hasta este viaje. **5.** Mamá, papá y yo no habíamos subido al monte Tibidabo hasta este viaje. **6.** Jaime no había conocido la Alhambra hasta este viaje. **7.** Tú no habías pasado Semana Santa en Sevilla hasta este viaje. **8.** Nosotros no habíamos conocido lugares tan impresionantes hasta este viaje. **9.** Yo no me había interesado tanto en la arquitectura gótica hasta este viaje. **10.** Vosotros no habíais ido a tantos restaurantes y discotecas hasta este viaje.

Actividad 11 **1.** Elena se habrá graduado para el año próximo. **2.** Alfredo y Armando se habrán mejorado antes de regresar a la universidad. **3.** Nosotros habremos ahorrado dinero antes de las vacaciones de invierno. **4.** Yo te habré dado tu regalo antes de tu fiesta de cumpleaños. **5.** Ud. y Laura se habrán mudado para mediados del mes. **6.** Tú habrás sacado un pasaporte para julio. **7.** Uds. habrán vuelto del centro comercial para las ocho. **8.** Vosotros habréis abierto una cuenta bancaria antes de empezar el nuevo trabajo.

Actividad 12 **1.** Su coche le habrá costado un ojo de la cara. **2.** Clara habrá escrito la carta. **3.** Felipe y Eduardo habrán ganado la regata. **4.** Uds. habrán tomado la merienda. **5.** Martín y yo no habremos entendido el motivo. **6.** Ud. no habrá hecho cola por mucho tiempo.

Actividad 13 **1.** Patricia y yo no habríamos salido. **2.** Sofía no habría roto su compromiso con su novio. **3.** Los turistas venezolanos no habrían hecho el viaje a California en autobús (no lo habrían hecho en autobús). **4.** Tú no te habrías cortado el pelo en la peluquería Melenas (no te lo habrías cortado). **5.** Ud. no habría creído lo que nos dijo Cecilia. (Ud. no lo habría creído.) **6.** Yo no me habría reído.

Actividad 14 **1.** El rancho (La estancia) habría sido muy grande. **2.** Los granjeros habrían tenido gallinas en un gallinero. **3.** Los campesinos habrían recogido cerezas y fresas. **4.** El paisaje del campo habría sido hermoso. **5.** La gente habría hecho un asado todos los domingos. **6.** Mi bisabuelo habría ido de pesca en el lago que quedaba cerca. **7.** Mi bisabuela habría cocinado frutas y verduras frescas de la cosecha. **8.** Habría habido caballos y vacas en el rancho (la estancia). **9.** Los granjeros habrían sembrado semillas en el huerto. **10.** Nos habría encantado la vida del rancho (de la estancia).

Actividad 15 **1.** A Lope Cernuda por haber dirigido «Plátanos y cerezas». **2.** A Ernesto del Olmo por haber compuesto la música de «Mosquitos mágicos». **3.** A Ela Pantoja y Roberto Campillo por haber escrito el guión de «Agua hervida». **4.** A Agustín Domingo por haber cantado en «Después de haber bailado». **5.** A Beatriz Perales por haber sido primera actriz en «Salchichas al sol». **6.** A Mateo de León y Diana Duque por haber producido «Grapadora en la mesa». **7.** A Silvia Siles por haber hecho la escenografía de «Narices al aire». **8.** A Memo Morado por haber actuado en «Langostas en el cielo». **9.** A Edit Revueltas por haber diseñado el vestuario de «Tijeras de poliéster». **10.** A Pepe del Oeste por haber maquillado a los actores de «Tamales quemados».

Actividad 16 *Answers will vary.*

Capítulo 8

Actividad 1 **1.** El correo electrónico fue leído por la recepcionista. **2.** Los formularios serán llenados por los empleados. **3.** El folleto ha sido preparado por el diseñador gráfico. **4.** La base de datos fue hecha por la programadora en su nuevo ordenador. **5.** El sitio Web será actualizado por el administrador de Web. **6.** Los billetes electrónicos fueron comprados por los agentes de viajes. **7.** La pantalla fue reparada por el técnico. **8.** Los problemas han sido resueltos por los gerentes.

Actividad 2 **1.** Las camas fueron subidas a los dormitorios por tres hombres. **2.** La alfombra de la sala fue corrida por la señora Pidal. **3.** Los cuadros fueron colgados en las paredes por Benita y Ramona. **4.** La secadora fue bajada al sótano por un cargador. **5.** El sillón azul fue colocado al lado de la ventana por el señor Pidal. **6.** Las lámparas fueron puestas en las mesas por la abuela.

Actividad 3 **1.** Se enchufará la nevera. **2.** Se encenderán las lámparas. **3.** Se guardarán las cajas. **4.** Se pondrá el sofá en la sala. **5.** Se colocará el lavaplatos en la cocina. **6.** Se meterán las sábanas en el armario. **7.** Se pondrán las sillas con la mesa del comedor. **8.** Se subirá el escritorio al dormitorio.

Actividad 4 **1.** Se buscan programadores de computadoras. **2.** Se prohíbe el fumar en los restaurantes. **3.** Se calculaban los impuestos. **4.** Se alquiló el condominio en la playa. **5.** Se entrega comida a la casa hasta la una de la mañana. **6.** Se paga con cheque o tarjeta de crédito. **7.** Se solicitarán gerentes. **8.** Se necesitan asesores bilingües.

Actividad 5 **1.** Mis amigos y yo hacemos una excursión al zoológico. **2.** Para llegar al zoológico, nosotros tomamos el autobús en la calle Azorín. **3.** Yo veo leones, tigres, leopardos y panteras. **4.** Los guardianes dan de comer a los animales. **5.** Los pandas comen bambú. **6.** Tú tiras cacahuetes a los elefantes. **7.** Un mono juega tirando plátanos. **8.** Vosotros compráis palomitas y refrescos.

Actividad 6 **1.** No sé. Cuando yo llegué, el cuarto ya estaba arreglado. **2.** No sé. Cuando yo llegué, el almuerzo ya estaba preparado.   **3.** No sé. Cuando yo llegué, la puerta ya estaba cerrada.   **4.** No sé. Cuando yo llegué, el microondas ya estaba apagado.   **5.** No sé. Cuando yo llegué, la mesa ya estaba puesta.   **6.** No sé. Cuando yo llegué, los vasos ya estaban rotos.   **7.** No sé. Cuando yo llegué, el fax ya estaba mandado.   **8.** No sé. Cuando yo llegué, las luces ya estaban prendidas.

Actividad 7   **1.** Tus papeles están estrujados. Sí, tengo mis papeles estrujados.   **2.** Esta torta está quemada. Sí, tiremos esta torta quemada.   **3.** Tus regalos están envueltos. Sí, traigo los regalos envueltos.   **4.** Tu informe está terminado. Sí, hoy entrego mi informe terminado.   **5.** Tus papeles están archivados. Sí, tengo mis papeles archivados.   **6.** La tortilla está recalentada. Sí, hoy sirvo la tortilla recalentada.

Actividad 8   **1.** Se venden periódicos y revistas aquí.
2. Se estaciona aquí.   **3.** Se dobla a la derecha.   **4.** Se entra por aquí.   **5.** Aquí se habla español.   **6.** Se cobran cheques de viajero.

Actividad 9   *Answers will vary.*

Actividad 10   *Answers will vary.*

Capítulo 9

Actividad 1   **1.** Sí, pasé el día hablando por teléfono celular.
2. Sí, pasaron el día tomando café en el cibercafé.   **3.** Sí, pasó el día durmiendo la siesta.   **4.** Sí, pasamos el día leyendo.   **5.** Sí, pasé el día oyendo las noticias.   **6.** Sí, pasamos el día imprimiendo los documentos.

Actividad 2   **1.** Pasé cuarenta y cinco minutos arreglándome.
2. Pasamos una hora y media andando en bicicleta.   **3.** Pasé dos horas escribiendo un informe.   **4.** Pasamos un par de horas comprando cosas en el centro comercial.   **5.** Pasamos una hora y cuarto vistiéndonos.   **6.** Pasé una hora viendo un documental.

Actividad 3   **1.** Los niños están acampando en la sierra.
2. Ricardo está nadando en el lago.   **3.** Lupe y yo estamos llenando la mochila.   **4.** Ester está desenvolviendo el saco de dormir.   **5.** Pablo está acostándose (se está acostando) en el saco de dormir.   **6.** Yo estoy observando las hormigas en el hormiguero.   **7.** Tú estás encendiendo el fuego para asar los perros calientes.   **8.** Pepe y Lucía están metiendo las pilas en la linterna.   **9.** Todos nosotros estamos quejándonos (nos estamos quejando) de las picaduras de los mosquitos.   **10.** Ud. está asustándose (se está asustando) al ver las arañas en la tienda de campaña.

Actividad 4   **1.** Estábamos leyéndolos. Los estábamos leyendo.
2. Uds. estarán haciéndolas. Uds. las estarán haciendo.
3. Estoy poniéndomelo. Me lo estoy poniendo.   **4.** Ud. estaba lavándoselo. Ud. se lo estaba lavando.   **5.** Estarás diciéndonoslos. Nos los estarás diciendo.   **6.** Rita está buscándolo. Rita lo está buscando.

Actividad 5   **1.** Los señores Sotomayor estaban registrándose. Los señores Sotomayor se estaban registrando.   **2.** El botones estaba subiéndoles el equipaje a unos huéspedes. El botones les estaba subiendo el equipaje a unos huéspedes.   **3.** Los mozos estaban sirviéndoles la cena a los clientes. Los mozos les estaban sirviendo la cena a los clientes.   **4.** El gerente estaba prendiendo el aire acondicionado.   **5.** La lavandera estaba devolviéndole el lavado a la señora Casona. La lavandera le estaba devolviendo el lavado a la señora Casona.   **6.** Los huéspedes del noveno piso estaban bajando en el ascensor.   **7.** Los turistas ingleses estaban tocando el timbre en la recepción.   **8.** Los cocineros estaban jactándose de los plátanos flameados que habían preparado.

Los cocineros se estaban jactando de los plátanos flameados que habían preparado.

Actividad 6   **1.** ¡Qué va! Sigue diciéndolos.   **2.** ¡Qué va! Siguen construyéndola.   **3.** ¡Qué va! Sigo leyéndola.   **4.** ¡Qué va! Siguen tocándolo.   **5.** ¡Qué va! Sigo asistiendo a los conciertos de jazz.   **6.** ¡Qué va! Seguimos jugando al fútbol en el estadio.

Actividad 7   **1.** Luisa estará viendo televisión a las dos y media.   **2.** Ud. estará duchándose a medianoche. (Ud. se estará duchando a medianoche.)   **3.** Mis amigos y yo estaremos muriéndonos de sueño a las cuatro. (Mis amigos y yo nos estaremos muriendo de sueño a las cuatro.)   **4.** Pablo y Ramona estarán jugando vídeojuegos a las doce y media.   **5.** Yo estaré oyendo música a la una y media.   **6.** Tú estarás comiéndote unos bocadillos a las tres. (Tú te estarás comiendo unos bocadillos a las tres.)   **7.** Uds. estarán enviándome un correo electrónico a las seis cuarenta (Uds. me estarán enviando un correo electrónico a las seis cuarenta.)   **8.** Vosotros estaréis bailando en una discoteca a la una.

Actividad 8   **1.** Llevo doce años pintando retratos.   **2.** Llevo unos meses usando estos pinceles.   **3.** Llevo varios años dibujando con modelos.   **4.** Llevo toda la vida dedicándome a la pintura.   **5.** La galería Olmo lleva un año colgando mis cuadros de paisajes.   **6.** Llevo poco tiempo interesándome en los murales.   **7.** Llevo nueve años trabajando en cerámica.
8. Llevo cinco años viviendo en Nueva York.   **9.** Mi esposa lleva un par de años ayudándome.   **10.** Llevo tres años escribiendo libros sobre el arte.   **11.** Llevo muchos años pintando autorretratos.   **12.** Llevo once meses exhibiendo en el Museo de Arte Moderno.

Actividad 9   **1.** están animando   **2.** está robando
3. estamos viendo   **4.** está marcando   **5.** están saliendo
6. está regateando   **7.** están pidiéndoles (les están pidiendo)
8. están entusiasmándose (se están entusiasmando)
9. están oyendo   **10.** está atrayendo

Actividad 10   **1.** ¡Estamos divirtiéndonos mucho! (¡Nos estamos divirtiendo mucho!)   **2.** Ud. estuvo corriendo (trotando) hasta que empezó a llover.   **3.** Siguen sirviendo la cena en el Hotel Palacio.   **4.** Voy conociendo Madrid poco a poco.   **5.** Mateo y Victoria estarán jugando al tenis toda la tarde.   **6.** Pedro y yo seguimos leyendo.

Actividad 11   *Answers will vary.*

Capítulo 10

Actividad 1   **1.** me despierto, despierto   **2.** aburría, se aburrían   **3.** se casaron, casó   **4.** nos paseamos, paseamos
5. tranquilizó, se tranquilizó   **6.** me divertí, divirtieron
7. me mareaba, mareaba   **8.** animamos, se anima
9. se asustaban, asustaban   **10.** se ofenden, ofenden

Actividad 2   **1.** ¿Uds. ya se despiertan solos? No, abuelita. Nos despierta mamá.   **2.** ¿Uds. ya se lavan el pelo solos? No, abuelita. Nos lava el pelo mamá. (Nos lo lava mamá.)
3. ¿Uds. ya se peinan solos? No, abuelita. Nos peina mamá.
4. ¿Uds. ya se atan los zapatos solos? No, abuelita. Nos ata los zapatos mamá. (Nos los ata mamá.)   **5.** ¿Uds. ya se preparan el desayuno solos? No, abuelita. Nos prepara el desayuno mamá. (Nos lo prepara mamá.)   **6.** ¿Uds. ya se acuestan solos? No, abuelita. Nos acuesta mamá.

Actividad 3   **1.** Marina y yo nos pusimos los jeans.
2. Arturo se puso un traje de baño.   **3.** Uds. se pusieron un impermeable.   **4.** Yo me puse un suéter de lana.
5. Víctor y Paz se pusieron un gorro.   **6.** Vosotros os pusisteis

una camiseta.   **7.** Tú te pusiste las sandalias.   **8.** Ud. se puso una chaqueta.

Actividad 4   **1.** Yo me pondré las medias.   **2.** Alicia se pondrá una blusa.   **3.** Nosotros nos pondremos los zapatos. **4.** Uds. se pondrán una camisa.   **5.** Los jefes se pondrán un traje.   **6.** Tú te pondrás una corbata.   **7.** Ud. se pondrá un cinturón.   **8.** Vosotros os pondréis una bufanda.

Actividad 5   **1.** Pilar y Luz se prueban el traje largo de lana. **2.** Yo me pruebo el abrigo de cuero.   **3.** Lorenzo se prueba el smoking de seda.   **4.** Uds. se prueban los zapatos de tacón alto. **5.** Tú te pruebas la blusa de algodón.   **6.** Antonio y Esteban se prueban la corbata de seda.   **7.** Nosotros nos probamos el chaleco de poliéster.   **8.** Vosotros os probáis los guantes de nailon.

Actividad 6   **1.** Miguel se rompió la pierna montando a caballo. **2.** Ana se quemó la mano cocinando.   **3.** El perro de Bernardo se perdió corriendo en las afueras.   **4.** Alicia se torció el tobillo patinando sobre hielo.   **5.** Todos nosotros nos enfermamos comiendo hamburguesas poco hechas.   **6.** Yo me hice daño cortando el césped.   **7.** Los hermanos de Anita se quebraron el dedo jugando al baloncesto.

Actividad 7   **1.** La actriz Ramona Taylor se lastimó en el rodaje de su nueva película.   **2.** El futbolista Diego Suárez se rompió el pie en el partido de hoy.   **3.** Unos turistas norteamericanos se cayeron en la escalera mecánica del metro.   **4.** Un carpintero se cortó la mano serrando madera.   **5.** Diez arqueólogos se hicieron daño en una excavación en las pirámides.   **6.** Un bombero se quemó apagando un incendio.   **7.** Los esposos se divorciaron después de veinte años de matrimonio.

Actividad 8   **1.** Vosotros os laváis el pelo todos los días. **2.** Yo me visto rápidamente por la mañana.   **3.** Uds. se duchan por la noche.   **4.** Carlos se afeita con una maquinilla de afeitar. **5.** Laura y Teresa se liman las uñas antes de ponerse el esmalte de uñas.   **6.** Tú te peinas con peine y cepillo.   **7.** Benjamín y yo nos arreglamos en el dormitorio.   **8.** Ud. se cepilla los dientes antes de maquillarse.

Actividad 9   **1.** Ud. quiere colocarse en una sucursal de la empresa. Ud. se quiere colocar en una sucursal de la empresa. **2.** Nosotros debemos despertarnos antes de las ocho. Nosotros nos debemos despertar antes de las ocho.   **3.** Vosotros pensáis reuniros en casa de Felipe esta noche. Vosotros os pensáis reunir en casa de Felipe esta noche.   **4.** Teresa necesita pesarse todas las semanas. Teresa se necesita pesar todas las semanas. **5.** Yo voy a irme de vacaciones en julio. Yo me voy a ir de vacaciones en julio.   **6.** Las señoras acaban de aprovecharse de las liquidaciones. Las señoras se acaban de aprovechar de las liquidaciones.   **7.** ¿Quieres sentarte en esta fila? ¿Te quieres sentar en esta fila?   **8.** Uds. tienen que secarse el pelo. Uds. se tienen que secar el pelo.

Actividad 10   **1.** Luisito está portándose mal. Luisito se está portando mal.   **2.** Los abuelos de Luisito están enfadándose. Los abuelos de Luisito se están enfadando.   **3.** Fernandito está escondiéndose en un armario. Fernandito se está escondiendo en un armario.   **4.** El tío de Fernandito está asustándose. El tío de Fernandito se está asustando.   **5.** Los gemelos están escapándose de su padre. Los gemelos se están escapando de su padre.   **6.** El padre de los gemelos está enojándose. El padre de los gemelos se está enojando.   **7.** Mari Carmen está ensuciándose con el helado. Mari Carmen se está ensuciando con el helado.   **8.** La madre de Mari Carmen está avergonzándose. La madre de Mari Carmen se está avergonzando.

Actividad 11   **1.** Se está apresurando para salir. Está apresurándose para salir.   **2.** Se están mudando a otro barrio.

Están mudándose a otro barrio.   **3.** Se están acercando a la escuela. Están acercándose a la escuela.   **4.** Se están paseando por el centro. Están paseándose por el centro.   **5.** Me estoy divirtiendo. Estoy divirtiéndome.   **6.** Nos estamos reuniendo en casa de Pepe. Estamos reuniéndonos en casa de Pepe. **7.** Se está vistiendo para ir a un baile. Está vistiéndose para ir a un baile.   **8.** Se está instalando en su nuevo apartamento. Está instalándose en su nuevo apartamento.

Actividad 12   **1.** Pruébese los dos. Pruébate los dos. **2.** Acuéstese temprano. Acuéstate temprano.   **3.** Dése prisa. Date prisa.   **4.** Póngase el impermeable. Ponte el impermeable. **5.** Diviértase mucho. Diviértete mucho.   **6.** Quédese otra semana entonces. Quédate otra semana entonces.

Actividad 13   **1.** No se levante todavía. No te levantes todavía. **2.** No se enferme. No te enfermes.   **3.** No se enfade con ella. No te enfades con ella.   **4.** No se despierte tarde. No te despiertes tarde.   **5.** No se duerma antes de terminar. No te duermas antes de terminar.   **6.** No se case con él. No te cases con él.   **7.** No se caiga. No te caigas.

Actividad 14   **1.** Niños, vístanse para salir.   **2.** Niños, cepíllense los dientes.   **3.** Niños, átense los cordones. **4.** Niños, pónganse serios.   **5.** Niños, lávense las manos. **6.** Niños, péinense.   **7.** Niños, levántense.   **8.** Niños, pruébense los zapatos.

Actividad 15   **1.** Niños, no se ensucien la cara.   **2.** Niños, no se hagan los sordos.   **3.** Niños, no se caigan patinando. **4.** Niños, no se olviden de guardar sus juguetes.   **5.** Niños, no se vayan del jardín.   **6.** Niños, no se quiebren el pie jugando al fútbol.   **7.** Niños, no se quejen tanto.   **8.** Niños, no se hagan daño.

Actividad 16   **1.** Marisol y yo nos hablamos por teléfono cuatro veces al día.   **2.** Jorge y yo nos entendemos perfectamente. **3.** María y yo nos vemos todos los días.   **4.** Consuelo y yo nos escribimos correos electrónicos.   **5.** Alicia y yo nos ayudamos con la tarea.   **6.** Victoria y yo nos prestamos la ropa. **7.** Claudia y yo nos queremos mucho.   **8.** Tú y yo nos tuteamos.

Actividad 17   **1.** Se conocieron en una fiesta.   **2.** Se llamaron a menudo.   **3.** Se escribieron mensajes por correo electrónico. **4.** Se hablaron constantemente.   **5.** Se compraron regalos. **6.** Se comprendieron muy bien.   **7.** Se dieron la mano. **8.** Se dijeron muchas cosas importantes.   **9.** Se hicieron promesas.   **10.** Se llegaron a querer.

Actividad 18   **1.** Ricardo se hizo (llegó a ser) millonario. **2.** Los arqueólogos se entusiasmaron al ver las ruinas. **3.** Magdalena se pone roja a menudo porque es muy tímida. **4.** Ellos se pusieron furiosos (se enfurecieron) al enterarse de la verdad.   **5.** ¡Carlitos se ha vuelto imposible!   **6.** Felisa está poniéndose muy gorda por la torta y el helado que come todos los días.   **7.** La región (La zona) se convirtió en un importante centro tecnológico (de tecnología).   **8.** Isabela se hizo (llegó a ser) programadora.

Actividad 19   **1.** con   **2.** en   **3.** de   **4.** de   **5.** en   **6.** a **7.** de   **8.** a   **9.** de   **10.** de   **11.** con   **12.** a   **13.** a   **14.** en

Actividad 20   **1.** Si no recuerdo mal, los Aranda se mudaron a Los Ángeles.   **2.** Ud. se equivoca. Lima es la capital de Perú, no de Ecuador.   **3.** Dos personas se quedaron ciegas a causa del accidente.   **4.** La niña se hace la dormida.   **5.** Juan Carlos ha enflaquecido (se ha puesto flaco).   **6.** Creíamos que íbamos a enloquecernos por el desorden de la casa.   **7.** Todos los habitantes están poniéndose furiosos por el número de robos en el barrio.   **8.** Diego se palidecía corriendo la última milla de la carrera. **9.** Te hiciste daño esquiando. **10.** Uds. se dieron prisa por llegar al aeropuerto. **11.** Se trata de hacer una base de datos primero.

Actividad 21 *Answers will vary.*

Capítulo 11

Actividad 1 **1.** Pero yo quiero que trabaje en el informe. **2.** Pero yo quiero que consigas empleo. **3.** Pero yo quiero que nos escriban. **4.** Pero yo quiero que siga nuestros consejos. **5.** Pero yo quiero que comamos fuera hoy. **6.** Pero yo quiero que vuelvas temprano. **7.** Pero yo quiero que duerman por la tarde. **8.** Pero yo quiero que pidamos taxi. **9.** Pero yo quiero que abran la tienda hoy. **10.** Pero yo quiero que entendamos. **11.** Pero yo quiero que piense en nosotros. **12.** Pero yo quiero que la oficina envíe el paquete. **13.** Pero yo quiero que cierres las ventanas. **14.** Pero yo quiero que nos divirtamos. **15.** Pero yo quiero que repitamos el vocabulario.

Actividad 2 **1.** Sí. Se alegra de que conozca a Pedro. **2.** Sí. Se alegra de que tengamos un día libre. (Sí. Se alegra de que Uds. tengan un día libre.) **3.** Sí. Se alegra de que le traiga flores. **4.** Sí. Se alegra de que construyan una casa. **5.** Sí. Se alegra de que salgamos juntos. **6.** Sí. Se alegra de que obedezca a su profesora. **7.** Sí. Se alegra de que componga música. **8.** Sí. Se alegra de que sea mañana. **9.** Sí. Se alegra de que haya reunión la semana que viene. **10.** Sí. Se alegra de que vayan a España.

Actividad 3 **1.** realices **2.** se acerquen **3.** comience **4.** dirija **5.** saquen **6.** recojamos **7.** se dedique **8.** entregues **9.** consiga **10.** organicen **11.** almuerce **12.** convenza **13.** venzan

Actividad 4 **1.** digamos **2.** aprenden **3.** se gradúe **4.** te quejas **5.** me matricule **6.** vayáis **7.** sale **8.** podemos **9.** sea **10.** haya **11.** están **12.** hagas **13.** sé **14.** consigue

Actividad 5 **1.** Laura espera perfeccionar su español. **2.** Ricardo y Beti prefieren visitar la catedral del Zócalo. **3.** Ud. debe conocer Taxco. **4.** Pablo y yo deseamos ir a Puebla. **5.** Tú prefieres hacer una excursión a la Ciudad Universitaria. **6.** Yo siento no poder quedarme más tiempo en la Ciudad de México. **7.** Uds. insisten en escaparse un par de días a Mérida. **8.** Todos nosotros nos alegramos de estar en Oaxaca.

Actividad 6 **1.** Laura espera que nosotros perfeccionemos nuestro español. **2.** Ricardo y Beti prefieren que Ud. visite la catedral del Zócalo. **3.** Ud. necesita que Leo conozca Taxco. **4.** Pablo y yo deseamos que Uds. vayan a Puebla. **5.** Prefieres que yo haga una excursión a la Ciudad Universitaria. **6.** Yo siento que nosotros no podamos quedarnos más tiempo en la Ciudad de México. **7.** Uds. insisten en que los amigos se escapen un par de días a Mérida. **8.** Todos nosotros nos alegramos de que tú estés en Oaxaca.

Actividad 7 **1.** Elena espera que sus cuñados tengan éxito. **2.** El señor Ayala les pide a sus suegros que vengan a verlos los domingos. **3.** La madrina se alegra que su ahijado saque buenas notas en la universidad. **4.** Los padres quieren que sus hijos se ganen la vida. **5.** A la señora Ayala le gusta que los bisabuelos sean felices en la tercera edad. **6.** Yo le aconsejo a la nieta que se haga arquitecta. **7.** Terencio le prohíbe a las ahijadas que vayan solas al extranjero. **8.** Tú sientes que tu cuñado no esté contento con el nuevo empleo. **9.** La suegra prefiere que los novios se muden con ella. **10.** Uds. les ruegan a los padrinos que acepten su regalo. **11.** Ricardo y yo necesitamos que los nietos nos den muchos besos y abrazos. **12.** Los hijos no dejan que sus padres trabajen demasiado manteniéndolos.

Actividad 8 **1.** te encuentres **2.** estamos **3.** puedas **4.** voy **5.** llegues **6.** pasen **7.** compren **8.** traigan

9. hace **10.** está **11.** llueve **12.** debes **13.** sé **14.** vas **15.** vas **16.** hay **17.** se despierten **18.** puedo **19.** tengo **20.** escribas **21.** viene

Actividad 9 **1.** Es malo que ellos vean el desorden. **2.** Es necesario que hagamos la limpieza del apartamento. **3.** Es importante que Lupe friegue las cacerolas. **4.** Es probable que Uds. recojan las cajas de pizza. **5.** Más vale que los padres traigan trapos y productos para la limpieza. **6.** Es dudoso que los padres se metan en todo esto. **7.** Es preciso que yo limpie el polvo. **8.** Es posible que María y Diana guarden su ropa sucia en la cómoda. **9.** Es mejor que tú quites las telarañas del techo. **10.** ¡Qué lástima que no nos relajemos en todo el día!

Actividad 10 **1.** No estoy seguro que Lorenzo siga enfermo. **2.** Es obvio que Teresa y Jesús se quieren mucho. **3.** No es cierto que Uds. tengan problemas con el coche. **4.** Es que Julia llega el sábado. **5.** No es seguro que Carmen sea de origen ruso. **6.** No es evidente que los niños estén aburridos. **7.** No creo que tú lo sepas todo. **8.** Es cierto que Martín renuncia a su puesto.

Actividad 11 **1.** Oye, Anita, insisto en que estudies para los exámenes finales. **2.** Oye, Miguel, me sorprende que no trabajes en la librería. **3.** Oye, Rebeca, más vale que escribas el informe para sociología. **4.** Oye, Tomás, es útil que practiques chino en el laboratorio de lenguas. **5.** Oye, Graciela, es importante que tomes apuntes en historia. **6.** Oye, Alfredo, te ruego que hagas la tarea. **7.** Oye, Carolina, espero que saques buenas notas. **8.** Oye, Ana, te prohíbo que juegues al béisbol todo el día.

Actividad 12 **1.** Es bueno que haya tantos adelantos tecnológicos. **2.** Preferimos usar la energía nuclear aún más. **3.** Todo el mundo se alegra (está contento) de tener la computadora. **4.** Es evidente que las guerras siguen estallando. **5.** Es probable que la contaminación del ambiente haga mucho daño. **6.** Es obvio que la gente quiere vivir en una sociedad democrática. **7.** Les aconsejamos a los líderes políticos que gasten el dinero con más responsabilidad. **8.** Ojalá que haya elecciones libres en todos los países. **9.** Es importante que haya más tecnología nueva en el siglo veintiuno.

Actividad 13 **1.** Clara siente que Uds. no hayan visto la exposición de arte. **2.** Dudamos que vosotros hayáis escrito la revista electrónica. **3.** Me alegro que Carlos se haya hecho ciudadano. **4.** Esperan que hayas visto la nueva película policíaca. **5.** Es una lástima que haya muerto el bisabuelo de Martín. **6.** Es mejor que las chicas no hayan dicho nada. **7.** Nos sorprende que haya habido un incendio en el metro. **8.** No piensan que Luz se haya puesto brava. **9.** No creen que me haya gustado el concierto.

Actividad 14 **1.** Me alegro que Julia y Paco se hayan casado. **2.** Es bueno que hayamos visto esos sitios Web. **3.** Ellos dudan que los Tigres hayan ganado el partido de fútbol. **4.** Esperamos que Fernando se haya hecho rico. **5.** ¿Está Ud. sorprendido/a que la familia Núñez se haya mudado? **6.** Ana no piensa que los chicos hayan roto la ventana.

Actividad 15 *Answers will vary.*

Capítulo 12

Actividad 1 **1.** se diera/diese **2.** encontrara/encontrase **3.** se pusieran/pusiesen **4.** supiéramos/supiésemos **5.** hubiera/hubiese **6.** siguieras/siguieses **7.** durmiera/durmiese **8.** viera/viese **9.** se reunieran/reuniesen **10.** oyéramos/oyésemos **11.** dijerais/dijeseis **12.** fueran/

fuesen **13.** construyeran/construyesen **14.** trajeras/trajeses **15.** se fuera/fuese

Actividad 2 **1.** Felipe les sugirió que fueran a una discoteca. **2.** Felipe esperaba que Angélica bailara con él y nadie más. **3.** Teodoro también deseaba que Angélica saliera con él. **4.** Angélica temía que los chicos tuvieran celos. **5.** Era posible que Felipe y Teodoro se pelearan por Angélica. **6.** Felipe no creía que fuera una buena idea ir a la discoteca. **7.** Felipe le propuso a Angélica que vieran una película. **8.** A Angélica le agradaba que Felipe y Teodoro la quisieran, ¡pero ella estaba enamorada de Julio!

Actividad 3 **1.** hubiera **2.** fuera **3.** pudiera **4.** se llevara **5.** cayera **6.** aprobaran **7.** quisiera

Actividad 4 **1.** fueran **2.** saliera **3.** acompañara **4.** jugara **5.** condujera **6.** trataran

Actividad 5 **1.** me hiciera **2.** siguiéramos **3.** tuviéramos **4.** trabajara **5.** nos casáramos **6.** fuéramos **7.** nos dedicáramos **8.** nos ayudáramos **9.** vivieran

Actividad 6 **1.** cortaras **2.** descongelaras **3.** regaras **4.** hicieras **5.** bañaras **6.** pusieras **7.** guardaras **8.** sacaras **9.** repararas

Actividad 7 **1.** mintiera **2.** rompiera **3.** tuviera **4.** hiciera **5.** invitaran **6.** tomara **7.** fueran **8.** metiera

Actividad 8 **1.** Ojalá que yo fuera de vacaciones en abril. **2.** Ojalá que Uds. recibieran un iPod. **3.** Ojalá que Diana no se quejara de todo. **4.** Ojalá que nuestro equipo ganara el campeonato. **5.** Ojalá que Bernardo y Marta no discutieran tanto. **6.** Ojalá que no te preocuparas por nada. **7.** Ojalá que tú y yo pudiéramos asistir al congreso en San Diego. **8.** Ojalá que vosotros nos invitarais a vuestra hacienda.

Actividad 9 **1.** Era bueno que Rebeca hubiera llegado a ser arquitecta. **2.** Nos gustó que las hermanas Cela hubieran hecho un viaje a Santo Domingo. **3.** Me extrañó que Uds. se hubieran quedado tanto tiempo. **4.** Era necesario que tú hubieras comprado una computadora nueva. **5.** Era importante que yo hubiera conocido Roma. **6.** Todos se alegraron que Juan y yo nos hubiéramos comprometido.

Actividad 10 **1.** Tú esperabas que ellos hubieran tenido éxito. **2.** Ellos temían que alguien me lo hubiera dicho. **3.** Sentíamos que Ud. no hubiera oído lo que pasó. **4.** Sarita dudaba que hubiéramos vuelto del campo. **5.** Me alegraba que hubiera hecho calor y sol. **6.** Ojalá que Uds. hubieran visto el sitio Web.

Actividad 11 **1.** puedo, visitaré **2.** ofrecen, aceptará **3.** saldremos, tenemos **4.** llama, diré **5.** pones, harán **6.** preguntan, sabrán **7.** vendremos, hay

Actividad 12 **1.** tuviera, haría **2.** vendrían, invitáramos **3.** vería, hubiera **4.** ganara, se compraría **5.** hiciera, saldríamos **6.** dormiría, se sintiera **7.** pudieras, resolverías **8.** saldrían, fuera **9.** supieran, dirían

Actividad 13 **1.** encontrara, me casaría **2.** besara, dejaría, me convertiría **3.** hubiera, notaría **4.** vinieran, comería **5.** mintiera, crecería **6.** diera, se despertaría **7.** tuviera, tendría

Actividad 14 **1.** fuera, gustaría **2.** hicieran, irían **3.** pudieran, se quedarían **4.** pasáramos, tomaríamos **5.** visitaras, probarías **6.** quisiera, conocería

Actividad 15 **1.** hubieran preguntado, habríamos/hubiéramos dicho **2.** habría/hubiera devuelto, hubiera visto **3.** se hubiera hecho, habría/hubiera estado **4.** habríamos/hubiéramos llamado, hubiéramos sabido **5.** hubiera jugado, habría/hubiera roto **6.** hubieras leído, habrías/hubieras entendido

Actividad 16 **1.** Pablo habría/hubiera asistido al teatro si hubiera vivido en la ciudad. **2.** Amelia habría/hubiera ordeñado las vacas si hubiera nacido en una finca. **3.** Pablo se habría/hubiera puesto más nervioso si hubiera oído tanto ruido todos los días. **4.** Amelia habría/hubiera respirado aire no contaminado si hubiera vivido en el campo. **5.** Pablo habría/hubiera tomado el metro y los taxis si hubiera trabajado en la ciudad. **6.** Amelia habría/hubiera aprendido a montar a caballo si hubiera pasado su vida en el campo. **7.** Pablo habría/hubiera comprado toda la comida en el supermercado si hubiera hecho la compra en la ciudad. **8.** Amelia habría/hubiera comido frutas y legumbres muy frescas si se hubiera criado en el campo. **9.** Pablo habría/hubiera llevado un traje, camisa y corbata si se hubiera ganado la vida trabajando en una empresa. **10.** Amelia habría/hubiera usado un sombrero de paja si hubiera cultivado la tierra.

Actividad 17 **1.** hubiera terminado, habría/hubiera podido **2.** hubiera planeado, habría/hubiera perdido **3.** hubiera hecho, habría/hubiera bailado **4.** hubiera gastado, habría/hubiera disfrutado **5.** hubiera manejado, me habría/hubiera atrasado **6.** se hubieran divertido, se habrían/hubieran quedado **7.** se hubiera acostado, habría/hubiera tenido

Actividad 18 **1.** Si Victoria hubiera tenido la llave, habría/hubiera abierto la maleta. **2.** Si Ud. hiciera un viaje este verano, ¿adónde iría? **3.** Si ellos hubieran tenido más cuidado, no se les habría/hubiera perdido su teléfono celular. **4.** Si Uds. doblan a la derecha en la esquina, verán el museo. **5.** Yo le haría caso a Roberto si diera buenos consejos. **6.** Si hubieras navegado más en la Red, habrías/hubieras encontrado el sitio Web.

Actividad 19 **1.** fuera **2.** vivieran **3.** tuviera **4.** pensara **5.** supiera **6.** oyeras **7.** dolieran **8.** comprendierais

Actividad 20 **1.** hubieran comido **2.** hubiera visto **3.** hubiera sido **4.** te hubieras divertido **5.** se hubiera hecho **6.** hubiera podido

Actividad 21 *Answers will vary.*

Capítulo 13

Actividad 1 **1.** manden **2.** aconseje **3.** llueva **4.** haya **5.** quieras **6.** sea **7.** prefiera **8.** digamos **9.** vaya

Actividad 2 **1.** Elena y Mario salieron del cibercafé antes de que nosotros entráramos en la zapatería. **2.** Ud. alquiló una película en la tienda de vídeos antes de que yo volviera de la farmacia. **3.** Uds. compraron los sellos en el supermercado antes de que Miguel pudiera ir al correo. **4.** Fernando y yo estacionamos en el centro comercial antes de que tú llegaras a la discoteca. **5.** Yo saqué la ropa de la tintorería antes de que Juana tuviera su cita en la peluquería. **6.** Tú fuiste a la joyería antes de que Arturo y Bárbara buscaran una librería. **7.** Vosotros llegasteis a la gasolinera antes de que Pedro y yo regresáramos de la universidad.

Actividad 3 **1.** sepa **2.** vino **3.** necesiten **4.** pudiera **5.** invitemos **6.** entramos **7.** terminó **8.** lleguen

Actividad 4 **1.** Los llamaré cuando llegue al aeropuerto. **2.** Consuelo puso la mesa una hora antes de que llegaran sus amigos. **3.** Hicieron cola en la taquilla después que almorzaron (después de almorzar). **4.** Ud. no quería ir de compras sin que nosotros fuéramos también. **5.** Háganlo como ellos quieran. **6.** Aunque hace frío debemos dar un paseo. **7.** Te presto el libro para que no tengas que sacarlo de la biblioteca. **8.** Carlos va a estudiar para su examen antes de jugar al tenis (antes que juegue al tenis).

Actividad 5 **1.** Tú quieres un apartamento que tenga dos baños. **2.** Marta necesita un apartamento donde haya aire acondicionado. **3.** Juana y yo buscamos un apartamento que esté cerca de la universidad. **4.** Uds. necesitan un apartamento que no cueste un ojo de la cara. **5.** Yo quiero un apartamento que no necesite renovación. **6.** Adela y Leonor desean un apartamento que sea moderno y fácil de limpiar. **7.** Vosotras buscáis un apartamento que dé a una calle poco transitada. **8.** Ud. necesita un apartamento donde quepan todos los fiesteros.

Actividad 6 **1.** sepa **2.** pueda **3.** comprenda **4.** me divierta **5.** sea **6.** tenga

Actividad 7 **1.** reúna **2.** sea **3.** quieras **4.** vaya **5.** tenga **6.** se enamore

Actividad 8 **1.** diera **2.** se esforzara **3.** permitiera **4.** compartiera **5.** invirtiera **6.** fuera **7.** pudiera **8.** hubiera **9.** dejara

Actividad 9 **1.** Mario y Carmen buscan una casa que tenga nueve cuartos. **2.** No hay ninguna comida que le guste. **3.** Yo quería un/a amigo/a que fuera conmigo a los museos. **4.** ¿No conoce Ud. a nadie que llegue antes de las tres? **5.** Rosa preparará el plato que escojamos. **6.** Necesitaban un/a secretario/a que trabajara los sábados. **7.** Tomaremos la clase con el/la profesor(a) que enseñe mejor. **8.** Yo tomaré el tren a la hora que llegue. **9.** Roberto buscaba un sitio Web que tuviera todos los datos necesarios. **10.** Nos quedaremos en el hotel que les guste. **11.** No había ningún cibercafé que estuviera abierto a la una de la mañana. **12.** Buscan a los programadores que trabajan los fines de semana.

Actividad 10 Answers will vary.

Capítulo 14

Actividad 1 **1.** Añada las patatas y cebollas peladas y picadas. **2.** Cocine a fuego lento. **3.** Espolvoree con sal. **4.** Bata los huevos. **5.** Ponga los huevos en la sartén. **6.** Haga dorar los huevos. **7.** Déle la vuelta a la tortilla con cuidado. **8.** No deje que se pegue la tortilla. **9.** Sirva en una fuente.

Actividad 2 **1.** Asistan a la reunión semanal en la oficina del director. **2.** Traigan la calculadora. **3.** Creen una base de datos. **4.** Envíen el correo electrónico. **5.** Sigan los consejos del gerente. **6.** Actualicen el sitio Web. **7.** Lean el manual sobre el programa de gráficas. **8.** Hagan copias de seguridad.

Actividad 3 **1.** Sí, búsquelo. No, no lo busque. **2.** Sí, fírmela. No, no la firme. **3.** Sí, llénelo. No, no lo llene. **4.** Sí, démela en pesos. No, no me la dé en pesos. **5.** Sí, selecciónela. No, no la seleccione. **6.** Sí, calcúlemelos. No, no me los calcule. **7.** Sí, ciérrela. No, no la cierre. **8.** Sí, cóbremelos. No, no me los cobre. **9.** Sí, pruébela. No, no la pruebe.

Actividad 4 **1.** Demos un paseo por la zona de la Plaza de Armas. Vamos a dar un paseo por la zona de la Plaza de Armas. **2.** Vamos de compras en el Jirón de la Unión. Vamos a ir de compras en el Jirón de la Unión. **3.** Conozcamos la Universidad de San Marcos. Vamos a conocer la Universidad de San Marcos. **4.** Hagamos una excursión a Machu Picchu. Vamos a hacer una excursión a Machu Picchu. **5.** Visitemos la catedral y unas iglesias de Cuzco. Vamos a visitar la catedral y unas iglesias de Cuzco. **6.** Quedémonos en Miraflores. Vamos a quedarnos en Miraflores.

Actividad 5 **1.** Cómo no. Démoselos. Cómo no. Vamos a dárselos. **2.** Cómo no. Saquémoslas. Cómo no. Vamos a sacarlas. **3.** Cómo no. Vamos al museo por la tarde. **4.** Cómo no. Caminemos por el parque. Cómo no. Vamos a caminar por el parque. **5.** Cómo no. Inscribámonos en la clase de computación. Cómo no. Vamos a inscribirnos en la clase de computación. **6.** Cómo no. Juguemos al tenis. Cómo no. Vamos a jugar al tenis. **7.** Cómo no. Conozcámoslo. Cómo no. Vamos a conocerlo. **8.** Cómo no. Enseñémoselo. Cómo no. Vamos a enseñárselo. **9.** Cómo no. Tumbémonos en la playa. Cómo no. Vamos a tumbarnos en la playa.

Actividad 6 **1.** Haced la torta, pero no le pongáis el glaseado todavía. **2.** Abrid las botellas de vino, pero no cortéis las rebanadas de naranja todavía. **3.** Sacad los platitos para las tapas, pero no preparéis el chorizo y el pulpo todavía. **4.** Poned la mesa, pero no coloquéis los claveles todavía. **5.** Salid a comprar aceitunas, pero no vayáis todavía. **6.** Removed la sangría, pero no la sirváis en un jarro todavía. **7.** Invitad a Pilar, pero no le digáis nada a Consuelo. **8.** Traed discos compactos, pero no traigáis vídeos.

Actividad 7 **1.** Da un paseo todos los días. **2.** Sal a divertirte. **3.** Toma una infusión de manzanilla. **4.** Tranquilízate escuchando música. **5.** No bebas mucha cafeína. **6.** No te pongas pesimista. **7.** Reúnete con tus amigos. **8.** No te preocupes por tonterías. **9.** Búscate otro novio más compasivo.

Actividad 8 **1.** Pórtate bien. **2.** No hagas payasadas. **3.** No seas terco. **4.** Deja al perro en paz. **5.** Recoge las migas de las galletas. **6.** No derrames el perfume de tu mamá. **7.** Hazme caso. **8.** No te encierres en el baño. **9.** Ven acá inmediatamente.

Actividad 9 **1.** Sed pacientes. **2.** Idos. **3.** Decid la verdad. **4.** No seáis desagradables. **5.** No os enfadéis. **6.** Escribid un e-mail. **7.** Asistid a la conferencia. **8.** Tocad el piano. **9.** Acostaos temprano.

Actividad 10 **1.** date prisa **2.** no te lastimes **3.** no te cortes el dedo **4.** ten cuidado **5.** no te rompas el pie **6.** no enciendas los fósforos **7.** conduce más lentamente **8.** ponte una armadura

Actividad 11 **1.** déjelo **2.** te mojes **3.** déle **4.** juegues **5.** hágale **6.** te quites **7.** tráigalo **8.** ven **9.** sal

Actividad 12 **1.** Sí, dáselos. **2.** Sí, mándenoslas (mándanoslas). **3.** Sí, entréguenmela. **4.** Sí, pónmelo. **5.** Sí, prepáreselos (prepáraselos). **6.** Sí, sírvanselo. **7.** Sí, explícamela. **8.** Sí, dígamelos.

Actividad 13 **1.** No, no se los des. **2.** No, no nos las mande(s). **3.** No, no me la entreguen. **4.** No, no me lo pongas. **5.** No, no se los prepare(s). **6.** No, no se lo sirvan. **7.** No, no me la expliques. **8.** No, no me los diga.

Actividad 14 **1.** Que los lea Manolo. **2.** Que las dibujen Terencio y Elena. **3.** Que los observe Paulina. **4.** Que los hagan los otros. **5.** Que las investigue Samuel. **6.** Que se dediquen a ellas mis amigos. **7.** Que lo escriba Celinda.

Actividad 15 **1.** Que ella le dé el cheque a Ud. **2.** Que se vayan. **3.** Que él le mande las tarjetas a ella. **4.** Que no se te pierda la cartera. **5.** Que vuelvan por la tarde. **6.** Que no se les acaben los refrescos.

Actividad 16 **1.** Cortarlos a tiritas. **2.** Calentar el aceite. **3.** Partirlos en trozos. **4.** Secar los tomates. **5.** Añadirlas a la salsa. **6.** Removerlo. **7.** Ponerla en una fuente.

Actividad 17 **1.** Hagan el favor de ir al laboratorio de lenguas. **2.** Tengan la bondad de aprender los diálogos de memoria. **3.** Favor de traer el diccionario. **4.** Tengan la bondad de matricularse si no lo han hecho. **5.** Háganme el favor de comprar el libro de texto y el cuaderno de trabajo. **6.** Favor de apuntarse en esta lista. **7.** Hagan el favor de hacer hincapié en los ejercicios de fonética todos los días. **8.** Tengan la bondad de buscar sitios Web en español. **9.** Favor de ver películas y leer periódicos en español.

Actividad 18 **1.** llamar **2.** Enviar/Mandar **3.** escribir
4. presentarse **5.** dirigirse **6.** adjuntar **7.** ponerse en contacto
8. concertar

Actividad 19 *Answers will vary.*

Capítulo 15

Actividad 1 **1.** Los españoles quisieron celebrar el santo del Rey Juan Carlos el 24 de junio. **2.** Uds. siempre procuraban ir de vacaciones en Semana Santa. **3.** Paco no pudo salir con su novia el Día de los Enamorados. **4.** Sueles preparar una barbacoa el Día de la Independencia. **5.** Alejandra y Pepita no consiguieron asistir a la Misa del Gallo este año. **6.** Los niñitos esperaban recibir muchos regalos lindos el Día de Reyes.
7. Debe haber unos desfiles grandes el Día de la Raza.
8. Decidí traerles flores y bombones a los tíos por el Año Nuevo.

Actividad 2 **1.** Sabíais nadar muy bien. **2.** Logré terminar el proyecto. **3.** Se prohíbe salir por esa puerta. **4.** Han ofrecido tocar un vals. **5.** Hacíamos limpiar la casa. **6.** No dejaste escuchar los discos compactos.

Actividad 3 **1.** en **2.** en **3.** a **4.** de **5.** a **6.** de **7.** a **8.** con **9.** de **10.** que

Actividad 4 **1.** Solíamos (Estábamos acostumbrados a) cenar a las nueve de la noche. **2.** ¿Por qué demoraron (tardaron) tanto en llamarnos? **3.** Patricia se negó a prestarle dinero a Diego.
4. Trate de pagar con una tarjeta de crédito. **5.** Vuelvan a cantar esa canción. **6.** Voy a asistir a la conferencia. **7.** Silvia amenazó con irse inmediatamente. **8.** Ellos sueñan con hacerse millonarios.

Actividad 5 **1.** Pedro llegó a (consiguió) hacerse presidente de la empresa. **2.** Consuelo presume de ser la mejor futbolista del equipo. **3.** El profesor obligó a cerrar los libros. **4.** Uds. se arrepintieron de perderse la boda. **5.** Yo no me acordé de recoger los pasteles. **6.** ¿Cómo es que comenzaste a (empezaste a) hacer la tarea a las dos de la mañana? **7.** No se permitía entrar en las salas de escultura. **8.** Están vacilando en invertir dinero en la compañía.

Actividad 6 **1.** Te llamaremos antes de salir. **2.** Viajaron a Ponce en auto sin parar. **3.** Niños, acuéstense después de cepillarse los dientes. **4.** Bernardo debe leer un libro en vez de mirar la televisión. **5.** Voy a estar en la biblioteca hasta volver a casa. **6.** Elena va a patinar con tal de que Daniel patine también. **7.** Invítelos en caso de verlos. **8.** Cuando llegamos (Al llegar) a la fiesta, empezamos (nos pusimos) a bailar.

Actividad 7 **1.** Mis padres toman sus vitaminas al desayunar.
2. Mi amigo Pablo y yo siempre salimos a trotar al acabar la tarea.
3. Al salir del trabajo, Teresa y Laura van al gimnasio.
4. Tú levantarás pesas al sentirte en forma. **5.** Vosotros camináis al terminar de almorzar. **6.** Al tomar café, yo no como pasteles. **7.** Llámenme al salir para la piscina.
8. Y al ir a la tienda de alimentos naturales, yo los avisaré.

Actividad 8 **1.** Los empleados se quejan al exigir demasiado el señor Montalbán. **2.** Al ver un problema grande, el señor Montalbán convoca una reunión. **3.** Los empleados se ponen gruñones al recibir el aviso de la reunión. **4.** En la reunión, todo el mundo se calló al entrar el señor Montalbán. **5.** El señor Montalbán se puso muy serio al dirigirse a sus empleados.
6. Pero al salir el señor Montalbán, todos empezaron a chismear.

Actividad 9 **1.** Sí, los oí ladrar. **2.** Sí, lo oí maullar. **3.** Sí, los oí despegar y aterrizar. **4.** Sí, las oí susurrar. **5.** Sí, los oí gritar. **6.** Sí, la oí roncar.

Actividad 10 **1.** Los vimos trotar. **2.** Os vimos hacer ejercicio.
3. Lo vimos entrar en la discoteca. **4.** La vimos dictar una conferencia. **5.** Los vimos hablar por teléfono celular. **6.** Te

vimos escanear los documentos. **7.** La vimos salir de la tienda de deportes.

Actividad 11 **1.** que **2.** para **3.** para **4.** que

Actividad 12 **1.** X **2.** de **3.** X **4.** de

Actividad 13 *Answers will vary.*

PARTE DOS

Capítulo 16

Actividad 1 **1.** el **2.** el **3.** el **4.** la **5.** el **6.** la **7.** la
8. el **9.** la **10.** la **11.** el **12.** la **13.** la **14.** el **15.** la
16. el **17.** el **18.** la **19.** el **20.** el

Actividad 2 **1.** la profesora **2.** la reina **3.** la artista
4. la abogada **5.** la princesa **6.** la gobernadora
7. la representante **8.** la bailarina **9.** la emperatriz
10. la actriz **11.** la estadista **12.** la holandesa **13.** la cliente
14. la atleta **15.** la programadora

Actividad 3 **1.** La señorita Galíndez se va de viaje de negocios el martes y volverá el jueves. **2.** No ponga la sartén en el lavaplatos. **3.** El inglés y el francés son las lenguas oficiales del Canadá. **4.** Beethoven nació el diez y seis de diciembre de mil setecientos setenta. **5.** Mis colores favoritos son el verde y el azul. **6.** Vamos a recoger (Recojamos) manzanas de ese manzano. **7.** El pájaro (ave) oficial de los Estados Unidos es el águila. **8.** ¿Les gustó más el crucero en el Mediterráneo o en el Caribe? **9.** El leer es tan agradable. **10.** Un frente tropical llegará mañana. **11.** Invertiremos nuestro capital en una compañía internacional. **12.** ¿Cómo se llaman los personajes de la novela? **13.** Al cámara se le perdió su cámara. **14.** En la película que vimos, los ángeles salvaron al bebé / a la bebé.
15. Los testigos hablaron con la víctima del accidente.

Actividad 4 **1.** guantes **2.** lavaplatos **3.** religiones
4. orígenes **5.** colores **6.** amistades **7.** reyes **8.** toses
9. martes **10.** irlandeses **11.** paréntesis **12.** luces **13.** tés

Actividad 5 **1.** vacas **2.** orangutanes **3.** elefantes
4. avestruces **5.** leones **6.** castores **7.** loros **8.** cóndores
9. delfines **10.** faisanes **11.** panteras **12.** tigres **13.** ovejas
14. monos

Actividad 6 **1.** Lucía pide guisantes. **2.** Yo prefiero los espárragos. **3.** Tú ordenas papas fritas. **4.** Claudia y Jesús quieren chiles. **5.** Nosotros tenemos ganas de comer aguacates.
6. Ud. y Luis piden frijoles. **7.** Ud. quiere camarones.

Actividad 7 **1.** los pianos **2.** las flautas **3.** las violas
4. los clarinetes **5.** los violonchelos **6.** los violines
7. las trompetas **8.** los trombones **9.** las arpas **10.** los oboes
11. los tambores **12.** las tubas

Actividad 8 **1.** la, las aceitunas **2.** el, los ensayos **3.** el, las aguas **4.** el, los árboles **5.** la, las sales **6.** el, los pasaportes
7. el, los volcanes **8.** la, las actividades **9.** el, los orígenes
10. el, los meses **11.** la, las serpientes **12.** el, los lápices
13. el, los franceses **14.** la, las veces **15.** el, los sacapuntas
16. el, los jugadores

Actividad 9 **1.** los ojos **2.** las mejillas **3.** las manos **4.** los labios **5.** los dientes **6.** el pelo **7.** el cuello **8.** las orejas

Actividad 10 **1.** X **2.** el **3.** el **4.** X **5.** X **6.** las **7.** X
8. el **9.** Las, la **10.** El **11.** X **12.** la **13.** Los, la **14.** la
15. La, la

Actividad 11 **1.** La familia Sánchez va a la Florida en la primavera. **2.** Florencia se puso los calcetines (las medias).
3. Dénos los libros de latín. **4.** A Juli y a Nicolás les encanta nadar. **5.** ¿Qué hicieron los turistas en el mar? **6.** Los gemelos se lavaron la cara. **7.** Elías sabe portugués, habla

italiano, lee ruso y aprende alemán.   **8.** El baile fue el sábado. Comenzó a las nueve y media de la noche.

Actividad 12   **1.** X, X   **2.** X   **3.** X, X   **4.** los   **5.** X   **6.** X   **7.** X, X

Actividad 13   **1.** El   **2.** un (al)   **3.** X   **4.** lo   **5.** del   **6.** Lo   **7.** del   **8.** las   **9.** X   **10.** X   **11.** las   **12.** el   **13.** un   **14.** el   **15.** los (unos)   **16.** al   **17.** las   **18.** la   **19.** unas   **20.** Un   **21.** lo   **22.** la   **23.** el   **24.** un   **25.** las (unas)   **26.** X   **27.** al   **28.** la   **29.** del   **30.** unas   **31.** la   **32.** un   **33.** unos   **34.** una   **35.** X

Actividad 14   **1.** un, unos mares   **2.** una, unas verdades   **3.** una, unas narices   **4.** un, unos paradores   **5.** un, unos olores   **6.** un, unos oboes   **7.** un, unas áreas   **8.** una, unas mochilas   **9.** un/a, unos/as jóvenes   **10.** un, unos papeles   **11.** un, unos irlandeses   **12.** un, unos paraguas   **13.** una, unas voces   **14.** un, unos desfiles   **15.** una, unas naciones   **16.** un, unos lavaplatos   **17.** una, unas sucursales   **18.** un, unos ascensores   **19.** un, unas hablas   **20.** un, unas aguas   **21.** un, unas aulas   **22.** un, unos mapas   **23.** un, unos programas   **24.** una, unas crisis

Actividad 15   **1.** un   **2.** un   **3.** unos   **4.** un   **5.** unas   **6.** una   **7.** unos   **8.** una   **9.** unos   **10.** unas   **11.** una   **12.** un

Actividad 16   **1.** X   **2.** un   **3.** X, X   **4.** X, X   **5.** X   **6.** un   **7.** X   **8.** X   **9.** un   **10.** X   **11.** X   **12.** X

Actividad 17   **1.** Concepción y Simón fueron al puesto de periódicos.   **2.** Yo fui al ayuntamiento.   **3.** Vosotros fuisteis al supermercado.   **4.** Ud. fue al parque de atracciones.   **5.** Lourdes fue a la iglesia.   **6.** Mi hermano fue a la bolsa.   **7.** Nosotros fuimos a la estación de tren.   **8.** Tú fuiste al centro comercial.   **9.** Uds. fueron al cibercafé.   **10.** Juan Diego fue a la facultad.

Actividad 18   **1.** Tú y yo volvimos del banco.   **2.** Mercedes y Julio salieron del cine.   **3.** Yo regresé de la librería.   **4.** Uds. volvieron de la tienda de vídeos.   **5.** Pedro salió del apartamento.   **6.** Tú regresaste de la galería de arte.   **7.** Vosotros salisteis del museo de ciencias naturales.   **8.** Ud. volvió del aeropuerto.

Actividad 19   **1.** ¿De quién es el almacén? Es del señor Acosta.   **2.** ¿De quién son los peines? Son de Adela y Matilde.   **3.** ¿De quién es el equipaje? Es de las turistas.   **4.** ¿De quién son los discos compactos? Son del pianista.   **5.** ¿De quién es este llavero? Es de la empleada.   **6.** ¿De quién son las sartenes? Son del cocinero.   **7.** ¿De quién son las raquetas? Son de estas tenistas.   **8.** ¿De quién es el reloj? Es del doctor Villanueva.

Actividad 20   **1.** la florería del señor Valle   **2.** la oficina del presidente   **3.** los discos de la programadora   **4.** el horario de la dentista   **5.** los empleados del doctor Arriaga   **6.** los sitios Web de los estudiantes   **7.** las conferencias de la profesora Salas   **8.** el proyecto del ingeniero   **9.** los hijos de los señores Manrique   **10.** el informe de la jefa

Actividad 21   *Answers will vary.*

Capítulo 17

Actividad 1   **1.** Están felices.   **2.** Estoy contento/a.   **3.** Se encuentra nerviosa.   **4.** Se siente deprimido.   **5.** Se encuentran tristes.   **6.** Estamos cansados/as.   **7.** Nos sentimos enfermos.

Actividad 2   **1.** Paco cree que Jacobo es listo.   **2.** La señora Alvarado piensa que Luisa es encantadora.   **3.** El profesor de cálculo encuentra a los hermanos inteligentes y trabajadores.   **4.** Nieves cree que Jacobo es sincero.   **5.** El señor Alvarado dice que Luisa es graciosa y generosa.   **6.** Las profesoras de computación encuentran a Jacobo serio y responsable.   **7.** Los hijos de los Alvarado creen que Luisa es independiente y simpática.   **8.** Todo el mundo dice que Jacobo y Luisa son corteses.

Actividad 3   **1.** arrogante   **2.** molesto   **3.** tacaños   **4.** tontos   **5.** mentirosa   **6.** desleales   **7.** engañosos   **8.** gruñones

Actividad 4   **1.** roja   **2.** amarillos   **3.** marrones   **4.** negros, rojos   **5.** amarillas, anaranjadas, verdes   **6.** negro   **7.** negro   **8.** morada   **9.** morados, grises

Actividad 5   **1.** mejor día   **2.** algunos discos compactos   **3.** muchos días   **4.** poemas renacentistas   **5.** ambas clases   **6.** ojos castaños   **7.** suficiente plata   **8.** peor decisión   **9.** teorías políticas

Actividad 6   **1.** ¡Qué absurda situación!   **2.** ¡Qué clima tan perfecto!   **3.** ¡Qué partido más emocionante!   **4.** ¡Qué paella tan rica!   **5.** ¡Qué ideas más estupendas!   **6.** ¡Qué problemas más complicados!   **7.** ¡Qué cariñosos niños!   **8.** ¡Qué reunión tan animada!

Actividad 7   **1.** primer   **2.** mala   **3.** grandes   **4.** buen   **5.** tercera   **6.** algún   **7.** ningún   **8.** San   **9.** gran   **10.** ninguna   **11.** algunas   **12.** Cualquier   **13.** tercer   **14.** mal

Actividad 8   **1.** mismo dentista   **2.** ciudad antigua   **3.** cosa cierta   **4.** medio portugués, medio mexicano   **5.** gran general   **6.** dramaturgo mismo   **7.** pura agua   **8.** persona única   **9.** Cierta empresa   **10.** vieja casa   **11.** varios libros, mismo tema   **12.** cualquier regalo

Actividad 9   **1.** Sí, es ruso.   **2.** Sí, son canadienses.   **3.** Sí, es israelí.   **4.** Sí, es costarricense.   **5.** Sí, es guatemalteco.   **6.** Sí, es japonés.   **7.** Sí, es india (hindú).   **8.** Sí, son egipcios.   **9.** Sí, es inglesa.   **10.** Sí, es coreano.   **11.** Sí, son franceses.

Actividad 10   **1.** Yo soy de origen estadounidense (norteamericano).   **2.** Teodoro e Irene son de origen salvadoreño.   **3.** Uds. son de origen coreano.   **4.** Gabriel es de origen vietnamés.   **5.** Adela y Rosa son de origen indio (hindú).   **6.** Vosotros sois de origen griego.   **7.** Tú eres de origen mexicano.   **8.** Ud. y yo somos de origen taiwanés.   **9.** Gualterio es de origen húngaro.

Actividad 11   **1.** buenos   **2.** españoles   **3.** recogidas   **4.** ingleses   **5.** frescos   **6.** rojos   **7.** rebajados   **8.** nuevos   **9.** magníficas   **10.** negros   **11.** caros   **12.** creativos

Actividad 12   **1.** Federico Felino es el mejor director de cine joven.   **2.** «El tango rojo» es su primer film doblado.   **3.** Será una gran película extranjera.   **4.** Hay diferentes efectos coreográficos.   **5.** Escribieron un guión inteligente.   **6.** Trabajaron en el film algunos intérpretes principales.   **7.** La película tiene un argumento interesante.   **8.** La película ganará un importante premio cinematográfico.

Actividad 13   **1.** frita, fritos   **2.** hecho, hechos   **3.** muertas, muertos   **4.** comida, comidas   **5.** metido, metidos   **6.** pagada, pagadas   **7.** dormido, dormido   **8.** hechas, hecha

Actividad 14   **1.** está echada   **2.** está parado   **3.** están sentados   **4.** está asomada   **5.** están arrodillados   **6.** están tirados   **7.** está inclinada

Actividad 15   **1.** Ya está bañado.   **2.** Ya están afeitados.   **3.** Ya está maquillada.   **4.** Ya estamos vestidos/as.   **5.** Ya estoy peinado/a.   **6.** Ya estamos duchados/as.   **7.** Ya estoy pintada.

Actividad 16   **1.** Ya están puestos.   **2.** Ya está servida.   **3.** Ya está preparado.   **4.** Ya están rotos.   **5.** Ya está cortado.   **6.** Ya está hecha.   **7.** Ya está frito.   **8.** Ya están pelados.

Actividad 17   **1.** Me gusta más la instrumental, pero me gusta la vocal también.   **2.** Prefiero los serios, pero me gustan los cómicos también. **3.** Prefiero comer en el chino, pero me gusta comer en el francés también. **4.** Prefiero el moderno, pero me gusta el viejo también. **5.** Me gusta más la privada, pero me gusta la estatal también. **6.** Prefiero las norteamericanas, pero me gustan las extranjeras también. **7.** Quiero vivir en la grande, pero me gusta vivir en la pequeña también. **8.** Me interesan más las políticas, pero me interesan las naturales también.

Actividad 18 **1.** Luisa es más astuta que Ana. Ana es menos astuta que Luisa. **2.** El museo de historia natural es mejor que el de arte. El museo de arte es peor que el de historia. **3.** Yo soy más inteligente que mi novio/a. Mi novio/a es menos inteligente que yo. **4.** Tu cuarto es más hermoso que el de Elena. El cuarto de Elena es menos hermoso que el tuyo. **5.** La película francesa es más aburrida que la inglesa. La película inglesa es menos aburrida que la francesa. **6.** Los cantantes son más talentosos que los bailarines. Los bailarines son menos talentosos que los cantantes.

Actividad 19 **1.** José habló más francamente que Consuelo. Consuelo habló menos francamente que José. José habló tan francamente como Consuelo. **2.** Los enfermeros trabajaron más cuidadosamente que los médicos. Los médicos trabajaron menos cuidadosamente que los enfermeros. Los enfermeros trabajaron tan cuidadosamente como los médicos. **3.** Virginia resolvió los problemas más fácilmente que Mario. Mario resolvió los problemas menos fácilmente que Virginia. Virginia resolvió los problemas tan fácilmente como Mario.

Actividad 20 **1.** La obra de teatro es tan divertida como la película. **2.** Las clases de física son tan fáciles como las clases de cálculo. **3.** Los documentales son tan artísticos como los reportajes. **4.** Los platos griegos son tan sabrosos como los platos húngaros. **5.** Esta actriz es tan célebre como ese actor. **6.** El arroz es tan bueno como el maíz.

Actividad 21 **1.** Alejandro manda tanto correo electrónico como Felipe. **2.** Miriam tiene tanta paciencia como Catalina. **3.** Ellos pasan tantas horas en línea como nosotros. **4.** Ella come tanta comida rápida como tú. **5.** Sus amigos ven tantos programas de realidad como Uds. **6.** Los asesores demuestran tanto interés en el proyecto como vosotros. **7.** A él le queda tanto dinero como a ti. **8.** Yo conozco tantos clubes de jazz como Marcos.

Actividad 22 **1.** Juan Pablo es el estudiante más aplicado. **2.** Daniel y Arturo son los estudiantes menos obedientes. **3.** Silvia es la estudiante más simpática. **4.** Irene y María son las estudiantes menos trabajadoras. **5.** Verónica es la estudiante más inteligente. **6.** Íñigo y Marisol son los estudiantes más habladores. **7.** Sergio es es el estudiante más encantador. **8.** Rosa y Jacinto son los estudiantes menos preparados.

Actividad 23 **1.** Sí. Es interesantísima. **2.** Sí. Es viejísimo. **3.** Sí. Son hermosísimas. **4.** Sí. Es grandísimo. **5.** Sí. Parece ferocísimo. **6.** Sí. Son simpatiquísimos. **7.** Sí. Son larguísimas. **8.** Sí. Es bellísimo.

Actividad 24 **1.** Allí se encuentra la plaza más imponente de la ciudad. **2.** Aquí ven el centro comercial más moderno del estado. **3.** En frente hay la universidad más conocida del país. **4.** Ésta es la calle más larga de la ciudad. **5.** En esta calle hay las tiendas más hermosas de la zona. **6.** Allí está la tienda de comestibles más estimada del barrio. **7.** Delante de nosotros hay el hotel más internacional del país. **8.** En este barrio se encuentran los restaurantes más concurridos de la ciudad. **9.** Aquí ven la casa más vieja de la ciudad. **10.** Pronto veremos el estadio más grande de la región.

Actividad 25 **1.** Es el poema más conocido de la literatura europea. **2.** Es la obra de teatro más presentada del año.

3. Es la comedia más aplaudida del teatro nacional. **4.** Es la novela más vendida de la literatura moderna. **5.** Es la tragedia más estimada de nuestro teatro. **6.** Es el poeta más respetado de su siglo. **7.** Es la novelista más leída del mundo. **8.** Es el dramaturgo más apreciado de nuestra época.

Actividad 26 **1.** Yo leo más que Ud. **2.** Ellos saben menos que nosotros. **3.** Ignacio se queja tanto como su mujer. **4.** Yo tengo más discos compactos que Federico. **5.** Eva ve menos películas que Margarita. **6.** Nosotros hacemos tantos viajes como ellos. **7.** Nosotros tenemos más de diez mil libros en nuestra biblioteca. **8.** El partido de fútbol fue más emocionante de lo que esperaban. **9.** Ruiz es el mejor programador de la compañía. **10.** Ésta es la playa más bella del país. **11.** Vosotros vivís en el barrio más elegante de la ciudad. **12.** A ella le gustó la película más que a nosotros. **13.** Rolando navega en la Red más que nadie. **14.** Uds. se reúnen más que nunca.

Actividad 27 *Answers will vary.*

Capítulo 18

Actividad 1 **1.** Estos libros de texto están bien escritos. Esos libros de texto están bien escritos. Aquellos libros de texto están bien escritos. **2.** Prefiero estos disquetes. Prefiero esos disquetes. Prefiero aquellos disquetes. **3.** Esta marca de agenda electrónica es conocida. Esa marca de agenda electrónica es conocida. Aquella marca de agenda electrónica es conocida. **4.** Me gusta este diccionario de español. Me gusta ese diccionario de español. Me gusta aquel diccionario de español. **5.** Usé esta calculadora de bolsillo. Usé esa calculadora de bolsillo. Usé aquella calculadora de bolsillo. **6.** Estas enciclopedias no tienen información sobre el tema. Esas enciclopedias no tienen información sobre el tema. Aquellas enciclopedias no tienen información sobre el tema.

Actividad 2 **1.** este **2.** Ese **3.** este **4.** aquel **5.** estas **6.** ese **7.** esas **8.** aquella **9.** Esta **10.** ese **11.** estas **12.** esos **13.** Este **14.** esta **15.** aquel **16.** ese **17.** esta

Actividad 3 **1.** Me gustó ésa más que aquélla. (Me gustó aquélla más que ésa.) **2.** Me gustaron aquéllos más que éstos. (Me gustaron éstos más que aquéllos.) **3.** Me gustó éste más que ése. (Me gustó ése más que éste.) **4.** Me gustaron ésas más que aquéllas. (Me gustaron aquéllas más que ésas.) **5.** Me gustó éste más que ése. (Me gustó ése más que éste.) **6.** Me gustaron éstos más que aquéllos. (Me gustaron aquéllos más que éstos.) **7.** Me gustó ésta más que ésa. (Me gustó ésa más que ésta.)

Actividad 4 **1.** No, no es suyo. Será de Martina. **2.** No, no son suyas. Serán de nosotros. **3.** No, no es suyo. Será de Enrique. **4.** No, no son suyos. Serán de Uds. **5.** No, no son suyas. Serán tuyas. **6.** No, no es suya. Será de la profesora Márquez. **7.** No, no es nuestra. Será de Eduardo.

Actividad 5 **1.** las maletas tuyas **2.** el equipaje de mano nuestro **3.** los cheques de viajero suyos **4.** la computadora portátil suya **5.** los maletines nuestros **6.** la mochila suya **7.** el pasaporte mío **8.** las visas vuestras **9.** los billetes electrónicos tuyos

Actividad 6 **1.** —¡Pero el mío es más moderno que el tuyo! **2.** —¡Pero los míos son más nuevos que los tuyos! **3.** —¡Pero la mía es más simpática que la tuya! **4.** —¡Pero la mía funciona mejor que la tuya! **5.** —¡Pero las mías son más interesantes que las tuyas! **6.** —¡Pero las mías son mejores que las tuyas! **7.** —¡Pero el mío es más inteligente que el tuyo!

Actividad 7 **1.** Los suyos estarán en la mesa. **2.** El mío estará en mi cartera. **3.** Las suyas estarán en la cómoda. **4.** Los nuestros estarán en el escritorio. **5.** La nuestra (La suya) estará en la computadora. **6.** Los nuestros estarán en el baño. **7.** La mía estará encima del piano.

Actividad 8 **1.** No, no se salen con la suya. **2.** No, no se sale con la suya. **3.** Sí, se sale con la suya. **4.** No, no se sale con la suya. **5.** No, no se salen con la suya. **6.** Sí, te sales con la tuya. **7.** Sí, os salís con la vuestra.

Actividad 9 **1.** Esto de la compañía es difícil de comprender. **2.** Eso de nuestro viaje tiene que resolverse. **3.** Vamos a tener que hablar de eso de comprar un coche nuevo. **4.** Un viejo amigo mío llega el sábado. **5.** ¿Cómo está tu familia / están los tuyos? **6.** Esperamos que gane nuestro equipo / que ganen los nuestros. **7.** Lo suyo es traer las flores. **8.** Lo mío es hacer copias.

Actividad 10 *Answers will vary.*

Capítulo 19

Actividad 1 **1.** nosotros/as **2.** Ud., él **3.** vosotras **4.** Uds., ellos, ellas **5.** yo **6.** Ud., ella **7.** vosotros/as **8.** tú **9.** Uds., ellas **10.** Ud., ella

Actividad 2 **1.** Yo trabajo de lunes a viernes, pero tú trabajas los fines de semana. **2.** Nosotros estudiamos en una universidad particular, pero Uds. estudian en una universidad estatal. **3.** Ellas viven en pleno centro, pero Ud. vive en las afueras. **4.** Tú vas de compras el sábado, pero nosotros vamos de compras el jueves. **5.** Él es abogado, pero yo soy profesor. **6.** Ellos escuchan música clásica, pero vosotros escucháis rock.

Actividad 3 **1.** para él **2.** contigo **3.** según tú **4.** por nosotros **5.** salvo yo **6.** sobre Ud. **7.** conmigo **8.** de vosotros **9.** para ellas **10.** por ti **11.** menos tú **12.** como yo **13.** en ella **14.** entre tú y yo

Actividad 4 **1.** Sí, vivo cerca de ellas. **2.** Sí, trabajaba en ella. **3.** Sí, logramos hablar sobre ellos. **4.** Sí, pagué un dineral por él. **5.** Sí, salí con ellos. **6.** Sí, hay mucho trabajo para ella. **7.** Sí, se casó con él. **8.** Sí, felicité a los jugadores por ella.

Actividad 5 **1.** No, con ellas, no. **2.** No, con él, no. **3.** No, para ella, no. **4.** No, por ella, no. **5.** No, para ellos, no. **6.** No, por él, no. **7.** No, con ellos, no. **8.** No, para ti, no.

Actividad 6 **1.** X **2.** a **3.** X **4.** al **5.** a **6.** A **7.** a **8.** X **9.** X **10.** X **11.** X **12.** X **13.** a **14.** a **15.** al **16.** A

Actividad 7 **1.** a **2.** a **3.** a **4.** a **5.** a **6.** X *(also* a*)* **7.** a **8.** A **9.** a **10.** a **11.** a **12.** a **13.** a

Actividad 8 **1.** No, no lo cambié. Voy a cambiarlo. **2.** No, no lo reparé. Voy a repararlo. **3.** No, no las pedí. Voy a pedirlas. **4.** No, no las llevé. Voy a llevarlas. **5.** No, no lo usé. Voy a usarlo. **6.** No, no lo arreglé. Voy a arreglarlo. **7.** No, no lo instalé. Voy a instalarlo.

Actividad 9 **1.** Piensa comprarlo. / Lo piensa comprar. **2.** Tiene que llenarlo. / Lo tiene que llenar. **3.** Trata de leerlas. / Las trata de leer. **4.** Prefiere conducirlo. / Lo prefiere conducir. **5.** Debe cargarla. / La debe cargar. **6.** Teme tenerlo. / Lo teme tener. **7.** Procura evitarlas. / Las procura evitar.

Actividad 10 **1.** la conozco **2.** los comprendo **3.** la llamo **4.** las busco **5.** lo llevo **6.** las conozco **7.** lo ayudo **8.** los veo

Actividad 11 **1.** Márquelos. / No los marque. **2.** Llámalo. / No lo llames. **3.** Recójanlos. / No los recojan. **4.** Sáltelas. / No las salte. **5.** Hazla. / No la hagas. **6.** Lánzala. / No la lances. **7.** Séalo. / No lo sea. **8.** Levántenlas. / No las levanten.

Actividad 12 **1.** Sí, lo he visto. **2.** No, no los he visto. **3.** Sí, la hemos visto. **4.** No, no los he visto. **5.** No, no las he visto. **6.** Sí, las hemos visto. **7.** Sí, lo he visto. **8.** No, no la he visto.

Actividad 13 **1.** Los arquitectos están empleándolo. Los arquitectos lo están empleando. **2.** Los constructores van cubriéndola. Los constructores la van cubriendo. **3.** Los dibujantes están dibujándolas. Los dibujantes las están dibujando. **4.** Los maestros de obras están echándolos. Los maestros de obras los están echando. **5.** Los frailes y las monjas siguen rezándolas. Los frailes y las monjas las siguen rezando. **6.** Los trabajadores siguen colocándolos. Los trabajadores los siguen colocando. **7.** Los albañiles van trayéndolas. Los albañiles las van trayendo. **8.** Los obreros están poniéndola. Los obreros la están poniendo.

Actividad 14 **1.** Tu calculadora de bolsillo la puse en tu mesa de trabajo. **2.** A los chicos los llevé al cine. **3.** Tu teléfono celular lo dejé en el jardín. **4.** A mis padres los vi en la sala. **5.** Tus libros los arreglé en tu oficina. **6.** Las cartas que escribiste las eché al correo. **7.** Tu abrigo lo colgué en el armario. **8.** Las galletas que compraste las comí.

Actividad 15 **1.** Te traje los refrescos. **2.** Nos dieron flores. **3.** Me mandó una tarjeta postal. **4.** Le dijeron los precios. **5.** Le ofrecimos el escritorio. **6.** Le preguntó la hora. **7.** Os expliqué mis ideas. **8.** Les recordaron el cumpleaños de Leo.

Actividad 16 **1.** A nosotros, a Uds. **2.** a mí, a ti **3.** a él, a ella **4.** A ti, a ellos **5.** A vosotros, a nosotros **6.** A ellas, a Ud.

Actividad 17 **1.** A tres jóvenes les suspenden el permiso de manejar. **2.** Los políticos nos ocultan los problemas económicos del país. **3.** Al pueblo le exigen más sacrificios. **4.** Nuestro país le va a comprar (va a comprarle) barcos a España. **5.** El gobierno les quita la visa a tres extranjeros.

Actividad 18 **1.** Le encantan esos perfumes. **2.** Nos interesan estas novelas. **3.** Les quedan unos exámenes. **4.** Te entusiasman las comedias. **5.** Os importan las ideas. **6.** Me hacen falta unas guías. **7.** Les fascinan estas materias. **8.** Le faltan unos cuadernos. **9.** Nos agradan sus planes.

Actividad 19 **1.** Nos van a importar sus problemas. **2.** No les va a quedar mucho dinero. **3.** Le va a encantar visitar a sus abuelos. **4.** No les va a sobrar comida. **5.** Os va a convenir viajar en tren. **6.** Te van a fascinar esos cuadros. **7.** Me van a entusiasmar sus obras. **8.** No le van a interesar esos programas.

Actividad 20 **1.** A él. **2.** Ellos. **3.** A ella no. **4.** Yo no. **5.** Nosotros sí. **6.** A Ud. **7.** A mí sí. **8.** Yo sí.

Actividad 21 **1.** (A mí) Me gustaría hacer un viaje a España. **2.** (A mí) Me encantaría visitar a mis parientes en Venezuela y Argentina. **3.** (A mí) Me interesaría ir de camping en Nuevo México o Arizona. **4.** Y (a mí) me fascinaría ver Italia. **5.** (A mí) Me entusiasmaría hacer deportes de agua. **6.** Nos convendría tomar una decisión lo antes posible. **7.** Tenemos suficientes sugerencias. ¡Echemos suertes! **8.** ¡Me toca a mí primero!

Actividad 22 **1.** Se nos acabó **2.** Se le perdieron **3.** Se me olvidó **4.** Se os quedó **5.** se te rompieron **6.** se les ocurrió **7.** se les cayeron

Actividad 23 **1.** Que no se les olvide asistir a la conferencia. **2.** Que no se le pierdan los anteojos. **3.** Que no se le acabe la paciencia. **4.** Que no se os queden los cheques de viajero en el hotel. **5.** Que no se le rompan las estatuillas de porcelana. **6.** Que no se te ocurran tales cosas. **7.** Que no se les caiga la torta de chocolate.

Actividad 24 1. ¿Se le perdió su cartera? No, se me había quedado en casa. 2. Se les están acabando los pasteles en la pastelería. ¿No se te ocurrió comprarlos esta mañana? 3. ¡Tengan cuidado! ¡Se les va a caer su iPod! ¡Se nos rompió ya! 4. Se me olvidó recoger (buscar) a Tere y a Leo. ¿No se te ocurrió que esperaban toda la noche?

Actividad 25 1. Me los dijeron. 2. Se los hemos puesto. 3. Está explicándosela. / Se la está explicando. 4. Os lo muestro. 5. ¿Te la darían? 6. Se los cuentas. 7. Nos las ha hecho. 8. Devuélvamelo. 9. Me las estaban enseñando. / Estaban enseñándomelas. 10. ¿A quién se lo vendiste? 11. Os la había escrito. 12. ¿Nos los prestarás? 13. Apréndanselas. 14. ¿Estáis preguntándoselo? / ¿Se lo estáis preguntando? 15. Se la pusieron. 16. Se los preparó. 17. Estará bajándomelo. / Me lo estará bajando. 18. Vendámosela. 19. Estuvimos trayéndoselos. / Se los estuvimos trayendo. 20. Te la apagaré.

Actividad 26 1. Van a traérmela. / Me la van a traer. 2. Acaba de decírtelo. / Te lo acaba de decir. 3. Vamos a hacérselos. / Se los vamos a hacer. 4. Acabo de ponéroslas. / Os las acabo de poner. 5. Va a mostrárselo. / Se lo va a mostrar. 6. Acabáis de comprárnosla. / Nos la acabáis de comprar. 7. Vas a contármelos. / Me los vas a contar. 8. Acabo de arreglárselas. / Se las acabo de arreglar. 9. Van a subírtela. / Te la van a subir. 10. Acabamos de dároslo. / Os lo acabamos de dar. 11. Vamos a describírselo. / Se lo vamos a describir. 12. Acaba de probársela. / Se la acaba de probar. 13. Va a limpiártelos. / Te los va a limpiar. 14. Acabo de encontrárselas. / Se las acabo de encontrar. 15. Van a pedírmela. / Me la van a pedir.

Actividad 27 1. —Papi, dámelos. —Sí, hijita, te los doy. 2. —Mami, cómpramelas. —Sí, hijita, te las compro. 3. —Juan, préstamela. —Sí, hermanita, te la presto. 4. —Amparo, cómpramelo. —Sí, hermanita, te lo compro. 5. —Abuelo, regálamelo. —Sí, hijita, te lo regalo. 6. —Elvira, sírvemelo. —Sí, hermanita, te lo sirvo. 7. —Tía, pónmelas. —Sí, hijita, te las pongo. 8. —Abuela, tráemela. —Sí hijita, te la traigo.

Actividad 28 1. a. Adela gave it to her (him, them, you). b. She (He, You) gave it to Adela. 2. a. The professors told it to you (him, her, them). b. You (They) told it to the professors. 3. a. The neighbor lent them to you (him, her, them). b. He (She, You) lent them to the neighbor. 4. a. My colleagues asked her (him, them, you) for them. b. They (You) asked my colleagues for them. 5. a. Laura returned it to you (her, him, them). b. He (She, You) returned it to Laura.

Actividad 29 1. —¿Sabes si las tiendas están abiertas? —No te lo sabría decir. (No sabría decírtelo). 2. No sé cómo Raúl se las apaña (arregla, compone). Cree que todo el mundo se la tiene jurada (que todos se la tienen jurada). 3. Cualquier estudiante que se porte mal tendrá que vérselas conmigo. 4. —¿Son ingenieros Ramón y Serena? —No, no lo son. Son programadores. —Creo que son muy inteligentes. —Sí, lo son. 5. Mariana no se pudo poner el abrigo, entonces se lo puse yo. 6. —¿Debo pedirles sus apuntes de historia a Alicia y a Pablo? —Pídeselos a él. No se los pidas a ella. 7. —Javier, por favor, préstame tus apuntes de física. —Pili, te los di el jueves. —Lo siento. Se me perdieron.

Actividad 30 *Answers will vary.*

Capítulo 20

Actividad 1 1. Veo al médico que tiene su consulta en aquel edificio. 2. Quiero ver la película que se rodó en Perú. 3. Me gustan más las revistas que se publican en Asunción. 4. Prefiero el restaurante que sirve comida del Caribe. 5. Voy a la peluquería que está en la calle del Conde. 6. Queremos comprar los libros que nos recomendó la profesora. 7. Uso el ordenador que me regalaron mis padres para Navidad. 8. Hablábamos con la secretaria que contratamos la semana pasada. 9. El mecánico que conoce el vecino repara mi coche. 10. Estoy leyendo la carta que me mandó Silvia ayer. 11. Mirián y Alejo van a la tienda de vídeos que queda al lado de la pizzería. 12. Escuchamos los discos compactos que Claudia nos prestó.

Actividad 2 1. La profesora que todos los estudiantes admiran. La profesora que enseña francés y español. La profesora que acaba de casarse. La profesora que conocen mis padres. 2. La casa que compraron Juana y Rafael. La casa que tiene patio y piscina. La casa que construyeron en 2005. La casa que es de ladrillos. 3. El regalo que mis hermanos y yo recibimos hace dos días. El regalo que nos mandaron mis tíos. El regalo que te enseñé ayer. El regalo que nos gustó tanto. 4. El restaurante que nuestros amigos cubanos abrieron el año pasado. El restaurante que sirve comida cubana auténtica. El restaurante que tiene fotos de La Habana. El restaurante que se encuentra en la Calle Ocho. 5. La senadora que era jefa de una empresa. La senadora que prometió reducir los impuestos. La senadora que es casada con un ingeniero. La senadora que eligieron hace dos años.

Actividad 3 1. Mis primos a quienes vi en Caracas hace dos años están de vacaciones en Estados Unidos. 2. La pintora a quien vieron en la exposición sólo pinta acuarelas. 3. La muchacha a quien le di un regalo ayer me dio las gracias hoy. 4. Los amigos a quienes llamamos a la una de la mañana no quisieron salir. 5. Los vecinos a quienes buscábamos se habían mudado. 6. El dependiente a quien Ud. conoció el año pasado ya no trabaja en esta tienda. 7. El señor a quien encontraste en la calle es mi profesor de cálculo.

Actividad 4 1. La señora Mora, quien se encarga de los archivos, es secretaria general de la universidad. 2. El profesor Uriarte, quien asistió a un congreso en Boston, enseña química. 3. Los estudiantes, quienes se graduán en junio, tienen que entregar una tesis. 4. La doctora Arrieta, quien figura en el tribunal de exámenes, tiene dos ayudantes de laboratorio. 5. Estos decanos, quienes planean el programa, trabajan en la Facultad de Ingeniería. 6. El rector de la universidad, quien dicta conferencias de ciencias políticas, es abogado. 7. Algunos estudiantes de medicina fueron a hablar con el profesor Quijano, quien estaba ya en el salón de actos. 8. La profesora Arenas, quien hace investigaciones de biología, se jubila el año que viene.

Actividad 5 1. a quien 2. quien 3. quienes 4. a quienes 5. quienes 6. a quien 7. a quien 8. quien

Actividad 6 1. los que 2. lo que 3. la que 4. lo que 5. lo que 6. el que 7. las que

Actividad 7 1. los cuales 2. lo cual 3. la cual 4. lo cual 5. lo cual 6. el cual 7. las cuales

Actividad 8 1. Éstas son las calles debajo de las cuales (debajo de las que) hay varias líneas de metro. 2. Allí ven la facultad cerca de la cual (cerca de la que) vivimos. 3. Allí está el cine en frente del cual (en frente del que) hay un restaurante. 4. Ven y te presento a los muchachos con quienes (con los cuales, con los que) solemos pasar los domingos aquí. 5. Ésta es la plaza en medio de la cual (en medio de la que) hay una exposición de arte. 6. Aquéllos son los edificios detrás de los cuales (detrás de los que) hay un mercado al aire libre. 7. El barrio hacia el cual (hacia el que) caminamos ahora es muy antiguo. 8. Éste es el río al otro lado del cual (al otro lado del que) se encuentran unas tiendas elegantes.

Actividad 9   **1.** en que   **2.** en el que   **3.** en que   **4.** en que   **5.** en el que   **6.** en los que   **7.** en que   **8.** en las que

Actividad 10   **1.** cuyas   **2.** cuyos   **3.** cuyo   **4.** cuya   **5.** cuyo   **6.** cuyas   **7.** cuya   **8.** cuyos

Actividad 11   **1.** Now you know the reason why I got angry. **2.** We used to live in a neighborhood where there were many shops.   **3.** There to the right is the door through which the actors enter and exit.   **4.** I don't understand the reasons why the union declared the strike.   **5.** My friends didn't tell me where they were going.   **6.** They're the hours during which Menchu does her homework.   **7.** Here's the newspaper stand behind which Sergio and Sol agreed to see/meet each other. **8.** Do you know the friends I went out with last night? **9.** I'll introduce you to the young man whose father was my marketing professor.   **10.** Raquela didn't invite us to her party, which surprised us.

Actividad 12   *Answers will vary.*

PARTE TRES

Capítulo 21

Actividad 1   **1.** alegremente   **2.** descuidadamente **3.** cruelmente   **4.** artísticamente   **5.** normalmente **6.** abiertamente   **7.** francamente   **8.** nerviosamente **9.** evidentemente   **10.** responsablemente   **11.** débilmente **12.** verdaderamente   **13.** torpemente   **14.** violentamente **15.** perspicazmente   **16.** burlonamente   **17.** comercialmente **18.** sagazmente   **19.** honradamente   **20.** humildemente **21.** difícilmente   **22.** admirablemente   **23.** estupendamente **24.** afectuosamente   **25.** vulgarmente

Actividad 2   **1.** Sí, lo explicó nerviosamente.   **2.** Sí, las pidió honestamente.   **3.** Sí, los contaron tristemente.   **4.** Sí, hablé furiosamente.   **5.** Sí, se quejó malhumoradamente.   **6.** Sí, contestamos incómodamente.   **7.** Sí, hablé distraídamente. **8.** Sí, habló incoherentemente.

Actividad 3   **1.** Pronunciaron las frases mal.   **2.** Trabajaron muy responsablemente.   **3.** Las cosas andaban bien. **4.** Quiero que mis hijos vivan felizmente.   **5.** Su última película fue muy interesante.   **6.** Patricia encontró esos problemas sumamente difíciles.   **7.** Encontramos el proyecto totalmente ridículo.   **8.** Mi madre está súper ocupada estos días.

Actividad 4   **1.** Martín y Fernando trabajan responsablemente. **2.** Celia canta maravillosamente.   **3.** Carmen y Pilar escriben hábilmente.   **4.** Paquito compone estupendamente.   **5.** Luisa estudia diligentemente.   **6.** Margarita pinta divinamente. **7.** Carla y Pedro viajan frecuentemente.   **8.** Alfonso juega enérgicamente.

Actividad 5   **1.** con inteligencia   **2.** con armonía   **3.** con elegancia   **4.** con diligencia   **5.** con cariño   **6.** con alegría **7.** con fuerza   **8.** con felicidad   **9.** con tristeza   **10.** con calor

Actividad 6   **1.** Ella bailó elegante y fácilmente.   **2.** Tú cantaste lenta y suavemente.   **3.** Uds. nos recibieron cariñosa y calurosamente.   **4.** Él contestó su correo electrónico oportuna y apasionadamente.   **5.** Nosotros hicimos la limpieza ligera y perezosamente.   **6.** Ud. les sirvió fiel y lealmente.   **7.** Yo le di consejos sabia y astutamente.   **8.** Vosotros os despedisteis deprimida y tristemente.

Actividad 7   **1.** ¿Ya fue al supermercado? Todavía no. No me he vestido todavía.   **2.** Vuelvo en seguida. Ven acá ahora mismo. **3.** Mariana no puede encontrar a su gato por ningún lado. ¡Mire

en lo alto! El gato está en el árbol.   **4.** ¿Están los chicos por aquí? Estarán en la casa. ¿Sabes si están arriba o abajo? Estarán escondidos detrás de algún mueble. Incluso puede que estén en el jardín.   **5.** ¿Está lejos la tienda de vídeos? No, está cerca. Y al lado hay una maravillosa heladería.

Actividad 8   **1.** Él escribe más sarcásticamente que tú.   **2.** Tú analizas el artículo menos críticamente que yo.   **3.** Ellos lo hacen tan fácilmente como nosotros.   **4.** Ana habla más francamente que Lucía.   **5.** Este niño juega menos alegremente que aquél.   **6.** Ella se expresa tan lógicamente como tú. **7.** Nosotros mandamos correo electrónico más frecuentemente que ellos.   **8.** Vosotros nos recibís tan afectuosamente como Pablo y Lucero.

Actividad 9   *Answers will vary.*

Capítulo 22

Actividad 1   **1.** a   **2.** X   **3.** a   **4.** X   **5.** al, a   **6.** a   **7.** A **8.** X   **9.** a

Actividad 2   **1.** de   **2.** X   **3.** X   **4.** del   **5.** X   **6.** de   **7.** de **8.** de

Actividad 3   **1.** Pensamos ir en avión.   **2.** Los recogeré en el aeropuerto.   **3.** Miguel es más alto que Juan en una cabeza. **4.** ¿Dice esto en serio o en broma?   **5.** Paula llegará en una semana.

Actividad 4   **1.** con leche   **2.** con llave   **3.** con cuerda   **4.** con gusto   **5.** con caramelos   **6.** con esfuerzo

Actividad 5   **1.** del   **2.** Con   **3.** a   **4.** en   **5.** en   **6.** con **7.** de   **8.** a   **9.** de   **10.** con   **11.** con   **12.** en   **13.** a   **14.** en **15.** de   **16.** a   **17.** de   **18.** de   **19.** Al   **20.** Al

Actividad 6   **1.** Fui al almacén por un par de zapatos.   **2.** La felicitamos por su cumpleaños.   **3.** Me duele (la espalda) por jugar al tenis por cuatro horas.   **4.** No lo terminó por pereza. **5.** Los veremos (verán) por la tarde.   **6.** Salieron por el puente más céntrico.   **7.** Iremos por salchicha y queso.   **8.** Tendré que hacerla por escrito.

Actividad 7   **1.** Por la fotografía.   **2.** Por el argumento. **3.** Por la dirección.   **4.** Por el guión.   **5.** Por el diálogo.

Actividad 8   **1.** Para ganar plata.   **2.** Para aprender mucho. **3.** Para ayudar a mamá y a papá.   **4.** Para demostrarle mi cariño.   **5.** Para perfeccionarlo.

Actividad 9   **1.** Para pasado mañana.   **2.** Para la semana entrante.   **3.** Para el martes.   **4.** Para finales del mes. **5.** Para el mes próximo.

Actividad 10   **1.** para, por, por, por   **2.** para, por   **3.** Para, Por **4.** por, para, Para, por, para   **5.** Para, para, por   **6.** por, Para, por, por, por   **7.** por, Por, Por, por   **8.** por, para, por

Actividad 11   **1.** Beatriz fue por la ensalada de fruta. Pagó treinta dólares por ella.   **2.** Carlos y Leo fueron por los refrescos. Pagaron cincuenta y cinco dólares por ellos.   **3.** Paula y yo fuimos por las servilletas. Pagamos siete dólares por ellas. **4.** Tú fuiste por los bocadillos. Pagaste ciento setenta y nueve dólares por ellos.   **5.** Yo fui por la torta. Pagué dieciocho dólares por ella.   **6.** Uds. fueron por el vino. Pagaron cuarenta y tres dólares por él.

Actividad 12   **1.** Mi informe está (queda) sin terminar. **2.** Puse (Coloqué) un libro sobre otro (encima de otro). **3.** Lo vi salir hacia atrás.   **4.** Vivió durante muchos años entre los indígenas.   **5.** Hace calor hasta en la sierra. **6.** Los inmigrantes sienten amor hacia su nuevo país.

7. Nos siguieron desde la puerta del cine.   8. Estoy leyendo un libro sobre Puerto Rico.

Actividad 13   **1.** c   **2.** c   **3.** c   **4.** a   **5.** a   **6.** b   **7.** a   **8.** b   **9.** b   **10.** c   **11.** c   **12.** a   **13.** a   **14.** b   **15.** a   **16.** c   **17.** c   **18.** c

Actividad 14   *Answers will vary.*

PARTE CUATRO

Capítulo 23

Actividad 1   **1.** ¿De qué se quejaba?   **2.** ¿En qué se interesan?   **3.** ¿De qué se jacta?   **4.** ¿Con quién se casará?   **5.** ¿En qué se fija?   **6.** ¿De quién se enamoró?   **7.** ¿Con quiénes soñó?

Actividad 2   A.   **1.** ¿De dónde es? ¿De qué nacionalidad es?   **2.** ¿Qué es? ¿Cuál es su profesión?   **3.** ¿Dónde trabaja? ¿Para qué (quiénes) trabaja?   **4.** ¿Dónde vive?   **5.** ¿Con quién es casado?   **6.** ¿Cuántos hijos tiene?
B.   **7.** ¿Dónde nació? ¿En qué país nació?   **8.** ¿De qué origen es? ¿De dónde son sus abuelos?   **9.** ¿Cuándo se mudó a Canadá? ¿Cuántos años tenía cuando se mudó a Canadá? ¿Adónde se mudó cuando tenía cuatro años?   **10.** ¿Qué estudia? ¿En qué hace sus estudios postgraduados? ¿Dónde estudia? ¿Dónde hace sus estudios postgraduados?   **11.** ¿Para qué estudia?   **12.** ¿Dónde vive? ¿Con quiénes vive?
C.   **13.** ¿Qué ganó?   **14.** ¿Qué es? ¿Dónde es un héroe nacional?   **15.** ¿Por quién fue condecorado? ¿Quién lo condecoró? ¿Qué le hizo el rey español?   **16.** ¿Cuántas bicicletas tiene?   **17.** ¿Cuál de sus bicicletas le gusta más? ¿De dónde es la bicicleta que le gusta más? ¿De qué color es la bicicleta que le gusta más?   **18.** ¿Qué quiere hacer?   **19.** ¿Adónde irá de vacaciones? ¿Para qué irá al Caribe?   **20.** ¿A quiénes llevará? ¿Cuántas hijas tiene?

Actividad 3   **1.** ¿Adónde piensas ir? ¿Dónde queda el centro comercial? ¿A cuál centro comercial piensas ir?   **2.** ¿Cuántas tiendas hay?   **3.** ¿Cuántos restaurantes y cafés hay?   **4.** ¿Cuántos pares de zapatos vas a comprar? ¿Qué vas a comprar?   **5.** ¿A quién necesitas comprarle un regalo? ¿Qué necesitas comprar?   **6.** ¿Cuánto tratarás de gastar?   **7.** ¿Qué le comprarás?/¿De qué será la blusa?   **8.** ¿Cuál color le gusta más?   **9.** ¿Cómo pagarás? ¿Con qué pagarás?   **10.** ¿Cómo vas a llegar al centro comercial?

Actividad 4   A.   **1.** Cuántas   **2.** Cuáles   **3.** Quién   **4.** Cómo   **5.** Cuántos   **6.** Por qué   **7.** Dónde   **8.** A qué
B.   **9.** de quién   **10.** Qué   **11.** Dónde   **12.** De qué   **13.** Cuál   **14.** Adónde   **15.** quién   **16.** Qué   **17.** qué, por qué   **18.** Por qué

Actividad 5   **1.** Dónde   **2.** Qué   **3.** Cuándo (A qué hora)   **4.** Quién   **5.** Adónde? (Cómo)   **6.** De dónde   **7.** Cuántas   **8.** Cuántos

Actividad 6   **1.** ¿De parte de quién?   **2.** ¿Dónde queda la casa?   **3.** ¿De quién es el coche?   **4.** ¿De qué color es el coche?   **5.** ¿A quién vas a llevar?   **6.** ¿A qué hora llegarán?   **7.** ¿Cuántos años tienes?   **8.** ¿A quiénes piensas ver?   **9.** ¿Cuándo será? (¿Qué día será?)   **10.** ¿Quiénes llegan?   **11.** ¿Cuánta plata gastaste? (¿Cuánto gastaste?)   **12.** ¿Qué tiempo hace?   **13.** ¿Cómo se encuentran (Tito y Josefa)? (¿Cómo están?)   **14.** ¿Hasta cuándo te quedas?   **15.** ¿Cuál quieres?

Actividad 7   **1.** ¿Cuánto tiene el río Iguazú de largo?   **2.** ¿Qué longitud tiene el río Amazonas?   **3.** ¿Cuánto mide el río Misisipí de largo?   **4.** ¿Cómo (Cuánto) es el lago Titicaca de ancho?   **5.** ¿Cuánto tiene el desierto Atacama de largo?   **6.** ¿Qué altura tiene el monte McKinley?   **7.** ¿Cuánto mide la cumbre Aconcagua de alto?

Actividad 8   **1.** Cuál (Cómo)   **2.** Qué   **3.** Cómo   **4.** Cuál   **5.** Cómo   **5.** Cuál   **7.** Qué

Actividad 9   **1.** ¿Para quién son estas rosas?   **2.** ¿Sobre qué hablaron los ingenieros?   **3.** ¿En qué oficina trabaja Celeste?   **4.** ¿Con cuántas personas fue Alberto?   **5.** ¿De quiénes son los CDs?   **6.** ¿Hacia dónde caminaba Fernando?   **7.** ¿Por dónde entró Jeremías?   **8.** ¿Con quién jugará al tenis Sol?   **9.** ¿En qué se metieron?   **10.** ¿De dónde vienen?

Actividad 10   **1.** ¿Aprenden Gustavo y Melinda francés?   **2.** ¿Trabaja Pepe en una tienda de vídeos?   **3.** ¿Toca Ud. piano?   **4.** ¿Se han vestido los niños?   **5.** ¿Jugará Cristóbal al béisbol?   **6.** ¿Se matriculó Elena anteayer?   **7.** ¿Deben Uds. quedarse unos días más?   **8.** ¿Está Ramona a dieta?

Actividad 11   **1.** ¿Son traviesos estos niños?   **2.** ¿Son bonitas las margaritas?   **3.** ¿Estaba descompuesto el televisor?   **4.** ¿Está abierto el museo?   **5.** ¿Es italiana la revista?   **6.** ¿Fueron robadas las joyas?   **7.** ¿Están rotos los pantalones?   **8.** ¿Es buena esta marca?   **9.** ¿Fue impresionante el espectáculo?

Actividad 12   **1.** No, Pedro no. Los compra Memo.   **2.** No, Domingo y Toni no. Nos llevan Salvador y Soledad.   **3.** No, Dora no. Las va a preparar Leonor.   **4.** No, Jorge no. Los traerá Miguel.   **5.** No, Carmen no. Piensa llevarlos Marcos.   **6.** No, nosotros no. Los harán Olivia y Nacho.   **7.** No, Jesús y Marta no. Los invitarás tú.   **8.** No, yo no. Se ocupa de ella Mari.

Actividad 13   **1.** Felipe me preguntó qué haría en la tarde.   **2.** Isabel me preguntó con quiénes había salido (salí).   **3.** Carlos me preguntó por qué no quería jugar al baloncesto.   **4.** Sol me preguntó a qué hora había vuelto (volví) a casa.   **5.** Claudio me preguntó para cuándo necesitaba escribir el informe.   **6.** Mi hermanita me preguntó cuándo la llevaba a una discoteca.   **7.** Mis primos me preguntaron por qué no les invitaba al parque de atracciones.   **8.** Mi mamá me preguntó por qué tenía dolor de cabeza.   **9.** Yo me pregunté a mí mismo/a por qué me había levantado (me levanté) de la cama hoy.   **10.** Mis amigos me preguntaron de dónde venía.   **11.** Mirián me preguntó cómo iba a llegar al centro.   **12.** Alejo me preguntó cuándo pensaba regresar a Madrid.

Actividad 14   *Answers will vary.*

Capítulo 24

Actividad 1   **1.** No, no fui nunca (jamás) a la Isla de Pascua.   **2.** No, no aprendimos chino tampoco.   **3.** No, nadie ha llamado esta tarde.   **4.** No, no va a tomar álgebra nunca más.   **5.** No leeré ni la novela ni el guión de la película.   **6.** No, ningún jefe (ninguno) renunció a su puesto.   **7.** No, no conoció a nadie por fin.   **8.** No, nunca limpio la casa los sábados.

Actividad 2   **1.** No queda nada de la comida.   **2.** No hay refrescos tampoco.   **3.** No bailan ni los chicos ni las chicas.   **4.** No canta bien ningún cantante.   **5.** No tiene ganas nadie de quedarse.   **6.** No dan fiestas divertidas nunca.

Actividad 3   **1.** ¡Qué va! Nadie te regaló dos millones de dólares.   **2.** ¡Qué va! Ninguna chica dice que eres un Adonis.   **3.** ¡Qué va! Nunca (Jamás) sacas una A en tus exámenes.   **4.** ¡Qué va! Los reyes de España no te mandaron nada.   **5.** ¡Qué va! Tú tampoco vas a la luna.   **6.** ¡Qué va! Conchita no va a salir contigo nunca más.   **7.** ¡Qué va! Tus padres no te van a regalar ni un Jaguar ni un Ferrari.

Actividad 4   **1.** nada, nadie   **2.** En la vida (Nunca, Jamás)
3. nada, algo   **4.** nunca   **5.** sino también   **6.** alguien
7. ningún otro momento   **8.** nadie   **9.** no solamente, sino
también   **10.** ninguna

Actividad 5   **1.** I can't stand her at all!   **2.** They're going to see
each other at the usual time.   **3.** They don't call her charming
for nothing.   **4.** Guillermo says he hasn't the slightest idea.
5. In the end all the arguing was useless.   **6.** What you're
saying has nothing to do with the present situation.   **7.** I think
the project is somewhat disorganized.   **8.** If Laura told you that
there must be a reason.

Actividad 6   **1.** No por nada renunció a su puesto.
2. Llamarán en cualquier momento.   **3.** Caminamos todo el día
por toda la ciudad.   **4.** Cualquiera podría ayudarnos con el
trabajo.   **5.** Toda avenida está embotellada (Todas las avenidas
están embotelladas) en las horas punta.   **6.** Hay ruinas romanas
por toda España.

Actividad 7   **1.** Aunque te querré para siempre, tengo que
decir ‹‹¡hasta nunca!››   **2.** Más vale algo que nada. (Algo es
algo.)   **3.** ¡Nada de ir a Marte antes de graduarte!
4. ¡Y aquí acaba el cuento de nunca acabar!   **5.** De algo lo/la
conozco. Será alguien.   **6.** ¡Haz lo que quieras! ¡Ve adónde
quieras! ¡Yo no te olvidaré nunca jamás!   **7.** ¿Este final? ¿Ese
final? Yo estoy contento/a con cualquiera de los dos.
8. Nada más. ¡Mañana será otro día!   **9.** No te dejaré por
nada del mundo.   **10.** No la puedo ver ni en pintura.
11. Nos reuniremos a la hora de siempre.   **12.** Dejen de llorar.
No sirve para nada.

Actividad 8   *Answers will vary.*

VOCABULARIO ESPAÑOL-INGLÉS

This Spanish-English Vocabulary contains all the words that appear in the text, with the following exceptions: (1) most close or identical cognates that do not appear in the thematic vocabulary lists; (2) most conjugated verb forms; (3) most diminutives and augmentatives; (4) most adverbs ending in **-mente;** (5) days of the week, months of the year, and most numbers; (6) subject, object, and demonstrative pronouns; (7) possessive and demonstrative adjectives. Only meanings used in the text are given.

Words containing **ch** and **ll** are alphabetized according to the individual letters of these consonant clusters. For example, words beginning with **ch** are found within the letter **c.** Also, **n** precedes **ñ** in alphabetical order.

The gender of nouns is indicated, except for masculine nouns ending in **-o** and feminine nouns ending in **-a.** Stem changes and spelling changes are indicated for verbs: **dormir (ue, u); llegar (gu); traducir (zc, j), comenzar (ie)(c).**

The following abbreviations are used in this vocabulary.

abbrev.	abbreviation	*m.*	masculine
adj.	adjective	*Mex.*	Mexico
adv.	adverb	*n.*	noun
coll.	colloquial	*pl.*	plural
f.	feminine	*p.p.*	past participle
fig.	figurative	*prep.*	preposition
gram.	grammatical term	*pron.*	pronoun
inf.	infinitive	*s.*	singular
inv.	invariable	*Sp.*	Spain
irreg.	irregular	*v.*	verb

A

a to; **a continuación** next; **¿a cuánto está?** what is the value (*of the dollar, peso*)?; **¿a cuántos estamos?** what is the date?; **a doble espacio** double-spaced; **a escondidas** stealthily, behind someone's back; **a espaldas** behind someone's back; **a finales de** at the end of; **a fuego lento** on low (heat), over low heat; **a la (mano) derecha/ izquierda** on the right/left; **a la inversa** the other way; **a la salida de** at the edge of (*a place*); upon leaving (*a* place); **a la vuelta de la esquina** around the corner; **a largo plazo** in the long run; **a lo largo de** *prep.* along; **a menudo** often; **a pesar de** in spite of; **a regañadientes** reluctantly; **a su juicio/parecer** in one's opinion; **a tiempo** on time; **a través de** through; **a veces** sometimes

abajo down; downstairs; underneath; **hacia abajo** downward

abierto/a (*p.p. of* **abrir**) open

abiertamente openly

abogado/a lawyer

aborrecer (zc) to hate

abrir (*p.p.* **abierto**) to open

abrazar (c) to hug, embrace

abrazo *n.* hug

abrelatas *m. inv.* can opener

abrigo overcoat, coat

abrocharse to button up (*one's shirt, coat*)

absoluto: en absoluto absolutely not; **superlativo absoluto** *gram.* absolute superlative

abstracto/a abstract

absurdo/a absurd

abuelo/a grandfather/grandmother

abuelos grandparents

aburrido/a bored; **ser** (*irreg.*) **aburrido/a** to be boring

aburrimiento boredom

aburrir to bore (*someone*); **aburrirse** to get bored

acá *adv.* here

acabar to finish; to end up; **acabar de** + *inf.* to have just (*done something*); **acabársele** to run out of; **cuento de nunca acabar** never-ending story

académico/a academic

acampar to camp

acaso: por si acaso just in case

accidente *m.* accident

acción *f.* action

aceite *m.* oil; **aceite de oliva** olive oil

aceituna olive

acento accent; accent mark

aceptar to accept

acerca de about, concerning

acercar (qu) to bring (*something*) closer, over; **acercarse (a)** to come closer, approach

acertar (ie) to be on target, guess right

acertijo riddle

aclarar to clarify

acoger (j) to welcome, receive (*someone*)

acomodador(a) *n* usher

acompañar to go with, accompany (*someone*)

acondicionado/a: aire (*m.*) **acondicionado** air-conditioning

aconsejar to advise

acontecimiento event

acordar (ue) to agree; **acordarse (de)** to remember

acostar (ue) to put (*someone*) to bed; **acostarse** to go to bed

acostumbrado/a accustomed, used to

acostumbrarse a + *inf.* to be accustomed to (*doing something*)

activo/a active; **construcción activa** *gram.* active construction; **voz** (*f.*) **activa** *gram.* active voice

actividad *f.* activity

acto act; **salón** (*m.*) **de actos** assembly hall

actor *m.* actor

actriz *f.* (*pl.* **actrices**) actress

actual current

actualizar (c) to update

actuar (actúo) to act, perform; to behave

acuarela watercolor (*painting*)

acuerdo: de acuerdo all right, okay; **estar** (*irreg.*) **de acuerdo (con)** to agree (with); **ponerse** (*irreg.*) **de acuerdo** to come to an agreement

adelante: hacia adelante toward the front

adelanto *n.* advance, progress

adentro inside

adivinar to guess

adjetival: cláusula adjetival *gram.* adjective clause

adjetivo *gram.* adjective; **adjetivo demostrativo** *gram.* demonstrative adjective; **adjetivo descriptivo** *gram.* descriptive adjective; **adjetivo posesivo** *gram.* possessive adjective

adjuntar to enclose (*in a letter*); to attach (*to an e-mail*)

administración *f.* administration; **administración de empresas** business administration

administrador(a) de web webmaster

administrar to administer

admirador(a) admirer

admirar to admire

admitir to admit

¿adónde? where (to)

Adonis *m. inv.* Adonis; handsome, young man (*from Greek mythology*)

aduanero/a customs agent

adverbial: cláusula adverbial *gram.* adverbial clause

adverbio *gram.* adverb

advertir (ie, i) to point out; to warn

aeropuerto airport

afectado/a affected

afecto affection

afectuoso/a affectionate

afeitar(se) to shave (oneself); **maquinilla de afeitar** electric razor

Afganistán Afghanistan

afgano/a Afghan

afición *f.* fondness, liking

aficionado/a *n.* fan

afirmar to confirm

afirmación *f.* sentence

afirmativo/a affirmative

afligir (j) to afflict

África Africa

africano/a African

afuera outside

afueras *f. pl.* the outskirts (*of town*)

agarrar to grab

agenda electrónica PDA

agente *m., f.* agent

agradarle to like (*something*)

agradecer (zc) to thank, be grateful

agregar (gu) to add

agua *f.* (*but* **el agua**) water; **agua de colonia** cologne; **agua mineral** mineral water; **agua pura** clean water; **deportes** (*m. pl.*) **de agua** water sports

aguacate *m.* avocado

aguafiestas *m., f. inv.* wet blanket, party pooper

aguantar to stand, tolerate

agudo/a: palabra aguda *gram. Spanish word with stress on the last syllable*

águila *f.* (*but* **el águila**) eagle

ahí there; **por ahí** around there

ahijado/a godson/goddaughter

ahogarse (gu) to drown

ahora now; **ahora mismo** right now; at once; **por ahora** for now

ahorrar to save (*money, time*)

ahorros (*m., pl.*): **cuenta de ahorros** savings account

aire *m.* air; **aire acondicionado** air conditioning; **aire puro** clean air; **al aire libre** *adj.* open-air; *adv.* outdoors; **bomba de aire** air pump; **narices** (*f., pl.*) **al aire** stuck-up (*lit.* noses in the air)

ajedrez *m.* chess

ajetreado/a hectic

ajetreo continuo hustle and bustle

ajo garlic; **diente** (*m.*) **de ajo** garlic clove

al (*contraction of* **a** + **el**) to the; **al aire libre** *adj.* open-air; *adv.* outdoors; **al contrario** on the contrary; **al día** per day; **al fin y al cabo** when all is said and done; **al final** in the end; **al final de** at the end of; **al fondo** *adv.* in the back; at the bottom; **al frente de** *prep.* at the head of; **al mes de** + *inf.* after a month of (*doing something*)

albañil *m., f.* bricklayer

alcanzar (c) to reach; to overtake

aldea small village

alegrarse to become happy; **alegrarse (de)** to be glad, happy (that)

alegre happy

alegría happiness

alejar to move (*something*) away; **alejarse (de)** to move away (from)

alemán German (*language*)

alemán, alemana *n., adj.* German

Alemania Germany

alfiler *m.* pin

alfombra carpet; rug; **limpiar la alfombra** to clean the carpet; **sacudir la alfombra** to shake the rug

álgebra *f.* (*but* **el álgebra**) algebra

algo something; anything; **algo +** *adj.* somewhat, a little **+** *adj.*, a little; **algo de +** *noun* a little **+** *noun*

algodón *m.* cotton

alguien someone, somebody; anyone

algún, alguno/a(s) some, any; **algún día** someday; **alguna vez** sometime; **algunas veces** sometimes; **de algún modo** somehow; **de alguna manera** somehow; **en/por algún lugar** somewhere; **en/por alguna parte** somewhere

alimentos *m., pl.* food; **alimentos naturales** health food

allá (over) there; **hacia allá** toward that place (far away); **por allá** around there (far away)

allí there; **allí arriba** up there; **hasta allí** up to there; **por allí** around there

alma *f.* (*but* **el alma**) soul

almacén *m.* department store

almacenar to store

almendra almond

almendro almond tree

almorzar (ue) (c) to have lunch

almuerzo lunch

alpinismo: hacer (*irreg.*) **alpinismo** to mountain climb

alquilar to rent

alrededores *m. pl.* surroundings

alto/a tall; high; **clase** (*f.*) **alta** upper class; **de alta costura** haute couture; **de alta tecnología** hi-tech; **de alta velocidad** high-speed; **de alto** in height; **de tacón alto** high-heeled; **en lo alto** up, up there, up high; **en voz alta** out loud; aloud; **hablar alto** to speak loudly

altura height

ama (*f.* [*but* **el ama**]) **de casa** housewife

amable kind, nice

amanecer (zc) to wake up in the morning

amarillo/a yellow

Amazonas *m. s.* Amazon (River)

ambos/as both

ambición *f.* ambition

ambiente (*m.*): **contaminación** (*f.*) **del ambiente** air pollution

ambiguo/a ambiguous

amenazar (c) (con) to threaten (to)

americano/a *n., adj.* American; **fútbol** (*m.*) **americano** football

Américas *f., pl.* Americas (North, Central, and South America)

amigo/a friend

amistad *f.* friendship

amor *m.* love; **carta de amor** love letter

ampliar (amplío) to expand

añadir to add

analfabetismo illiteracy

análisis *m.* analysis

analizar (c) to analyze

anaranjado/a *adj.* orange

ancho/a wide; **ancho/a de espaldas** wide-shouldered; **de ancho** in width

anchura width

anciano/a *n.* old man/lady

andaluz(a) Andalusian

andamio scaffolding

andar *irreg.* to walk; **andar a gatas** to crawl; **andar bien** to go well; **andar con cuidado** to be careful; **andar en bicicleta** to ride a bike, go bike riding

andorrano/a Andorran

anfiteatro amphitheater

anfitrión, anfitriona host, hostess

ángel *m.* angel

anillo ring

animar to cheer (*someone up*); **animarse** to cheer up; to feel like (*doing something*)

animado/a excited; lively

ánimo courage; energy

animal *m.* animal

aniversario anniversary

año year; **año escolar** school year; **Año Nuevo** New Year; **el año pasado** last year; **cumplir años** to have a birthday; **tener** (*irreg.*)... **años** to be ... (years old)

anoche *adv.* last night

anochecer *m.* nightfall

anotar to note, jot down

antártico/a *adj.* Antarctic

Antártida *n.* Antarctic

ante *prep.* before; in front of; **ante todo** above all; first of all

anteayer *adv.* day before yesterday

anteojos *m. pl.* eyeglasses

anterior previous; preceding

anteriormente formerly

antes *adv.* before; **antes de** *prep.* before; **antes (de) que** *conj.* before; **lo antes posible** as soon as possible; **mucho antes** a long time before

antiguo/a old; former

Antillas *f. pl.* Antilles (Islands)

antillano/a Antillean, from the Antilles

antipático/a unpleasant, unfriendly

antropología anthropology

anunciar to announce

anuncio announcement; advertisement

apagar (gu) to put out, extinguish; to turn off, shut off

apagado/a (turned) off, out

apañárselas to manage, to get by

aparato appliance; **aparato eléctrico** (electrical) appliance; **aparato multimedia** multimedia device

aparcar (qu) to park

aparecer (zc) to appear

apartado de correos P.O. box

apartamento apartment

apasionado/a passionate

apdo. *abbrev. for* **apartado** (P.O.) box

apenas hardly, scarcely

aplacar (qu) quench

aplaudido/a applauded, praised, celebrated

aplaudir to applaud

aplausos *m. pl.* applause

aplicado/a diligent; studious

apócope *gram.* apocope

apoderarse (de) to take possession (of)

apoyarse (contra) to lean (against)

apreciado/a esteemed

aprender to learn; **aprender a +** *inf.* to learn to (*do something*)

aprendizaje *m.* learning

apresurarse to hurry
apretar (ie) to squeeze; to be tight
aprobar (ue) to pass (an exam)
apropiado/a appropriate, correct
aprovechar(se) (de) to take advantage (of)
apto. *abbrev. for* **apartamento** apartment
apuntarse (a) to register, sign up (for); **apuntarse en** to put one's name down (*on a list*)
apuntes *m. pl.* (class) notes
aquel, aquella *dem. adj.* that (*over there*); **aquél, aquélla** *dem. pron.* that one (*over there*)
aquello *dem. pron.* that; that thing
aquellos/as *dem. adj.* those (*over there*); **aquéllos/as** *dem. pron.* those (ones) (*over there*)
aquí *adv.* here; **aquí cerca** near here; **desde aquí** from here; **por aquí** around here
Arabia Saudita Saudi Arabia
araña spider
árbitro umpire
árbol *m.* tree
arbusto bush
arca *f. (but* **el arca***)* ark; **arca de Noé** Noah's ark
archivado/a filed (*papers*)
archivar to file (*papers*)
archivo archives; filing cabinet; *pl.* files
área *f. (but* **el área***)* area
arepas *f. pl. Venezuelan dish of fried or baked corn cakes*
argamasa mortar
Argelia Algeria
argelino/a Algerian
argentino/a Argentinean, Argentine
argumento plot
árido/a dry
aritmético/a arithmetical
arma *f. (but* **el arma***)* arm, weapon
armadura suit of armor
armar to set up, put together
armario closet
armiño ermine
armonía harmony
armónicamente harmoniously
arpa *f. (but* **el arpa***)* harp
arqueología archeology
arqueólogo/a archeologist
arquitecto/a architect
arquitectura architecture
arrancar (qu) to pull up/out (*weeds*); to start up (*a vehicle*)
arrastrar to drag
arrebatarle to snatch, grab (*something from someone*)
arreglado/a straightened up
arreglar to arrange; to fix; to straighten up; **arreglarse** to get ready (*to go out*); to fix (*hair, clothing*); **arreglárselas** to manage, get by
arrepentirse (ie, i) (de) to regret, repent
arriba up; upstairs; above; **allí arriba** up there; **hacia arriba** upward
arrodillado/a kneeling (down)
arrodillarse to kneel (down)
arrogante arrogant
arroz *m.* rice
arte *f. (but* **el arte***)* art; **bellas artes** fine art
Ártico Arctic

ártico/a artic
artículo (newspaper) article; **artículo (in)definido** *gram.* (in)definite article; **artículo neutro** *gram.* neuter article
artista *m., f.* artist
artístico/a artistic
asado/a roast(ed)
asar to roast
ascender (ie) to go up, climb; to promote
ascenso raise (*in salary*)
ascensor *m.* elevator
aseo hygiene
aserrar (ie) to saw
así in this way; like that; **así que** therefore, consequently, so
asiático/a Asian
asiento seat
asistente/a assistant
asistir a to attend
asomar to appear, stick one's head out of (*a window*)
aspiradora vacuum cleaner; **pasar la aspiradora** to vacuum
aspirina aspirin
astuto/a astute
asunto issue; affair
asustar to frighten (*someone*); **asustarse** to get frightened, scared
atar to tie; **atarse** to tie (*one's shoes, belt, and so on*)
Atacama: Desierto Atacama Atacama Desert (Chile)
atacar (qu) to attack
ataque *m.* attack; **ataque de nervios** panic attack
atardecer *m.* dusk
ataúd *m.* coffin
Atenas Athens
atención *f.* attention; **llamar atención** to attract attention
atento/a attentive
aterrizaje *m.* landing (*airplane*)
aterrizar (c) to land (*airplane*)
atleta *m. f.* athlete
atónito/a astonished
atracción (*f.*): **parque** (*m.*) **de atracciones** theme park
atraer *irreg.* to attract
atrás behind; back; **hacia atrás** backward; toward the rear; **para atrás** backwards; to the back
atrasarse to be late; to fall behind
atravesar (ie) to cross
atreverse (a) to dare (*to do something*)
atribuir (y) to attribute
aula *f. (but* **el aula***)* classroom; lecture hall
aumentar to increase
aun even
aún still, yet
aunque although, even, though
ausentarse (de) to go away (from)
australiano/a Australian
austriaco/a Austrian
auténtico/a authentic
auto car
autobús *m. s.* bus; **parada de autobuses** bus stop

automático/a: cajero automático ATM
autopista highway
autor(a) autor
autorretrato self-portrait
auxiliar: verbo auxiliar *gram.* auxiliary verb
avanzar (c) to advance
avda. *abbrev. for* avenida avenue
ave *f.* (*but* el ave) bird
avenida avenue
avergonzarse (ue) (c) (de) to be ashamed (of)
avería breakdown (*car*)
averiguar (güe) to find out
avestruz *m.* (*pl.* avestruces) ostrich
avión *m.* airplane; billete (*m.*)/boleto de avión
   plane ticket
avisar to advise; to inform
aviso notice
¡ay! *interj.* ah!; ouch!
ayer yesterday
ayuda help *n.*
ayudante *m., f.* assistant
ayudar to help
ayuntamiento town hall
azteca *m., f.* Aztec
azúcar *m.* sugar
azul *m., f.* blue; príncipe (*m.*) azul prince
   charming

B

bahamiano/a Bahamian
bailar to dance
bailarín, bailarina dancer
baile *m.* dance; baile de etiqueta formal ball; baile
   de gala big dance
bajo *adv.* under; below; bajo juramento under
   oath; bajo llave under lock and key
bajo/a short; low; en voz baja in a low voice;
   quietly; Países (*m. pl.*) Bajos Netherlands
bajamar *f.* low tide
bajar (a) to go down (to); to lower; to download
   (*computer*)
balear *m., f.* Balearic
Baleares *f. pl.* Balearic Islands
balón *m.* ball
baloncesto basketball
bambú *m.* (*pl.* bambúes) bamboo
banca electrónica electronic/online banking
bancario/a: cuenta bancaria bank account
banco bank; trámite (*m.*) de banco bank
   transaction; sucursal (*f.*) del banco bank branch
banda sonora sound track (*of a movie*)
bandeja tray; bandeja de plata silver platter
banquero/a banker
bantú (*pl.* bantúes) Bantu
bañar to bathe (*someone*); bañarse to take a bath,
   bathe
bañera bathtub
baño bath(room); cuarto de baño bathroom; traje
   (*m.*) de baño bathing suit
bar *m.* bar
barato/a cheap
barbaridad *f.* atrocity
barcelonés, barcelonesa from Barcelona

barco boat; ship
barrer to sweep
barrio neighborhood
barro clay
base *f.* base; base de datos data base
básquetbol *m.* basketball
bastante *adv.* enough; quite, rather; quite a lot
bastón cane
basura trash, garbage; correo basura junk mail
Batalla Naval Battleship (*board game*)
bate *m.* bat
batería battery; cargar (gu) la batería to charge
   the battery
batir to beat
baúl *m.* (car) trunk
bebé *m., f.* baby
beber to drink
bebida drink
beca scholarship
béisbol *m.* baseball
belga *m., f.* Belgian
Bélgica Belgium
bello/a beautiful; Bella Durmiente Sleeping
   Beauty; bellas artes fine art
berenjena eggplant
besar to kiss
beso kiss
bibliografía bibliography
biblioteca library
bibliotecario/a librarian
bicicleta bicycle, bike; andar (*irreg.*)/montar en
   bicicleta to ride a bike, go bike riding
bien *adv.* well; andar (*irreg.*) bien to go well; caerle
   (*irreg.*) bien to make a good impression on
   someone; llevarse bien (con) to get along (with)
bienes *m. pl.* goods
bilbaíno/a from Bilbao
bilingüe bilingual
billete *m.* ticket; billete de avión plane ticket;
   billete de lotería lottery ticket; billete
   electrónico e-ticket
biográfico/a biographical
biología biology
bisabuelo/a great-grandfather, great-grandmother;
   m. pl. great-grandparents
bisnietos *m. pl.* great-grandchildren
bizcocho cake
blanco/a white
Blancanieves *f. s.* Snow White
blusa blouse
bocadillo sandwich
boda wedding
bodega grocery store
bogotano/a from Bogotá
boleto de avión plane ticket
bolígrafo pen
boliviano/a Bolivian
bolsa purse; (grocery) bag; bolsa de valores stock
   exchange; la Bolsa stock market;
bolsillo: calculadora de bolsillo pocket calculator
bomba de aire air pump
bombero/a fireman, firewoman
bombones *m. pl.* chocolates
bonaerense *m., f.* from Buenos Aires
bondad (*f.*): tener (*irreg.*) la bondad to be kind
   enough (*to do something*)

bonito/a pretty
boquiabierto/a astounded; speechless
borde (*m.*): **al borde** on the verge
borrar to erase
bosque *m.* forest
bostezar (c) to yawn
bota boot
botella bottle
botones *m. inv.* bellhop
Brasil Brazil
brasileño/a Brazilian
bravo/a angry, furious; **mar** (*f.*) **brava** very rough sea
brazo arm; **tener** (*irreg.*) **en brazos** to hold
Bretaña: Gran Bretaña Great Britain
breve *adj.* short, brief
brillante brilliant
brillar to shine
brindar (por) to drink a toast (to)
británico/a British
bucear to scuba dive
buen, bueno/a *adj.* good; **buenas tardes** good afternoon/evening; **de buen humor** in a good mood; **de buena fe** in good faith; **lo bueno** the good thing, news; **hacer** (*irreg.*) **buen/mal tiempo** to be good/bad weather; **por las buenas o por las malas** whether one likes it or not
bueno *interj.* well
bufanda scarf
buganvilla bougainvillea
buhardilla attic
bulevar *m.* boulevard
burlarse (de) to laugh (at); to make fun (of)
burlón, burlona mocking *adj.*
busca *n. m.* beeper; *n. f.* search
buscar (qu) to look for
buzón *m.* mailbox

C

c/ *abbrev. for* **calle** *f.* street
caballo horse; **a caballo** on horseback; **montar a caballo** to ride horseback
caber *irreg.* to fit
cabeza head; **dolor** (*m.*) **de cabeza** headache; **lavarse la cabeza** to wash one's hair
cabo: al fin y al cabo when all is said and done
cacahuete *m.* peanut
cacerola saucepan
cachapas *f. pl. Venezuelan corn "pancakes"*
cachemir(a) from Kashmir
Cachemira Kashmir
cada each; every
cadena de restaurantes restaurant chain
caer *irreg.* to fall; **caerle bien/mal** to make a good/bad impression on someone; **caerse** to fall down; **caérsele a uno** to drop; **no tener** (*irreg.*) **dónde caerse muerto** to not have a penny to one's name
café *m.* coffee; coffeehouse, café
cafeína caffeine
cafetería cafeteria
caja box; **caja de herramientas** toolbox; **caja de juguetes** toy chest

cajero/a cashier; **cajero automático** ATM
cajón *m.* drawer (*furniture*); crate
calcetín *m.* sock (*Sp.*)
calculadora (de bolsillo) (pocket) calculator
calcular to calculate; to work out; to compute
cálculo calculus
calentar (ie) to heat
caliente hot; **perro caliente** hot dog
callar to become quiet
calle *f.* street
calmar to calm (*someone*) down; **calmarse** to calm down
calor heat; warmth; **hacer** (*irreg.*) **calor** to be hot (*weather*); **tener** (*irreg.*) **calor** to be, feel hot
caluroso/a warm, affectionate; hot
cama bed; **hacer** (*irreg.*) **la cama** to make the bed
cámara (digital) (digital) camera
camarero/a waiter, waitress
camarón *m.* shrimp
cambiar to change; to cash (*checks*); **cambiar de idea** to change one's mind
cambio *n.* change
Camboya Cambodia
camboyano/a Cambodian
caminar to walk
camino path; route; way; **en camino** on the way, along the way; in route
camisa shirt
camiseta T-shirt
campamento camp, campground
campanada strike of the clock
campaña campaign; **tienda de campaña** tent
campeón, campeona champion
campeonato championship
campesino/a farmer
camping (*m.*): **ir** (*irreg.*) **de camping** to go camping
campo country; countryside; field
campus *m.* (university) campus
canadiense *m., f.* Canadian
canal *m.* channel
Canarias *f. pl.* Canary Islands
canario/a from the Canary Islands
cancha field, court (*sports*)
canción *f.* song
candidato/a candidate
canicas *f. pl.* marbles
cansado/a tired
cansancio tiredness, weariness
cansarse to get tired
cantante *m., f.* singer
cantar to sing
cántaros (*m. pl.*): **llover (ue) a cántaros** to rain cats and dogs
capa layer
capataz *m., f.* foreman, forewoman
capaz (*pl.* **capaces**) capable, able
capital *f.* capital (city); *m.* capital (*money*)
capítulo chapter
cara face; **costarle (ue) un ojo de la cara** to cost an arm and a leg
caro/a expensive
carácter *m.* character (*trait*)
característico/a characteristic
caramelo (piece of) candy
caraqueño/a from Caracas

carcajadas (*f. pl.*): **reírse (i, i) (me río) a carcajadas** to laugh one's head off
carecer (zc) to lack
cargador(a) mover
cargar (gu) to load, upload; to charge (*a battery*)
Caribe *m.* Caribbean
caridad *f.* charity
cariño affection; **con cariño** affectionately
cariñoso/a *adj.* affectionate, loving
carioca *m., f.* from Rio de Janeiro
carnaval *m.* carnival
carne *f.* meat
carnet (*m.*) **de conducir** driver's license
carnicería butcher shop
carpeta briefcase
carpintero/a carpenter
carrera race; career; course of study
carretera highway
carro car
carta letter; menu; **carta de amor** love letter; **carta de despedida** farewell letter; **carta de odio** hate mail; **cartas** (playing) cards
cartel *m.* poster
cartera wallet; purse
cartero/a mail carrier
casa house; home; **ama** (*f.* [*but* **el ama**]) **de casa** housewife
casado/a married; **recién casado/a** newlywed
casarse (con) to get married (to)
casa house
cáscara peel (*of fruit*)
casi *adv.* almost; **casi nada** hardly; **casi nunca** hardly ever
caso: en caso de in case; **hacerle** (*irreg.*) **caso** to pay attention (*to someone*)
castaña chestnut
castaño chestnut tree
castaño/a light brown (*eyes, hair*)
castigar (gu) to punish
castillo castle
castor *m.* beaver
casualidad (*f.*): **por casualidad** by chance
catalán *m.* Catalan (*language*)
catedral *f.* cathedral
categoría category
católico/a Catholic; **Reyes** (*m. pl.*) **Católicos** Ferdinand and Isabel (*Spanish monarchs*)
catolicismo Catholicism
causa cause; **a causa de** because of
cazuela (sauce)pan
cebolla onion
celebración *f.* celebration
celebrar to celebrate
célebre famous, well-known
celos *m. pl.* jealousy; **tener** (*irreg.*) **celos** to be jealous
celular: teléfono celular cell phone
cena dinner, supper
cenar to have dinner
centavo cent
centésimo one-hundredth
céntrico/a centrally located
centro downtown; **centro comercial** mall; **centro de tecnología** tech center; **en pleno centro** in the middle of downtown
cepillarse to brush

cepillo brush
cerámica *s.* ceramics, pottery
cerca *adv.* close, nearby; **aquí cerca** near here; **cerca de** near; **cerca de** + *número* about, approximately + *number*
cereal *m.* cereal
ceremonia ceremony
cereza cherry
cerezo cherry tree
cerilla match (*fire*)
cero zero
cerrado/a closed
cerrar (ie) to close
certidumbre *f.* certainty
cerveza beer
césped *m.* lawn; grass
cesta basket
chaleco vest
chalet *m.* country house
champiñón *m.* mushroom
champú *m.* shampoo
chantajista *m., f.* blackmailer
chaqueta jacket
charada *s.* charades
charlar to chat
charol *m.* patent leather
cheque *m.* check; **cheque de viajero** traveler's check
chico/a boy, girl
chicle *m.* gum
chile *m.* chili (pepper)
chileno/a Chilean
chino Chinese (*language*)
chino/a Chinese
chismear to gossip
chismes *m. pl.* gossip
chocar (qu) (con/contra) to run (into), collide (with)
chocolate *m.* chocolate; **helado de chocolate** chocolate ice cream; **torta de chocolate** chocolate cake
choque *m.* collision, wreck
chorizo sausage
chufa tiger nut
chuleta (*meat*) chop; **chuleta de cordero** lamb chop; **chuleta de ternera** veal chop
cibercafé *m.* cyber café
cielo sky; **poner** (*irreg.*) **el grito en el cielo** to scream bloody murder
ciencia science; *pl.* (*academic discipline*) science; **ciencia ficción** science fiction; **ciencias naturales** natural science; **ciencias políticas** political science; **ciencias sociales** social sciences
ciento hundred; **por ciento** percent
cierto/a true; certain; **de cierta manera** in a certain way; **por cierto** certainly
cimiento: echar los cimientos to lay the foundation
cine *m.* movie theater; **director(a) de cine** film director; **ir** (*irreg.*) **al cine** to go to the movies
cinematográfico/a *adj.* cinematographic, film, movie
cínico/a cynical
cinturón *n.* belt; **cinturón de seguridad** seatbelt
ciruela plum
ciruelo plum tree
cirujano/a surgeon
cisne *m.* swan
cita appointment

ciudad *f.* city; **ciudad universitaria** university campus

ciudadano/a citizen

civil: **estado civil** marital status

claridad *f.* clarity; **con claridad** clearly

clarinete *m.* clarinet

claro *interj.* of course; **claro que sí** *interj.* of course; **claro que no** *interj.* of course not

claro/a clear

clase *f.* class; **clase alta** upper class; **compañero/a de clase** classmate; **sala de clase** classroom

clásico/a classical, classic

cláusula *gram.* clause; **cláusula adjetival** *gram.* adjective clause; **cláusula adverbial** *gram.* adverbial clause; **cláusula principal/ independiente** *gram.* main clause; **cláusula relativa** *gram.* relative clause; **cláusula subordinada/dependiente** *gram.* dependent clause

clave (*f.*): **clave personal** PIN (personal identification number)

clavel *m.* carnation

cliente/a client

clima *m.* climate; weather

cobrar to charge; to cash (*checks*)

cobre *m.* copper

cocer (ue) (z) to cook

coche *m.* car; **coche descapotable** convertible; **coche todo terreno** all-terrain vehicle (ATV)

cochecito toy car

cocido/a cooked

cociente intelectual *m.* IQ

cocina kitchen; cuisine; **libro de cocina** cookbook

cocinado/a cooked

cocinar to cook

cocinero/a cook, chef

código code

codo elbow

coger (j) to take; to grasp; to catch

cohete *m.* rocket

cola: hacer (*irreg.*) **cola** to stand in line

colaborar to collaborate

colchón *m.* mattress

colección *f.* collection

coleccionar to collect

colega *m., f.* colleague

colegio school

colgar (ue) (gu) to hang

collar *m.* necklace

colocar (qu) to put, place; **colocarse** to get a job

colombiano/a Colombian

colonia: agua (*f.* [*but* **el agua**]) **de colonia** cologne

coloquio discussion

color *m.* color

columna column

columpio *n.* swing

coma *f.* comma; **coma** *m.* coma

comedia comedy

comedor *m.* dining room

comentar to comment

comentario comment

comenzar (ie) (c) to begin

comer to eat; **comerse** to eat (*something*) up; **comerse de envidia** to be consumed by envy

comercial: **centro comercial** mall

comercio business

comestible (*m.*): **tienda de comestibles** grocery store

cometa *f.* kite; *m.* comet

comida food; meal; **comida rápida** fast food

comité *m.* committee

como like, as; **como si nada** as if it were nothing at all

¿cómo? how?; what?

cómoda dresser

cómodo/a comfortable

compacto/a: **disco compacto** CD

compadecer (zc) to feel sympathy for

compañero/a companion, friend; **compañero/a de clase** classmate; **compañero/a de cuarto** roommate

compañía company

comparación *f.* comparison

comparativo/a comparative

comparecer (zc) (ante) to appear (before) (*a judge*)

compartir to share

complemento directo/indirecto *gram.* direct/ indirect object

completo/a complete; **por completo** completely

componer (*like* **poner**) to compose; to repair; **componérselas** to manage, get by

composición *f.* composition

compositor(a) composer

compra: hacer (*irreg.*) **la compra** to do the shopping; **ir** (*irreg.*) **de compras** to go shopping

comprar to buy

comprender to understand

comprobar (ue) to prove

comprometerse to get engaged

comprometido/a engaged

compromiso agreement; engagement

compuesto/a: **condicional compuesto** *gram.* conditional perfect; **futuro compuesto** *gram.* future perfect; **infinitivo compuesto** *gram.* compound infinitive

computación *f.* computer science

computadora computer; **computadora portátil** laptop (computer)

común: **por lo común** usually

con with; **con cariño** affectionately; **con claridad** clearly; **con cuidado** careful; **con diligencia** diligently; **con el fin de** with the aim of; **con fuerza** forcefully

concentrarse to concentrate (*on something*)

concepto concept

concertar (ie) to arrange

concierto concert

concluir (y) to conclude

concordancia agreement

concreto concrete

concurrido/a busy, much frequented

condicional *m. gram.* conditional (tense); **condicional compuesto/perfecto** *gram.* conditional perfect

condominio condominium

cóndor *m.* condor

conducir *irreg.* to drive; **carnet** (*m.*) **de conducir** driver's license

conductor(a) driver

conferencia lecture; conference; **dar** (*irreg.*) **una conferencia** to deliver a lecture; **dictar conferencias** to deliver lectures; **sala de conferencias** lecture hall

conferenciante *m., f.* lecturer

confesar (ie) to confess

confiar (confío) (en) to trust; to rely (on); to confide (in)

confirmar to confirm

conforme: estar (*irreg.*) **conforme (con)** to agree (with)

confuso/a confusing

congreso conference

conjetura guess

conjugado/a *gram.* conjugated

conjunción *f. gram.* conjunction

conjunto group

conmigo with me

conmover (*like* **mover**) to move (*emotionally*)

conocer (zc) to know

conocido/a (well-)known

consecuencia: por consecuencia consequently

conseguir (*like* **seguir**) to get, acquire, obtain; **conseguir** + *inf.* to succeed in (*doing something*), manage (*to do something*); to get (*to do something*)

consejo piece of advice

consentir (*like* **sentir**) **en** + *inf.* to consent, agree to (*do something*)

conservatorio conservatory

considerar to consider

consigo with him, her, you (*form. s., pl.*), them; **consigo mismo/a** with himself, herself, yourself (*form. s.*); **consigo mismos/as** with yourselves (*form., pl.*); themselves

consiguiente: por consiguiente consequently

consistir en to consist of

construcción *f.* construction; **construcción activa/pasiva** *gram.* active/passive construction

constructor(a) builder

construir (y) to build

consulta (doctor's) office; **libro de consulta** reference book

consultar consult

consultor(a) consultant

consultorio (doctor's) office

contabilidad *f.* accounting

contacto: ponerse (*irreg.*) **en contacto** to get in touch

contador(a) accountant

contaminación (*f.*) **del ambiente** environmental pollution

contaminado/a polluted

contar (ue) to count; to tell, relate, recount (*a story*); **contar con** to count on (*someone*)

contemporáneo/a contemporary, modern

contener (*like* **tener**) to contain

contenido content

contento/a happy

contestar to answer

contigo with you (*fam. sing.*)

continente *m.* continent

continuación (*f.*): **a continuación** next

continuar (continúo) to continue

continuo/a: ajetreo continuo hustle and bustle

contra *prep.* against; **en contra de** against

contracción *f. gram.* contraction

contradecir (*like* **decir**) to contradict

contraer (*like* **traer**) to contract

contrario/a: al contrario on the contrary

contraste *m.* contrast

contratado/a hired

contrato contract

contribuir (y) to contribute

controlar to control

convalecer (zc) to convalesce, recover

convencer (z) to convince

convenir (*like* **venir**) to agree; to be suitable, fitting

conversación *f.* conversation

convertir (ie, i) to convert; **convertirse en** to become

convocar (qu) to call (*a meeting*)

copa: sombrero de copa top hat

copia copy; **hacer** (*irreg.*) **copias** to (photo)copy

copiar to (photo)copy; **copiar (en los exámenes)** to cheat (on exams)

corazón *m.* heart

corbata tie

cordero lamb; **chuleta de cordero** lamb chop

cordón *m.* lace, string

Corea del Norte North Korea

Corea del Sur South Korea

coreano/a Korean

coreográfico/a choreographic

coro choir, chorus

corona crown

correcto/a correct, right

corregir (i, i) (j) to correct

correo mail; post office; **apartado de correos** P.O. box; **correo basura** junk mail; **correo de voz** voice mail; **correo electrónico** e-mail; **echar al correo** to mail

correr to run; **correr las cortinas** to draw the curtains; **correrse** to move over, make room for

corresponder a to correspond to

corrida de toros bullfight

corriente: cuenta corriente checking account

cortacésped *m.* lawnmower

cortar to cut; **cortar a tiritas** to cut into strips; **cortarse** to cut oneself

corte (*m.*): **Corte Inglés** *department store chain in Spain*

cortés *m., f.* courteous

cortina curtain; **correr las cortinas** to draw the curtains

corto/a short; **cuento corto** short story

cosa thing

cosecha harvest

coser to sew

cosmopolita *m., f.* cosmopolitan

cosquillas *f. pl.* tickling; **hacerle** (*irreg.*) **cosquillas** to tickle (someone)

costado side; **por los cuatro costados** on both sides (*of the family*)

costar (ue) to cost; **costarle un ojo de la cara** to cost an arm and a leg; **costar un dineral** to cost a fortune

costarricense *m., f.* Costa Rican

costura: de alta costura haute couture

crear to create

creativo/a creative

crecer (zc) to grow

crédito: tarjeta de crédito credit card

creer (y) (*p.p.* **creído**) to think, believe
criar (crío) to raise, bring up
crisis *f. inv.* crisis
cristal (*m.*): **zapatilla de cristal** glass slipper
cristalino/a crystal clear
crítico/a *n.* critic (*person*); *adj.* critical
crucigrama *m.* crossword puzzle
cruzar (c) to cross
cuaderno notebook; **cuaderno de trabajo** workbook
cuadro *n.* painting
cual: el/la cual *rel. pron.* which; who; *rel. pron.* **los/las cuales** which; who; **lo cual** *neut. rel. pron.* which; **ser** (*irreg.*) **tal para cual** to be two of a kind
¿cuál? which?; what?
cualidad *f.* quality
cualquier *adj.* any
cualquiera *pron.* anyone; either
cuando *conj.* when
¿cuándo? when?; **¿desde cuándo?** how long?
cuanto: en cuanto *conj.* as soon as; **en cuanto a** *prep.* regarding
¿cuánto/a? how much?; **¿cuántos/as?** how many?; **¿a cuánto está?** what is the value (*of the dollar, peso*)?; **¿a cuántos estamos?** what is the date?
cuarto room; **compañero/a de cuarto** roommate; **cuarto de baño** bathroom
cuarto/a *adj.* fourth; *n. m.* one fourth
cuatro four; **trabajar por cuatro** to work like a slave
cubano/a Cuban
cubierto/a (*p.p. of* **cubrir**) covered
cubrir (*p.p.* **cubierto**) to cover
cuenta account; bill; **cuenta bancaria** bank account; **cuenta corriente** checking account; **cuenta de ahorros** savings account; **darse** (*irreg.*) **cuenta (de)** to realize; **por su cuenta** on one's own; **tener** (*irreg.*) **en cuenta** to keep in mind
cuento story; **cuento corto** short story; **cuento de hadas** fairy tale; **cuento de nunca acabar** never-ending story
cuero leather
cuerpo body
cuesta *n.* slope
cuestión *f.* matter, question
cuidado care; **andar** (*irreg.*) **con cuidado** to be careful; **con cuidado** careful; **(tener [*irreg.*]) cuidado (de)** (to be) careful (to)
cuidadoso/a careful
cuidar to take care of (*someone*); **cuidarse** to take care of (*oneself*)
culpa blame; **por culpa de** because of, through the fault of; **tener** (*irreg.*) **la culpa (de)** to be guilty (of)
culpable guilty
cultivar to cultivate, farm
cumbre *f.* (mountain) top
cumpleaños *m. inv.* birthday
cumplir to fulfill, carry out; **cumplir años** to have a birthday, to turn (*years old*); **cumplir con su deber** to do one's duty, do what one is supposed to do
cuñado/a brother-in-law, sister-in-law
cura *m.* priest
curioso/a curious
currículum vitae *m.* résumé, CV

cursar to take (*a class, course*)
cursivo/a: letra cursiva italics
curso course; **fin** (*m.*) **de curso** end of the (school) year
cuyo/a whose

D

damas *f. pl.* checkers
danés, danesa Danish
daño: hacer(se) (*irreg.*) **daño** to hurt (oneself)
dar *irreg.* to give; **dar escalofrío** to make (*someone*) shudder; **dar gato por liebre** to put something over on someone; **dar las gracias** to thank; **dar gritos** to shout; **dar la mano** to shake hands; **dar la vuelta** to turn (*something*) over; **dar un paseo** to take a walk; **dar una conferencia** to deliver a lecture; **darse cuenta (de)** to realize; **darse prisa** to hurry
dardos *m. pl.* darts
dato fact, piece of information; *pl.* data; **base de datos** data base
de of; from; **de algún modo** somehow; **de alguna manera** somehow; **de alta costura** haute couture; **de alta tecnología** hi-tech; **de alta velocidad** high-speed; **de alto** in height; **de ancho** in width; **de buen humor** in a good mood; **de buena fe** in good faith; **de cierta manera** in a certain way; **de día** during the day, by day; **¡de eso nada, monada!** *interj.* none of that!; no way!; **de fondo** background; **de inmediato** immediately; **de la noche** at night; **de largo** in length; **de memoria** (*to learn, know*) by heart; **de modo que** so that; **de nada** you're welcome; don't mention it; **de ningún modo** in no way; **de ninguna manera** in no way; **de noche** at night; during the night; **de repente** suddenly; **de tacón alto** high-heeled; **de todas formas** at any rate
debajo de *prep.* under
deber to owe; **deber** + *inf.* should, ought to (*do something*); must (*do something*), to be supposed to (*do something*)
deber *n. m.* duty; **cumplir con su deber** to do one's duty, do what one is supposed to do
débil weak
década decade
decaer (*like* **caer**) to decline, weaken, deteriorate
decente decent
decidir to decide; **decidirse a** to decide to
décimo/a tenth
decir *irreg.* (*p.p.* **dicho**) to say; to tell; **decir adentro** to say to oneself; **es decir** that's to say
decisión *f.* decision; **tomar una decisión** to make a decision
declarar to declare; **declarar una huelga** to call a strike (*labor*)
decorado *n.* scenery, set
dedicar (qu) to dedicate; **dedicarse a** to devote oneself to
dedo finger
deducir *irreg.* to deduce; to deduct
defecto defect
defender (ie) to defend
definido/a: artículo definido *gram.* definite article

dejar to let, allow; **dejar + inf.** to let, allow (*something happen*); **dejar + noun (en)** to leave (*something*) behind/(in a place); **dejar en paz** to leave alone; **dejar de + inf.** to stop (*doing something*)

del *contraction of* **de + el** of the; from the

delante de *prep.* in front of

delfín *m.* dolphin

delgado/a thin

delineante *m., f.* draftsperson

demás: los/las demás the others; the rest; **por lo demás** furthermore

demasiado *adv.* too, too much

democracia democracy

demócrata *m., f.* Democrat

demorar (en) to delay, put off, take a long time (to)

demostrar (ue) to show

demostrativo/a *gram.* demonstrative

dentista *m., f.* dentist

dentro de *prep.* inside of; **dentro de nada** in a moment

dentista *m., f.* dentist

depender to depend

dependiente: cláusula dependiente *gram.* dependent clause

dependiente/a *n.* clerk

deporte *m.* sport; **deportes de agua** water sports; **hacer** (*irreg.*) **deportes** to play, participate in sports; **practicar (qu) deportes** to play, practice sports; **revista de deportes** sports magazine; **sección** (*f.*) **de deportes** sports section; **tienda de deportes** sporting goods store

deportivo/a: coche (*m.*) **deportivo** sports car

depósito: depósito de artículos perdidos lost and found; **depósito de gasolina** fuel tank

deprimido/a depressed

deprimirse to get depressed

derecho law (*profession*); right (*legal*); (straight) ahead

derecho/a right; **a la (mano) derecha** on the right

derivar to derive

derramar to spill

desabrochar(se) to undo (*one's article of clothing*)

desaparecer (zc) to disappear

desatar(se) to untie (*one's shoes, laces*)

desayunar to have breakfast

desayuno breakfast

descansar to rest

descapotable: coche descapotable convertible

descargar (*like* **cargar**) to download

descender (ie) to go down

descolgar (*like* **colgar**) to hang up

descomponer (*like* **poner**) to break (down), malfunction

descompuesto/a (*p.p. of* **descomponer**) broken, in disrepair

desconectar to disconnect

descongelar to defrost

desconocer (*like* **conocer**) to be ignorant of

describir (*p.p.* **descrito**) to describe

descripción *f.* description

descriptivo/a: adjetivo descriptivo *gram.* descriptive adjective

descrito/a (*p.p. of* **describir**) described

descubierto/a (*p.p. of* **descubrir**) discovered

descubrir (*like* **cubrir**) to discover

descuento discount

descuidado/a careless; untidy

desde from; since; **desde aquí** from here; **¿desde cuándo?** how long?

desdecir (de) (*like* **decir**) to fall short, be unworthy (of)

desear to want

desenchufar to unplug

desenredar to solve, unravel (*a mystery*)

desentendido/a: hacerse (*irreg.*) **el/la desentendido/a** to play innocent

desenvolver (*like* **volver**) to unroll

desfile *m.* parade

desgracia: por desgracia unfortunately

desgraciado/a *n., adj.* unlucky (person)

deshacer (*like* **hacer**) to undo

deshecho/a (*p.p. of* **deshacer**) undone

desierto desert; **Desierto Atacama** Atacama Desert (Chile)

desilusionado/a disappointed

desleal disloyal

deslizarse (c) to slip

desmayarse to faint

desobedecer (*like* **obedecer**) to disobey

desolado/a devastated

desorganizado/a unorganized

despacio *adv.* slowly

despedida: carta de despedida farewell letter

despedir (*like* **pedir**) to fire, dismiss; **despedirse (de)** to say good-bye (to)

despegar (gu) to take off (*airplane*)

despegue *m.* takeoff (*airplane*)

despejado/a clear (*sky*)

despejar to clear up

despertador *m.* alarm clock

despertar (ie) to wake (*someone*) (up); **despertarse** to wake up

despistado/a confused

después *adv.* after, afterward; **después de** *prep.* behind; after

destinatario/a addressee

destruir (y) to destroy

desván *m.* attic

detalle *m.* detail

detective (privado) *m., f.* (private) detective

detener (*like* **tener**) to stop, bring to a halt; to detain; **detenerse** to stop, come to a halt

detrás *adv.* behind; **detrás de** *prep.* behind; **por detrás** behind (*someone's*) back/the back of (*something*)

deuda debt

devolver (*like* **volver**) to return, give back (*something*)

día *m.* day; **al día** per day; **algún día** someday; **de día** during the day, by day; **Día de la Raza** Columbus Day (October 12); **día de por medio** every other day; **Día de Reyes** Epiphany (January 6); **día feriado** holiday; **todos los días** every day

diablo devil

diablura: hacer (*irreg.*) **diabluras** to make mischief

diálogo dialogue

diario/a daily

dibujante *m., f.* draftsperson

dibujar to draw

diccionario dictionary

dicho (*p.p. of* **decir**) said; told
dictar conferencias to deliver lectures
dictador(a) dictator
diente *m.* tooth; **cepillarse/limpiarse los dientes** to brush one's teeth; **diente de ajo** garlic clove
dieta: estar (*irreg.*) **a dieta** to be on a diet
diferencia difference
diferenciar to differentiate
diferente different
difícil difficult
difundir to publicize; to broadcast; to spread
digital: cámara digital digital camera
diligencia: con diligencia diligently; **hacer** (*irreg.*) **las diligencias** to run errands
Dinamarca Denmark
dineral *m.* fortune; **costar (ue) un dineral** to cost a fortune
dinero money
dirección *f.* address; (film) directing *n.*; **dirección electrónica** e-mail (address); Internet address
directo/a: complemento directo *gram.* direct object; **imperativo directo** *gram.* direct question, imperative
director(a) de cine film director; **director(a) ejecutivo/a** executive director; **director(a) de orquesta** orchestra conductor
dirigir (j) to direct; to lead; to conduct; **dirigirse a** to address oneself, speak to (*someone*)
disco compacto CD
discoteca disco(theque)
disculpa: pedir (i, i) disculpas to apologize
disculparse to apologize
discurso speech
discutir to discuss, argue
diseñador(a) designer
diseñar to design
disfraz *m.* (*pl.* **disfraces**) costume, disguise
disfrazarse (c) to disguise oneself
disfrutar to enjoy
disponerse (*like* **poner**) **a** + *inf.* to get ready to (*do something*)
dispuesto/a (*p.p. of* **disponer**) *adj.* ready; willing
disquete *m.* diskette
distinguir (distingo) to distinguish
distinto/a different
distraer (*like* **traer**) to distract; to amuse, entertain
distraído/a distracted
distribuir (y) to distribute
divertido/a fun
divertir (ie, i) to amuse; **divertirse** to have a good time
dividir to divide
divino/a wonderful
divorciarse to get divorced
doblado/a dubbed
doblar to turn; to change direction; to dub (*film*)
doble: a doble espacio double-spaced
doctor(a) doctor
documental *m.* documentary
documento document
dólar *m.* dollar
doler (ue) to hurt, ache
dolor *m.* pain, ache; **dolor de cabeza** headache; **dolor de estómago** stomachache; **dolor de muelas** toothache
doméstico/a: labores (*f. pl.*) **domésticas** housework

dominar to dominate; to have command (*of a language*)
dominicano/a Dominican; **República Dominicana** Dominican Republic
dominio command, grasp (*of a language*)
dominó *s.* dominoes
don *m.* gift; talent; *title of respect used with a man's first name*; **ser** (*irreg.*) **un don nadie** to be a nobody; **tener** (*irreg.*) **el don de gentes** to have charm, be charming; to get along well with people
donar to donate
donde where
¿dónde? where?
doña *title of respect used with a woman's first name*
dorar to brown
dormir (ue, u) to sleep; **dormirse** to fall asleep; **dormirse en los laureles** to rest on one's laurels; **saco de dormir** sleeping bag
dormitorio bedroom
dos two; **en un dos por tres** in a jiffy
dramático/a dramatic
dramaturgo/a playwright
dramón *m.* sob story
ducharse to take a shower
dudar to doubt; **dudar en** to hesitate over (about)
dudoso/a doubtful
dueño/a owner
dulce *adj.* sweet; *n. m. pl.* candy; **dulce** (*m.*) **de leche** *a sweet caramel spread popular in Argentina*
duque *m.* duke
duquesa duchess
durante *adv.* during
durar to last
durazno peach
durmiente: Bella Durmiente Sleeping Beauty

E

e and (*used instead of* **y** *before words beginning with stressed* **i** *or* **hi,** *except* **hie-**)
echar to throw; **echar al correo** to mail; **echar los cimientos** to lay the foundation; **echar suertes** to draw lots, flip a coin; **echarse** to lie down; **echarse a** + *inf.* to begin to (*do something*); **echárselas de** + *adj.* to boast of being (*something*)
economía *s.* economics; economy
económico/a economic
economista *m., f.* economist
ecoturismo ecotourism
ecuatorial: Guinea Ecuatorial Equatorial Guinea
ecuatoriano/a Ecuadorian
edad *f.* age; **Edad Media** *s.* Middle Ages; **tercera edad** old age, golden years
edificio building
editor(a) editor
editorial: casa editorial publisher, publishing house
efecto effect; **efectos coreográficos** choreography; **efectos especiales** special effects
efectuar (efectúo) to effect; to carry out, execute
eficazmente efficiently

eficientemente efficiently
egipcio/a Egyptian
Egipto Egypt
ejecutivo/a: director(a) ejecutivo/a executive
  director
ejemplo example; **por ejemplo** for example
ejercer (z) to exercise (*a right*); to practice
  (*a profession*); to exert
ejercicio exercise; **hacer** (*irreg.*) **ejercicio** to
  exercise; **hacer los ejercicios** to do the exercises
  (*school work*)
elección *f.* election
electricista *m., f.* electrician
eléctrico/a: aparato eléctrico (electrical) appliance
electrónico/a: agenda electrónica PDA; **banca**
  electrónica electronic (online) banking; **billete**
  (*m.*) **electrónico** e-ticket; **correo electrónico**
  e-mail; **dirección** (*f.*) **electrónica** e-mail (address);
  Internet address; **mensaje** (*m.*) **electrónico** e-mail
  (*message*); **revista electrónica** e-zine (*Internet*
  magazine)
elefante *m.* elephant
elegante elegant
elegir (j) to choose, elect
elemento element
email *m.* e-mail
embarcar (qu) to embark, go on board
embargo: sin embargo however; nevertheless
embellecer (zc) to beautify, embellish
embotellado/a blocked, jammed (*streets*)
embotellamiento traffic jam
emocionado/a moved (*emotionally*), touched
emocionante moving; thrilling
emocionar to move, touch, excite; **emocionarse**
  to become excited; to be moved, touched,
  to be/get excited
empeñarse en + *inf.* to insist on (*doing something*);
  to persist in (*doing something*); to be determined
  (*to do something*)
emperador *m.* emperor
emperatriz *f.* empress
empezar (ie) (c) (a) to begin (to)
empleado/a employee
emplear to use
empleo employment; job
empresa firm; business; **administración** (*f.*) **de**
  empresas business administration; **empresa de**
  alta tecnología hi-tech business; **empresa**
  familiar family business; **sucursal** (*f.*) **de**
  empresa business/company branch
empujar to push
en in; on; **en algún lugar** somewhere; **en alguna**
  parte somewhere; **en camino** on the way;
  en caso de in case; **en contra de** against; **en**
  cuanto *conj.* as soon as; **en cuanto a** *prep.*
  regarding; **en fin** anyway; **en forma** fit, in shape;
  en lo alto up, up there, up high; **en lugar de**
  instead of; **en ningún lugar** nowhere; **en punto**
  on the dot (*time*); **en serio** seriously; **en un dos**
  por tres in a jiffy; **en voz alta** out loud; aloud; **en**
  voz baja in a low voice; quietly; **hablar en serio**
  to be serious
enamorarse (de) to fall in love (with)
enano/a dwarf
encantador(a) charming
encantar to like very much; to love

encargar (gu) to put in charge, entrust; to order
  (*something*)
encender (ie) to turn on (*an appliance*); to light;
  encender el fuego to turn on the flame; to light
  the fire
encerrar (ie) to lock in; to contain; **encerrarse (en)**
  to shut oneself up (in)
enchufar to plug (*something*) in
enciclopedia encyclopedia
encima *adv.* on top; **encima de** *prep.* on; upon;
  on top of
encoger (*like* **coger**) to shrink; **encogerse de**
  hombros to shrug one's shoulders
encontrar (ue) to find; **encontrarse** + *adj.* to
  feel + *adj.*
encuesta survey
enemigo/a enemy
energía energy; **energía nuclear** nuclear energy
enérgico/a energetic
enfadado/a angry
enfadar to make (*someone*) angry; **enfadarse**
  (con) to become angry, get angry (with)
enfático *gram.* emphatic (*pronoun*)
enfermo/a *n.* sick (person); *adj.* sick
enflaquecer (zc) to lose weight, grow thinner
enfrente *adv.* opposite, facing; **enfrente de** across
  from
enfurecer (zc) to make furious; **enfurecerse** to
  become angry
engañoso/a deceitful
enloquecer (zc) to drive crazy; **enloquecerse** to
  go crazy
enojado/a angry
enojar to make (*someone*) angry; **enojarse (con)**
  to become angry, get angry (with)
enorme enormous
enredarse to get entangled, involved
enriquecer (zc) to enrich
ensalada salad; **ensalada de fruta** fruit salad
ensayar to rehearse
ensayo essay; rehearsal
ensuciar to make dirty; **ensuciarse** to get dirty
entender (ie) to understand
enterarse (de) to find out (about)
enternecer (zc) to soften; to move (*emotionally*)
entonces *adv.* then, next; afterward; **para entonces**
  by then; **por aquel entonces** at that time
entrada entrance; entry, way in; ticket (*to a*
  performance); **entrada principal** main door;
  forzar (ue) (c) una entrada to break in
entrar (en, a) to go/come in; to enter
entre *prep.* between; among; **por entre** through
entregar (gu) to hand, turn in/over; to deliver
entrometido/a *n.* busybody; *adj.* meddling
entrenador(a) trainer
entrevista interview
entrevistar to interview
entristecer (zc) to sadden
entusiasmar to excite, thrill, stir
entusiasmo: con entusiasmo enthusiastically
entusiasta *m., f.* enthusiast
envejecer (zc) to grow old
enviado/a sent
enviar (envío) to send
envidia envy; **comerse/morirse (ue, u)**
  (*p.p.* **muerto**) **de envidia** to be consumed by envy

envolver (*like* **volver**) to wrap (up)
envuelto/a (*p.p. of* **envolver**) wrapped
época era, time (*period*)
equipaje *m.* luggage
equipo team
equivocado/a mistaken; wrong
equivocarse (qu) (de) to be mistaken, wrong (about)
es decir that's to say
escalar to climb
escalera ladder; stairs; **escalera mecánica** escalator
escalofrío shiver *n.;* **dar** (*irreg.*) **escalofrío** to make (*someone*) shudder
escampar to stop raining, clear up
escanear to scan
escaparse to escape; to get away; **escaparse por un pelo** to have a narrow escape, to escape by the skin of one's teeth
escayolado/a in a (plaster) cast
escena scene
escenario stage
escenografía scenery, setting
escocés, escocesa Scottish
Escocia Scotland
escoger (j) to choose
escolar (*adj.*): **año escolar** school year
esconder to hide; **esconderse** to hide (oneself)
escondido/a hidden; **a escondidas** stealthily, behind someone's back
escondite *m.* hide and seek
escribir (*p.p.* **escrito**) to write
escrito/a (*p.p. of* **escribir**) written; **por escrito** in writing; **sobre gustos no hay nada escrito** to each his own
escritor(a) writer
escritorio desk
escuchar to listen (to)
escuela school
escultor(a) sculptor
escultura sculpture (*general*); (piece of) sculpture
esforzarse (ue) (c) en/por + *inf.* to strive (*to do something*); to try (hard) (*to do something*)
esfuerzo effort
esmalte (*m.*) **de uñas** nail polish; **ponerse** (*irreg.*) **el esmalte de uñas** to polish one's nails
esmoquin *m.* tuxedo
espacio: a doble espacio double-spaced
espaguetis *m. pl.* spaghetti
espalda back; **a espaldas** behind (*someone's*) back; **ancho de espaldas** wide-shouldered
español(a) *n.* Spaniard; *adj.* Spanish
espárragos *m., pl.* asparagus
especial special; **efectos especiales** special effects
especialista *m., f.* specialist
espécimen *m.* specimen
espectáculo show
espejo mirror
espera: sala de espera waiting room
esperanza hope
esperar to hope, expect, wait
espía *m., f.* spy
espiar (espío) to spy
espinacas *f., pl.* spinach
espionaje *m.* spying, espionage; **película de espionaje** spy film
espléndido splendid

espolvorear to sprinkle (*cooking*)
esposo/a husband, wife
esquiar (esquío) to ski
esquina corner
establecer (zc) to establish
establo stable
estación *f.* season; station
estacionar to park (*a car*)
estadio stadium; **tribuna del estadio** grandstand
estadista *m., f.* statesman, stateswoman
estadística statistic
estado state; **estado civil** marital status; **golpe** (*m.*) **de estado** coup d'etat
estadounidense *adj. m., f.* U.S.
estafar to swindle, cheat, trick
estallar to break out (*war*)
Estambul Istanbul
estancia *n.* stay
estantería shelf
estar *irreg.* to be; **estar a dieta, régimen** to be on a diet; **estar a punto de** + *inf.* to be about to (*do something*); **estar conforme (con)** to agree (with); **estar de acuerdo (con)** to agree (with); **estar de luto** to be in mourning; **estar de vacaciones** to be on vacation; **estar de vuelta** to be back; **estar en contra** to be against; **estar en forma** to be in shape; **estar hecho/a una lástima** to be a sorry sight, in a sad state; **estar hecho/a una sopa** to be soaking wet; **estar mojado/a hasta los huesos** to be soaking wet; **estar muy pagado/a de sí mismo/a** to be very satisfied with oneself; **estar para** + *inf.* to be ready to (*do something*); **estar por** to be in favor of, in the mood for (*something*)
estatal *adj.* state
estatua statue
estatuilla figurine; **estatuilla de porcelana** china figurines; **estatuilla del Óscar** Oscar
estatura height; **estatura media** medium height
estéreo stereo
estilo style
estimado/a esteemed, respected
estómago: dolor (*m.*) **de estómago** stomachache
estornudar to sneeze
estremecer (zc) to shake, startle
estrenado/a debuted
estropeado/a damaged; broken
estructura structure
estrujar to crush, crumple
estudiante *m., f.* student
estudiar to study
estudios (*m., pl.*) **posgraduados** graduate studies
estupendo/a fantastic; great
etiqueta: baile (*m.*) **de etiqueta** formal ball
Europa Europe; **Europea Oriental** East Europe
europeo/a European
evaluar (evalúo) to evaluate
evidente evident
evitar to avoid
exacto/a exact
exactitud *f.* accuracy
exagerar to exaggerate
examen *m.* exam, test; **copiar en los exámenes** to cheat on exams; **pasar el examen por los pelos** to barely get through an exam; **tribunal** (*m.*) **de exámenes** board of examiners

exasperar to exasperate, make (*someone*) lose patience; **exasperarse** to get exasperated, lose one's patience

excavación *f.* excavation

excelente excellent

exclamación *f.* exclamation

excursión *f.* trip, excursion; **hacer** (*irreg.*) **una excursión** to go on an outing

excusa excuse; **poner** (*irreg.*) **excusas** to make excuses

exhibir to exhibit

exigir (j) to demand

éxito success; **peldaños** (*m. pl.*) **del éxito** ladder of success; **tener** (*irreg.*) **éxito** to be successful

expandir to expand

expansión *f.* expansion

expectativa expectation

experiencia experience

experimentar to experience

experimento experiment

explicación *f.* explanation

explicar (qu) to explain

explosión *f.* explosion

explotar to exploit; to develop

exponer (*like* **poner**) to exhibit

exposición *f.* exhibit, exhibition

expresar to express

expresión *f.* expression; **expresión impersonal** *gram.* impersonal expression; **expresión indefinida** *gram.* indefinite expression; **expresión negativa** *gram.* negative expression

extinguir (extingo) to extinguish

extrañar to surprise

extranjero abroad, overseas

extranjero/a foreign

F

fábrica factory; **gerente** (*m., f.*) **de fábrica** factory manager

fabricar (qu) to make; to manufacture

fabuloso/a fabulous

fácil easy; **lo fácil** the easy thing

facultad *f.* department (*academic*)

faisán *m.* pheasant

faja cummerbund

fallecer (zc) to die

falta: hacer (*irreg.*) **falta** to be necessary

faltar to be missing; to be lacking; **faltar** + *noun* to have (something) left; **faltar (a)** to miss, be absent (from); **faltar** + *tiempo* **para** + *hora* it's (*time*) until (*hour*)

fama name, reputation

familiar *adj.* family; **empresa familiar** family business; **reunión** (*f.*) **familiar** family reunion

famoso/a famous

fanfarrón, fanfarrona braggart

fantasma *m.* ghost

fantástico/a: novela fantástica fantasy novel

farmacia pharmacy

faro headlight

fascinar to fascinate

favor: favor de please; **hacer** (*irreg.*) **el favor de** + *inf.* to do (*someone*) the favor of (*doing something*); **por favor** please

favorecer (zc) to favor

favorito/a favorite

fax *m.* fax

fe *f.* faith; **de buena fe** in good faith

fecha date; **fecha de nacimiento** birth date

felicidad *f.* happiness; **felicidades** *interj.* congratulations

felicitar to congratulate

feliz (*pl.* **felices**) happy

femenino/a feminine

feriado/a: día (*m.*) **feriado** holiday

feroz (*pl.* **feroces**) fierce, ferocious

festival *m.* festival

fiarse (me fío) (de) to trust

ficción (*f.*): **ciencia ficción** science fiction

fiebre *f.* fever

fiesta party

fiestero/a partier

figurar en to figure among, be listed in; **figurarse** to imagine, suppose

fijarse (en) to notice; to pay attention (to)

fila row

Filadelfia Philadelphia

Filipinas Philippines

filipino/a Philippine

film *m.* film, movie

filmar to film

filosofía philosophy

fin *m.* end; **al fin y al cabo** when all is said and done; **con el fin de** with the aim of; **de fin de curso** end of the (school) year; **en fin** anyway; **fin de semana** weekend; **por fin** finally

final *m. n.* ending, end; *adj.* final; **a finales de** at the end of; **al final** in the end; **al final de** at the end of; **para finales de** at the end of

finca farm

fingir (j) to pretend

finlandés, finlandesa Finnish

Finlandia Finland

firmar to sign

física *n. s.* physics

físico/a *n.* physicist

físico/a *adj.* physical; **lo físico** physical traits

flameado/a flambéed

flauta flute

flechazo love at first sight

florentino/a from Florence (Italy)

flor *f.* flower

florería florist (*shop*)

florero vase

folleto brochure

fondo fund (*banking*); **al fondo** in the back; at the bottom; **de fondo** background

fontanero/a plumber

footing (*m.*): **hacer** (*irreg.*) **footing** to jog

forma form; **de todas formas** at any rate; **en forma** fit, in shape

formación (*f.*) **profesional** occupational training

formal formal; **imperativo formal** *gram.* formal command

formarse to form, be formed

formular *gram.* to form, formulate

formulario form (*paper*)

forrado/a lined

fortalecer (zc) to fortify
forzar (ue) (c) una entrada to break in
fósforo match (*fire*)
foto(grafía) *f.* photo(graph)
fotografía photography
fotografiar (fotografío) to photograph
fractura fracture; break
fraile *m.* monk
francés *m.* French (*language*)
francés, francesa French
Francia France
franco/a frank
frasco small bottle, flask
frecuente frequent
fregar (ie) (gu) to scour; to clean
freír (i, i) (frío) (*p.p.* **frito, freído**) to fry
frenar to brake
frenético/a frantic
frente *n. f.* forehead; *m.* (weather, military) front
frente: al frente de *prep.* at the head of; **frente a** *prep.* in front of; opposite
fresa strawberry
fresco (*n.*): **hacer** (*irreg.*) **fresco** to be cool (*weather*)
fresco/a fresh
frío (*n.*): **hacer** (*irreg.*) **frío** to be cold (*weather*); **tener** (*irreg.*) **frío** to be, feel cold
frío/a cold
frito/a (*p.p. of* **freír**) fried; **estar** (*irreg.*) **frito/a** to be done for; **papas** (*f. pl.*) **fritas** French fries
fruta fruit; **ensalada de fruta** fruit salad; **jugo de fruta** fruit juice
fuego fire; heat (*cooking*); **a fuego lento** on low (heat), over low heat; **encender (ie) el fuego** to turn on the flame; to light the fire
fuente *f.* serving dish
fuera *adv.* outside; out; **fuera de** *prep.* outside; **por dentro y por fuera** inside and outside
fuerte *adj.* strong; *adv.* loud
fuerza: con fuerza forcefully
fumar to smoke; *n. m.* smoking
funcionar to work, function (*machine*)
furioso/a furious
fútbol *m.* soccer; **fútbol americano** football
futbolista *m. f.* soccer/football player
futuro future; *gram.* future (tense); **futuro compuesto/perfecto** *gram.* future perfect

G

gafas *f. pl.* (eye)glasses
gaita (*Sp.*) *s.* bagpipes
gala: baile (*m.*) **de gala** big dance
galería gallery
Gales Wales
galés, galesa Welsh
galleta cookie
gallina chicken
gallinero chicken coop
gallo: misa del gallo midnight mass
gambas *f. pl.* shrimp
gana wish; *pl.* urge, desire; **darle** (*irreg.*) **la gana** to feel like (*doing something*); **de mala gana** reluctantly; **tener** (*irreg.*) **ganas (de)** to feel like (*doing something*)

ganar to earn; to win; **ganar plata** to make money; **ganarse la vida** to earn a living
garaje *m.* garage
gasolina gas; **depósito de gasolina** fuel tank
gasolinera gas station
gastar to spend; to waste
gatas (*f. pl.*): **andar** (*irreg.*) **a gatas** to crawl
gato (car) jack
gato/a cat; **dar** (*irreg.*) **gato por liebre** to put something over on someone
gaveta drawer
gemelos *m. pl.* twins
gemir (i, i) to groan; to moan
general *n.* general (military); *adj.* general; **por lo general** generally; **secretario/a general** registrar
generoso/a generous
genial brilliant
gente *f. s.* people; **tener** (*irreg.*) **el don** (*m.*) **de gentes** to have charm, be charming; to get along well with people
gentilicio name of the inhabitants of country or city
gerente *m., f.* manager; **gerente de fábrica** factory manager
gerundio *gram.* gerund, present participle
gibraltareño/a Gibraltarian
gimnasia *s.* gymnastics
gimnasio gymnasium
Ginebra Geneva
gira tour; excursion
glaseado icing (*cake*)
gobernador(a) governor
gobernar (ie) to govern
gobierno government
gol *m.* goal (*soccer*); **marcar (qu) un gol** to score a goal
golpe (*m.*) **de estado** coup d'etat
gordo/a fat; **premio gordo** grand prize
gorro cap
gótico/a Gothic
gozar (c) to enjoy
grabar to record; to carve
gracias *f., pl.* thanks; **dar** (*irreg.*) **las gracias** to give thanks
gracioso/a funny; witty
grados *m. pl.* degrees (*temperature*)
graduación *f.* graduation
graduarse (me gradúo) to graduate
gráficas *f., pl.* graphics
gráfico *n.* graph
gráfico/a *adj.* graphic
Gran Bretaña Great Britain
gran, grande big, large; great; older
granizar (c) to hail
granjero/a farmer
grapadora stapler
Grecia Greece
griego/a Greek
gripe *f.* flu
gris gray
gritar to shout
grito scream *n.*; **dar** (*irreg.*) **gritos** to shout; **poner** (*irreg.*) **el grito en el cielo** to scream bloody murder
grueso/a thick; **mar** (*f.*) **gruesa** rough sea
gruñir to grunt
gruñón, gruñona grumpy, grouchy
grupo group

guante *m.* glove; baseball mitt, glove
guapo/a good-looking, handsome
guardar to put away
guardián, guardiana watchman, watchwoman
guatemalteco/a Guatemalan
guerra war
guía *f.* guide(book); *m., f.* (tour) guide; **guía telefónica** phonebook
guiar (guío) to guide
Guinea Ecuatorial Equatorial Guinea
guineoecuatoriano/a Equatorial Guinean
guión *m.* script
guionista *m., f.* scriptwriter
guisante *m.* pea
guitarra guitar
gustar to be pleasing
gusto pleasure; taste; **sobre gustos no hay nada escrito** to each his own

H

haba *f.* (*but* **el haba**) bean
habanero/a from Havana
haber *irreg.* to have *auxiliary verb with past participle; impersonal verb* there + *forms of* to be; **habérselas con** to be up against; to face; to deal with; **haber que** + *inf.* to be necessary to do (*something*)
hábil skillful
habitación *f.* room
habitante *m., f.* inhabitant
hablador(a) *n.* speaker; *adj.* talkative
hablar to speak; **hablar alto** to speak loudly; **hablar en serio** to be serious; **ni hablar** *interj.* nothing doing
hacer *irreg.* to make; to do; **hace** + *period of time* + **que** + *present tense* to have been (*doing something for a period of time*; **hace** + *time* time ago; **hacer buen/mal tiempo** to be good/bad weather; **hacer calor** to be hot (*weather*); **hacer cola** to stand in line; **hacer copias** to (photo)copy; **hacer deportes** to play, participate in sports; **hacer diabluras** to make mischief; **hacer ejercicio** to exercise; **hacer el favor de** + *inf.* to do (*someone*) the favor of (*doing something*); **hacer falta** to need (*something*); **hacer footing** to jog; **hacer fresco** to be cool (*weather*); **hacer frío** to be cold (*weather*); **hacer hincapié** to emphasize; **hacer juego (con)** to match; **hacer la compra** to do the shopping; **hacer las diligencias** to run errands; **hacer las maletas** to pack (one's suitcases); **hacer los ejercicios** to do the exercises (*school work*); **hacer preguntas** to ask questions; **hacer sol** to be sunny; **hacer viento** to be windy; **hacer una excursión** to take a (field)trip; **hacerle caso (a)** to pay attention (*to someone*); **hacerle cosquillas** to tickle (someone); **hacerse** to become, make oneself; **hacerse el tonto** to play dumb; **hacerse el/la** + *adj.* to pretend to be (*something*); **hacer(se) daño** to hurt (oneself); **hacerse el/la desentendido/a** to play innocent; **hacerse los sordos** to turn a deaf ear; **hacérsele tarde** to get, grow late; **hacía** + *period of time* + **que** + *imperfect tense* to had been (*something for a period of time*)
hacha *f.* (*but* **el hacha**) axe

hacia toward; **hacia abajo** downward; **hacia adelante** toward the front; **hacia allá** toward that place (far away); **hacia arriba** upward; **hacia atrás** backward; toward the rear; **mirar hacia el futuro** to look ahead
hacienda ranch
hada (*f.* [*but* **el hada**]): **cuento de hadas** fairy tale
haitiano/a Haitian
halcón *m.* falcon
hambre *f.* hunger; **morir (ue, u)** (*p.p.* **muerto/a**) **de hambre** to be starving; **tener** (*irreg.*) **hambre** to be, feel hungry
hamburguesa hamburger
harina flour
hasta *adv.* even; *prep.* until; **estar** (*irreg.*) **mojado/a hasta los huesos** to be soaking wet; **hasta allí** up to there; **hasta nunca** good riddance; **hasta pronto** see you soon; **hasta que** *conj.* until
hay there is, there are
hebreo Hebrew
hecho *n.* fact
hecho/a (*p.p. of* **hacer**): **estar** (*irreg.*) **hecho/a una lástima** to be a sorry sight, in a sad state; **estar** (*irreg.*) **hecho/a una sopa** to be soaking wet; **hecho/a a la medida** tailor-made; **hecho/a a mano** hand-made; **trato hecho** it's a deal
heladería ice cream parlor
helado de chocolate chocolate ice cream
helar (ie) to freeze
herido/a *n.* casualty, injured person
hermano/a brother, sister
hermoso/a beautiful
héroe *m.* hero
heroína heroine
herramienta: caja de herramientas toolbox
hervir (ie, i) to boil
hielo ice; **patinar sobre el hielo** to ice-skate
hierba: mala hierba weed
hierbajo weed
hijo/a son, daughter; *m. pl.* children
hincapié (*m.*): **hacer** (*irreg.*) **hincapié** to emphasize
historia history
historiador(a) historian
historial *m.* curriculum vitae; medical record
histórico/a historical; **novela histórica** historical novel
Holanda Holland
holandés, holandesa Dutch
holgazán, holgazana lazy
hombre *m.* man; **hombre de negocios** businessman
hombro shoulder; **encogerse (j) de hombros** to shrug one's shoulders
hondureño/a Honduran
honesto/a honest
honrado/a honest; respectable
hora hour; time; **horas punta** rush hour; **media hora** half an hour; **ser** (*irreg.*) **hora de** to be time to
horario schedule
horchata *sweet drink made from rice (Mex.) or tiger nuts (Sp.)*
hormiga ant
hormiguero anthill
horno oven; **al horno** baked
hospital *m.* hospital
hotel *m.* hotel

hoy today

huelga strike (labor); declarar una huelga to call a strike

huésped(a) guest (at a hotel)

hueso bone; estar (irreg.) mojado/a hasta los huesos to be soaking wet

huevo egg

huir (y) to flee

humedecer (zc) to dampen, moisten

humilde humble

humor m. mood; sentido del humor sense of humor

húngaro/a Hungarian

Hungría Hungary

huracán m. hurricane

I

idea idea; cambiar de idea to change one's mind

identidad f. identity

idioma m. language

iglesia church

igualdad f. equality

iluso/a n. dreamer; adj. gullible

imaginarse to imagine; to suppose

impedir (i, i) to prevent

imperativo directo gram. direct command; imperativo formal gram. formal command; imperativo negativo gram. negative command

imperfecto gram. imperfect tense; imperfecto progresivo gram. imperfect progressive

impermeable m. raincoat

impersonal: expresión (f.) impersonal gram. impersonal expression

imponente imposing; impressive

imponer (like poner) to impose

importar to matter, be important; meterse en lo que no le importa to butt into someone else's business

importante important

impresionado/a impressed

impresionante impressive

impresionista m., f. impressionist (art)

impreso/a (p.p. of imprimir) printed

impresora printer

imprimir to print

impuesto n. tax

impuesto/a adj. (p.p. of imponer) imposed

incendio fire

inclinarse to bend over

incluir (y) to include

inclusive adv. even

incoherente incoherent

incómodo/a uncomfortable; embarrassed

indefinido/a: artículo indefinido gram. indefinite article

independiente independent; cláusula independiente gram. independent (main) clause

indicar (qu) to indicate

indicativo gram. indicative (mood, tense)

indio/a Indian

indirecto/a: complemento indirecto gram. indirect object; mandato indirecto gram. indirect command; pregunta indirecta gram. indirect question

indonesio/a Indonesian

inducir (irreg.) to induce

industria industry

inesperado/a unexpected

infinitivo gram. infinitive; infinitivo compuesto gram. compound infinitive

inflación f. inflation

influir (y) to influence

información f. information

informática computer science

informe m. report

informar to inform

infusión f. infusion, tea

ingeniería engineering

ingeniero/a engineer

Inglaterra England

inglés m. English (language)

inglés, inglesa n., adj. English; Corte Inglés department store chain in Spain

iniciar to begin, start; to initiate; iniciar la sesión to log on

inmediato/a immediate; de inmediato immediately

inmigrante m., f. immigrant

inocente innocent

inolvidable unforgettable

inquilino/a tenant

inscribir (p.p. inscrito) to register, enroll

inscrito/a (p.p. of inscribir) registered

insistir (en) to insist (on)

insolente insolent

instalar to install; instalarse en to move in

instrucción f. instruction

instrumento instrument; instrumento musical musical instrument

intelectual: cociente (m.) intelectual IQ

inteligencia intelligence

inteligente intelligent

intención f. intention

intenso/a intense

intentar + inf. to try, attempt to (do something)

intercambio n. exchange

interés m. interest; tener (irreg.) interés en + inf. to be interested in (doing something)

interesado/a n. interested person, party

interesante interesting

interesar to interest

interferencia interference

internacional international

intérprete m., f. interpreter

interrogativo/a: palabra interrogativa gram. question word, interrogative

interrumpir to interrupt

introducción f. introduction

introducir irreg. to introduce

inútil useless

inválido/a disabled, handicapped

inverso/a opposite; a la inversa the other way

invertir (ie, i) to invest

investigación f. investigation

investigar (gu) to investigate

invierno winter

invitado/a n. guest (at a party)

invitar (a) to invite (to)

involucrar to involve; involucrarse to be, get involved

ir *irreg.* to go; **ir al cine** to go to the movies; **ir de compras** to go shopping; **ir de pesca** to go fishing; **ir de vacaciones** to go on vacation; **irse** to go away

Irak Iraq

iraní *m., f.* (*pl.* **iraníes**) Iranian

iraquí *m., f.* (*pl.* **iraquíes**) Iraqi

Irlanda Ireland

irlandés, irlandesa Irish

irritar to irritate; **irritarse** to get irritated

isla island; **Isla de Pascua** Easter Island (Chile)

israelí *m., f.* (*pl.* **israelíes**) Israeli

italiano/a Italian

itinerario itinerary

izquierdo/a left; **a la (mano) izquierda** on the left

jactarse de to boast about

jamaicano/a Jamaican

jamás never; **nunca jamás** never ever; never again; no more; **jamás de los jamases** never ever

japonés *m.* Japanese

japonés, japonesa *n. adj.* Japanese

jarabe *m.* syrup

jardín *m.* garden; yard

jarra jug; mug

jarro jug; jug full

jazz *m.* jazz

jeans *m. pl.* jeans

jefe/a boss; **jefe/a de redacción** editor-in-chief

Jordania Jordan

jordano/a Jordanian

joven *n. m., f.* young man, young woman; *adj.* young

joyas *f., pl.* jewelry

joyería jewelry store

jubilarse to retire

judaísmo Judaism

judío/a Jew; Jewish

juego game; **hacer** (*irreg.*) **juego (con)** to match; **Juegos Olímpicos** Olympics, Olympic Games

juez *m. f.* judge

jugador(a) player

jugar (ue, u) (gu) (a) to play (*a game, sport*)

jugo juice; **jugo de fruta/naranja** fruit/orange juice

juguete *m.* toy; **caja de juguetes** toy chest

juicio: a mi juicio in my opinion

juntar to join

junto *adv.* close; **junto a** close to, right next to

juntos/as *adj.* together

juramento: bajo juramento under/upon oath

jurar to judge; **tenérsela** (*irreg.*) **jurada a uno/a** to have it in for someone

juventud *f.* youth

kilómetro kilometer

Kosovo Kosova

kosovano/a Kosovar

kuwaití (*pl.* **kuwaitíes**) Kuwaiti

L

laberinto labyrinth

labio lip; **pintarse los labios** to put on lipstick

laboratorio laboratory; **laboratorio de lenguas** language lab

labores (*f. pl.*) **domésticas** housework

lado side; **al lado** *adv.* next door; **al lado de** *prep.* next to; **en/por algún lado** somewhere; **en/por ningún lado** nowhere; **por todos lados** everywhere; **por un lado..., por otro** on the one hand ..., on the other hand

ladrar to bark

ladrillo brick

ladrón, ladrona thief

lago lake

lamentarse (de) to complain (about); to regret

lámpara lamp

lana wool

langosta lobster

lanzar (c) to throw

lápiz *m.* (*pl.* **lápices**) pencil

largo/a long; lengthy; **a largo plazo** in the long run; **a lo largo de** *prep.* along; **de largo** in length

lástima pity; **estar** (*irreg.*) **hecho/a una lástima** to be a sorry sight, in a sad state; **¡qué lástima!** what a pity!

lavarse la cabeza to wash one's hair

lastimar(se) to hurt (oneself)

laurel (*m.*): **dormirse** (*irreg.*) **en los laureles** to rest on one's laurels

lavado *n.* wash

lavandero/a laundry worker

lavaplatos *m. inv.* dishwasher

lavar to wash (*someone, something*); **lavar la ropa** to do the laundry; **lavarse** to wash up; **lavarse el pelo** to shampoo one's hair

leal loyal

leche *f.* milk; **dulce** (*m.*) **de leche** *a sweet caramel spread popular in Argentina*

leer (y) (*p.p.* **leído**) to read

legumbre *f.* vegetable

lejos *adv.* far off, far away; **lejos de** *prep.* far from

lengua language; **laboratorio de lenguas** language lab; **mala lengua** vicious tongue

lento/a slow; **a fuego lento** on low (heat), over low heat

león *m.* lion

leona lioness

leopardo leopard

letra cursiva italics

levantar to raise, pick up; **levantar pesas** to lift weights; **levantarse** to get up, rise

ley *f.* law

libanés, libanesa Lebanese

Líbano Lebanon

libertad *f.* liberty

libertador(a) liberator

libra pound

libre free; **al aire libre** *adj.* open-air; *adv.* outdoors; **libre mercado** free market

librería bookstore

libreta notebook

libro book; **libro de cocina** cookbook; **libro de texto** textbook; **libro de consulta** reference book

licencia license

líder *m., f.* leader

liebre *m.* hare; **dar** (*irreg.*) **gato por liebre** to put something over on someone

ligero/a light

limarse las uñas to file one's nails

limeño/a from Lima (Peru)

limón *m.* lemon

limosina limousine

limpiaparabrisas *m. inv.* windshield wiper

limpiar to clean; **limpiar el polvo** to dust; **limpiarse las uñas** to remove the polish from one's nails; **limpiarse los dientes** to brush one's teeth

limpieza *n.* cleaning; **producto para la limpieza** cleaning product

línea line

linterna flashlight

lío mess; *pl.* trouble; **meterse en un lío** to get into a mess

liquidación sale, liquidation

lista *n.* list; **pasar lista** to take attendance

listo/a ready; clever, responsible; **preparados, listos, ya** ready, set, go

literario/a literary

literatura literature

llamar to call; **llamar a la puerta** to knock (on a door); **llamar la atención** to attract attention; **llamarse** to be named, called

llano/a: palabra llana *gram. Spanish word with stress on next-to-last syllable*

llave *f.* key; **bajo llave** under lock and key

llavero key ring

llegada *n.* arrival; **a nuestra llegada** upon our arrival

llegado/a: recién llegado/a new arrival; newly arrived

llegar (gu) to arrive; **llegar a** + *inf.* to get to (*do something*); to succeed in (*doing something*); **llegar a ser** to become

lleno/a full; **mar llena** high tide

llenar to fill (up, out)

llevar to wear; to carry; **llevar** + *time* + *gerund* to have been (*doing something*) for (*time*); **llevar a** to lead to; **llevarse bien/mal (con)** to get along / not get along (with); *Lo que el viento se llevó Gone with the Wind*

llorar to cry

llover (ue) to rain; **llover a cántaros** to rain cats and dogs

lloviznar to sprinkle

lluvia rain

lo bueno the good thing, news; **lo de siempre** the same old story; **lo fácil** the easy thing; **lo físico** physical traits; **lo mismo** *pron.* the same (thing)

loco/a *n.* crazy person; madman, madwoman; *adj.* crazy, mad

locutor(a) announcer; presenter

lógico/a logical

login *m.* log-in

logon *m.* log-on

logoff *m.* log-off

lograr + *inf.* to succeed in (*doing something*)

londinense *m., f.* Londoner

Londres London

longitud *f.* longitude

loro parrot

lotería lottery; **billete** (*m.*) **de lotería** lottery ticket

lucir (zc) to wear; to sport, show off

luego then, afterward; **luego que** as soon as

lugar *m.* place; room, space; **en/por algún lugar** somewhere; **en/por ningún lugar** nowhere; **en primer lugar** in the first place; **en lugar de** instead of; **tener** (*irreg.*) **lugar** to take place

lujoso/a luxurious

luna moon

luto: estar (*irreg.*) **de luto** to be in mourning

luz *f.* light; **luz piloto** pilot (light); **luz roja** red light; **traje** (*m.*) **de luces** bullfighter's costume

M

madera wood

madre *f.* mother

madrileño/a from Madrid

madrina godmother

madrugar (gu) to get up early

maestro/a *n.* teacher; **maestro/a de obras** master builder

maestro/a (*adj.*): **obra maestra** masterpiece

mágico/a magic

magnífico/a magnificent

magnitud *f.* magnitude; dimension

maíz *m.* corn; **palomitas** (*f. pl.*) **de maíz** popcorn

mal *adv.* badly, poorly; **caerle** (*irreg.*) **mal** to make a bad impression on someone; **llevarse mal (con)** to not get along (with); **menos mal (que)** thank goodness, it's a good thing (that); **pasarlo mal** to have a bad time; **portarse mal** to behave badly; **quedarle mal** to look bad (*on someone, something*); **salir** (*irreg.*) **mal** to turn, come out badly

mal, malo/a *adj.* bad; **de mala gana** reluctantly; **hacer** (*irreg.*) **mal tiempo** to be bad weather; **mala hierba** weed; **mala lengua** vicious tongue; **por las buenas o por las malas** whether one likes it or not

malagueño/a from Málaga

malcriado/a ill-mannered

maldecir (*like decir*) to curse

maleta suitcase; **hacer** (*irreg.*) **las maletas** to pack

maletero (car) trunk

maletín *m.* briefcase

malgache *m., f.* from Madagascar

malhumorado/a in a bad mood

Mallorca Majorca

mallorquín, mallorquina Majorcan

maltés, maltesa Maltese

Malvinas *f. pl.* Falkland Islands

malvinense *m., f.* from the Falkland Islands

malvinero/a from the Falkland Islands

mami *f.* mom, mommy

mancha spot; stain

mandar to send; to order; **mandar a** + *inf.* to order to (*do something*)

mandato *gram.* command

manejar to drive; **permiso de manejar** driving permit/license

manera way; **de alguna manera** somehow; **de cierta manera** in a certain way; **de manera que** so that; **de ninguna manera** in no way

mano *f.* hand; **a la mano derecha/izquierda** on the right/left; **dar** (*irreg.*) **la mano** to shake hands; **hecho/a a mano** hand-made

mantel *m.* tablecloth

mantener (*like* **tener**) to maintain; **mantenerse en forma** to stay in shape

manual *n. m.* manual

manzana apple; (street) block

manzanilla chamomile tea

manzano apple tree

mañana tomorrow; **pasado mañana** day after tomorrow

mapa *m.* map

maquillado/a made-up

maquillar to put makeup (*on someone*); **maquillarse** to put on makeup

máquina machine; **máquina de lavar** washing machine

maquinilla de afeitar electric razor

mar *m. and f.* sea; **mar brava** very rough sea; **mar gruesa** rough sea; **mar llena** high tide; **mar rizada** choppy sea

maravilla marvel, wonder

maravilloso/a marvelous, wonderful

marca brand

marcar (qu) to dial; to mark; to score (*a goal*)

marcha: ponerse (*irreg.*) **en marcha** to get to work

marear to make dizzy; **marearse** to get, feel dizzy

margarita daisy

marido husband

marino/a *adj.* marine

mariscos *m. pl.* shellfish

marketing *m.* marketing

marrón brown

marroquí *m., f.* Moroccan

Marruecos Morocco

mártir *m., f.* martyr

más more; **más vale que** it's better that; **nunca más** never again; no more

mascar (qu) to chew

masculino/a masculine

masticar (qu) to chew

matar to kill; **matar de aburrimiento** to bore to death

matemáticas *f. pl.* mathematics

materia (school) subject

matrícula tuition; **placa de matrícula** license plate

matricularse to register

maullar to meow

maullido *n.* meow

maya Mayan

mayor older; oldest; greater; greatest

mecánico/a mechanic

mecánico/a *adj.* mechanical; **escalera mecánica** escalator

mecedora rocking chair

mecer (z) to rock

mediador(a) mediator

mediados (*m. pl.*): **a/para mediados de** about the middle of

medianoche *f.* midnight

mediante by means of

media sock (*L.A.*); stocking (*Sp.*)

médico/a *n.* (medical) doctor

medicina medicine

medieval Medieval

medido/a: hecho/a a la medida tailor-made

medio *n.* half; middle; *adv.* half

medio/a *adj.* half; middle; average; **de porte** (*m.*) **medio** (*person*) of medium build; **día** (*m.*) **de por medio** every other day; **Edad** (*f.*) **Media** *s.* Middle Ages

mediodía *m.* midday, noon

medir (i, i) to measure

Mediterráneo *n.* Mediterranean (Sea)

mediterráneo/a *adj.* Mediterranean

mejilla cheek

mejor better; best

mejorar(se) to improve (oneself)

melocotón *m.* peach

melocotonero peach tree

memoria memory; **de memoria** (*to learn, know*) by heart

mencionar to mention

menor younger; **no tener la menor idea** to not have any idea (*about something*)

menos *adv.* less; least; *prep.* except, but; minus; **a menos que** *conj.* unless; **lo menos posible** as little as possible; **por lo menos** at least

mensaje *m.* message; **mensaje electrónico** e-mail (message)

mentir (ie, i) to lie

mentiroso/a *n.* liar; *adj.* lying

menudo: a menudo often

mercadeo marketing

mercado market; **mercado al aire libre** open-air market; **libre mercado** free market

merecer (zc) to deserve

merendar (ie) to have (an afternoon) snack, a picnic

merienda snack

mes *m.* month; **al mes de** + *inf.* after a month of (*doing something*)

mesa table; **poner** (*irreg.*) **la mesa** to set the table

meteorológico/a: pronóstico meteorológico weather forecast

meter to put in; to insert; **meterse a** + *inf.* to start to (*do something*); **meterse en** to get involved in; **meterse en lo que no le importa** to butt into someone else's business; **meterse en un lío** to get into a mess

método method

metro meter; subway; **parada de metro** subway station

metropolitano/a metropolitan; **Metropolitana** Metropolitan (Opera)

mexicano/a Mexican

mezquita mosque

microondas *m. inv.* microwave

miedo fear; **tener** (*irreg.*) **miedo** to be afraid

miembro member

mientras while

migas *f. pl.* crumbs

mil *m.* (a) thousand; **mil millones** *m. pl.* (a) billion

milagro miracle

milésimo one-thousandth

milla mile

millón *m.* million

millonario/a millionaire

mimado/a spoiled (*person*)

mineral: agua (*f.* [*but* **el agua**]) **mineral** mineral water

minuto minute

mío/a(s) *poss. adj.* my; *poss. pron.*(of) mine
mirar to look at
misa del gallo midnight mass
Misisipí *m.* Mississippi (River)
mismo *adv.* even: **ahora mismo** right now; at once; **lo mismo** *pron.* the same (thing); **por lo mismo** for that very reason
mismo/a *adj.* same; *emphasis with noun or pronoun*: **(yo/tú) mismo/a** myself/yourself, **(tú) mismo/a** yourself, *and so on*; **consigo mismo/a** with himself, herself, yourself (*form. s.*); **consigo mismos/as** with yourself (*form. s., pl.*); themselves
misterio mystery
mochila backpack; knapsack
moda fashion; style; **de moda** in style
modelo *n., adj* model; *n. m., f.* model (*person*)
módem *m.* modem
modismo idiom
modista *m., f.* fashion designer
modo way, manner; *gram.* (verb) mode; **de algún modo** somehow; **de modo que** so that; **de ningún modo** in no way; **ni modo** no way
mojado/a wet; **estar** (*irreg.*) **mojado/a hasta los huesos** to be soaking wet
mojarse to get wet
molestar to annoy, bother; **molestarse** to get annoyed
molesto/a annoying
momento moment
monada: ¡de eso nada, monada! *interj.* None of that!, No way!
moneda coin
monja nun
mono monkey
monstruo monster
montaña mountain; **montaña rusa** roller coaster
montar to set up, mount; to ride; **montar a caballo** to ride horseback; **montar en bicicleta** to ride a bike, go bike riding
monte *m.* mountain
montura frame (*eyeglasses*)
moqueta carpet (*Sp.*)
morado/a purple
moreno/a brunette
morir(se) (ue, u) (*p.p.* **muerto**) to die; **morirse de envidia** to be consumed by envy; **morir de hambre** to be starving; **morirse de risa** to die laughing
mortero mortar
mosca: por si las moscas just in case
moscovita *m., f.* from Moscow
Moscú Moscow
mosquito mosquito
mostrador *m.* counter
mostrar (ue) to show
motivo motive; **por motivo de** on account of
moto *f.* (*abbrev. of* **motocicleta**) motorcycle
motocicleta motorcycle
mover (ue) to put in motion; **moverse** to move, stir, budge
móvil: teléfono móvil cell phone
movimiento movement
mozo/a server (*restaurant*)
muchacho/a boy, girl
mucho *adv.* a lot, much; very
mucho/a *adj.* a lot (of); *pl.* many

mudarse to move (*change residence*)
mueble *m.* piece of furniture; *pl.* furniture; **tienda de muebles** furniture store
muela tooth; molar; **dolor** (*m.*) **de muelas** toothache
muerto/a (*p.p. of* **morir**) **no tener** (*irreg.*) **dónde caerse muerto** to not have a penny to one's name
mujer *f.* woman; wife; **mujer policía** policewoman
muleta crutch
multa fine
multimedia: aparato multimedia multimedia equipment
multiplicar (qu) to multiply
multitud *f.* crowd
muñeca doll
mural *m.* mural
museo museum
música music
musical: instrumento musical musical instrument
músico/a musician

N

nacer (zc) to be born
nacido/a born; **recién nacido/a** newborn
nacimiento: fecha de nacimiento birth date
nación *f.* nation
nacional national
nacionalidad *f.* nationality
nacionalista *m., f.* nationalist
nada *pron.* nothing, (not) anything; *adv.* at all; **¡de eso nada, monada!** *interj.* None of that!, No way!; **de nada** you're welcome; **dentro de nada** in a moment; **más que nada** more than anything; **más vale algo que nada** something's better than nothing; **nada de eso** nothing of the sort; **nada de nada** nothing at all; **nada más** that's all; **no conocer (zc) de nada** to not know (*someone*) from Adam; **no servir (i, i) para nada** to be useless; **no tener** (*irreg.*) **nada de** + *noun* to not have any _____ at all; **por nada** you're welcome; **por nada del mundo** for nothing in the world; **sobre gustos no hay nada escrito** to each his own; **tener** (*irreg.*) **en nada** to think very little of, take no notice of (*something, someone*)
nadar to swim
nadie no one, nobody; **nadie más** nobody else; **no ser** (*irreg.*) **nadie para quejarse** to have no right to complain; **ser** (*irreg.*) **un don nadie** to be a nobody
nailón *m.* nylon
nanosegundo nanosecond
naranja orange (*fruit*); **jugo de naranja** orange juice
naranjo orange tree
nariz *f.* (*pl.* **narices**) nose; **narices al aire** stuck-up (*lit.* noses in the air)
narración *f.* narration
narrador(a) narrator
natación *n., f.* swimming
natalidad *f.* birth rate
natural natural; **alimentos** (*m. pl.*) **naturales** health food; **ciencias** (*f. pl.*) **naturales** natural science
naval: Batalla Naval Battleship (*board game*)

navegar (gu) en la Red to surf, navigate the Web
Navidad *f.* Christmas
necesario/a necessary
necesidad *f.* necessity
necesitar to need; **necesitar** + *inf.* to have to (*do something*)
negar (gu) to deny
negativo/a negative; **imperativo/mandato negativo** *gram.* negative command; **palabra negativa** *gram.* negative word
negocios *m. pl.* business; **hombre** *m.* **de negocios** businessman
negro/a black; **verlo todo negro** to be pessimistic
neocelandés, neocelandesa New Zealander
neoyorquino/a New Yorker
nervios (*m. pl.*): **ataque** (*m.*) **de nervios** panic attack; **crisis** (*f.*) **de nervios** panic attack; **tener** (*irreg.*) **los nervios en punta** to be on edge
neutro/a: artículo neutro *gram.* neuter article
nervioso/a nervous
neutro/a neuter
nevar (ie) to snow
nevera freezer
ni nor; **ni... ni...** neither . . . nor . . . ; **ni hablar** *interj.* nothing doing; **ni modo** nothing doing; **ni siquiera** not even; **ni uno** not even one; **no tener** (*irreg.*) **ni idea** to not have the slightest idea
nieto/a grandson, granddaughter; *m., pl.* grandchildren
nieve *f.* snow
ningún, ninguna no, none; **bajo ningún concepto** under no circumstance; **de ningún modo** in no way; **de ninguna manera** in no way; **en/por ningún lugar** nowhere; **en/por ninguna parte** nowhere
niñez *f.* childhood
niño/a boy, girl; *m. pl.* children
no no; not; **claro que no** *interj.* of course not; **ya no** no longer
Nóbel: Premio Nóbel Nobel prize
noche *f.* night; **de noche** at night; during the night; **de/por la noche** at night; **esta noche** tonight; **toda la noche** all night
nochebuena Christmas Eve
nocturno/a *adj.* night
Noé Noah; **arca** (*f.* [*but* **el arca**]) **de Noé** Noah's ark
nombre *m.* name
norte *m.* north
Norteamérica North America
norteamericano/a North American
noruego/a Norwegian
Noruego Norway
nota grade (*in class*)
noticia piece of news; *pl.* news
noticiero newscast
novela novel; **novela fantástica** fantasy novel
novelista *m., f.* novelist
noveno/a ninth
novio/a boyfriend, girlfriend; fiancé(e); groom, bride
nube (*f.*): **poner** (*irreg.*) **por las nubes** to praise to the skies
nuclear: energía nuclear nuclear energy
nuevo/a: Año Nuevo New Year; **Nueva York** New York; **Nueva Zelanda** New Zealand
número number

nunca never; **casi nunca** hardly ever; **cuento de nunca acabar** never-ending story; **hasta nunca** good-bye forever; **nunca jamás** never again, no more; **nunca más** never again; no more

O

obedecer (zc) to obey
obediente obedient
objeto object; **con el objeto de** in order to; **objeto de valor** valuable object; **oficina de objetos perdidos** lost and found
obligar (gu) a + *inf.* to force to (*do something*); to compel to (*do something*)
oboe *m.* oboe
obra work; **maestro/a de obras** master builder; **obra de teatro** play; **obra literaria** literary work
obrero/a worker, laborer
observación *f.* observation
observar to observe
obtener (*like* **tener**) to obtain
obvio/a obvious
océano ocean
octavo/a eighth
ocultar to hide
ocupación *f.* occupation
ocupado/a busy
ocuparse de to take care of
ocurrir to happen
ocurrírsele to dawn on (*someone*); to get the idea of
odiar to hate
odio hate; **carta de odio** hate mail
oeste *m.* west
ofender to offend; to insult; to hurt (*someone*); **ofenderse** to get offended; to get insulted; to feel hurt
oferta *n.* offer
oficina office; **oficina de objetos perdidos** lost and found
ofrecer (zc) to offer; **ofrecerse a** + *inf.* to offer to (*do something*)
oído *n.* (inner) ear
oír (y) to hear
ojalá (que) I wish (that); I hope (that)
ojo eye; **costarle (ue) un ojo de la cara** to cost an arm and a leg
oler (ue) (huelo) to smell
olímpico/a: Juegos Olímpicos Olympics, Olympic Games
oliva: aceite (*m.*) **de oliva** olive oil
olor *m.* odor
olvidar(se) (de) to forget
onceavo one-eleventh
opción *f.* option
opinar to think
opinión *f.* opinion
oponer (*like* **poner**) to oppose; **oponerse (a)** to oppose, be against
oportuno/a timely; appropriate
optativa *n.* elective (*subject*)
oración *f.* sentence
orangután *m.* orangutan
orden *m.* order, tidiness; *f.* order, command; **poner** (*irreg.*) **en orden** to straighten up

ordenador *m.* computer (*Sp.*)
ordenar to clean up; to order
ordeñar to milk
oreja (outer) ear
organizar (c) to organize
oriental: Europea Oriental East Europe
origen *m.* origin
oro gold *n.* oro; **Ricitos de Oro** Goldilocks
orquesta orchestra; **director(a) de orquesta** conductor; **orquesta sinfónica** symphony orchestra
ortodoncista orthodontist
ortografía *n.* spelling
ortográfico/a *adj.* spelling
Óscar: estatuilla del Óscar Oscar (*trophy*); **premio Óscar** Oscar (*award*)
oscuro/a dark
oso bear
ostra oyster
otoño fall (*season*)
otro/a other; another
oveja sheep

P

paciente *n., adj. m., f.* patient
Pacífico Pacific (Ocean)
padecer (zc) to suffer; to endure
padre *m.* father
padrino godfather; *pl.* godparents
pagado/a: estar (*irreg.*) **muy pagado/a de sí mismo/a** to be very satisfied with oneself
página page
paisaje *m.* landscape
país *m.* country; **Países Bajos** Netherlands
paja straw
pájaro bird
pakistaní (*pl.* **pakistaníes**) Pakistani
palabra word; **palabra aguda** *gram. Spanish word with stress on the last syllable;* **palabra interrogativa** *gram.* question word, interrogative; **palabra llana** *gram. Spanish word with stress on next-to-last syllable*
palacio palace
palco box (seats) (*in a theater*)
palidecer (zc) to turn pale
pálido/a pale
palomitas (*f. pl.*) **de maíz** popcorn
pan *m.* bread
panadero/a baker
panameño/a Panamanian
panda *m.* panda (bear)
pandilla gang
pantalla screen
pantalones *m. pl.* pants
pantera panther
papá *m.* dad, daddy
papa potato; **papas fritas** French fries
papel *m.* paper; role, part (*in a play, movie*)
papelería stationary store
papi *m.* daddy
paquete *m.* package
par *m.* pair
para *prep.* (intended) for; by (*deadline*); to (*a place*); **para** + *inf.* (in order) to (*do something*); **para atrás**

backwards; to the back; **para entonces** by then; **para finales de** at the end of; **para que** *conj.* so that; **¿para qué?** for what purpose?
parabrisas *m. inv.* windshield
parachoques *m. inv.* bumper
parada *n.* stop; **parada de autobuses** bus stop; **parada de metro** subway station
parador *m. state-run hotel housed in a historical building* (*Sp.*)
paraguas *m. inv.* umbrella
paraguayo/a Paraguayan
parar to stop; **pararse** to stand up (*L.A.*)
parecer (zc) to seem; **a su parecer** in one's opinion; **parecer** + *inf.* to seem to (*do something*); **parecerse (a)** to resemble
pared *f.* wall
pareja couple
paréntesis *m. inv.* parentheses
pariente *m., f.* relative
parisiense Parisian
parque *m.* park; **parque de atracciones** theme park
parte *f.* part; **de parte de** on behalf of; **en/por alguna parte** somewhere; **en/por ninguna parte** nowhere; **por su parte** as far as one is concerned; **por todas partes** everywhere
participante *m., f.* participant
participar to participate
participio *gram.* participle; **participio pasado** *gram.* past participle; **participio presente** *gram.* present participle, gerund
partido game; match
partir to break; to cut; to divide
pasado/a *adj.* last; *n.* past; **participio pasado** *gram.* past participle; **pasado mañana** day after tomorrow
pasajero/a passenger
pasaporte *m.* passport
pasar to spend; to pass; to happen; to run (*a red light*); **pasar a ser** to become; **pasar la aspiradora** to vacuum; **pasar lista** to take attendance; **pasarlo bien/mal** to have a good/bad time
pasatiempo pastime, hobby
pascua: Isla de Pascua Easter Island
pasear to walk, take a walk; **pasearse** to stroll
paseo *n.* stroll, walk; avenue; **dar** (*irreg.*) **un paseo** to take a walk
pasivo/a: construcción pasiva *gram.* passive construction; **voz** (*f.*) **pasiva** *gram.* passive voice
paso step; footstep
pastelería pastry shop
pastel *m.* cake; pie
pastilla pill
patata potato (*Sp.*)
patinar to skate; **patinar sobre el hielo** to ice-skate
patineta scooter
patrocinado/a sponsored
pavimentar to pave
payasada: hacer (*irreg.*) **payasadas** to clown around
paz *f.* peace; **dejar en paz** to leave alone
peatón, peatona pedestrian
pedazo piece; **hacer** (*irreg.*) **pedazos a** to destroy
pedir (i, i) to ask for; to order; **pedir disculpas** to apologize
pegar (gu) to stick (*to something*); to hit (*someone*)

peinar to comb (*someone's*) hair; **peinarse** to comb one's hair

peine *m.* comb

pelado/a peeled

pelar to peel

peldaños (*m. pl.*) **del éxito** ladder of success

pelear to fight

película movie

peligro danger

peligroso/a dangerous

pelo hair; **escaparse por un pelo** to have a narrow escape, to escape by the skin of one's teeth; **lavarse el pelo** to shampoo one's hair; **pasar el examen por los pelos** to barely get through an exam; **tomarle el pelo** to pull someone's leg; **traído/a por los pelos** far-fetched

pelota ball

peluquero/a hairdresser (*person*)

peluquería hairdresser (*salon*)

peña rock

pendiente *adj.* pending; *n., m., pl.* earrings; **todo está pendiente** it's all up in the air

pensamiento thought

pensar (ie) to think; **pensar + *inf.*** to intend, plan (*to do something*)

peor worse

pequeño/a small

pera pear

peral *m.* pear tree

percepción *f.* perception

perder (ie) to lose; to miss (*a train, bus, and so on*); **perderse** to get lost

perecer (zc) to perish

pereza laziness

perezoso/a lazy

perfeccionar to perfect

perfecto/a perfect; **condicional perfecto** *gram.* conditional perfect; **futuro perfecto** *gram.* future perfect; **perfecto de subjuntivo** *gram.* present subjunctive

perfume *m.* perfume

periódico newspaper

perla pearl

permanecer (zc) to remain, stay

permiso de manejar driving permit/license

permitir to permit, allow

perro/a dog; alone; **perro caliente** hot dog

perseguir (*like* **seguir**) to pursue; to persecute; to aim for

personaje *m.* character

personal: aseo personal personal hygiene; **clave** *f.* **personal** PIN (personal identification number)

personalidad *f.* personality

perspectiva perspective

perspicaz *f.* perceptive

persuadir (a) to persuade (to)

pertenecer (zc) to belong

pesar to weigh; **a pesar de** in spite of; **pesarse** to weigh oneself

pesas *f. pl.* weights; **levantar pesas** to lift weights

pesca: ir (*irreg.*) **de pesca** to go fishing

pescado fish (*cooked*)

pescar (qu) to fish

pesimista *m., f.* pessimist

peso weight; *monetary unit in some Latin American countries;* **bajar de peso** to lose weight

pestaña eyelash

petróleo petroleum; oil

pez *m.* (*pl.* **peces**) fish (*animal*)

pianista *m., f.* pianist

picado/a chopped

picadura (insect) bite

picante hot, spicy; **pimienta picante** hot pepper

picar (qu) to chop

picnic (*m.*): **hacer** (*irreg.*) **un picnic**

pie *m.* foot; **a pie** on foot; **ponerse** (*irreg.*) **de pie** to stand up (*Sp.*)

piel *f.* skin

pierna leg

pieza piece; **pieza de repuesto** spare part

pila battery

piloto *adj., inv.:* **apartamento piloto** model apartment; **luz** (*f.*) **piloto** pilot (light)

pimienta pepper (*spice*); **pimienta picante** hot pepper

pimiento pepper (*vegetable*)

pincel *m.* paintbrush

pinchazo blowout

pintar to paint; **pintarse** to put on makeup; **pintarse los labios** to put on lipstick

pintor(a) painter

pintura painting

pirámide *f.* pyramid

Pirineos Pyrenees (Mountains)

pisar to stand on; to step on

piscina (swimming) pool

piso floor (*of a building*)

pista hint, clue; (running) track; (skating) rink; **seguir** (*irreg.*) **la pista** to follow the lead, trail

pizarra (chalk) board

placa (de matrícula) license plate

planchar to iron

plan *m.* plan

planeta *m.* planet

planilla de retiro withdrawal form, slip

plata silver; money; **bandeja de plata** silver platter; **ganar plata** to earn money

plátano banana

platicar (qu) to chat

plato plate, dish; dish (*recipe*); **plato principal** main course

playa beach

plaza town square

plazo period (*of time*); **a corto/largo plazo** in the short/long run

pleno: en pleno centro in the middle of downtown

plomo: soldadito de plomo tin soldier

pluma feather

plumón *m.* down (*feather*)

pluscuamperfecto *gram.* pluperfect

plusmarquista *m., f.* record holder, record breaker

pobre *n. m., f.* poor person; *adj.* poor

pobreza poverty

pocilga pigsty

poco *adv.* little; **hace poco** not too long ago; **poco a poco** little by little; **por poco** almost

poco/a *adj.* little; *pl.* few; **poco/a transitado/a** with little traffic

poder *irreg.* can, to be able to

poema *m.* poem

poesía poetry

poeta *m., f.* poet

polaco/a Polish

policía *m., f.* police officer; *f.* police (force)

policíaco/a *adj.* police

poliéster *m.* polyester

política *n. s.* politics

político/a *n.* politician; *adj.* political; **ciencias** (*f. pl.*) **políticas** political science

pollo chicken

Polonia Poland

polvo dust; **limpiar el polvo** to dust

poner *irreg.* (*p.p.* **puesto**) to put; **poner al horno** to put in the oven; **ponerse el esmalte de uñas** to polish one's nails; **poner el grito en el cielo** to scream bloody murder; **poner en orden** to straighten up; **poner excusas** to make excuses; **poner la mesa** to set the table; **poner por las nubes** to praise to the skies; **ponerse** to put on (*clothing*); **ponerse** + *adj.* to become + *adj.*; **ponerse a** + *inf.* to begin to (*do something*); **ponerse al tanto** to catch up on the news; **ponerse de acuerdo** to come to an agreement; **ponerse de pie** (*Sp.*) to stand up; **ponerse de rodillas** to kneel; **ponerse en contacto** to get in touch; **ponerse en marcha** to get going

por by; for; through, around; along, by way of; because of; times, by; **por ahí** around there; **por ahora** for now; **por algún lado/lugar/sitio** somewhere; **por alguna parte** somewhere; **por allá** around there (far away); **por allí** around there; **por aquel entonces** at that time; **por aquí** around here; **por casualidad** by chance; **por ciento** percent; **por cierto** certainly; **por completo** completely; **por consecuencia** consequently; **por consiguiente** consequently; **por culpa de** because of, through the fault of; **por dentro y por fuera** inside and outside; **por desgracia** unfortunately; **por detrás** behind (*someone's*) back/the back of (*something*); **por ejemplo** for example; **por entre** through; between; **por eso** therefore; **por escrito** in writing; **por favor** please; **por fin** finally; **por la mañana/tarde** in the morning/afternoon (evening); **por la noche** at night; **por las buenas o por las malas** whether one likes it or not; **por lo común** usually; **por lo demás** furthermore; **por lo general** generally; **por lo menos** at least; **por lo mismo** for that very reason; **por lo pronto** for the time being; **por lo tanto** therefore; **por lo visto** apparently; **por los cuatro costados** on both sides (of the family); **por medio de** by means of; **por motivo de** on account of; **por nada** you're welcome; **por nada del mundo** for nothing in the world; **por ningún lugar** nowhere; **por ninguna parte** nowhere; **por poco** almost; **¿por qué?** why?; **por si acaso** just in case; **por su cuenta** on one's own; **por su parte** as far as one is concerned; **por supuesto** of course; **por todas partes** everywhere; **por último** finally; **por un lado..., por otro** on the one hand . . ., on the other

porcelana: estatuilla de porcelana china figurine

porcentaje *m.* percentage

portaaviones *m. inv.* aircraft carrier

portarse bien/mal to behave well/badly

portátil: computadora portátil laptop (computer)

porte *m.*: **de porte medio** (*person*) of medium build

porteño/a from Buenos Aires

portugués, portuguesa Portuguese

pos: en pos de *prep.* after

poseer (*p.p.* **poseído**) to have, possess

posesión *f.* possession

posesivo: adjetivo posesivo *gram.* possessive adjective

posgraduado/a *adj.* graduate

posibilidad *f.* possibility

posponer (*like* **poner**) to postpone

pospuesto/a (*p.p. of* **posponer**) postponed

postal: (tarjeta) postal postcard

posteriormente subsequently

practicar (qu) to practice; **practicar deportes** to play, practice sports

preceder to precede

precio price

precioso/a lovely, beautiful; precious

preciso precise; clear; **es preciso (que)** it's necessary (that)

precolombino pre-Columbian

predecir (*like* **decir**) (*p.p.* **predicho**) predicted

predicho/a (*p.p. of* **predecir**) predicted

preferencia preference

preferir (ie, i) to prefer

pregunta question; **hacer** (*irreg.*) **preguntas** to ask questions; **pregunta indirecta** *gram.* indirect question

preguntar to ask (a question)

preguntón, preguntona *n.* busybody; *adj.* nosy; inquisitive

premio prize, award; **premio gordo** grand prize; **Premio Nóbel** Nobel Prize; **premio Óscar** Oscar (award)

prender to turn on

prensa press

preocupación worry

preocupado/a worried

preocupar to worry someone; **preocuparse (por)** to worry (about)

preparado/a prepared; ready; **preparados, listos, ya** ready, set, go

preparar to prepare; **prepararse** to get ready

preposición *f. gram.* preposition

preposicional *gram.* prepositional (*pronoun*)

presencia presence

presentador(a) presenter

presentar(se) to present (oneself)

presente *m.* present; *gram.* present (tense); **present perfecto** *gram.* present perfect; **tener** (*irreg.*) **presente** to keep in mind

presidencial presidential

presidente *m., f.* president

prestado/a: pedir (i, i) prestado to borrow (*something*)

préstamo loan

prestar to lend; to borrow

presumir de to boast about

pretender + *inf.* to try (*to do something*)

pretérito *gram.* preterite (tense)

prevalecer (zc) to prevail

prevenir (*like* **venir**) to prevent; to warn

prever (*like* **ver**) to foresee

previsto/a (*p.p. of* **prever**) foreseen

primavera spring

primer, primero/a first; **en primer lugar** in the first place
primo/a cousin
princesa princess
principal main, principal; **actor** (*m.*) **principal** lead actor; **cláusula principal** *gram.* main, independent clause; **entrada principal** main door; **plato principal** main course
prisa: darse (*irreg.*) **prisa** to hurry; **tener** (*irreg.*) **prisa** to be in a hurry
privado/a private; **detective privado** *m., f.* private detective
privatizar (c) to privatize
probabilidad *f.* probability
probar (ue) to try; to test; **probarse** to try on
problema *m.* problem
procurar + *inf.* to try (*to do something*)
producir (*irreg.*) to produce
producto para la limpieza cleaning product
profe *m., f.* (*abbrev. of* **profesor[a]**) professor
profesional: formación (*f.*) **profesional** occupational training
profesor(a) professor
profundo/a deep
programa *m.* program
programador(a) programmer
programar to program
progresivo/a *gram.* progressive (tense)
progreso progress
prohibir (prohíbo) to forbid; to prohibit
promesa promise
prometer to promise (to)
pronombre *m. gram.* pronoun
pronóstico forecast; **pronóstico meteorológico** weather forecast
pronto soon; **hasta pronto** see you soon; **por lo pronto** for the time being; **tan pronto como** as soon as
pronunciar to pronounce
propina tip
propio/a *adj.* own
proponer (*like* **poner**) to propose; to suggest
propuesto/a (*p.p. of* **proponer**) proposed; suggested
proseguir (*like* **seguir**) to proceed; to pursue
prosperar to prosper
prosperidad *f.* prosperity
proteger (j) to protect
protestante *m., f.* protestant
protestantismo Protestantism
provenir (*like* **venir**) **de** to originate from
provincia province
próximo/a next
proyecto project
prueba test; quiz
publicar (qu) to publish
público *adj.* public, *n.* audience
pueblo town; village; people
puente *m.* bridge
puerta door; **llamar/tocar (qu) a la puerta** to knock (on a door)
puerto port
puertorriqueño/a Puerto Rican
puesto job; position
puesto/a (*p.p. of* **poner**) put; placed
pulpo octopus
pulsar to press, push (*a button*)

pulsera bracelet
punta: horas (*f. pl.*) **punta** rush hour; **tener** (*irreg.*) **los nervios en punta** to be on edge
punto point; **en punto** on the dot (*time*); **estar a punto de** + *inf.* to be about to (*do something*)
puñetazo punch
puro/a pure; sheer; **agua** (*f.* [*but* **el agua**] **pura** clean water; **aire** (*m.*) **puro** clean air; **pura verdad** (*f.*) absolute/plain truth

Q

que that
¿qué? what?
¡qué + *adj.*! how + *adj.*!; **¡qué lástima!** what a pity!
quebrado *n.* fraction
quebradura fracture
quebrar (ie) to break
quedar to remain, be left; to be (located); **quedar a** + *time* to meet at (*time*); **quedar en** + *inf.* to agree to (*do something*); **quedarle bien/mal** to look good/bad (*on someone, something*); **quedarse** to stay, remain (*in a place*); **quedarse con** to keep, hold onto
quejarse (de) to complain (about)
quemar(se) to burn (oneself)
querer (*irreg.*) to want; to love
querido/a dear
queso cheese
quien(es) who, whom
¿quién(es)? who?, whom?; **¿de quién?** whose?
química chemistry
quinto/a fifth
quiosco kiosk
quitar to take away; to remove; **quitarse** to take off (*clothing*)
quizá(s) perhaps, maybe

R

radio *m.* radio (*apparatus*); *f.* radio (*medium*)
ramillete *m.* bouquet
rancho ranch
rapidez *f.* speed; quickness
rápido/a fast; quickly; **comida rápida** fast food
raqueta racquet
rascacielos *m. inv.* skyscraper
rayado/a scratched
raza race, ethnicity; **Día** (*m.*) **de la Raza** Columbus Day (October 12)
razón *f.* reason; **tener** (*irreg.*) **razón** to be right; **no tener razón** to be wrong
reacción *f.* reaction
reaccionar to react
realidad (*f.*): **en realidad** in fact
realista *m., f.* realist
realizar (c) to realize, achieve; to carry out; to accomplish
realmente really
rebanada slice
recado message
recaer (*like* **caer**) to fall again
recalentar (ie) to warm up, reheat

recargar (gu) to charge (*a battery*)
recaudar to collect
recepción *f.* reception
recepcionista *m., f.* receptionist
receta recipe; prescription
rechazar (c) to reject; to turn down
recibir to receive; to get
recibo receipt
recién newly; just; recently; **recién casado/a** newlywed; **recién llegado/a** new arrival; newly arrived; **recién nacido/a** newborn
reciente recent
recíproco/a reciprocal
reclamar to demand
recoger (*like* **coger**) to collect; to gather; to pick up
recomendar (ie) to recommend
reconocer (zc) to recognize
recordar (ue) to remember; to remind
recostarse (ue) to lie down
rector(a) president (*university*)
recuerdo memory
Red *f.* Web, Internet; **navegar (gu) en la Red** to surf, navigate the Web
redacción (*f.*): **jefe/a de redacción** editor-in-chief
redondo/a round
reducir (*irreg.*) to reduce
reemplazar to replace
referirse (ie, i) (a) to refer (to)
reflexivo/a *gram.* reflexive
refrán *m.* proverb
refresco soft drink
regalar to give (*as a gift*)
regalo gift
regañadientes: a regañadientes reluctantly
regar (ie) (gu) to water
regata boat race
regatear to haggle, bargain; to dribble (*a ball*)
regazo lap
régimen regime; diet; **estar** (*irreg.*) **a régimen** to be on a diet
región *f.* region
registrarse to check in
regresar to come back, return
rehacer (*like* **hacer**) to redo
rehecho/a (*p.p. of* **hacer**) redone
reina queen
reinar to reign; to prevail
reino: Reino Unido United Kingdom
reír(se) (i, i) (me río) to laugh; **reírse a carcajadas** to laugh one's head off
relación *f.* relationship
relajarse to relax
relámpago lightning; **visita relámpago** quick visit
relativo/a: cláusula relativa *gram.* relative clause; **pronombre** (*m.*) **relativo** *gram.* relative pronoun
religión *f.* religion
reloj *m.* watch
relucir (zc) to shine; glitter
remitir to remit; to send
remontar (a) to date back (to)
remover (ue) to stir
renacentista *adj. m., f.* Renaissance
Renacimiento *n. m.* Renaissance
renovación *f.* renovation

renunciar (a) to give up (*something*); to quit; to resign
reñir (i, i) to scold; to quarrel
reparar to repair
repasar to review
repente: de repente suddenly
repetir (i, i) to repeat; to have a second helping
repipí *m., f. sl.* brat (*Sp.*)
reponerse (*like* **poner**) to get well
reportaje *m.* report
reportero/a reporter
representante *m., f.* representative
representar to represent
reproducir (*like* **producir**) to reproduce
República Dominicana Dominican Republic
republicano/a Republican
repuesto: pieza de repuesto spare part
requisito requirement
resbalar to slip, slide
resbalón *m.* slide
rescate *m.* ransom
reservación *f.* reservation
resfriarse (me resfrío) to catch cold
residencia (university) dorm
resistir to resist; to stand, endure
resolver (ue) (*p.p.* **resuelto**) to solve; to resolve; to decide; **resolverse a** + *inf.* to resolve, decide to (*do something*)
respecto a about, concerning
respetado/a respected
respirar to breathe
resplandecer (zc) to shine; to blaze; to glow
responder to respond, answer
responsabilidad *f.* responsibility
responsable responsible, reliable
respuesta answer
restablecer (zc) to reestablish
restar to subtract
restaurante *m.* restaurant
resultado result
resumen *m.* summary
retener (*like* **tener**) to retain
retiro: planilla de retiro withdrawal form, slip
retrato portrait
reunión *f.* meeting; **reunión familiar** family reunion
reunir (reúno) to join; to gather; **reunirse (con)** to get together (with)
reventón blowout (*Sp.*)
revista magazine; **revista de deportes** sports magazine; **revista electrónica** e-zine (*Internet magazine*)
revolver (*like* **volver**) to turn over; to stir
revuelto/a (*p.p. of* **revolver**) turned over
rey *m.* king; **Día de Reyes** Epiphany (January 6); **Reyes Católicos** Ferdinand and Isabel (*Spanish monarchs*)
rezar (c) to pray
Ricitos de Oro Goldilocks
rico/a rich; good, delicious
ridículo/a ridiculous
río river
risa: morirse (ue, u) de risa to die laughing
rizado/a: mar (*f.*) **rizada** choppy sea
robar to steal
rodaja slice (*of an orange*)

rodaje *m.* filming, shooting (*of a film*)
rodar (ue) to roll; to film
rodilla knee; **ponerse** (*irreg.*) **de rodillas** to kneel
roer (y) to gnaw
rogar (ue) (gu) to beg; to ask
rojo/a red; **luz** (*f.*) **roja** red light
Roma Rome
romano/a Roman
romántico/a romantic
romper (*p.p.* **roto**) to break; to crack; to tear (*clothing*); **romper con** to break up with
roncar (qu) to snore
ronquidos *m. pl.* snoring
ropa clothes, clothing; **lavar la ropa** to do the laundry; **tienda de ropa** clothing store
rosa rose
rosado/a pink
roto/a (*p.p. of* **romper**) broken
rubí *m.* (*pl.* **rubíes**) ruby
rubio/a blond(e)
ruido noise
ruinas *f. pl.* ruins
Rumania Romania
rumano/a Romanian
ruso Russian (*language*)
ruso/a *n, adj.* Russian; **montaña rusa** roller coaster

sábana sheet
saber *irreg.* to know; **saber** + *inf.* to know how to (*do something*)
sabio/a wise
sabroso/a tasty
sacapuntas *m. inv.* pencil sharpener
sacar (qu) to take out; to get
saco jacket; **saco de dormir** sleeping bag
sacrificio sacrifice
sacudir to shake; **sacudir los muebles** to dust (the furniture)
sagaz *m., f.* wise
sal *f.* salt
sala living room; exhibition hall, gallery; **sala de clase** classroom; **sala de conferencias** lecture hall; **sala de espera** waiting room
salchicha sausage (link)
salida exit; **a la salida de** at the edge of (*a place*); upon leaving (*a place*)
salir *irreg.* to leave; to go out; to rise (*the sun*); **salir bien/mal** to turn, come out well/badly; **salir con la suya** to get one's way
salón (*m.*) **de actos** assembly hall
salpimentar to season, spice
salsa sauce
saltamontes *m. inv.* grasshopper
salud *f.* health
saludar to greet
salvadoreño/a Salvadorian
salvar to save
salvavidas *m., f. inv.* lifeguard; *m. inv.* life preserver
salvo *adv.* except
sandalia sandal
sándwich *m.* sandwich
sánscrito Sanskrit

san, santo/a saint; **Semana Santa** Holy Week
santiaguino/a from Santiago
sapo toad
sarape *m.* serape, shawl; blanket (*Mex.*)
sarcástico/a sarcastic
sartén *f.* frying pan
satisfacer *irreg.* (*p.p.* **satisfecho**) to satisfy
satisfecho/a (*p.p. of* **satisfacer**) satisfied
saudí, saudita Saudi Arabian; **Arabia Saudita** Saudi Arabia
saxofón *m.* saxophone
secador *m.* hair dryer
secadora (clothes) dryer
secar (qu) to dry; **secarse el pelo** to dry one's hair
sección (*f.*) section; **de deportes** sports section
secretario/a secretary; **secretario/a general** registrar
secreto secret
sed *f.* thirst
seda silk
seducir *irreg.* to tempt; to charm
seguida: en seguida right away
seguido/a de followed by
seguir (i, i) to follow; to continue
según according to
segundo/a second
seguridad (*f.*): **cinturón** (*m.*) **de seguridad** seatbelt
seguro/a sure, certain; true
seleccionar to select, choose
sello stamp
selva jungle
semana week; **fin** (*m.*) **de semana** weekend; **semana entrante** next week; **semana que viene** next week; **Semana Santa** Holy Week
semanal weekly
sembrar (ie) to plant
semilla seed
Sena *m.* (river) Seine (France)
senado senate
senador(a) senator
sencillez *f.* simplicity
señal *f.* signal; sign; **señal de tráfico** road sign
señalar to signal
señor *m.* Mr.; man; sir
señora Mrs.; lady, woman; ma'am
señorita Miss; young lady, young woman
sentado/a seated, sitting
sentar (ie) to seat, sit; **sentarse** to sit down
sentido del humor sense of humor
sentimiento *n.* feeling
sentir (ie, i) to regret, be sorry; to feel; **sentirse** to feel; **sentirse en forma** to feel fit
séptimo/a seventh
ser *irreg.* to be; **llegar (gu) a ser** to become; **pasar a ser** to become; **ser tal para cual** to be two of a kind; **ser un don nadie** to be a nobody
serbio/a Serbian
serie *f. s.* series
serio/a serious; **en serio** seriously
serpiente *f.* serpent, snake
serrar (ie) to saw
servicio de metro subway (service)
servilleta napkin
servir (i, i) to serve; **no servir para nada** to be useless; **servir de** to serve as; **servirse de** to use
sesión session; **iniciar la sesión** to log on
sevillano/a from Seville

sí yes; **claro que sí** *interj.* of course
sicología psychology
sicólogo psychologist
siempre always; **lo de siempre** the usual (thing); **para siempre** forever
siento: lo siento I'm sorry
sierra mountain range; mountains
siesta nap; **dormir (ue, u) la siesta** to take a nap
siglo century
significado meaning
significar to mean
signo sign
siguiente *adj.* next
silenciador *m.* muffle
silla chair
sillón *m.* armchair
simpático/a nice; pleasant
simple simple; mere
sin without; **sin embargo** however; nevertheless
sinagoga synagogue
sincero/a sincere
sindicato (labor) union
sinfonía symphony
sinfónico/a: orquesta sinfónica symphony orchestra
sino *conj.* but (rather); **sino también** but also
sinónimo synonym
siquiera: ni siquiera not even
Siria Syria
sirio/a Syrian
sistema *m.* system
sitio place; room, space; **en/por algún sitio** somewhere; **en/por ningún sitio** nowhere; **sitio web** Web site
smoking *m.* tuxedo
sobrar to be left (over); **sobrarle** to have more than enough (*of something*)
sobre *n.* envelope; *prep.* above, about; **sobre gustos no hay nada escrito** to each his own
sobremesa after-dinner conversation
sobresaltado/a startled
sobrevolar (ue) to fly over
sobrino/a nephew, niece
social: ciencias (*f. pl.*) **sociales** social sciences
socio/a associate, partner; member
sociología sociology
sofá *m.* sofa, couch
software *m.* software
sol *m.* sun; **hacer sol** to be sunny; **tomar el sol** to sunbathe
sólo *adv.* only
solo/a *adj.* alone, by oneself; single
soldadito de plomo tin soldier
soldado soldier
soler (ue) + *inf.* to be used to, accustomed to (*doing something*); to usually (*do something*)
solicitar to ask for; to request
sollozar (c) to sob
sombra shadow
sombrero hat; **sombrero de copa** top hat; **sombrero de paja** straw hat
sonar (ue) to ring; to sound
sondeo poll
sonido sound
sonoro/a: banda sonora sound track (*of a movie*)
sonreír(se)(*like* **reír**) to smile

sonrisa *n.* smile
sopa: estar hecho/a una sopa to be soaking wet
soportar to stand, put up with
sordo/a deaf; **hacerse** (*irreg.*) **el sordo** to turn a deaf ear
sorprender to surprise; **sorprenderse** to be surprised
sorpresa *n.* surprise
sostener (*like* **tener**) to sustain
sótano basement
suave soft
subir to go up; to climb; to raise; to upload
subjuntivo *gram.* subjunctive (mood)
subordinado/a: cláusula subordinada *gram.* dependent clause
subrayar to underscore, underline
suceder to happen
suceso event
sucio/a dirty
sucursal *f.* branch; **sucursal de empresa** business/company branch; **sucursal del banco** (bank) branch
Sudáfrica South Africa
sudafricano/a South African
sudamericano/a South American
sudanés, sudanesa Sudanese
Suecia Sweden
sueco/a Swedish
suegro/a father-in-law, mother-in-law
sueldo salary
suelo floor
sueño dream
suerte *f.* luck; **echar suertes** to draw lots, flip a coin; **tener (mala) suerte** to be (un)lucky
suficiente *adj.* enough; **lo suficiente** *adv.* enough
sufrir to suffer
sugerencia suggestion
sugerir (ie, i) to suggest
Suiza Switzerland
suizo/a Swiss
sujeto *gram.* subject
sumamente extremely
sumar to add
superficie *f.* surface
superlativo *gram.* superlative
supermercado supermarket
suponer (*like* **poner**) to suppose
supuesto: por supuesto of course
sur *m.* south; **Corea del Sur** South Korea; **Vietnám del Sur** South Vietnam
surgir (j) to arise
suspender to suspend
sustantivo *gram.* noun
sustituir (y) to substitute
susto fright, scare
susurrar to whisper
suyo/a *poss. adj.* your (*form.*); his, her, its, their; *poss. pron.* (of) yours (*form.*); (of) his, hers; (of) theirs

T

tabla chart
tabú *m.* (*pl.* **tabúes**) taboo
tacaño/a mean; stingy

tacón: de tacón alto high-heeled
tailandés, tailandesa Thai
Tailandia Thailand
taiwanés, taiwanesa Taiwanese
tal such, such a; **con tal de que** *conj.* provided
(that); **¿qué tal?** how are you?; **ser** (*irreg.*) **tal para**
cual to be two of a kind; **tal como** just as; **tal vez**
perhaps, maybe
talento talent
talentoso/a talented
taller *m.* workshop
tamal *m.* tamale
tambor *m.* drum
Támesis *m.* (River) Thames
tampoco neither, not either
tan *adv.* so; as, such; **tan… como** as . . . as; **tan**
pronto como as soon as
tanque *m.* tank
tanto *adv.* so much; **ponerse** (*irreg.*) **al tanto** to
catch up on the news; **por lo tanto** therefore;
tanto como as much as
tanto/a as much; so much; such a; *pl.* so many; as
many; **tanto/a(s)… como** as much/
many . . . as
taquilla ticket office; box office
tardar to take/be a long time; **tardar** + *time* to take
(*time*); **tardar en** + *inf.* to delay in (*doing*
something); to take a long time to (*do some-*
thing)
tarde *n. f.* afternoon; evening; **buenas tardes** good
afternoon/evening; **de la tarde** in the afternoon/
evening; **por la tarde** in/during the afternoon/
evening
tarde *adv.* late; **hacérsele tarde** to get, grow late;
más tarde later
tardón, tardona slow poke
tarea homework
tarjeta (post)card; **tarjeta de crédito** credit card;
tarjeta postal postcard
taxi *m.* taxi
té *m.* tea
teatro theater; **obra de teatro** play
techo roof; ceiling
tecla key (on a piano, keyboard)
técnico/a technician
tecnología technology; **de alta tecnología**
hi-tech
tecnológico/a technological
telaraña cobweb
tela material; cloth
tele (*abbrev. for* **televisión** [*f.*]) television
telefónico/a *adj.* telephone; **guía telefónica** phone
book
teléfono telephone; **teléfono celular/móvil** cell
phone
telenovela soap opera
televidente *m., f.* T.V. viewer
televisión *f.* television
televisor *m.* television set
telón *m.* curtain
tema *m.* theme; topic
temblar to tremble
temer + *inf.* to be afraid to (*to do something*)
temperatura temperature
tempestad *f.* storm
temprano early

tener *irreg.* to have; **no tener dónde caerse muerto**
to not have a penny to one's name; **no tener**
nada de + *noun* to not have any _____ at all;
no tener ni idea to not have the slightest idea; **no**
tener razón to be wrong; **tener… años** to be . . .
(years old); **tener calor** to be, feel hot; **tener celos**
to be jealous; **tener cuidado** to be careful; **tener el**
don de gentes to have charm, be charming,
to get along well with people; **tener en brazos**
to hold; **tener en cuenta** to keep in mind; **tener**
en nada to think very little of, take no notice of
(*something, someone*); **tener éxito** to be successful;
tener frío to be, feel cold; **tener ganas (de)** + *inf.*
to feel like (*doing something*); **tener hambre** to be,
feel hungry; **tener interés en** + *inf.* to be interested in (*doing something*); **tener la bondad** to be
kind enough (*to do something*); **tener la culpa (de)**
to be guilty (of); **tener los nervios en punta** to be
on edge; **tener lugar** to take place; **tener miedo**
to be afraid; **tener presente** to keep in mind;
tener prisa to be in a hurry; **tener que** + *inf.*
to have to (*do something*); **tener razón** to be right;
tener vergüenza to be embarrassed **tenérsela**
jurada a uno/a to have it in for someone
tenis *m.* tennis; **zapato de tenis** tennis shoe
tenista *m., f.* tennis player
teoría theory
tercer, tercero/a third
tercio one-third
terciopelo velvet
terco/a stubborn
terminar to finish, end; **terminar de** + *inf.* to stop
ternera veal; **chuleta de ternera** veal chop
terremoto earthquake
terreno: coche todo terreno all-terrain vehicle (ATV)
terror *m.* terror
tesis *f.* thesis
testigo *m., f.* witness
texto text(book); **libro de texto** textbook
tía aunt
tibio/a tepid, lukewarm
tiempo time; *gram.* tense; weather; **a tiempo** on
time; **hacer buen/mal tiempo** to be good/bad
weather
tienda store; **tienda de comestibles** grocery store;
tienda de deportes sporting goods store; **tienda**
de muebles furniture store; **tienda de ropa**
clothing store
tierra land
tigre *m., f* tiger
tigresa tiger
tijeras *f. pl.* scissors
timbre *m.* bell; **tocar (qu) el timbre** to ring
the bell
tímido/a shy
tintorería drycleaner
tío uncle; *pl.* uncles; aunt(s) and uncle(s)
típico/a typical
tipo type; guy
tirar to throw; **tirarse** to jump; to throw oneself;
to lie down
tirita strip; **cortar a tiritas** to cut into strips
titular *m.* headline
titularse to be titled
título title
toalla towel

tobillo ankle
tocar (qu) to touch; to play (*a musical instrument*); **tocar a la puerta** to knock (at a door); **tocar el timbre** to ring the bell; **tocarle a uno** to be someone's turn; to be up to someone
todavía still; yet; **todavía no** not yet
todo *adv.* entirely; completely
todo/a *n.* everything; whole; all; *adj.* all; every; each; **ante todo** above all; first of all; **por todas partes** everywhere; **todo está pendiente** it's all up in the air; **todos los días** every day; **una vez por todas** once and for all
tomar to take; to drink; to drink (*alcohol*); **tomarle el pelo** to pull someone's leg; **tomar sol** to sunbathe; **tomar una decisión** to make a decision
tomate *m.* tomato
tontería silly thing; nonsense
tonto/a silly; stupid; **hacerse el tonto** to play dumb
torcer(se) (ue) (z) to twist
tormenta storm
toro bull; **corrida de toros** bullfight
torpe clumsy
torpeza clumsiness
torre *f.* tower
torta cake (*Sp.*); **torta de chocolate** chocolate cake
tortilla potato and egg omelet (*Sp.*)
tos *f.* cough
toser to cough
tostado/a: pan (*m.*) **tostado** toast
trabajar to work; **trabajar por cuatro** to work like a slave
trabajador(a) hard-working
trabajo work; **cuaderno de trabajo** workbook
tradicional traditional
traducción *f.* translation
traducir (zc, j) *irreg.* to translate
traer *irreg.* to bring
tráfico traffic; **señal** (*f.*) **de tráfico** road sign
tragar (gu) to swallow
trago (*alcoholic*) drink
traje *m.* suit; **traje de baño** bathing suit; **traje de luces** bullfighter's costume
trámite *m.* procedure; **trámite de banco** bank transaction
tranquilizar (c) to calm someone down; **tranquilizarse** to calm down; to stop worrying
transformarse en to become
transitado/a busy; **poco/a transitado/a** with little traffic
transmitir to transmit
tranvía *m.* streetcar
trapo cleaning rag
tras *prep.* after
trasnochador(a) night owl
trasnochar to stay up late/all night; to go to bed very late
tratar (de) to try (to)
trato hecho it's a deal
través: a través de through
travieso/a mischievous
tremendo/a tremendous, terrible
tren *m.* train; **estación** (*f.*) **de trenes** train station
trepar to climb
tres three; **en un dos por tres** in a jiffy
tribuna stand; **tribuna del estadio** grandstand
tribunal (*m.*) **de exámenes** board of examiners

trigo wheat
triste sad
tristeza sadness
trombón *m.* trombone
trompeta trumpet
trompetista *m., f.* trumpet player
tronar (ue) to thunder
tropezar (ie) (c) to trip; to stumble
trotamundos *m., f. inv.* globetrotter
trotar to jog; to travel (around) (*Sp.*)
trozo piece
trueno thunder
tulipán *m.* tulip
tumbarse to lie down
tunecino/a Tunisian
Túnez Tunisia
turco/a Turkish
turista *m., f.* tourist
turístico/a *adj.* tourist
Turquía Turkey
tuyo/a *poss. adj.* your (*fam. s.*); *poss. pron.* (of) yours (*fam. s.*)

U

Ucrania Ukraine
ucraniano/a Ukrainian
últimamente lately; recently
último/a last; latest; **las últimas** the latest news; **por último** finally; **últimos de** at the end of (*month, year*)
único/a only; unique; **Reino Unido** United Kingdom
universidad *f.* university
universitario/a *adj.* university; **ciudad universitaria** university campus
uña (finger)nail; **esmalte** (*m.*) **de uñas** nail polish; **limarse las uñas** to file one's nails; **limpiarse las uñas** to remove the polish from one's nails
urgirle (j) + *inf.* to be urgent for someone (*to do something*)
uruguayo/a Uruguayan
usar to use; to wear
uso *n.* use
útil useful
utilizar (c) to use
uva grape

V

vaca cow
vacaciones *f. pl.* vacation; **estar** (*irreg.*) **de vacaciones** to be on vacation; **ir** (*irreg.*) **de vacaciones** to go on vacation
vacilar en + *inf.* to hesitate over (*doing something*)
vacío/a empty
vale *n. m.* gift certificate
valer (g) to be worth; **más vale algo que nada** something's better than nothing; **más vale que** it's better that; **valerse de** to use
valenciano/a from Valencia

valiente brave

valla fence; hurdle (*sports*)

valle *m.* valley

valor *m.* value; **bolsa de valores** stock exchange; **objeto de valor** valuable object

vals *m.* (*pl.* **valses**) waltz

vámonos let's go

vanidad *f.* vanity

vaqueros *m. pl.* jeans

variar (varío) to vary

varios/as *pl.* several

vasco Basque (*language*)

vaso (*drinking*) glass

vecindad *f.* neighborhood

vecino/a neighbor

vegetación *f.* vegetation

veinteavo one twentieth

velero sailboat

velocidad *f.* speed; **de alta velocidad** high-speed

vencedor(a) *adj.* winning

vencer (z) to conquer, overcome; to win

vendaje *m.* bandage

vender to sell

venezolano/a Venezuelan

venir *irreg.* to come

venta sale

ventana window

ventanilla small window; (car) window

ver (*irreg.*) (*p.p.* **visto**) to see; **no los puedo ver** I can't stand them; **verlo todo negro** to be pessimistic

verano summer; **escuela de verano** summer school; **vacaciones** (*f., pl.*) **de verano** summer vacation

veras: de veras really

verdad *f.* truth; **de verdad** really; **pura verdad** absolute/plain truth

verdadero/a *adj.* true

verde green

verdura vegetable

vereda path

vergüenza shame; **tener** (*irreg.*) **vergüenza** to be embarrassed

vestíbulo lobby

vestido *n.* dress

vestido/a *adj.* (*p.p. of* **vestir**) dressed

vestir (i, i) to dress (someone); **vestirse** to dress, get dressed

vestuario wardrobe

vez *f.* (*pl.* **veces**) time; **a veces** sometimes; **alguna vez** sometime; **algunas veces** sometimes; **de una vez por todas** once and for all; **en vez de** instead of; **otra vez** again; **tal vez** perhaps, maybe; **una vez por todas** once and for all

viajar to travel

viajero/a traveler; **cheque** (*m.*) **de viajero** traveler's check

vicio vice

víctima victim

vida life; **ganarse la vida** to earn a living

videojuego video game

viejo/a old; former

viento wind; **hacer** (*irreg.*) **viento** to be windy; *Lo que el viento se llevó* Gone with the Wind

vietnamés, vietnamesa *n., adj.* Vietnamese

vietnamita *adj., m., f.* Vietnamese

vínculo link

vino wine

violento/a violent

violín *m.* violin

violinista *m., f.* violinist

violonchelo *m. inv.* cello

visita visit; **visita relámpago** quick visit

visitar to visit

visto/a (*p.p. of* **ver**) seen; **por lo visto** apparently

vitae: currículum (*m.*) **vitae** résumé, CV

vitamina vitamin

vivir to live

vocero/a spokesperson

volante *m.* steering wheel

volar (ue) to fly

volcán *m.* volcano

volcar (ue) (qu) to knock over; **volcarse** to get knocked over

vólibol *m.* volleyball

voluntario/a volunteer

volver (ue) (*p.p.* **vuelto**) to return; **volver a** + *inf.* to do (*something*) again; **volverse** + *adj.* to go, become + *adj.*

voz *f.* voice; **correo de voz** voice mail; **en voz alta** out loud; aloud; **en voz baja** in a low voice; quietly; **voz activa** *gram.* active voice

vuelo flight

vuelta: a la vuelta de la esquina around the corner; **dar** (*irreg.*) **la vuelta** to turn (*something*) over; **estar** (*irreg.*) **de vuelta** to be back

vuelto/a (*p.p. of* **volver**) returned

vulgar common; vulgar

web *m.* Web; **administrador(a) de web** webmaster; **sitio web** Web site

ya already; **preparados, listos, ya** ready, set, go; **ya no** no longer; not anymore

yemení *m., f.* (*pl.* **yemeníes**) Yemeni

yendo *present participle of* ir

York: Nueva York New York

zapatería shoe store

zapatilla de cristal glass slipper

zapato shoe; **(des)atarse los zapatos** to (un)tie one's shoelaces; **zapato de tenis** tennis shoe

Zelanda: Nueva Zelanda New Zealand

zócalo town square (*Mex.*)

zoológico *n.* zoo

INDEX

Note: *In accordance with the latest spelling reforms of the Spanish Real Academia de la Lengua this index does not treat* **ch** *and* **ll** *as separate letters of the alphabet.*

in progressive tenses, 124, 130
position of object pronoun
with, 123
position of reflexive pronoun
with, 123
with verbs of perception, 123
-gir verbs, 33
-guir verbs, 33–34
gustar, 318
verbs usually with indirect object
pronoun, 318

H

haber (auxiliary verb), 99, 118
in perfect tenses, 99, 104, 108,
109–110, 118
hacer
hace + *expression of time* + **que,** 5
hacerse *to become,* 152, *pretend to
be,* 154

I

-iar verbs, 30
imperative: *see* commands
imperfect tense, 66–67, 71, 79
compared with preterite tense, 71
hacía + *expression of time* + **que** +
imperfect, 79
imperfect + **desde hacía** +
expression of time, 79
irregular forms, 66
indefinite article, 253–254
indefinite words, 395, 396–397
indirect object pronouns, 314–316,
318–319, 322
forms, 314–316
position, 314–316
other uses, 322
infinitive
adjective + **de** + *infinitive,* 231
after prepositions, 225
after verbs of perception, 229
al + *infinitive,* 226–227
conjugated verb + *infinitive,* 219–220
conjugated verb + *preposition* +
infinitive, 221–222
preceded by **que,** 230
information questions, 374–375
interrogative words, 374–375
ir, 11
-ir verbs
formation of, 4
irregular, 9–12, 416–422
regular, 4, 411
spelling changes, 33–34, 414–416
stem-changing, 25–26, 412–414

L

llegar a ser *to become,* 152
llevar
in progressive tenses, 130
lo, 306, 330
lo de, 252
lo + *long-form possessive adjective,*
295
neuter article, 252

N

negative words and expressions,
389–390, 392–395
no
tag: **¿no?,** 383
with negative words, 389
with subject pronouns, 393
noun clauses, 163–164, 178
nouns
gender, 234–239
number, 241–243
numbers
arithmetic operations, 404–405
cardinal, 400–401
days, dates, and years, 402–403
fractions and percentages, 405
ordinal, 402
telling time, 403–404
use of period and comma, 401

O

object pronouns
direct, 306–308
double, 324–325
indirect, 314–316, 318–319, 322
other uses, 322–323
verbs usually used with, 318–319
position with commands, 213
special uses, 330

P

para, 362–363
compared with **por,** 364–365
passive constructions
passive voice, 113
por (agent phrase), 113, 118
se constructions, 115–116
past participle, 98–99, 104, 108,
109–110, 275
uses, 99, 104, 108, 109–110, 118,
275

past perfect tense, 104, 183
perfect tenses
conditional perfect, 109–110
future perfect, 108
haber as auxiliary verb of, 99, 104,
108, 109–110, 118
past participle, 98–99, 104, 108,
109–110, 118, 275
past perfect, 104
position of object pronouns, 99
present perfect, 99
personal **a,** 303–305, 356, 390
poner, 9
ponerse to become, 152
por, 363–364
agent phrase in passive, 113, 118
compared with **para,** 364–365
possession, 257–258
possessive adjectives, 292–293
possessive pronouns, 295
prepositions
a, 356–357
con, 360–361
de, 358–359
en, 360
other simple prepositions, 369
para and **por,** 362–365
preceding interrogative
words, 375
pronouns after, 301, 340
sets of prepositions and
compound prepositions,
370–371
present participle (gerund), 122–123
present perfect tense, 99, 174
present tense
formation of, 2–4
irregular forms, 9–12
spelling changes, 33–34
stem changes, 18–19, 25–26
uses of, 5–6
preterite tense
compared with imperfect
tense, 71
formation of, 49–50
irregular forms, 59–60
spelling changes, 50–52
stem changes, 51–52
probability
expressed by conditional, 93
expressed by conditional
perfect, 110
expressed by future, 90
expressed by future perfect, 108
progressive tenses, 124–126, 130
seguir and **ir** with gerund, 126
with **llevar,** 130
with reflexive pronouns, 142
pronouns
after prepositions, 301
demonstrative, 290–291
direct object, 306–308